Test Kitchens Staff: Julia Dowling and Diane Hogan

Charles Walton IV, Senior Foods Photographer; Tina Evans, Photographer

Assistant Foods Editors: Denise Gee, Andria Scott Hurst, and Jodi Jackson Loe

J. Savage Gibson, Photographer; Leslie Byars Simpson, Senior Photo Stylist

Southern Living

1995 ANNUAL RECIPES

Library of Congress Catalog Number: 79-88364
ISBN: 0-8487-1453-9
ISSN: 0272-2003

Manufactured in the United States of America
First printing 1995

Cover: *Coconut-Lemon Cake (page 319),*
    Orange Cake (page 320)
Back Cover: *(clockwise from top) Summery Chicken Salad*
    (page 138), Honey Angel Biscuits with Honey Butter
    (page 138); Oranges in Grand Marnier (page 142), Spirited
    Raspberries (page 142), Blueberry Cordial (page 142),
    Rumtopf (page 142); Late-Night Pasta Chez Frank
    (page 228); Manny and Isa's Key Lime Pie (page 118)
Page 1: *Grilled Turkey Breast With Cranberry Salsa (page 252)*
Page 4: *Chocolate-Raspberry Shortcake (page 99)*

Southern Living®

Executive Editor: Elle Barrett
Foods Editor: Dana Adkins Campbell
Associate Foods Editor: Kaye Mabry Adams
Assistant Foods Editors: Denise Gee, Andria Scott Hurst,
    Jodi Jackson Loe, Jackie Mills, R.D.
Editorial Coordinator: Susan Hawthorne Nash
Test Kitchens Director: Patty Vann
Assistant Test Kitchens Director: Peggy Smith
Test Kitchens Staff: Julia Dowling, Judy Feagin,
    Diane Hogan, Vanessa McNeil Ward, Vie Warshaw
Editorial Assistants: Karen Brechin, Wanda Stephens
Senior Foods Photographer: Charles Walton IV
Photographers: Tina Evans, J. Savage Gibson
Senior Photo Stylist: Leslie Byars Simpson
Photo Services: Tracy Underwood
Production Manager: Kenner Patton
Assistant Production Manager: Vicki Weathers

Oxmoor House, Inc.

Editor-in-Chief: Nancy Fitzpatrick Wyatt
Senior Editor, Editorial Services: Olivia Kindig Wells
Art Director: James Boone

Southern Living® 1995 Annual Recipes

Senior Foods Editor: Susan Carlisle Payne
Assistant Foods Editor: Whitney Wheeler Pickering
Copy Editor: Donna Baldone
Editorial Assistant: Stacey Geary
Production and Distribution Director: Phillip Lee
Associate Production Manager: Theresa L. Beste
Production Coordinator: Marianne Jordan Wilson
Production Assistant: Valerie L. Heard
Editorial Consultant: Jean Wickstrom Liles
Indexer: Mary Ann Laurens
Designer and Illustrator: Carol Middleton

TABLE OF CONTENTS

OUR YEAR AT SOUTHERN LIVING — 10

JANUARY — 13

Ever-Changing Chili: Make It Mild Or Make It Wild — 14
High-Yield Stocks — 17
What's For Supper? After-Christmas Casserole — 19
Celebrate In A New Light — 20
Appetizers On The Cheesy Side — 21
Super Spud Toppers — 22
Living Light: Tighten Your Belt — 23
Serve These Casseroles On The Side — 26
Southern Living Hall Of Fame: Savannah Style — 27
Old Favorites Made New: Mama's Cooking Just Got Better — 28
From Our Kitchen To Yours — 30
Lively Lemons Add Zing — 31
Quick & Easy: Make A Break For It — 32
Seasonal Sensation — 34
Just Dip It! — 35
Delicious Indulgence — 36

FEBRUARY — 41

Flat-Out Winners — 42
From Our Kitchen To Yours — 44
Homemade Made Easy — 45
Quick & Easy: Curry In A Hurry — 46
Fresh From The Vine — 47
Spinach On The Side — 48
Batter Up — 49
Fools For Fudge — 50
Living Light: One Meal Three Ways — 52
What's For Supper? Chances Are It's Chicken — 54
Soda's The Secret — 55
Company Coming? No Problem — 56
Breakfast At Brennan's – By The Book — 57
Bake A Bread Bowl — 58

MARCH — 59

Glorious Goat Cheese — 60
Searing Heat, Subtle Flavors — 64
Simple Salads Made Sensational — 66
From Our Kitchen To Yours — 67
Quick & Easy: Build A Meal — 68
What's For Supper? Dinner On A Shoestring — 70

A Touch O' Irish — 70
Out Of Africa — 71
Southern Living Hall Of Fame: To Market, To Market — 72
Sourdough Made Simple — 77
Living Light: Bake It Light — 78
Beignets For Breakfast — 80

APRIL — 81

Sweet Stalks Of Spring — 82
Quick & Easy: Nontaxing Standbys — 84

Spring Celebrations Special Section — 85

Dinner On The Lawn — 85
Say "I Do" To Great Food — 88
Bubble Over — 90
Happy Anniversary — 91
Stir Up Some Fun — 93
Spring's Best Salads — 94
Easy Things Come In Small Packages — 96

Shortcakes Deliciously Layered — 98
Easter Sunday Brunch — 100
PB & J For Easter — 101

Share in the seasons and celebrations of the South as you journey through our pages. Discover new flavors or snuggle up with comforting classics. And along the way, you'll find timesaving tips, surefire substitutes, tricks of the trade, and gift-giving ideas from folks across our land.

A Memorable Passover	102
Lamb – Texas Style	104
From Our Kitchen To Yours	105
Living Light: Low-Fat Catch	106
What's For Supper? Something Good To Talk About	108

MAY 113

When Smoke Gets In Your Eyes	114
From Our Kitchen To Yours	116
Hometown Favorites	117
Spring For Rhubarb	119
Southern Living Hall Of Fame: The Nashville Cookbook	120
What's For Supper? Dinner On The Ground	121
Living Light: Light And Lazy	122
Quick & Easy: True Confessions (Of The Food Kind)	125
Hooked On Tuna	126
Dinner's A Done Deal	128
A Taste Of La Paz	130
Not-So-Ordinary Spaghetti	131
Garden Club Vegetable Favorites	132
Start With Buttermilk	134

Menu For Mom	135
An Oatmeal Cookie Sampler	136

JUNE 137

Hats Off To Summer Entertaining	138
Finger Foods: The Balancing Act	140
Beverages For A Crowd	140
Cordially Yours	141
Give Them A Worldly Send-Off	142
Slices Of Summer	143
The Big Grill: Chicken Sandwiches	153
Down By The River	154
From Our Kitchen To Yours	156
Quick & Easy: A Delightful Mix-up	157
Winning Ways Of Southern Cooks	158
Shreds Of Garden Goodness	159
Open A Can Of Promises	160
Living Light: Light Night Out	161
Polenta's Not So Posh	164
Peanuts, Popcorn, And . . .	166
What's For Supper? Mix And Match	165
Pudding Is Child's Play	167
Say Hello To Dessert	168

JULY 169

Tomatoes – Nature's Crimson Declaration Of Summer	170
Summer Suppers® Special Section	173
A Midsummer Night's Theme: Casual Yet Elegant	173
A Taste Of Southern Elegance	175
Easy Weekend Entertaining	176
Fresh From The Garden	179
The Best Sides Of Summer	179
Notable Totables	182
Fast Alfresco	183
Picnic Panache	184
Living Light: Herbal Light	189
Quick & Easy: Catch A Wave	191
Sizzling Kabobs	192
What's For Supper? King Ranch Chicken	193
From Our Kitchen To Yours	194
Peaches: A Bushel And A Peck	195
Eggplant For Everyone	196
Consuming Kudzu	198

AUGUST 199

Mind Your Teas & Cubes	200
Living Light: Low-Cal Tropical	202
Cooking In Austin	205
A Taste Of Red Hot Success	206
From Our Kitchen To Yours	208
Quick & Easy: Reel In A Fresh Catch	209
What's For Supper? Weekday Solutions	210
Feast Without Meat	211
Pantry Shape-up	212
Winning Snacks	214
Southern Living Hall Of Fame: One Of A Kind	215
Cool Off With Cucumbers	216
Can-Do Tomatoes	217
French Bread Fix-ups	218
Yogurt: The Key Ingredient	219

SEPTEMBER 225

Food Of Our Native Fathers	226
Chefs' Whisk-And-Tell Secrets	228
Living Light: Seasoned With A Southern Accent	230

Eat Your Greens 233
In Pursuit Of Perfect Fried
    Chicken 234
Ribs, Ribs, Ribs 236
A Family Cookout 237
Toast To Touchdown 238
Appetizers That Score Big 239
Peppers Aplenty 240
What's For Supper? BBQ ASAP 242
Southern Living Hall Of Fame:
    The Texas Experience 243
Quick & Easy: Snacks Cool For
    After School 244
Start With Biscuit Mix 245
From Our Kitchen To Yours 246

OCTOBER 247

Fabulous Fruitcake 248
Autumn In A Jar 250
Living Light: Do Yourself
    A Flavor 252
Perfect Baked Paella 254
What's For Supper? Casseroles
    For Any Occasion 255
Dinner In A Piecrust 256
More Cluck, Less Buck 261
Hash Things Out 262
Southern Comfort Food 263
Earthy Delights 264
Top Chops 266
Beyond Pepperoni 267
A Pleasing Risotto 269
Freezer-Easy Potatoes 269
Heads Up 270
Common Scents 271
Quick & Easy: These Cookies
    Take The Cake 272
Scare Up A Halloween Party 273
From Our Kitchen To Yours 274

NOVEMBER 275

Grab A Cup And A Conversation 276

Holiday Dinners® Special
    Section 279

    Company's Cooking 279
    Breakfast Made Beautiful 281
    Great Beginnings 283
    Try Lamb This Season 284
    Wine And Dine 286
    Ten Years Later, Ten
        Times Easier 286

Dressed For Success 288
Sweet On Sweet Potatoes 290
On A Roll 292
Holiday Greenery 301
Cranberry Options 301
Classic Endings 302
Special Delivery 304

Thanksgiving, Southern Style 305
What's For Supper? Calm In
    The Kitchen 308
Southern Living Hall Of Fame:
    Party Potpourri 309
Living Light: Wrap And Roll 310
Quick & Easy: Fast Dishes For
    Busy Days 311
These Recipes Cut The Mustard 312
Use Your Nog In . . . 313
From Our Kitchen To Yours 314

DECEMBER 315

Kentucky Traditions 316
The 12 Doughs Of Christmas 320
Crème Brûlée 323

It's All In The Game 325
An Enchanted Evening 326
Merry Mousse 327
Angel Wings And Southern
    Things 328
Living Light: Seasons
    Teachings 330
Not A Creature Was Stirring 332
Sip Into Something
    Comfortable 337
A Craving For Chicken And
    Dumplings 338
Rebuilding The Reuben 338
Tacos Many Ways 339
What's For Supper? Pause
    For Pasta 340
Sensational Sides 341
Southern Boy Makes
    Good 342
From Our Kitchen To Yours 343

RECIPE INDEX SECTION 344

METRIC EQUIVALENTS 368

A warm welcome into Southern kitchens, this collection of nearly 1,000 treasured recipes is indexed by title, month, main ingredient, and food category from appetizers to desserts. So, whether you're looking for recipes that are quick-and-easy or elegant, intimate or crowd-pleasing, the timeless hospitality of the South is at your fingertips.

OUR YEAR AT SOUTHERN LIVING®

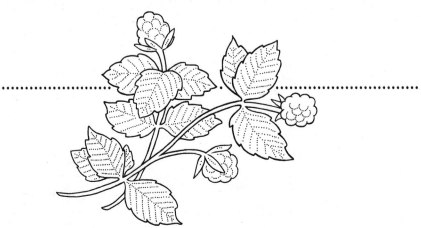

Your many letters and recipes tell us that SOUTHERN LIVING® must meet a wide variety of tastes and cooking needs.

Our Foods Staff members come from several Southern states, and our different backgrounds, interests, and family situations help us offer something special to each of you.

For us, *Southern Living® 1995 Annual Recipes* isn't just a must-have cookbook in our own homes. It's also a scrapbook of our year in food, bringing you the gamut of our region's best dishes.

From the first low-fat menu toasting the New Year to the last bite of December's most indulgent dessert, you'll find recipes sure to be favorites long after 1995 is just a memory.

This year we expanded the foods section in several areas you've told us are important to you. This was the first year we've focused monthly on solving the routine dinnertime dilemma. The easy weeknight recipes you sent for our new column, "What's For Supper?" made our job easy. In addition we created a new special section – "Spring Celebrations" – bursting with fresh, colorful ideas for entertaining friends and relatives.

This year we focused more than ever on food indigenous to our region.

The South's bounty blossoms in April's rich strawberry shortcake and peaks with July's brilliant tomatoes, best eaten simply on white bread with mayonnaise, salt, and pepper in the lauded tomato sandwich. Our pages introduce you to goat cheese at a North Carolina farm and whisk you to Maryland for a traditional crab feast. We take you to Georgia to meet some blue-ribbon home cooks and to visit with a stellar gathering of Southern chefs to learn their secrets. And we spotlight no-cook picnic ideas from one of our favorite spots on the Florida Gulf Coast, Seaside.

Yes, it was a very good year. And now, with a turn of these pages, you can visit any month of our calendar you choose. Thanks for inviting us into your kitchen. We hope to see more of your recipes soon. Keep in touch.

Dana Adkins Campbell
Foods Editor

1995's Best Recipes

We gather almost every day for taste-testing. There we scrutinize our recipes and declare favorites.

Recipes prepared by our Test Kitchens Staff must be tasted, retested, if necessary, and "passed" before being published. After gaining our stamp of approval, we assign each recipe an in-house rating. It's rare for a recipe to receive our highest rating – a three – but when it does, it's extra special. We'd like to share the eight recipes that received the honor this year. You won't want to miss them as you use this cookbook.

HEAVENLY SMOKED BRISKET
recipe, page 114

The key ingredient for this recipe is . . . napkins. Have plenty on hand. Submitted by Sam D. Morrison, Jr. of Alexandria, Louisiana, Heavenly Smoked Brisket will have juice dribbling down your chin while it runs down your forearm. Marinated in a blend that includes brown sugar and Cajun seasoning, and slowly smoked for five hours over hickory wood chunks, this is a recipe for down-home Southern barbecue. And although smoking may seem like an intimidating technique, a first-timer from our Test Kitchens described it as "easy, easy."

BURK'S FARM-RAISED CATFISH FRY
recipe, page 158

Bessie Burk of Rome, Georgia, won the 1980 National Catfish Recipe Contest with this recipe. Buttermilk, cornmeal, and peanut oil lend a Southern accent to this fish fry. Start making this recipe a day ahead, and after the catfish marinates overnight, you'll have only a few minutes of kitchen duty to prepare the night's meal. A prize-winning recipe in our kitchen, too, Burk's Farm-Raised Catfish Fry is a great catch for a quick supper.

SESAME-CRUSTED SALMON WITH GINGER VINAIGRETTE
recipe, page 162

The highest-rated salmon recipe we've ever published, Sesame-Crusted Salmon With Ginger Vinaigrette, came to us from chefs Anne Quatrano and Clifford Harrison at Bacchanalia in Atlanta. Sesame oil, honey, soy sauce, fresh ginger, and red pepper jazz up the vinaigrette. Drizzle it over the salmon's crusted coating, and you've got a dynamic duo.

GRILLED TURKEY BREAST WITH CRANBERRY SALSA
recipe, page 252; photograph, page 1

Julia Downey of Houston submitted this light recipe with the "big-as-Texas" taste. All-time favorite flavors, turkey and cranberries, are made over and slimmed down in Grilled Turkey Breast With Cranberry Salsa. Grilling browns the meat quickly, while locking in the flavor and natural juices. The cranberry salsa – with its jalapeños – packs a festive kick. And with a calorie count at just over 300 and only 16% of its calories from fat, this dish alone is reason to celebrate.

GRILLED SHIITAKES
recipe, page 265

Dale Glennon of Florence, Alabama, defines quick and easy cooking with this recipe for Grilled Shiitakes. The woodsy flavor and meaty texture of shiitakes make them a hearty substitute for meat in your favorite recipe. And grilled, these earthy morsels pair up nicely with anything from a noontime sandwich to a steak dinner. The recipe is a cinch to prepare and requires only a handful of ingredients.

CREAM CHEESE POUND CAKE
recipe, page 304

Each Christmas Eddy McGee, a postal worker from Elkin, North Carolina, delivers more than the mail. He brings sweet buttery flavored Cream Cheese Pound Cake to special friends. Simple to make, his recipe calls for only seven ingredients – all kitchen staples – and is hot out of the oven in about one hour. Sure to become a tried-and-true favorite in your home, this classic pound cake rates our "first-class" stamp.

TEE'S CORN PUDDING
recipe, page 318

A classic Southern side dish, Tee's Corn Pudding is rich with Bluegrass tradition. Sharing a love of the Kentucky countryside and its bounty, Sissy Nash of Louisville and daughter, Kathy Nash Cary, work to create a treasured part of their holiday feast. Submitted by Sissy, her mother's recipe will win raves for its creamy goodness at your family's table as well.

CRAB-STUFFED LOBSTER TAILS
recipe, page 326

A celebration dinner need not mean eating out. With our recipe for Crab-Stuffed Lobster Tails, you can turn a home-cooked meal into a memorable occasion. The ingredients will cost about the same as a nice restaurant meal, but you'll savor the results. The combination of lobster, crabmeat, and Garlic-Butter Sauce is sure to rate highly in your kitchen, too.

OUR STYLE

With each new year come resolutions. And the Foods Staff always has the same – to meet your needs by publishing top-quality recipes with high standards. These standards extend to our simple-to-use recipe format that makes it easier than ever to follow directions.

We use bullets (•) to highlight each step and **boldfaced** terms to help you follow recipe procedures. In addition, we often offer helpful hints and cooking tips. You'll find these just below the recipe title, before the ingredients.

We offer you an option to reduce calories, fat, or sodium when you see a heart-shaped symbol (♥) with a note following recipes. Each version is tested so we know how the lightened one compares with the original. The heart symbol also highlights the nutritional analysis on "Living Light" recipes.

We hope keeping your resolutions will be a breeze with our easy-to-follow recipes and emphasis on healthful options.

> Bullets (•) highlight the separation of paragraphs.

> A heart-shaped symbol gives healthier alternatives to lighten selected recipes and also highlights the nutritional analysis on "Living Light" recipes.

SWISS-ONION DIP

With only 5 ingredients, this dip takes only minutes to assemble, and is so easy your teenager could make it for a party without any help from you.

1 (10-ounce) package frozen chopped onion, thawed
3 cups (12 ounces) shredded Swiss cheese
1 cup mayonnaise or salad dressing
1 tablespoon coarse-grained Dijon mustard
⅛ teaspoon pepper

• **Drain** onion on paper towels.
• **Combine** onion and remaining ingredients. Spoon mixture into a 1-quart baking dish.
• **Bake** at 325° for 25 minutes or until bubbly and lightly browned. Serve dip with melba toast rounds. **Yield:** 4 cups.

♥ To reduce fat and calories in the dip, substitute reduced-fat mayonnaise for regular mayonnaise.
Kathy Sellers
Nashville, Tennessee

> Frequently, we'll suggest helpful hints and cooking tips.

> **Boldfaced** terms help you quickly read the steps in the recipe.

> Short paragraphs group the directions for each step.

JANUARY

EVER-CHANGING CHILI
MAKE IT MILD OR MAKE IT WILD

Texans haven't single-handedly roped and tied
the chili market; readers from all over the South sent us creative
results of their culinary experiments. The only thing
that these versions have in common is their humble beginnings:
meat, tomatoes, and chile peppers or powder. After that,
it's uncharted territory. So explore and enjoy.

CHILI VERDE
(pictured on page 38)

¾ pound beef chuck roast, cut into
  1-inch cubes
¾ pound pork loin or shoulder
  roast, cut into 1-inch cubes
1 large onion, chopped
1 large green pepper, chopped
1 clove garlic, minced
2 tablespoons olive oil, divided
2 (16-ounce) cans whole tomatoes,
  undrained and chopped
2 (4½-ounce) cans chopped green
  chiles, undrained
1 cup Burgundy or other dry
  red wine
1 cup salsa
¼ cup chopped fresh cilantro
2 beef bouillon cubes
1 tablespoon brown sugar
3 tablespoons lemon juice
Hot cooked rice
Garnish: fresh cilantro sprigs

• **Combine** first 5 ingredients. Cook
half of mixture in 1 tablespoon olive oil
in a large Dutch oven over medium-
high heat, stirring constantly, until
browned. Remove from Dutch oven;
set aside. Repeat procedure with remaining meat mixture and 1 tablespoon olive oil.
• **Combine** meat mixture, tomatoes,
and next 7 ingredients. Bring to a boil;
cover, reduce heat, and simmer 1 hour
or until meat is tender, stirring occasionally. Serve over rice, and garnish, if
desired. **Yield:** 11 cups.

Fran Pointer
Kansas City, Missouri

BODACIOUS CHILI
(pictured on page 38)

*With such a long list of ingredients,
the name is obviously appropriate. But
none of the items are terribly unusual
or expensive, and it's easy to make. The
flavor? Well, the name again applies.*

2 pounds boneless beef chuck
  roast, cut into 1-inch
  cubes
2 large onions, chopped
3 stalks celery, sliced into 1-inch
  pieces
1 large green pepper, coarsely
  chopped
1 large sweet red pepper, coarsely
  chopped
1 cup sliced fresh mushrooms
2 jalapeño peppers, seeded and
  chopped
4 cloves garlic, minced
3 tablespoons olive oil
2 tablespoons cocoa
2 tablespoons chili powder
1 teaspoon ground cumin
1 teaspoon dried oregano
1 teaspoon paprika
1 teaspoon ground turmeric
½ teaspoon salt
½ teaspoon ground cardamom
¼ teaspoon pepper
1 tablespoon molasses
½ cup Burgundy or other dry
  red wine
2 (16-ounce) cans whole tomatoes,
  undrained and chopped
1 (16-ounce) can kidney beans,
  drained
1 (15-ounce) can chick-peas
  (garbanzo beans),
  drained
Spicy Sour Cream Topping
Shredded Cheddar cheese

• **Cook** first 8 ingredients in olive oil in
a large Dutch oven over medium-high
heat, stirring constantly, until meat
browns. Drain and return meat mixture to Dutch oven.
• **Stir** in cocoa and next 13 ingredients.
Bring mixture to a boil; cover, reduce
heat, and simmer 1½ hours, stirring
occasionally. Serve with Spicy Sour
Cream Topping and shredded cheese.
Yield: 12 cups.

Spicy Sour Cream Topping

1 (8-ounce) carton sour cream
⅓ cup salsa
2 tablespoons mayonnaise
1 teaspoon chili powder
½ teaspoon onion powder
½ teaspoon curry powder
Dash of ground red pepper
1 tablespoon lemon juice
1 teaspoon Dijon mustard

● **Combine** all ingredients; cover and chill. Serve with chili. **Yield:** 1⅔ cups.
Peggy Huffstetler
Lebanon, Tennessee

OUT WEST CHILI

Robert Follett uses pure ground chile peppers (not chili powder, which is a spice blend). Check your produce section or gourmet shops for dried chile peppers, and grind them in your blender or food processor (remove seeds first). Robert's chili is quite thick and could be rolled up in a flour tortilla, burrito style.

4 slices bacon
2½ pounds beef chuck roast, cut into ½-inch cubes
1 medium onion, chopped
2 cloves garlic, finely chopped
2 (6-ounce) cans tomato paste
1 (4½-ounce) can chopped green chiles, undrained
¼ cup masa harina
5 tablespoons ground red chile peppers (not chili powder) *
1½ teaspoons salt
1½ teaspoons ground cumin
¾ teaspoon dried or ¼ teaspoon ground Mexican or regular oregano
4 cups water
1 (15-ounce) can pinto beans, drained
Condiments: shredded cheeses, chopped onion, sour cream

● **Cook** bacon in a large Dutch oven until crisp; remove bacon, reserving 1½ tablespoons drippings in pan. Crumble bacon, and set aside.
● **Cook** beef, onion, and garlic in drippings, stirring constantly, until meat browns.
● **Add** tomato paste and next 7 ingredients to pan, stirring until blended. Bring mixture to a boil; reduce heat, and simmer 1½ hours, stirring mixture occasionally.
● **Stir** in bacon and beans, and simmer 30 additional minutes. Serve chili with desired condiments. **Yield:** 8 cups.

* Substitute 5 dried red chile peppers for ground peppers. Remove seeds, and process peppers in an electric blender until ground.
Robert Follett
Park City, Utah

Bowl of red, pot of fire, stroke of genius.

Those Texan cattle drivers were really onto something when they created chili in the late 1800s. But the spicy sustenance they offered from chuck wagons was much simpler than today's recipes.

BLAND OR BLISTERING?

How do you know before trying a recipe whether you can handle the heat? Here are a few hot tips.

■ Ground chile *peppers* pack more heat than ground chili *powder*, which is actually a blend that includes ground peppers. So the powder will be milder than pure peppers.

■ The heat is hidden in the seeds and inner membranes of dried and fresh chile peppers. Remove and discard both to cool off things a bit.

■ If you know you can't take much heat, try using a little less chile pepper, chili powder, and red or black pepper. Taste toward the end of the cooking time when the flavors have had time to blend; then add more of those ingredients if you want to liven it up.

■ So you followed these tips and it's *still* too hot? Toss in some chunks of raw potato, and simmer 15 minutes. Remove the potato, and hopefully you'll remove some of the heat.

BLACK BEAN CHILI MARSALA

1 large onion, chopped
2 cloves garlic, minced
3 tablespoons vegetable oil
1 (2½-pound) boneless beef
    chuck roast, trimmed and
    chopped
1 (29-ounce) can tomato sauce
2 (6-ounce) cans tomato paste
1 cup Marsala wine *
1 cup water
2 or 3 (4-ounce) cans sliced
    mushrooms, drained
3 to 4 tablespoons chili powder
2 teaspoons seasoned salt
1 teaspoon freshly ground pepper
2 (15-ounce) cans black beans,
    undrained
Hot cooked rice
Garnish: strips of lime rind or
    cilantro sprigs

• **Cook** onion and garlic in oil in a Dutch oven over medium-high heat, stirring constantly, until tender. Add chopped roast and next 8 ingredients.
• **Bring** mixture to a boil. Cover, reduce heat, and simmer 1 hour, stirring occasionally.
• **Add** beans, and cook until thoroughly heated. Serve chili over rice. Garnish, if desired. **Yield:** 12 cups.

* Substitute 1 cup dry white wine plus 1½ tablespoons brandy for Marsala.
Walter C. Lund
Miami, Florida

GREEK CHILI

You may read this recipe and question boiling the ground beef in water instead of browning it. But we followed Judy Ring's directions and came up with the same unusually smooth texture she does.

4 cups water
2 pounds lean ground beef
2 medium onions, chopped
2 (15-ounce) cans tomato
    sauce
4 cloves garlic, finely chopped
3 tablespoons chili powder
2 teaspoons ground cinnamon
1½ teaspoons salt
1 to 1½ tablespoons ground
    allspice
1 teaspoon ground cumin
½ teaspoon ground red pepper
2 bay leaves
2 tablespoons white vinegar
2 tablespoons Worcestershire
    sauce

• **Bring** water to a boil in a large Dutch oven or stockpot. Add beef, and boil 30 minutes, stirring occasionally until it crumbles. Remove and discard fat from top of mixture, if desired.
• **Stir** in onion and remaining ingredients. Bring to a boil; reduce heat, and simmer 2 hours. Remove and discard bay leaves. **Yield:** 10 cups.

Judy Ring
Newport, Kentucky

NOW, THATSA CHILI

Italian sausage and Italian-style tomatoes give this version a subtle twist.

2 pounds lean ground beef
1 pound hot Italian link sausage,
    casings removed
1 large onion, chopped
½ cup sliced fresh mushrooms
1½ tablespoons minced fresh
    garlic
¼ cup chili powder
2 to 3 tablespoons ground cumin
2 (16-ounce) cans Italian-style
    tomatoes, undrained and
    chopped
1 (16-ounce) can kidney beans,
    drained
1 (6-ounce) can tomato paste
⅔ cup beer
¼ cup chopped fresh parsley
¼ cup Burgundy or other dry red
    wine
¼ cup Dijon mustard
1 tablespoon dried oregano
1 tablespoon dried basil
1 teaspoon salt
1 teaspoon pepper
2 tablespoons lemon juice
Condiments: shredded cheese,
    chopped green onions, salsa,
    sour cream

• **Cook** beef and sausage in a large Dutch oven, stirring until meat crumbles and browns. Drain and return to Dutch oven.

SECOND TIME AROUND

■ Spoon chili over a baked potato as a topping.

■ Serve chili over hot cooked spaghetti or noodles – Cincinnati style.

■ Open a snack-size bag of corn chips, and spoon some chili over chips – state-fair style.

■ Use it atop hot dogs. (It beats the canned stuff any day.)

■ Split open cornbread or biscuits, and top with chili.

■ Pull out the inside of a round bread loaf, leaving a bread "shell" or "bowl," and fill the shell with chili.

■ Spoon into miniature baked pastry shells, and sprinkle with cheese.

■ Line a bowl with a warm flour tortilla; then add chili.

■ Serve chili over rice.

■ Mix with melted process cheese, and use as a dip for tortilla chips.

• **Add** onion, mushrooms, and garlic; cook about 3 minutes, stirring constantly. Stir in chili powder and remaining ingredients (except condiments).

• **Bring** to a boil; reduce heat, and simmer 1 to 2 hours, stirring occasionally. Serve with desired condiments. **Yield:** 11 cups.

John C. Justice
Birmingham, Alabama

HIGH-YIELD STOCKS

....

Great Southern cooks have *always* known that homemade gravies, soups, and sauces are only as good as the stock from which they're made. Water and a few inexpensive ingredients can be the beginning of a wonderful meal.

Stocks are usually made by slowly simmering meaty bones and vegetables until they have yielded most of their flavor to the water in which they've been cooked. The liquid is then strained off, and the stock is either served as a hearty broth or used as a delicate foundation for other flavorings in soups and sauces.

Here are methods for making three basic stocks: beef, chicken, and fish. Although they take a long time to make, once preparation has begun, they require little supervision. And each batch yields ample quantities that can be refrigerated or frozen in small containers for future use.

QUICK FULL-BODIED STOCK

2 (14½-ounce) cans ready-to-serve chicken or beef broth
1 large carrot, scraped and sliced
1 medium onion, sliced
1 bay leaf
3 or 4 sprigs fresh parsley

• **Remove** solidified fat from top of broth, if necessary, and discard. Combine broth and remaining ingredients in a medium saucepan.

• **Bring** mixture to a boil over medium heat; cover, reduce heat, and simmer 25 minutes.

• **Pour** mixture through a large wire-mesh strainer into a bowl, discarding solids. Cool stock slightly. Cover and chill up to 2 days, or freeze up to 1 month. **Yield:** 2 cups.

BEEF STOCK

5 pounds beef or veal bones
2 large carrots, quartered
2 large onions, quartered
4 stalks celery, quartered
4 quarts water, divided
3 tablespoons tomato paste
6 or 8 sprigs fresh parsley
3 or 4 sprigs fresh thyme
4 whole cloves
½ teaspoon black peppercorns
1 bay leaf
2 cloves garlic, crushed

• **Place** first 4 ingredients in a large roasting pan; bake at 500° for 1 hour, turning occasionally.

• **Transfer** mixture to a large stockpot; discard drippings from roasting pan. Set aside.

• **Add** 1 quart water to roasting pan; bring to a boil over medium-high heat, stirring to loosen pieces that cling to bottom. Pour into stockpot; add remaining 3 quarts water, tomato paste, and remaining ingredients to stockpot.

• **Bring** to a boil; cover, reduce heat, and simmer 2 hours.

• **Line** a large wire-mesh strainer with a double layer of cheesecloth; place in a large bowl. Pour stock through strainer, discarding solids. Cool stock slightly.

• **Cover** and chill; remove and discard solidified fat from top of stock. Store stock in refrigerator up to 2 days, or freeze up to 1 month. **Yield:** 2 quarts.

RED CHILE SAUCE

2 cups Beef Stock, divided (see recipe)
2 cloves garlic
¼ cup coarsely chopped onion
¼ cup chili powder
1½ tablespoons peanut oil
2 tablespoons all-purpose flour
½ cup tomato sauce
½ teaspoon salt
¼ teaspoon dried oregano
¼ teaspoon ground cumin
⅛ teaspoon ground cloves
⅛ teaspoon ground cinnamon

• **Position** knife blade in food processor bowl; add ¼ cup stock, garlic, and next 4 ingredients. Process until smooth, stopping once to scrape down sides.

• **Transfer** to a heavy saucepan; cook over medium-high heat 2 minutes. Stir in remaining stock, tomato sauce, and remaining ingredients.

• **Bring** to a boil; reduce heat, and simmer 10 minutes or until thickened. Cover and chill up to 3 days or freeze up to 3 months. **Yield:** 1½ cups.

BURNED BOURBON WITH MOLASSES SAUCE

⅓ cup bourbon
4 cups Beef Stock (see recipe)
¾ cup port wine
1 tablespoon molasses
2 tablespoons butter or margarine

• **Bring** bourbon to a boil over medium heat in a long-handled saucepan. Remove from heat; ignite and let stand until flames disappear. Combine bourbon and next 3 ingredients in a heavy saucepan.

• **Bring** to a boil; reduce heat, and simmer 50 minutes or until reduced to about ¾ cup. Remove from heat.

• **Add** butter, 1 teaspoon at a time, stirring until blended. Serve with beef or pork tenderloin. **Yield:** about ¾ cup.

Charles Walton IV
Birmingham, Alabama

CHICKEN STOCK

4 pounds chicken pieces
1 pound chicken wings
4 quarts water
2 onions, peeled and quartered
4 stalks celery with tops, cut into
    2-inch pieces
4 carrots, scraped and cut into
    2-inch pieces
1 large bay leaf
6 sprigs fresh parsley
1 tablespoon fresh thyme or
    1 teaspoon dried thyme
6 sprigs fresh dill or ½ teaspoon
    dried dillweed
½ teaspoon black peppercorns

• **Combine** first 3 ingredients in a large stockpot; bring to a boil, skimming the surface to remove excess fat and foam.
• **Add** onion and remaining ingredients. Return to a boil; reduce heat, and simmer, uncovered, 2 hours, skimming surface to remove excess fat, if necessary. Cool.
• **Line** a large wire-mesh strainer with a double layer of cheesecloth; place in a large bowl. Pour stock through strainer; reserve chicken for other uses, and discard remaining solids. Cool stock slightly.
• **Cover** and chill stock. Remove and discard solidified fat from top of stock. Cover stock, and chill up to 2 days, or freeze up to 1 month. **Yield:** 2 quarts.

CURRY SAUCE

½ cup butter or margarine
⅔ cup finely chopped onion
2 Granny Smith apples, unpeeled,
    cored, and chopped
1 cup sliced mushrooms
⅔ cup all-purpose flour
⅔ cup golden raisins
3 to 4 tablespoons curry powder
½ teaspoon freshly ground pepper
½ teaspoon ground ginger
2 bay leaves
3 cups milk
2 cups Chicken Stock (see recipe)
Juice of 1 lemon
6 cups chopped cooked chicken
Hot cooked rice

• **Melt** butter in a Dutch oven over medium-high heat; add onion, apple, and mushrooms, and cook, stirring constantly, until tender.
• **Stir** in flour and next 5 ingredients. Cook 1 minute, stirring constantly. Gradually add milk and stock; cook, stirring constantly, 10 minutes.

• **Stir** in lemon juice and chicken; cook mixture until thoroughly heated.
• **Remove** and discard bay leaves. Spoon sauce over rice; serve with shredded coconut, chopped cashews, and chutney, if desired. **Yield:** 10 cups.

Louise Jackson
Shreveport, Louisiana

STOCK TIPS

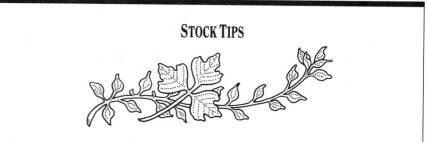

When making stock, the goal is to produce a strong foundation that's clear and distinctly flavored. You'll want to follow these few cardinal rules when making stock.

■ Use a heavyweight stockpot that can hold from 10 to 20 quarts of liquid.

■ To produce a more flavorful stock, cut all vegetables in pieces, remove excess fat from bones, and crack large bones.

■ When making beef stock, roast bones and vegetables in the oven only until golden; overbrowning will damage the stock's flavor and color.

■ If making fish stock, use the heads, bones, and trimmings from any mild whitefish; avoid oily, strong-flavored fish, such as salmon and mackerel, as they will yield a milky, bitter-tasting stock.

■ In order to coax maximum flavor from meat, bones, and vegetables, begin cooking these ingredients in a cold liquid. If the ingredients have been browned first, allow them to cool slightly before adding them to the cold cooking liquid.

■ It's best to bring stock to a boil slowly; then reduce heat and simmer gently throughout cooking time. Rapid boiling will produce a murky, unpalatable stock. Gentle simmering, on the other hand, extracts flavors from ingredients and produces a relatively clear, well-flavored stock.

■ To achieve a clear stock, it's important to carefully skim the fat and foam from the surface of the mixture as it rises to the top during cooking. To make the skimming easier, vegetables and "aromatics" (seasonings) are best added after about one-fourth of the cooking time has elapsed. Once the vegetables are added, do not skim the fat again unless necessary.

■ As a stock simmers, its flavor becomes more pronounced; therefore, you should only add salt after stock is finished cooking.

■ In a hurry? Simmering with aromatic vegetables for 30 minutes or so gives canned broth a tremendous flavor boost.

FISH STOCK

2 leeks
6 to 9 sprigs fresh parsley
1 large bay leaf
4 sprigs fresh basil
4 sprigs fresh rosemary
3 sprigs fresh thyme
2 (2- x ½-inch) strips lemon
   rind
2 (2- x ½-inch) strips orange
   rind
2 tablespoons margarine
1 medium onion, sliced
½ carrot, sliced
2 stalks celery with leaves, coarsely
   chopped
3 pounds fish bones and shrimp
   shells
6 whole peppercorns
2 quarts water
1 cup Chablis or other dry white
   wine
½ teaspoon salt

• **Remove** roots, outer leaves, and green tops of leeks, reserving 2 pieces of tops. Split white portion in half lengthwise, and wash; set aside. Trim reserved green pieces; place parsley and next 6 ingredients on top of 1 green piece; top with other green piece of leek, and tie with string. Set bouquet garni aside.
• **Melt** margarine in a stockpot over medium heat. Add leek, onion, carrot, and celery; cook, stirring constantly, until tender. Add bouquet garni, bones, and next 3 ingredients. Bring to a boil; cover, reduce heat, and simmer 35 minutes.
• **Line** a wire-mesh strainer with a double layer of cheesecloth; place in a bowl. Pour stock into strainer; discarding solids. Stir in salt; cool stock slightly.
• **Cover** and chill stock. Remove and discard solidified fat from top of stock. Cover stock, and chill up to 2 days, or freeze up to 1 month. **Yield:** 1½ quarts.

SHRIMP BISQUE

1 pound unpeeled medium-size
   fresh shrimp
3 tablespoons butter or margarine
3 tablespoons all-purpose flour
1 medium onion, chopped
2 stalks celery
2 cloves garlic, crushed
1 sweet red pepper, coarsely
   chopped
4 cups Fish Stock (see recipe)
1 (8-ounce) can tomato sauce
2 or 3 dashes of hot sauce
1 bay leaf
¼ teaspoon paprika
Garnish: fresh chives

• **Peel** shrimp and devein, if desired; set aside.
• **Melt** butter in a Dutch oven over medium heat; add flour, stirring until smooth. Cook, stirring constantly, 5 minutes, or until golden.
• **Stir** in onion, celery, and garlic; cook, about 3 minutes, stirring constantly. Stir in sweet red pepper; cook 1 minute. Gradually add stock and next 4 ingredients.
• **Bring** to a boil, stirring occasionally. Reduce heat, and simmer 5 minutes.
• **Add** shrimp; cook 5 minutes or until shrimp turn pink. Remove and discard bay leaf. Spoon into individual bowls; garnish, if desired. **Yield:** 6½ cups.

Marie Davis
Charlotte, North Carolina

WHAT'S FOR SUPPER?

AFTER-CHRISTMAS CASSEROLE

. . . .

Your holiday guests are gone, the decorations are down, and the house is back to normal. All that remains are wonderful memories and the leftover ham and turkey. Ham-and-Turkey Spaghetti is easy to prepare. And our Test Kitchens staff has waved its magic wand once again – lowering the calories by substituting some reduced-fat products, yet keeping the flavor rich and creamy.

HAM-AND-TURKEY SPAGHETTI

Just add your favorite green vegetable and a salad to this entrée, and you've got a complete meal.

1 (8-ounce) package thin
   spaghetti, uncooked
2 tablespoons butter or
   margarine
6 green onions, sliced
1½ cups sliced fresh mushrooms
1½ cups chopped cooked
   ham
1½ cups chopped cooked turkey
   or chicken
1 (12-ounce) carton nonfat
   cottage cheese
1 (8-ounce) carton reduced-fat
   sour cream
2 tablespoons milk
¼ teaspoon salt
¼ teaspoon celery salt
¼ to ½ teaspoon pepper
1 cup (4 ounces) shredded
   reduced-fat sharp Cheddar
   cheese

• **Cook** spaghetti according to package directions; drain and set aside.
• **Melt** butter in a skillet over medium-high heat; add green onions and mushrooms, and cook, stirring constantly, until crisp-tender. Add ham and turkey; toss gently. Set mixture aside.
• **Combine** cottage cheese, sour cream, milk, salt, celery salt, and pepper in a large bowl; add spaghetti and meat mixture. Toss gently. Spoon mixture into a lightly greased 13- x 9- x 2-inch baking dish.
• **Cover** and bake at 350° for 45 minutes. Uncover; sprinkle with shredded cheese. Bake 5 additional minutes. **Yield:** 8 servings.

Sharlie G. Rigby
Batesville, Arkansas

CELEBRATE IN A NEW LIGHT

Resolve to celebrate New Year's Eve at home this year. Invite a couple of treasured friends to a quiet celebration by the firelight. You'll avoid the crowds, the noise, and another calorie-laden holiday meal. Our celebration menu, with only 466 calories and 6.3 fat grams, lets you say "cheers" without reservations.

NEW YEAR'S EVE MENU
Serves Four

Country Crab Cakes
Rosemary-Roasted Potatoes
Steamed Asparagus
Strawberry-Champagne Sorbet

COUNTRY CRAB CAKES

3 ounces thinly sliced country ham, trimmed
¼ cup egg substitute
1 tablespoon baking powder
1 teaspoon Old Bay seasoning
1 tablespoon chopped fresh parsley
1 tablespoon reduced-sodium Worcestershire sauce
1 tablespoon reduced-fat mayonnaise
2 slices white bread
1 pound fresh lump crabmeat, drained
Vegetable cooking spray
Lemon slices

• **Place** ham in a large nonstick skillet, overlapping slices as needed. Add water to cover. Cook over high heat 3 minutes. Remove ham, and drain. Finely chop ham; set aside.
• **Combine** egg substitute and next 5 ingredients in a large bowl; set aside.
• **Remove** crusts from bread; discard crusts. Tear bread into ½-inch pieces; add bread and ham to egg substitute mixture. Let stand until liquid is absorbed. Stir well. Fold in crabmeat, and shape into 8 patties.
• **Cook** patties in a nonstick skillet coated with cooking spray until lightly browned, turning once. Serve with lemon slices. **Yield:** 4 servings.

♥ Per serving: Calories 194 (25% from fat)
Fat 5.3g (0.5g saturated) Cholesterol 99mg
Sodium 1103mg Carbohydrate 8.7g
Fiber 0.3g Protein 26.4g

ROSEMARY-ROASTED POTATOES

3 large baking potatoes, unpeeled
Olive oil-flavored cooking spray
¼ teaspoon salt
1½ teaspoons dried rosemary
½ teaspoon freshly ground pepper

• **Wash** potatoes, and pat dry; cut into ¼-inch slices. Arrange slices into 4 rows on a baking sheet coated with cooking spray, overlapping half of each slice with the next. Sprinkle with salt.
• **Combine** rosemary and pepper; sprinkle potato with half of mixture. Set remaining mixture aside.
• **Bake** at 375° for 20 minutes; turn potato over. Coat with cooking spray, and sprinkle with remaining rosemary mixture. Bake 20 additional minutes. **Yield:** 4 servings.

♥ Per serving: Calories 110 (7% from fat)
Fat 0.9g (0g saturated) Cholesterol 0mg
Sodium 157mg Carbohydrate 23.3g
Fiber 2.6g Protein 3.1g

STRAWBERRY-CHAMPAGNE SORBET

½ cup sugar
½ cup water
1 (10-ounce) package frozen strawberries, thawed and undrained
2 tablespoons lemon juice
1½ cups champagne
Fresh whole strawberries

• **Combine** sugar and water in a heavy saucepan; cook over medium heat, stirring constantly, until sugar dissolves. Remove sugar syrup from heat; cool.
• **Place** thawed strawberries in container of an electric blender or food processor; process until smooth. Pour through a wire-mesh strainer into an 8-inch square pan, pressing with back of spoon against the sides of the strainer to squeeze out juice. Discard pulp and seeds. Stir lemon juice, sugar syrup, and champagne into strawberry puree. Cover and freeze at least 4 hours.

- **Position** knife blade in food processor bowl; add frozen mixture, and process until smooth. Return to pan, and freeze until firm. Repeat processing procedure, and return mixture to pan; freeze until firm.
- **Spoon** into glasses, and serve with fresh strawberries. **Yield:** 3 cups.

♥ Per ½-cup serving: Calories 127 (0% from fat)
Fat 0g (0g saturated) Cholesterol 0mg
Sodium 4mg Carbohydrate 22.1g
Fiber 0.4g Protein 0.4g

APPETIZERS ON THE CHEESY SIDE

....

If saying "Cheese!" makes you smile, you'll be grinning from ear to ear when you bite into these cheese-packed appetizers. Even the straight-faced won't be able to turn these morsels down.

Each easy-to-make selection takes advantage of a different kind of cheese. You'll be able to find all of them at the cheese counter of large supermarkets or cheese shops. Fontina cheese might be the only scarce one – if you can't find it in your grocery store, substitute Swiss instead.

OREGANO CHEESE PUFFS

Fontina cheese contains about 45% butterfat, so it's smooth in texture and is packed with a creamy rich flavor – definitely worth a try.

¾ cup milk
3 tablespoons butter or margarine
¾ cup all-purpose flour
½ teaspoon salt
⅛ teaspoon pepper
3 large eggs
½ cup (2 ounces) shredded fontina cheese, divided
1½ teaspoons dried oregano

- **Bring** milk and butter to a boil in a medium saucepan. Reduce heat to low; add flour, salt, and pepper all at once, stirring vigorously until mixture leaves sides of pan and forms a smooth ball. Remove from heat, and cool 5 to 10 minutes.
- **Add** eggs, one at a time, beating with a wooden spoon after each addition. Stir in ¼ cup cheese and oregano. Drop by level tablespoonfuls onto greased baking sheets.
- **Bake** cheese puffs at 400° for 18 minutes. Sprinkle with remaining cheese, and bake 2 to 3 additional minutes. Serve immediately. **Yield:** 2½ dozen.

Valerie Stutsman
Norfolk, Virginia

MEXICAN PINWHEELS

If you want to dress up these pinwheels, spoon a tablespoon or two of salsa onto each individual plate. Place three pinwheels on top of the salsa, and serve it as a seated appetizer.

2 cups (8 ounces) shredded Cheddar cheese
½ cup sour cream
1 (8-ounce) package cream cheese, softened
1 (4½-ounce) can chopped green chiles, drained
1 (2¼-ounce) can sliced ripe olives, drained
⅔ cup chopped green onions
1 clove garlic, pressed
¼ teaspoon seasoned salt
8 (8-inch) flour tortillas
Salsa

- **Combine** first 8 ingredients. Spread ½ cup mixture over each tortilla; roll up tortillas, jellyroll fashion. Wrap each separately in plastic wrap.
- **Chill** up to 8 hours.
- **Unwrap** each roll and cut into 12 slices. Secure pinwheels with wooden picks, if desired. Serve with salsa. **Yield:** 8 dozen.

Note: Rolls may be frozen up to 1 month. To serve, thaw and slice.

MARINATED CHEESE

To make these appetizers ahead of time, marinate the cheese overnight in the refrigerator. You can also toast the bread slices a day ahead and store at room temperature wrapped in towels. Assemble the cheese and crostini ("little crusts") right before your party.

¾ pound fresh mozzarella cheese in brine
1 (8-ounce) bottle olive oil vinaigrette
1 clove garlic, crushed
¼ teaspoon freshly ground pepper
1 French baguette, cut into thin slices
Garnish: cherry tomato slices, fresh basil, or parsley sprigs

- **Remove** cheese from brine; discard brine. Cut cheese into ¼-inch-thick slices. Place cheese in a single layer in a shallow dish.
- **Combine** vinaigrette, garlic, and pepper; pour over cheese. Cover and chill 8 hours.
- **Place** bread slices on a baking sheet. Bake at 350° for 8 minutes or until lightly toasted, turning once.
- **Drain** cheese. Place one cheese slice on each bread slice. Garnish, if desired. **Yield:** 20 appetizer servings.

Note: To reduce costs, use one 8-ounce package mozzarella cheese, and cut into ¼-inch-thick slices.

FRIED STUFFED JALAPEÑO PEPPERS

Using canned peppers makes for quick work. When frying, let the oil return to the specified temperature before adding the next batch.

1 (10-ounce) can whole pickled
    jalapeño peppers, drained
⅔ cup pimiento cheese
¾ cup all-purpose flour, divided
¼ cup plus 2 tablespoons
    cornmeal, divided
¼ teaspoon salt
¼ teaspoon pepper
1 cup buttermilk
Vegetable oil

• **Cut** stems from peppers. Remove seeds, using a small sharp knife (do not split peppers). Stuff each with pimiento cheese. Cover and chill at least 2 hours.
• **Combine** ¼ cup flour, 2 tablespoons cornmeal, and next 3 ingredients; set batter aside.
• **Combine** remaining ½ cup flour and ¼ cup cornmeal.
• **Dip** stuffed peppers in batter; dredge in flour mixture.
• **Pour** oil to depth of 2 to 3 inches in a Dutch oven; heat to 375°. Fry peppers, a few at a time, 1 to 2 minutes on each side or until golden. Drain on paper towels. **Yield:** about 12 appetizers.

DeLea Lonadier
Montgomery, Louisiana

SUPER SPUD TOPPERS

....

Pump up your potatoes with these tasty toppings, and turn ordinary baked potatoes into super spuds.

When shopping, buy medium (6- to 8-ounce) or large (8- to 10-ounce) baking potatoes. For a tenderer skin, lightly coat potatoes with oil before baking. If you're pressed for time, microwave potatoes, pricking or piercing the skins before cooking to prevent bursting.

CRABMEAT-TOPPED POTATOES

4 large baking potatoes
1 tablespoon butter or margarine
¼ cup chopped green pepper
¼ cup chopped green onions
1 (8-ounce) package cream cheese,
    softened
1 (6-ounce) can crabmeat, drained
¼ cup milk
½ cup sour cream
½ teaspoon ground white
    pepper
¼ teaspoon garlic powder

• **Scrub** potatoes; prick several times with a fork.
• **Bake** potatoes at 400° for 1 hour or until done.
• **Melt** butter in a large skillet; add green pepper and green onions, and cook over medium-high heat, stirring constantly, until tender.
• **Add** cream cheese, crabmeat, and milk. Cook over low heat, stirring constantly, until mixture is smooth.
• **Remove** from heat; add sour cream, white pepper, and garlic powder. Serve over split baked potatoes. **Yield:** 4 servings.

Tricia Chaffin
Little Rock, Arkansas

GUMBO POTATOES

4 large baking potatoes
½ cup chopped onion
¼ cup chopped celery
1 tablespoon vegetable oil
2 cups chopped cooked chicken
¼ teaspoon salt
¼ teaspoon pepper
1 (10¾-ounce) can condensed
    chicken gumbo, undiluted
2 tablespoons ketchup
2 tablespoons prepared
    mustard

• **Scrub** potatoes; prick several times with a fork.
• **Bake** potatoes at 400° for 1 hour or until done.
• **Cook** onion and celery in oil in a skillet over medium-high heat, stirring constantly, until tender. Stir in chicken and next 5 ingredients; simmer 15 minutes, stirring occasionally. Serve over split baked potatoes. **Yield:** 4 servings.

Janice M. France
Louisville, Kentucky

BLACK-EYED PEA-SPINACH-STUFFED POTATOES

(pictured on page 39)

6 large baking potatoes
1 (10-ounce) package frozen
    chopped spinach, thawed
1 (15½-ounce) can black-eyed
    peas, drained
1 (16-ounce) can whole tomatoes,
    drained and chopped
½ cup chopped sweet red pepper
¼ cup finely chopped onion
1 tablespoon chopped fresh
    cilantro
3 tablespoons lime juice
1 tablespoon olive oil
1 clove garlic, minced
½ teaspoon ground cumin
¼ teaspoon salt
Dash of hot sauce (optional)
Garnish: fresh cilantro sprigs

• **Scrub** potatoes; prick several times with a fork.
• **Bake** potatoes at 400° for 1 hour or until done.
• **Press** spinach between paper towels to remove excess moisture.
• **Combine** spinach and next 10 ingredients; stir in hot sauce, if desired. Serve over split baked potatoes. Garnish, if desired. **Yield:** 6 servings.

ROSEMARY-BAKED POTATOES

Savor the lemony-pine herb flavor in Rosemary-Baked Potatoes. They taste so good, you'll never miss the butter and sour cream.

4 medium baking potatoes
8 fresh rosemary sprigs
Vegetable oil
1 tablespoon plus 1 teaspoon coarse sea salt

• **Scrub** potatoes, and pat dry. Cut each potato in half lengthwise, cutting to, but not through, the opposite side. Place 2 rosemary sprigs in center of each potato; fold halves back together. Rub potato skins with vegetable oil; sprinkle potatoes evenly with sea salt. Wrap in foil.
• **Bake** at 400° for 1 hour or until done. **Yield:** 4 servings.

CINNAMON-APPLE SWEET POTATOES

4 medium-size sweet potatoes
1½ cups finely chopped cooking apples
½ cup orange juice
¼ cup sugar
1½ teaspoons cornstarch
½ teaspoon ground cinnamon
½ teaspoon grated orange rind

• **Scrub** potatoes; prick several times with a fork.
• **Place** sweet potatoes on a baking sheet, and bake at 375° for 1 hour or until done.
• **Combine** chopped apple, orange juice, sugar, cornstarch, cinnamon, and orange rind in a 2-quart baking dish.
• **Cover** and microwave at HIGH 3 minutes; uncover.
• **Stir** mixture, and microwave at HIGH 2 additional minutes or until sauce thickens. Serve over split baked sweet potatoes. **Yield:** 4 servings.
Sara A. McCullough
Zavalla, Texas

TIGHTEN YOUR BELT

The frenzied holiday season is over. After spending more than you should and eating more than you thought possible, welcome January with these low-fat, inexpensive, quick-to-fix entrées.

BEAN-AND-HOMINY SOUP

3 (15½-ounce) cans Great Northern beans, undrained
1 (15½-ounce) can hominy, undrained
1 (14½-ounce) can no-salt-added stewed tomatoes, undrained
1 (11½-ounce) can bean with bacon soup, undiluted
1 (10-ounce) can diced tomatoes and green chiles, undrained
1 (11-ounce) can whole kernel yellow corn, undrained
2 cups water
2 bay leaves
1 tablespoon dried cilantro
1 teaspoon ground cumin
1 cup (4 ounces) shredded reduced-fat sharp Cheddar cheese

• **Combine** all ingredients except cheese in a large Dutch oven. Bring to a boil; cover, reduce heat, and simmer 30 minutes. Remove and discard bay leaves; sprinkle each serving evenly with shredded cheese. **Yield:** 12 cups.
Anne S. Miller
Longwood, Florida

♥ Per 1½-cup serving: Calories 326 (24% from fat)
Fat 6.2g (1.6g saturated) Cholesterol 10mg
Sodium 714mg Carbohydrate 28.1g
Fiber 7.8g Protein 15.9g

SWEET POTATO-AND-SAUSAGE SOUP

½ pound reduced-fat smoked sausage, cut into ½-inch slices
1 medium-size sweet potato, peeled and cut into ½-inch cubes
1 cup coarsely shredded cabbage
½ cup chopped green pepper
½ cup chopped celery
½ cup chopped onion
1 (16-ounce) can no-salt-added tomatoes, undrained and chopped
1 (15½-ounce) can crowder peas, undrained
1 (13¾-ounce) can ready-to-serve, no-salt-added, fat-free beef-flavored broth
¼ teaspoon hot sauce

• **Combine** all ingredients in a large Dutch oven; bring to a boil over medium-high heat. Cover, reduce heat, and simmer 30 minutes or until potato is tender. **Yield:** 7 cups.
Dorothy J. Callaway
Thomasville, Georgia

♥ Per serving: Calories 310 (34% from fat)
Fat 11.9g (5.2g saturated) Cholesterol 30mg
Sodium 886mg Carbohydrate 36.5g
Fiber 2.4g Protein 15.9g

CHANGE YOUR EATING HABITS FOR GOOD

Beverly Gianna of New Orleans changed her eating habits for good after a weeklong stay at a health spa five years ago. Here she shares some tips she's learned along the way.

■ Drinking water will not cause you to rust. Drink it throughout the day instead of sodas.

■ Who needs health clubs when there's a car to wash, a garden to tend, and housework to do? Even scrubbing the bathtub can be rejuvenating.

■ When your favorite dinner is a toss-up between restaurant fare or carryout, watching your weight can be a challenge. Check with a restaurant to see if the menu includes healthful entrées or if you can request a dish prepared in a certain way.

■ Ask for half orders of a dish if you know you'll eat the entire serving before anything has a chance to reach a doggy bag.

■ Instead of a big noon meal, have several "mini-meals" throughout the day. Keep a stash of bottled water, yogurt, and fresh fruit at work for a midday break.

■ Eat healthy foods; forget about empty high-fat calories, and losing weight will be a welcome by-product.

BEEF HASH

Hash is the perfect way to use leftover roast beef. If you don't have any leftovers, buy 5 ounces of lean deli roast beef.

1 cup cubed cooked lean beef
1 cup peeled, cubed potato
½ cup chopped onion
1 tablespoon chopped fresh parsley
¼ teaspoon salt
¼ teaspoon pepper
2 teaspoons vegetable oil
⅓ cup skim milk

• **Combine** first 6 ingredients.
• **Cook** mixture in hot oil in a large nonstick skillet over medium-high heat 10 minutes or until mixture is browned and potatoes are tender, stirring occasionally. Stir in milk; cover, reduce heat, and simmer 5 minutes. **Yield:** 2 servings.

Suzan L. Wiener
Spring Hill, Florida

♥ Per serving: Calories 282 (30% from fat)
Fat 9.4g (1.7g saturated) Cholesterol 63mg
Sodium 366mg Carbohydrate 21.5g
Fiber 2.1g Protein 26.9g

LEMON-ROASTED CHICKEN

Always roast chicken with the skin on. The skin keeps the chicken moist, and the fat won't absorb into the meat. Be sure to remove the skin before serving.

1½ teaspoons salt
2 teaspoons freshly ground pepper
2 to 3 teaspoons dried rosemary, crushed
1 (3-pound) broiler-fryer
1 medium lemon, cut in half

• **Combine** first 3 ingredients; set aside.
• **Loosen** skin from chicken breast by running fingers between the two; rub 1 teaspoon seasoning mixture under skin. Rub remaining seasoning mixture over outside of chicken. Place chicken in a heavy-duty, zip-top plastic bag; seal and store in refrigerator 8 hours.

• **Remove** chicken from bag. Insert lemon halves in cavity; tie ends of legs together with string. Lift wing tips up and over back, and tuck under bird. Place chicken, breast side down, in a lightly greased shallow pan.
• **Bake** at 450°, turning over every 15 minutes, for 50 minutes or until a meat thermometer registers 180°. Let chicken stand 10 minutes. Remove skin before serving. **Yield:** 4 servings.

Clay Nordan
Birmingham, Alabama

♥ Per 3-ounce serving without skin:
Breast meat:
Calories 116 Fat 2g Cholesterol 72mg
Drumstick meat:
Calories 132 Fat 3g Cholesterol 79mg
Thigh meat:
Calories 150 Fat 7g Cholesterol 81mg

SALMON BURGERS

1 (15-ounce) can pink salmon, undrained
1 large egg, lightly beaten
½ cup unsalted saltine cracker crumbs
¼ cup finely chopped onion
¼ cup finely chopped celery
½ teaspoon baking powder
Vegetable cooking spray
½ cup nonfat mayonnaise
2 tablespoons lemon juice
½ teaspoon dried dillweed
¼ teaspoon pepper
¼ teaspoon hot sauce
6 onion sandwich rolls, split
6 tomato slices
1 cup shredded lettuce

• **Drain** salmon, reserving liquid; remove and discard skin and bones. Flake salmon with a fork.
• **Combine** salmon and next 5 ingredients. Add 1 to 2 tablespoons reserved liquid, stirring until mixture sticks together. Shape into 6 patties, and set aside.
• **Coat** a large nonstick skillet with cooking spray; add salmon patties, and cook over medium heat about 4 minutes on each side or until lightly browned. Keep warm.

• **Combine** mayonnaise and next 4 ingredients; spread on cut sides of rolls. Place a salmon patty on bottom half of each roll; top each with a tomato slice, lettuce, and top half of bun. **Yield:** 6 servings.

♥ Per serving: Calories 322 (22% from fat)
Fat 7.9g (1.5g saturated) Cholesterol 84mg
Sodium 793mg Carbohydrate 41.7g
Fiber 0.5g Protein 21.6g

CHICKEN NOODLE SALAD

Be sure you buy the low-fat version of ramen noodles. Regular ramen noodles can have as much as 17 fat grams in a 3-ounce package.

1 (3-ounce) package low-fat Oriental-flavored ramen noodle soup mix
2 cups water
1 stalk celery, chopped
1 large carrot, scraped and chopped
3 green onions, chopped
½ cup chopped green pepper
½ cup cooked chopped chicken breast meat
1 tablespoon reduced-fat mayonnaise
2 teaspoons low-sodium soy sauce
1 teaspoon lemon juice
¼ teaspoon ground red pepper

• **Remove** seasoning packet from soup mix; set aside.
• **Bring** water to a boil; stir in noodles, and cook 3 minutes; drain and set aside.
• **Combine** seasoning packet from soup mix, celery, and next 8 ingredients in a medium bowl. Gently stir in cooked noodles. Cover and chill. **Yield:** 4 cups.

Ann Winniford
Dallas, Texas

♥ Per 2-cup serving: Calories 281 (16% from fat)
Fat 5.1g (0.8g saturated) Cholesterol 39mg
Sodium 1,121mg Carbohydrate 39.9g
Fiber 2.6g Protein 19.8g

Cary Shackelford, a chef from Chattanooga, Tennessee, with food professionals Richard R. Arnold and Marguerite Moses, R.D., have won the American Culinary Federation's National School Lunch Challenge. Entrants were faced with the dilemma of creating tasty, economical, low-fat dishes that the average 8-year-old would love. Here's one of Cary's kid-approved recipes.

Turkey Taco Salad: Brown 1 pound ground skinless turkey in a large nonstick skillet, stirring until it crumbles. Drain turkey, and pat dry with paper towels. Wipe pan drippings from skillet with a paper towel. Return browned turkey to skillet. Stir in 1 (1¼-ounce) package taco seasoning mix and ¾ cup water; cook turkey mixture 10 minutes, stirring often. On each of four plates, layer 1½ cups baked tortilla chips, ½ cup shredded lettuce, one-fourth of turkey mixture, ¼ cup shredded reduced-fat American cheese, ¼ cup fresh, chopped tomato, 1 tablespoon salsa, and 1 tablespoon nonfat sour cream. **Yield:** 4 servings.

MAMMA MIA PASTA

6 ounces wheel-shaped (rotelle) pasta, uncooked
4 cloves garlic, minced
1 medium onion, finely chopped
2 teaspoons olive oil
1 (14½-ounce) can no-salt-added whole tomatoes, undrained and chopped
1 tablespoon tomato paste
2 teaspoons sugar
2 teaspoons dried oregano
1 teaspoon dried basil
¼ teaspoon salt
¼ teaspoon freshly ground pepper
¼ cup freshly grated Parmesan cheese
½ cup (2 ounces) shredded part-skim mozzarella cheese, divided

• **Cook** pasta according to package directions, omitting salt and oil; drain pasta, and set aside.
• **Cook** garlic and onion in olive oil in a large skillet over medium heat until tender. Add tomatoes and next 6 ingredients; cook 5 minutes.
• **Add** Parmesan cheese and ¼ cup mozzarella cheese, stirring until cheese melts. Pour over cooked pasta. Sprinkle with remaining ¼ cup mozzarella cheese. **Yield:** 3 servings.

Caroline Wallace Kennedy
Newborn, Georgia

♥ Per serving: Calories 389 (22% from fat)
Fat 9.6g (2.8g saturated) Cholesterol 16mg
Sodium 479mg Carbohydrate 59.2g
Fiber 2.8g Protein 17.4g

SERVE THESE CASSEROLES ON THE SIDE

....

Finding a new vegetable recipe to please even your most finicky relatives is often a challenge. Here we share an assortment sure to pass the test. These recipes offer a variety of flavor combinations that perfectly complement roasted meats and poultry.

CREAMY RICE AND SQUASH CASSEROLE

Tomatoes, basil, and Parmesan cheese accent this recipe with Italian-style flavor.

¼ cup plus 1 tablespoon butter or margarine, divided
2 cups chopped yellow squash
1 cup chopped onion
2 (14½-ounce) cans diced tomatoes, drained
¼ cup all-purpose flour
2 cups chicken broth
4 cups cooked rice
½ cup whipping cream
1 tablespoon dried basil
1 tablespoon dried parsley flakes
¼ teaspoon pepper
¼ cup grated Parmesan cheese

• **Melt** 1 tablespoon butter in a large skillet over medium-high heat; add squash, onion, and tomatoes, and cook until squash is tender, stirring often. Set vegetables aside.
• **Melt** remaining ¼ cup butter in a medium saucepan over low heat; add flour, stirring until smooth. Cook 1 minute, stirring constantly. Gradually add chicken broth; cook over medium heat, stirring constantly, until mixture is thickened.
• **Stir** in vegetables, rice, and next 4 ingredients. Pour into a lightly greased

11- x 7- x 1½-inch baking dish. Sprinkle with cheese.
• **Bake** at 350° for 30 minutes or until mixture is thoroughly heated. **Yield:** 8 to 10 servings.

Lorraine Brownell
Salisbury, North Carolina

FRENCH ONION CASSEROLE

Your family will think the creamy sauce in this casserole was hard to make – only you will know that you relied on canned products.

3 medium-size sweet onions
2 tablespoons butter or margarine
1 (8-ounce) package fresh mushrooms, sliced
2 cups (8 ounces) shredded Swiss cheese, divided
1 (10¾-ounce) can cream of mushroom soup, undiluted
1 (5-ounce) can evaporated milk
2 teaspoons soy sauce
6 (½-inch-thick) slices French bread
¼ cup finely chopped fresh parsley

• **Cut** onions crosswise into ¼-inch slices; cut each of the slices in half.
• **Melt** butter in a large skillet over medium-high heat; cook onion and mushrooms, stirring constantly, until tender.
• **Spoon** mixture into a lightly greased 2-quart baking dish. Sprinkle with 1 cup cheese.
• **Combine** soup, milk, and soy sauce; pour over cheese. Top with bread slices, and sprinkle with remaining 1 cup cheese and parsley.
• **Cover** and chill 4 to 8 hours. Remove baking dish from refrigerator, and let stand at room temperature 30 minutes.
• **Cover** and bake at 375° for 30 minutes. Uncover and bake 15 to 20 additional minutes or until thoroughly heated. Let stand 5 minutes before serving. **Yield:** 6 servings.

Ellie Wells
Lakeland, Florida

SWISS VEGETABLE MEDLEY

The French fried onions make this dish a family favorite.

1 (16-ounce) bag frozen broccoli, carrots, and cauliflower, thawed and drained
1 (10¾-ounce) can cream of celery soup, undiluted
⅓ cup sour cream
1 (4-ounce) jar diced pimientos, drained
¼ teaspoon pepper
1 cup (4 ounces) shredded Swiss cheese, divided
1 (2½-ounce) can French fried onions, divided

• **Combine** broccoli, soup, sour cream, pimiento, and pepper. Stir in ½ cup cheese and half of onions. Spoon mixture into a lightly greased 1½-quart baking dish.
• **Cover** and bake at 350° for 40 to 45 minutes. Uncover and sprinkle with remaining cheese and onions. Bake 5 additional minutes. **Yield:** 4 to 6 servings.

Miriam C. Colimore
Cockeysville, Maryland

CASSEROLES FOR A CROWD

Casseroles are easy to double or triple. But before preparing extra food to serve guests, consider:

■ **Your time.** If you increase a recipe's size, allow more time for preparation, chilling, and cooking.

■ **Your equipment.** Be sure your food processor, blender, mixer, mixing bowls, and cookware can handle increased amounts.

■ **Your ingredients.** Don't automatically increase seasoning – it doesn't take much to permeate an entire dish. Taste and adjust.

SAVANNAH STYLE

Savannah represents the South well. Its historic homes and
buildings and time-honored recipes are Southern traditions you'll want
to read about in this cookbook.

To help folks enjoy a little of this venerable city in Georgia no matter where they live, the local Junior League captures both the region's history and recipes in *Savannah Style*. The efforts must have been successful because this book's reputation has traveled far. Rumor has it that a man bought a copy at a thrift store in China. He liked it so much that he wrote to inquire about ordering more.

CASSEROLE OF BLACK BEANS

*Savannah enjoys the influence of
its Caribbean neighbors to the south
with foods like black beans.*

1   pound dried black beans
6   cups water
1½ cups coarsely chopped
      onion
1½ cups coarsely chopped
      celery
1   carrot, scraped and chopped
2   cloves garlic, minced
1   tablespoon finely chopped
      fresh parsley
1½ tablespoons salt
½   teaspoon freshly ground
      pepper
¼   teaspoon dried oregano
2   bay leaves
Dash of ground red pepper
¼   cup butter or margarine
¼   cup dark rum (optional)
Sour cream

● **Sort** and wash beans; place in a Dutch oven. Add 6 cups water; bring to a boil over high heat. Remove from heat; cover and let stand 1 hour.
● **Add** onion and next 9 ingredients. Bring to a boil; cover, reduce heat to low, and simmer 2 hours. Remove and discard bay leaves.
● **Spoon** bean mixture into a lightly greased 3-quart casserole. Stir in butter and rum, if desired.
● **Cover** and bake at 350° for 1 hour or until beans are tender. Serve with a slotted spoon. Top each serving with sour cream. **Yield:** 8 servings.

SAVANNAH RED RICE

2   (16-ounce) cans whole
      tomatoes, undrained
6   slices bacon
½   cup chopped onion
½   cup chopped celery
¼   cup chopped green
      pepper
2   cups long-grain rice,
      uncooked
2   teaspoons salt
1   teaspoon sugar
¼   teaspoon pepper
⅛   teaspoon hot sauce

● **Place** tomatoes in container of an electric blender; process until smooth, and set aside.
● **Cook** bacon in a large skillet until crisp; remove bacon, reserving 1½ tablespoons drippings in skillet. Crumble bacon, and set aside.
● **Cook** onion, celery, and green pepper in bacon drippings over medium- high heat until tender; stir in pureed tomatoes, rice, and remaining ingredients. Cook mixture over medium heat 10 minutes.
● **Spoon** into a lightly greased 3-quart baking dish.
● **Cover** and bake at 350° for 1 hour. **Yield:** 8 servings.

MEMMIE'S SPOONBREAD

1½ cups boiling water
1   cup cornmeal
1   teaspoon salt
2   tablespoons butter or
      margarine
1   cup milk
2   large eggs, lightly beaten
2   teaspoons baking powder

● **Pour** water over cornmeal gradually, stirring until smooth. Add salt and butter, stirring until blended; cool 10 minutes. Gradually stir in milk and eggs. Add baking powder, stirring until blended. Pour mixture into a lightly greased 1½-quart baking dish.
● **Bake** at 375° for 40 minutes or until lightly browned. **Yield:** 4 to 6 servings.

OLD FAVORITES MADE NEW

MAMA'S COOKING JUST GOT BETTER

Some of Mama's recipes have changed a bit over time. Old standbys have been updated and redefined from generations past to better fit today's lifestyle. But the secret ingredient – love – remains generously sprinkled throughout.

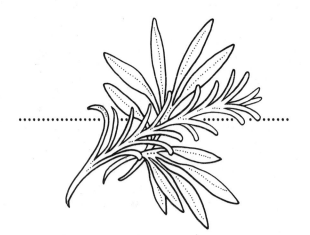

■ As a child of the fifties, **Mary Beth House** describes her mother as a combination of "Donna Reed, Harriet Nelson, and June Cleaver." Mary Beth shares her mother's definition of and recipe for Standing Rib Roast.

"One evening as Mother was fixing a standing rib roast, I asked, 'What is the difference between a standing rib roast and a sitting rib roast?' In her flippant manner, Mother answered, 'It's all in the way the cow is slaughtered; some stand up and some sit down.' Years later, when I studied cuts of meat in home economics class, I felt very important being able to explain the difference in these two roasts. I could not understand why everyone was laughing. After all, my mother would *never* lie to me. It was with great embarrassment that I finished that course."

STANDING RIB ROAST

1 (5- to 6-pound) rib roast (3 ribs)
Steamed new potatoes (optional)
Steamed carrots (optional)
Garnishes: fresh sage sprigs, fresh
    rosemary sprigs

● **Place** roast, fat side up, on a rack in a shallow roasting pan. Insert meat thermometer, making sure it does not touch fat or bone.
● **Bake** at 350° for 2 hours or until meat thermometer registers 145° (medium-rare) or 160° (medium). Let stand 10 minutes before slicing. If desired, serve with new potatoes and carrots, if desired. Garnish, if desired. **Yield:** 8 to 10 servings.

Mary Beth House
Chapel Hill, North Carolina

■ **Sunny Tiedemann** started collecting recipes 37 years ago, as a young bride. Like other family favorites, Crunchy Crisp Salad has changed a bit over time. Light mayonnaise, balsamic vinegar, and white wine Worcestershire sauce have replaced the original dressing ingredients. Instead of croutons, this main-dish salad is topped with cheese crackers.

CRUNCHY CRISP SALAD

1 to 2 cloves garlic
½ teaspoon salt
½ cup reduced-fat mayonnaise
1 tablespoon balsamic or red wine
    vinegar
1 teaspoon lemon juice
½ teaspoon white wine
    Worcestershire sauce
4 cups torn salad greens
3 tomatoes, coarsely chopped
2 cups chopped cooked
    chicken
1 cup bite-size square cheese
    snack crackers
Garnish: tomato slices

● **Crush** garlic in a bowl. Add salt, and continue crushing until blended. Stir in mayonnaise and next 3 ingredients; cover and chill at least 1 hour.
● **Combine** salad greens, tomato, and chicken. Just before serving, add crackers and dressing; toss. Serve immediately. Garnish, if desired. **Yield:** 4 servings.

Ruth "Sunny" F. Tiedemann
Bartlesville, Oklahoma

■ "My grandmother and I have spent a lot of time in her South Carolina kitchen," writes 12-year-old **Tara Hallowell**. "I remember pulling up a chair to the counter to watch, always asking if I could help. We make French toast, pancakes, or scrambled eggs. Little by little, Grandma has taught me how to bake brownies, cookies, and cakes. I have done a few recipes all by myself."

Tara and her grandmother, Carolyn, are a great team. Whenever they're in the same kitchen, the two manage to create some special moments. Tara's favorite thing is baking. "One of my favorites is Marble Pound Cake. I think I make a pretty good one." Carolyn types the recipes prepared by the young chef, placing a copy of each in a notebook for safekeeping.

MARBLE POUND CAKE

This recipe uses a nontraditional method of adding and beating ingredients for this cake. We tested it in our kitchens, and it works well for this cake.

3 cups sifted cake flour
2 cups sugar
1 tablespoon baking powder
1 teaspoon salt
1½ cups shortening
¾ cup milk
6 large eggs
2 teaspoons vanilla extract
½ cup chocolate syrup

• **Combine** all ingredients except chocolate syrup in a large mixing bowl; beat at low speed with an electric mixer until blended. Beat at high speed 10 minutes.
• **Combine** 1 cup batter and chocolate syrup; set aside.
• **Divide** remaining batter in half; pour one portion into a greased and floured 12-cup Bundt or 10-inch tube pan. Spoon half of reserved chocolate batter on top; repeat layers. Gently swirl batter with a knife.
• **Bake** at 350° for 1 hour; cover loosely with aluminum foil after 50 minutes to prevent excess browning. Cool in pan on wire rack 10 to 15 minutes; remove from pan, and let cool completely on a wire rack. **Yield:** one 10-inch cake.

Carolyn Hallowell
Hilton Head Island, South Carolina

■ It took only a few minutes of leafing through her paternal grandmother's favorite recipes for **Leslie Griffin** to recognize that the more things change, the more they stay the same.

Berry Shrub, traditionally made from a fresh fruit syrup, is still as refreshing as the day Leslie's grandmother first recorded its ingredients many years ago.

BERRY SHRUB

Make this summer recipe year-round. Frozen berries work as well as fresh.

2 quarts fresh or frozen
    strawberries, raspberries,
    blackberries, or dewberries,
    thawed
2 cups white vinegar
Sugar
Water
Crushed ice
Garnish: fresh mint sprigs

• **Place** berries in a large stainless steel or glass bowl. Add vinegar, and cover tightly with cheesecloth. Let stand at room temperature 3 days, stirring gently each day.
• **Pour** mixture carefully through a large wire-mesh strainer into a 4-cup liquid measuring cup (do not crush berries). Discard berries, and measure juice. Place juice in a large heavy saucepan, adding 1 cup sugar for every 1 cup of juice.
• **Bring** juice mixture to a boil over medium heat. Reduce heat, and simmer mixture 5 minutes. Cool juice mixture completely, and store berry syrup in an airtight container in the refrigerator.
• **Dilute** each 1 cup berry syrup with 1½ cups water, and serve over crushed ice. Garnish, if desired. **Yield:** 5½ cups syrup (with frozen berries) to 7½ cups syrup (with fresh berries).

Leslie Griffin
Cleveland, Mississippi

KIDS IN THE KITCHEN

Make sure that when your children are grown they remember favorite recipes from childhood as do the people featured on these pages. One way to ensure fond memories is to invite your kids into the kitchen – not just to eat, but also to cook. Here are a few pointers to keep in mind when children help with the cooking.

■ Ask your child to join you when planning a recipe or menu. Even finicky eaters will more likely eat what they've helped plan and prepare.

■ When children are 5 or 6, they're ready to help with simple tasks like stirring ingredients, counting vanilla wafers for banana pudding, or punching the buttons on the microwave. Attention spans are often short, so keep tasks simple.

■ Preteens will enjoy assembly-line tasks such as using a biscuit cutter, threading a kabob, or decorating cookies. Teens want to know why you're doing certain procedures, so be ready with answers.

■ As you begin your culinary field trip, teach your child the importance of food safety: Wash hands before cooking, make sure there's plenty of counter space to avoid mishaps, and wipe up spills when they happen. Use caution around sharp knives and hot pans, and keep pot handles turned toward the cooktop to prevent accidents.

■ Cleanup can be just as fun as cooking when you do it together. Form an assembly line for washing and drying bowls and pans, and show your youngster where ingredients should be put away.

FROM OUR KITCHEN TO YOURS

A resolution for the New Year: to prepare good weeknight suppers in

30 minutes or less with minimal cleanup. It isn't easy to juggle schedules, cope with

mounds of laundry, and prepare a home-cooked meal. To avoid that nightly dose

of fast food or restaurant fare, rely on time-savers like convenience products. If you have

a similar goal, try these survival tactics on how to make home cooking easier.

WHY DIDN'T I THINK OF THAT?

■ To easily cut a cake into layers, wrap a long piece of unflavored dental floss or sewing thread around the circumference of the cake, halfway between the top and the bottom; cross ends of floss, and pull, separating the cake into two layers.

■ Having difficulty separating cream-filled chocolate sandwich cookies? The secret to success: Slip a hot knife between one of the chocolate cookies and the filling.

■ To prevent piecrust edges from overbrowning, cut the bottom from a disposable aluminum foil piepan, leaving the rim and sides intact. When the crust is light golden and the filling isn't quite done, place the foil ring on top to slow down the browning process. The foil rim can be used again and again.

■ Who says biscuits have to be round? Pat out biscuit dough in a square, grab a chef's knife, and make 2-inch cuts one way, turn the knife and make 2-inch cuts the other way. Baking square biscuits saves a bunch of time.

TRIED-AND-TRUE TIME-SAVERS

■ For a small amount of grated onion, squeeze a piece of onion through a garlic press.

■ To crush cookies without a food processor, place cookies in a heavy-duty plastic bag, and roll with a rolling pin or pound with a meat mallet.

■ Thinly slice or cut foods into small pieces, and they'll cook faster.

■ Double a recipe so you'll have a heat-and-eat supper to serve another day.

■ Use diced, ready-cut, or precut canned tomatoes in most any recipe calling for chopped tomatoes.

■ Purchase precut produce. Look for convenient bags of spinach, broccoli flowerets, baby or shredded carrots, celery hearts, and ready-to-use lettuces and slaw mixes in the produce section of your local supermarket.

■ Replace 1 tablespoon chopped fresh herbs with 1 teaspoon dried herbs.

■ Substitute an equal amount of ready-to-serve, reduced-sodium chicken broth for homemade chicken stock.

■ Use prepackaged frozen chopped onion and green pepper instead of fresh.

■ Use refrigerated pasta. It cooks faster than the dried variety. Boil-in-bag rice takes half the time of regular rice.

■ Buy precut packaged meats for marinating and stir-frying.

■ Keep sauces, such as salsas, marinades, pestos, mustards, and flavored vinegars, on hand to add flavor to simple dishes.

■ Plan for leftovers. Cook roasts, ham, soups, and stews – any food that will guarantee enough extras to reheat for future meals.

■ For easy cleanup, coat the grater, knife blade of a food processor, and beaters of an electric mixer with vegetable cooking spray before using.

■ Cook more pasta than you need. Drain, toss the excess pasta lightly with olive oil, and store it in a zip-top plastic bag in the refrigerator up to three days. Reheat, if desired, by placing the pasta in boiling water just until pasta is thoroughly heated.

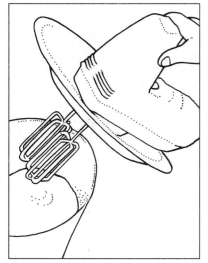

Use a pastry blender to slice hard-cooked eggs and butter and to chop canned tomatoes.

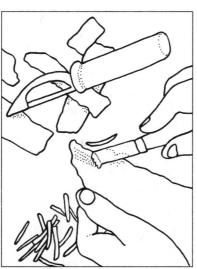

To quickly shave or shred fresh Parmesan cheese, use a vegetable peeler or a zester.

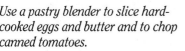

Avoid splatters when mixing by punching holes in a paper plate; insert beaters, and keep the surface of plate even with the top of the bowl.

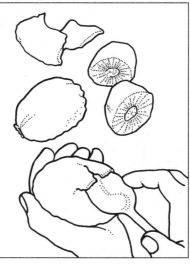

To peel kiwifruit, trim off ends; insert a spoon under the skin with the bowl facing the flesh. Rotate the spoon around the fruit.

LIVELY LEMONS ADD ZING

....

Lemon is one of our most versatile flavoring ingredients. Replace your usual condiments with these versions, and add some zest to your recipes.

LEMON VINEGAR

1 medium lemon
1 cup white vinegar
1 cup dry white vermouth

● **Remove** yellow portion of rind from lemon; reserve lemon for other uses. Cut rind into thin strips.
● **Combine** rind, vinegar, and vermouth in a 2½-cup jar.
● **Cover** mixture, and let stand at room temperature 10 days, shaking occasionally. Serve vinegar with seafood. **Yield:** 2 cups.

Orange Vinegar: Substitute 1 medium orange for lemon, and proceed with as directed.

Lemon Vinaigrette: Combine 3 tablespoons olive oil and 1 tablespoon Lemon Vinegar in a jar. Cover tightly, and shake vigorously. Serve with green salad.

Nora Henshaw
Okemah, Oklahoma

LEMONY BARBECUE SAUCE

½ cup ketchup
1 teaspoon grated lemon rind
2 teaspoons lemon juice
2 teaspoons Worcestershire sauce
2 teaspoons prepared mustard
Dash of garlic powder

● **Combine** all ingredients. Use as a basting or dipping sauce for chicken, beef, or pork. **Yield:** about ⅔ cup.

LEMONY TARTAR SAUCE

½ cup mayonnaise or salad
    dressing
2 tablespoons finely chopped green
    onions
2 tablespoons sweet pickle relish
1 teaspoon grated lemon rind
2 teaspoons lemon juice

● **Combine** all ingredients. Serve sauce with seafood or as a sandwich spread. **Yield:** ⅔ cup.

LEMON BASTING SAUCE

1½ lemons, peeled, sectioned, and
    finely chopped
2 tablespoons white wine vinegar
½ cup olive oil
2 teaspoons dried thyme
¼ teaspoon cracked peppercorns

● **Combine** all ingredients in a small bowl. Cover and store in refrigerator up to 1 week or freeze up to 3 months. Use as a basting sauce for fish or chicken or toss hot cooked pasta with sauce. **Yield:** about 1 cup.

LEMON MAYONNAISE

⅓ cup egg substitute
1 tablespoon grated lemon rind
½ teaspoon sugar
½ teaspoon dry mustard
¼ teaspoon salt
Dash of paprika
2 tablespoons lemon juice
3 or 4 drops of hot sauce
1 cup vegetable oil

● **Combine** first 8 ingredients in food processor bowl or container of an electric blender. Process 20 seconds, stopping once to scrape down sides. Gradually pour oil in a slow, steady stream through food chute with processor running. Process 30 seconds or until thickened. **Yield:** 1½ cups.

LEMON SQUEEZERS

16 (6-inch) squares cheesecloth
2 lemons, halved
Sprigs of fresh flat leaf parsley,
    mint, or other herb (optional)

● **Divide** cheesecloth squares into 4 stacks. Place 1 lemon half, cut side down, in center of each stack.
● **Gather** ends of cheesecloth, and tie together with string. Tie ends again, inserting a sprig of herb under string, if desired. **Yield:** 4 squeezers.

LEMON BUTTER

½ cup butter or margarine,
    softened
1 tablespoon grated lemon rind
½ teaspoon dried oregano
¼ teaspoon dried parsley flakes
¼ teaspoon garlic salt
Dash of pepper

● **Combine** all ingredients, and spoon onto plastic wrap. Shape mixture into a 1-inch diameter log by folding plastic wrap over mixture and rolling, working quickly to keep mixture from melting. Seal log in plastic wrap; chill 4 hours. Serve with fish, poultry, or vegetables. **Yield:** ½ cup.

Jan O'Donnell
Memphis, Tennessee

LEMON-MINT SUGAR

2 cups sugar
3 tablespoons grated lemon rind
2 tablespoons dried mint flakes
¼ teaspoon salt

● **Combine** all ingredients; spread in a thin layer in a 15- x 10- x 1-inch jelly-roll pan.
● **Bake** sugar mixture at 200° for 15 minutes. Cool in pan.
● **Place** mixture in container of an electric blender. Process to a fine powder. Store in an airtight container up to 6 months. Serve with hot or iced tea or fresh fruit. **Yield:** 2 cups.

MAKE A BREAK FOR IT

....

If you have a few eggs on hand, a fast and hearty meal is simply an open refrigerator door away.

CRABMEAT BRUNCH SCRAMBLE

¼ cup butter or margarine
1 (6-ounce) package ready-to-serve
    frozen crabmeat, thawed and
    drained
2 tablespoons sliced green onions
8 large eggs, lightly beaten
½ cup reduced-fat sour cream
2 tablespoons grated Parmesan
    cheese
½ teaspoon salt
⅛ teaspoon pepper
3 English muffins, split, toasted,
    and buttered

● **Melt** butter in a large skillet; add crabmeat and green onions. Cook over medium-high heat, stirring constantly, until onions are tender; set crabmeat mixture aside.
● **Combine** eggs and next 4 ingredients. Add to crabmeat mixture.
● **Cook,** without stirring, until mixture begins to set on bottom. Draw a spatula across bottom of pan to form large curds. Continue cooking until eggs are thickened but still moist; do not stir constantly.
● **Serve** immediately over English muffin halves. **Yield:** 6 servings.

Tricia Chaffin
Little Rock, Arkansas

QUICHE CASSEROLE

6 slices whole wheat bread, torn
¼ teaspoon garlic powder
1 (26-ounce) carton frozen quiche
  filling with ham, thawed
1 medium-size sweet red pepper,
  seeded and cut into rings

• **Place** bread evenly into a lightly
greased 11- x 7- x 1½-inch baking
dish; set aside.
• **Stir** garlic powder into quiche filling;
pour over bread.
• **Bake** at 400° for 20 minutes; top
with pepper rings, and bake 5 additional minutes. Let casserole stand 5
minutes before serving. **Yield:** 4 to 6
servings.

DILL-CHEESE-HAM OMELET

6 large eggs, lightly beaten
¼ cup milk
¼ teaspoon curry powder
½ teaspoon dried dillweed
2 teaspoons Worcestershire sauce
Vegetable cooking spray
½ cup chopped green onions
½ cup chopped cooked ham
½ cup (2 ounces) shredded
  Cheddar cheese
¼ cup (1 ounce) shredded Havarti
  cheese

• **Combine** first 5 ingredients; set
aside.
• **Coat** a 10-inch omelet pan or nonstick skillet with cooking spray; add
green onions, and cook over medium
heat until tender.
• **Add** egg mixture. As egg mixture
starts to cook, gently lift the edges of
omelet with a spatula, and tilt pan so
that the uncooked portion will flow
underneath. Top with chopped ham
and cheeses.
• **Cover** and cook 3 minutes or until
omelet is set.
• **Fold** omelet in half; serve immediately. **Yield:** 4 servings.

Tom Maze
Petersburg, Virginia

"EGGSTRA" INFORMATION

STORING EGGS
■ Avoid washing eggs before storing
them; you may end up removing
their protective coating and they
won't stay fresh as long.

■ An egg's shelf life in the refrigerator is about 10 days.

■ Unsure of an egg's age? Place it
in a pan of cold water. If it lies on
its side, it's fresh; if it tilts at an
angle, it's about three to four days
old; if it stands upright, it's about
10 days old; if it floats, toss it!

■ Avoid placing eggs near odorifer-
ous foods, such as onions – they'll
absorb those odors right through
their shells.

COOKING EGGS
■ An easy way to separate several
egg yolks from their whites: Use
a kitchen funnel.

■ Salt toughens eggs – add it to
your dish after it's prepared, not
while cooking. In addition, salted
butter can cause fried or scrambled
eggs to stick to a pan; use vegetable
oil or unsalted butter instead.

■ Add a teaspoon of salt or a tablespoon of vinegar to water before
hard-cooking the eggs to make
them easier to peel.

■ Plunge hard-cooked eggs into
cold water while they're hot to

prevent a greenish ring from forming around egg yolks.

■ When cooking an egg in a
microwave, first remove it from
the shell and pierce its yolk;
otherwise, it'll explode!

■ Scrambled eggs get a boost from
¼ teaspoon cornstarch per egg
(makes them fluffier); 1 tablespoon
sour cream per 2 eggs (makes them
rich and creamy); or 1 teaspoon
sherry per egg (adds a delightful
flavor).

COUNTING CALORIES
■ To reduce calories, fat, and
cholesterol, use fewer egg yolks and
more egg whites. All you'll miss is
the color.

■ Egg substitutes? They're an
obvious health benefit because
they're cholesterol free and are
lower in calories. They also can
be used as a substitute in dishes like
omelets, casseroles, and yes, even
desserts, with the exception of the
more delicate baked goods.

■ Calories? One large egg = 80;
1 egg white = 20; 1 egg yolk = 60.

■ Though eggs often get a bad
rap, let's not forget they provide
protein, iron, vitamins A and D,
and other nutrients. They also
cook up in a snap and leave you
time to tackle other projects.

TEX-MEX EGG BURRITOS

1 pound ground hot pork sausage
12 large eggs, lightly beaten
1 (4½-ounce) can chopped green
    chiles, drained
8 (8-inch) flour tortillas, warmed
Picante sauce
Shredded Cheddar cheese
Sliced jalapeño peppers (optional)

● **Brown** sausage in a large skillet, stirring until it crumbles; drain. Add eggs and chiles to sausage.
● **Cook,** without stirring, until mixture begins to set on bottom. Draw a spatula across bottom of pan to form large curds. Continue cooking until eggs are thickened but still moist; do not stir constantly.
● **Spoon** egg mixture evenly down center of tortillas; top each with picante sauce, cheese, and jalapeño peppers, if desired. Fold opposite sides over filling. Serve immediately. **Yield:** 8 servings.

Georgana McNeil
Houston, Texas

CHEESE-CHIVE SCRAMBLED EGGS

6 large eggs, lightly beaten
2 tablespoons water
¼ teaspoon seasoned salt
Dash of pepper
2 tablespoons butter or margarine
3 ounces reduced-fat cream cheese,
    cut into ¼-inch cubes and
    softened
1 tablespoon frozen chopped
    chives, thawed

● **Combine** first 4 ingredients.
● **Melt** butter in a large nonstick skillet over medium heat, tilting pan to coat bottom.
● **Add** egg mixture to pan; top with cream cheese and chives.
● **Cook,** without stirring, until mixture begins to set on bottom. Draw a spatula across bottom of pan to form large curds. Continue cooking until eggs are thickened but still moist; do not stir constantly. **Yield:** 4 to 6 servings.

Linda Sutton
Winston-Salem, North Carolina

SEASONAL SENSATION

What could be better on a wintry eve than

a steamy cup of Sugar-and-Spice Hot Chocolate paired

with Scottish Shortbread?

SCOTTISH SHORTBREAD

Agnes Hunter Dauphinée, a native of Scotland, shares her mother's recipe for Scottish Shortbread.

1 cup butter, softened
1 cup margarine, softened
1 cup sifted powdered sugar
4 cups all-purpose flour
½ teaspoon baking powder
¼ teaspoon salt

● **Beat** butter and margarine at medium speed with an electric mixer until creamy; gradually add sugar, beating well.
● **Combine** flour, baking powder, and salt; add to butter mixture. Mix at low speed until well blended.
● **Turn** dough out onto a well-floured surface; knead 10 times. Shape on a cookie sheet into a 15- x 10-inch rectangle. Pierce dough with a fork at 2-inch intervals.
● **Bake** at 300° for 1 hour or until shortbread is golden. Cut immediately into 2½- x 1-inch pieces. Cool on pan 10 minutes; remove to a wire rack to cool completely. **Yield:** 5 dozen.

Agnes Hunter Dauphinée
Trussville, Alabama

SUGAR-AND-SPICE HOT CHOCOLATE

¼ cup cocoa
⅓ cup sugar
½ teaspoon ground cinnamon
¼ teaspoon ground nutmeg
⅛ teaspoon salt
½ cup hot water
3½ cups milk
1 teaspoon vanilla extract
Garnishes: whipped cream,
    ground cloves

● **Combine** first 5 ingredients in a large saucepan; stir in hot water.
● **Bring** mixture to a boil over medium heat, stirring constantly; reduce heat, and simmer 2 minutes.
● **Add** milk, and cook until thoroughly heated, stirring constantly (do not boil). Remove from heat; add vanilla, stirring with a wire whisk until frothy. Garnish, if desired. **Yield:** 4 servings.

Charlotte Pierce
Greensburg, Kentucky

JUST DIP IT!

....

Fondue, the party rage of the sixties, is making a nineties comeback. The idea is age-old: Just heat a flavored mixture, dip a bite-size piece of food into it, and enjoy.

Fondue pots have been updated, and convenience products make preparation easier.

Want to try the latest fondue revival? Shop for new designs in fondue pots and chafing dishes. Or check yard sales for the tried-and-true avocado- or mustard-colored versions. A small slow cooker or even a saucepan over a burner works, too. For fondue forks, use either table forks, wooden picks, or skewers.

CARAMEL FONDUE

3 (14-ounce) packages caramels, unwrapped
⅓ to ½ cup milk
1 (8-ounce) container soft cream cheese

• **Combine** caramels, ⅓ cup milk, and cream cheese in a large Dutch oven; cook over low heat, stirring constantly, until caramels melt and mixture is smooth. Add additional milk if mixture is too thick for dipping.
• **Spoon** mixture into a fondue pot or chafing dish. **Yield:** 4 cups.

Carolyn Look
El Paso, Texas

PEPPERMINT FONDUE

1 cup sifted powdered sugar
2 tablespoons cornstarch
2 cups whipping cream
¼ teaspoon peppermint extract
1 or 2 drops of red liquid food coloring

• **Combine** sugar and cornstarch in a heavy saucepan; gradually stir in whipping cream. Bring to a boil over medium heat, stirring constantly.
• **Remove** from heat, and stir in flavoring and coloring. Spoon into a fondue pot or chafing dish. **Yield:** 2 cups.

CHOCOLATE PLUNGE

2 cups light corn syrup
1½ cups whipping cream
3 (12-ounce) packages semisweet chocolate morsels

• **Combine** corn syrup and whipping cream in a heavy saucepan; bring mixture to a boil.
• **Remove** from heat; add chocolate morsels, stirring until smooth. Spoon into a fondue pot or chafing dish. **Yield:** 7 cups.

Mary Pappas
Richmond, Virginia

PUB FONDUE

1 (10¾-ounce) can Cheddar cheese soup, undiluted
¾ cup beer
2 cups (8 ounces) shredded mild Cheddar cheese
2 teaspoons prepared mustard
1 teaspoon Worcestershire sauce

• **Combine** soup and beer in a heavy saucepan; bring to a boil over medium heat, stirring constantly. Gradually add shredded cheese and remaining ingredients, stirring constantly, until cheese melts. Spoon into a fondue pot or chafing dish. **Yield:** 2½ cups.

NACHO FONDUE

3 (11-ounce) cans nacho cheese soup, undiluted
3 cups (12 ounces) shredded Monterey Jack cheese
1½ cups salsa
¾ cup milk

• **Combine** all ingredients in a heavy saucepan; cook over medium heat, stirring constantly, until cheese melts. Spoon into a fondue pot or chafing dish. **Yield:** 7½ cups.

Sandra J. Enwright
Winter Park, Florida

DUNKING MORSELS

SAVORY
French or pumpernickel bread cubes
Breadsticks
Raw vegetables
Tortilla or corn chips
Cubes of cooked ham

SWEET
Pound cake cubes
Angel food cake cubes
Fruit slices or chunks (apple, pear, pineapple, banana)
Whole small fruits (strawberries, grapes, cherries)
Shortbread cookies
Marshmallows

DELICIOUS INDULGENCE

Caramel. The very word stirs thoughts of rich, buttery sweetness. Each of these reader recipes presents an opportunity to indulge in this favorite flavor.

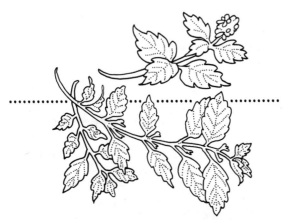

EASY CARAMEL-CHOCOLATE STICKY BUNS

1 (15-ounce) can coconut-pecan frosting
1 cup pecan halves
2 (10-ounce) cans refrigerated buttermilk biscuits
20 chocolate kisses, unwrapped

• **Spread** frosting in bottom of a lightly greased 9-inch square baking pan. Arrange pecan halves over frosting. Set aside.
• **Separate** biscuits; flatten each to about ¼-inch thickness. Place a chocolate kiss to one side of center of each biscuit. Fold biscuit in half, forming a semi-circle; press edges gently to seal in chocolate kiss. Repeat procedure with remaining biscuits and chocolate kisses. Arrange over pecans, flat sides down.
• **Bake** at 375° for 28 to 30 minutes or until lightly browned. Cool in pan on a wire rack 5 minutes; invert onto serving plate, and serve immediately. **Yield:** 20 servings.

Doris J. Phillips
Fayetteville, Arkansas

CARAMEL ICE CREAM DESSERT

1⅓ cups all-purpose flour
⅔ cup quick-cooking oats, uncooked
⅔ cup firmly packed brown sugar
⅔ cup chopped pecans or walnuts
⅔ cup butter or margarine, melted
1 cup firmly packed brown sugar
½ cup butter or margarine
¼ cup evaporated milk
½ gallon vanilla ice cream, softened

• **Combine** first 4 ingredients, and stir in melted butter; press mixture firmly into a lightly greased 15- x 10- x 1-inch jellyroll pan.
• **Bake** at 350° for 12 minutes or until lightly browned; remove cookie to wire rack. Cool and crumble.
• **Combine** 1 cup brown sugar, ½ cup butter, and evaporated milk in a heavy saucepan. Bring to a boil over medium heat, stirring constantly; boil 3 minutes. Cool caramel sauce.
• **Sprinkle** half of crumbs into bottom of a lightly greased 10-inch springform pan. Drizzle with half of caramel sauce. Spread ice cream over sauce. Drizzle with remaining caramel sauce; sprinkle with remaining crumbs.
• **Cover** and freeze until firm. **Yield:** 12 servings.

Becky Haney
Winston-Salem, North Carolina

CARAMEL DESSERT BISCUITS

2 cups sugar, divided
3 cups boiling water
½ cup butter or margarine
1 teaspoon vanilla extract
¼ teaspoon salt
2¾ cups biscuit and baking mix
¼ cup sugar
⅔ cup milk

• **Sprinkle** 1 cup sugar in a heavy Dutch oven; place over low heat. Cook, stirring constantly, until sugar melts (sugar will clump first) and syrup is light golden. Gradually add boiling water to syrup, stirring until sugar crystals dissolve.
• **Add** remaining 1 cup sugar, butter, vanilla, and salt to syrup. Bring to a boil; boil 2 minutes. (Mixture will be a thin syrup.) Pour mixture into a 13- x 9- x 2-inch baking pan; set aside.
• **Combine** biscuit mix and ¼ cup sugar; add milk, stirring with a fork until dry ingredients are moistened. Turn dough out onto a lightly floured surface; knead lightly 3 or 4 times.
• **Roll** dough to ½-inch thickness; cut with a 2½-inch round cutter, and place on syrup mixture.
• **Bake** at 350° for 20 to 25 minutes or until biscuits are golden. Serve with ice cream. **Yield:** 8 servings.

Connie Reeves
McGregor, Texas

Nourish body and soul with made-from-scratch Chicken Noodle Soup (recipe, page 45).

You don't have to head west for a jewel of a chili. Lasso a bowl of Bodacious Chili (foreground), topped with spice-spiked sour cream, or Chili Verde, made with a double dose of meat right in your own kitchen. (Recipes begin on page 14.)

Above: *The peppery cream cheese in Tortilla Bites (recipe, page 42) helps this appetizer turn any get-together into a fiesta.*

Loaded with goodness and a snap to prepare, Black-Eyed Pea-Spinach-Stuffed Potatoes (recipe, page 22) are a meal in themselves.

Cola and cream make a rich sauce for Soda Pop Pears (recipe, page 55), a fun dessert for all ages.

FEBRUARY

FLAT-OUT WINNERS

For ease of preparation and versatility, these recipes using tortillas really stack up. And you'll see that the round, thin pancakes, made from corn or wheat flour, can do *almost* anything.

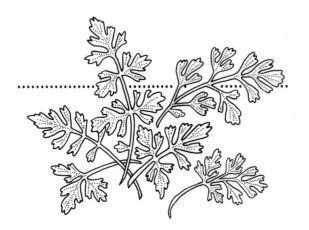

Fresh Salsa

1 small purple onion, quartered
2 jalapeño peppers, seeded and quartered
2 cloves garlic
¼ cup chopped fresh cilantro
2 tablespoons fresh lime juice
1 teaspoon salt
1 (14½-ounce) can diced tomatoes, drained

• **Position** knife blade in food processor bowl; add first 6 ingredients. Pulse six times or until finely chopped.
• **Combine** onion mixture and tomatoes. Cover and store in refrigerator up to one week. **Yield:** 2 cups.

Wendy Kitchens
Charlotte, North Carolina

SPICY CHICKEN QUESADILLAS
(pictured on page 39)

4 skinned and boned chicken breast halves, cut into ¼-inch thick strips
1 (1¼-ounce) package taco seasoning mix
2½ cups (10 ounces) shredded Monterey Jack cheese
⅔ cup picante sauce
1 medium-size sweet red pepper, chopped
10 (10-inch) flour tortillas
Melted butter

• **Combine** chicken and taco seasoning mix in a heavy-duty, zip-top plastic bag; toss to coat. Cover and chill 1 hour.
• **Place** chicken in a 15- x 10- x 1-inch jellyroll pan.
• **Broil** chicken 5½ inches from heat (with electric oven door partially opened) 5 minutes.
• **Cool** chicken, and cut breasts into bite-size pieces.
• **Combine** chicken, cheese, picante sauce, and sweet red pepper, stirring well. Set aside.
• **Brush** one side of each tortilla with melted butter; place 2 tortillas, buttered side down, on a lightly greased baking sheet. Top each tortilla with about 1 cup chicken mixture,

TORTILLA BITES
(pictured on page 39)

Cajun-style blackened seasoning provides the spice accent for this make-ahead appetizer.

1 pound unpeeled large fresh shrimp
¼ cup Cajun blackened seasoning for seafood
1 (8-ounce) package cream cheese, softened
½ teaspoon ground red pepper
¼ teaspoon salt
2 cloves garlic, crushed
Vegetable cooking spray
1 large sweet red pepper
6 (8-inch) flour tortillas
18 large fresh spinach leaves
1 medium avocado, peeled, seeded, and thinly sliced (optional)
Fresh Salsa

• **Peel** shrimp, and devein, if desired; cut shrimp in half, lengthwise. Combine shrimp and blackened seasoning in a heavy-duty, zip-top plastic bag; toss to coat. Chill 1 hour.

• **Combine** cream cheese and next 3 ingredients; set aside.
• **Thread** shrimp onto skewers.
• **Coat** food rack with cooking spray; place rack on grill over medium-hot coals (350° to 400°). Place shrimp and sweet red pepper on rack.
• **Cook,** covered with grill lid, about 10 minutes, turning shrimp once and red pepper occasionally.
• **Remove** shrimp from grill when done; remove shrimp from skewers, and set aside.
• **Remove** red pepper from grill when skin is blistered and black. Remove and discard skin and seeds; cut pepper into thin strips. Set aside.
• **Spread** cream cheese mixture evenly on one side of each tortilla. Place 3 spinach leaves on half of the cream cheese. Top spinach evenly with shrimp, red pepper strips, and avocado slices, if desired. Roll each tortilla tightly, starting at spinach side.
• **Cut** each tortilla crosswise into 5 portions, and secure each portion with a wooden pick. Cover and store in refrigerator. Serve with Fresh Salsa. **Yield:** 30 appetizers.

spreading to edges of tortilla. Top each with another tortilla, buttered side up.
• **Bake** at 375° for 10 minutes or until golden. Cut into wedges. Repeat with remaining tortillas and chicken mixture. Serve immediately. **Yield:** 5 main-dish servings or 30 appetizers.

Note: Quesadillas can be cooked on the cooktop in a hot cast-iron skillet or griddle. Cook, one at a time, 3 minutes on each side.

Amy Cromwell
Atlanta, Georgia

CARNE GUISADA BURRITOS

Assemble these generously stuffed flour tortillas just before serving so that they don't get soggy.

⅓ cup vegetable oil
2 pounds round steak, cut into
   ¾-inch pieces
2 or 3 jalapeño peppers
2 medium tomatoes, chopped
1 medium onion, finely chopped
¼ cup chopped fresh cilantro
½ teaspoon salt
12 (10-inch) flour tortillas
Garnish: sour cream

• **Heat** vegetable oil in a Dutch oven over medium-high heat; add steak pieces. Cook 3 to 4 minutes, stirring constantly.
• **Seed** peppers, if desired; chop.
• **Add** peppers, tomato, and next 3 ingredients. Cover, reduce heat, and simmer 1 hour or until meat is tender.
• **Heat** tortillas according to package directions, or prepare homemade tortillas (on page 44).
• **Spoon** about ⅓ cup meat mixture down center of each tortilla, using a slotted spoon; reserve tomato gravy in skillet. Roll up each tortilla.
• **Place** 2 rolled tortillas, seam side down, on each plate; spoon tomato gravy over tortillas. Garnish, if desired. **Yield:** 6 servings.

Corn and flour tortillas are as important to Mexican cuisine as biscuits are to Southern cooking.

At Fonda San Miguel restaurant in Austin, Texas, Chef Miguel Ravago gives you a peek at the traditional method of shaping and cooking tortillas by hand. If you can't make it to Austin, turn to "From Our Kitchen to Yours" on the next page for Chef Ravago's recipe for making flour tortillas. Or cruise by the dairy case at most any supermarket, and you'll find an ample selection of corn and flour tortillas in a variety of sizes.

APPLE CHIMICHANGAS

Filled tortillas are folded like an envelope and crisped in the oven.

1 (8-ounce) package dried apples
1½ cups water
3 tablespoons butter or margarine
½ cup sugar
1 teaspoon ground cinnamon
¼ teaspoon freshly ground
   nutmeg
2 tablespoons lemon juice
6 (8-inch) flour tortillas
Butter-flavored cooking spray
Toppings: vanilla ice cream, caramel
   sauce, toasted chopped pecans
   (optional)

• **Combine** apples and water in a large saucepan. Bring to a boil, reduce heat, and simmer 20 minutes or until tender.
• **Add** butter and next 4 ingredients; cook until butter melts. Set aside.
• **Heat** tortillas according to package directions; coat both sides of each tortilla with cooking spray.
• **Spoon** about ⅓ cup apple mixture down center of each tortilla. Fold in sides of tortilla to enclose filling, forming a rectangle. Secure with a wooden pick, and place folded side down on a lightly greased baking sheet.
• **Bake** chimichangas at 450° for 10 minutes or until golden. Serve chimichangas warm, and add toppings, if desired. **Yield:** 6 servings.

From Our Kitchen to Yours

It's convenient to toss a package of commercial flour tortillas into the grocery cart. But it's also fun to make hot-off-the-grill tortillas, and nothing beats the taste of fresh tortillas. All-purpose flour, shortening, and a rolling pin are basically all you need.

For recipes that use these home-made tortillas, see "Flat-Out Winners" on page 42.

FLOUR TORTILLAS

3 cups all-purpose flour
1 teaspoon baking powder
1½ teaspoons salt
½ cup shortening
¾ cup warm water

• **Combine** first 4 ingredients in a large mixing bowl, and beat at medium speed with an electric mixer until blended.
• **Add** water gradually in a steady stream, beating until blended.
• **Let** dough stand 15 minutes.
• **Divide** dough into equal portions, depending on the size tortillas you need. Coat hands with shortening, and roll each portion into a ball, coating ball completely with shortening.
• **Place** each dough ball between two sheets of wax paper, and roll dough into a thin circle.
• **Heat** an ungreased cast-iron skillet or griddle over medium-high heat. Cook tortillas, one at a time, about 1 minute on each side or until lightly browned and beginning to puff. Remove from skillet, and wrap in foil to keep warm. **Yield:** 20 (6-inch), 10 (8-inch), or six 10-inch tortillas.

TORTILLA TUTORIAL

Flour tortillas, Mexico's everyday bread, are traditionally made by hand. The staff at Fonda San Miguel restaurant in Austin, Texas, showed us how they make and cook hundreds of the thin, floppy rounds, which resemble very thin pancakes. It looks so easy, and it is. To speed up their time-consuming process, we used an electric mixer and reduced the restaurant's recipe to a family-size amount.

TORTILLA PRIMER
■ Flour tortillas cook quickly; have three or four balls of dough rolled and ready to cook.

■ To keep a round shape, roll ball into a disk between two sheets of wax paper. Starting from the center, roll out in all directions. If the dough springs back at any time, let it stand 2 to 3 minutes, and roll again.

■ Trim any odd-shaped tortillas into even circles with kitchen shears.

■ Remove top sheet of wax paper. Invert tortilla onto hot skillet, peeling away remaining wax paper.

■ When placed in the skillet, the tortilla should sizzle slightly. After about 1 minute, tiny bubbles will appear on the upper surface, and the bottom will be dry, pale, and sprinkled with brown spots; turn tortilla and cook the other side 1 minute. Do not overcook or the tortilla will become stiff.

■ To make ahead, stack cooled tortillas between sheets of wax paper, place in heavy-duty, zip-top plastic bags, and chill up to two days or freeze up to six months.

■ Always reheat tortillas; cold ones will crack when you roll them. To warm, stack six tortillas, and wrap in aluminum foil. Bake at 325° for 10 to 15 minutes. Or place the stack in an unsealed, heavy-duty zip-top plastic bag, and microwave at HIGH 30 to 45 seconds or until thoroughly heated. If the tortillas are very dry, pat each one between dampened hands before stacking.

KITCHEN COLLECTIBLES
And for the cook who has everything but . . .

■ A **tortilla press** flattens dough in a snap. Just place the ball of dough on the bottom plate, lower the upper plate, and press to flatten. A cast-iron tortilla press is available by calling Pendery's at 1-800-533-1870.

■ To warm and soften tortillas, wet the lid of a terra-cotta **tortilla warmer** with water, and stack tortillas in the container. Cover and place in a 250° oven for 10 to 12 minutes. Tortilla warmers are available in 7-inch (item #22746263) or 8-inch (item #22837518) diameter from Williams-Sonoma. To order, call 1-800-541-2233.

■ Press and bake a homemade tortilla in less than 2 minutes with an **electric tortilla maker.** The Tortilla Chef (item #22528554) is available from Williams-Sonoma. To order, call 1-800-541-2233.

HOMEMADE MADE EASY

We've redefined "scratch" – it's a creative choice, not a chore.

The word "homemade" can cause cooks to beam proudly or to hide in

the shadows. If you've been timid about your cooking

skills, you're not alone. But now you can proudly take the spotlight

with these easy recipes. Whether there're just a few ingredients or

an extensive list, the results are a triumph for the cook.

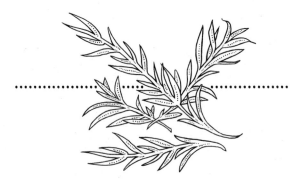

CHICKEN NOODLE SOUP
(pictured on page 37)

1 (3½- to 4-pound) broiler-fryer, halved
2 stalks celery, halved
1 large onion, quartered
1 carrot, scraped and halved
1 turnip, peeled and halved
2 cloves garlic, crushed
1¼ teaspoons salt
¾ teaspoon pepper
¼ teaspoon dried tarragon
4 cups water
3 cups chicken broth
4 ounces medium egg noodles, uncooked
1 large onion, chopped
2 stalks celery, sliced
2 carrots, scraped and sliced
½ teaspoon salt
½ teaspoon pepper
¼ teaspoon tarragon

• **Combine** first 11 ingredients in a large Dutch oven, and bring mixture to a boil over high heat. Reduce heat; cook 45 minutes or until chicken is tender.
• **Remove** chicken from broth, reserving broth; set chicken aside to cool slightly.
• **Pour** broth through a wire-mesh strainer into a large bowl; discard cooked vegetables. Remove and discard fat from broth; return broth to Dutch oven.
• **Cook** noodles according to package directions, omitting salt and fat; drain and set aside.
• **Skin** and bone chicken; chop chicken meat, and set aside.
• **Add** chopped onion, sliced celery, and sliced carrot to chicken broth; bring to a boil over high heat. Reduce heat; simmer 15 minutes.
• **Stir** in chopped chicken and noodles; add ½ teaspoon salt and remaining ingredients. Cook until thoroughly heated. **Yield:** 10 cups.

QUICK YEAST ROLLS

You can have these wonderful yeast rolls ready in about an hour – in time to serve with dinner.

2 packages active dry yeast
½ cup warm milk (105° to 115°)
1 cup milk
2 tablespoons sugar
2 tablespoons vegetable oil
1 teaspoon salt
1 large egg, lightly beaten
4 cups all-purpose flour, divided

• **Combine** yeast and ½ cup warm milk in a 2-cup liquid measuring cup; let stand 5 minutes.
• **Combine** yeast mixture, 1 cup milk, and next 4 ingredients in a large bowl. Gradually add 1 cup flour, stirring until smooth. Gradually stir in enough remaining flour to make a soft dough. Place in a well-greased bowl, turning to grease top.
• **Cover** and let stand in a warm place (85°), free from drafts, 15 minutes.
• **Punch** dough down; cover and let stand in a warm place (85°), free from drafts, 15 minutes.
• **Turn** dough out onto a floured surface; knead 3 or 4 times. Divide dough into 24 pieces; shape into balls. Place in 2 greased 9-inch square pans. Cover and let stand in a warm place (85°), free from drafts, 15 minutes.
• **Bake** at 400° for 15 minutes or until golden. **Yield:** 2 dozen.

THESE ROLLS ARE TOPS

After rolls are shaped and have risen, brush with a glaze of:

■ A whole egg or egg yolk beaten with a little water to make the rolls shiny and golden

■ An egg white-water mixture to hold toppings like poppy seeds and sesame seeds

---

SURPRISE PULL-APART BISCUITS

3 (10-ounce) cans refrigerated
   biscuits
3 ounces cooked ham, cut into 60
   small cubes
4 ounces Cheddar cheese, cut into
   60 small cubes
2 teaspoons dried Italian seasoning
½ cup butter or margarine, melted
½ teaspoon grated onion
¼ teaspoon garlic powder

• **Cut** biscuits into quarters. Wrap each
quarter around a ham or cheese cube,
and roll in Italian seasoning. Arrange
biscuits in a lightly greased 10-cup
Bundt pan.
• **Combine** butter and remaining ingredients; drizzle over biscuits.
• **Bake** at 350° for 30 minutes or until
golden, covering loosely with aluminum foil after 20 minutes, if necessary, to prevent overbrowning. Cool
on a wire rack 10 minutes; invert onto
a platter. **Yield:** one 10-inch loaf.

ORANGE BUTTER CAKE

2 cups all-purpose flour
1 cup graham cracker crumbs
1 cup firmly packed light brown
   sugar
½ cup sugar
1 teaspoon baking powder
1 teaspoon baking soda
¼ teaspoon salt
1 teaspoon ground cinnamon
1 cup butter, softened
1 tablespoon grated orange
   rind
1 cup orange juice
3 large eggs, lightly beaten
Tropical Cheese Spread (optional)

• **Combine** first 12 ingredients in a
large mixing bowl; beat at low speed
with an electric mixer until blended.
Beat at high speed 3 minutes. Pour
batter into 2 greased and floured 8½- x
4½- x 3-inch loaf pans.
• **Bake** at 350° for 45 minutes or until
a wooden pick inserted in center comes
out clean. Cool in pans on wire racks
10 minutes; remove from pans, and let
cool completely on wire racks. Frost
with Tropical Cheese Spread, if desired. **Yield:** 2 loaves.

Tropical Cheese Spread

1 cup chopped dried mixed fruit
¾ cup water
2 tablespoons Grand Marnier or
   other orange-flavored liqueur
2 (8-ounce) packages cream cheese,
   softened
½ cup orange marmalade

• **Combine** first 3 ingredients in a small
saucepan; bring to a boil over medium
heat. Cover, reduce heat, and simmer 8
minutes or until fruit is soft. Drain well.
• **Beat** cream cheese at medium speed
with electric mixer until light and
fluffy; add marmalade, and beat until
blended. Fold in fruit. **Yield:** 3½ cups.
Dorsella Utter
Louisville, Kentucky

OATMEAL-CHOCOLATE
MORSEL COOKIES

1 (18.25-ounce) package yellow
   cake mix with pudding
1 cup regular oats, uncooked
1 cup raisins
1 cup semisweet chocolate morsels
1 cup chopped pecans
⅓ cup vegetable oil
½ teaspoon vanilla extract
3 large eggs, lightly beaten

• **Combine** all ingredients; stir well.
• **Drop** dough by rounded teaspoonfuls 2 inches apart onto a lightly
greased cookie sheet.
• **Bake** at 350° for 8 to 10 minutes. Remove to wire racks to cool. **Yield:** 6
dozen.

Cammie Middleton
Red Oak, Texas

CURRY IN A HURRY

....

When you're in a pinch to prepare a
fast, flavorful meal, reach for curry powder. It'll quickly brighten a dish with
exotic color and flavor, while leaving
a warm "I've-been-cooking-all-day"
aroma lingering in your kitchen.

CURRIED TUNA MELTS

1 (6-ounce) can water-packed
   tuna, drained and flaked
3 hard-cooked eggs, chopped
¼ cup chopped green onions
⅓ cup reduced-calorie mayonnaise
½ teaspoon curry powder
¼ teaspoon salt
¼ teaspoon pepper
8 slices rye bread
1 cup (4 ounces) shredded
   Monterey Jack cheese

• **Combine** first 7 ingredients; spread
evenly onto 4 bread slices. Sprinkle
cheese evenly over tuna mixture, and
top each with a bread slice.
• **Heat** a large nonstick skillet over
medium heat. Add sandwiches; grill 2
minutes on each side or until cheese
melts and sandwiches are golden. Serve
immediately. **Yield:** 4 servings.
Trey Byrnes
Birmingham, Alabama

ALOHA SHRIMP SALAD

6 cups water
2 pounds unpeeled medium-size
   fresh shrimp
1 cup finely chopped celery
1 (20-ounce) can unsweetened
   pineapple chunks, drained
⅓ cup raisins
½ cup reduced-calorie mayonnaise
2 teaspoons curry powder

• **Bring** water to a boil; add shrimp,
and cook 3 to 5 minutes or until

shrimp turn pink. Drain; rinse with cold water. Peel shrimp, and devein, if desired.

• **Combine** shrimp, celery, and remaining ingredients. Cover and chill at least 1 hour before serving. Serve on leaf lettuce or in pita bread. **Yield:** 3 to 4 servings.

CURRIED CHICKEN SKILLET DINNER

2 teaspoons brown sugar
2 teaspoons curry powder
½ teaspoon salt
½ teaspoon dry mustard
¼ teaspoon pepper
4 skinned and boned chicken breast halves, cut into bite-size pieces
1 (14½-ounce) can ready-to-serve chicken broth
1½ cups orange juice
1¼ cups long-grain rice, uncooked
1 (10-ounce) package frozen English peas

• **Combine** first 5 ingredients; sprinkle 1 tablespoon seasoning mixture over chicken, tossing to coat. Reserve remaining seasoning mixture.
• **Bring** chicken broth, orange juice, rice, and reserved seasoning mixture to a boil in a large nonstick skillet. Add chicken; cover, reduce heat, and simmer 15 minutes.
• **Stir** in peas; cover and simmer 10 minutes or until liquid is absorbed. **Yield:** 4 servings.

CURRIED CORN AND SWEET RED PEPPERS

3 tablespoons butter or margarine
¼ cup chopped sweet red pepper
1 (15¼-ounce) can whole kernel corn, drained
1 teaspoon curry powder
⅛ teaspoon salt
⅛ teaspoon pepper
¼ cup whipping cream

• **Melt** butter in a medium skillet; add red pepper, and cook, stirring constantly, until tender. Stir in corn and next 3 ingredients; cook 3 minutes, stirring often. Stir in whipping cream; cook, stirring constantly, just until thoroughly heated. Serve alone or over chicken breasts or sliced pork tenderloin. **Yield:** 3 to 4 servings.

Leanne McMullen
Natchez, Mississippi

FRESH FROM THE VINE

....

When you toast the fruits of the vine, you're probably referring to wine. But here's a different approach. These recipes place plump, pearly grapes in dishes ranging from appetizers to side dishes.

When you buy grapes at the supermarket, use them quickly. They'll keep just under a week, unwashed, in a plastic bag in the refrigerator. Wash grapes well and dry with paper towels just before using them. And remember to purchase an extra bunch as a snack for the cook.

HONEYED GRAPES

¼ cup honey
¼ cup loosely packed fresh mint leaves, chopped
1 pound seedless red grapes
1 pound seedless green grapes

• **Combine** honey and mint in a large bowl. Set aside.
• **Remove** and discard grape stems. Wash grapes; drain and pat dry with paper towels. Add grapes to honey mixture; toss gently to coat. Cover and chill at least 2 hours. **Yield:** 6 servings.

Edith Askins
Greenville, Texas

WHAT'S CURRY?

....

■ Often called "the poor man's saffron," homemade curry powder is a hot and spicy mainstay in Far Eastern kitchens. Its milder, gentler Western cousin, standard commercial curry powder, is often popular with Southerners who like their spice to bite back a bit. Want even more kick to your curry? Reach for Madras or West Indian blends, which are available at most gourmet grocers.

■ Curry powder is a finely ground, aromatic blend of up to 20 spices, including any combination of cardamom, chiles, cinnamon, cloves, coriander, cumin, fennel seeds, fenugreek, mace, nutmeg, red and black pepper, poppy and sesame seeds, saffron, tamarind, turmeric (which gives the mix its rich yellow color), and more.

■ Curry powder complements bland stews, vegetables, poultry, lamb, beef, seafood – you name it. And why not do as many South Carolinians do? Use it to perk up chicken salad.

■ Curry powder should be stored in an airtight container in a dry spot about two months. After that, it may begin to lose its characteristic pungency.

BLUE CHEESE-PECAN GRAPES

1 (4-ounce) package crumbled
   blue cheese
1 (3-ounce) package cream cheese,
   softened
¼ pound seedless green grapes
1 cup finely chopped pecans,
   toasted

• **Combine** cheeses in a small mixing bowl; beat at medium speed with an electric mixer until smooth. Cover and chill at least 1 hour.
• **Remove** and discard grape stems. Wash grapes; drain and pat dry with paper towels. When completely dry, wrap each grape with enough cheese mixture to cover. Roll in pecans; cover and chill at least 1 hour. **Yield:** about 2 dozen.

Jim Green
Birmingham, Alabama

CARIBBEAN GRAPES

1½ pounds black grapes
1 (8-ounce) carton sour cream
2 tablespoons sugar
1 tablespoon light rum
¼ teaspoon ground cinnamon
⅓ cup chopped almonds or
   macadamia nuts, toasted

• **Remove** and discard grape stems. Wash grapes; drain and pat dry with paper towels. Cut grapes in half; remove and discard seeds; set grape halves aside.
• **Combine** sour cream and next 3 ingredients; stir until sugar dissolves. To serve, spoon sour cream mixture over grape halves, and sprinkle with chopped almonds. **Yield:** 6 servings.

Charlotte Scott
Simpsonville, South Carolina

WILD RICE WITH GRAPES

2 tablespoons butter or margarine,
   divided
2 tablespoons sliced almonds
¼ cup chopped green onions
1 (14½-ounce) can ready-to-serve
   chicken broth
3 tablespoons water
½ teaspoon salt
¼ teaspoon pepper
⅔ cup wild rice, uncooked
½ cup seedless green grapes, cut
   in half
½ cup seedless red grapes, cut
   in half

• **Melt** 1 tablespoon butter in a large saucepan; add almonds, and cook, stirring constantly, until golden. Remove almonds from pan; set aside.
• **Melt** remaining 1 tablespoon butter in saucepan; add green onions, and cook, stirring constantly, until tender. Add broth and next 3 ingredients.
• **Bring** to a boil; stir in rice. Return to a boil; cover, reduce heat, and simmer 1 hour or until tender. Drain any excess liquid. Stir in grapes. To serve, sprinkle rice mixture with almonds. **Yield:** 4 servings.

Karen Lapidus
Huntsville, Alabama

SPINACH ON THE SIDE

....

Move over macaroni and cheese – make way for spinach! That Popeye guy sure knew a winner when he saw it. These spinach side dishes will win you over, too.

No need to worry about selecting and cleaning your greens. Our recipes use convenient frozen chopped spinach that you can keep in your freezer.

When buying frozen spinach, avoid limp or damp packages – a sign that the vegetable has defrosted at least once.

SPINACH PIE WITH MUENSTER CRUST

3 (10-ounce) packages frozen
   chopped spinach, thawed
2 (6-ounce) packages Muenster
   cheese slices
1 small onion, finely chopped
1 cup reduced-fat cottage
   cheese
3 large eggs, lightly beaten
⅓ cup grated Parmesan cheese
½ teaspoon salt
¼ teaspoon pepper
Garnish: pimiento strips

• **Drain** spinach well, pressing between layers of paper towels, and set spinach aside.
• **Cut** 2 or 3 cheese slices into small triangles, and reserve for garnish. Cover bottom and sides of a lightly greased 9-inch pieplate with remaining Muenster slices, overlapping cheese as needed.
• **Combine** spinach, onion, and next 5 ingredients; spoon into cheese-lined pieplate.
• **Bake** at 350° for 45 minutes or until pie is set. Cool 10 minutes before serving. Garnish, if desired. **Yield:** 6 to 8 servings.

Note: To bake pie in a 9-inch pieplate, assemble pie, and place on a baking sheet. Bake as directed. The baking sheet will catch any oil that might run over during baking.

Michelle Stockhaus
Lorton, Virginia

SPINACH-ARTICHOKE BAKE

2 (10-ounce) packages frozen
   chopped spinach
¼ cup butter or margarine
½ cup finely chopped onion
1 (14½-ounce) can artichoke
   hearts, drained and quartered
1 (16-ounce) carton sour
   cream
¼ teaspoon salt
¼ teaspoon pepper
½ cup freshly grated Parmesan
   cheese, divided

- **Cook** spinach according to package directions; drain well, pressing between layers of paper towels; set aside.
- **Melt** butter in a large skillet over medium heat. Add onion; cook until tender. Gently stir in spinach, artichoke hearts, and next 3 ingredients; stir in ¼ cup Parmesan cheese.
- **Spoon** into a lightly greased 1½-quart casserole; sprinkle with remaining Parmesan cheese.
- **Bake** at 350° for 25 to 30 minutes. **Yield:** 6 servings.

Edith Peacock
Natchez, Mississippi

SPINACH SQUARES

2 (10-ounce) packages frozen chopped spinach, thawed
1 cup cooked rice
¼ cup sliced green onions
1 cup (4 ounces) shredded Swiss cheese
1 (10¾-ounce) can cream of mushroom soup, undiluted
3 large eggs, lightly beaten
⅛ teaspoon salt
⅛ teaspoon pepper
⅛ teaspoon dried basil
⅛ teaspoon dried oregano
¼ cup soft breadcrumbs
2 tablespoons grated Parmesan cheese
1 tablespoon butter, melted

- **Drain** spinach well, pressing between layers of paper towels.
- **Combine** spinach and next 3 ingredients in a large bowl; set aside. Combine mushroom soup and next 5 ingredients; add to spinach mixture, stirring well. Spoon into a lightly greased 8-inch square baking dish.
- **Combine** breadcrumbs, Parmesan cheese, and melted butter; sprinkle over spinach mixture.
- **Bake** at 325° for 30 minutes or until thoroughly heated. Let stand 10 minutes before cutting into squares; serve immediately. **Yield:** 6 servings.

Valerie Stutsman
Norfolk, Virginia

SPINACH CORNBREAD

1 (10-ounce) package frozen chopped spinach, thawed
1 (6-ounce) package Mexican cornbread mix
½ teaspoon salt
½ cup butter or margarine, melted
¾ cup cottage cheese
1 cup chopped onion
4 large eggs, lightly beaten

- **Drain** spinach well, pressing between layers of paper towels. Place spinach in a bowl; add cornbread mix and remaining ingredients, stirring until blended. Pour into a lightly greased 8-inch square baking dish.
- **Bake** at 400° for 30 minutes or until lightly browned. Serve immediately. **Yield:** 9 servings.

Sandra Stewart
Northport, Alabama

BATTER UP

....

It's a cold morning – it'll take more than hot cereal to lure your family from the warmth of their covers. But whether you're the chef or the sleepyhead, these quick-and-easy muffins will have your crew bounding to the table.

SAUSAGE MUFFINS

Serve these savory muffins either for breakfast or with salad and soup.

½ pound ground pork sausage
2 cups all-purpose flour
2 tablespoons sugar
1 tablespoon baking powder
¼ teaspoon salt
1 cup milk
1 large egg, lightly beaten
¼ cup butter or margarine, melted
½ cup (2 ounces) shredded Cheddar cheese
Vegetable cooking spray

- **Brown** sausage in a large skillet, stirring until it crumbles; drain. Set sausage aside.
- **Combine** flour and next 3 ingredients; make a well in center.
- **Combine** milk, egg, and butter; add to dry mixture, stirring just until moistened. Stir in sausage and cheese.
- **Place** paper baking cups in muffin pans, and coat lightly with cooking spray. Spoon batter into cups, filling two-thirds full.
- **Bake** at 375° for 20 minutes or until golden. Remove from pans immediately. **Yield:** 1 dozen.

Ethyl C. Jernegan
Savannah, Georgia

MUFFIN "MUSTS"

■ Remember to stir dry and wet ingredients just until batter holds together, usually no more than about 15 seconds. Don't worry about a few lumps.

■ The less muffin batter is beaten, the better. Overbeating results in muffins that are tough with undesirable tunnels inside.

■ If all the cups are not used when filling the muffin pan with batter, pour some water or place an ice cube into the empty cups to keep the pan from buckling.

■ Muffins are done when tops are domed and dry to the touch, sides have slightly pulled away from cups, and a wooden pick inserted in the center comes out clean.

■ Muffins are best eaten fresh the day they are made, but they freeze well, too. Cover muffins, and store up to one month.

KEY LIME MUFFINS

The fresh lime flavor of these muffins makes them the perfect choice to serve with a cup of tea.

2 cups all-purpose flour
1 cup sugar
1 tablespoon baking powder
½ teaspoon salt
⅓ cup milk
2 large eggs, lightly beaten
¼ cup vegetable oil
1 teaspoon grated lime rind
¼ cup Key lime juice

• **Combine** first 4 ingredients in a large bowl, and make a well in the center of mixture.
• **Combine** milk and remaining ingredients; add to dry ingredients, stirring just until moistened. Spoon into lightly greased muffin pans, filling three-fourths full.
• **Bake** muffins at 400° for 18 minutes or until lightly browned. Remove muffins from pan immediately. **Yield:** 1 dozen.

Clairiece Gilbert Humphrey
Charlottesville, Virginia

FUDGE BROWNIE MUFFINS

Pantry ingredients become a lunchbox treat or an after-school snack.

½ cup butter or margarine
¼ cup cocoa
2 large eggs, lightly beaten
1 cup sugar
1 teaspoon vanilla extract
¾ cup all-purpose flour
1 teaspoon ground cinnamon
¼ cup chopped pecans
Vegetable cooking spray
Semisweet chocolate morsels

• **Place** butter and cocoa in a 2-cup liquid measuring cup; microwave at HIGH 1 minute or until butter melts. Set aside.
• **Combine** eggs, sugar, and vanilla in a medium bowl. Add butter mixture, flour, cinnamon, and chopped pecans, stirring just until blended.

• **Place** paper baking cups in muffin pan, and coat lightly with cooking spray. Spoon batter into cups, filling two-thirds full. Sprinkle each muffin with 6 to 8 chocolate morsels.
• **Bake** at 350° for 20 minutes or until done. Remove from pan immediately. **Yield:** about 10 muffins.

Note: For miniature muffins, place baking cups into miniature (1¾-inch) muffin pans, and coat lightly with cooking spray. Spoon batter into baking cups, filling each two-thirds full. Sprinkle each muffin with 2 or 3 chocolate morsels. Bake at 350° for 13 to 15 minutes. Remove from pans immediately. **Yield:** 30 miniature muffins.

Elizabeth A. Cooper
Fort Worth, Texas

FOOLS FOR FUDGE

....

Chocoholics can always find a reason to indulge in fudge. And here's one more to savor.

So, fudge lovers enjoy. We've included recipes for all tastes, from buttermilk to peanut butter.

MINT FUDGE

2 cups sugar
⅓ cup cocoa
Pinch of salt
⅔ cup milk
2 tablespoons light corn syrup
¼ cup butter or margarine
¼ teaspoon peppermint extract
1 cup sifted powdered sugar
3 to 4 teaspoons milk
3 drops of peppermint extract
1 or 2 drops of green liquid food coloring

• **Combine** first 5 ingredients in a heavy 3-quart saucepan; bring mixture to a boil over medium heat, stirring constantly. Cover and boil 3 minutes.

• **Remove** lid; cook until mixture reaches soft ball stage or candy thermometer registers 234°. Remove from heat; cool 10 minutes.
• **Add** butter and ¼ teaspoon peppermint extract; beat until mixture thickens and begins to lose its gloss.
• **Pour** mixture into a buttered 8-inch square pan or dish. Cool and cut into squares.
• **Place** squares at least ½-inch apart on a wax-paper lined baking sheet; set aside.
• **Combine** powdered sugar and remaining ingredients, stirring until blended.
• **Place** mixture in a heavy-duty, zip-top plastic bag; seal. Snip a tiny hole in one corner of bag; drizzle over fudge. **Yield:** 1¼ pounds.

DOUBLE-GOOD FUDGE

Vegetable cooking spray
1 (16-ounce) package powdered sugar, sifted
1 cup chunky peanut butter
¼ cup plus 2 tablespoons milk
½ teaspoon vanilla extract
½ cup butter or margarine
1 (16-ounce) package powdered sugar, sifted
¼ cup milk
½ cup cocoa
1 teaspoon vanilla extract

• **Coat** eight 4-ounce shallow baking dishes with vegetable cooking spray; set aside.
• **Combine** 1 package powdered sugar, peanut butter, and ¼ cup plus 2 tablespoons milk in a large microwave-safe bowl, stirring well. Add ½ teaspoon vanilla; stir until smooth. Cover with wax paper and microwave at HIGH 2 to 3 minutes. Spread evenly into prepared dishes.
• **Place** butter in a separate microwave-safe bowl. Microwave at HIGH 1 minute or until melted. Stir in 1 package powdered sugar, ¼ cup milk, and cocoa.
• **Cover** with wax paper, and microwave at MEDIUM HIGH (70% power) 2 to 3 minutes. Add 1 teaspoon

vanilla; stir until smooth. Spread chocolate mixture evenly over peanut butter layers; cool. **Yield:** 3¼ pounds.

Note: The two layers of fudge may be poured into a buttered 9-inch square pan or dish, if desired.

CREAMY MOCHA FUDGE

1½ tablespoons instant coffee
    granules
1½ tablespoons hot water
3 cups (18 ounces) semisweet
    chocolate morsels
1 (14-ounce) can sweetened
    condensed milk
¼ cup chopped pecans, toasted

● **Dissolve** coffee granules in hot water in a large saucepan; add chocolate morsels and sweetened condensed milk. Cook over low heat, stirring constantly, until morsels melt.
● **Spread** into a lightly buttered 8-inch square pan or dish; sprinkle evenly with ¼ cup chopped pecans. Gently press pecans into fudge. Cover and chill until firm. Store loosely covered at room temperature. **Yield:** about 2 pounds.

Creamy Almond Fudge: Omit coffee granules and hot water. Add ½ teaspoon almond extract, and substitute toasted almonds for chopped pecans.

PEANUT BUTTER FUDGE

½ cup butter or margarine
5 cups sugar
1 (12-ounce) can evaporated
    milk
1 (18-ounce) jar creamy peanut
    butter
1 (7-ounce) jar marshmallow
    cream

● **Butter** sides and bottom of a large Dutch oven, leaving excess butter in pan. Add sugar and evaporated milk, stirring mixture well. Bring mixture to a boil over medium heat, stirring occasionally.

● **Cook,** stirring constantly, until mixture reaches soft ball stage or candy thermometer registers 234°. Remove from heat; add peanut butter and marshmallow cream, beating with a wooden spoon until blended.
● **Pour** into a buttered 13- x 9- x 2-inch baking pan or dish; cool. **Yield:** about 2 pounds.

Linda Creek
Jasper, Tennessee

WHITE CHOCOLATE FUDGE

2 (3-ounce) packages cream cheese,
    softened
1 (16-ounce) package powdered
    sugar, sifted
1½ teaspoons vanilla extract
1 (12-ounce) white chocolate-
    flavored baking bar, melted
1 cup chopped pecans, toasted

● **Beat** cream cheese at medium speed with an electric mixer until fluffy; gradually add sugar, beating well.
● **Add** vanilla and melted white chocolate to cream cheese mixture, stirring until blended. Stir in chopped pecans.
● **Spread** into a buttered 8-inch square baking pan or dish. Cover and store in refrigerator. **Yield:** 2 pounds.

Jean Williams
Hurtsboro, Alabama

FIVE POUNDS OF CHOCOLATE FUDGE

2 (12-ounce) packages semisweet
    chocolate morsels (4 cups)
1 cup butter or margarine
1 (7-ounce) jar marshmallow
    cream
4½ cups sugar
1 (12-ounce) can evaporated milk
Butter or margarine
2 tablespoons vanilla extract
1½ cups chopped pecans, toasted

● **Combine** first 3 ingredients in a large mixing bowl; set aside.
● **Combine** sugar and evaporated milk in a buttered Dutch oven.

● **Cook** over medium heat, stirring constantly, until mixture reaches soft ball stage or candy thermometer registers 234°; pour over chocolate morsels mixture. Beat at high speed with an electric mixer or wooden spoon until mixture thickens and begins to lose its gloss. Stir in vanilla and pecans.
● **Spread** into a buttered 15- x 10- x 1-inch jellyroll pan. Cover and chill until firm. Store in an airtight container at room temperature. **Yield:** 5 pounds.

Mrs. R. D. Walker
Garland, Texas

FUDGE FACTS & FANTASY

■ Making fudge from granulated sugar can be tricky. To prevent graininess, coat the saucepan with butter before adding ingredients, or cover the pan with a lid for a few minutes when the ingredients come to a boil.

■ Another trick is knowing how long to beat the fudge before you pour it into a pan. Most recipes say to beat the mixture until it thickens and begins to lose its gloss. However, do not beat the mixture too long, or the fudge will harden in the saucepan.

■ For Valentine's Day giving, check cooking shops for heart-shaped containers. Pour fudge into a small heart-shaped glass container. After the fudge is gone, the dish is perfect for holding pins or change.

■ To shape Five Pounds of Chocolate Fudge, left, into one large heart, use a two-piece, heart-shaped tube pan. Don't use the bottom piece of the pan that has the tube attached. Instead, cut a piece of cardboard into a heart shape to fit to use as the base, and cover the cardboard with aluminum foil.

BUTTERMILK FUDGE

2 cups sugar
1 cup buttermilk
½ cup butter or margarine
1 teaspoon baking soda
2 tablespoons light corn syrup
Butter or margarine
1 teaspoon vanilla extract
¾ cup chopped pecans,
    toasted

• **Combine** first 5 ingredients in a buttered Dutch oven.
• **Cook** over medium heat, stirring constantly, until mixture reaches soft ball stage or candy thermometer registers 234°; remove from heat. Cool to 180°. Stir in vanilla.
• **Beat** at high speed with an electric mixer until mixture thickens and begins to lose its gloss. Stir in pecans.
• **Pour** into a buttered 8-inch square pan or dish; cool. **Yield:** 1¼ pounds.

Terri Abbott
Bartlesville, Oklahoma

SOUR CREAM FUDGE

2 cups sugar
Pinch of salt
1 (8-ounce) carton sour cream
Butter or margarine
2 tablespoons butter or
    margarine
½ cup chopped pecans, toasted
    (optional)

• **Combine** first 3 ingredients in a buttered heavy saucepan.
• **Cook** over medium heat, stirring constantly, until mixture reaches soft ball stage or candy thermometer registers 234°. Remove from heat; stir in 2 tablespoons butter.
• **Beat** at high speed with an electric mixer until mixture thickens and begins to lose its gloss (4 to 5 minutes). Stir in pecans, if desired.
• **Pour** into a buttered 8-inch square baking pan or dish; cover and chill until firm. Store in an airtight container at room temperature. **Yield:** 1¼ pounds.

Joella Whitley
Baytown, Texas

living *light*
ONE MEAL THREE WAYS

Pork tenderloin and broccoli are a canvas for a multitude of flavor possibilities. Planning dinner around pork tenderloin practically guarantees a low-fat meal. With just 5 fat grams per 3-ounce serving, it's a refreshing alternative to the same old fish or chicken. Pair it with fresh broccoli, add pasta, rice, or potatoes, and dinner's a done deal.

HONEY-MUSTARD PORK TENDERLOIN

2 (¾-pound) pork tenderloins,
    trimmed
Vegetable cooking spray
¼ cup honey
2 tablespoons apple cider vinegar
1 tablespoon Dijon mustard
½ teaspoon paprika

• **Place** tenderloins on a rack coated with cooking spray; place rack in broiler pan, and set aside.
• **Combine** honey and remaining ingredients; spoon one-third of honey mixture over tenderloins; set remaining honey mixture aside.
• **Bake** tenderloins at 350° for 30 minutes or until a meat thermometer inserted in thickest portion registers 160°, basting occasionally with remaining honey mixture. Cut tenderloins into thin slices. **Yield:** 6 servings.

Marie A. Davis
Charlotte, North Carolina

♥ Per serving: Calories 183 (21% from fat)
Fat 4.3g (1.4g saturated) Cholesterol 64mg
Sodium 121mg Carbohydrate 12g
Fiber 0g Protein 22.9g

BROCCOLI AND WALNUT SAUTÉ

1½ pounds fresh broccoli
½ cup water
2 tablespoons balsamic vinegar
2 teaspoons cornstarch
1 teaspoon chicken bouillon
    granules
1 clove garlic, minced
1 cup thin onion strips (cut
    vertically)
½ cup thin strips sweet red
    pepper
2 teaspoons vegetable oil
¼ cup chopped walnuts,
    toasted

• **Remove** and discard broccoli leaves and tough ends of stalks; cut broccoli into flowerets. Peel broccoli stems, and thinly slice. Set broccoli aside.
• **Combine** water and next 3 ingredients; set cornstarch mixture aside.
• **Cook** garlic, onion, red pepper, and broccoli in oil in a large skillet over medium heat, stirring mixture constantly, 3 minutes or until broccoli is crisp-tender.
• **Add** cornstarch mixture to vegetable mixture, and bring to a boil, stirring

constantly. Cook 1 minute, stirring constantly.

- **Spoon** into a serving dish; sprinkle with walnuts. **Yield:** 6 servings.

Edith Askins
Greenville, Texas

♥ Per serving: Calories 94 (43% from fat)
Fat 5.1g (0.4g saturated) Cholesterol 0mg
Sodium 33mg Carbohydrate 10.5g
Fiber 4.3g Protein 4.6g

APPLE-MUSHROOM PORK TENDERLOIN

2 (¾-pound) pork tenderloins, trimmed *
¾ cup all-purpose flour
½ teaspoon salt
¼ teaspoon pepper
Vegetable cooking spray
1 clove garlic, minced
1 cup sliced fresh mushrooms
¾ cup frozen apple juice concentrate, thawed and undiluted

- **Cut** each tenderloin crosswise into 6 medaillons. Place medaillons, cut side down, between 2 sheets of heavy-duty plastic wrap; flatten medaillons to ¼-inch thickness, using a meat mallet or rolling pin.
- **Combine** flour, salt, and pepper; coat pork slices with flour mixture.
- **Coat** a large nonstick skillet with cooking spray; place skillet over medium heat until hot.
- **Arrange** pork in skillet, and cook until browned on both sides.
- **Remove** pork from pan; set aside. Add garlic and mushrooms; cook 30 seconds, stirring constantly. Add apple juice concentrate and pork; simmer 3 minutes until thoroughly heated. **Yield:** 6 servings.

* You can substitute 6 skinned and boned chicken breast halves for pork tenderloins.

♥ Per serving: Calories 275 (14% from fat)
Fat 4.2g (1.4g saturated) Cholesterol 74mg
Sodium 253mg Carbohydrate 32.5g
Fiber 0.6g Protein 25.7g

LEMON BROCCOLI

2 tablespoons grated lemon rind
¼ teaspoon salt
¼ teaspoon freshly ground pepper
1½ pounds fresh broccoli
2 tablespoons lemon juice

- **Combine** first 3 ingredients; set lemon rind mixture aside.
- **Remove** and discard broccoli leaves and tough ends of stalks; cut broccoli into spears.
- **Arrange** broccoli in a steamer basket over boiling water. Cover and steam 5 minutes or until crisp-tender.
- **Arrange** broccoli on a serving platter. Sprinkle with lemon rind mixture and lemon juice. **Yield:** 6 servings.

Rublelene Singleton
Scotts Hill, Tennessee

♥ Per serving: Calories 33 (8% from fat)
Fat 0.4g (0g saturated) Cholesterol 0mg
Sodium 128mg Carbohydrate 6.7g
Fiber 3.6g Protein 3.4g

SESAME PORK TENDERLOIN

¼ cup reduced-sodium soy sauce
¼ cup orange juice
2 tablespoons honey
1 tablespoon peeled, minced fresh ginger
1 clove garlic, minced
2 (¾-pound) pork tenderloins, trimmed
1½ tablespoons toasted sesame seeds
¼ cup Burgundy or other dry red wine
¼ cup ready-to-serve reduced-sodium, fat-free chicken broth
2 teaspoons cornstarch
2 tablespoons water

- **Combine** first 5 ingredients in a shallow dish, and add tenderloins. Cover and chill 8 hours, turning meat occasionally.
- **Remove** tenderloins from marinade; reserve marinade. Place tenderloins in roasting pan. Sprinkle with sesame seeds.

- **Bake** at 350° for 30 minutes or until a meat thermometer inserted in thickest portion registers 160°. Slice and keep warm.
- **Combine** marinade, wine, and broth in a saucepan. Bring to a boil, reduce heat, and simmer 5 minutes. Strain sauce mixture, if desired.
- **Combine** cornstarch and water. Stir into sauce mixture, and bring to a boil. Boil 1 minute, stirring constantly. Serve with pork. **Yield:** 6 servings.

Carol Barclay
Portland, Texas

♥ Per serving: Calories 186 (26% from fat)
Fat 5.3g (1.5g saturated) Cholesterol 64mg
Sodium 370mg Carbohydrate 9.6g
Fiber 0.1g Protein 23.9g

THE ART OF GOOD LIVING

Suzanne Engelmann of Jupiter, Florida, practices what she calls "the art of good living." For her, enjoying fresh foods and getting daily exercise bestows a feeling of fitness. Here she shares her tips for a healthful lifestyle.

- The best food is fresh. Cut out fast and prepackaged food for 10 days. Your palate will sharpen, and you'll enjoy flavors more.

- Have a heaping bowl of fresh vegetables each day. Toss fresh herbs into a green salad, and forgo a rich dressing. A simple dressing of balsamic vinegar and olive oil is all you need.

- Slow down and savor the textures and flavors of each meal. You'll end up eating less and enjoying your food more.

- Collect a file of tasty, easily prepared recipes that use fresh ingredients; frozen prepackaged foods will become less appealing.

GARLIC BROCCOLI

1½ pounds fresh broccoli
1½ teaspoons dark sesame oil
1½ teaspoons vegetable oil
½ teaspoon dried crushed red
     pepper
2 cloves garlic, minced
¼ cup reduced-sodium soy
     sauce
1 tablespoon sugar
1 tablespoon lemon juice
1 tablespoon water

• **Remove** and discard broccoli leaves and tough ends of stalks; cut broccoli into spears.
• **Arrange** broccoli in a steamer basket over boiling water. Cover and steam 5 minutes or until crisp-tender. Remove from heat; keep warm.
• **Heat** sesame and vegetable oils in a small saucepan until hot but not smoking; remove from heat.
• **Add** crushed red pepper, and let stand 10 minutes.
• **Add** garlic and next 4 ingredients, stirring to dissolve sugar.
• **Toss** broccoli spears gently with oil mixture just before serving. Serve hot or cold. **Yield:** 6 servings.

Patsy Bell Hobson
Liberty, Missouri

♥ Per serving: Calories 88 (25% from fat)
Fat 2.7g (0.2g saturated) Cholesterol 0mg
Sodium 357mg Carbohydrate 14.5g
Fiber 3.9g Protein 4.4g

BROCCOLI BITES

■ When buying fresh broccoli, look for a firm bunch with dark green, tightly clustered flowerets. If they are yellowish-green or wilted, or if the stem is slippery, the broccoli is overmature.

■ One bunch of broccoli equals about one-and-a-half pounds. Store in refrigerator, unwashed, up to four days in an airtight bag.

CHANCES ARE IT'S CHICKEN

....

Mornings are always the same: a good-bye kiss and the question "What do you want for supper?" Chances are the answer will be *chicken*. If this is the typical scene at your house, then you're in luck. Here are four recipes from Southern neighbors.

CHICKEN AND RICE

¾ cup long-grain rice, uncooked
2 (10¾-ounce) cans cream of
     chicken soup, undiluted
1 (1-ounce) envelope onion soup
     mix
½ cup milk
6 chicken breast halves, skinned

• **Spread** rice in a lightly greased 13- x 9- x 2-inch baking dish; set aside.
• **Combine** soup, soup mix, and milk, stirring until smooth; set aside ½ cup. Spoon remainder of soup mixture evenly over rice. Top with chicken, meaty side up; spoon remaining ½ cup soup mixture over chicken.
• **Cover** and bake at 300° for 2 hours. **Yield:** 6 servings.

Karen Steenwyks
Brewton, Alabama

SWISS CHICKEN

6 skinned and boned chicken
     breast halves
⅛ teaspoon garlic powder
⅛ teaspoon pepper
6 (4-inch-square) slices Swiss
     cheese
1 (10¾-ounce) can cream of
     chicken soup, undiluted
¼ cup milk
2 cups herb-seasoned stuffing mix
¼ cup butter or margarine,
     melted

• **Place** chicken in a greased 13- x 9- x 2-inch baking dish; sprinkle with garlic powder and pepper. Top each breast with a cheese slice; set aside.
• **Combine** soup and milk, stirring until smooth; pour over chicken. Sprinkle with stuffing mix, and drizzle with butter.
• **Cover** and bake at 350° for 50 minutes or until chicken is done. **Yield:** 6 servings.

Deborah S. Price
Baxley, Georgia

CHICKEN POT PIE

1 (2½-pound) broiler-fryer
2 quarts water
1 teaspoon salt
⅓ cup butter or margarine
1 cup chopped onion
1 cup chopped celery
1 cup chopped carrot
1 small potato, peeled and
     chopped
½ cup frozen English peas, thawed
½ cup all-purpose flour
1 cup half-and-half
1 teaspoon salt
½ teaspoon pepper
½ (15-ounce) package refrigerated
     piecrusts
1 teaspoon all-purpose flour

• **Combine** first 3 ingredients in a Dutch oven, and bring to a boil; cover, reduce heat, and simmer 1 hour. Remove chicken, reserving broth. Skin, bone, and chop chicken; set aside. Skim fat from broth, reserving 2 cups broth.
• **Melt** butter in a large skillet. Add chopped onion and next 4 ingredients; cook, stirring constantly, 10 minutes or until carrot is tender. Add flour, stirring until smooth. Gradually add reserved broth and half-and-half; cook over medium heat, stirring constantly, until thickened and bubbly. Stir in chicken, 1 teaspoon salt, and pepper. Pour into a lightly greased 11- x 7- x 1½-inch baking dish; set aside.
• **Unfold** 1 piecrust, and press out fold lines; sprinkle with 1 teaspoon flour, spreading over surface.

• **Roll** pastry into a 12- x 8-inch rectangle; place floured side down over filling. Fold edges under and crimp; cut slits in top to allow steam to escape.
• **Bake** at 400° for 30 minutes or until golden, covering edges with aluminum foil after 20 minutes to prevent excessive browning. **Yield:** 6 servings.

Note: Use cookie cutters to cut out chicken shapes from remaining refrigerated piecrust, if desired. Place on top of pie before baking.

Judy Wilson
Salem, Virginia

CHICKEN LASAGNA BAKE

8 ounces lasagna noodles, uncooked
1 (10¾-ounce) can cream of chicken soup, undiluted
1 cup canned ready-to-serve chicken broth
½ teaspoon salt
2 (3-ounce) packages cream cheese, softened
1 cup cottage cheese
½ cup sour cream
½ cup mayonnaise or salad dressing
⅓ cup chopped onion
⅓ cup chopped green pepper
⅓ cup chopped pimiento-stuffed olives, drained
¼ cup finely chopped fresh parsley
3 cups chopped cooked chicken
½ cup fine, dry breadcrumbs
1 tablespoon butter or margarine, melted

• **Cook** lasagna according to package directions; drain. Rinse with cold water; drain again, and set aside.
• **Combine** soup, broth, and salt, stirring until smooth; set aside.
• **Combine** cream cheese and next 3 ingredients in a large mixing bowl; beat at medium speed with an electric mixer 1 minute or until smooth. Stir in onion and next 3 ingredients. Set cream cheese mixture aside.
• **Layer** half each of lasagna noodles, cream cheese mixture, soup mixture, and chopped chicken in a lightly greased 13- x 9- x 2-inch baking dish. Repeat layers. Combine breadcrumbs and butter; sprinkle over top.
• **Bake** at 375° for 25 to 30 minutes. **Yield:** 12 servings.

❤ To reduce fat and calories, substitute ready-to-serve, fat-free chicken broth, reduced-fat cream cheese, reduced-fat cottage cheese, reduced-fat sour cream, and reduced-fat mayonnaise.

Melinda Padgett
Little Rock, Arkansas

SODA'S THE SECRET

....

When soda pop pops up in a recipe, you know it's fun. Dispel the elegant character of poached pears by simmering them in a liter of cola.

Even kids love the fun of cooking with soda. One reader sent in the recipe that streamlines old-fashioned cola cake by starting with a chocolate cake mix. And don't forget the entrée. In the recipe below, flank steak marinates in a southwestern-inspired mix of lemon-lime soda, cilantro, and jalapeño peppers. From entrée to dessert, soda's the secret to these recipes.

LEMON-LIME FLANK STEAK

1 (12-ounce) can lemon-lime carbonated beverage (1½ cups)
¼ cup chopped fresh cilantro
¼ cup lime juice
¼ cup vegetable oil
2 cloves garlic, minced
2 jalapeño peppers, unseeded and finely chopped
1 (1½-pound) flank steak
Vegetable cooking spray
Salt

• **Combine** first 6 ingredients in a 2-quart shallow dish, stirring well; add flank steak, turning to coat. Cover and chill 8 hours, turning meat occasionally.
• **Remove** steak from marinade; discarding marinade.
• **Coat** grill rack with cooking spray, and place on grill. Cook steak, covered with grill lid, over medium-hot coals (350° to 400°) about 7 minutes on each side or to desired degree of doneness. Remove steak from grill, and sprinkle evenly with salt. To serve, cut steak diagonally across grain into thin slices. **Yield:** 4 servings.

SODA POP PEARS
(pictured on page 40)

6 pears
1 liter (about 4 cups) cola-flavored carbonated beverage
⅓ cup whipping cream
2 (8-ounce) packages reduced-fat cream cheese, softened
⅓ cup sour cream
¼ cup whipping cream
2 tablespoons sugar
2 teaspoons vanilla extract
Garnish: fresh mint sprigs

• **Peel** pears, leaving stems intact; cut a thin slice from bottom of each pear.
• **Place** pears and cola in a large Dutch oven; bring to a boil. Cover, reduce heat, and simmer 30 minutes or until pears are tender. Cool pears and cola in Dutch oven.
• **Remove** pears; set aside. Bring cola to a boil, and cook over medium-high heat until cola is reduced to 1 cup. Add ⅓ cup whipping cream, and boil 1 minute.
• **Beat** cream cheese in a large mixing bowl at medium speed with an electric mixer until fluffy; add sour cream, ¼ cup whipping cream, sugar, and vanilla, beating well.
• **Spread** cream cheese mixture evenly in center of 6 plates; stand 1 pear on cream cheese mixture on each plate, and top with cola sauce. Garnish, if desired. **Yield:** 6 servings.

Donna Ellis
Speedwell, Tennessee

QUICK CHOCOLATE COLA CAKE

1 (18.25-ounce) package devil's
    food cake mix without
    pudding
1 (3.9-ounce) package chocolate
    instant pudding mix
4 large eggs
½ cup vegetable oil
1 (10-ounce) bottle cola-flavored
    carbonated beverage
    (1¼ cups)
Chocolate-Cola Frosting

• **Combine** cake mix, pudding mix,
eggs, and oil in a large mixing bowl;
beat at low speed with an electric mixer
until blended; set aside.
• **Bring** cola to a boil in a small
saucepan over medium heat. With
mixer on low speed, gradually pour hot
cola into cake batter. Increase speed to
medium; beat 2 minutes.
• **Pour** batter into a greased and
floured 13- x 9- x 2-inch baking pan.
• **Bake** at 350° for 30 minutes or until
a wooden pick inserted in center comes
out clean. Cool in pan on a wire rack
10 minutes.
• **Spread** warm Chocolate-Cola Frosting over top of warm cake; let cake
cool completely on wire rack. **Yield:** 15
servings.

Chocolate-Cola Frosting

½ cup butter or margarine
¼ cup plus 2 tablespoons
    cola-flavored carbonated
    beverage
3 tablespoons cocoa
1 (16-ounce) package powdered
    sugar, sifted
1 teaspoon vanilla extract
1 cup chopped pecans,
    toasted

• **Combine** first 3 ingredients in a large
saucepan; cook over medium heat, stirring constantly, until butter melts. (Do
not boil.) Remove from heat; add powdered sugar and vanilla, stirring until
smooth. Stir in pecans. **Yield:** about
2¼ cups.

Meredith Bennett
Joiner, Arkansas

COMPANY COMING? NO PROBLEM

....

Dinner guests are due in 15 minutes,
and you're still shuffling pots on all
four burners. When the doorbell rings,
you plant a smile on your face and pre-
tend to be relaxed. Oh, what fun.

Put those four pots away, and pick
up this easy dinner menu instead. You
can walk in the door at 5, sort the mail
or walk the dog, and still serve a beautiful dinner to company at 7. We
promise.

You can pick up dessert on the way
home, but on a weekend or when you
have some extra time, you can try your
hand at homemade. Zesty Black-Eyed
Pea Relish has more oomph if chilled
longer, but it's still good after just an
hour or so.

A MEAL WITHOUT MADNESS
Serves Four

Flank Steak-and-Spinach Pinwheels
Zesty Black-Eyed Pea Relish
Toasted Rice and Pasta
Bakery Dessert

FIVE STEPS TO SIMPLICITY

■ Stir together Zesty Black-Eyed Pea
Relish, and chill. (You can walk the
dog or sort the mail now.)

■ Assemble Flank Steak-and-Spinach
Pinwheels (just three ingredients), and
place pinwheels on a broiler pan.

■ Put Toasted Rice and Pasta on cooktop to cook.

■ Broil pinwheels.

■ Spoon rice and pasta in center of
plates. Top with chilled relish and
pinwheels.

FLANK STEAK-AND-SPINACH PINWHEELS
(pictured on page 147)

1 (1¼- to 1½-pound) flank steak
1 (10-ounce) package frozen
    spinach, thawed and well
    drained
¼ cup grated Parmesan cheese
Garnish: fresh flat-leaf parsley

• **Trim** excess fat from steak; make
shallow diagonal cuts on one side of
steak. Place steak between two sheets
of heavy-duty plastic wrap; pound to
⅜-inch thickness, using a meat mallet
or rolling pin.
• **Place** spinach on cut side of steak,
and sprinkle evenly with grated Parmesan cheese. Starting at narrow end, roll
up steak, and secure with wooden picks
at 1-inch intervals. Cut into 1-inch
slices (leaving picks in steak), and place
pinwheels on a lightly greased rack;
place rack in a broiler pan.
• **Broil** pinwheels 5½ inches from heat
(with electric oven door partially
opened) 5 to 7 minutes on each side or
until done. Remove wooden picks, and
serve immediately. Garnish, if desired.
Yield: 4 servings.

Heather Riggins
Nashville, Tennessee

ZESTY BLACK-EYED PEA RELISH
(pictured on page 147)

2 (15½-ounce) cans black-eyed
    peas, rinsed and drained
1 cup chopped celery
1 green pepper, chopped
1 large tomato, peeled and
    chopped
2 cloves garlic, minced
2 green onions, sliced
1 (4-ounce) jar sliced mushrooms,
    drained
1 (4-ounce) jar diced pimiento,
    drained
1 (8-ounce) bottle Italian salad
    dressing
½ teaspoon pepper
3 slices bacon, cooked and
    crumbled (optional)
3 green onions, sliced (optional)

• **Combine** first 10 ingredients in a large bowl, tossing gently. Cover and chill at least 3 hours, stirring occasionally. (Relish will be ready after 1 hour, but will have more flavor with longer chilling.)
• **Drain** mixture, and, if desired, stir in bacon and 3 sliced green onions. **Yield:** 7 cups.

Note: Combine 1 cup leftover Zesty Black-Eyed Pea Relish and 1 cup cooked chilled rice for Hopping John Salad.

Lilann Taylor
Savannah, Georgia

TOASTED RICE AND PASTA
(pictured on page 147)

1½ cups long-grain rice, uncooked
4 ounces angel hair pasta or vermicelli, uncooked and broken into 1½-inch pieces
2 tablespoons vegetable oil
1 large onion, chopped
2 (14½-ounce) cans ready-to-serve chicken broth
¼ cup chopped fresh parsley

• **Cook** rice and pasta in oil in a Dutch oven over medium heat, stirring constantly, 3 to 5 minutes or until golden. Add onion, and cook 3 minutes.
• **Stir** in broth; bring to a boil. Cover, reduce heat to low, and cook 15 to 17 minutes.
• **Stir** in parsley, and serve immediately. **Yield:** 4 to 6 servings.

Mrs. Harland J. Stone
Ocala, Florida

BREAKFAST AT BRENNAN'S – BY THE BOOK

Dinner by candlelight at a white-tablecloth restaurant is often the choice for a special occasion. But in New Orleans, who needs to wait for sunset? "Breakfast at Brennan's" has been a be-all, end-all, budget-busting celebration in that city for decades.

Now, that tradition has been captured in a keepsake cookbook. After thumbing through reminiscent pages of the family history, you can choose from more than 200 recipes to try in your own kitchen. We picked an "eye-opening" champagne punch. The Brennans created this morning wake-up drink in honor of their late cellar master, Herman Funk. It's a Brennan's tradition.

While you sip, peruse other courses from appetizers to desserts. As the book's title implies, you can either begin *or* end your day there – *Breakfast at Brennan's and Dinner, Too.*

MR. FUNK OF NEW ORLEANS

The cookbook gives a recipe for one, but we knew you'd want to share it with friends, so we've adapted it for four to six.

1 (750-milliliter) bottle champagne, chilled
2½ cups cranberry juice drink, chilled
⅓ to ½ cup peach schnapps
Garnish: fresh whole strawberries

• **Combine** first 3 ingredients; pour into stemmed glasses. Garnish, if desired. **Yield:** about 6 cups.

BAKE A BREAD BOWL

Transform packaged bread or dough into showcase bowls for salads, stews, chili, or condiments. Our quick-and-easy instructions show you how.

Cornbread Bowls: Coat a baking sheet with butter-flavored cooking spray. Invert two 10-ounce custard cups several inches apart on baking sheet; coat outside of cups with cooking spray. Separate 1 (11½-ounce) can refrigerated cornbread twists at perforations. Flatten each strip to a 2-inch width. Cover the outside of each custard cup with strips, cutting away excess and moistening edges as needed to seal strips together. Bake at 400° for 10 to 12 minutes. Cool on a wire rack before removing from baking sheet. Remove bowls from custard cups. Use to serve stews or chili. **Yield:** two 10-ounce bowls.

French Bread Bowls: Coat a baking sheet with butter-flavored cooking spray. Invert two 10-ounce custard cups several inches apart on baking sheet; coat outside of cups with cooking spray. Unroll 1 (11-ounce) can refrigerated crusty French bread dough. Cut crosswise into 2 portions. Mold 1 portion of dough around outside of custard cup, allowing edges to extend straight onto baking sheet on two sides. Cut each long extended edge of dough from center to ½ inch from custard cup, forming two flaps. Cross flaps and fold back over custard cup. Repeat procedure with remaining portion of dough and second custard cup. Bake at 400° for 10 minutes. Cool 5 minutes; remove bread from custard cups and baking sheet. Invert on a wire rack; cool completely. Use for serving chicken, tuna, and vegetable salads or thick stews. **Yield:** two 10-ounce bowls.

Lahvosh Cracker Bread Bowl: Coat a baking sheet with butter-flavored cooking spray. Invert a 1½- to 2-quart glass bowl on baking sheet; spray outside with cooking spray. Mist both sides of 1 (16-inch) soft lahvosh cracker bread lightly with water. Gently mold bread around outside of bowl, allowing edges to extend out from bowl onto baking sheet. Bake at 400° for 10 to 12 minutes. Cool completely on a wire rack before removing bread from baking sheet. Remove bread bowl from bowl. Use for serving salads. **Yield:** one 1½- to 2-quart bowl.

Phyllo Bowls: Thaw 8 sheets frozen phyllo dough. Coat a baking sheet with butter-flavored cooking spray. Invert two 10-ounce custard cups several inches apart on baking sheet; coat outside of cups with cooking spray. Cut phyllo sheets in half crosswise. Layer 8 half sheets on one custard cup, coating top of each with cooking spray and turning slightly so that corners of pastry fan out onto baking sheet. Mold phyllo sheets around outside of custard cup. Repeat procedure with remaining 8 half sheets on second custard cup. Bake bowls at 400° for 7 minutes. Cool bowls completely on a wire rack before removing from baking sheet. Remove bowls from custard cups. Use bowls for serving fruit or vegetable salads. **Yield:** two 10-ounce bowls.

Puff Pastry Bowls: Thaw 1 (17¼-ounce) package frozen puff pastry sheets. Coat a baking sheet with butter-flavored cooking spray. Invert two 10-ounce custard cups several inches apart on baking sheet; coat outside of cups with cooking spray. Mold 1 puff pastry sheet around outside of cup, allowing edges to extend out from bowl onto baking sheet. Trim edges of dough, leaving a 1½-inch rim around bowl on baking sheet. Repeat procedure with remaining puff pastry sheet and cup. Bake at 400° for 10 to 12 minutes. Cool completely on a wire rack before removing pastry from baking sheet. Remove bowls from custard cups. Use for serving pudding, fruit salad, or a thick stew. **Yield:** two 10-ounce bowls.

Wonton Wrapper Bowl: Pour vegetable oil to depth of 4 inches into a Dutch oven; heat oil to 350°. Place 1 wonton wrapper on the surface of oil. Immediately submerge wrapper in oil by pressing the wrapper down in the center with the bottom of a wire whisk or bowl of a small ladle (bottom should be 1 to 1½ inches in diameter). Fry 1 minute or until golden. Remove with tongs; drain upside down on paper towels. Use for serving salad dressings, dips, or sauces.

MARCH

GLORIOUS GOAT CHEESE

At Celebrity Dairy, nestled in the North Carolina countryside south of Greensboro, the weathered barn is full of goats and hay and life. There Fleming and Brit Pfann operate North Carolina's only licensed goat dairy where the 100-goat farm produces 150 to 200 pounds of goat cheese weekly. If you've never eaten this versatile cheese, sometimes referred to as chèvre, try these dishes from the Pfanns – they're *great*.

CELEBRITY CHICKEN BREASTS

1 (6-ounce) package long-grain
    and wild rice mix
6 ounces fresh goat cheese (chèvre)
¼ teaspoon garlic powder
¼ teaspoon dried basil
¼ teaspoon pepper
6 skinned and boned chicken
    breast halves
2 ounces fresh goat cheese (chèvre)
2 tablespoons water
¾ cup crushed corn flakes cereal
Garnishes: tomato wedges and
    fresh basil

• **Cook** rice according to package directions; set aside to cool.
• **Combine** 6 ounces cheese and next 3 ingredients, stirring until blended. Add 1 cup cooked rice mix, stirring well; set aside.

• **Place** each breast half between 2 sheets of heavy-duty plastic wrap; flatten each to ¼-inch thickness, using a meat mallet or rolling pin.
• **Spoon** about ¼ cup cheese-rice mixture onto center of each chicken breast half. Fold edges of chicken to center to enclose mixture, and secure with a wooden pick.
• **Combine** 2 ounces of cheese and water, stirring until smooth and the consistency of sour cream. Spread mixture on all surfaces of chicken bundles; coat with crushed corn flakes cereal. Place chicken bundles, seam side down, on a lightly greased baking sheet.
• **Bake** chicken at 375° for 25 minutes. Remove and discard wooden picks; serve warm chicken bundles over remaining rice mix. Garnish, if desired.
Yield: 6 servings.

FEARRINGTON HOUSE GOAT CHEESE AND BLACK-EYED PEA SALAD

This dish, featuring Celebrity Dairy chèvre, is a favorite at Fearrington House Restaurant near Chapel Hill, North Carolina.

1 (6-inch) log fresh goat cheese
    (chèvre)
¼ cup olive oil
½ teaspoon dried thyme
½ teaspoon dried tarragon
½ pound dried black-eyed peas
3 cups water
1 small smoked ham hock
1 bay leaf
2 cloves garlic, minced
½ teaspoon salt
1 purple onion, cut into
    ¼-inch-thick slices
1 sweet red pepper, seeded and cut
    into ¼-inch strips
¼ cup dry breadcrumbs
Leaf lettuce
7 cups mixed salad greens
Vinaigrette

• **Cut** cheese with dental floss into 6 (1-inch) rounds. Place in a small baking dish; drizzle olive oil over cheese, and sprinkle with thyme and tarragon. Cover and chill 8 hours.
• **Sort** and rinse peas; place in a large saucepan. Add 3 cups water and next 4 ingredients; bring to a boil. Cover, reduce heat, and simmer 40 minutes or until peas are just tender. Remove ham hock; set aside. Drain peas; set aside. Remove and discard bay leaf. Cut meat from ham hock. Chop meat, and return to peas; set aside.
• **Cook** onion and red pepper strips, covered with grill lid, over medium-hot coals (350° to 400°) 10 to 15 minutes, turning once; set aside.
• **Coat** the bottom and outside of each goat cheese round with breadcrumbs; place on a nonstick baking sheet.
• **Bake** at 350° for 10 minutes.
• **Arrange** leaf lettuce on a platter; top with mixed salad greens, pea mixture, grilled onion slices, and grilled red pepper strips. Drizzle with Vinaigrette. Top with warm goat cheese rounds.
Yield: 6 servings.

Vinaigrette

⅓ cup red wine vinegar
1 teaspoon dry mustard
1 teaspoon dried oregano
1 teaspoon dried thyme
2 teaspoons honey
1 cup olive oil

• **Position** knife blade in food processor bowl; add first 5 ingredients, and pulse 3 or 4 times. With food processor running, pour olive oil through food chute in a slow, steady stream; process until blended. **Yield:** 1¼ cups.

CREAMED ASPARAGUS ON TOAST

1½ pounds fresh asparagus
8 ounces fresh goat cheese (chèvre)
2½ teaspoons chopped fresh dill
6 slices whole wheat bread
Garnish: lemon zest

• **Snap** off tough ends of asparagus. Remove scales from stalks with a vegetable peeler, if desired. Cover and cook asparagus in a small amount of boiling water 6 minutes or until crisp-tender; drain, reserving ¾ cup cooking liquid. Set asparagus aside.
• **Place** cheese in a saucepan; gradually add ½ cup cooking liquid, whisking with a wire whisk until smooth. Cook mixture over medium heat until sauce is thoroughly heated; stir in dill. Add additional cooking liquid, if desired, for a thinner consistency.
• **Cut** bread slices in half diagonally, and place on a baking sheet. Bake at 350° for 5 minutes or until lightly toasted. Arrange toast on a platter; top with asparagus and sauce. Garnish, if desired. **Yield:** 6 servings.

A new breed of Southern cheesemakers milks sophisticated tastes with a little help from their (barnyard) friends.

Celebrity Dairy features 12 varieties of goat cheese, including fresh logs, seasoned spreadables, and herbed cheese marinated in olive oil. All is sold to gourmet grocers and restaurants in Chapel Hill, Raleigh, and Durham. The Pfanns' products are also available at farmers markets in Carrboro and at Fearrington Village near Chapel Hill. Like most commercial goat cheese, theirs sells from $7 to $12 a pound.

The couple share a deep affection for goats and a love for their work. Goats, say the "ambassadors of goat cheese" as the Pfanns call themselves, are "very affectionate and intelligent – they love to be around people. Most livestock aren't so interesting," Fleming says. And most farm animals aren't named after such celebrities as Benjamin Franklin, Tallulah Bankhead, and Shirley Chisolm, either. "We have a lot of fun naming our goats," Fleming says.

But with the fun comes a lot of hard work. She readily admits that working such long hours, especially from March until Thanksgiving – the peak of milking season – can be backbreaking.

There's daily feeding, milking, pasteurizing, adding yogurt cultures, separating curds and whey, forming and wrapping cheese, cleaning, marketing, delivering, maintaining grounds, checking on the baby goats, and gathering eggs in the hen house. "Vacations? *Hah!*" Fleming muses.

As a highlight of their pastoral profession, one Sunday a month the Pfanns offer a casual goat cheese dinner on their 215-acre, walnut tree-shaded property. It features comparative cheese tastings, a dinner showcasing their goat cheese, and a barn tour.

If you can't make it to North Carolina for one of their dinners, you can enjoy the next best thing with their recipes. For a listing of other Southern goat cheesemakers, turn to page 63.

GOAT CHEESE 101

No two goat cheeses are exactly alike. From state to state, country to country, you taste subtle, sometimes even strong, differences.

As opposed to the French varieties, American-style goat cheese is younger (usually two to four weeks old) and milder (except for aged varieties, which can be quite pungent). Like cheeses made with cow's milk, goat cheeses come in a variety of shapes, sizes, and styles. Here are a few of the most common styles.

■ **Soft fresh,** the most widely available, is found in both a soft, creamy form (fromage blanc) or in plain, sliceable logs, like the variety that's popular in Montrachet, France. Soft fresh goat cheeses are often rolled in herbs, decorated with flowers, or marinated in oil and spices. An edible ash, often used in France as a protective coating, is used less in America, replaced by breathable plastic wrap.

■ **Semisoft** goat cheese comes in fresh or aged varieties. The types include plain or seasoned goat mozzarella or Jack.

■ **Surface-ripened** goat cheeses have smooth surface molds and include styles like goat blue, Camembert, and Brie.

■ **Hard-aged** goat cheeses range from crumbly feta to hard, grating cheeses like white Cheddar.

ITS USES

Goat cheese makes a versatile substitute in a variety of dishes from lasagna to cheesecake. Fresh goat cheese can be used as a substitute for cream cheese in most recipes, but the goat cheese is much lighter and cleaner in taste.

Serve chèvre spread on toast, mixed with sugar and rum and layered on fruit, stuffed inside pasta, or melted on pizza or sandwiches. Use it in soups or desserts.

It's easier to slice a log of goat cheese when it's at room temperature; it will crumble when cold. **Tip:** For even slicing, use a string of dental floss instead of a knife.

HEALTH BENEFITS

Goat cheese is more easily digestible than other cheeses. It contains 20% fewer calories, more than twice the protein, and at least 30% less fat than cream cheese.

BUYING AND STORING

■ Store goat cheese in the coldest part of the refrigerator; it'll remain unchanged for up to three weeks. After this time, mold may grow on the surface, but after it's scraped off, the cheese isn't harmful to eat (although its flavor will be intensified). For best results, remove cheese from refrigerator about one hour before serving.

■ Avoid storing goat cheese in a sealed plastic bag – excess moisture encourages the growth of foreign mold. Instead, use wax paper to wrap; the cheese will be able to breathe and age properly. **Tip:** Refrigerator-dried goat cheese can be grated and used like Parmesan.

■ For more lengthy storage, consider freezing chèvre. As long as the cheese is in good condition and tightly wrapped (either in heavy-duty plastic wrap or aluminum foil), its flavor, texture, and moisture content will remain unchanged.

■ Goat cheese is higher in price than cow's milk cheese because of the scarcity of goat's milk. The average goat produces only two to three quarts of milk daily, while a cow produces between 10 and 20.

BUTTERNUT SQUASH SOUP

1 (2½-pound) butternut squash, peeled, seeded, and cut into 1-inch chunks
3 cups water
2 medium onions, chopped
1 large sweet red pepper, seeded and finely chopped
2 cloves garlic, pressed
3 tablespoons vegetable oil
1 teaspoon ground cumin
1 teaspoon ground coriander
1 teaspoon ground ginger
1 teaspoon dry mustard
1 teaspoon curry powder
½ teaspoon salt
1 cup orange juice
1 teaspoon lemon juice
⅛ teaspoon ground red pepper
¼ cup fresh goat cheese (chèvre)
¼ cup water

● **Combine** squash and 3 cups water in a large saucepan. Bring to a boil over medium-high heat; cover, reduce heat, and simmer 10 minutes or until squash is tender. Drain, reserving cooking liquid; set both aside.

● **Cook** chopped onion, chopped sweet red pepper, and garlic in oil in a Dutch oven over medium-high heat, stirring constantly, 10 minutes or until tender.

● **Add** cumin, coriander, ginger, mustard, curry powder, and salt, stirring mixture well.

● **Combine** half of squash and half of cooked onion mixture in container of an electric blender; process until smooth, stopping once to scrape down sides.

● **Pour** blended squash mixture into another container. Repeat procedure with remaining squash and onion mixture, return blended squash mixture to Dutch oven.

● **Add** orange juice, lemon juice, ground red pepper, and cooking liquid to squash mixture. Cook over medium heat, stirring constantly, until thoroughly heated.

● **Combine** cheese and ¼ cup water, stirring until mixture is smooth and the consistency of sour cream. Dollop mixture onto the center of each serving. **Yield:** 7 cups.

POPPY SEED CAKE

Though the idea of goat cheese in this cake may surprise you, trust us – you'll love the sweet, mildly tangy flavor.

½ cup fresh goat cheese (chèvre)
¾ cup water
1 (18.25-ounce) package yellow cake mix
1 (3.4-ounce) package vanilla instant pudding mix
1 cup all-purpose flour
4 large eggs
½ cup vegetable oil
½ cup bourbon
¼ cup poppy seeds

• **Combine** cheese and water in a small bowl, stirring until mixture is smooth and the consistency of sour cream. Set aside.

• **Combine** cake mix, pudding mix, and flour in a large mixing bowl, stirring until blended. Add cheese mixture, eggs, vegetable oil, and bourbon; beat at low speed with an electric mixer until moistened. Beat mixture at medium speed 2 minutes, scraping down sides of bowl occasionally.

• **Stir** in poppy seeds; spoon batter into a well-greased 12-cup Bundt pan.

• **Bake** at 350° for 55 minutes or until a wooden pick inserted in center comes out clean. Cool in pan on a wire rack 10 minutes; remove from pan, and cool completely on wire rack.

• **Serve** with fruit preserves or ice cream. **Yield:** one 10-inch cake.

GOAT CHEESE ACROSS THE SOUTH

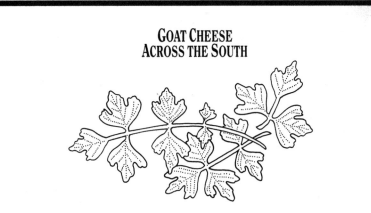

These Southern grade-A licensed goat dairy farms offer plain and flavored, fresh and aged goat cheese.

ALABAMA

■ **Fromagerie Belle Chèvre,** 26910 Bethel Road, Elkmont, 35620 (20 miles northwest of Huntsville); (205) 423-2238. Features a variety of fresh goat cheese. Operated since 1988. Mail order available.

■ **Sweet Home Farm,** 27107 Schoen Road, Elberta, 36530 (18 miles northeast of Gulf Shores); (334) 986-5663. Offers a selection of fresh and aged cow's and goat's milk cheese. Operated since 1987. Mail order is available in cold months only.

LOUISIANA

■ **Chicory Farm,** P.O. Box 25, Mount Hermon, 70450 (80 miles north of New Orleans); (504) 877-4550. Offers a variety of aged farmstead European-style cheese made from cow's, goat's, and sheep's milk. Operated since 1990. Mail order available.

MARYLAND

■ **Brentland Farm & Goat Dairy Corporation,** 7550 Brentland Road, Welcome, 20693 (35 miles south of Washington, D.C.); (301) 934-1818. Offers pasteurized grade-A goat's milk and a small amount of fresh goat cheese. Operated since 1977. No mail order.

NORTH CAROLINA

■ **Celebrity Goat Dairy,** 2106 Mount Vernon-Hickory Mountain Road, Siler City, 27344 (1 hour south of Greensboro); (919) 742-5176. Features a variety of fresh goat cheese. Operated since 1990. No mail order.

SOUTH CAROLINA

■ **Split Creek Farm,** 3806 Centerville Road, Anderson, 29625 (10 miles south of Clemson); (803) 287-3921. Offers a variety of fresh and semiaged goat's milk cheese. Operated since 1986. Mail order available.

TEXAS

■ **Larsen Farms,** H.C. 01, Box 98B, Dripping Springs, 78620 (between Austin and San Antonio); (210) 833-5192. Offers a variety of fresh goat cheese. Operated since 1987. No mail order available.

■ **Mozzarella Company,** 2944 Elm Street, Dallas, 75226; (214) 741-4072 or 1-800-798-2954. Features a variety of aged and fresh cow's and goat's milk cheese. Operated since 1982. Mail order available.

WEST VIRGINIA

■ **Brier Run Farm,** H.C. 32, Box 73, Birch River, 26610 (approximately 70 miles northeast of Charleston); (304) 649-2975. Offers a variety of fresh, certified organic goat cheese. Operated since 1985. Mail order available.

Searing Heat, Subtle Flavors

....

Why would you even *want* to blacken and blister vegetables in an intensely hot oven? Because an ordinary recipe becomes sublime when you roast the ingredients first.

Roasting imparts a depth of flavor that you can't achieve with any other method of cooking. The extreme heat caramelizes the natural sugars in vegetables, saturating them with a sweet, smoky flavor.

So, cooks, preheat your ovens. Take the time for roasting. You'll be generously rewarded for your efforts with extraordinary flavor.

ROASTED TOMATO SALSA

12 Roma tomatoes
2 cloves garlic, unpeeled
1 small onion, quartered
1 medium jalapeño pepper
1½ tablespoons olive oil
1 teaspoon ground cumin
¼ teaspoon salt
3 tablespoons fresh lime juice
¼ cup chopped fresh cilantro

•Toss first 4 ingredients with olive oil; spread vegetables in a 13- x 9- x 2-inch pan. Broil 5½ inches from heat (with electric oven door partially opened) 10 minutes or until vegetables are charred; cool.
•Remove and discard tomato cores. Remove and discard stem (but not seeds) from pepper. Peel garlic, discarding skins.
•Position knife blade in food processor bowl; add roasted vegetables. Pulse 4 times or until vegetables are coarsely chopped. Stir in cumin and remaining ingredients. Serve with tortilla chips or as a sauce with Roasted Chiles Rellenos (see recipe). **Yield:** 3 cups.

Stanlay Webber
Winston-Salem, North Carolina

ROASTED TOMATILLO SALSA

2½ pounds fresh tomatillos
6 cloves garlic, unpeeled
4 large jalapeño peppers
2 large onions, quartered
2½ tablespoons vegetable oil
½ to ¾ teaspoon salt
½ teaspoon freshly ground pepper
½ cup chopped fresh cilantro
½ cup whipping cream

•Remove and discard tomatillo husks; rinse tomatillos.
•Toss tomatillos and next 3 ingredients in vegetable oil; spread vegetables in a 13- x 9- x 2-inch pan.
•Bake at 500° for 15 minutes or until vegetables are charred; cool. Remove and discard stems (but not seeds) from peppers. Peel garlic, discarding skins. Drain tomatillos, discarding any liquid.
•Position knife blade in food processor bowl; add roasted vegetables. Pulse 4 times in processor or until vegetables are coarsely chopped.
•Pour mixture into a bowl; stir in salt and remaining ingredients. Serve with Roasted Chiles Rellenos (see recipe), tortilla chips, or grilled chicken. **Yield:** 4 cups.

Sandy San Jose
Richmond, Texas

ROASTED CHILES RELLENOS

Use Anaheim or poblano peppers for this recipe.

10 large long green chile peppers
2½ cups (10 ounces) shredded Longhorn cheese
3 large eggs, separated
¼ teaspoon salt
2 tablespoons all-purpose flour
Vegetable oil
Roasted Tomato Salsa or Roasted Tomatillo Salsa (see recipes)

•Wash and dry peppers; place on an aluminum foil-lined baking sheet.
•Broil 5½ inches from heat (with electric oven door partially opened) about 5 minutes on each side or until peppers look blistered.
•Place peppers in a heavy-duty, zip-top plastic bag immediately; seal and let stand 10 minutes. Peel peppers, leaving stems intact; split one side of peppers. Remove and discard membranes and seeds; set aside.
•Spoon cheese evenly into center of peppers. Close pepper over cheese; set aside.
•Beat egg yolks; set aside. Beat egg whites and salt in a small mixing bowl at high speed with an electric mixer until soft peaks form. Add egg yolks and flour, beating well; set aside.
•Pour oil to depth of 1 inch into a large, heavy skillet; heat to 350°.
•Dip filled peppers into egg mixture.
•Fry peppers 1½ to 2 minutes on each side or until golden. Drain on paper towels. Serve with Roasted Tomato Salsa or Roasted Tomatillo Salsa. **Yield:** 5 main-dish or 10 appetizer servings.

Hilda Marshall
Bealeton, Virginia

ROASTED VEGETABLES

4 small yellow squash, cut into 1-inch slices
4 small zucchini, cut into 1-inch slices
2 large purple or sweet onions, quartered
2 tablespoons olive oil
2 teaspoons dried oregano
½ to ¾ teaspoon salt
½ teaspoon pepper
2 large sweet red peppers, seeded and cut into ½-inch strips
2 large sweet yellow peppers, seeded and cut into ½-inch strips
2 tablespoons balsamic vinegar
¼ cup chopped fresh parsley

•Toss first 3 ingredients with olive oil; spread mixture in a large roasting pan, and sprinkle with oregano, salt, and pepper.
•Bake at 500° for 10 minutes. Add pepper strips; toss gently. Bake 10

additional minutes or until vegetables are tender and begin to char.
- **Place** in a serving bowl; cool slightly. Add vinegar and parsley; toss gently. **Yield:** 6 to 8 servings.

Ann Beckham
Macon, Georgia

ROASTED ONION SALAD

5   medium onions, unpeeled and
    cut into ½-inch-thick slices
¼   cup olive oil
8   cups mixed baby lettuces
½   cup chopped walnuts, toasted
1   (4-ounce) package crumbled
    blue cheese
Garlic Vinaigrette

- **Arrange** onion slices in a lightly greased roasting pan. Drizzle evenly with olive oil.
- **Bake** at 500° for 10 minutes or until onion slices are lightly charred; cool. Remove and discard outer skin of onion slices. Set onion slices aside.
- **Combine** lettuces, walnuts, and blue cheese; toss gently. Top with roasted onion slices; drizzle with Garlic Vinaigrette. **Yield:** 8 servings.

Garlic Vinaigrette

4   cloves garlic
2   shallots
¼   cup chopped fresh parsley
½   teaspoon dried crushed red
    pepper
½   teaspoon salt
½   teaspoon freshly ground black
    pepper
2   tablespoons white wine vinegar
⅔   cup olive oil

- **Position** knife blade in food processor bowl; add garlic and shallots, and pulse 3 or 4 times. Add parsley and next 4 ingredients; process 20 seconds, stopping once to scrape down sides.
- **Pour** olive oil through food chute in a slow, steady stream with processor running, and process until blended. **Yield:** 1 cup.

W. N. Cottrell II
New Orleans, Louisiana

CREAM OF ROASTED SWEET RED PEPPER SOUP
(pictured on page 73)

8   large sweet red peppers
6   cloves garlic, minced
1   small onion, chopped
3   tablespoons butter or margarine,
    divided
2   (14½-ounce) cans ready-to-serve
    chicken broth
2   cups dry white wine
1   bay leaf
½   teaspoon salt
¼   teaspoon pepper
2   tablespoons all-purpose flour
1½ cups whipping cream
Garnish: fresh basil, cut into thin
    strips

- **Place** peppers on an aluminum foil-lined baking sheet; broil 5½ inches from heat (with electric oven door partially opened) about 5 minutes on each side or until peppers look blistered.
- **Place** roasted peppers in a heavy-duty, zip-top plastic bag immediately; seal and let stand 10 minutes. Peel peppers; remove and discard stem and seeds. Set roasted peppers aside.
- **Cook** minced garlic and chopped onion in 1 tablespoon butter in a Dutch oven over medium heat until crisp-tender. Add chicken broth and next 4 ingredients; bring to a boil. Reduce heat, and simmer 30 minutes. Pour broth mixture through a large wire-mesh strainer into a large container, reserving solids. Remove and discard bay leaf. Set broth mixture aside.
- **Position** knife blade in food processor bowl; add reserved solids and roasted peppers. Process 30 seconds or until mixture is smooth, stopping once to scrape down sides; set pepper puree aside.
- **Melt** remaining 2 tablespoons butter in Dutch oven over low heat; add flour, stirring until smooth. Cook 1 minute, stirring constantly. Gradually add broth mixture; cook over medium heat, stirring constantly, until thickened and bubbly (about 3 minutes). Stir in pepper puree. Gradually stir in whipping cream. Cook over low heat until thoroughly heated. Garnish, if desired. **Yield:** 8 cups.

Nicholas Rutyna
San Antonio, Texas

HOT TIPS FOR ROASTING

- Stay close to the kitchen. When you're cooking at 500°, there's a fine line between roasted and burned. Vegetables should only have highlights of charring. If they're completely black, then you've gone too far.

- Use a heavy baking pan for roasting. A thin pan may warp under the high heat. Select a pan with sides; the vegetables will lose some water during roasting. Make sure the pan is large enough so that vegetables are not crowded. If not directly exposed to heat, the vegetables won't brown.

- Most vegetables need to be coated with oil before roasting to ensure even browning and to keep them from sticking together. Peppers can be roasted without oil, but make sure that you line the pan with aluminum foil for easy cleanup.

- Always roast with the pan uncovered or the vegetables will be steamed, not roasted. If covered, they will not develop the characteristic brown color and caramelized flavor.

- The pan will be extremely hot when you take it out of the oven, so have some heavy oven mitts close-by. Know where you are going to put the pan before you take it out of the oven.

Simple Salads Made Sensational

....

Celebrate spring's arrival with salads. These recipes are based on some familiar ingredients, like cauliflower and spinach. What's new, however, is the way these salads are arranged. For some tips on another salad basic that's anything but boring, see "From Our Kitchen to Yours" on the next page, and rediscover greens.

MARINATED ARTICHOKE SALAD

For this salad presentation, we cooked fresh artichokes and opened them up like a flower, then spooned the Curry Mayonnaise and salad on top. For ease, use canned artichokes in the salad. Short on time? Serve this salad on a bed of lettuce.

4 medium fresh artichokes
4 to 6 Roma tomatoes, sliced
Curry Mayonnaise
Marinated Artichoke Hearts

● **Hold** artichokes by the stem; wash by plunging up and down in cold water. Cut off stem end; trim about ½ inch from top of each artichoke. Remove any loose bottom leaves.
● **Arrange** artichokes in a steamer basket over boiling water. Cover and steam 25 minutes or until tender. Drain and chill until cool.
● **Spread** artichoke leaves apart to reach center; press down gently to flatten. Cut off yellow leaves; remove fuzzy thistle (choke) with a spoon, and discard. Place an artichoke on each serving plate; repeat procedure with remaining artichokes.
● **Arrange** tomato slices on artichoke leaves. Dollop Curry Mayonnaise in center, and top with Marinated Artichoke Hearts. **Yield:** 4 servings.

Curry Mayonnaise

1 cup mayonnaise
¼ cup sour cream
1 tablespoon lemon juice
1 tablespoon grated onion
½ teaspoon curry powder

● **Combine** all ingredients, stirring until blended. **Yield:** 1¼ cups.

Marinated Artichoke Hearts

1 (14-ounce) can quartered artichoke hearts, rinsed and drained
1 tablespoon sugar
2 tablespoons lemon juice
2 tablespoons olive oil
2 tablespoons water
¼ teaspoon garlic powder
¼ teaspoon dried oregano
¼ teaspoon dried tarragon

● **Combine** all ingredients; cover and chill 8 hours. **Yield:** 1½ cups.
Myrt Pfannkuche
Pell City, Alabama

CAULIFLOWER-ENGLISH PEA SALAD

The traditional cauliflower and pea salad takes on a new look when cradled in a bed of radicchio, red leaf cabbage, or red-tipped lettuce. Serve the Creamy Dressing on the side so you can see the shapes and colors of the vegetables.

1 head cauliflower, separated into flowerets
1 bunch radishes, thinly sliced
2 stalks celery, diagonally sliced
½ cup sliced fresh mushrooms
1 (10-ounce) package frozen English peas, thawed and drained
1 large head radicchio
Creamy Dressing
Garnish: chopped fresh chives

● **Combine** first 5 ingredients.
● **Arrange** radicchio leaves on 6 salad plates. Spoon vegetable mixture evenly inside leaves.

● **Spoon** Creamy Dressing beside vegetables; garnish, if desired. **Yield:** 6 servings.

Creamy Dressing

1½ cups mayonnaise
1 (3-ounce) package cream cheese, softened
1 teaspoon salt-free lemon-and-herb seasoning

● **Combine** all ingredients, stirring until well blended. **Yield:** 1½ cups.
Carroll Quisenberry
Childress, Texas

SPINACH SALAD WITH THE BLUES

Spoon the salad dressing on the plate, and arrange the salad on top. To shred fresh spinach, roll several leaves together. Use kitchen scissors or a sharp knife to cut the roll at ¼-inch intervals.

½ cup chopped walnuts
⅓ cup olive oil
¼ cup white wine vinegar
1 tablespoon prepared mustard
1 teaspoon sugar (optional)
1 (10-ounce) bag fresh spinach, washed, trimmed, and shredded
1 head Belgian endive, washed and trimmed
2 Red Delicious apples, cored and thinly sliced
1 (4-ounce) package crumbled blue cheese

● **Spread** walnuts in a shallow pan. Bake at 350° for 5 minutes, stirring occasionally. Set aside.
● **Combine** olive oil, vinegar, mustard, and, if desired, sugar in a jar. Cover tightly, and shake vigorously. Pour evenly onto 6 salad plates.
● **Arrange** spinach on top of dressing.
● **Arrange** endive leaves and thin apple slices evenly beside shredded spinach.
● **Sprinkle** with walnuts and blue cheese. **Yield:** 6 servings.
Agnes L. Stone
Ocala, Florida

From Our Kitchen to Yours

Today an army of salad greens – leaf lettuce, curly endive, escarole, radicchio, romaine, and watercress – keeps salads from being boring. Here's a primer.

....

Remember when bland, crunchy iceberg was the sole lettuce in the grocery store? Now there's a variety of lettuces available, and it's easy to toss together a combination of them to bring color, texture, and flavor to the table. Here are a few tips.

GREENS GALORE

■ Lettuce grows in many sizes and shapes. There are four general classifications of lettuce – Boston, iceberg, red or green leaf, and romaine.

■ Combine tangy greens with those milder in flavor, crisp greens with tender varieties, and pale greens with those flashier in color.

■ Large-leaf greens offer more leaf for your money and take less time to wash. (Rule of thumb: 1 pound iceberg, leaf lettuce, or romaine yields about 6¼ cups torn pieces; 1 pound endive yields only about 4¼ cups.)

■ Familiar round **iceberg,** which stores easily and holds its texture well, is tossed in more salads than any other lettuce. It is the mildest in flavor of all greens and works well with flavor-packed ones. Try combining iceberg or other mild-flavored greens (Bibb, romaine, red or green leaf, and spinach) with bitter greens (Belgian and curly endive, escarole, frisee, and radicchio).

■ **Arugula** has dark-green leaves and a pungent flavor which adds a spicy taste when combined with sweet or bitter greens.

■ The spear-shaped leaves of **Belgian endive** are pale green, almost white, with slightly ruffled, pale-yellow edges. **Curly endive** has large, lacy (almost prickly), dark-green outer leaves and tender, pale-green inner ones. Their textures are crisp. Pair Belgian endive with a sweet, creamy dressing. Mix curly endive with other bitter greens; top with a robust vinaigrette.

■ **Escarole** has dark-green outer leaves that are loosely packed and slightly furled. It has a bitter flavor with a slightly sweet edge and is excellent in mixed green salads.

■ **Frisee,** lettuce with frilly light-green leaves, firm white ribs, and a light-yellow central core, is the least bitter of all.

■ Developed in Italy, **radicchio** is a delicacy. Beautifully veined leaves are any shade from bright red to maroon, and the head ranges from the size of a golf ball to a grapefruit.

■ **Watercress,** a member of the mustard family, has a peppery flavor. Its 5- to 6-inch sprigs have crisp, succulent stems and tender green leaves.

THE BASICS

■ Look for fresh, crisp greens with firm, unblemished leaves. Choose compact heads that give slightly when squeezed.

■ Greens last longer if they're washed as soon as you get home.

■ To clean tight heads of greens, such as iceberg lettuce, tap the core end of the head firmly against a counter; then pull or twist out the core. Rinse lettuce, core end up, under cool, running water, spreading the edges of the leaves so water runs between them. Drain, core end down. Wrap loosely in paper towels, place in a zip-top plastic bag, and store in refrigerator up to two weeks.

■ To clean leafy greens, cut off the bottom to separate leaves, and soak in cold water 10 minutes. Drain, whisk away water in a salad spinner, and store in refrigerator up to one week in zip-top plastic bags with a few paper towels to absorb any remaining moisture. (Squeeze out as much air as possible before sealing the bag.)

IT'S IN THE BAG

Precut greens trim time, not money. Ready-to-use packages of spinach, lettuces, and slaw mixes cost only pennies more and need just a quick wash. A 1-pound bag of garden salad (mostly iceberg, carrots, and red cabbage) serves five for about 32 cents per serving; a 1-pound head of iceberg serves four for about 24 cents per serving.

If you don't need to serve a lot of people, try the mixed salads, such as the Mediterranean salad (romaine, radicchio, and endive), which serves three for about 75 cents per serving.

Choose the prepackaged bags carefully; some ingredients look wilted before the sell-by date.

BUILD A MEAL

· ·

Let's engage in some constructive play with these dishes, shall we?

Here's the game: Match any of the following entrées with any of our suggested Base Hits (see box). No matter how you mix and match, you'll wind up with quick, inventive meals.

ITALIAN CHICKEN AND ARTICHOKES

1 (12-ounce) jar marinated
    artichoke hearts, undrained
2 cloves garlic, minced
6 skinned and boned chicken
    breast halves
1 (10¾-ounce) can cream of
    chicken soup, undiluted
1 (8-ounce) carton sour cream
½ cup (2 ounces) shredded
    mozzarella cheese
¼ cup grated Parmesan cheese
¼ cup Chablis or other dry white
    wine
¼ teaspoon salt
¼ teaspoon pepper

• **Drain** artichokes, reserving marinade in a large nonstick skillet. Cut artichokes in half, and set aside. Add garlic to skillet, and bring to a boil over medium heat.
• **Add** chicken to skillet; cook 10 minutes, turning once. Remove chicken from skillet; drain and discard marinade and drippings from pan. Wipe clean with paper towels.
• **Combine** soup and next 6 ingredients in skillet; return chicken to skillet. Cover and cook over medium heat 5 minutes or until chicken is tender. Add artichokes; cover and cook 2 minutes or until thoroughly heated. **Yield:** 6 servings.

Debbie Collard Estes
Vine Grove, Kentucky

BASE HITS

■ **Basmati or long-grain American basmati:** Boil 1 cup rice in 1¾ to 2 cups water (1 teaspoon butter and ½ teaspoon salt, optional). Stir once; cover with tight-fitting lid, reduce heat, and simmer 15 to 20 minutes. Remove from heat; let stand covered 5 minutes. Serves 4.

■ **Cornbread:** Preheat oven to 400°. Combine 7½ ounces cornbread mix and ½ cup milk; bake in lightly greased 8-inch cast-iron skillet or nonstick baking pan for 16 to 18 minutes. Serves 4.

■ **Couscous:** Melt 2 tablespoons butter in 1½ cups boiling salted water or broth. Add 1 cup couscous. Cover and remove from heat. Let stand 5 minutes. Turn into serving dish, and fluff with fork. Serves 4.

■ **French bread:** Slice 1 medium loaf in half lengthwise; lightly coat cut sides of bread with butter. Broil 5½ inches from heat, 2 to 3 minutes or until browned. Serves 4.

■ **Instant brown rice:** Boil 1¾ cups water; stir in 2 cups rice. Return to boil, and reduce heat to low; cover and simmer 5 minutes. Remove from heat and stir; cover. Let stand 5 minutes. Fluff rice with fork. Serves 4.

■ **Instant premium long-grain rice:** Boil 2¼ cups water, and stir in 1 (7-ounce) package rice. Cover and remove from heat. Let stand 5 minutes. Fluff rice with fork. Serves 4.

■ **Pasta** (dried varieties, excluding herbed or flavored ones): Boil 2 quarts water, and add salt, if desired. Add 7 to 8 ounces pasta, and cook 6 to 8 minutes or until pasta reaches desired tenderness. Drain pasta well. Serves 4.

■ **Pasta** (refrigerated varieties): Add 9 ounces pasta to 3 quarts boiling water. Boil gently 2 to 3 minutes or until pasta is tender, stirring occasionally. Serves 3.

EASY SHRIMP CREOLE

6 cups water
2 pounds unpeeled medium-size
    fresh shrimp *
1 medium-size sweet red pepper,
    seeded and chopped
1 medium-size green pepper,
    seeded and chopped
2 cloves garlic, minced
2 tablespoons olive oil
2 (14½-ounce) cans Cajun-style
    stewed tomatoes, undrained
Garnish: chopped green onions

• **Bring** water to a boil; add shrimp, and cook 3 to 5 minutes or until shrimp turn pink. Drain well, and rinse with cold water.
• **Peel** shrimp, and devein, if desired; set aside.
• **Cook** peppers and garlic in olive oil in a large skillet over medium-high heat, stirring constantly, until tender. Add tomatoes; bring to a boil. Reduce heat, and simmer 8 minutes. Add shrimp; cook 2 minutes or until thoroughly heated. Garnish, if desired. **Yield:** 4 servings.

* You can substitute 2 (12-ounce) packages medium-size frozen shrimp for fresh. Cook according to package directions; drain.

Susan Bellan
Baton Rouge, Louisiana

SWEET PEPPERY SAUSAGE

1 pound Italian sausage, sliced into ¾-inch pieces
Vegetable cooking spray
1 medium onion, sliced into ¼-inch rings
1 tablespoon olive oil
2 cloves garlic, minced
1 sweet red pepper, cut into ¼-inch strips
1 sweet yellow pepper, cut into ¼-inch strips
1 cup sliced fresh mushrooms
1 cup dry white vermouth
1 teaspoon dried basil
1 teaspoon dried oregano

• **Cook** sausage in a nonstick skillet coated with cooking spray; drain well, and set aside.
• **Cook** onion in olive oil 2 minutes; add garlic and next 3 ingredients. Cook over medium heat, stirring constantly, 4 minutes or until vegetables are crisp-tender. Add sausage and vermouth. Cook over high heat until liquid is reduced by half. Stir in basil and oregano. **Yield:** 4 servings.

Lyn DelCaro
Louisville, Colorado

PORK CACCIATORE

2 (¾-pound) pork tenderloins, cut into ½-inch-thick medaillons
2 to 4 tablespoons olive oil
2 medium-size green peppers, seeded and cut into 1-inch pieces
2 medium onions, cut into 1-inch pieces
1 (8-ounce) can tomato sauce
1 cup water
½ teaspoon dried oregano
¼ teaspoon salt
¼ teaspoon ground nutmeg
¼ teaspoon pepper
1 (4-ounce) can sliced mushrooms, drained

• **Brown** pork medaillons in olive oil in a large skillet over medium heat; remove pork, reserving drippings in skillet. Set pork aside.

• **Add** peppers and onion to drippings in skillet; cook over medium heat until lightly browned.
• **Return** pork to skillet; add tomato sauce and next 5 ingredients.
• **Bring** mixture to a boil; reduce heat, and simmer 15 minutes. Add mushrooms, and cook 5 additional minutes. **Yield:** 6 servings.

Caroline Wallace Kennedy
Newborn, Georgia

BEEF BURGUNDY

1 pound beef sirloin steak, cut into 2-inch strips
2 tablespoons olive oil
1 cup scraped and thinly sliced carrot
¼ cup chopped green onions
½ cup sliced fresh mushrooms
1 tablespoon all-purpose flour
½ teaspoon salt
¼ teaspoon pepper
¼ teaspoon dried thyme
½ cup Burgundy or other dry red wine
½ cup beef broth

• **Brown** beef in oil in a large skillet or Dutch oven over medium-high heat about 2 minutes or until meat is browned. Remove beef with a slotted spoon, reserving drippings in skillet; set beef aside.
• **Add** carrot and green onions to reserved drippings in skillet; cook over medium-high heat until crisp-tender. Add mushrooms; cook 2 minutes. Reduce heat; stir in flour and next 3 ingredients. Gradually add wine and broth, stirring constantly.
• **Return** beef strips to skillet; simmer 10 minutes or until meat is tender. **Yield:** 4 servings.

Michelle Ettenger
Alpharetta, Georgia

MEXICAN STACK-UP

1 pound ground beef
1 medium onion, chopped
1 green pepper, seeded and chopped
2 (8-ounce) cans tomato sauce
1 (1¼-ounce) package taco seasoning mix
¾ cup water
Condiments: chopped tomato, shredded Cheddar cheese, sliced olives, sour cream, and chopped green onions

• **Cook** first 3 ingredients in a large skillet over medium-high heat, stirring constantly, until meat crumbles; drain well. Return beef mixture to skillet; add tomato sauce, taco seasoning mix, and water. Bring mixture to a boil; reduce heat, and simmer 10 minutes.
• **Top** beef mixture with desired condiments. **Yield:** 4 to 6 servings.

Jennifer Simpson
Brownwood, Texas

VEGETARIAN SAUTÉ

1 medium onion, chopped
1 medium-size green pepper, seeded and chopped
1 medium zucchini, chopped
2 cloves garlic, minced
2 tablespoons olive oil
1 (14½-ounce) can chili-style stewed tomatoes, undrained
1 (15-ounce) can dark red kidney beans, rinsed and drained
½ teaspoon dried oregano
¼ teaspoon salt
¼ teaspoon pepper
½ cup (2 ounces) shredded Cheddar cheese

• **Cook** first 4 ingredients in olive oil in a large skillet over medium-high heat 5 minutes or until tender.
• **Stir** in tomatoes and next 4 ingredients; cook until thoroughly heated. Sprinkle with Cheddar cheese. **Yield:** 4 servings.

Valerie Stutsman
Norfolk, Virginia

DINNER ON A SHOESTRING

....

Who isn't interested in saving a little money these days – and the grocery store is a good place to start. You probably learned long ago that ground beef is a real bargain. It's most likely at the top of your grocery list each week. For a leaner choice and a few cents more per pound, look for ground chuck specials.

These three recipes using this versatile meat won't break your budget or your back. Team any one of them with a salad, and announce "supper's ready."

CAROLINA GUMBO

1 pound lean ground beef
1 large onion, chopped
1 (16-ounce) package frozen white corn, thawed
1 (15½-ounce) can Great Northern beans, drained
3 (14½-ounce) cans stewed tomatoes, undrained
1 (10-ounce) package frozen sliced okra, thawed
2 tablespoons chili powder
Hot cooked rice
Hot sauce (optional)

• **Brown** ground beef and onion in a Dutch oven, stirring until beef crumbles. Drain, rinse with hot water, and return to Dutch oven.
• **Stir** in corn and next 4 ingredients. Bring mixture to a boil over medium heat, stirring occasionally; cover, reduce heat, and simmer 20 minutes, stirring occasionally.
• **Serve** over rice. Sprinkle with hot sauce, if desired. **Yield:** 1½ quarts.
Dawn Poston
Elkin, North Carolina

MOZZARELLA TAMALE

2 pounds lean ground beef
½ cup finely chopped onion
½ cup finely chopped green pepper
1 (1¼-ounce) package chili seasoning mix
2 (14½-ounce) cans stewed tomatoes, undrained
1 cup (4 ounces) shredded Cheddar cheese
1 cup (4 ounces) shredded mozzarella cheese
1 (2¼-ounce) can sliced ripe olives, drained
1 (6-ounce) package cornbread mix

• **Brown** ground beef, onion, and green pepper in a large nonstick skillet or Dutch oven, stirring until beef crumbles; drain. Return beef mixture to skillet.
• **Stir** in chili seasoning mix and tomatoes. Bring to a boil over medium heat; cover, reduce heat, and simmer 15 minutes, stirring occasionally.
• **Stir** in cheeses and olives; spoon mixture into a lightly greased 13- x 9- x 2-inch baking dish.
• **Prepare** cornbread mix according to package directions; spoon mixture in 1-inch-wide strips diagonally over meat mixture.
• **Bake** tamale at 425° for 15 minutes or until cornbread is golden. **Yield:** 6 to 8 servings.
Vernice P. Garrett
Texas City, Texas

BURGER BOAT

1½ pounds lean ground beef
¼ cup chopped green pepper
¼ cup chopped green onions
1 (10¾-ounce) can cream of mushroom soup, undiluted
1 cup water
½ teaspoon salt
½ teaspoon pepper
¼ teaspoon garlic powder
1 (16-ounce) loaf French bread
½ cup (4 ounces) shredded sharp Cheddar cheese

• **Brown** ground beef, green pepper, and green onions in a large nonstick skillet, stirring until beef crumbles; drain. Return mixture to skillet.
• **Add** soup and next 4 ingredients. Bring to a boil over medium-high heat, stirring constantly. Reduce heat, and simmer 15 minutes, stirring occasionally; set aside.
• **Cut** a wedge of bread from the top of the bread loaf. Remove pieces of bread from inside of loaf, leaving a 1-inch shell.
• **Position** knife blade in food processor bowl; add bread pieces and wedge. Process until crumbs are fine and uniform in size; spread evenly on a baking sheet.
• **Bake** bread shell and crumbs at 350° until lightly toasted; cool.
• **Stir** 1½ cups toasted breadcrumbs into ground beef mixture; reserve any extra breadcrumbs for other uses.
• **Spoon** meat mixture into bread shell; top with cheese.
• **Bake** at 350° for 15 minutes or until cheese melts. (For a softer loaf, wrap in aluminum foil before baking.) **Yield:** 4 servings.
Carol S. Noble
Burgaw, North Carolina

A TOUCH O' IRISH

....

On St. Patrick's Day, Irish expatriate Marge Kinsella says only *three*-leaf clovers – shamrocks – are magical for her family.

"Not those *four*-leaf clovers," dismisses the Austin, Texas, restaurateur in her Irish brogue. "Shamrocks represent the Holy Trinity – the *real* spirit of Ireland."

So does the Emerald Restaurant, a friendly, authentic recreation of an Irish inn. Housed in a 1927 limestone cottage in the Texas Hill Country, it's been run since 1981 by Marge, husband Paul, son and chef Paul John, son

David, and daughters Michelle and Margaret Mary.

The 65-seat restaurant features generous servings of fine Irish and Continental cuisine: Pride of Erin – Roast Duck in Brandied Cherry Sauce, Dalton Feast – Quail With Irish Dressing, Dublin Lawyer – Lobster in Irish Whiskey, St. Patrick's Delight – Monkfish Seasoned With Irish Mustard, and other delectables, including two warm and winning ways to celebrate St. Patrick's: Irish stew and soda bread.

EMERALD ISLE STEW

1 (4½-pound) leg of lamb *
1 (1-pound) trimmed lean
    boneless beef top sirloin steak,
    cut into 1-inch cubes
1 tablespoon vegetable oil
1 pound onions, chopped
1 clove garlic, minced
¾ cup stout beer
4 bay leaves
1 (10½-ounce) can condensed beef
    broth, undiluted
1 tablespoon salt
1 teaspoon pepper
2 cups water
¾ pound carrots, cut into
    ¼-inch slices
1 pound new potatoes, cut into
    ¾-inch cubes
2 to 3 teaspoons dried tarragon
3 tablespoons all-purpose flour
¼ cup water
1 (17¼-ounce) package frozen
    puff pastry, thawed

• **Remove** meat from lamb bone; cut into 1-inch cubes. Set bone aside.
• **Brown** all sides of beef and lamb cubes in oil in a large Dutch oven over medium-high heat, stirring beef and lamb occasionally.
• **Add** lamb bone, onion, and next 7 ingredients; bring to a boil. Cover, reduce heat, and simmer 30 minutes.
• **Remove** lamb bone; add carrot, potato, and tarragon. Cover and simmer 30 minutes. Remove and discard bay leaves.
• **Combine** flour and ¼ cup water; stir until mixture is smooth. Slowly add flour mixture to stew, stirring constantly. Cook over medium heat 3 minutes or until thickened and bubbly.
• **Cut** puff pastry into shapes with a 5-inch shamrock cookie cutter. Place pastry shamrocks on an ungreased baking sheet.
• **Bake** at 400° for 5 minutes or until lightly browned.
• **Spoon** stew into individual bowls; top each with shamrock puff pastry. **Yield:** 3½ quarts.

∗ You can substitute 3 pounds trimmed lean boneless beef top sirloin steak, cut into 1-inch cubes, for lamb.

Note: For the stout beer, we used Guinness.

IRISH SODA BREAD

6 cups all-purpose flour
1 tablespoon baking powder
1½ teaspoons baking soda
2 teaspoons salt
1 tablespoon plus 1 teaspoon sugar
2½ cups buttermilk
2 tablespoons butter, melted
1½ cups raisins

• **Combine** first 5 ingredients in a large bowl; set aside.
• **Combine** buttermilk, butter, and raisins; add to flour mixture, stirring until moistened.
• **Turn** dough out onto a well-floured surface, and knead until smooth and elastic (about 5 minutes). Place on a greased baking sheet.
• **Press** dough evenly into a 1½-inch-thick circle.
• **Bake** at 325° for 1 hour or until bread sounds hollow when tapped. Remove to a wire rack; cool 5 minutes. Cut into wedges. **Yield:** one 12-inch round loaf.

OUT OF AFRICA

....

Take your family on a flavor safari while you pump up the volume of your Lenten vegetables. Ordinary potatoes, beans, and carrots become exotic Ethiopian fare when they're prepared with fresh ginger and hot chile peppers. Serve with a lentil salad and lots of heavy, crusty bread to sample the Ethiopian experience.

YATAKLETE KILKIL
(yah-TAH-kla-TAY keel-keel)

1½ quarts water
1 teaspoon salt
6 small potatoes, peeled and cut
    into 1-inch cubes
3 large carrots, scraped and cut
    into 1-inch pieces
½ pound green beans, cut into
    2-inch pieces
3 small onions, quartered and
    separated
1 large green pepper, cut into
    strips
3 chile peppers, seeded and
    chopped
¼ cup vegetable oil
2½ teaspoons minced fresh ginger
2 cloves garlic, minced
1 teaspoon salt
¼ to ½ teaspoon pepper
6 green onions, cut into 2-inch
    pieces

• **Bring** water to a boil in a Dutch oven. Add salt and next 3 ingredients; cook 5 minutes. Remove from heat; drain vegetables, and rinse with cold water. Drain again; set vegetables aside.
• **Cook** onion and peppers in oil in pan, stirring constantly, 5 minutes or until crisp-tender. Stir in ginger and next 3 ingredients. Add vegetables and green onions, tossing gently to coat.
• **Cover** and cook over low heat 8 additional minutes or until vegetables are tender, stirring mixture occasionally. **Yield:** 4 servings.

TO MARKET, TO MARKET

This cookbook combines the charm of the South with the bounty of the Midwest, and in particular, the spirit (bourbon) of Kentucky. While selecting recipes from *To Market, To Market,* we found a fat pig – he prances and jigs through the illustrations on the subject dividers of this clever Owensboro, Kentucky, Junior League cookbook.

This book also boasts menu ideas from a Derby party to a gathering for Owensboro's barbecue festival.

We weren't surprised to discover that many of the recipes from this 344-page book have been sent to *Southern Living* by readers. The following selections offer a few more reasons to try this cookbook.

BUCK'S TATERS

6 large baking potatoes
4 small onions, thinly sliced
Seasoned salt
Pepper
6 tablespoons butter or
    margarine

● **Peel** potatoes, if desired.
● **Slice** each potato crosswise at ¼-inch intervals, cutting to, but not through, opposite side. Carefully insert onion slices into potato cuts.
● **Sprinkle** each potato with seasoned salt and pepper; dot each with 1 tablespoon butter or margarine.
● **Wrap** each potato in aluminum foil; place on baking sheet.
● **Bake** potatoes at 400° for 1 hour. **Yield:** 6 servings.

HOT CURRIED FRUIT

This favorite side dish doubles as a dessert when served over ice cream or pound cake.

1 (29-ounce) can pear halves,
    drained
1 (29-ounce) can peach halves,
    drained
1 (20-ounce) can pineapple
    chunks, drained
2 (17-ounce) cans apricot halves,
    drained
½ cup butter or margarine,
    softened
1 cup firmly packed brown sugar
1 tablespoon cornstarch
1½ teaspoons curry powder

● **Place** first 4 ingredients in a 13- x 9- x 2-inch baking dish.
● **Combine** butter and remaining ingredients; spoon over fruit.
● **Bake** at 325° for 1 hour, basting occasionally with cooking liquid.
● **Serve** with a slotted spoon. **Yield:** 8 to 10 servings.

Note: You can prepare casserole and chill it up to 2 days in advance; bake according to directions just before serving.

FIBBER McGEE COOKIES

1 cup butter or margarine,
    softened
1⅓ cups sugar
1⅓ cups firmly packed brown
    sugar
2 large eggs
1 teaspoon vanilla extract
1¾ cups all-purpose flour
1 teaspoon baking soda
3½ cups quick-cooking oats,
    uncooked
1½ cups salted peanuts, coarsely
    chopped
1 cup (6 ounces) semisweet
    chocolate morsels

● **Beat** butter at medium speed with an electric mixer until creamy; gradually add sugars, beating at medium speed until blended. Add eggs, one at a time, beating just until yellow disappears; stir in vanilla. Set aside.
● **Combine** flour and soda; stir into butter mixture, mixing well. Stir in oats and remaining ingredients, mixing well (mixture will be crumbly). Drop by teaspoonfuls onto ungreased baking sheets.
● **Bake** at 350° for 10 to 12 minutes. Let stand 1 minute; remove to wire racks to cool. **Yield:** 5½ dozen.

Roasting peppers until they're nearly black is the surprising key to the delicate flavor of Cream of Roasted Sweet Red Pepper Soup (recipe, page 65).

Above: *Seared Scallops With Tomato-Mango Salsa (recipe, page 122) captures the colorful flair of the tropics.*
Left: *Some upscale twists on a down-home favorite include topping Basic Polenta with Sausage and Peppers; Garlic and Mushrooms; Tomato, Basil and Cheese; and fresh rosemary and sage sprigs. (Recipes begin on page 164.)*

Dinner is smooth sailing for the busy cook with quick and easy Oven-Fried Catfish, Baked Hush Puppies, and Green Bean Slaw. (Recipes begin on page 106.)

SOURDOUGH MADE SIMPLE

....

If you've ever wanted to bake sourdough bread but were intimidated by the procedure, it's time to reconsider. Freshly baked bread not only smells wonderful, it assumes a prized position on the dinner menu. There's no substitute for that fresh-from-the-oven texture and aroma. Here are some ideas that will have you baking in no time.

Made-from-scratch bread is always a welcome gift. To have homemade Potato Sourdough Bread at a moment's notice, bake several loaves when you have extra time, and freeze them up to a month. To freeze, wrap cooled bread in aluminum foil, and seal tightly in a heavy-duty, zip-top plastic bag; then label and date. Thaw foil-wrapped bread at room temperature two to three hours.

POTATO SOURDOUGH STARTER

¾ cup sugar
3 tablespoons instant potato flakes
1 package active dry yeast
1 cup warm water (120° to 130°)
Starter Food

• **Combine** first 3 ingredients in a small mixing bowl. Stir in warm water. Cover with plastic wrap; pierce wrap 4 or 5 times with point of a sharp knife. Store in refrigerator 3 to 5 days.
• **Remove** starter from refrigerator; let stand at room temperature 1 hour.
• **Stir** well. Remove 1 cup starter; use in a recipe or give to a friend.
• **Prepare** 1 recipe Starter Food, and stir into remaining starter; let stand, uncovered, 8 to 12 hours. Cover with plastic wrap; pierce wrap 4 or 5 times with a sharp knife. Store in refrigerator 3 to 5 days. Each time starter is used, repeat the feeding procedure. Use all starter or discard after 4 feedings. **Yield:** 3½ cups.

Starter Food

¾ cup sugar
3 tablespoons instant potato flakes
1 cup warm water (120° to 130°)

• **Combine** all ingredients, and use to feed starter as directed.

POTATO SOURDOUGH BREAD DOUGH

6 cups bread flour
⅓ cup sugar
1 package active dry yeast
1 tablespoon salt
½ cup vegetable oil
1 cup Potato Sourdough Starter (see recipe)
1½ cups warm water (120° to 130°)

• **Combine** first 4 ingredients in a large bowl; gradually stir in oil and remaining ingredients.
• **Turn** dough out onto a floured surface; knead lightly 4 or 5 times. Place in a well-greased bowl, turning to grease top.
• **Cover** and let rise in a warm place (85°), free from drafts, 2 hours or until doubled in bulk. **Yield:** 6 cups.

Potato Sourdough Bread: Punch dough down, and divide in half; shape each portion into a loaf. Place in a lightly greased 9- x 5- x 3-inch loafpan. Brush tops with 2 tablespoons melted butter; cover and let rise in a warm place (85°), free from drafts, 1 hour or until doubled in bulk. Bake at 350° for 25 minutes or until loaves sound hollow when tapped. Remove bread from pans immediately; cool on wire racks. **Yield:** 2 loaves.

Potato Sourdough Rolls: Punch dough down, and divide in half; shape each portion into 12 balls. Place in a greased 8-inch round pan. Brush tops with 2 tablespoons melted butter. Cover; let rise in a warm place (85°), free from drafts, 1 hour or until doubled in bulk. Bake at 350° for 15 minutes or until golden. **Yield:** 2 dozen.

POTATO SOURDOUGH CINNAMON ROLLS

Bake Potato Sourdough Cinnamon Rolls in a recyclable aluminum pan so the lucky recipient won't have containers to return. Wrap the pan with colored plastic wrap, and secure with brightly colored ribbon.

1 recipe Potato Sourdough Bread Dough (see recipe)
½ cup butter or margarine, softened
½ cup firmly packed brown sugar
1 tablespoon ground cinnamon
½ cup raisins
3 cups sifted powdered sugar
1½ teaspoons vanilla extract
5 to 6 tablespoons milk

• **Divide** dough in half. Roll each portion into a 12- x 10-inch rectangle. Spread each rectangle with ¼ cup softened butter to within ½ inch of edge. Sprinkle each with ¼ cup brown sugar, 1½ teaspoons cinnamon, and ¼ cup raisins.
• **Roll** dough, jellyroll fashion, starting with long side and pressing firmly to eliminate air pockets; pinch seams to seal. Cut into 12 (1-inch) slices; place slices, cut side down, in 2 greased 13- x 9- x 2-inch baking pans.
• **Cover** and let rise in a warm place (85°), free from drafts, 1 hour or until doubled in bulk.
• **Bake** at 350° for 20 minutes or until golden.
• **Combine** powdered sugar and remaining ingredients; drizzle over rolls. **Yield:** 2 dozen.

Marie Davis
Charlotte, North Carolina

BAKE IT LIGHT

Muffins, breads, and cookies are completely unforgiving. You take out the fat, and the flavor goes with it. But some of our enterprising readers have used a little kitchen alchemy to lighten the fat content and heighten the flavor in these baked goodies. Indulge in these low-fat breads and desserts that don't sacrifice flavor.

GRANOLA MUFFINS

If there's a way to make a delicious fat-free muffin at home, we haven't found it yet. Rather than offer a recipe for a fat-free hockey puck, we decided on these low-fat Granola Muffins.

1½ cups reduced-fat biscuit and baking mix
1 cup firmly packed brown sugar
1 teaspoon ground cinnamon
1 cup oats and honey granola cereal with almonds
½ cup raisins
1 large egg, lightly beaten
¾ cup skim milk
1 tablespoon vegetable oil
Vegetable cooking spray

• **Combine** first 3 ingredients in a bowl; stir in cereal and raisins. Make a well in center; set aside.

• **Combine** egg, milk, and oil; add to flour mixture, stirring just until moistened. (Batter will be thin.)
• **Coat** muffin cups with cooking spray; spoon batter into cups, filling three-fourths full.
• **Bake** at 375° for 15 to 20 minutes or until golden. **Yield:** 16 muffins.

Note: For oats and honey granola cereal with almonds, we used Quaker 100% Natural Oats & Honey Cereal.

Amanda E. Anglin
Magnolia, Mississippi

♥ Per muffin: Calories 140 (21% from fat)
Fat 3.3g (0.7g saturated) Cholesterol 14mg
Sodium 153mg Carbohydrate 25.1g
Fiber 0.6g Protein 2.5g

FRUITY BANANA BREAD

Vegetable cooking spray
⅓ cup margarine
¾ cup sugar
½ cup egg substitute
1¾ cups all-purpose flour
2¾ teaspoons baking powder
1 cup mashed ripe banana
¾ cup coarsely chopped mixed dried fruit

• **Coat** an 8½- x 4½- x 3-inch loafpan with cooking spray; set aside.
• **Beat** margarine at medium speed with an electric mixer until margarine is creamy; gradually add sugar, beating well. Add egg substitute, beating until blended.
• **Combine** flour and baking powder; add to butter mixture. Beat at low speed until blended. Stir in mashed banana and dried fruit. Pour batter into prepared loafpan.
• **Bake** at 350° for 1 hour or until a wooden pick inserted in center of loaf comes out clean. Cool in pan on a wire rack 10 minutes; remove from pan, and cool completely on a wire rack. **Yield:** 1 loaf.

Hilda Marshall
Bealeton, Virginia

♥ Per ½-inch slice: Calories 149 (22% from fat)
Fat 3.8g (0.7g saturated) Cholesterol 0mg
Sodium 54mg Carbohydrate 27.3g
Fiber 0.7g Protein 2.3g

DON'T TRY THIS AT HOME

You've probably heard that it's a good idea to replace the fat in your muffin and bread recipes with applesauce, yogurt, or prune puree. We don't recommend the switch. You can end up with anything from rubbery bread to concrete muffins. But if the original recipe is printed using these ingredients, it usually means that it's been tested, and you should get good results.

ENGLISH MUFFIN BREAD

3½ to 3¾ cups all-purpose flour,
    divided
1 cup whole wheat flour
½ cup oat bran
2 teaspoons salt
1 package rapid-rise yeast
1 cup skim milk
1 cup water
3 tablespoons reduced-calorie
    margarine
Vegetable cooking spray
2 tablespoons cornmeal

• **Combine** 1½ cups all-purpose flour
and next 4 ingredients in a large mixing bowl, and set aside.

• **Combine** skim milk, water, and margarine in a 4-cup liquid measuring cup.
Microwave at HIGH 2 minutes; pour
over flour mixture. Beat mixture at
medium speed with an electric mixer 2
minutes. Gradually stir in 2 cups all-
purpose flour. Turn dough out onto a
lightly floured surface; if dough is
sticky, knead in remaining ¼ cup flour.

• **Cover** dough with a large bowl; let
rest 10 minutes.

• **Coat** 2 (8½- x 4½- x 3-inch) loafpans
with cooking spray; sprinkle evenly
with cornmeal. Divide dough in half;
shape each portion into a loaf, and
place in pan.

• **Cover** pans, and let dough rise in a
warm place (85°), free from drafts, 1
hour or until doubled in bulk.

• **Bake** at 400° for 25 minutes. Remove loaves from pans, and cool on a
wire rack. **Yield:** 2 loaves.

Ann Roberts
Fayetteville, Arkansas

♥ Per ½-inch slice: Calories 77 (10% from fat)
Fat 0.9g (0.1g saturated) Cholesterol 0mg
Sodium 154mg Carbohydrate 14.6g
Fiber 1g Protein 2.5g

LIGHTEN UP

LIGHT SPREADS

At less than 3 fat grams per
tablespoon, you can easily afford to
top your bread with one of these
spreads. Stretch the calories in blue
cheese by mixing it with fat-free
cream cheese for a piquant sandwich
or cracker spread. Reduced-fat
cream cheese makes a low-calorie
base for Raisin-Nut Spread and
Strawberry Spread. Choose either
one to make the morning's bagels,
English muffins, waffles, or pancakes
special.

Blue Cheese Spread: Combine
1 (8-ounce) package fat-free cream
cheese, softened; ¼ cup crumbled
blue cheese; 2 tablespoons finely
chopped onion; 1 tablespoon skim
milk; and 1 tablespoon reduced-
sodium Worcestershire sauce. **Yield:**
1¼ cups.

Mary Pappas
Richmond, Virginia

Raisin-Nut Spread: Combine
4 ounces reduced-fat cream cheese,
softened; 3 tablespoons honey; and
¼ teaspoon ground cinnamon. Stir
in 3 tablespoons chopped raisins and
3 tablespoons chopped pecans.
Yield: ¾ cup.

Cindy Quebe
Greenville, Texas

Strawberry Spread: Combine
4 ounces reduced-fat cream cheese,
softened, and ¼ cup strawberry
preserves. **Yield:** ¾ cup.

OH, NUTS!

There's no getting around it – nuts
are packed with fat. But their flavor
is so wonderful that most people
can't give them up. Just so you'll
know what you're getting yourself
into, here's the skinny on the fat in
nuts. All values are for 1 ounce of
shelled nuts, which is equal to
about ¼ cup.

Almonds: With approximately 15
fat grams and 167 calories, almonds
are one of the lower fat nuts.

Hazelnuts: These sweet, made-for-
baking nuts have nearly 18 fat
grams and 180 calories.

Macadamia Nuts: These expensive, delicious nuts rate high on the
fat scale. At 21 fat grams and 200
calories, they're best saved for very
special occasions.

Peanuts: A handful has more than
14 fat grams and 164 calories.
(They have the same number of
calories even if you float them in
diet cola.)

Pecans: The Southern favorite
weighs in at 19 fat grams and 190
calories.

Walnuts: Snack on a handful of
these, and you'll have consumed
182 calories and 16 fat grams,
about one-fourth of the total you
should have for an entire day.

CHOCOLATE-HAZELNUT BISCOTTI

*For the same number
of calories as a rice cake, you can
have a slice of biscotti.*

2 large eggs
⅔ cup sugar
1 tablespoon Frangelico or other
   hazelnut-flavored liqueur
2 cups sifted cake flour
1½ teaspoons baking powder
¼ teaspoon salt
1½ tablespoons cocoa
⅔ cup hazelnuts, chopped and
   toasted
Vegetable cooking spray

• **Beat** eggs at medium speed with an electric mixer until foamy. Gradually add sugar, beating at high speed until mixture is thick and pale. Add liqueur, beating until blended. Combine flour and next 3 ingredients; fold into egg mixture. Fold in nuts. Cover and chill 30 minutes.
• **Coat** a cookie sheet with cooking spray. Divide dough into 3 portions, and spoon portions onto cookie sheet 2 inches apart. Shape each portion of dough into an 8- x 1½-inch strip. Cover and chill 30 minutes; reshape dough, if necessary.
• **Bake** at 375° for 20 minutes or until lightly browned. Remove to wire racks to cool. Cut diagonally into ½-inch-thick slices. Lay slices flat on a cookie sheet. Bake at 375° for 5 minutes; turn slices over, and bake 5 additional minutes. Remove to wire racks to cool. **Yield:** 3½ dozen.

*Andy Lorber
Atlanta, Georgia*

♥ Per cookie: Calories 50 (30% from fat)
Fat 1.7g (0.2g saturated) Cholesterol 11mg
Sodium 17mg Carbohydrate 7.9g
Fiber 0.1g Protein 1g

MINI SWISS CHEESE LOAVES

*Fill Mini Swiss Cheese Loaves
with turkey or chicken for
lunch, or serve them as a savory
bread with dinner.*

1 package active dry yeast
¼ cup warm water (105°
   to 115°)
2⅓ cups all-purpose flour,
   divided
2 tablespoons sugar
1 teaspoon salt
¼ teaspoon baking soda
1 (8-ounce) carton plain nonfat
   yogurt
1 large egg
1 cup (4 ounces) shredded
   reduced-fat Swiss cheese
Vegetable cooking spray
2 teaspoons sesame seeds,
   toasted

• **Combine** yeast and warm water in a 1-cup liquid measuring cup; let stand 5 minutes.
• **Combine** yeast mixture, 1 cup flour, sugar, and next 4 ingredients in a large mixing bowl.
• **Beat** at low speed with an electric mixer 30 seconds. Beat at high speed 2 minutes, scraping bowl occasionally.
• **Stir** in remaining flour and cheese, mixing well.
• **Divide** batter evenly among 8 (5- x 3- x 2-inch) loafpans coated with cooking spray; sprinkle evenly with sesame seeds.
• **Cover** and let rise in a warm place (85°), free from drafts, 1 hour. (Batter may not double in bulk.)
• **Bake** at 350° for 25 minutes or until golden. Remove from pans; serve warm, or cool on a wire rack. **Yield:** 8 loaves.

Note: For reduced-fat Swiss cheese, we used Alpine Lace.

*Shannon Arrington
Woodland, Alabama*

♥ Per loaf: Calories 226 (20% from fat)
Fat 4.9g (2.3g saturated) Cholesterol 38mg
Sodium 380mg Carbohydrate 34.2g
Fiber 1.3g Protein 10.7g

BEIGNETS FOR BREAKFAST

• •

Warning: Never wear black while eating beignets. The powdered sugar will dust your clothes.

But these traditional New Orleans yeast pastries served warm are definitely worth the floating cloud of sugar that sifts onto your lap. With the first delicious bite, a puff of warm air escapes. And with the last bite, lick the sugar from your fingers.

Invite a friend to join you. Make some café au lait. And, be sure you all wear white.

FRENCH MARKET BEIGNETS

*With warm beignets, café au lait,
and a classic movie, you'll live life
New Orleans style . . . easy.*

1 package active dry yeast
1 cup warm water (105° to 115°)
¾ cup canned evaporated milk
¼ cup sugar
1 teaspoon salt
1 large egg, lightly beaten
4 to 4½ cups all-purpose flour
Vegetable oil
Sifted powdered sugar

• **Combine** yeast and warm water in a 2-cup liquid glass measuring cup; let stand 5 minutes.
• **Combine** yeast mixture, evaporated milk, and next 3 ingredients. Gradually stir in enough flour to make a soft dough. Cover and chill 8 hours.
• **Turn** dough out onto a well-floured surface; knead 5 to 6 times. Roll dough into a 15- x 14-inch rectangle; cut into 2½-inch squares.
• **Pour** oil to depth of 3 to 4 inches into a Dutch oven; heat to 375°. Fry 3 to 4 beignets at a time, 1 minute on each side or until golden. Drain on paper towels; sprinkle with powdered sugar. **Yield:** 2½ dozen.

APRIL

Sweet Stalks Of Spring

Celebrate the season with the crisp flavor of asparagus.

These firm, tall stalks with a light brush of lavender against a palate

of rich green are showcased in recipes that welcome spring.

GARLICKY PASTA WITH ASPARAGUS, TOMATOES, AND SHRIMP

Asparagus isn't the main attraction in this dish, but it provides a distinctive color and flavor accent. And yes, the recipe calls for a whole head of garlic. Don't worry: The long baking greatly mellows its pungent flavor.

1 pound fresh asparagus
1 pound unpeeled medium-size fresh shrimp
1 large head garlic
1½ tablespoons olive oil, divided
6 plum tomatoes, quartered
6 ounces fusilli or corkscrew pasta
2 teaspoons lemon juice
1 teaspoon dried Italian seasoning
1 teaspoon dried thyme
¼ teaspoon salt
¼ teaspoon pepper
¼ to ½ cup shredded fresh Parmesan cheese

● **Snap** off tough ends of asparagus; remove scales from stalks with a knife or vegetable peeler, if desired. Cut asparagus into 2-inch pieces, and set aside.

● **Peel** shrimp, and devein, if desired; set aside.

● **Slice** ¼ inch from top of garlic head; place on aluminum foil. Drizzle garlic with 2 teaspoons olive oil. Seal foil around garlic. Bake at 425° for 10 minutes. (Leave garlic in oven.)

● **Place** tomato in a 13- x 9- x 2-inch baking pan; drizzle with remaining 2½ teaspoons olive oil. Place in oven with garlic. Bake, without stirring, 20 minutes or until tomato wrinkles and begins to brown.

● **Place** asparagus and shrimp over tomato. Bake with garlic 10 minutes or until shrimp turn pink and asparagus is tender. Remove garlic and pan from oven. Set tomato mixture aside. Unwrap garlic; cool 5 minutes.

● **Cook** pasta in a large saucepan according to package directions; drain. Return to saucepan.

● **Separate** garlic cloves; squeeze out soft pulp. Add garlic pulp, lemon juice, and next 4 ingredients to pasta; toss gently. Add tomato mixture; toss gently. Serve with Parmesan cheese. **Yield:** 4 servings.

Lora Sheridan
Winston-Salem, North Carolina

CREAMY ASPARAGUS-AND-CHICKEN SOUP

4 chicken breast halves (about 1¾ pounds)
4 cups water
1 medium onion, quartered
2 large stalks celery, cut into 1-inch pieces
1½ teaspoons salt
¼ teaspoon pepper
1½ pounds fresh asparagus
2 cups half-and-half
2 tablespoons butter or margarine
¼ teaspoon salt
¼ teaspoon pepper
Garnish: chopped fresh parsley

● **Combine** first 6 ingredients in a 3-quart saucepan. Bring to a boil over medium-high heat; cover, reduce heat, and simmer 35 minutes or until chicken is tender.

● **Remove** chicken, reserving broth and vegetables in saucepan. Let chicken cool slightly. Remove and discard bones and skin; cut chicken into bite-size pieces. Set aside.

● **Snap** off tough ends of asparagus; remove scales from stalks with a knife or vegetable peeler, if desired. Cut asparagus into 2-inch pieces; add to reserved chicken broth and vegetables.

● **Bring** to a boil over medium-high heat; cover, reduce heat, and simmer 10 minutes or until asparagus is tender. Cool 10 minutes.

● **Pour** about one-third of asparagus mixture into container of an electric blender; process until smooth, stopping once to scrape down sides. Pour puree into a large container; repeat procedure twice with remaining asparagus mixture. Return all puree to saucepan.

● **Add** chicken, half-and-half, and next 3 ingredients to asparagus puree; cook over medium heat about 5 minutes or until thoroughly heated, stirring occasionally. Garnish, if desired. **Yield:** 8½ cups.

Lilann Taylor
Savannah, Georgia

MARINATED ASPARAGUS WITH PROSCIUTTO

Prosciutto is cured Italian ham sliced paper thin. If you can't find it, ask a butcher to slice regular ham as thinly as possible.

2   pounds fresh asparagus
¾   cup vegetable oil
¼   cup white wine vinegar
2   tablespoons Dijon mustard
2   tablespoons honey
2   teaspoons dried tarragon
¼   pound prosciutto or thinly
      sliced ham, cut into
      thin strips

• **Snap** off tough ends of asparagus; remove scales from stalks with a knife or vegetable peeler, if desired.
• **Cover** and cook asparagus in a small amount of boiling water 4 minutes or until crisp-tender; drain. Plunge into ice water to stop the cooking process; drain. Place in a shallow baking dish; set aside.
• **Combine** oil and next 4 ingredients in a jar. Cover tightly, and shake vigorously. Pour over asparagus; cover and chill at least 2 hours.
• **Remove** asparagus, reserving marinade; arrange asparagus on a platter. Top with prosciutto, and drizzle with reserved marinade. **Yield:** 8 servings.
Gwyneth A. Jones-Rader
Ellicott City, Maryland

ASPARAGUS STIR-FRY

Peanut oil is recommended for stir-frying because it can stand higher temperatures than other oils before it begins to smoke or taste "off."

1½ pounds fresh asparagus
1   tablespoon peanut oil
¾   cup chicken broth, divided
1   tablespoon cornstarch
1   teaspoon sugar
2   tablespoons soy sauce
1   (2-ounce) package cashews,
      coarsely chopped and toasted
      (about ½ cup)

Fresh-from-the-earth asparagus confirms our hopes that warmer weather and sun-filled days have returned.

When you're selecting your asparagus at the market, follow these tips to be sure you buy the best stalks.

■ Select stalks with smooth and tightly closed tips. (Frayed tips indicate the asparagus isn't fresh.)

■ Check that the stalks in a bunch are all about the same diameter. If some are large and some pencil thin, they'll need different cooking times.

■ After washing asparagus, hold each end of the stalk, and bend it, letting it snap where it naturally breaks. Discard the larger end.

• **Snap** off tough ends of asparagus; remove scales from stalks with a knife or vegetable peeler, if desired. Diagonally cut into 1-inch pieces; set aside.
• **Cook** asparagus in oil in a large skillet over medium-high heat 2 minutes, stirring constantly. Add ¼ cup chicken broth to skillet; cover and cook 4 minutes or until crisp-tender.
• **Combine** remaining ½ cup chicken broth and next 3 ingredients, stirring until smooth. Add to asparagus mixture, stirring constantly.
• **Bring** to a boil, and boil 1 minute, stirring constantly. Sprinkle with cashews, and serve immediately. **Yield:** 4 to 6 servings.

Kathy Sellers
Nashville, Tennessee

ASPARAGUS WITH GARLIC CREAM

1   (8-ounce) carton sour cream
2   tablespoons milk
1   tablespoon white wine vinegar
1   tablespoon olive oil
1 to 2 cloves garlic, minced
⅛   teaspoon salt
⅛   teaspoon freshly ground pepper
2   pounds fresh asparagus
Garnish: chopped fresh chives

• **Stir** together first 7 ingredients. Cover and chill at least 2 hours.
• **Snap** off tough ends of asparagus; remove scales from stalks with a knife or vegetable peeler, if desired.
• **Cover** and cook asparagus in a small amount of boiling water 4 minutes or until crisp-tender; drain. Plunge into ice water to stop the cooking process; drain. Cover and chill.
• **Place** a small bowl in the center of a large bowl. Stand asparagus between bowls. Place garlic cream in small bowl. Garnish, if desired. **Yield:** 16 to 20 appetizer servings or 8 side-dish servings.
Fran Baker
Rockledge, Florida

NONTAXING STANDBYS

....

Missing receipts, canceled checks, itemized deductions, bulging bank statements, blurry vision, ringing telephones . . . grrrr . . . .

Need a tax break? We thought so.

Try penciling in one or all of these painless recipes. After beating the April 15 deadline, you'll be relieved to know that none of these recipes is too taxing.

OREGANO CHICKEN

¼ cup butter or margarine, melted
¼ cup lemon juice
2 tablespoons Worcestershire sauce
2 tablespoons soy sauce
2 teaspoons dried oregano
1 teaspoon garlic powder
6 skinned and boned chicken breast halves

• **Combine** first 6 ingredients. Place chicken in an ungreased 11- x 7- x 1½-inch baking dish. Pour half of butter mixture over chicken.
• **Bake** at 375° for 15 minutes, and pour remaining butter mixture over chicken.
• **Bake** 15 additional minutes. Transfer chicken to a serving platter. **Yield:** 6 servings.

Note: Remove excess fat from pan drippings with a fat separator, and serve the pan drippings over hot cooked rice, if desired.

Georgia M. Olvey
Fayetteville, Georgia

EGGPLANT PARMESAN

1 (1½-pound) eggplant, peeled and sliced into ¼-inch-thick slices
½ cup grated Parmesan cheese, divided
2 cups (8 ounces) shredded part-skim mozzarella cheese, divided
1½ cups spaghetti sauce, divided
Vegetable cooking spray

• **Layer** half of eggplant, ¼ cup Parmesan cheese, ¾ cup mozzarella, and half of spaghetti sauce in a 2-quart shallow baking dish coated with cooking spray. Repeat with remaining eggplant, Parmesan cheese, ¾ cup mozzarella, and spaghetti sauce.
• **Bake** at 350° for 35 minutes; sprinkle with remaining ½ cup mozzarella cheese, and bake 5 additional minutes. **Yield:** 6 servings.

Gloria Stricklin
Winter Haven, Florida

BAKED MUSHROOM RICE

¼ cup butter or margarine, melted
1 cup long-grain rice, uncooked
1 (10½-ounce) can condensed chicken broth, undiluted
1 (10½-ounce) can condensed French onion soup, undiluted
1 (2½-ounce) jar sliced mushrooms, drained

• **Combine** all ingredients in an ungreased 2-quart baking dish.
• **Cover** and bake at 350° for 1 hour. **Yield:** 4 servings.

COWBOY COFFEE CAKE

2 (11-ounce) cans refrigerated buttermilk biscuits
¼ cup butter or margarine, melted
⅓ cup firmly packed brown sugar
⅓ cup chopped pecans
1 teaspoon ground cinnamon

• **Arrange** biscuits in a lightly greased 9-inch round cakepan, overlapping edges.
• **Combine** butter and remaining ingredients; spread evenly over biscuits.
• **Bake** at 350° for 22 minutes or until golden. Serve warm. **Yield:** one 9-inch coffee cake.

James Michelinie
Louisville, Kentucky

RICH BROWNIES

1 (10¼-ounce) package fudge brownie mix
½ cup miniature marshmallows
½ cup semisweet chocolate morsels
½ cup chopped pecans

• **Prepare** brownie mix according to package directions, folding marshmallows, chocolate morsels, and pecans into batter. Spread batter evenly into a greased 8-inch square baking pan.
• **Bake** at 350° for 24 minutes or until done. Cool in pan on a wire rack; cut into squares. **Yield:** 16 brownies.

COOK QUICK

■ Use two sets of measuring cups so you can measure consecutive ingredients without repeatedly washing or wiping out the measure. Use nonstick skillets, saucepans, and baking pans, which are easier to clean.

■ Use a microwave for thawing foods quickly or for shortcuts such as softening or melting margarine.

■ Cooked rice stores well, offering a fast side dish or base to a one-dish meal. Store it in the refrigerator up to one week or in the freezer as long as three months.

Spring Celebrations

DINNER ON THE LAWN

Southern hospitality is in full bloom. Swing into the season with menus, recipes, and tips that are guaranteed to make your party a success. For Dick and Inez Thompson of Bay St. Louis, Mississippi, their expansive front porch and the shady sweep of lawn that overlooks the Jordan River make the perfect backdrop for a family get-together. We offer two menus varied enough to please any palate. Either lawn party menu is the perfect way to kick off a season of spring celebrations.

LAWN PARTY MENUS

BAYOU MENU
Serves Eight

Cajun Blackened Filet Mignon
Stuffed Shrimp With
Hollandaise Sauce
Cooked Rice
Steamed Asparagus
Key Lime Pies

HERB LOVER'S MENU
Serves Eight

Pita Bread Salad
Lemon-Herb Grilled Chicken
Garlic-Roasted Potatoes
Grilled Fruit With
Honey Yogurt

CAJUN BLACKENED FILET MIGNON

1 (1½-pound) beef tenderloin, trimmed
Vegetable cooking spray
2 tablespoons Cajun blackened seasoning
1 (8-ounce) carton reduced-fat sour cream
¼ cup prepared horseradish
1 (16-ounce) sourdough baguette, cut into 24 slices and toasted
¼ cup sliced green onions

• **Spray** all sides of beef with cooking spray; sprinkle with seasoning, and spray again.
• **Heat** a cast-iron or ovenproof heavy skillet over medium-high heat 3 to 5 minutes; add beef, and cook 3 to 4 minutes on each side.
• **Bake** at 400° for 15 minutes or until a meat thermometer inserted in thickest portion of meat registers 145° (medium-rare). Let stand 10 minutes. Cut into 24 slices; set aside.
• **Combine** sour cream and horseradish; set horseradish sauce aside.
• **Place** a slice of tenderloin on each toasted baguette slice. Top with horseradish sauce; sprinkle evenly with green onions. **Yield:** 24 appetizers.

STUFFED SHRIMP WITH HOLLANDAISE SAUCE

24 unpeeled jumbo fresh shrimp
¼ cup butter, divided
1 medium onion, finely chopped
½ sweet red pepper, finely chopped
½ green pepper, finely chopped
2 cloves garlic, minced
2 tablespoons Cajun or Creole seasoning
½ cup fine, dry breadcrumbs
1 large egg, lightly beaten
⅓ cup mayonnaise
1 pound frozen crawfish tails, thawed and chopped
2 tablespoons lemon juice
2 tablespoons Chablis or other dry white wine
Hollandaise Sauce

• **Peel** shrimp, leaving the tails on; devein shrimp, if desired. Butterfly shrimp by making a deep slit down the back of each from the large end to the tail, cutting to, but not through, the inside curve of shrimp. Set aside.
• **Melt** 2 tablespoons butter in a large saucepan; add onion and next 3 ingredients. Cook over medium-high heat until vegetables are tender, stirring often. Stir in seasoning and breadcrumbs; set aside.
• **Combine** egg, mayonnaise, and crawfish; stir into onion mixture.
• **Stuff** slit in each shrimp with about 3 tablespoons crawfish mixture; arrange on an aluminum foil-lined 15- x 10- x 1-inch jellyroll pan.
• **Melt** remaining 2 tablespoons butter in a small saucepan; add lemon juice and wine. Drizzle over shrimp.
• **Bake** shrimp at 400° for 20 minutes. Serve with Hollandaise Sauce. Yield: 6 to 8 servings.

Hollandaise Sauce

1 cup egg substitute
½ teaspoon salt
¼ cup lemon juice
1 cup butter, softened and divided
1 teaspoon grated lemon rind

• **Combine** egg substitute and salt in a heavy saucepan; cook over medium heat, stirring constantly with a wire whisk. Gradually add lemon juice, beating constantly with whisk.
• **Remove** from heat; add ½ cup butter, 2 tablespoons at a time, beating well after each addition. (The butter should not simply melt; it should be worked into the sauce mixture with the whisk.)
• **Pour** mixture into container of an electric blender. With blender on high, drop remaining ½ cup butter, 2 tablespoons at a time, into blender. Blend mixture until smooth; stir in lemon rind.
• **Return** to saucepan to keep warm, and place pan in larger pan filled with hot water. Yield: 2 cups.

KEY LIME PIES

⅔ cup fresh lime juice
2 (14-ounce) cans sweetened condensed milk
1 tablespoon grated lime rind
2 or 3 drops of green liquid food coloring (optional)
2 (6-ounce) chocolate-flavored crumb crusts
6 egg whites
½ teaspoon cream of tartar
¾ cup sugar
1 teaspoon vanilla extract

• **Stir** lime juice gradually into sweetened condensed milk; stir in lime rind and food coloring, if desired. Spoon evenly into crusts; set aside.
• **Beat** egg whites and cream of tartar at high speed with an electric mixer until foamy.
• **Add** sugar gradually to mixture, 1 tablespoon at a time, beating until stiff peaks form and sugar dissolves (2 to 4 minutes). Add vanilla, beating mixture until blended. Spread meringue evenly over pies.
• **Bake** at 325° for 25 to 28 minutes. Cool pies on wire racks; chill thoroughly. Yield: 2 pies.

PITA BREAD SALAD

4 (6-inch) pita rounds
1 bunch fresh parsley, finely chopped
4 medium tomatoes, finely chopped
1 large green pepper, seeded and finely chopped
1 bunch green onions, finely chopped
1 medium cucumber, peeled, seeded, and finely chopped
3 cloves garlic, minced
⅓ cup fresh lemon juice (about 2 large lemons)
⅓ cup olive oil
2 tablespoons finely chopped fresh mint
¼ teaspoon salt
¼ teaspoon pepper
2 cups shredded romaine lettuce
4 ounces feta cheese, crumbled (1 cup)

• **Cut** each pita round into 6 wedges, and separate each wedge into 2 triangles. Place triangles in a single layer on a baking sheet.
• **Bake** at 400° for 10 minutes or until crisp and brown. Cool completely; place pita triangles in a zip-top plastic bag, and set aside.
• **Combine** chopped parsley and next 10 ingredients; toss gently. Cover and chill 1 hour.
• **Toss** parsley mixture with lettuce; sprinkle with feta cheese. Serve with toasted pita triangles. Yield: 6 to 8 servings.

Shirley Awood Glaab
Hattiesburg, Mississippi

LEMON-HERB GRILLED CHICKEN

1 cup vegetable oil
¾ cup lemon juice
¼ cup honey
2 tablespoons dried oregano
1 tablespoon dried rosemary
1 teaspoon salt
½ teaspoon pepper
4 cloves garlic
2 whole chickens, quartered
   and skinned

• **Combine** all ingredients except chicken in container of an electric blender, and process mixture until smooth, stopping occasionally to scrape down sides.
• **Place** chicken in a heavy-duty, zip-top plastic bag; pour oil mixture over chicken. Seal bag, and marinate chicken in refrigerator at least 8 hours.
• **Drain** and discard marinade.
• **Cook** chicken, covered with grill lid, over medium-hot coals (350° to 400°) about 35 minutes or until meat thermometer inserted in thickest part of chicken registers 180°, turning occasionally. **Yield:** 8 servings.

GARLIC-ROASTED POTATOES

3 pounds small round red
   potatoes
¼ cup olive oil
6 cloves garlic, minced
2 tablespoons dried rosemary,
   crushed
¾ teaspoon salt
½ teaspoon pepper

• **Pierce** each potato with a fork. Coat potatoes with olive oil; place in a 13- x 9- x 2-inch baking dish. Sprinkle with minced garlic and remaining ingredients; toss to coat.
• **Bake** potatoes at 400° for 50 minutes or until potatoes are tender. **Yield:** 8 servings.

Donna Ellis
Speedwell, Tennessee

GRILLED FRUIT WITH HONEY YOGURT

1 (8-ounce) carton vanilla yogurt
2 tablespoons honey
1 fresh pineapple
4 bananas
4 peaches
4 pears

• **Combine** yogurt and honey; cover and chill.
• **Peel**, core, and cut pineapple into ¾-inch wide spears. Peel bananas, and cut each in half lengthwise and then crosswise.
• **Cut** peaches in half, and remove pit. Cut pears in half, and remove core. Grill peaches and pears, covered with grill lid, over medium-hot coals (350° to 400°) about 10 minutes.
• **Add** banana and pineapple to grill in a grill basket.
• **Grill** 10 additional minutes or until fruit reaches desired degree of doneness.
• **Serve** grilled fruit with yogurt mixture. **Yield:** 8 servings.

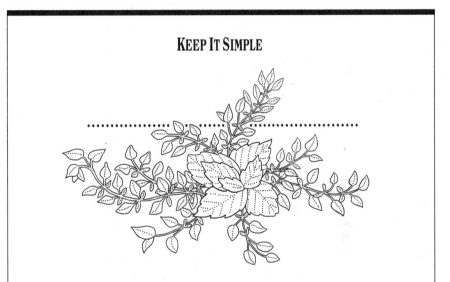

KEEP IT SIMPLE

■ The trick to outdoor entertaining is to keep it simple. Choose foods that will stand up to the heat. Prepare dishes that look good when served on a buffet. For easy cleanup, use paper plates, cups, and napkins.

■ Arrange seating for dining in a shady area. If children are invited, plan some entertainment for them. Hang a tire from a tree for a swing, give them a ball, or teach them to play croquet. Plan for the party to end before dark or have outdoor lighting available. Have citronella candles or bug spray on hand in case insects are a problem.

■ Prepare as many foods ahead as you can. **For the Bayou Menu,** cook the filet mignon and prepare the horseradish sauce early in the day. Slice the beef and assemble the Cajun Blackened Filet Mignon appetizer just before guests arrive. Make stuffing and stuff shrimp the morning of the party; cover and chill. Bake them 30 minutes before you plan to serve dinner. Make Key Lime Pies the morning of the party, and chill. **For the Herb Lover's Menu,** toast pita bread triangles the day before the party, and store in a zip-top plastic bag. Marinate chicken the night before.

SAY "I DO" TO GREAT FOOD

....

When Mary Katherine Luckie of Birmingham, Alabama, asked us to help with a bridal shower and cooking demonstration for her bride-to-be friend Lizzie Barnes, we jumped at the chance. Just about any new bride could use a little kitchen savvy. Here's a checklist of what to do.

First, plan a great-tasting but easy-to-do menu. Then, make up a grocery list of just what you'll need for the recipe demonstration. Do as much as possible ahead for the demonstration. And most importantly, practice before the big day (see "Demo Details" on facing page).

A MENU FOR THE CLASS
Serves Eight

Cucumber Canapés
Fresh Mint Tea
Creamy Ham-and-Chicken Lasagna
Rolls With Garlic Butter
Jeweled Congealed Fresh Fruit
Party Tarts

CUCUMBER CANAPÉS

First, define canapé: They're little sandwiches with no top. You can decorate them for a gorgeous presentation. Cucumbers, pastry, or bread may be used as the base of the appetizer. This recipe is so easy you may have time to show the entire process to the group.

3 cucumbers, unpeeled
1 (8-ounce) container cream cheese
    with chives
6 cherry tomatoes
Garnish: fresh dill sprigs

• **Remove** and discard thin strips of peel from cucumbers lengthwise, at equally spaced intervals, using a citrus stripper or fork, if desired. (This is for decoration.) Cut the cucumbers into ½-inch slices. Scoop out and discard a small amount of pulp from each cucumber slice, using a melon baller or spoon. Pipe or dollop a small amount of cream cheese with chives into each cucumber slice.
• **Cut** cherry tomatoes into thin slices, and arrange slices on top of cream cheese. Garnish, if desired. **Yield:** about 3 dozen appetizers.

FRESH MINT TEA
(pictured on page 146)

Our bride-to-be enjoyed learning how to make the garnish for the beverage. First, slice a lemon into rounds. Cut from the edge of each lemon round to the center, being careful not to cut the membranes at the center of the lemon. Slide the lemon slice onto the rim of the glass, and insert a sprig of fresh mint.

4 cups boiling water
8 regular-size tea bags
2 cups sugar
⅔ cup fresh lemon juice
1 cup fresh mint leaves, coarsely
    chopped
Crushed ice
Garnishes: lemon slices, fresh mint
    sprigs

• **Pour** boiling water over tea bags; cover and steep 5 minutes. Remove tea bags, squeezing them gently; discard. Let tea cool.
• **Combine** sugar and lemon juice in a medium saucepan, and cook over medium heat, stirring constantly, until mixture boils and sugar dissolves. Remove mixture from heat, and stir in chopped mint; cool.
• **Pour** mixture through a wire-mesh strainer into a pitcher, discarding solids. Stir in tea, and serve over crushed ice. Garnish, if desired. **Yield:** 1½ quarts.

CREAMY HAM-AND-CHICKEN LASAGNA
(pictured on page 146)

Instead of demonstrating this recipe, we talked through it. The recipe calls for bone-in chicken breasts because they're less expensive, but you can substitute boneless breasts. After boiling the noodles, place them on wax paper coated with vegetable cooking spray.

2 bone-in chicken breast halves
2 cups chopped cooked ham
9 lasagna noodles, uncooked
Vegetable cooking spray
1 tablespoon butter or
    margarine
1 (8-ounce) package sliced fresh
    mushrooms
⅓ cup butter or margarine
⅓ cup all-purpose flour
3 cups milk
1½ cups freshly grated Parmesan
    cheese
½ cup whipping cream
¾ teaspoon dried basil or 2
    teaspoons chopped fresh basil
½ teaspoon salt
¼ teaspoon freshly ground
    pepper
Garnishes: chopped fresh parsley,
    paprika

• **Place** chicken breasts in a saucepan; add water to cover. Bring to a boil over high heat; cover, reduce heat to medium, and cook 45 minutes or until chicken is tender. Drain and let cool slightly.
• **Remove** and discard skin from chicken; remove meat from bones, discarding bones. Chop chicken into bite-size pieces, and place in a large bowl; add chopped ham.
• **Cook** lasagna noodles according to package directions; drain. Place wax paper on a baking sheet; coat wax paper with cooking spray. Place cooked noodles in a single layer on wax paper; cover with additional wax paper coated with cooking spray. Continue layering noodles and wax paper. Set aside.
• **Melt** 1 tablespoon butter in a large skillet over medium-high heat; add

mushrooms, and cook, stirring constantly, until tender. Drain and stir into meat mixture; set aside.

- **Melt** ⅓ cup butter in skillet; add flour and cook 1 minute, stirring constantly. Gradually stir in milk; cook, stirring constantly, about 3 minutes or until bubbly. Stir in cheese and next 4 ingredients; cook until cheese is melted and mixture is thickened. Add chicken mixture to cheese mixture; stir well.
- **Coat** a 2-quart shallow baking dish with cooking spray. Spread one-fourth of meat mixture into dish; top with 3 lasagna noodles. Repeat layers with remaining meat mixture and noodles, ending with meat mixture.
- **Cover** and bake at 350° for 30 minutes. Remove from oven, and let stand 10 minutes before serving. Garnish, if desired. **Yield:** 8 servings.

♥ To save 187 calories and 11 fat grams per serving, substitute reduced-fat ham for regular; cook mushrooms in vegetable cooking spray instead of butter; substitute 2¾ cups skim milk for 3 cups whole milk; and reduce whipping cream to ¼ cup. The analysis for the lightened version is:

Per serving: Calories 367 (39% from fat)
Fat 15.9g (6.2g saturated)   Cholesterol 57mg
Sodium 856mg   Carbohydrate 28.2g
Fiber 0.7g   Protein 28g

GARLIC BUTTER

(pictured on page 146)

For this recipe, demonstrate how to use a garlic press. Just place the garlic in the gadget, and squeeze.

1   cup butter, softened
2 to 3   cloves garlic, pressed
1   teaspoon dried Italian
    seasoning

- **Combine** all ingredients; beat at high speed with an electric mixer until creamy. Cover and chill until firm. Serve with Italian rolls or French bread. **Yield:** 1 cup.

JEWELED CONGEALED FRESH FRUIT

(pictured on page 146)

This recipe was the hit of our party. Demonstrate unmolding it so the group feels comfortable doing it. Insert a flat knife between the salad and edge of the Bundt pan to break the suction. Flip the salad (still in pan) onto a lettuce-lined plate. If it won't come out, place hot towels around the pan for a minute or two, and try again.

1   pint strawberries, hulled and
    halved
3   envelopes unflavored gelatin
4½   cups unsweetened pineapple
    juice, divided
2   (15¼-ounce) cans pineapple
    tidbits, drained
2   (11-ounce) cans mandarin
    oranges, drained
1   grapefruit, peeled, sectioned,
    and well drained
1   cup fresh blueberries
1   cup seedless green grapes
Lettuce leaves
Poppyseed dressing

- **Arrange** strawberry halves, cut side up, in the bottom of a lightly greased 12-cup Bundt pan. Set aside.
- **Sprinkle** gelatin over ½ cup pineapple juice in a small saucepan; stir and let stand 1 minute. Cook over low heat, stirring until gelatin dissolves (about 2 minutes). Combine gelatin mixture and remaining 4 cups pineapple juice in a large bowl.
- **Pour** about ½ cup pineapple juice mixture over strawberries in Bundt pan; chill until firm.
- **Chill** remaining pineapple juice mixture until consistency of unbeaten egg white. Stir in pineapple tidbits and remaining fruit; spoon into Bundt pan. Chill until firm.
- **Line** a large serving plate with lettuce leaves.
- **Unmold** fruit mold onto lettuce leaves. Cut with an electric knife, and serve with poppyseed dressing. **Yield:** 10 to 12 servings.

DEMO DETAILS

- Do as much cutting, chopping, measuring, and preparing as possible ahead.

- Inexpensive wicker trays make quick work of organizing the demonstration. You'll need one tray per recipe.

- Arrange utensils on each tray in order of usage – this helps you keep your place and stay organized while demonstrating. Keep a copy of the recipe on the tray.

- Plan the step(s) you want to show in advance for each recipe; it's impossible to do every one start to finish.

- Before the demonstration, practice in front of someone you trust. If you feel like you're running out of air, then you're probably talking too fast.

- Don't worry if you make a mistake – new cooks need to know that great cooks make mistakes, too. Take questions while you work. Ask members of the audience to come up and help you.

- Ask a helper to move trays or hand extra utensils to the demonstrator.

PARTY TARTS

(pictured on page 146)

For ease, substitute pie filling or pudding. To make lemon tarts, fill two dozen tart shells with one 11¼-ounce jar lemon curd.

½ (15-ounce) package refrigerated
    piecrusts
⅔ cup sugar
¼ cup all-purpose flour
2 tablespoons cocoa
Dash of salt
2 egg yolks
1 cup milk
1 tablespoon butter or margarine
¼ teaspoon almond extract
½ cup whipping cream
1 tablespoon powdered sugar
Garnishes: chocolate shavings,
    toasted sliced almonds

• **Unfold** pastry, and roll to ⅛-inch thickness on a lightly floured surface. Cut 24 circles, using a 2½-inch round cutter.
• **Press** circles into ungreased miniature (1¾-inch) muffin pans, using a tart tamper or back of spoon. Prick pastry with a fork.

• **Bake** at 425° for 4 to 5 minutes. Cool in pans on wire racks.
• **Combine** ⅔ cup sugar and next 3 ingredients in a saucepan.
• **Combine** egg yolks and milk, stirring with a wire whisk; add to sugar mixture. Add butter, stirring well.
• **Cook** over medium heat, stirring constantly, until mixture thickens and boils. Remove from heat, and stir in almond extract. Cool chocolate mixture.
• **Beat** whipping cream until foamy; add powdered sugar, beating until soft peaks form.
• **Fill** each tart shell with chocolate mixture. Pipe or dollop each tart with sweetened whipped cream. Garnish, if desired. **Yield:** 2 dozen.

BUBBLE OVER

· · · · · · · · · · · · · · · · · · · ·

Warning: You're going to fall for these drinks. They masquerade as hard chunks of ice, but they're really slushy in the glass.

The basic ingredients – fruit juice, soft drinks, and other spirited ingredients – are stirred together and frozen until needed. Just before serving, pour a bubbly beverage over the frozen mixture, and stir until slushy.

AMARETTO SLUSH

1 (46-ounce) can pineapple juice
3 cups amaretto
1 (12-ounce) can frozen pink
    lemonade concentrate, thawed
    and undiluted
1 (6-ounce) can frozen pink
    lemonade concentrate, thawed
    and undiluted
⅓ cup lemon juice
1 (3-liter) bottle lemon-lime
    carbonated beverage, chilled

• **Combine** first 5 ingredients in a large plastic container.
• **Cover** and freeze at least 8 hours, stirring twice during freezing process. To serve, combine equal portions of frozen mixture and lemon-lime beverage, stirring well. Cover and store any remaining frozen mixture in freezer. Serve immediately. **Yield:** 6 quarts.
Elizabeth A. Crawley
New Orleans, Louisiana

PIÑA COLADA SLUSH

1 (46-ounce) can pineapple juice
2 (12-ounce) cans frozen
    lemonade concentrate, thawed
    and undiluted
3 cups water
2 cups light rum
1 (15-ounce) can cream of
    coconut
1 (3-liter) bottle lemon-lime
    carbonated beverage,
    chilled

• **Combine** first 5 ingredients in a large plastic container.
• **Cover** and freeze at least 8 hours, stirring twice during freezing process. To serve, combine equal portions of frozen mixture and lemon-lime beverage, stirring well. Cover and store any remaining frozen mixture in freezer. Serve immediately. **Yield:** 6 quarts.
Linda Janca
Mount Mourne, North Carolina

PUNCH FOR A BUNCH

8 cups water, divided
1½ cups sugar
1 (7½-ounce) bottle frozen lemon
    juice, thawed
1 (6-ounce) can frozen orange
    juice concentrate, thawed and
    undiluted
2 (6-ounce) cans unsweetened
    pineapple juice (1½ cups)
1 (2-liter) bottle ginger ale,
    chilled

• **Combine** 2 cups water and sugar in a medium saucepan. Bring to a boil, reduce heat, and simmer 20 minutes. Cool. Stir in remaining 6 cups water and fruit juices.

• **Cover** and freeze at least 8 hours, stirring twice during freezing process.

• **Remove** from freezer 30 minutes before serving. Break into chunks; add ginger ale, and stir until slushy. **Yield:** 5 quarts.

Lynn L. Williams
Lexington, Virginia

FROZEN MARGARITA PUNCH

4 (12-ounce) cans frozen limeade
  concentrate, thawed and
  undiluted
3 quarts water
3 cups Triple Sec or other orange-
  flavored liqueur
3 cups tequila
2 (2-liter) bottles lemon-lime
  carbonated beverage

• **Combine** first 4 ingredients.

• **Cover** and freeze at least 8 hours, stirring twice during freezing process.

• **Remove** from freezer 30 minutes before serving. Break into chunks; add lemon-lime carbonated beverage, and stir until mixture is slushy. **Yield:** 2½ gallons.

HAPPY ANNIVERSARY

....

Remember your beautiful spring wedding? Has it been a year, four years, 10 or more? Don't wait for the silver or golden years to toast your union. Gather friends and family for a celebration of love, and share memories as you create new ones.

ANNIVERSARY PARTY MENU
Serves Eight

Marinated Bourbon Steak
Rosemary Biscuits
Marinated Vegetable Medley
Blue Cheese Spread
Sesame Shrimp
Miniature Orange Éclairs
Orange-Pecan Truffles
Petits Fours from the Bakery

MARINATED BOURBON STEAK
(pictured on page 110)

½ cup bourbon
2 tablespoons lemon juice
2 teaspoons brown sugar
½ teaspoon cracked black pepper
2 (1-inch) beef top loin strip
  steaks, trimmed (about
  1½ pounds)

• **Combine** first 4 ingredients in a shallow dish; add steaks, turning to coat. Cover and chill 4 hours, turning steaks occasionally.

• **Remove** steaks from marinade; discard marinade.

• **Cook,** covered with grill lid, over hot coals (400° to 500°) 8 minutes on each side or until a meat thermometer inserted in thickest part of the steak registers 160°.

• **Slice** and serve with Rosemary Biscuits and mayonnaise. **Yield:** 8 appetizer servings.

ROSEMARY BISCUITS
(pictured on page 110)

4 cups biscuit and baking
  mix
1½ teaspoons dried rosemary,
  crushed
1⅓ cups milk
¼ cup butter or margarine,
  melted

• **Combine** biscuit mix and rosemary in a large bowl. Add milk, stirring with a fork until dry ingredients are moistened. Turn dough out onto a lightly floured surface, and knead lightly 3 or 4 times.

• **Roll** dough to ½-inch thickness; cut with a 2-inch round cutter, and place on a lightly greased baking sheet.

• **Bake** at 450° for 8 minutes or until lightly browned. Brush with melted butter. **Yield:** 3 dozen.

MARINATED VEGETABLE MEDLEY

2 cups baby carrots
1 teaspoon salt
1 pound Sugar Snap peas,
  trimmed
1 small cauliflower, cut into
  flowerets
½ pound fresh mushrooms, halved
½ cup olive oil
½ cup white wine vinegar
1 tablespoon sugar
1 teaspoon dried Italian seasoning
1 teaspoon spicy brown mustard
Lettuce leaves

• **Combine** carrots and salt in a large saucepan; add water to cover. Bring to a boil; cover, reduce heat, and simmer 7 minutes. Remove carrots, reserving boiling water in pan. Plunge carrots into ice water to stop the cooking process; drain carrots, and place in a 13- x 9- x 2-inch dish.

• **Add** peas to boiling water; cover and cook 3 minutes or until crisp-tender. Drain and plunge into ice water to stop the cooking process. Drain peas, and place in a separate container; chill until ready to serve.

• **Add** cauliflower and mushrooms to carrots; set aside.

• **Combine** olive oil and next 4 ingredients in a small saucepan; bring to a boil, stirring constantly. Pour over vegetables, tossing gently.

• **Cover** and chill 8 hours, tossing occasionally. Just before serving, add peas; toss gently. Drain and spoon vegetables into a lettuce-lined bowl to serve. **Yield:** 18 to 20 appetizer servings or 8 salad servings.

BLUE CHEESE SPREAD

1 (8-ounce) package cream cheese, softened
1 (4-ounce) package blue cheese
¾ cup chopped pecans, toasted and divided
Garnish: pecan halves

• **Position** knife blade in food processor bowl; add cream cheese and blue cheese. Process 20 seconds or until mixture is blended. Stir in ½ cup chopped pecans.
• **Line** a 1½-cup bowl with plastic wrap, and press cream cheese mixture into bowl. Cover and chill 8 hours.
• **Unmold** cheese; remove plastic wrap. Roll outside edge of cheese mold in remaining ¼ cup chopped pecans. Garnish, if desired. Serve with apple slices and grapes. **Yield:** 1½ cups.

SESAME SHRIMP

1½ pounds unpeeled large fresh shrimp
3 tablespoons cornstarch
2 tablespoons reduced-sodium teriyaki sauce
1 tablespoon water
2 teaspoons grated fresh ginger
¼ teaspoon salt
⅓ cup sesame seeds, toasted
⅓ cup fine, dry breadcrumbs
Vegetable oil

• **Peel** shrimp, and devein, if desired; set shrimp aside.
• **Combine** cornstarch and next 4 ingredients; set aside.
• **Combine** toasted sesame seeds and breadcrumbs. Dip each shrimp into cornstarch mixture; coat with sesame seed mixture.
• **Pour** oil to depth of 3 inches into a Dutch oven; heat to 365°. Fry shrimp, 8 to 10 at a time, 1 minute or until golden. Drain on paper towels. **Yield:** 8 appetizer servings.

MINIATURE ORANGE ÉCLAIRS

¾ cup whipping cream
1 tablespoon powdered sugar
1 drop of yellow liquid food coloring
1 drop of red liquid food coloring
24 ladyfingers
⅓ cup Grand Marnier or other orange-flavored liqueur
½ cup fudge sauce
Garnishes: orange rind strips, orange slice wedges, fresh mint

• **Beat** whipping cream until foamy; add sugar and food coloring, beating until soft peaks form. Set aside.
• **Separate** ladyfinger halves. Brush bottom halves with liqueur; spread evenly with whipped cream mixture. Cover with top halves of ladyfingers. Drizzle about 2 teaspoons fudge sauce on each éclair. Garnish, if desired. **Yield:** 2 dozen.

Bess Feagin
Memphis, Tennessee

ORANGE-PECAN TRUFFLES

8 (1-ounce) squares semisweet chocolate
⅓ cup butter or margarine
½ cup orange marmalade
½ cup chopped pecans, toasted
2 tablespoons Grand Marnier or other orange-flavored liqueur *
1 cup finely chopped pecans

• **Combine** chocolate and butter in top of a double boiler; bring water to a boil. Reduce heat to low; cook until chocolate melts, stirring occasionally.
• **Remove** from heat; stir in marmalade, ½ cup chopped pecans, and liqueur. Cool slightly; cover and chill until firm (at least 2 hours).
• **Shape** mixture into ¾-inch balls; roll in 1 cup finely chopped pecans. (Mixture tends to stick to hands.) Place in paper or foil bonbon cups.

• **Store** candy in airtight containers in refrigerator up to 3 weeks or freeze up to 12 months. Serve cold. **Yield:** 3 dozen.

* You can substitute 2 tablespoons orange juice for liqueur.

Louise W. Mayer
Richmond, Virginia

YOU CAN DO IT, TOO

UP TO THREE WEEKS AHEAD:
■ Make and freeze Orange-Pecan Truffles.
■ Order petits fours from local bakery.
■ Select photographs and music.

UP TO TWO DAYS AHEAD:
■ Make Blue Cheese Spread; cover and chill.
■ Bake Rosemary Biscuits, and store in zip-top plastic bags.

THE DAY BEFORE:
■ Peel and devein shrimp.
■ Make Marinated Vegetable Medley; cover and chill.
■ Prepare Miniature Orange Éclairs; cover and chill.

THE DAY OF THE PARTY:
■ Marinate steak, and prepare as directed.
■ Pick up petits fours at bakery.
■ Remove Orange-Pecan Truffles from freezer, and arrange on a serving tray.
■ Drain Marinated Vegetable Medley, and spoon into a lettuce-lined bowl. Place Blue Cheese Spread and Miniature Orange Éclairs on serving trays.
■ Decorate with selected photographs.
■ Turn on music, and celebrate.

STIR UP SOME FUN

....

You just heard your teenager say the gang wants to watch a movie at your house – tonight. What will you serve that ravenous group?

Don't fret. When we found these dips and a spread that require only seven ingredients or less, we knew that relief was just around the corner. And the best thing about these munchies? Your teen can make them without any help from you – they're that easy. (Just remember to include a few extra fresh veggies, crackers, and chips.)

BUTTERY HAM SPREAD

1 cup butter or margarine, softened
1 (8-ounce) package cream cheese, softened
2 (5-ounce) cans tender chunk ham, drained and flaked
2 tablespoons chopped green onions
1 tablespoon lemon juice
¼ teaspoon salt
⅛ teaspoon pepper

• **Combine** butter and cream cheese in a large mixing bowl; beat at medium speed with an electric mixer until creamy. Add ham and remaining ingredients, mixing well. Serve with assorted crackers. **Yield:** 4 cups.

Sue-Sue Hartstern
Louisville, Kentucky

QUICK HUMMUS

1 or 2 cloves garlic
1 (15-ounce) can garbanzo beans, drained
¼ cup tahini
2 tablespoons lemon juice
2 tablespoons water
¼ teaspoon salt

• **Position** knife blade in food processor bowl; add garlic. Pulse 2 or 3 times or until garlic is chopped.
• **Add** garbanzo beans and remaining ingredients; process until smooth. Serve with assorted raw vegetables. **Yield:** 1⅓ cups.

PESTO DIP

1 (3½-ounce) jar pesto
1 cup plain nonfat yogurt
⅓ cup chopped dried tomatoes

• **Combine** all ingredients; cover and chill. Serve with assorted raw vegetables. **Yield:** 1⅓ cups.

BLACK BEAN DIP

1 (15-ounce) can black beans, drained
1 (8-ounce) can tomato sauce
½ cup (2 ounces) shredded Cheddar cheese
1 teaspoon chili powder
Garnish: shredded Cheddar cheese

• **Combine** beans and tomato sauce in a small saucepan; bring to a boil over medium heat, stirring occasionally. Remove from heat.
• **Mash** beans with a potato masher or back of spoon.
• **Add** ½ cup cheese and chili powder; cook, stirring constantly, until cheese melts. Garnish, if desired. Serve dip warm with toasted pita triangles and fresh vegetables. **Yield:** 2 cups.

Elza Reeves
Louisville, Kentucky

ONE-MINUTE SALSA

1 (10-ounce) can diced tomatoes and green chiles, undrained
1 (14½-ounce) can stewed tomatoes, undrained
½ to 1 teaspoon pepper
½ teaspoon garlic salt

• **Combine** all ingredients in container of an electric blender; process 30 seconds. Serve salsa with tortilla chips. **Yield:** 3 cups.

Debbie Jones
Lewisville, Texas

SWISS-ONION DIP

1 (10-ounce) package frozen chopped onion, thawed
3 cups (12 ounces) shredded Swiss cheese
1 cup mayonnaise or salad dressing
1 tablespoon coarse-grained Dijon mustard
⅛ teaspoon pepper

• **Drain** onion on paper towels.
• **Combine** onion and remaining ingredients. Spoon mixture into a 1-quart baking dish.
• **Bake** at 325° for 25 minutes or until bubbly and lightly browned. Serve dip with melba toast rounds. **Yield:** 4 cups.

♥ To reduce fat and calories in the dip, substitute reduced-fat mayonnaise for regular mayonnaise.

Kathy Sellers
Nashville, Tennessee

EASY GUACAMOLE

2 ripe avocados, peeled and
　　mashed
¼ cup picante sauce
1½ teaspoons lemon juice
½ teaspoon garlic salt

● **Combine** all ingredients. Serve with tortilla chips. **Yield:** 1 cup.

Carol Muto
Richardson, Texas

FRESH FRUIT DIP

1 (8-ounce) carton sour cream
1 tablespoon sugar
½ teaspoon pumpkin pie spice
¼ teaspoon vanilla extract

● **Combine** all ingredients; cover and chill. Serve dip with apple slices or other assorted fresh fruit. **Yield:** 1 cup.

Laura Butler
Charlotte, North Carolina

TIPS ON DIPS

■ Don't settle on an ordinary bowl to serve your dip. Consider hollowing out firm-textured vegetables like sweet peppers, whole cabbage heads, or artichokes. Fruits such as cantaloupe, honeydew melon, or pineapple work well also. Or hollow out large bread rounds.

■ Potato chips and celery are not the only dip scoopers. Use your imagination, and shop your local grocery for unusual crackers, pita bread triangles, colored tortilla chips, and bagel chips. Try different vegetable dippers like sweet peppers, snow peas, or baby corn.

SPRING'S BEST SALADS

....

Luscious, creamy salads, complemented by crispy, crunchy greens, will satisfy most everyone.

To create a classical setting, use planters and pedestals from local garden shops. Line the planters with plastic wrap before filling with salads. Architectural elements and white china add a finishing touch.

CRAB LOUIS

1 cup mayonnaise or salad dressing
¼ cup chili sauce
¼ cup chopped green onions
1 teaspoon lemon juice
¼ teaspoon salt
¼ cup whipping cream, whipped
1 head iceberg lettuce, shredded
2 pounds fresh crabmeat, drained
　　and flaked *
2 large tomatoes, cut into wedges
4 hard-cooked eggs, cut into
　　wedges

● **Combine** first 5 ingredients in a large bowl. Fold in whipped cream; set dressing aside.
● **Place** shredded lettuce in a serving bowl or on a platter; arrange crabmeat, tomato wedges, and egg wedges on lettuce. Spoon 2 tablespoons dressing over salad; serve with remaining dressing. **Yield:** 8 to 10 servings.

* You can substitute 2 pounds imitation crab, 2 pounds peeled cooked shrimp, or 1 pound of each for the fresh crabmeat.

Jeanne S. Hotaling
Augusta, Georgia

HAM-AND-POTATO SALAD

1 pound small round red potatoes, cut into ½-inch wedges (about 3 cups)
1 (16-ounce) package frozen mixed vegetables
⅓ cup mayonnaise or salad dressing
⅓ cup sour cream
½ cup sliced green onions
1 teaspoon pepper
½ teaspoon salt
3 cups chopped cooked ham (about 1 pound)

● **Cook** potato, covered, in boiling water to cover 10 minutes or until tender (do not overcook); drain and set aside.
● **Cook** mixed vegetables according to package directions; drain vegetables, and set aside.
● **Combine** mayonnaise and next 4 ingredients in a large bowl. Gently stir in potato, vegetables, and ham. Cover and chill at least 8 hours. **Yield:** 6 to 8 servings.

Charlotte Pierce
Greensburg, Kentucky

CHERRY-COLA SALAD

2 (16-ounce) cans pitted dark, sweet cherries, undrained
¾ cup amaretto
¾ cup orange juice
2 (3-ounce) packages black cherry-flavored gelatin
1 (12-ounce) can cola-flavored carbonated beverage (1½ cups)
1 (8-ounce) package reduced-fat cream cheese, softened
½ cup reduced-fat mayonnaise
2 tablespoons milk
1 cup chopped walnuts, toasted

● **Drain** cherries; reserve ¾ cup cherry liquid. Spoon cherries into an 11- x 7- x 1½-inch dish; set aside.
● **Bring** reserved liquid, amaretto, and orange juice to a boil in a large

saucepan over medium heat; add gelatin, stirring 2 minutes or until gelatin dissolves. Cool 10 minutes.

• **Add** cola to gelatin mixture; chill to consistency of unbeaten egg white.

• **Pour** gelatin mixture over cherries; cover and chill until firm.

• **Beat** cream cheese at low speed with an electric mixer until creamy; add mayonnaise and milk, beating until smooth. Stir in walnuts.

• **Spread** cream cheese mixture evenly over gelatin. Cover and chill at least 3 hours. **Yield:** 12 servings.

H. W. Asbell
Tallahassee, Florida

GINGERED FRUIT SALAD

1 (8-ounce) package cream cheese, softened
⅓ cup orange juice
2 tablespoons sugar
½ teaspoon ground ginger
3 cups green grapes, halved
3 cups strawberries, hulled and halved
3 Granny Smith apples, cored and chopped
1 (11-ounce) can mandarin oranges, drained

• **Combine** first 4 ingredients in a small bowl, blending well.

• **Combine** grapes and next 3 ingredients in a large bowl. Pour dressing over fruit, and toss gently. Serve immediately. **Yield:** 8 servings.

Peggy H. Amos
Martinsville, Virginia

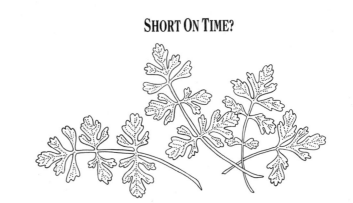

SHORT ON TIME?

You can entertain with a salad bar. Just prepare a bowl of mixed salad greens and offer a variety of toppings on the side. Here are some suggested additions.

■ Marinated vegetables
■ Miniature corn
■ Shredded carrot
■ Sliced radishes
■ Chopped green, sweet red, or sweet yellow pepper

■ Broccoli and cauliflower flowerets
■ Chopped onion
■ Sliced hard-cooked eggs
■ Chopped ham or turkey
■ Croutons
■ Shredded cheese
■ Nuts

Don't forget the salad dressings, crackers or breadsticks, and beverages.

MARINATED TOMATO AND BRIE SALAD

1 (15-ounce) mini Brie
4 large tomatoes, seeded and cut into ½-inch cubes
1 cup fresh basil, cut into ⅛-inch-wide strips
3 to 4 cloves garlic, crushed
½ cup olive oil
¼ teaspoon salt
½ teaspoon freshly ground pepper
Garnish: fresh basil
Toasted Italian bread slices

• **Remove** and discard rind from Brie; cut into ½- to ¾-inch cubes.

• **Combine** Brie, tomato, and next 5 ingredients; cover and let stand at room temperature 1 hour. Garnish, if desired. Serve salad with bread slices. **Yield:** 8 servings.

Rublelene Singleton
Scotts Hill, Tennessee

BROCCOLI SALAD

½ cup raisins
2 pounds broccoli, cut into flowerets
1 cup purple seedless grapes, halved
3 green onions, thinly sliced
⅔ cup mayonnaise
2 tablespoons tarragon vinegar
¼ cup slivered almonds, toasted
8 slices bacon, cooked and crumbled

• **Soak** raisins in hot water 5 minutes; drain.

• **Combine** raisins and next 3 ingredients in a large bowl. Combine mayonnaise and vinegar; stir into broccoli mixture. Cover and chill.

• **Stir** in almonds and bacon just before serving. **Yield:** 6 to 8 servings.

Ruth J. Carnes
Victoria, Texas

EASY THINGS COME IN SMALL PACKAGES

....

Once you follow our simple how-to se-crets, these intriguing appetizers and desserts are all wrapped up with some-where to go – your next spring party. The treats start with pastry products you buy at the grocery store, and the magic is in the assembly.

TEXAS FIRECRACKERS
(pictured on page 109)

True to their name, these appetizers start with a little sizzle, and when you discover the peppers inside, they end with a nice "pow."

2 (22-ounce) jars pepperoncini salad peppers, drained *
6 ounces Monterey Jack cheese with peppers, cut into 24 (1½- x ¼- x ¼-inch) rectangles
1 (6-ounce) skinned and boned chicken breast half, cooked and cut into 24 strips
24 sheets frozen phyllo pastry, thawed
Butter-flavored cooking spray
48 fresh long chives (optional) **

• Select 24 (2-inch-long) salad pep-pers; set others aside for garnish.
• Remove and discard stems and seeds from peppers; drain thoroughly on paper towels.
• Stuff each pepper with 1 piece Mon-terey Jack cheese and 1 chicken strip; set aside.
• Spray both sides of 4 phyllo sheets with cooking spray; stack. Cut stacked phyllo in half lengthwise and then crosswise.

• Place 1 pepper on each phyllo stack, at one long end. Starting with long end, roll phyllo around pepper. Twist ends to seal. Place on a baking sheet. Repeat with remaining phyllo and stuffed peppers.
• Bake at 375° for 20 minutes or until golden. Tie twisted ends of pastry with chives, if desired. Serve immediately. Yield: 2 dozen.

* Substitute 24 (2-inch) banana pep-pers for pepperoncini salad peppers. Roast peppers at 400° until charred (about 12 minutes). Cool completely; remove and discard stems and seeds.

** Slice the green portion of green onions lengthwise and substitute for chives.

Note: Freeze unbaked Texas Firecrack-ers in an airtight container up to 3 months. To serve, bake as directed, and tie with chives, if desired.

Carol Barclay
Portland, Texas

FRIED WONTON ENVELOPES
(pictured on page 109)

Carol Barclay always serves these with her own Guacamole Dip, but you can buy guacamole in the dairy case to save time.

1 (8-ounce) package Monterey Jack cheese with peppers, cut into 1- x 1- x ½-inch pieces
24 small wonton wrappers
Vegetable cooking spray
Vegetable oil
Guacamole Dip (optional)

• Place 1 cheese cube in center of each wonton wrapper. Moisten edges of wrapper with water. Fold corners of wrapper to center, enclosing filling and overlapping edges slightly.
• Place on sheets of wax paper sprayed with cooking spray; cover with addi-tional wax paper to prevent drying out.

• Pour oil to depth of 3 inches into a Dutch oven; heat to 350°. Fry won-tons, 3 or 4 at a time, until golden on each side, turning once. Drain on paper towels. Serve immediately with Guacamole Dip, if desired. Yield: 2 dozen.

Guacamole Dip

2 large ripe avocados, peeled and mashed
3 tablespoons fresh lime juice
½ teaspoon salt
1 tablespoon chopped fresh cilantro or ½ teaspoon dried coriander
2 tablespoons finely chopped green onions
3 tablespoons mayonnaise or salad dressing

• Combine all ingredients; cover and chill. Yield: 1¼ cups.

Carol Barclay
Portland, Texas

APPETIZING APPETIZERS

■ When making appetizers, the most helpful tools in the kitchen are as basic as sharp knives and large baking sheets to help you cut and cook efficiently.

■ For serving pieces, concentrate on varying size, shape, and height of containers to add interest to a buffet table.

■ Remember to provide plenty of napkins for sticky fingers, and try to avoid messy foods that are apt to drip as guests eat them.

■ In a hurry? Steps in an appetizer recipe can often be done ahead and then assembled just before the party.

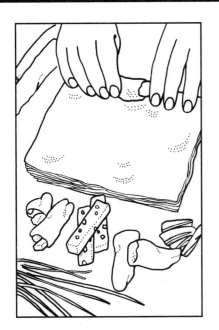

For Texas Firecrackers, stuff each pepper with a piece of cheese and chicken, and roll – it's that simple.

There's no need to cut pastry for Fried Wonton Envelopes. Just fold wrappers around cheese, and fry.

Pull up the sides of Chocolate-Raspberry Bags to enclose morsel mixture, pinching "neck" to seal.

CHOCOLATE-RASPBERRY BAGS
(pictured on page 109)

This dessert is great to serve to company. It's always easy to make ahead, or it can even be done at the last minute, if necessary, and it never fails to impress your guests. The pastry bags hold two flavors of chocolate morsels.

1 (10-ounce) package frozen raspberries in light syrup, thawed and undrained
1¼ cups sifted powdered sugar, divided
1 (17¼-ounce) package frozen puff pastry sheets, thawed
1 cup raspberry-flavored chocolate morsels or semisweet chocolate morsels
1 cup white chocolate or vanilla-milk morsels
1 cup chopped pecans

• **Combine** raspberries and 1 cup powdered sugar in container of an electric blender; process until smooth, stopping once to scrape down sides.
• **Pour** raspberry mixture through a large wire-mesh strainer into a bowl, discarding seeds. Cover and chill.
• **Roll** each pastry sheet on a lightly floured surface into a 12-inch square; cut each sheet of pastry into 4 squares.
• **Combine** chocolate morsels, white chocolate morsels, and pecans; place evenly in middle of each pastry square. Reserve some morsel mixture for garnish, if desired. Pull up sides of pastry to enclose morsel mixture; twist ends just above morsels, pinching to seal at "neck" and spreading open top edges of pastry. Place filled bags on an ungreased baking sheet.
• **Bake** at 425° for 20 minutes, covering loosely with aluminum foil after 10 minutes to prevent excess browning.
• **Spoon** raspberry sauce evenly onto dessert plates; set aside. Sprinkle baked pastries with remaining ¼ cup powdered sugar, and place a pastry bag in center of each plate on sauce. Sprinkle reserved morsel mixture on sauce. Serve immediately. **Yield:** 8 servings.

Note: You can assemble the pastry bags up to 4 hours before baking them; cover with plastic wrap, and chill. Substitute caramel sauce for raspberry sauce. For puff pastry sheets, we used Pepperidge Farm.

SHORTCAKES DELICIOUSLY LAYERED

Take dinner from boring to beautiful. It's all in the construction. After sampling our easy-to-assemble shortcakes, you'll be ready to create some combinations of your own. Let dinner get vertical; then see how it all stacks up.

HAM STROGANOFF ON CHEESY ONION BISCUITS

Use leftover or deli ham to make this creamy topping for a savory shortcake. Add a tossed green salad and supper is ready.

2 tablespoons butter or margarine
2 cups chopped cooked ham
¼ cup finely chopped onion
1 (10¾-ounce) can cream of chicken soup, undiluted
½ cup milk
1 (8-ounce) carton sour cream
⅛ teaspoon pepper
Cheesy Onion Biscuits

● **Melt** butter in a heavy skillet over medium-high heat; add ham and onion, and cook, stirring constantly, until onion is tender.
● **Stir** in soup and milk; cover and cook over medium heat 3 to 4 minutes. Stir in sour cream and pepper; cook over low heat until mixture is thoroughly heated. Serve between split Cheesy Onion Biscuits. **Yield:** 4 servings.

Lea Davis
Dallas, Texas

Cheesy Onion Biscuits

2 cups all-purpose flour
3 tablespoons instant nonfat dry milk powder
4 teaspoons baking powder
¾ teaspoon salt
⅓ cup butter or margarine
½ cup grated Parmesan cheese
2 tablespoons finely chopped green onions
¾ cup water

● **Combine** first 4 ingredients in a large bowl; cut in butter with pastry blender or fork until mixture is crumbly.
● **Stir** in Parmesan cheese and green onions. Add water, stirring with a fork until dry ingredients are moistened.
● **Turn** biscuit dough out onto a lightly floured surface, and knead lightly 5 or 6 times.
● **Roll** to ½-inch thickness; cut with a 3-inch round cutter. Place on a lightly greased baking sheet.
● **Bake** at 400° for 15 minutes or until lightly browned. **Yield:** 8 biscuits.

Charlotte Pierce
Greensburg, Kentucky

CHEESY CHICKEN SHORTCAKES

We added green chiles for a mild Southwestern flavor. For more fire, serve with hot salsa or dried crushed red peppers.

6 ounces process cheese spread
⅓ cup chicken broth
1½ cups chopped cooked chicken
1 (4½-ounce) can chopped green chiles, undrained
Cornmeal Biscuits

● **Combine** cheese and chicken broth in a medium saucepan; cook over medium heat, stirring constantly, until cheese melts.
● **Stir** in chicken and chiles; cook until thoroughly heated. Serve over Cornmeal Biscuits. **Yield:** 2½ cups.

Suzan Wiener
Spring Hill, Florida

Cornmeal Biscuits

1½ cups all-purpose flour
½ cup yellow cornmeal
2 teaspoons baking powder
½ teaspoon baking soda
½ teaspoon salt
¼ cup butter or margarine
¾ cup plus 2 tablespoons buttermilk
1 egg white, lightly beaten

● **Combine** first 5 ingredients in a bowl; cut in butter with pastry blender until mixture is crumbly. Add buttermilk, stirring with a fork until dry ingredients are moistened. Turn dough out onto a lightly floured surface, and knead lightly 5 or 6 times.
● **Roll** dough to ½-inch thickness; cut with a 2½-inch round cutter, and place on a lightly greased baking sheet. Brush tops with egg white.
● **Bake** at 450° for 12 minutes or until lightly browned. **Yield:** 1 dozen.

Joel Allard
San Antonio, Texas

CREAMED SHRIMP ON PECAN-CORNMEAL ROUNDS

Mix and match recipes for flavorful layers. We paired these two with delicious results.

1 pound unpeeled medium-size
    fresh shrimp
¼ cup butter or margarine
½ cup chopped onion
½ cup chopped sweet red or green
    pepper
1 (10¾-ounce) can cream of
    mushroom soup, undiluted
½ cup water
¼ teaspoon ground black
    pepper
⅛ teaspoon ground red pepper
Pecan-Cornmeal Rounds
Garnish: fresh parsley sprigs

• **Peel** shrimp, and devein, if desired; set aside.
• **Melt** butter in a heavy skillet over medium-high heat; add onion and chopped pepper. Cook 2 minutes or until vegetables are crisp-tender. Stir in soup and next 3 ingredients. Bring to a boil, stirring constantly. Add shrimp, reduce heat, and simmer 10 minutes or until shrimp turn pink.
• **Place** a plain Pecan-Cornmeal Round on plate, and top with shrimp mixture and a pecan-topped round. Garnish, if desired. **Yield:** 4 servings.

Pat Gindrup
Conroe, Texas

Pecan-Cornmeal Rounds

¾ cup plus 2 tablespoons butter,
    softened
1½ cups all-purpose flour
½ cup yellow cornmeal
2 tablespoons sugar
¾ teaspoon salt
1 egg, lightly beaten
¾ cup chopped pecans
4 pecan halves (optional)

• **Beat** butter at medium speed with an electric mixer until creamy. Add flour and next 4 ingredients; mix at low speed until blended. Stir in chopped pecans. Wrap dough in plastic wrap; chill 1 hour.

• **Turn** dough out onto a lightly floured surface. Roll to ½-inch thickness. Cut into 8 shapes with a 3-inch daisy-shaped or round cutter. Place on a lightly greased baking sheet. Press a pecan half in the center of half the rounds, if desired.
• **Bake** at 350° for 20 minutes or until rounds are lightly browned; remove from pan, and cool rounds on wire racks. **Yield:** 8 rounds.

Edith Askins
Greenville, Texas

CHOCOLATE-RASPBERRY SHORTCAKE
(pictured on page 4)

½ cup butter or margarine,
    softened
1¼ cups sugar
2 large eggs, separated
1¼ cups sifted cake flour
2 teaspoons baking powder
¼ teaspoon salt
⅓ cup cocoa
⅔ cup milk
1 teaspoon vanilla extract
2 tablespoons seedless raspberry
    jam
2 tablespoons Chambord or other
    raspberry-flavored liqueur
2 cups whipping cream
¼ cup sifted powdered sugar
3 cups fresh raspberries
Garnish: fresh mint sprigs

• **Grease** two 9-inch round cakepans; line with wax paper, and grease wax paper. Set aside.
• **Beat** butter at medium speed with an electric mixer 2 minutes or until creamy; add sugar gradually, beating well. Add egg yolks, one at a time, beating until blended after each addition.
• **Combine** flour and next 3 ingredients; add to butter mixture alternately with milk, beginning and ending with flour mixture. Beat at low speed until blended after each addition. Stir in vanilla.
• **Beat** egg whites at high speed with an electric mixer until stiff peaks form; gently fold into batter. Pour batter into prepared pans.

• **Bake** at 350° for 18 minutes or until a wooden pick inserted in center comes out clean. Cool in pans on wire racks 10 minutes. Remove from pans; cool completely on wire racks.
• **Cook** jam in a small saucepan over low heat until melted; stir in liqueur. Set jam mixture aside.
• **Beat** whipping cream at medium speed with an electric mixer until foamy; gradually add powdered sugar, beating until soft peaks form.
• **Place** one cake layer on a serving plate; brush with half of jam mixture. Arrange half of raspberries over jam. Spread half of whipped cream over raspberries.
• **Top** with second cake layer; brush with remaining jam mixture. Spread remaining whipped cream over jam mixture; arrange remaining raspberries on top. Garnish, if desired. **Yield:** one 9-inch shortcake.

Mattie Scott
Birmingham, Alabama

YUMMY COCONUT BISCUITS

Layer pineapple or mango chunks and sweetened whipped cream with this great biscuit for a shortcake.

2 cups all-purpose flour
¾ cup flaked coconut, toasted
2 tablespoons sugar
1 tablespoon baking powder
½ teaspoon salt
⅓ cup shortening
1 cup milk
½ teaspoon vanilla extract

• **Combine** first 5 ingredients in a large bowl; cut in shortening with pastry blender until mixture is crumbly.
• **Combine** milk and vanilla; add to dry ingredients, stirring until dry ingredients are moistened (dough will be sticky).
• **Drop** dough, 2 tablespoons at a time, onto a lightly greased baking sheet.
• **Bake** at 450° for 10 minutes or until biscuits are golden. **Yield:** about 1 dozen.

Suzan Wiener
Spring Hill, Florida

ORANGE-STRAWBERRY SHORTCAKE

2 pints fresh strawberries, sliced
2 (11-ounce) cans mandarin
   oranges, drained
½ cup sugar
1½ tablespoons Triple Sec or
   other orange-flavored liqueur
2 cups biscuit and baking mix
⅔ cup milk
1 tablespoon sugar
1½ teaspoons ground cinnamon
2 cups whipping cream
½ cup sifted powdered sugar
¼ cup sour cream

• **Combine** first 4 ingredients, stirring until sugar dissolves. Cover and chill 2 hours.
• **Combine** biscuit and baking mix and next 3 ingredients; stir with a fork until dry ingredients are moistened. Turn out onto a lightly floured surface; knead 4 or 5 times. Place dough on a lightly greased baking sheet; press into a 7- x ¾-inch round.
• **Bake** at 425° for 15 minutes or until done. Carefully remove from pan; cool on a wire rack.
• **Beat** whipping cream until foamy; gradually add powdered sugar, beating until soft peaks form. Add sour cream, and beat until stiff peaks form.
• **Split** biscuit round in half horizontally. Place bottom half on a serving dish. Drain fruit, reserving 2 tablespoons liquid. Spoon two-thirds of fruit on bottom round; drizzle with reserved liquid. Spoon half of the whipped cream mixture over fruit. Add top biscuit round. Top mixture with remaining fruit and whipped cream. **Yield:** 8 servings.

Joyce Ogletree
Newnan, Georgia

EASTER SUNDAY BRUNCH

....

Colored eggs, fresh flowers, and whimsical bunnies set the tone for our brunch gathering. Add your favorite ham to our menu for an easy party.

SUNDAY EGG CASSEROLE

2 tablespoons butter or margarine
4 tablespoons dry sherry, divided
1 pound fresh mushrooms, sliced
1 (10¾-ounce) can cream of
   chicken soup, undiluted
1 (8-ounce) carton sour cream
2 tablespoons all-purpose flour
½ teaspoon salt
½ teaspoon pepper
1 tablespoon finely chopped onion
1 (2-ounce) jar chopped pimiento,
   drained
1 (10-ounce) package frozen
   English peas, thawed and
   drained
14 hard-cooked eggs, cut
   lengthwise into 4 wedges
1 (8-ounce) can sliced water
   chestnuts, drained
1 cup fresh breadcrumbs (2 slices
   bread)
1 tablespoon butter or margarine,
   melted

• **Melt** 2 tablespoons butter in a large skillet; add 2 tablespoons sherry and mushrooms, and cook over medium heat 5 minutes or until mushrooms are tender. Drain well; set aside.
• **Combine** remaining 2 tablespoons sherry, soup, and next 6 ingredients in a medium saucepan. Cook 2 minutes or until mixture is bubbly; stir in mushrooms and peas.
• **Arrange** egg wedges and water chestnuts in bottom of a lightly greased 13- x 9- x 2-inch baking dish. Pour soup mixture evenly over top.
• **Combine** breadcrumbs and melted butter. Sprinkle over soup mixture.

• **Bake** at 375° for 20 minutes or until top is golden. **Yield:** 6 to 8 servings.

Brenda Russell
Signal Mountain, Tennessee

BERRY-CITRUS TWIST

2 quarts fresh strawberries, halved
2 fresh pineapples, peeled, cored,
   and cut into chunks *
½ cup orange marmalade
¼ cup orange juice
2 tablespoons lemon juice
½ cup fresh or frozen blueberries

• **Combine** strawberries and pineapple in a bowl; set aside.
• **Combine** orange marmalade, orange juice, and lemon juice; pour over fruit, and toss gently. Stir in blueberries just before serving. **Yield:** 10 cups.

* Substitute 2 (20-ounce) cans pineapple chunks in juice, drained, for fresh.

Ruth Sherrer
Fort Worth, Texas

HOT CROSS BUNS

4¼ to 4¾ cups all-purpose flour,
   divided
⅔ cup sugar
1 (¼-ounce) envelope rapid-rise
   yeast
1 teaspoon salt
1 teaspoon ground nutmeg
¼ teaspoon ground cinnamon
1 cup milk
¼ cup water
⅓ cup unsalted butter, cut up
2 large eggs
⅔ cup currants
⅓ cup chopped, mixed candied
   fruit
1 tablespoon all-purpose flour
1 egg white, slightly beaten
1 cup sifted powdered sugar
1 to 1½ tablespoons milk
½ teaspoon vanilla extract

• **Combine** 2½ cups flour, sugar, yeast, salt, nutmeg, and cinnamon in a large mixing bowl, stirring well. Set aside.

- **Combine** 1 cup milk, water, and butter in a saucepan; cook over medium heat, stirring constantly, just until butter melts. Cool 5 minutes (to 130°).
- **Pour** milk mixture into flour mixture; beat at low speed with an electric mixer until dry ingredients are moistened. Add eggs; beat at medium speed 3 minutes. Gradually stir in enough remaining flour to make a soft dough.
- **Turn** dough out onto a well-floured surface; knead until smooth and elastic (about 8 minutes). Place in a well-greased bowl, turning to grease top.
- **Cover** and let rise in a warm place (85°), free from drafts, 1 hour (won't quite be doubled in bulk).
- **Punch** dough down, and turn out onto a floured surface. Combine currants, candied fruit, and 1 tablespoon flour, stirring to coat. Knead about one-fourth of fruit mixture at a time into dough until all fruit mixture is evenly dispersed.
- **Divide** dough into 15 equal portions; shape each portion into a ball. Place balls in a greased 13- x 9- x 2-inch pan; cover and let rise in a warm place 1 hour or until doubled in bulk. Gently brush tops with beaten egg white.
- **Bake** at 375° for 16 minutes or until buns are deep golden and sound hollow when tapped. Cool 10 minutes in pan on a wire rack.
- **Combine** powdered sugar, 1 to 1½ tablespoons milk, and vanilla; pipe evenly on top of warm buns, forming a cross. **Yield:** 15 buns.

Velma Kestner
Berwind, West Virginia

SPARKLING CRANBERRY PUNCH

1 (2-liter) bottle lemon-lime carbonated beverage, chilled
1 (48-ounce) bottle cranberry-apple juice drink, chilled
1½ cups white grape juice, chilled

- **Combine** all ingredients. Serve immediately over ice, if desired. **Yield:** 1 gallon.

Louise Mimbs
Birmingham, Alabama

PB & J FOR EASTER

....

Peanut butter and jelly still make a great pair, so we thought peanut butter and jelly beans must be even better. Not in a sophisticated manner, of course, but in the realm of fun food. Our readers have turned this favorite combination into Easter cookies, candies, and a snack we couldn't resist – Bunny Trail Mix.

But the quickest way to taste this new PB&J combination? A bag of jelly beans, a jar of peanut butter, and a spoon.

BUNNY TRAIL MIX

1 cup (6 ounces) butterscotch-flavored morsels
½ cup chunky peanut butter
4 cups granola cereal
1 cup jelly beans (about 8 ounces)

- **Line** bottom of a 13- x 9- x 2-inch pan with wax paper; set aside.
- **Combine** butterscotch morsels and peanut butter in a large heavy saucepan; cook over low heat, stirring constantly, until melted.
- **Add** cereal, stirring well; press mixture into prepared pan. Cover and chill until firm.
- **Break** into pieces; stir in jelly beans. Store in an airtight container at room temperature. **Yield:** 8 cups.

Mildred Bickley
Bristol, Virginia

EASTER BASKET AND EGGS

1 (20-ounce) package refrigerated sliceable sugar cookie dough
1 (20-ounce) package refrigerated sliceable peanut butter cookie dough
1 (8-ounce) package cream cheese, softened
½ cup creamy peanut butter
1 (16-ounce) package powdered sugar, sifted
1 teaspoon vanilla extract
1 cup flaked coconut
Few drops of green food coloring
6 (7-ounce) packages small jelly beans

- **Cut** sugar cookie dough into ¼-inch-thick slices; place on lightly greased cookie sheets. Bake at 350° for 9 minutes or until lightly browned. Cool on wire racks.
- **Press** peanut butter cookie dough into a lightly greased 13-inch pizza pan. Bake at 350° for 18 minutes or until browned. Cool on a wire rack.
- **Beat** cream cheese and peanut butter at medium speed with an electric mixer until creamy. Gradually add powdered sugar, beating until well blended. Stir in vanilla.
- **Spread** frosting on small cookies (eggs) and large cookie (basket).
- **Combine** coconut and food coloring in a jar. Cover with lid, and shake until evenly tinted.
- **Press** black and brown jelly beans into frosting on large cookie for "basket weave." Sprinkle green coconut on cookie for "grass." Press colored jelly beans onto small cookies to decorate "Easter eggs." **Yield:** 30 small cookies and 1 large cookie.

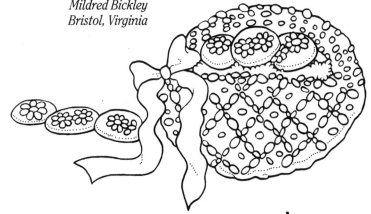

BIRD'S NESTS

Remember the old favorite – ooey, gooey rice cereal squares? Emily Chastain dressed it up for Easter by shaping it into nests filled with jelly bean "eggs."

3½ cups crisp rice cereal
1 cup flaked coconut
1 cup miniature marshmallows
1 cup chunky peanut butter
½ cup firmly packed brown sugar
⅓ cup light corn syrup
1 teaspoon vanilla extract
5 tablespoons chunky peanut butter
1 (7-ounce) package small jelly beans

• **Combine** cereal and coconut in a large bowl; set aside.
• **Combine** marshmallows and next 3 ingredients in a saucepan; cook over medium heat, stirring constantly, until smooth. Remove from heat; stir in vanilla. Pour over cereal and coconut, stirring to coat evenly.
• **Shape** mixture into 1½-inch balls; make indentation in center of each ball with thumb. Spoon about ½ teaspoon peanut butter into each indentation; place 3 jelly beans on peanut butter. **Yield:** 2½ dozen.

Emily Chastain
San Antonio, Texas

NEED A QUICK FAVOR?

■ Make "bean bags" for your child's school party by filling colored plastic wrap with jelly beans and tying with curling ribbon.

■ Fill a new cup and saucer or mug with coffee- or cappuccino-flavored jelly beans for a java lover. (Check candy stores or gourmet shops for the sweets.)

A MEMORABLE PASSOVER

....

"Passover is a great time for people who like to cook," says Liz Berek of Austin, Texas. "It's an opportunity to try new things, yet celebrate tradition – a lot like Thanksgiving."

Pesach, as the holiday is known in Hebrew, celebrates the Israelites' escape from Egyptian slavery. "It's a festive time with lots of wine and laughter. Almost everyone enjoys observing Passover for its wonderful rituals."

Here she shares her favorite holiday recipes with us. All can be used with nonkosher products.

PASSOVER BRISKET

1 (4-pound) beef brisket, well trimmed
2 cloves garlic, thinly sliced
1 tablespoon Kosher for Passover-labeled vegetable oil
2 carrots, scraped and finely chopped
1 stalk celery, finely chopped
3 medium onions, finely chopped
2 tablespoons brown sugar
2 teaspoons salt
½ teaspoon paprika
¼ teaspoon pepper
4 bay leaves, crumbled
10 peppercorns
¾ cup condensed Kosher for Passover-labeled chicken broth, undiluted
¾ cup water

• **Cut** 1-inch-wide slits in brisket, and insert garlic slices into slits just under the surface.
• **Heat** oil in a large Dutch oven over high heat; add brisket, and cook, turning until browned on all sides. Remove from pan.
• **Reduce** heat; add carrot, celery, and onion. Cook, stirring constantly,

5 minutes or until onion is tender. Return brisket to Dutch oven.
• **Combine** brown sugar and next 5 ingredients; sprinkle over brisket. Add broth and water, and bring to a boil. Cover, reduce heat to low, and simmer 2 hours or until tender, turning once.
• **Remove** brisket and peppercorns from pan, reserving pan drippings; slice brisket, and discard peppercorns. Pour drippings over brisket or serve them separately. **Yield:** 8 to 10 servings.

Note: To remove excess fat, cover and chill brisket in broth 8 hours; then skim off fat. Reheat brisket in pan drippings.

TZIMMES

This Passover dish (pronounced SIM-ihs) is one of the most traditional.

2 (12-ounce) packages pitted prunes
3 cups boiling water
2 medium onions, chopped
1 tablespoon Kosher for Passover-labeled vegetable oil
5 medium sweet potatoes (about 3 pounds), peeled and cut into 1-inch pieces
1 pound carrots, scraped and sliced
1 cup orange juice
1 cup honey
2 whole cloves
1½ teaspoons salt
1 teaspoon ground cinnamon
1 teaspoon minced fresh ginger
½ teaspoon pepper
½ teaspoon ground nutmeg

• **Combine** prunes and boiling water in a large bowl; let stand 30 minutes. Drain prunes, reserving liquid.
• **Cook** onion in oil in a large oven-proof stockpot over medium-high heat, stirring constantly, until tender. Place prunes, sweet potato, and carrot over onion.
• **Combine** reserved liquid, orange juice, and remaining ingredients; pour over vegetables.
• **Cover** and bake at 350° for 2 hours or until vegetables are tender, stirring occasionally. **Yield:** 8 servings.

PREPARING FOR PASSOVER

"The best tip for keeping your kitchen kosher during Passover is *talk to your rabbi*," Liz Berek of Austin, Texas, advises. "Kosher standards can vary greatly from congregation to congregation." Though the preparation or "kashering" can be time-consuming, it all helps in understanding and appreciating religious freedom, she says.

For her Ashkenazic congregation and others, the core of Passover observance revolves around a set of dietary laws restricting them from eating or owning *hametz* – forbidden foods including wheat, barley, oats, rye, leaveners, rice, corn, and legumes. Sephardic congregations, however, will differ in opinion on what is forbidden during Passover. At all times, though, all congregations view pork and shellfish as nonkosher, and they always store and prepare meat and dairy foods separately. A different set of dishes and cooking utensils is also required.

"The most important thing is to set up a kosher kitchen and look for the "Kosher for Passover" label on certain oils, stocks, wines, and starches," Liz says. "Beyond that, your congregation or local Jewish organization will have lots of helpful information."

Kosher for Passover differs from other kosher products. Check with your rabbi for local stores that carry these products.

Here are a couple of sources for more on kosher living.

■ **Kosher Notions** (8881 West Pico Blvd., Suite 2, Los Angeles, CA 90035) offers a catalog of kitchenware for keeping kitchens kosher. Many are labeled "Milk," "Meat," and "Pareve" (neutral).

■ The Union for Traditional Judaism sponsors **"The Kosher Nexus,"** an entertaining, informative newsletter that keeps its readers posted on the "latest and greatest in the world of Kashrut." Write The Union for Traditional Judaism, 241 Cedar Lane, Teaneck, NJ 07666; or call 1-800-843-8825.

BURNT SUGAR SPONGE CAKE WITH BERRY SAUCE

¼ cup water
½ teaspoon lemon juice
1½ cups sugar
Kosher for Passover-labeled vegetable cooking spray, margarine, or vegetable oil
9 large eggs, separated
¼ cup fresh orange juice
¾ cup Kosher for Passover-labeled potato starch
¼ cup matzo cake meal
½ teaspoon salt
¼ cup sugar
Powdered sugar, sifted
Berry Sauce

● **Combine** first 3 ingredients in a small heavy saucepan; cook over low heat until sugar dissolves, stirring occasionally. Increase heat to high, and boil 7 to 9 minutes or until mixture is caramel colored. (Do not overcook.)
● **Pour** immediately into a 15- x 10- x 1-inch jellyroll pan coated with cooking spray; cool until hard. Break into pieces.

● **Position** knife blade in food processor bowl; add caramel pieces. Process until it becomes a fine powder.
● **Combine** caramel powder and egg yolks; beat at high speed with an electric mixer until smooth and thickened. Add orange juice, and beat until blended.
● **Combine** potato starch and cake meal; sift together 3 times. Gradually add starch mixture to yolk mixture, mixing well; set aside.
● **Combine** egg whites and salt in a large mixing bowl. Beat at high speed until foamy. Gradually add ¼ cup sugar, beating until stiff but not dry.
● **Stir** one-third egg white mixture into cake batter; fold in remaining egg white mixture. Pour into an ungreased 10-inch tube pan, spreading evenly.
● **Bake** at 325° for 45 to 55 minutes or until cake springs back when lightly touched. Invert pan, and cool cake completely.
● **Loosen** cake from sides of pan, using a narrow metal spatula; remove from pan. Sprinkle with powdered sugar, and serve with Berry Sauce. **Yield:** one 10-inch cake.

Berry Sauce

2 cups Kosher for Passover-labeled sweet red wine
½ cup water
1 teaspoon grated orange rind
¼ cup fresh orange juice
1 cup sugar
7 whole cloves
5 peppercorns
1 (2½-inch) stick cinnamon
2 cups sliced fresh strawberries
2 cups fresh blueberries

● **Combine** first 8 ingredients in a small saucepan; bring to a boil over high heat, and cook 10 minutes.
● **Pour** through a wire-mesh strainer into a medium bowl, discarding spices. Add fresh berries; cover and chill. **Yield:** 4 cups.

Note: For sweet red wine, we used Mogen David Concord Wine.

LAMB–TEXAS STYLE

You might think that nothing can live on this land of dust and more dust, but look a little closer. The movement you see between the twisted mesquite is probably a flock of sheep.

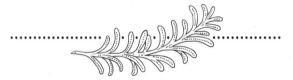

The flocks live well in West Texas, providing the locals a major source of income with their wool and, in the spring, lamb. Ranchers and chefs of the region have discovered numerous ways to prepare this plentiful meat. Sample these recipes, and find out just how good lamb can be – Texas style.

GRILLED LAMB WITH MANGO SALSA

Occasionally you can find boneless leg of lamb; if you can't, ask your butcher to remove the bone from a leg of lamb.

1   teaspoon cumin seeds
1   teaspoon coriander seeds
1   cup olive oil
½   cup Chablis or other dry white wine
¼   cup tequila
2   tablespoons fresh lime juice
2   tablespoons minced fresh garlic
2   tablespoons chopped fresh cilantro
2   jalapeño peppers, seeded and finely chopped
½   teaspoon salt
½   teaspoon freshly ground pepper
1   (4- to 4½-pound) boneless leg of lamb
Mango Salsa
Garnish: fresh cilantro sprigs

• **Cook** cumin seeds in a heavy skillet, stirring constantly, until browned; remove from heat, and crush. Repeat procedure with coriander seeds.

• **Combine** crushed cumin and coriander seeds, olive oil, and next 8 ingredients in a large heavy-duty, zip-top plastic bag or a large shallow dish. Add lamb, turning to coat. Seal bag or cover dish, and chill 8 hours, turning occasionally.

• **Cook** lamb, without grill lid, over medium-hot coals (350° to 400°) about 40 minutes or until meat thermometer inserted in thickest portion of meat registers 150° (medium-rare) or to desired degree of doneness, turning meat once.

• **Cut** lamb into thin slices; serve with Mango Salsa. Garnish, if desired. **Yield:** 8 servings.

Mango Salsa

4   medium mangoes, peeled and chopped
¼   cup chopped celery
¼   cup finely chopped green onions
¼   cup chopped sweet yellow or sweet red pepper
1   jalapeño pepper, seeded and minced
⅓   cup chopped fresh cilantro
¼   cup honey
¼   cup olive oil
2   tablespoons fresh lime juice
¼   teaspoon salt

• **Combine** first 6 ingredients in a small bowl. Combine honey and remaining ingredients; pour over mango mixture. Toss gently to coat; cover and chill 30 minutes. **Yield:** about 4 cups.

Sue Sims
San Angelo, Texas

GRILLED LAMB WITH SWEET PEPPER RELISH

Grill an extra sweet pepper or two with the lamb. Cut off the top, remove seeds, and use to serve Sweet Pepper Relish.

4   (8-ounce) lamb rib sections (2 ribs per section)
¼   teaspoon salt
¼   teaspoon garlic powder
¼   teaspoon pepper
½   teaspoon chopped fresh basil
½   teaspoon chopped fresh rosemary
Sweet Pepper Relish
Garnish: fresh herbs

• **Trim** fat from rib sections, and set lamb aside.

• **Combine** salt, garlic powder, and pepper, and sprinkle over lamb. Press basil and rosemary evenly onto lamb rib sections.

• **Cook,** covered with grill lid, over medium-hot coals (350° to 400°) 12 minutes on each side or until meat thermometer registers 150° (medium-rare) to 160° (medium). Serve with Sweet Pepper Relish. Garnish, if desired. **Yield:** 4 servings.

Sweet Pepper Relish

2   sweet red peppers, cut into thin strips
2   sweet yellow peppers, cut into thin strips
¾   cup firmly packed brown sugar
8   serrano chile peppers, seeded and cut into thin strips

• **Combine** all ingredients. Cover and chill 8 hours.

• **Place** mixture in a small saucepan; bring to a boil over medium-low heat, stirring constantly. Reduce heat, and simmer 40 minutes, stirring frequently. Cool. **Yield:** 1 cup.

Gert Rausch
Austin, Texas

FROM OUR KITCHEN TO YOURS

....

We've discovered a couple of winners – Grilled Lamb with Mango Salsa and Grilled Lamb with Sweet Pepper Relish. These recipes, on the facing page, received high ratings, and their easy preparation and elegant appearance ranked them even higher. And if you're skeptical about how to cook with lamb, here are a few hints.

SEASONING SENSATIONS

A wide variety of seasonings enhances lamb's flavor. Seasoned with cumin, jalapeño, and cilantro, Grilled Lamb with Mango Salsa echoes the flavors of both the Southwest and South Florida. Add curry powder for a hint of the flavors of India. Or prepare lamb Greek style, using oregano, mint, and garlic. Following are several suggested seasonings and easy ways to use them.

■ Season lamb with allspice, basil, bay leaf, caraway, cilantro, cinnamon, cloves, coriander, curry, dill, garlic, ginger, marjoram, mint, mustard, oregano, paprika, parsley, pepper, rosemary, or thyme.

■ Rub a mixture of the herbs or spices on lamb before broiling, grilling, or roasting.

■ Cut several small slits in the lamb's surface, and insert slivers of garlic.

■ Make a marinade using dry wine or sherry and seasonings, or try a commercial teriyaki marinade.

■ Stir together a combination of herbs and broth; brush on the meat during cooking.

■ Combine a few herbs with a fruit jelly or pepper jelly, and spread over lamb before roasting.

■ Soak fresh or dried herbs, such as, basil, oregano, sage, or thyme in water for about one hour; shake dry, and place on hot coals just before adding lamb to the grill.

■ Mix equal amounts of mint jelly and orange marmalade; serve with lamb.

■ Prepare a béarnaise sauce, and serve with lamb chops or steaks.

COOKING CLASS

The American Lamb Council recommends broiling or grilling 1-inch-thick chops, steaks, and kabob cubes about 4 inches from heat source for 8 to 10 minutes (160° medium). For roasting larger cuts, follow the guidelines in the cooking chart on this page, and use a meat thermometer to ensure that the lamb reaches the desired degree of doneness (150° medium-rare, 160° medium). Be sure not to overcook meat; lamb should be pink and juicy inside.

COOKING FOR TWO

Believe it or not, a leg of lamb can feed two people. Instead of having leftovers, divide the large cut into usable portions.

Ask the butcher to remove the sirloin section of the leg before boning it and to slice this portion into 1-inch-thick steaks. Have the remaining portion boned and butterflied (spread out flat to resemble a butterfly shape). Ask that the butterflied section be cut into four portions and labeled top round, sirloin, shank, and bottom round.

From the top round, you'll have a 1- to 1½-pound roast that can be cut into 1-inch-thick fillets, if desired. Cut the sirloin portion into cubes for kabobs, fondue, or stir-frys. Cut the shank portion into cubes for soup or stew. And cut the bottom round portion into strips for stroganoff or fajitas. Package, label, and freeze these cuts of meat for several ready-to-go future meals.

STORAGE SAVVY

CUTS	REFRIGERATE UP TO	FREEZE UP TO
Ground lamb	1 day	4 months
All other lamb cuts	2 days	9 months
Cooked lamb	4 days	Not recommended

COOKING SAVVY

CUT	OVEN TEMPERATURE	APPROXIMATE COOKING TIME (MINUTES PER POUND)
Leg, bone-in (5 to 7 pounds)	325°	20 (medium-rare); 25 (medium)
Leg, bone-in (7 to 9 pounds)	325°	16 to 18 (medium-rare); 20 (medium)
Leg, boneless (4 to 7 pounds)	325°	30 (medium-rare); 32 to 34 (medium)
Shoulder, boneless	325°	36 to 38 (medium-rare); 40 (medium)
Rib roast, rack	375°	30 (medium-rare); 31 to 33 (medium)
Sirloin roast, boneless	325°	45 (medium-rare); 50 (medium)
Crown roast, unstuffed (2 to 3 pounds)	375°	21 to 24 (medium-rare); 30 (medium)

LOW-FAT CATCH

Trout and catfish are a busy cook's dream. They taste best when prepared fresh, simply, and quickly. Whether you prefer your catch oven-fried, sautéed, grilled, or baked, we've discovered the low-fat way to do it. We've even cut the fat in the trimmings, including low-calorie versions of slaw, hush puppies, and seafood sauces.

GRILLED TROUT

You can substitute any fresh herb for the tarragon in this recipe.

¼ cup olive oil
¼ cup fresh tarragon
¼ cup lemon juice
½ teaspoon salt
2 (2-pound) dressed trout
4 sprigs fresh tarragon
1 lemon, sliced
Vegetable cooking spray

• **Combine** olive oil and tarragon in a small saucepan. Cook over very low heat 20 minutes; pour mixture through a wire-mesh strainer, discarding solids.
• **Combine** oil mixture, lemon juice, and salt, whisking to blend. Brush half of mixture inside each trout. Place 2 sprigs tarragon and 2 lemon slices inside each trout.
• **Place** trout in a large baking dish. Pour remaining oil mixture over trout. Cover and chill 2 hours.
• **Place** trout in a grill basket coated with cooking spray. Cook, covered with grill lid, over hot coals (400° to 500°) 5 minutes on each side. **Yield:** 4 servings.

♥ Per serving: Calories 233 (46% from fat) Fat 11.6g (1.8g saturated) Cholesterol 83mg Sodium 185mg Carbohydrate 0.7g Fiber 0g Protein 29.9g

Baked Trout: Prepare trout as directed, and bake at 350° for 30 minutes or until fish flakes easily when tested with a fork. Do not turn trout during baking.

Poached Trout: Place tarragon sprigs and lemon slices inside each trout. Wrap each trout in three layers of cheesecloth; set aside. Combine 4 cups water and 2 cups dry white wine in a fish poacher or oblong Dutch oven; bring to a boil over high heat. Reduce heat, and add fish to wine mixture. Cover and simmer 20 minutes or until fish flakes easily when tested with a fork. Remove and discard cheesecloth. Prepare olive oil and lemon juice mixture as directed in Grilled Trout recipe and serve with the fish.

OVEN-FRIED CATFISH
(pictured on page 76)

Try this recipe using any type of whitefish fillets.

¾ cup crushed corn flakes cereal
¾ teaspoon celery salt
¼ teaspoon onion powder
¼ teaspoon paprika
Dash of pepper
Vegetable cooking spray
4 (6-ounce) skinless farm-raised catfish fillets, halved

• **Combine** first 5 ingredients; set aside. Spray all sides of fish with cooking spray, and coat with corn flake mixture. Arrange fillets in a single layer on a baking sheet coated with cooking spray. Spray tops of fillets with cooking spray.
• **Bake** at 350° for 30 minutes or until fish flakes easily when tested with a fork. **Yield:** 4 servings.

Note: After trying Chef Chris Dupont's Molasses Catfish at his Cafe Dupont in Springville, Alabama, we adapted his creamy molasses sauce recipe to serve with this Oven-Fried Catfish. For a special touch, add 2 tablespoons chopped toasted pecans to the corn flake mixture in the recipe above, and proceed as directed. While the fish bakes, combine ¾ cup dry white wine and ¼ cup molasses. Cook 15 minutes or until mixture reduces to ⅓ cup. Stir in 2 tablespoons whipping cream. Spoon sauce evenly over catfish fillets. This sauce will add 5 fat grams and 100 calories to the nutritional analysis (below) of each serving, but it's worth the indulgence.

Edith Askins
Greenville, Texas

♥ Per serving: Calories 247 (33% from fat) Fat 8.7g (1.6g saturated) Cholesterol 77mg Sodium 673mg Carbohydrate 14g Fiber 0.2g Protein 25.5g

MAKE YOUR CATCH COUNT

FISH SUBSTITUTIONS

When a particular fresh fish is unavailable, purchase another with similar characteristics. Substitute one of comparable oil content, texture, and firmness. Lean fish has a mild-flavored, light-colored flesh; however, its low percentage of fat causes the flesh to dry out easily during cooking. Moist heat methods of cooking, such as baking or poaching, are best. Lean fish are ideal for grilling if basted often.

You can interchange lean, light-colored fish, but there will be subtle differences in color, flavor, and texture. The fat content makes the flesh of a fish darker, richer, and stronger flavored than lean fish. Because the fat moistens the flesh during cooking, fat fish is great for broiling, grilling, and smoking. The textures of both fish categories can be either firm or soft and delicate. For grilling, it's easier to handle a firm-textured fish, like grouper, salmon, snapper, swordfish, or tuna.

Following are types of fish that have similar characteristics.

■ Light-colored flesh, delicate-flavored lean fish: flounder, grouper, halibut, orange roughy, redfish, sea bass, sole, and tilefish

■ Light-colored flesh, moderate-flavored lean fish: mahimahi, red snapper, sea trout (speckled trout), shark, and swordfish

■ Light-colored flesh, firm-textured fat fish: amberjack, croaker, mullet, and pompano

■ Dark-colored flesh, firm-textured fat fish: bluefish, king and Spanish mackerel, salmon, and tuna

FISHING GUIDE

Look for these characteristics when you shop for whole fish: bright, clear, full, and often protruding eyes; bright-red or pink gills; firm elastic flesh which springs back when gently pressed with a finger; shiny skin; firmly attached scales; fresh mild odor; and fresh-cut appearance for fillets.

■ Make the fish market your last stop when shopping. Fish should go straight home to the bottom shelf or the meat keeper of your refrigerator, where temperatures are coldest.

■ Trust your nose: Good-quality fresh fish has the aroma of the sea – not the boat bottom.

■ "Dressed" fish has the gills and viscera removed. A 2-pound dressed fish will yield about 1 pound of cooked fish.

■ Keep seafood refrigerated until just before you cook it, and use it within two days of purchase.

■ To avoid cross-contamination of food, don't cut raw and cooked seafood on the same surface. Always wash cutting board in hot, soapy water after each use to avoid contamination of the next food.

■ Always spray the grill basket with vegetable cooking spray before grilling.

■ To make oven-fried fish extra crispy, lightly coat the top of the breaded fillets with vegetable cooking spray just before you bake them.

■ To bone a cooked trout, run a knife along the entire length of the backbone of the fish. Lift off the top fillet, including the bones and tail, and place trout skin side down on a plate. Lift the bones away from the top fillet, being careful to remove all of them in one piece. Remove the tail from the top fillet. Remove the head from the bottom fillet, and you're ready to eat.

■ If a fish bone gets caught in your throat, eat a piece of bread. As you swallow, it will take the bone with it.

FISHING FOR CONDIMENTS

If you like your fish with a little something on the side, give one of these low-fat extras a try.

Tartar Sauce: Combine 1 cup reduced-fat mayonnaise, 2 tablespoons sweet pickle relish, 1 tablespoon chopped fresh parsley, 1 tablespoon finely chopped onion, and 1 tablespoon chopped pimiento-stuffed olives in a bowl; cover and chill. **Yield:** 1¼ cups.
Mary Pappas
Richmond, Virginia

Red Seafood Sauce: Combine 1 (12-ounce) bottle chili sauce, 2 tablespoons prepared horseradish, and 1 tablespoon lemon juice; cover and chill. **Yield:** 1¼ cups.

Cucumber-Dill Salsa: Peel, seed, and finely chop 2 cucumbers and 1 large tomato; place in a small bowl. Stir in ¼ cup sliced green onions, 3 tablespoons chopped fresh dill, 1 tablespoon lemon juice, ¼ teaspoon salt, and ¼ teaspoon pepper. **Yield:** 2½ cups.

GREEN BEAN SLAW
(pictured on page 76)

½ pound fresh green beans
¼ small onion, cut into thin strips (about ¼ cup)
½ cup thin sweet red pepper strips
1 medium cucumber, peeled, seeded, and cut into thin strips
2½ tablespoons tarragon or other herb vinegar
2 tablespoons fat-free cream cheese
1 tablespoon skim milk
1 teaspoon sugar
¼ teaspoon salt
¼ teaspoon pepper

• **Wash** beans; remove ends. Cook in boiling water 8 minutes or until crisp-tender; drain. Plunge into ice water to stop the cooking process; drain.
• **Combine** beans, onion, red pepper, and cucumber; toss gently, and set aside.
• **Combine** vinegar and remaining ingredients, stirring until smooth. Pour dressing over bean mixture; toss gently. Cover and chill thoroughly before serving. **Yield:** 4 cups.

♥ Per 1-cup serving: Calories 49 (3% from fat)
Fat 0.2g (0.5 saturated) Cholesterol 3mg
Sodium 241mg Carbohydrate 9.1g
Fiber 1.8g Protein 3.7g

BAKED HUSH PUPPIES
(pictured on page 76)

1 cup yellow cornmeal
1 cup all-purpose flour
1 tablespoon baking powder
1 teaspoon sugar
1 teaspoon salt
⅛ teaspoon ground red pepper
2 large eggs, lightly beaten
¾ cup milk
¼ cup vegetable oil
½ cup finely chopped onion
Vegetable cooking spray

• **Combine** first 6 ingredients in a large bowl; make a well in center of mixture. Set dry mixture aside.
• **Combine** eggs and next 3 ingredients, stirring well; add to dry mixture, stirring just until dry ingredients are moistened.
• **Coat** miniature muffin pans with cooking spray. Spoon about 1 tablespoon batter into each muffin cup. (Cups will be about three-fourths full.)
• **Bake** at 425° for 15 minutes or until done. Remove from pans, and serve immediately. **Yield:** 3 dozen.

Millie Givens
Savannah, Georgia

♥ Per hush puppy: Calories 55 (40% from fat)
Fat 2.4g (0.2g saturated) Cholesterol 13mg
Sodium 71mg Carbohydrate 6.9g
Fiber 0.4g Protein 1.3g

LIGHT NOTES

After having two children, Danell Sims of Paint Rock, Texas, decided it was time to launch a new, healthy lifestyle. She's been able to keep her family and herself fit for almost 10 years. Here's how.

■ **Cook ethnic.** Her Italian dishes based on pasta and Mexican dishes made from beans and rice don't use meat or high-fat cheeses and, therefore, don't have as much fat.

■ **Shop the perimeter of the grocery store.** Buy vegetables, fruits, and low-fat dairy products. Stay away from processed foods, but don't overlook all of the new reduced-fat products.

■ **Cook smart.** In some recipes, you can substitute 2 egg whites for 1 egg. Use balsamic vinegar as a fat-free flavor booster for marinades, sauces, and salad dressings.

SOMETHING GOOD TO TALK ABOUT

....

There's talk going around in Chesapeake, Virginia, that if you see Michele Harrington at your door, she may – just may – be bringing you some of her Sausage-and-Bean Dinner. It's her way of saying "Congratulations" or "I'm sorry." She's so generous that she doesn't mind us sharing her answer to that inevitable question "What's for supper?"

SAUSAGE-AND-BEAN DINNER

If you're serving a crowd, spoon this entrée over hot cooked rice or pasta.

1 pound reduced-fat smoked sausage, cut into ¼-inch slices
1 large green pepper, seeded and chopped
1 medium onion, chopped
1 tablespoon vegetable oil
2 (14½-ounce) cans stewed tomatoes, undrained
1 (16-ounce) can pink beans, drained
1 (16-ounce) can pinto beans, drained
1 (15-ounce) can Great Northern beans, drained
½ teaspoon garlic powder

• **Brown** sausage in a Dutch oven over medium-high heat; remove sausage, and set aside. Discard drippings.
• **Cook** pepper and onion in oil in Dutch oven over medium heat, stirring constantly, until tender.
• **Add** cooked sausage, tomatoes, and remaining ingredients. Bring mixture to a boil; reduce heat, and simmer 30 minutes. **Yield:** 10 cups.

Michele C. Harrington
Chesapeake, Virginia

These pretty packages have good cooking all wrapped up. Open (clockwise from bottom) Chocolate-Raspberry Bags, Texas Firecrackers, and Fried Wonton Envelopes with Guacamole Dip, and discover a hidden treasure inside. (Recipes begin on page 96.)

Left: *Pineapple and rum impart the flavor of the islands into Jamaican Chicken Sandwich with Red Cabbage Slaw (recipe, page 153).*

Far left: *Pair Marinated Bourbon Steak with Rosemary Biscuits (recipes, page 91) for a savory combination worthy of a celebration.*

Above: *Luna Notte's Risotto Primavera (recipe, page 163) is a creamy low-fat takeoff of the traditional Italian specialty.*

Break for a cup of coffee and a slice of paradise with Manny and Isa's Key Lime Pie (recipe, page 118).

MAY

WHEN SMOKE GETS IN YOUR EYES

Head to any barbecue fete below the Mason-Dixon line and you'll *see* it. And *smell* it. And *taste* it. Just imagining that smoky, woody, slow-cooked, mouth-watering, crisp-tender, juicy, seasoned-to-sultriness manna (need we say more?) has us reaching for the nearest napkins.

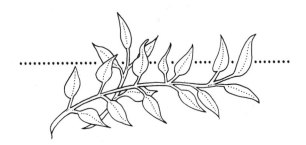

SMOKED SALMON

Hickory or fruitwood chips
2 teaspoons onion powder
¼ teaspoon salt
¼ teaspoon pepper
1 (1½-pound) salmon fillet with skin

• **Soak** wood chips in water at least 30 minutes.
• **Combine** onion powder, salt, and pepper; rub fillet with mixture. Cover and chill 30 minutes.
• **Prepare** charcoal fire in smoker; let burn 15 to 20 minutes.
• **Drain** chips, and place on coals. Place water pan in smoker; add water to pan to depth of fill line.
• **Place** fillet, skin side down, on upper food rack; cover with smoker lid.
• **Cook** 1½ hours or until fish flakes easily when tested with a fork. **Yield:** 4 servings.

Sylvia D. Ellis
San Antonio, Texas

CITRUS-MARINATED SMOKED SHRIMP

Hickory or fruitwood chips
2 pounds unpeeled jumbo fresh shrimp
1 (6-ounce) can frozen orange juice concentrate, thawed, undiluted, and divided
¼ cup honey
2 tablespoons water
1 tablespoon chopped fresh basil
1 tablespoon chopped fresh thyme

• **Soak** wood chips in water at least 30 minutes.
• **Peel** shrimp, and devein, if desired.
• **Combine** ¼ cup orange juice concentrate, honey, and next 3 ingredients.
• **Place** shrimp in a shallow dish or large heavy-duty, zip-top plastic bag; pour orange juice mixture over shrimp, stirring to coat. Cover or seal, and chill 1 hour.
• **Prepare** charcoal fire in smoker; let burn 15 to 20 minutes.
• **Drain** chips, and place on coals. Place water pan in smoker; add remaining orange juice concentrate to pan.
• **Remove** shrimp from marinade; pour marinade into water pan. Add water to pan to depth of fill line.
• **Thread** shrimp onto skewers, and place on upper and lower food racks. Cover with smoker lid.
• **Cook** 45 minutes to 1 hour. **Yield:** 8 appetizer servings.

Charlie Gagne
Birmingham, Alabama

HEAVENLY SMOKED BRISKET

½ cup firmly packed dark brown sugar
2 tablespoons Cajun seasoning
2 tablespoons salt
1 tablespoon lemon-pepper seasoning
2 tablespoons Worcestershire sauce
1 (5- to 6-pound) beef brisket, untrimmed
Hickory wood chunks

• **Combine** first 5 ingredients. Place brisket in a large shallow dish. Spread sugar mixture evenly on both sides of brisket. Cover and chill at least 8 hours.
• **Soak** wood chunks in water 1 hour.
• **Prepare** charcoal fire in smoker; let burn 15 to 20 minutes.
• **Drain** wood chunks, and place on coals. Place water pan in smoker; add water to pan to depth of fill line.
• **Remove** brisket from marinade; place on lower food rack. Pour remaining marinade over meat. Cover with smoker lid.
• **Cook** 5 hours or until thermometer inserted in thickest portion registers 170°. **Yield:** 12 servings.

Sam D. Morrison, Jr.
Alexandria, Louisiana

. . . you couldn't be happier. You know what wondrous food awaits.

Though there are many ways and many foods to smoke, we've decided to offer truly outstanding poultry, seafood, and meat recipes tested only on water smokers (what most use at home). For more on the basics of smoking, see "From Our Kitchen to Yours" on the next page. And for the inside track on flavor enhancers such as hearty wood chunks and chips and liquids such as beer, fruit juice, and wine, see our suggestions below.

Although smoking has been used in food preservation for centuries, it's now valued almost exclusively for the unique woody flavor and ring of deep color it gives to whatever is smoked.

That's why it's important to select a good wood for flavor. Hickory is available almost everywhere, but you can find other woods at gourmet grocery stores and through mail-order sources. Here are a few to consider.

BEST WOOD BETS
■ **Alder** is delightful with fish, especially salmon.

■ **Fruitwoods (apple, cherry, peach)** offer a subtle sweetness that pampers poultry, seafood, and many vegetables.

■ **Hickory** gives a rich, full-bodied flavor to meats and poultry; may overpower seafood and vegetables.

■ **Maple** is milder in flavor than hickory and works well with poultry.

■ **Oak** has a less assertive flavor than hickory and works well with ham.

■ **Pecan** has a milder flavor than hickory and works well with a variety of meats and poultry.

WOODS TO AVOID
■ **Evergreens (pine, cedar, firs, spruce)** contain noxious resins that discolor foods and ruin their flavors.

■ **Mesquite** is not ideal for prolonged smoking because it can leave a bitter flavor in the smoked food.

CHIPS AND CHUNKS
■ Wood chips and chunks should always be presoaked in water or another liquid (wine, fruit juice, or beer) before being used to smoke. Chips need to soak only about 30 minutes, while heftier chunks of wood should soak at least an hour.

■ For a mild smoke taste, two handfuls of chips or chunks on the fire should be enough; for a smokier taste, replenish the chips or chunks as the smoke lessens (usually every 30 minutes).

■ Wood chips work best when smoking for less than two hours;

for extended cooking periods, opt for the longer-burning chunks.

■ Unshelled walnuts or pecans work nicely, too. Crack them and soak for at least an hour before adding them to the fire.

LIQUID ASSETS
■ **Water pan enhancers:** Add 1 to 2 cups wine, beer, or fruit juice to the smoker's water pan to help "steam" additional flavor into the food. But be careful when using alcoholic beverages; if the water evaporates, the pan may catch on fire. Watch it closely. Herbs, such as dill, basil, and sage, added to the water pan can impart wonderful flavors.

■ **Injectors:** Inject 4 to 6 ounces of commercial or homemade marinade into meat or poultry to keep the meat juicy. Look for commercial injectors at cookware specialty shops and department stores. For meat and poultry try Worcestershire sauce, melted garlic butter, pineapple syrup, soy or teriyaki sauce, or orange juice. For fish and vegetables try lemon juice, melted butter, or white wine.

SOUTHERN SPARERIBS

1 (12-ounce) can beer
¼ cup soy sauce
2 tablespoons brown sugar
2 tablespoons chili sauce
2 tablespoons ketchup
2 tablespoons lemon juice
1 teaspoon onion powder
½ teaspoon salt
¼ teaspoon pepper
1 (4-pound) rack pork
     spareribs
Hickory wood chunks

• **Combine** first 9 ingredients. Place ribs in a shallow dish; pour beer mixture over ribs, turning to coat. Cover and chill 8 hours.
• **Soak** chunks in water 1 hour.
• **Prepare** charcoal fire in smoker; let burn 15 to 20 minutes.
• **Drain** wood chunks, and place on coals. Place water pan in smoker.
• **Remove** ribs from marinade; pour marinade into water pan. Add water to pan to depth of fill line.
• **Place** ribs on lower food rack; cover with smoker lid.
• **Cook** 5 hours or until done. **Yield:** 6 servings.

Jane Cooper
Washington Court House, Ohio

SMOKY HERB CHICKEN

Hickory or fruitwood chips
1½ teaspoons dried oregano
1 tablespoon dried rosemary
1 tablespoon dried tarragon
1 tablespoon salt
1½ teaspoons pepper
1½ teaspoons onion powder
1½ teaspoons garlic powder
1½ teaspoons paprika
6 chicken quarters
½ cup olive oil
6 sprigs fresh sage

• **Soak** wood chips in water at least 30 minutes.
• **Combine** oregano and next 7 ingredients; set dried herb mixture aside.
• **Brush** chicken with olive oil; rub with dried herb mixture, coating all sides.

Place chicken in a 15- x 10- x 1-inch jellyroll pan.
• **Broil** 5½ inches from heat (with electric oven door partially open) 10 minutes on each side.
• **Prepare** charcoal fire in smoker; let burn 15 to 20 minutes.
• **Drain** chips, and place on coals. Place water pan in smoker; add sage and water to pan to depth of fill line.
• **Place** chicken on food racks; cover with smoker lid.
• **Cook** 2½ hours or until thermometer inserted in thickest portion registers 180°. **Yield:** 6 servings.

FROM OUR KITCHEN TO YOURS

....

There are many variables that affect cooking in a water smoker: outside temperature, wind, quality of charcoal, size of wood chunks or chips, and the internal temperature of the smoker. Cooking times provide general guidelines on how long to smoke. Check the smoker every one to two hours to know when to add additional charcoal, wood chunks, and water.

The color of the meat isn't always a good measure of doneness, especially for pork and poultry. The outside of white meat is a pinkish red while the inside is often pink, even though it's done. Follow our tested recipes or the manufacturer's directions, and use a meat thermometer for larger cuts. Internal temperatures for cooked meat and poultry are the same as if you roasted them in a conventional oven. Beef should be cooked to 145° (medium-rare); lamb, 150° (medium-rare); pork, 160° (medium); whole poultry or poultry quarters, halves, or thighs, 180°; poultry breast, 170°.

The next time you fire up the smoker, follow these tips.

■ **Soaking the wood:** Use large wood chunks for meat and poultry that will cook several hours. Presoak wood chunks for about an hour; soaking longer saturates the wood, creating a more intense flavor. Because wood chips burn faster than chunks, they are more suitable for the short-term smoking of fish and seafood. They'll need soaking only about 30 minutes. For a subtle smokiness, start with two or three pieces of wood. Use six or seven pieces for a more intense flavor.

■ **Starting the fire:** Arrange charcoal briquets in a shallow, pyramid-shaped pile. (As a rule, 8 pounds of charcoal is enough to cook up to 4 pounds of boneless meat.) Squirt briquets with liquid starter, and let soak 1 to 2 minutes. Carefully light and let burn 15 to 20 minutes or until center coals are coated with gray ash; then add the soaked chunks. The black coals around the outside will ignite gradually as the fire spreads and the center coals cool, keeping the temperature stabilized.

■ **Filling the water pan:** Pour liquid (water, juice, or marinade) into the water pan up to the fill line and add flavor enhancers like fresh herbs and orange slices (see page 115 for more flavor-enhancing ideas). This amount of liquid should last two to three hours. The water should simmer, not boil. If you hear a sizzling sound, it's past time to refill the water pan. Don't allow the water pan to run dry. (When adding water, be sure to use hot tap water; adding cold water can increase cooking time by as much as 25%.)

■ **Adding the food:** Remove grill rack from grill; coat with cooking spray to prevent sticking. Place rack on grill; add meat, poultry, or seafood.

■ **Maintaining the temperature:** The internal temperature of the smoker should be between 170° and 250°. (If the smoker doesn't have a built-in thermometer or if the thermometer isn't accurate, place an oven thermometer inside on the food rack.) It takes about 45 minutes for the temperature to reach 170°. If the temperature is too low (145° or below), open the vents or side door; added ventilation makes briquets burn faster and hotter. If the temperature rises above 250°, close the vents. Resist the temptation to peek once the temperature is correct. Each quick look adds about 15 minutes to the cooking time. When checking the water level after two to three hours, notice the internal temperature. If it has dropped below 170°, use long-handled tongs to add more charcoal briquets through the side door. For the long-term smoking recipes, add two handfuls of charcoal three times. When the smoke begins to subside, it's time to add more soaked wood chunks.

■ **Cleaning the smoker:** The coals and water pan remain very hot after food is removed. Wait until the next day to clean the smoker. Line the charcoal pan and the water pan with heavy-duty aluminum foil for easy cleanup. Dump the coals, wash the water pan and food rack with warm soapy water, and wipe the smoker clean.

HOMETOWN FAVORITES

Do you like discovering quirky eats particular to certain towns – those edible oddities that make a place famous? Sometimes you not only get lucky enough to try (and love) the trademark dish, but to walk away with the recipe. Following is a sampling from some well-known eateries sure to become your favorites.

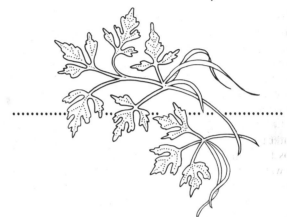

■ The fried cheese and marinara sauce craze may have swept fern bars in the eighties, but Charlie Gitto Jr. of **Charlie Gitto's** "on the Hill" in St. Louis, Missouri, gets credit for an even tastier version – Toasted Ravioli, – a mistake-turned-clever invention. Supposedly, a cook dropped some ravioli into breadcrumbs by accident, and rather than toss it out, he deep fried it to a golden brown. The term "toasted" remains a mystery, however. You can easily make these at home with frozen or refrigerated ravioli from your supermarket.

ST. LOUIS TOASTED RAVIOLI
(pictured on page 223)

2 tablespoons milk
1 large egg, lightly beaten
¾ cup dry Italian-seasoned
    breadcrumbs
½ teaspoon salt (optional)
½ (27.5-ounce) package frozen
    cheese-filled ravioli, thawed *
Vegetable oil
Grated Parmesan cheese
Spaghetti or pizza sauce

● **Combine** milk and egg in a small bowl. Place breadcrumbs and salt, if desired, in a shallow bowl. Dip ravioli in milk mixture, and coat with breadcrumbs.
● **Pour** oil to depth of 2 inches into a Dutch oven; heat to 350°.
● **Fry** ravioli, a few at a time, 1 minute on each side or until golden. Drain on paper towels.
● **Sprinkle** with Parmesan cheese, and serve immediately with warm spaghetti or pizza sauce. **Yield:** about 2 dozen appetizers.

* You can substitute refrigerated fresh ravioli for frozen ravioli. Vary the flavor by using sausage, chicken, Italian, or other filling varieties.

■ Charles Stevens of Columbus, Georgia's **Dinglewood Pharmacy**, has served his patrons this hot dog smothered with chili for nearly 50 years. The name may be misleading; there are no scrambled eggs. The assembly makes it a Scrambled Dog.

DINGLEWOOD PHARMACY'S SCRAMBLED DOG

Charles Stevens won't share his secret chili recipe, so use canned chili or your own recipe.

12 hot dogs
12 hot dog buns
3 (15-ounce) cans chili without beans
1 (6-ounce) jar prepared mustard
1 (10-ounce) jar sweet salad cubes
1½ cups chopped onion
2 cups (8 ounces) shredded Cheddar cheese
2 cups oyster crackers

• **Cook** hot dogs according to package directions; drain.
• **Place** hot dogs in buns; arrange on individual serving plates.
• **Cut** each into six pieces. Top evenly with warm chili and next 4 ingredients; sprinkle evenly with crackers. **Yield:** 12 servings.

■ In addition to growing and squeezing their own Key limes, Manny and Isa Ortiz of Islamorada, Florida, also make their own pastry from scratch. But here the owners of **Manny and Isa's** give some shortcuts.

MANNY AND ISA'S KEY LIME PIE
(pictured on page 112)

½ (15-ounce) package refrigerated piecrusts
1 teaspoon all-purpose flour
5 large eggs, separated
1 (14-ounce) can sweetened condensed milk
½ cup fresh or bottled Key lime juice
¼ teaspoon cream of tartar
⅓ to ½ cup sugar

• **Unfold** piecrust, and press out fold lines; sprinkle with flour, spreading over surface. Place crust, floured side down, in a 9-inch pieplate; fold edges under, and flute. Prick bottom and sides of piecrust generously with fork.
• **Bake** at 450° for 9 to 11 minutes; cool on a wire rack.
• **Combine** yolks, condensed milk, and lime juice in a heavy nonaluminum saucepan. Cook over low heat, stirring constantly, 10 minutes or until mixture thickens and boils. Pour into piecrust.
• **Beat** egg whites and cream of tartar at high speed with an electric mixer until foamy. Add sugar gradually to whites, 1 tablespoon at a time, beating until stiff peaks form and sugar dissolves (about 2 to 4 minutes).
• **Spread** meringue over warm filling, sealing to edge of pastry.
• **Bake** at 325° for 25 to 28 minutes. **Yield:** one 9-inch pie.

■ **Weidmann's Restaurant** in Meridian, Mississippi, offers something for everyone – it's part hunting lodge, local museum, Bavarian tavern, and Southern diner. But the main attraction of this eclectic eatery is the Black Bottom Pie. It's a puff of bourbon-spiked cream separated from crispy gingersnap crust by a silky ribbon of rich chocolate.

WEIDMANN'S BLACK BOTTOM PIE

1½ cups gingersnap crumbs (about 26 cookies)
⅓ cup butter or margarine, melted
½ cup sugar
¼ cup cornstarch
2 cups milk
4 large egg yolks, beaten
1 teaspoon vanilla extract
1 (1-ounce) square unsweetened chocolate
1 envelope unflavored gelatin
2 tablespoons cold water
1 tablespoon meringue powder
¼ cup cold water
½ cup sugar, divided
2 tablespoons bourbon
¾ cup whipping cream, whipped
Grated unsweetened chocolate

• **Combine** gingersnap crumbs and butter, and press mixture into a 9-inch pieplate.
• **Bake** at 375° for 6 to 8 minutes; cool completely.
• **Combine** ½ cup sugar, cornstarch, and milk in a heavy saucepan. Cook over medium heat, stirring constantly, 8 to 10 minutes or until mixture thickens and boils. Boil 1 minute, stirring constantly. Remove from heat.
• **Stir** about one-fourth of hot mixture gradually into yolks; add to remaining hot mixture, stirring constantly. Stir in vanilla.
• **Melt** chocolate in a small heavy saucepan over low heat, stirring often; set aside.
• **Sprinkle** gelatin over 2 tablespoons cold water; stir and let stand 1 minute. Add gelatin to milk mixture in saucepan. Cook over low heat, stirring constantly, 2 minutes or until gelatin dissolves.
• **Add** 1 cup milk mixture to melted chocolate, stirring with a wire whisk until smooth. Spread over crust. Cool remaining milk mixture.
• **Beat** meringue powder, ¼ cup cold water, and 2 tablespoons sugar at high speed with an electric mixer 5 minutes. Gradually add remaining 6 tablespoons sugar, beating until stiff peaks form (about 3 minutes).
• **Fold** remaining milk mixture and bourbon into meringue mixture; spread over chocolate mixture in crust. Cover and chill pie at least 4 hours.
• **Spread** whipped cream over pie; sprinkle with grated chocolate. **Yield:** one 9-inch pie.

BOUDIN AT ITS BEST

Although the recipe isn't in this story, there's one more hometown favorite to discover: Cajun boudin. Sample this spicy rice sausage at roadside stands across South Louisiana; our top pick is the Boudin King restaurant in Jennings.

SPRING FOR RHUBARB

....

Vegetable gardening enthusiasts praise rhubarb in the seasonal parade of homegrown bounty. And fans of the celery-like plant watch its ruby-colored spikes push through the warm earth, then eagerly wait to harvest the tender bunches. They know the pink stalks will perform well in a myriad of recipes. Versatile rhubarb also waits year-round in your grocer's freezer.

RHUBARB-RASPBERRY PEAR PIE

1 (12-ounce) package frozen rhubarb
1 (12-ounce) package frozen, unsweetened raspberries *
2½ cups peeled and chopped fresh pears (about 3 medium)
1¼ cups sugar
⅓ cup all-purpose flour
1½ teaspoons grated orange rind
½ tablespoon ground cinnamon
1 (15-ounce) package refrigerated piecrusts
1 teaspoon all-purpose flour
1 large egg, lightly beaten
1 tablespoon milk
1 teaspoon sugar
Garnish: fresh raspberries

• **Thaw** and drain frozen rhubarb and raspberries.
• **Combine** rhubarb, raspberries, and next 5 ingredients in a large bowl; set aside.
• **Unfold** 1 piecrust, and press out fold lines; sprinkle with 1 teaspoon flour, spreading over surface. Place, floured side down, in a 9-inch deep-dish pieplate. Trim off excess pastry around edges. Spoon in fruit mixture.
• **Roll** remaining piecrust on a lightly floured surface to press out fold lines. Cut 6 flowers with a 1½-inch flower-shaped cutter and 3 leaves with a

1½-inch leaf-shaped cutter; set aside. Cut remaining pastry into ¼-inch-wide strips, and arrange in a lattice design over fruit.
• **Combine** pastry scraps, and roll into 3 thin ropes; braid ropes, and place along rim of piecrust. Stack 2 flowers together, alternating petals; repeat procedure with remaining flowers. Arrange flowers and pastry leaves on top of pie.
• **Combine** egg and milk; brush over pastry lattice, flowers, and braided rim. Sprinkle with 1 teaspoon sugar.
• **Bake** at 425° for 30 minutes. Cover edges with aluminum foil; bake 30 additional minutes. (If pie runs over, place on baking sheet, and continue baking.) Cool on a wire rack. Garnish, if desired. Serve with ice cream or frozen yogurt. **Yield:** one 9-inch deep-dish pie.

* You can substitute 12 ounces frozen, unsweetened whole strawberries for raspberries.

Elizabeth R. Drawdy
Spindale, North Carolina

STRAWBERRY-RHUBARB CRISP

3 cups fresh stalks or frozen sliced rhubarb, thawed
1 quart fresh strawberries, mashed
2 tablespoons lemon juice
1 cup sugar
⅓ cup cornstarch
2 cups all-purpose flour
1 cup sugar
1 teaspoon baking powder
1 teaspoon baking soda
½ teaspoon salt
1 cup butter or margarine
1½ cups buttermilk
2 large eggs, lightly beaten
1 teaspoon vanilla extract
¼ cup butter or margarine, melted
¾ cup all-purpose flour
¾ cup sugar

• **Combine** first 3 ingredients in a saucepan; cover and cook over medium heat 5 minutes.

• **Combine** 1 cup sugar and cornstarch; gradually stir into rhubarb mixture. Bring mixture to a boil, stirring constantly; boil 1 minute. Remove from heat; set aside.
• **Combine** 2 cups flour and next 4 ingredients; cut in 1 cup butter with a pastry blender until mixture is crumbly. Add buttermilk, eggs, and vanilla; stir with a fork until dry ingredients are moistened.
• **Spread** half of batter evenly into a greased 13- x 9- x 2-inch baking dish. Spoon rhubarb mixture evenly over batter, and drop remaining batter by tablespoonfuls over filling.
• **Combine** ¼ cup melted butter and remaining ingredients; sprinkle mixture over batter.
• **Bake** at 350° for 40 to 45 minutes. Cool on a wire rack. Cut into squares. **Yield:** 15 servings.

Ellie Wells
Lakeland, Florida

RULES FOR RHUBARB

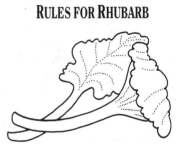

Enjoy the plentiful supply of fresh rhubarb you'll find in most Southern supermarkets this season.

■ Choose firm, crisp stalks that are cherry-red or pink in color.

■ Avoid wilted stalks. They'll be stringy and less flavorful.

■ Oversize stalks might be tough.

■ Remember, only the stalks are edible; rhubarb leaves can be toxic.

THE NASHVILLE COOKBOOK

The Nashville Cookbook samples the tastes of historic Nashville and the Cumberland plateau region. Published by the Nashville Area Home Economics Association in 1976, the book forged ahead of its time by including a section devoted to healthy cooking. With more than 100,000 copies published, this cookbook has generated over $20,000 for restoration and preservation projects within the Nashville area, including the School for the Blind and the Ronald McDonald House.

The book opens with a chapter called "Specialties of the Region," which features recipes from the historic Maxwell House Hotel. Collector prints and historic references keep you close to Tennessee's roots.

GOLD NUGGET CHICKEN

A delicious surprise awaits you when you cut into this attractive bundle.

8 skinned and boned chicken breast halves
8 to 10 ounces sharp Cheddar cheese, cut into 8 equal pieces
2 large eggs, lightly beaten
¾ cup dry breadcrumbs
1 chicken-flavored bouillon cube
1 cup boiling water
½ cup margarine, divided
½ cup chopped onion
½ cup chopped green pepper
2 tablespoons all-purpose flour
1 teaspoon salt
½ teaspoon pepper
3 cups cooked rice
1 (4-ounce) can sliced mushrooms, drained
1 (2-ounce) jar diced pimiento, drained
Garnish: fresh oregano sprigs

• **Place** chicken between two sheets of heavy-duty plastic wrap, and flatten to ¼-inch thickness, using a meat mallet or rolling pin. Place a piece of cheese in center of each breast; fold over all sides of breast, enclosing cheese, and secure with wooden picks.
• **Dip** chicken bundles in egg, draining excess; dredge in breadcrumbs, coating all sides.
• **Combine** bouillon cube and boiling water; set aside.
• **Melt** ¼ cup margarine in a large skillet over medium-high heat. Cook chicken bundles on both sides until browned; remove from skillet.
• **Melt** remaining ¼ cup margarine in skillet; add onion and green pepper, and cook, stirring constantly, until tender.
• **Add** flour; cook 1 minute, stirring constantly.
• **Add** salt, pepper, and bouillon to skillet; cook, stirring constantly, until thickened.
• **Add** cooked rice, mushrooms, and pimiento; pour into a lightly greased 13- x 9- x 2-inch baking dish. Place chicken bundles on top.
• **Bake** at 400° for 20 minutes. Garnish, if desired. **Yield:** 8 servings.

CHICKEN ON EGG BREAD

Nashville cooks often rely on this dish for easy entertaining. You can substitute your favorite cornbread for the Egg Bread.

3 tablespoons butter or margarine
2 tablespoons finely chopped celery
2 tablespoons finely chopped onion
3 tablespoons all-purpose flour
2 cups chicken broth
¾ cup whipping cream
¼ teaspoon salt
Egg Bread
3 cups coarsely chopped cooked chicken
Freshly ground pepper

• **Melt** butter in a large skillet over medium-high heat; add celery and onion, and cook, stirring constantly, until tender.
• **Add** flour; cook, stirring constantly, 1 minute. Gradually add chicken broth, whipping cream, and salt; bring to a boil, stirring constantly. Reduce heat, and simmer until slightly thickened (about 3 minutes). Remove from heat, and keep warm.

• **Cut** Egg Bread into wedges or squares; slice in half horizontally. Top with chicken and sauce. Sprinkle with pepper. **Yield:** 6 servings.

Egg Bread

1 cup milk
1 cup water
2¼ cups yellow cornmeal, divided
3 large eggs
1 teaspoon salt
2 cups buttermilk
1 teaspoon baking soda
2 tablespoons shortening

• **Combine** milk and water in a large saucepan; bring to a boil over high heat. Reduce heat, and stir in 2 cups cornmeal. Remove from heat.
• **Beat** eggs at high speed with an electric mixer until foamy; add salt, and beat until light and fluffy.
• **Combine** buttermilk and soda; add to cornmeal mixture with egg mixture, and beat until smooth.
• **Place** shortening in a 10-inch cast-iron skillet; place skillet in a 400° oven for 5 minutes. Pour melted shortening into cornmeal mixture, stirring well. Add remaining ¼ cup cornmeal, stirring until smooth. Pour mixture into hot skillet.
• **Bake** at 400° for 25 to 30 minutes or until firm. Remove from skillet immediately. **Yield:** 6 to 8 servings.

DINNER ON THE GROUND

....

Planting flowers, raking winter's leaves, and trimming overgrown shrubs – these are just some of the activities planned for one special Saturday in May at many Southern cemeteries. The next day, families return to pay homage to past loved ones with baskets full of food and flowers on Decoration Day. It's like a mini reunion – a time to reminisce, tell those "remember when" stories, and share wonderful food.

CHICKEN-SQUASH CASSEROLE

1 (2½- to 3-pound) broiler-fryer chicken
2 pounds yellow squash, cut into ¼-inch-thick slices
½ cup water
2 large carrots, scraped and shredded
1 medium onion, finely chopped
1 (8-ounce) carton sour cream
1 (10¾-ounce) can cream of mushroom soup, undiluted
½ teaspoon salt
¼ teaspoon pepper
1½ cups chicken-flavored one-step stuffing mix
¼ cup butter or margarine, melted

• **Cook** chicken in a Dutch oven in boiling water to cover 45 minutes or until tender; drain. Cool chicken; skin and bone. Cut meat into bite-size pieces.
• **Combine** squash and water in a medium saucepan; bring to a boil. Cover, reduce heat, and simmer 8 minutes or until tender; drain between paper towels.
• **Combine** squash, carrot, and onion; toss gently, and set aside.
• **Combine** sour cream and next 3 ingredients in a large bowl. Add chicken and squash mixture to sour cream mixture, stirring to blend.
• **Spoon** mixture into a lightly greased 13- x 9- x 2-inch baking dish.
• **Combine** stuffing mix and butter; sprinkle over casserole.
• **Bake** at 350° for 25 minutes or until bubbly. **Yield:** 8 servings.

Note: For chicken-flavored one-step stuffing mix, we used Stove Top One-Step Stuffing Mix.

Dorothy Burgess
Huntsville, Texas

HAMBURGER-BEAN BAKE

1 pound ground beef
1 large onion, chopped
1 green pepper, chopped
1 (31-ounce) can pork and beans
1 (16-ounce) can kidney beans, drained
1 (15¼ -ounce) can lima beans, drained
¼ to ½ cup firmly packed brown sugar
1 cup ketchup
1 tablespoon prepared mustard

• **Brown** ground beef, onion, and green pepper in a Dutch oven, stirring until beef crumbles; drain.
• **Combine** beef mixture, pork and beans, and remaining ingredients; spoon into a lightly greased 3-quart baking dish.
• **Cover** and bake at 350° for 1 hour and 15 minutes. **Yield:** 8 servings.

Girland Branstetter
Middletown, Missouri

living *light*
LIGHT AND LAZY

Springtime heralds a craving for food that's as carefree as
the season. When you want to get out of the kitchen and into the
great outdoors, these easy recipes make it happen in a hurry.

CHICKEN TOSTADAS
(pictured on page 148)

1 pound skinned and boned
    chicken breast halves, cut into
    ¾-inch cubes
½ cup fresh lime juice
4 (8-inch) flour tortillas
½ teaspoon salt
¼ teaspoon pepper
Vegetable cooking spray
1 cup picante sauce
2 tablespoons finely chopped fresh
    cilantro
2 tablespoons reduced-fat sour
    cream
4 cups shredded lettuce
2 medium tomatoes, chopped
6 fresh mushrooms, sliced

• **Place** chicken in a shallow dish or
heavy-duty, zip-top plastic bag; pour
lime juice over chicken. Cover or seal,
and chill 30 minutes.
• **Place** tortillas on a baking sheet; bake
at 350° for 3 to 5 minutes or until
tortillas are lightly browned and crisp.
Set aside.
• **Remove** chicken from lime juice, discarding juice. Sprinkle chicken with salt
and pepper.
• **Coat** a nonstick skillet with cooking
spray; place over medium heat until
hot. Add chicken, and cook 4 minutes
or until done, stirring often.
• **Stir** in picante sauce, cilantro, and
sour cream. Return to a simmer, and
cook 5 minutes, stirring occasionally.

• **Place** tortillas on serving plates;
spoon chicken mixture evenly onto
tortillas; top with lettuce, tomato, and
mushrooms. Cut into wedges, and
serve immediately. **Yield:** 4 servings.
Claudia Vance
Tuscaloosa, Alabama

♥ Per serving: Calories 314 (18% from fat)
Fat 6.1g (1.5g saturated) Cholesterol 69mg
Sodium 1210mg Carbohydrate 32.4g
Fiber 2.7g Protein 32.1g

SEARED SCALLOPS WITH TOMATO-MANGO SALSA
(pictured on page 75)

*Scallops should smell sweet, not fishy.
They cook very quickly and will become
tough and chewy if overcooked.*

1 medium tomato, finely
    chopped
¾ cup finely chopped mango
3 tablespoons finely chopped
    purple onion
2 tablespoons finely chopped fresh
    basil
2 tablespoons red wine vinegar
1 tablespoon capers
1 tablespoon olive oil
12 sea scallops
¼ teaspoon salt
¼ teaspoon pepper
¼ avocado, sliced
Garnish: fresh basil sprigs

• **Combine** first 6 ingredients. Cover
and chill salsa at least 30 minutes.
• **Heat** olive oil in a skillet over
medium-high heat until hot. Add scallops; cook 3 minutes or until scallops
are opaque, turning once. Remove
scallops from skillet; sprinkle with salt
and pepper.
• **Arrange** scallops, salsa, and avocado
slices evenly on plates. Garnish, if desired. **Yield:** 2 servings.

Note: Scallops may be threaded on
skewers and grilled. Cook, covered
with grill lid, over hot coals (400° to
500°) 3 to 5 minutes on each side or
until scallops are opaque.
Joe R. Farralt
Muskogee, Oklahoma

♥ Per serving: Calories 246 (40% from fat)
Fat 11.2g (1.7g saturated) Cholesterol 30mg
Sodium 782mg Carbohydrate 21.7g
Fiber 2.9g Protein 17g

GARLIC-AND-HERB CHEESE GRITS

*Serve this flavorful 10-minute
side dish with grilled or broiled
beef or chicken.*

4 cups ready-to-serve, reduced-
    sodium, fat-free chicken
    broth
1 cup quick-cooking grits
1 (5-ounce) package light garlic-
    and-herb soft, spreadable
    cheese
¼ teaspoon freshly ground
    pepper

• **Bring** chicken broth to a boil in a
medium saucepan over high heat;
gradually stir in grits. Cook, stirring
constantly, 5 to 7 minutes or until
thickened.
• **Remove** from heat; stir in cheese and
pepper. Serve immediately. **Yield:**
5 cups.

♥ Per ¾-cup serving: Calories 161 (24% from fat)
Fat 4.1g (3g saturated) Cholesterol 12mg
Sodium 112mg Carbohydrate 23.7g
Fiber 1.3g Protein 5.1g

LENTIL BURGERS

Even the beef lovers will like this vegetable burger recipe.

1 cup dried lentils
2½ cups water
¼ cup ketchup
¼ teaspoon garlic powder
1 small onion, chopped
1 cup quick-cooking oats, uncooked
1 large egg
½ teaspoon salt
1 tablespoon whole wheat flour
2 tablespoons vegetable oil
8 hamburger buns
Tomato slices
Lettuce leaves
Pickle slices

● **Combine** lentils and water in a saucepan; bring to a boil over medium-high heat. Cover, reduce heat, and simmer 25 minutes. Cook, uncovered, 10 minutes or until water is absorbed and lentils are tender.
● **Stir** ketchup and next 5 ingredients into lentils.
● **Shape** into 8 patties; sprinkle with flour. Cover and chill 1 hour.
● **Pour** 1 tablespoon oil in a skillet. Fry 4 patties over medium-high heat 1 to 2 minutes on each side or until golden. Drain on paper towels. Repeat procedure with remaining 1 tablespoon oil and 4 patties.
● **Place** a patty on bottom half of each bun; top with tomato, lettuce, and pickles; add top half of bun. **Yield:** 8 servings.

Note: You can freeze cooked lentil patties in an airtight container. Bake thawed patties at 350° for 12 minutes or until thoroughly heated.

Leonard Loria
Birmingham, Alabama

♥ Per serving: Calories 316 (24% from fat)
Fat 8.4g (0.8g saturated) Cholesterol 41mg
Sodium 359mg Carbohydrate 47.5g
Fiber 4.3g Protein 12.9g

YOU'LL NEVER MISS THE MEAT

EARTHY DELIGHTS

Portabello mushrooms taste better than they look. Their hearty flavor makes them a top choice for meatless meals. Give them a try with these easy recipes.

■ **Microwave Portabello Mushrooms:** Place a whole portabello mushroom in a microwave-safe dish, and cover with heavy-duty plastic wrap. Microwave at HIGH 3 to 4 minutes or until tender. Transfer mushroom to a baking sheet; sprinkle with feta cheese. Broil 5½ inches from heat 1 to 2 minutes. Enjoy the mushroom alone or over pasta. **Yield:** 1 serving.

■ **Grilled Portabello Mushrooms:** Cut a portabello mushroom into ½-inch-thick slices. Toss with olive oil to coat, and sprinkle lightly with garlic salt. Cook, covered with grill lid, over hot coals (400° to 500°) 3 minutes on each side. Drizzle with balsamic vinegar. **Yield:** 1 serving.

■ **Sautéed Portabello Mushrooms:** Cook 2 garlic cloves, minced; 1 green pepper, thinly sliced; and 1 portabello mushroom, cut into thin strips, in 1 tablespoon olive oil 2 minutes, stirring constantly. Add ½ cup white wine, and cook 2 additional minutes. Remove from heat; stir in ¼ teaspoon salt and ¼ teaspoon freshly ground pepper. Spoon mushroom mixture over fettuccine. Serve with grated Parmesan cheese. **Yield:** 1 serving.

BOCA BURGERS

We've tried a lot of vegetable burgers, but few come close to the Boca Burger. This meatless, low-calorie, fat-free burger is the brainchild of Max Shondor of Boca Raton, Florida.

Most vegetable burgers are so spongy they bounce back when you bite into them, but not this one. It's textured like a real hamburger and has a beefy, charcoal-grilled flavor.

The burgers are available in fat-free Original Flavor, 99% fat-free Hint of Fresh Garlic, and 98% fat-free Chef Max's Favorite. They're prebaked and can be grilled, microwaved, or heated in a skillet.

The hard part is finding Boca Burgers. But Max has recently quadrupled his production, cranking out about 1.5 million burgers a month.

The Clintons have a direct line to Shondor's plant. The White House wolfed down 7,500 Boca Burgers in one six-month period.

Look for Boca Burgers in the freezer section of your grocery store and in health food stores across the South. And if you just can't find them, try Lentil Burgers instead.

OPEN-FACE EGGPLANT SANDWICHES

Tahini (tuh-HEE-nee) is a thick paste made from ground sesame seeds. Look for it next to the peanut butter at most grocery stores.

¼ cup plain low-fat yogurt
1½ tablespoons tahini
1½ tablespoons water
1 tablespoon lemon juice
1 clove garlic, minced
Vegetable cooking spray
½ teaspoon fennel seeds
½ teaspoon ground cumin
¼ teaspoon ground red
      pepper
1 small eggplant, cut into
      ½-inch-thick slices (about
      ¾ pound)
¼ cup hickory-flavored barbecue
      sauce
1 small onion, sliced and separated
      into rings
1 small green pepper, cut into
      rings
1 clove garlic, pressed
¼ cup dry red wine
1 medium tomato, sliced
4 (1-inch-thick) slices French
      bread, toasted

• **Combine** first 5 ingredients; set yogurt mixture aside.
• **Coat** a 12-inch cast-iron or large electric skillet with cooking spray; heat over high heat until hot. Add fennel seeds, cumin, and red pepper; cook, stirring constantly, until toasted.
• **Brush** one side of each eggplant slice with barbecue sauce. Place slices, brushed side down, in skillet, and brush top sides with remaining sauce.
• **Cook** eggplant 1 to 2 minutes or until browned. Turn slices, and push to one side of skillet.
• **Add** onion, pepper, and pressed garlic; cook 1 to 2 minutes or until vegetables are slightly tender and eggplant is blackened, stirring frequently.
• **Add** wine; cover, reduce heat, and simmer 2 minutes. Remove vegetables from skillet; keep warm.
• **Add** tomato slices to skillet; cook 1 minute on each side. Remove from skillet.

• **Place** 2 bread slices on each serving plate; top evenly with vegetables. Drizzle with yogurt mixture. Serve immediately. **Yield:** 2 sandwiches.

Julie A. Young
Houston, Texas

♥ Per serving: Calories 377 (25% from fat)
Fat 10.9g (1.7g saturated) Cholesterol 3mg
Sodium 598mg Carbohydrate 61g
Fiber 7.6g Protein 12.6g

BREAKING BAD HABITS

■ Once you make a change, don't revert to your old eating habits. Forget the days when you ate four hamburgers just for lunch.

■ Limit high-calorie foods you love, but don't eliminate them. Don't deprive yourself and then binge.

■ You can still eat large servings, but be selective in your choices. A heaping plateful of green beans has fewer calories than one chocolate chip cookie.

■ Lettuce leaves and yogurt do not make a dinner menu. Include lots of variety in your meals and don't deprive yourself of all your favorite foods.

■ Become a quality eater, not a quantity eater. Learn to appreciate the flavors of food and experiment with new recipes.

■ If a bad habit resurfaces, visualize health goals. The long-term rewards of a fit, healthy body hold strong appeal when compared with a few minutes of indulgence.

■ A word of caution: You can't fight genetics. Work with what you've got, and do the best you can with it.

APRICOT-YOGURT TORTONI

Randy Coleman freezes tortoni between each layering. We found that if you're careful you can assemble the dessert all at once and then freeze it.

1 (12-ounce) package reduced-fat
      vanilla wafers, crushed
½ gallon nonfat frozen vanilla
      yogurt, softened and
      divided
1 teaspoon almond extract
Vegetable cooking spray
1 (18-ounce) jar apricot
      preserves
1 (17-ounce) can apricot halves in
      light syrup, undrained
1 (2.25-ounce) package sliced
      almonds, toasted

• **Combine** wafer crumbs, 1¼ cups yogurt, and almond extract; divide mixture in half.
• **Coat** a 13- x 9- x 2-inch dish with cooking spray. Spoon half of wafer mixture evenly into dish; spread remaining yogurt over top. Spread apricot preserves over yogurt; top with remaining wafer mixture.
• **Cover** and freeze at least 8 hours. Cut dessert into squares; top evenly with apricots and a small amount of syrup. Sprinkle with almonds. **Yield:** 15 servings.

Randy Coleman
San Angelo, Texas

♥ Per serving: Calories 278 (17% from fat)
Fat 5.3g (0.2g saturated) Cholesterol 0mg
Sodium 88mg Carbohydrate 51.5g
Fiber 0.9g Protein 6.5g

TRUE CONFESSIONS (OF THE FOOD KIND)

Today we're busier than ever. And these days convenience products – bottled spaghetti sauce, boxed biscuit mixes, canned chicken, and the like – prevail in even our Foods Staff's pantries. And no doubt about it; they're tasting better than ever. Here we 'fess up and share some of our favorite convenience foods recipes.

PAPRIKA CHICKEN

1 tablespoon margarine
4 skinned and boned chicken breast halves
1 (10¾-ounce) can reduced-sodium cream of mushroom soup
1 tablespoon paprika
½ teaspoon dried tarragon
½ teaspoon salt
½ teaspoon ground red pepper
⅓ cup reduced-fat sour cream
Hot cooked egg noodles
Chopped fresh parsley

● **Melt** margarine in a large nonstick skillet over medium-high heat; add chicken, and cook until browned on both sides.
● **Combine** soup and next 4 ingredients; add to skillet, turning chicken to coat. Cover and cook over medium heat 8 minutes or until chicken is done.
● **Remove** chicken; keep warm. Stir sour cream into pan drippings, and cook 1 minute.
● **Place** chicken on noodles; top with sour cream mixture. Sprinkle with parsley. **Yield:** 4 servings.

Denise Gee
Birmingham, Alabama

QUICK CHICKEN AND DUMPLINGS

1⅔ cups reduced-fat biscuit mix
½ teaspoon dried rosemary
1½ teaspoons chopped fresh parsley or ½ teaspoon dried parsley flakes
⅔ cup skim milk
2 (16-ounce) cans fat-free ready-to-serve chicken broth
1 (10-ounce) can white chicken in water
2 teaspoons chopped fresh parsley

● **Combine** first 3 ingredients in a large bowl; make a well in center of mixture. Add milk, stirring just until moistened.
● **Bring** chicken broth to a boil in a large Dutch oven over medium-high heat. Drop biscuit mixture by tablespoonfuls into broth. Cook, uncovered, 10 minutes. Cover, reduce heat, and simmer 10 minutes. Add chicken, and cook 1 minute. Sprinkle with parsley. Serve immediately. **Yield:** 2 to 3 servings.

Jodi Jackson Loe
Birmingham, Alabama

EASY MEAT LOAF

2 (8-ounce) cans tomato sauce, divided
2 slices sandwich bread, torn into small pieces
1 large egg, lightly beaten
½ teaspoon salt
½ teaspoon pepper
1 cup chopped onion
1 (1-ounce) envelope dry onion soup mix
3 pounds ground chuck

● **Combine** 1 can tomato sauce and next 6 ingredients in a large bowl. Let mixture stand 10 minutes or until bread is softened.
● **Combine** beef and tomato sauce mixture; shape into a 12- x 5-inch loaf. Place on a lightly greased rack; place rack in broiler pan.
● **Bake** at 350° for 1½ hours. Pour remaining can tomato sauce over meat loaf, and bake 5 additional minutes. **Yield:** 10 to 12 servings.

Peggy Smith
Birmingham, Alabama

MACARONI-CHEESE-BEEF CASSEROLE

1 (7.25-ounce) package macaroni and cheese dinner
1 pound lean ground beef
2 (14½-ounce) cans stewed tomatoes, drained
1 cup (4 ounces) shredded reduced-fat sharp Cheddar cheese

● **Prepare** macaroni and cheese dinner according to package directions; set aside.
● **Brown** ground beef in a skillet, stirring until it crumbles; drain and pat dry with paper towels.
● **Combine** macaroni and cheese dinner, beef, and tomatoes in a lightly greased 1½-quart baking dish.
● **Bake** at 350° for 15 minutes. Sprinkle with cheese, and bake 5 additional minutes. **Yield:** 4 servings.

Karen Brechin
Birmingham, Alabama

BLACK, WHITE, AND RED ALL OVER SOUP

1 (15½-ounce) can white hominy, rinsed and drained
1 (15-ounce) can black beans, rinsed and drained
1 (14½-ounce) can chili-style diced tomatoes, undrained
1 (14½-ounce) can ready-to-serve chicken broth
1 teaspoon chopped fresh cilantro
½ teaspoon chili powder
½ teaspoon ground cumin

• **Combine** all ingredients in a large saucepan; cook over medium heat until thoroughly heated, stirring occasionally. **Yield:** 5½ cups.

Julia Dowling
Birmingham, Alabama

SOUTHWESTERN VEGGIE PIZZA

1 (10-ounce) Italian bread shell
1 carrot, scraped and chopped
1 zucchini, sliced
1 clove garlic, minced
1 tablespoon olive oil
1 (11-ounce) jar black bean dip
½ cup salsa, drained
1 cup (4 ounces) shredded Monterey Jack cheese with peppers

• **Bake** bread shell on a baking sheet at 350° for 5 minutes; set aside.
• **Cook** carrot, zucchini, and garlic in olive oil in a skillet over medium heat, stirring constantly, 3 to 5 minutes or until crisp-tender; drain.
• **Spread** bean dip over bread shell; top with salsa and vegetables.
• **Bake** at 350° for 5 minutes; sprinkle with cheese. Bake 5 additional minutes or until cheese melts and pizza is thoroughly heated. **Yield:** 2 to 3 servings.

Note: For the Italian bread shell, we used Boboli.

Susan Dosier
Birmingham, Alabama

BLACK BEANS AND YELLOW RICE

1 (5-ounce) package saffron rice mix
1 (15-ounce) can black beans
3 tablespoons fresh lime juice
1 teaspoon chili powder
½ teaspoon cumin
2 tablespoons chopped fresh cilantro, divided
Garnishes: sour cream, sliced green onions, fresh cilantro

• **Cook** rice mix according to package directions; keep warm.
• **Drain** beans, reserving 2 tablespoons liquid. Combine beans, reserved liquid, lime juice, chili powder, and cumin in a saucepan.
• **Cook** over medium heat until thoroughly heated; stir in 1 tablespoon cilantro. Serve beans over rice; sprinkle with remaining cilantro. Garnish, if desired. **Yield:** 3 to 4 servings.

Dana Adkins Campbell
Birmingham, Alabama

ITALIAN CHEESE BREADSTICKS

1 (11-ounce) can refrigerated breadsticks
2 teaspoons dried Italian seasoning
1½ teaspoons garlic powder
¾ cup (3 ounces) shredded mozzarella cheese

• **Twist** breadsticks, and place on a baking sheet. Sprinkle with Italian seasoning and garlic powder.
• **Bake** at 350° for 10 to 13 minutes; sprinkle with cheese, and bake 5 additional minutes or until cheese melts and breadsticks are done. Serve with spaghetti sauce and Ranch-style salad dressing for dipping. **Yield:** 6 servings.

Jennifer Cobble
Birmingham, Alabama

CINNAMON ICE CREAM

1 teaspoon ground cinnamon
1 quart vanilla ice cream, softened
Fudge sauce
Garnish: cinnamon sticks

• **Stir** together cinnamon and ice cream. Scoop into individual servings, and top with fudge sauce. Garnish, if desired. **Yield:** 4 servings.

Andria Scott Hurst
Birmingham, Alabama

HOOKED ON TUNA

．．．．．．．．．．．．．．．．．．．

Not many menus are planned around this budget staple. But take another look at its potential. If you put a little imagination into familiar dishes that usually don't involve tuna, a renaissance occurs. We wouldn't exactly call the following recipes gourmet, but they do show that canned tuna has taste-pleasing potential.

HOT TUNA MELTS

If you're hooked on coffee shop tuna salad sandwiches, you'll love these heated versions.

1 (6-ounce) can solid white tuna in spring water, drained and flaked
⅓ cup mayonnaise
¼ cup sliced pimiento-stuffed olives, drained
3 hard-cooked eggs, chopped
3 tablespoons sweet pickle relish, drained
2 tablespoons finely chopped onion
2 English muffins, split and lightly toasted
4 (1-ounce) slices sharp Cheddar cheese

- **Combine** first 6 ingredients, stirring well. Spoon evenly onto muffin halves; place on a baking sheet.
- **Broil** 5½ inches from heat (with electric oven door partially opened) 2 minutes. Top each with a cheese slice; broil 1 minute or until cheese melts. **Yield:** 4 servings.

Southwestern Tuna Melts: Prepare tuna mixture as directed, substituting 2 to 4 tablespoons chopped pickled jalapeño peppers for olives. Omit English muffins. Lightly brush one side of 4 (6-inch) flour tortillas with ¾ teaspoon melted butter; place, buttered side up, on an ungreased baking sheet, and bake at 400° for 3 minutes. Turn tortillas over, and bake 1 additional minute. Spread buttered sides evenly with tuna mixture; broil as directed for 1 minute. Top each with a cheese slice; broil 1 minute or until cheese melts.

CREAMED CHIPPED TUNA

Instead of the usual jar of dried beef, open a can of tuna for this convenient entrée.

4 frozen puff pastry shells *
3 tablespoons butter or margarine
¼ cup finely chopped onion
3 tablespoons all-purpose flour
2 cups milk
2 (6-ounce) cans solid white tuna in spring water, drained and flaked
2 hard-cooked eggs, sliced
1 cup (4 ounces) shredded Swiss cheese
½ cup frozen English peas, thawed
¼ teaspoon salt
½ teaspoon freshly ground pepper
1 tablespoon finely chopped fresh parsley

- **Bake** pastry shells according to package directions; set aside.
- **Melt** butter in a heavy saucepan over low heat; add onion and cook, stirring constantly, 2 minutes or until onion is tender.
- **Stir** in flour; cook 1 minute, stirring constantly. Gradually add milk, stirring constantly with a wire whisk. Cook, stirring constantly, until mixture is thickened.
- **Stir** in tuna and next 5 ingredients, and cook, stirring constantly, until cheese melts.
- **Spoon** tuna mixture over pastry shells; sprinkle with parsley. **Yield:** 4 servings.

* Substitute 4 slices toast, cut in half, for pastry shells.

Carol Richard
Birmingham, Alabama

TUNA NACHOS

To make a lighter version, use baked tortilla chips, reduced-fat cheese, and light sour cream.

1 (10-ounce) bag tortilla chips
1 (8-ounce) package shredded colby-Monterey Jack cheese blend
2 (6-ounce) cans solid white tuna in spring water, drained and flaked
1 cup chopped tomato
¼ to ½ cup sliced pickled jalapeño peppers
½ cup sliced green onions
Salsa
Guacamole
Sour cream
Garnish: pickled jalapeño pepper slices

- **Arrange** chips in a single layer, overlapping edges, in a 15- x 10- x 1-inch jellyroll pan or on ovenproof plates. Sprinkle evenly with 1 cup cheese, tuna, tomato, jalapeño peppers, and sliced green onions. Top with remaining cheese.
- **Bake** at 375° for 8 minutes or until cheese melts. Top nachos with salsa, guacamole, and sour cream. Garnish, if desired. **Yield:** 8 appetizer servings or 4 main-dish servings.

Pam Hamby
St. Petersburg, Florida

TUNA TAPENADE

Tuna makes a lower fat substitute for the traditional amount of ripe olives in this Mediterranean-inspired appetizer spread.

1 (8-ounce) carton fresh mushrooms, chopped
2 tablespoons olive oil
⅓ cup chopped onion
2 cloves garlic, chopped
½ teaspoon dried thyme
1 tablespoon lemon juice
1 (6-ounce) can solid white tuna in spring water, drained
¼ teaspoon salt
½ teaspoon freshly ground pepper
½ (8-ounce) package cream cheese, softened
2 tablespoons sliced ripe olives
2 tablespoons capers
2 tablespoons chopped fresh parsley

- **Cook** mushrooms in olive oil in a heavy skillet over medium-high heat, stirring constantly, 5 minutes.
- **Add** onion, garlic, and thyme; reduce heat to medium, and cook until onion is tender.
- **Add** lemon juice, and cook until liquid is absorbed.
- **Position** knife blade in food processor bowl; add mushroom mixture, tuna, salt, and pepper. Pulse 4 times.
- **Add** cream cheese, and pulse 4 times or until blended. Shape mixture into a mound on a serving plate; top with olives, capers, and parsley. Serve spread with toasted baguette slices or melba toast. **Yield:** 1½ cups.

Z. Stiff
Birmingham, Alabama

TUNA BURGERS

For a smokier flavor, try using hickory-flavored water-packed tuna.

3 tablespoons butter or margarine, melted
1 tablespoon lemon juice
2 drops of hot sauce
⅛ teaspoon pepper
3 (6-ounce) cans solid white tuna in spring water, drained and flaked
2 cups soft breadcrumbs
3 large eggs, lightly beaten
1 teaspoon Worcestershire sauce
1 medium onion, finely chopped
2 tablespoons dried parsley flakes
1 teaspoon lemon-pepper seasoning
½ teaspoon onion powder
½ teaspoon garlic powder
1 teaspoon cracked black pepper
½ teaspoon dried thyme
4 kaiser rolls, split
Lettuce leaves
Tomato slices

• **Combine** first 4 ingredients, and set mixture aside.
• **Combine** tuna and next 6 ingredients; shape into 4 patties. Brush patties lightly with half of butter mixture.
• **Combine** onion powder and next 3 ingredients; sprinkle evenly on sides of patties.
• **Heat** remaining butter mixture in a skillet; add patties and cook 4 minutes on each side or until done.
• **Place** each patty on a roll with lettuce and tomato slices; serve with mayonnaise, tartar sauce, or sweet pickle relish. **Yield:** 4 servings.

Note: To blacken patties, remove food rack from grill, and place a cast-iron skillet directly on hot coals; heat at least 5 minutes. (Do not add remaining butter mixture.) Add patties, and cook 3 minutes on each side. Remove from heat, and drizzle with remaining butter mixture.

Kimberly R. Diamondidis
Germantown, Maryland

DINNER'S A DONE DEAL

....

It's been another hectic day, and the kids would be delighted with drive-through fast food again. But you want a home-cooked meal. We have a solution. Turn off your tired brain, and pick one of these menus. We even made your shopping list, so no thinking is necessary. And tell the kids to chill out – it's fun food (with an adult twist for you).

BURGERS AT HOME
Serves Four

Brie-Mushroom Burgers
Parmesan-Zucchini Fries
Tangy Fruit Shake

GROCERY LIST
■ 1½ pounds lean ground beef
■ 2 medium onions
■ 6 ounces Brie
■ ¼ pound fresh mushrooms
■ 4 hamburger buns with sesame seeds
■ 1 container fine, dry breadcrumbs
■ 2 medium zucchini
■ 3 (8-ounce) cartons nonfat peach or blueberry yogurt
■ 3 small bananas
■ Orange-flavored breakfast beverage crystals
■ Check staples: Worcestershire sauce, dry mustard, salt, pepper, butter, eggs, olive oil, vegetable oil, Parmesan cheese

BRIE-MUSHROOM BURGERS

Brie brings sophistication to an ordinary burger. If the kids don't like it, slip Cheddar into theirs, and enjoy your gourmet version alone.

1½ pounds lean ground beef
3 tablespoons grated onion
2 teaspoons Worcestershire sauce
¾ teaspoon dry mustard
¼ teaspoon freshly ground pepper
6 ounces Brie
2 tablespoons butter or margarine
1 cup sliced fresh mushrooms
1 medium onion, sliced
4 hamburger buns with sesame seeds
Olive oil
Garnish: fresh parsley sprigs

• **Combine** first 5 ingredients; shape into 8 (6-inch) patties; set aside.
• **Set** one-third of Brie aside. Cut remaining Brie into 4 pieces, and place 1 piece on each of 4 patties. Top with remaining patties, and seal edges. Cover and chill.
• **Melt** butter in a large nonstick skillet over medium heat. Add mushrooms and onion; cook until tender, stirring often. Remove from heat; add remaining 2 ounces cheese to skillet, stirring until cheese melts. Remove from skillet, and keep warm.
• **Cook** patties in skillet over medium heat 8 minutes, turning once. Remove from skillet, and keep warm.
• **Brush** cut sides of buns with olive oil; place buns, cut side down, in skillet, and cook until lightly browned.
• **Place** bottom half of each bun on a plate; top with a patty, and spoon mushroom mixture over meat. Cover with bun tops; garnish, if desired. **Yield:** 4 servings.

Note: Grill burgers, covered with lid, over medium-hot coals (350° to 400°) 7 to 8 minutes on each side. Toast buns on grill as well.

Lilann Taylor
Savannah, Georgia

PARMESAN-ZUCCHINI FRIES

Yes, you may finally get your kids to eat zucchini – one of those vegetables on their "yuck list."

1 cup fine, dry breadcrumbs
1 cup grated Parmesan cheese
½ teaspoon salt
2 medium zucchini
2 large eggs, lightly beaten
Vegetable oil

• **Combine** first 3 ingredients; set aside.
• **Cut** zucchini into thin strips; dip into beaten egg, and dredge in breadcrumb mixture.
• **Pour** oil to depth of 2 to 3 inches into a Dutch oven or heavy saucepan; heat to 375°. Fry zucchini in oil until golden. Drain on paper towels. Serve immediately. **Yield:** 4 to 6 servings.

Mrs. L. D. Fulton
Sturgis, Mississippi

TANGY FRUIT SHAKE

It's the old "hide-the-fruit" in the dessert trick again.

3 (8-ounce) cartons nonfat peach or blueberry yogurt
3 small bananas
¼ cup orange-flavored breakfast beverage crystals
2¼ cups water
Ice

• **Combine** 1 carton yogurt, 1 banana, 1 tablespoon plus 1 teaspoon beverage crystals, and ¾ cup water in container of an electric blender or food processor; process until smooth.
• **Add** enough ice to bring yogurt mixture to 3-cup level; process until smooth, stopping once to scrape down sides. Repeat twice with remaining ingredients. Serve immediately. **Yield:** 7½ cups.

Zoe Cassimus
Birmingham, Alabama

NOT-YOUR-USUAL TACO SALADS
Serves Six

Mexican Chicken Tortilla Salads
Baked Pears à la Mode

GROCERY LIST

■ 1 (8-ounce) package Monterey Jack cheese (shredded, if available)
■ 1 (8-ounce) carton sour cream
■ 1 small bunch cilantro or parsley
■ 1 (12-ounce) jar pickled jalapeño peppers
■ 6 skinned and boned chicken breast halves
■ 1 head leaf lettuce
■ 1 (10-ounce) bag tortilla chips
■ 3 Roma tomatoes
■ 2 (16-ounce) cans pear halves
■ Almond or coconut macaroons or amaretti cookies
■ Vanilla ice cream
■ Check staples: mayonnaise, garlic, honey, butter

MEXICAN CHICKEN TORTILLA SALADS

Fresh cilantro and a wonderful creamy sauce brushed on the chicken give the typical taco salad a lift.

¼ cup mayonnaise, divided
¾ cup (3 ounces) shredded Monterey Jack cheese
3 tablespoons sour cream
2 tablespoons chopped fresh cilantro or parsley
1 tablespoon finely chopped pickled jalapeño peppers
1 clove garlic, minced
6 skinned and boned chicken breast halves
1 (10-ounce) bag tortilla chips
1 head leaf lettuce, shredded
3 Roma tomatoes, sliced
Garnishes: sour cream, cilantro

• **Combine** 3 tablespoons mayonnaise, shredded cheese, and next 4 ingredients. Set aside.
• **Place** chicken between two sheets of heavy-duty plastic wrap, and flatten to ¼-inch thickness, using a meat mallet or rolling pin.
• **Brush** both sides of chicken lightly with remaining mayonnaise; place on a rack in broiler pan.
• **Broil** 5½ inches from heat (with electric oven door partially opened) 5 minutes on each side.
• **Spread** cheese mixture evenly on top of chicken.
• **Broil** 5 additional minutes or until mixture is browned; keep warm.
• **Layer** chips, lettuce, and tomato on individual plates; top with chicken. Garnish, if desired. **Yield:** 6 servings.

La Juan Coward
Jasper, Texas

❤ Reduce fat and calories by using reduced-fat mayonnaise and reduced-fat sour cream.

BAKED PEARS À LA MODE

Sneak in a little fruit with the ice cream. Add the sweet crunch of crumbled cookies, and you might even feel like you're getting a cone.

2 (16-ounce) cans pear halves, drained *
½ cup honey
½ cup butter or margarine, melted
1 cup crumbled almond or coconut macaroons or amaretti cookies
Vanilla ice cream

• **Arrange** pears in an 11- x 7- x 1½-inch baking dish. Set aside.
• **Combine** honey and butter; pour over pears.
• **Bake** at 350° for 20 minutes. Sprinkle cookie crumbs over pears; bake 10 additional minutes. Serve warm with ice cream. **Yield:** 6 servings.

* Substitute 6 pears, peeled, cored, and quartered lengthwise for canned. Bake at 350° for 30 minutes or until tender. Remove from oven, sprinkle with cookie crumbs, and bake 10 additional minutes.

Gwen Louer
Roswell, Georgia

A Taste of La Paz

....

"We're not a cookie-cutter version of a Mexican restaurant chain; each of our locations has its own character and style," says La Paz Restaurante Cantinas co-founder Tom Nickoloff, a Southern California native. As a child, Tom shunned lemonade and instead hawked avocados at a neighborhood stand. "It worked," he recalls.

So did the idea of Southwestern cuisine presented in an Arizona-soaked atmosphere – the concept behind La Paz (meaning "the peace"). By 1979, when the first La Paz opened in Atlanta, Southeasterners were crying out for a change from Burrito Combo No. 12. Now we get quesadillas stuffed with salmon and goat cheese; poblano chiles with spinach and Monterey Jack cheese; soft tacos filled with shredded pork; and red chile tortillas paired with roasted corn and zucchini, to name just a few.

And with the changes came more La Paz locations now in Asheville, Birmingham, Charlotte, Destin, Knoxville, and Nashville.

NORTHERN NEW MEXICAN VEGETABLE QUESADILLA WITH ROASTED SALSA

Calabacitas
6 (8- to 10-inch) flour tortillas
3 cups (12 ounces) shredded
     Monterey Jack cheese
Roasted Salsa

• **Spoon** Calabacitas evenly over half of each tortilla; sprinkle evenly with cheese. Fold tortillas in half.
• **Cook** filled quesadillas in a large non-stick skillet over high heat 1 minute on each side or until tortillas are slightly browned and cheese melts. Cut each quesadilla into 3 triangles, and serve with Roasted Salsa. **Yield:** 6 servings.

Calabacitas

Calabacita means "little squash."

1 cup finely chopped
     zucchini
1 cup finely chopped yellow
     squash
½ cup chopped sweet red pepper
½ cup chopped Anaheim or New
     Mexican pepper
½ cup chopped purple onion
1 cup frozen whole kernel corn,
     thawed
1 tablespoon chopped poblano
     pepper
1 tablespoon chopped fresh
     cilantro
1 teaspoon salt
1 clove garlic, minced

• **Combine** all ingredients in a large bowl. **Yield:** 4 cups.

Roasted Salsa

Be sure to wear rubber gloves when seeding peppers. The peppers can burn your hands.

1 large tomato
3 large poblano peppers
1 tablespoon olive oil
1 cup chopped purple onion
2 cloves garlic, minced
1 canned chipotle pepper in
     Adobo sauce
1 (14.5-ounce) can whole
     tomatoes, undrained
½ teaspoon salt
½ teaspoon ground
     coriander
½ teaspoon ground cumin
1 teaspoon red wine vinegar

• **Place** tomato and poblanos on a baking sheet lined with aluminum foil.

TORTILLAS PACKING FLAVOR

Want to find the red chile and pesto flour tortillas made popular at La Paz restaurants? Then look to Léona Medina-Tiede in Chimayó, New Mexico.

Her family-run company, Léona's de Chimayó, offers 12-count packages of high-quality traditional 8-inch flour tortillas that are heftier – 13 ounces more – than traditional commercial varieties. You'll find savory red chile, jalapeño, piñon (pine nut), onion, garlic, and pesto tortillas, as well as sweet varieties like chocolate, banana, apple-cinnamon, raspberry, strawberry, and blueberry.

Single-flavor packs of 10 tortillas are $2.50, while assorted packs are $3 a dozen. (Prices exclude shipping and handling.)

For more mail-order details, write to Léona's de Chimayó, Manzana Center, Highway 76, Chimayó, NM 87522; or call 1-800-453-6627.

Broil 5½ inches from heat (with electric oven door partially opened) about 5 minutes on each side or until skin looks blistered.

• **Place** peppers in a heavy-duty, zip-top plastic bag; seal and let stand 10 minutes. Peel peppers; remove and discard membranes and seeds. Set aside.

• **Heat** oil in a skillet over medium-high heat until hot. Add onion and garlic; cook until tender, stirring constantly. Set aside.

• **Remove** membranes and seeds from chipotle pepper; set aside.

• **Position** knife blade in food processor bowl; add roasted tomato and poblanos, onion mixture, chipotle, canned tomatoes, and remaining ingredients. Pulse 6 or 7 times or until slightly chunky.

• **Pour** mixture into a large saucepan, and bring to a boil. Reduce heat, and simmer mixture 15 minutes. Cool. **Yield:** 3 cups.

GRILLED SALMON QUESADILLA WITH CUCUMBER SALSA

1 (8-ounce) salmon fillet
4 (8- to 10-inch) flour
    tortillas
1 cup (4 ounces) shredded
    Monterey Jack cheese
2 ounces goat cheese,
    crumbled
2 jalapeño peppers, seeded and
    sliced
Cucumber Salsa

• **Cook** salmon, covered with grill lid, over medium-hot coals (350° to 400°) 5 to 6 minutes on each side or until done. Cool; flake with a fork.

• **Spoon** flaked salmon evenly over half of each tortilla. Top evenly with cheeses and pepper slices. Fold tortillas in half.

• **Cook** tortillas in a large nonstick skillet over high heat 1 minute on each side or until tortillas are slightly browned and cheese melts. Cut each quesadilla into 3 triangles, and serve with chilled Cucumber Salsa. **Yield:** 4 servings.

Cucumber Salsa

1 large cucumber, chopped
1 clove garlic, minced
1 tablespoon finely chopped
    poblano pepper
1 tablespoon finely chopped purple
    onion
1 tablespoon finely chopped sweet
    red pepper
1 tablespoon finely chopped sweet
    yellow pepper
1 tablespoon finely chopped fresh
    cilantro
1 teaspoon olive oil
¼ teaspoon salt
⅛ teaspoon pepper

• **Combine** all ingredients; cover and chill. **Yield:** 1¼ cups.

CUCUMBER SALSA: NOT JUST FOR TEX-MEX

La Paz's cooling, yet sweetly peppery Cucumber Salsa is delicious with Grilled Salmon Quesadilla and other Tex-Mex entrées, but it's also great with other summertime dishes. Try this easy-to-prepare salsa to add fresh flavor and vivid color to the following:

■ Hot dogs
■ Fresh tomato sandwiches
■ Cold pasta salads
■ Tuna or chicken salads or sandwiches
■ Grilled chicken or fish
■ Yogurt (as a cooling condiment for spicy chicken or meat)
■ Tomato soup (for an easy gazpacho)
■ Omelets
■ Sliced turkey
■ Tomato aspic
■ Green salads
■ Black-eyed peas and rice (for an inventive variation of that Southern favorite hopping John)

NOT-SO-ORDINARY SPAGHETTI

....

Spaghetti's not just for meatballs anymore. Put your noodles to good use in salads, casseroles, and soups. When preparing spaghetti, allow two ounces per side-dish serving and four ounces for each main-dish serving. If you're serving spaghetti chilled, rinse it with cold water after cooking to keep the strands from clinging to each other.

CHEESY FLORENTINE BAKE

6 ounces spaghetti, uncooked
1 (10-ounce) package frozen
    chopped spinach, thawed
2 large eggs, lightly beaten
1 (14-ounce) jar spaghetti
    sauce, divided
1 cup grated Parmesan cheese,
    divided
½ cup cottage cheese
¼ teaspoon ground nutmeg

• **Cook** spaghetti according to package directions; drain.

• **Drain** spinach well, pressing between layers of paper towels.

• **Combine** eggs, spaghetti, ½ cup spaghetti sauce, and ¾ cup Parmesan cheese. Spoon mixture into a lightly greased 9-inch square baking pan.

• **Combine** spinach, cottage cheese, and nutmeg; spoon over spaghetti mixture. Spread with remaining spaghetti sauce.

• **Bake** at 350° for 30 minutes. Sprinkle with remaining ¼ cup Parmesan cheese; bake 5 additional minutes. Let stand 5 minutes before slicing. **Yield:** 6 servings.

Joy Knight Allard
San Antonio, Texas

CASSEROLE SPAGHETTI

As one parent stated during taste testing of this recipe, "Kids will vacuum up this recipe."

1½ pounds ground chuck
1 green pepper, chopped
1 large onion, chopped
½ cup chopped celery
2 cloves garlic, crushed
1 (10¾-ounce) can cream of mushroom soup, undiluted
¾ cup water
1 (16-ounce) can tomatoes, undrained and chopped
2 tablespoons chili powder
½ teaspoon salt
¼ teaspoon pepper
1 (8-ounce) package spaghetti, uncooked
2 ounces sharp Cheddar cheese, cut into ½-inch cubes
1 (5-ounce) jar pimiento-stuffed olives, drained
¾ cup (3 ounces) shredded sharp Cheddar cheese

• **Cook** first 5 ingredients in a Dutch oven, stirring until meat crumbles; drain well, and return mixture to Dutch oven.
• **Stir** in soup and next 5 ingredients.
• **Bring** to a boil over medium heat. Cover, reduce heat, and simmer 1 hour, stirring occasionally.
• **Cook** spaghetti according to package directions; drain.
• **Stir** spaghetti, cheese cubes, and olives into meat sauce. Spoon mixture into a lightly greased 11- x 7- x 1½-inch baking dish.
• **Cover** and bake at 325° for 20 minutes or until thoroughly heated. Sprinkle with ¾ cup shredded cheese, and bake, uncovered, 10 additional minutes. **Yield:** 6 to 8 servings.

Note: Casserole Spaghetti may be prepared ahead, omitting shredded cheese. Cover and chill 8 hours. Remove from refrigerator; let stand at room temperature 30 minutes. Cover and bake at 325° for 45 minutes or until thoroughly heated. Uncover and sprinkle with shredded cheese; bake 10 additional minutes.

MEDITERRANEAN SALAD

For a new twist, use fusilli (spiral-shaped noodles) in place of spaghetti. We liked both versions a lot.

1 (8-ounce) package spaghetti, uncooked
1 (6-ounce) jar marinated artichoke hearts, drained and coarsely chopped
1 (4-ounce) can sliced ripe olives, drained
1 cup frozen English peas, thawed
1 medium-size sweet red pepper, chopped
1 small zucchini, chopped
½ small purple onion, thinly sliced
½ cup freshly grated Parmesan cheese
½ cup mayonnaise or salad dressing
½ cup Italian salad dressing
1 teaspoon dried parsley flakes
½ teaspoon dried dillweed
½ teaspoon coarsely ground pepper

• **Cook** spaghetti according to package directions; drain. Rinse with cold water, and drain.
• **Combine** artichokes and next 6 ingredients in a large bowl. Add spaghetti, tossing well.
• **Combine** mayonnaise and next 4 ingredients, stirring with wire whisk; add to spaghetti mixture, and stir well. Cover and chill. **Yield:** 8 servings.

Janice Rinks
Bluff City, Tennessee

GARDEN CLUB VEGETABLE FAVORITES

....

Gardeners love to share their harvest and their favorite vegetable dishes and casserole recipes, too. As any garden club authority would advise, fresh from the backyard is always best, but we found it interesting that these recipes also work well with frozen or market vegetables.

LIMA BEAN CASSEROLE

"This is my momma's recipe and we usually had it with either turkey or ham for a special occasion." – Freda Wilkins

2 cups water
4 cups fresh, shelled baby lima beans *
4 slices bacon
2 tablespoons all-purpose flour
3 tablespoons brown sugar
1½ teaspoons salt
¼ teaspoon pepper
1½ tablespoons dry mustard
1½ tablespoons lemon juice
½ cup dry breadcrumbs
2 tablespoons butter, melted
½ cup (2 ounces) shredded medium Cheddar cheese

• **Bring** water to a boil in a medium saucepan. Add lima beans; return to a boil. Reduce heat, and simmer 20 minutes or until tender; drain, reserving 1 cup liquid (add water to make 1 cup, if necessary). Place lima beans in a lightly greased 8-inch square baking dish; set aside.
• **Cook** bacon in a large skillet until crisp; remove bacon, reserving 2 tablespoons drippings in skillet. Crumble bacon, and set aside.
• **Heat** bacon drippings in skillet; add flour, stirring until smooth. Cook 1

minute, stirring constantly. Gradually add reserved bean liquid; cook over medium heat, stirring constantly, until mixture is thickened. Stir in brown sugar and next 4 ingredients. Pour sauce over beans. Combine breadcrumbs and butter; sprinkle over top.

• **Bake** at 350° for 25 minutes; sprinkle with cheese. Bake 5 additional minutes or until cheese melts. Sprinkle crumbled bacon over top. **Yield:** 6 servings.

* Substitute 2 (10-ounce) packages frozen baby lima beans for fresh. Simmer 14 to 16 minutes or until beans are tender.

Freda Wilkins
Wilmington, North Carolina

VEGETABLES IN WINE SAUCE CASSEROLE

"I use this year-round whenever I want something different. It's great served with ham or veal. I would also serve it in the fall with roast beef and roasted potatoes." – Harriet Rieman

1   pound small, fresh boiling
     onions, peeled
3   cups 1-inch carrot pieces
1   quart water
1¾ teaspoons salt, divided
4   cups 1-inch celery pieces
⅓   cup butter or margarine
½   cup all-purpose flour
½   teaspoon dry mustard
⅛   teaspoon pepper
2   cups half-and-half
⅔   cup dry white wine
¼   cup grated Parmesan
     cheese

• **Combine** onion, carrot, water, and 1 teaspoon salt in a large saucepan or Dutch oven.
• **Bring** to a boil. Cover, reduce heat, and simmer 10 minutes.
• **Add** celery; return to a boil. Cover, reduce heat, and simmer 10 minutes. Remove from heat; drain. Set aside.
• **Melt** butter in a heavy saucepan over low heat; add flour, remaining ¾ teaspoon salt, mustard, and pepper, stirring until smooth. Cook 1 minute,

stirring constantly. Gradually add half-and-half; cook over medium heat, stirring constantly, until mixture is very thick. Gradually stir in wine, and remove from heat. Pour over vegetables, stirring to combine.
• **Pour** into a lightly greased 2-quart shallow baking dish; sprinkle with Parmesan cheese.
• **Bake** at 350° for 30 minutes or until bubbly. **Yield:** 8 to 10 servings.

Harriet Rieman
Wilmington, North Carolina

HEALTHY SALAD

"We're all so conscious of low-fat foods these days that this makes a smart and delicious salad. I have served it with grilled chicken breasts to make a light meal." – Katherine Goslee

2   medium carrots, scraped and
     grated
2   medium apples, cored and
     grated
10 medium radishes, grated
2   cups shredded red cabbage
4   stalks celery, thinly
     sliced
½   cup chopped fresh
     parsley
½   cup raisins
Honey-Lemon Dressing
Romaine lettuce leaves
3   tablespoons chopped dry-roasted
     peanuts

• **Combine** first 7 ingredients in a large bowl.
• **Pour** Honey-Lemon Dressing over top, stirring gently to coat.
• **Cover** and chill at least 2 hours.
• **Spoon** onto a serving platter lined with romaine lettuce. Sprinkle with peanuts; serve immediately. **Yield:** 8 servings.

Honey-Lemon Dressing

½   cup corn oil
⅓   cup lemon juice
1   tablespoon honey
½   teaspoon salt

• **Combine** all ingredients in container of an electric blender, and process 15 seconds.
• **Cover** and chill at least 1 hour. **Yield:** ¾ cup.

Katherine Goslee
Wilmington, North Carolina

SPECIAL PEAS

"I love this recipe because it dresses up peas and provides an interesting way to use iceberg lettuce. I would serve it with dinner or, even better, at an afternoon luncheon in lieu of a traditional garden salad." – Jane Maloy

2   pounds fresh unshelled English
     peas *
½   cup chopped purple onion
¼   cup seeded and chopped sweet
     red pepper
2   tablespoons butter, melted
2   cups coarsely shredded iceberg
     lettuce
½   teaspoon salt
¼   teaspoon pepper
¼   teaspoon dried tarragon

• **Shell** peas; rinse well, and drain.
• **Cook** peas, onion, and red pepper in butter in a large saucepan over medium-high heat, stirring constantly, 6 minutes or until peas are crisp-tender. Reduce heat; gently stir in lettuce and remaining ingredients.
• **Cover** peas, and simmer 5 minutes. Serve immediately. **Yield:** 4 servings.

* Substitute 1 (10-ounce) package frozen English peas for fresh.

Jane Maloy
Wilmington, North Carolina

START WITH BUTTERMILK

The tangy goodness of buttermilk shouldn't be limited to just cornbread and biscuits. These recipes, including a soup, salad, and some desserts, offer fresh ideas for this Southern staple.

ORANGE-BUTTERMILK SALAD

"This very light dish can be made the day before and is always a hit. People cannot believe it's made with buttermilk." – Juanita B. Hutto

1 (20-ounce) can unsweetened crushed pineapple, undrained
1 (6-ounce) package orange-flavored gelatin
2 cups buttermilk
1 (8-ounce) container frozen whipped topping, thawed
1 cup chopped pecans, toasted
Lettuce leaves

● **Bring** pineapple and liquid to a boil in a medium saucepan. Remove from heat; stir in gelatin. Stir until gelatin dissolves; cool.
● **Add** buttermilk to pineapple mixture; cover and chill until mixture is the consistency of unbeaten egg white. Fold in whipped topping and chopped pecans.
● **Spoon** mixture into a lightly oiled 9-cup mold; cover and chill until mixture is firm.
● **Unmold** onto a lettuce-lined plate. **Yield:** 14 to 16 servings.

Juanita B. Hutto
Mechanicsville, Virginia

CHILLED CUCUMBER-BUTTERMILK SOUP

5 (7- to 8-inch-long) cucumbers (about 2¾ pounds)
½ teaspoon salt
6 green onions, chopped
½ cup chopped fresh parsley
1 tablespoon chopped fresh dill
1 quart buttermilk
1 (16-ounce) carton sour cream
¼ cup lemon juice
¼ teaspoon salt
¼ teaspoon ground white pepper
Garnishes: thinly sliced cucumber, fresh parsley

● **Peel** cucumbers; cut in half lengthwise, and scoop out seeds. Place cucumber shells on a paper towel; sprinkle ½ teaspoon salt evenly over both sides of cucumber. Let stand 30 minutes. Drain; coarsely chop.
● **Combine** cucumber, green onions, and next 7 ingredients. Place one-third of mixture in container of an electric blender; process 1 minute or until smooth. Pour into a 3-quart container. Repeat procedure twice with remaining mixture. Cover and chill at least 3 hours. Garnish, if desired. **Yield:** 2¼ quarts.

Fran Jackson
Kansas City, Missouri

BUTTERMILK BREAD PUDDING WITH BUTTER-RUM SAUCE

1 (16-ounce) loaf unsliced French bread
¼ cup butter or margarine
1 quart buttermilk
1 cup raisins
2 large eggs, lightly beaten
1⅓ cups firmly packed light brown sugar
1 tablespoon vanilla extract
Butter-Rum Sauce

● **Tear** bread into 1-inch pieces; reserve 7½ cups. Set aside remaining bread for other uses.
● **Melt** butter in a 13- x 9- x 2-inch baking pan in 350° oven.
● **Combine** 7½ cups bread pieces, buttermilk, and raisins in a large bowl; set aside.
● **Combine** eggs, brown sugar, and vanilla, whisking well.
● **Add** egg mixture to bread mixture, stirring gently. Pour into pan of melted butter.
● **Bake** at 350° for 1 hour. Serve warm or cold with Butter-Rum Sauce. **Yield:** 10 to 12 servings.

Butter-Rum Sauce

½ cup butter or margarine, softened
½ cup sugar
1 egg yolk
¼ cup water
3 tablespoons rum

● **Combine** first 4 ingredients in a small saucepan, stirring well.
● **Cook** over medium heat until sugar dissolves and sauce begins to thicken (about 10 minutes). Stir in rum. **Yield:** ¾ cup.

Marie Davis
Charlotte, North Carolina

BUTTERMILK-LEMON PUDDING CAKE WITH BLUEBERRY SAUCE

⅔ cup sugar
¼ cup all-purpose flour
½ cup fresh lemon juice
¼ cup butter or margarine, melted
3 large eggs, separated
1 tablespoon grated lemon rind
1½ cups buttermilk
¼ cup sugar
Powdered sugar
Blueberry Sauce
Garnish: lemon rind curls

• **Combine** ⅔ cup sugar and flour in a large bowl; stir in lemon juice, melted butter, egg yolks, lemon rind, and buttermilk. Set aside.
• **Beat** egg whites at high speed with an electric mixer until foamy. Gradually add ¼ cup sugar, 1 tablespoon at a time, beating until stiff peaks form and sugar dissolves (2 to 4 minutes).
• **Fold** egg white mixture into buttermilk mixture; pour into a greased 9- x 5- x 3-inch loafpan, and place loafpan in a 13- x 9- x 2- inch baking pan. Add hot water to baking pan to depth of 1½ inches.
• **Bake** at 350° for 1 hour and 10 minutes, shielding with aluminum foil after 40 minutes. Carefully remove loafpan; cool on a wire rack 15 minutes. Dust with powdered sugar. Serve over warm Blueberry Sauce, and garnish, if desired. **Yield:** 6 to 8 servings.

Blueberry Sauce

¼ cup sugar
2 teaspoons cornstarch
¼ cup water
2 tablespoons lemon juice
¼ teaspoon ground cinnamon
2 cups fresh or frozen blueberries

• **Combine** all ingredients in a medium saucepan; cook over medium-low heat, stirring constantly, until mixture boils and thickens. **Yield:** 1 cup.

Linda Magers
Clemmons, North Carolina

MENU FOR MOM

....

When the sun is rising on Mother's Day, Dad and the kids are in charge of waking Mom with a specially prepared breakfast. Don't fret – with this menu, the whole family will enjoy Mom's special day.

So the timing works out right, bake the muffins first, and then bake the quiche. Start the hash browns the last 10 minutes.

MOTHER'S DAY BREAKFAST
Serves Four

Sealed With a Quiche
Convenient Hash Browns
Speedy Blueberry Muffins
Orange Juice

SEALED WITH A QUICHE

1 small onion, chopped
1 tablespoon vegetable oil
½ (15-ounce) package refrigerated piecrusts
¾ cup chopped ham (6 ounces)
1 (26-ounce) package frozen three-cheese quiche filling, thawed

• **Cook** onion in oil in a skillet over medium-high heat, stirring constantly, until tender.
• **Fit** piecrust in a 9-inch deep-dish pieplate according to package directions. Press edges with a fork, or fold edges under, and crimp edges of piecrust, if desired.
• **Place** onion and ham in bottom of piecrust; add quiche filling.
• **Bake** at 375° for 50 to 55 minutes or until a knife inserted in center of quiche comes out clean. Let quiche stand 5 minutes before serving. **Yield:** 4 to 6 servings.

Byron Hurst
Birmingham, Alabama

CONVENIENT HASH BROWNS

During the last 10 minutes of baking time for the quiche, get this started so it can be served warm.

3 tablespoons vegetable oil
½ (24-ounce) bag frozen hash browns with onions and peppers
½ teaspoon dried Italian seasoning
¾ teaspoon paprika

• **Heat** oil in large nonstick skillet or griddle over medium heat until hot. Carefully add hash browns to form a single layer. Sprinkle layer with Italian seasoning and paprika.
• **Cover** and fry hash browns 10 minutes, stirring thoroughly after 5 minutes. **Yield:** 4 servings.

SPEEDY BLUEBERRY MUFFINS

You'll need to make these first. While they're baking, prepare Sealed With a Quiche, and set it aside. When the muffins are ready, remove from oven, reduce the temperature, wait a few minutes, and bake the quiche.

1 (14-ounce) package blueberry muffin mix with real blueberries
½ cup milk
1 large egg

• **Rinse** blueberries thoroughly with cold water; drain and set aside.
• **Combine** muffin mix, milk, and egg until moistened (batter will be slightly lumpy).
• **Fold** blueberries gently into batter. Spoon batter into greased muffin pans, filling two-thirds full.
• **Bake** at 400° for 18 to 21 minutes. Remove from pans. **Yield:** 8 muffins.

AN OATMEAL COOKIE SAMPLER

. . . .

Homemade cookies always score high marks with family and friends, and these recipes will get you at least four stars. Filled with nuts, raisins, and other yummy ingredients, these oatmeal cookies will melt even the hardest heart. Mix up a batch today and see for yourself.

TOASTED OATMEAL COOKIES

¾ cup butter or margarine
2 cups quick-cooking oats, uncooked
1 cup firmly packed brown sugar
1 large egg
1 teaspoon vanilla extract
½ cup all-purpose flour
1 teaspoon ground cinnamon
½ teaspoon baking soda
½ teaspoon salt
1 cup coarsely chopped pecans

• **Melt** butter in a skillet over medium heat; cook until lightly browned, stirring occasionally. (Be sure you do not burn butter.)
• **Add** oats and cook, stirring constantly, 5 minutes or until oats are golden. Cool.
• **Combine** sugar, egg, and vanilla in a large bowl.
• **Combine** flour and next 4 ingredients; stir in toasted oats. Add to sugar mixture, stirring well.
• **Drop** dough by rounded teaspoonfuls 3 inches apart onto ungreased cookie sheets.
• **Bake** at 350° for 12 minutes or until golden. Cool on cookie sheets 5 minutes; remove to wire racks to cool completely. **Yield:** 3½ dozen.

Agnes Stone
Ocala, Florida

CRISPY OATMEAL-TOFFEE LIZZIES

1 cup butter-flavored shortening
1 cup sugar
1 cup firmly packed brown sugar
2 large eggs
1 tablespoon milk
1 teaspoon vanilla extract
2 cups all-purpose flour
1 teaspoon baking soda
1 teaspoon salt
2 cups quick-cooking oats, uncooked
2 cups (12 ounces) semisweet chocolate morsels
¾ cup almond brickle chips
½ cup chopped pecans

• **Beat** shortening at medium speed with an electric mixer until fluffy; gradually add sugars, beating well. Add eggs, one at time, beating until blended after each addition. Add milk and vanilla, beating until blended.
• **Combine** flour, baking soda, and salt; gradually add to shortening mixture, beating at low speed until blended. Stir in oats and remaining ingredients; cover and chill 1 hour.
• **Shape** dough into 1¼-inch balls; place 2 inches apart on lightly greased cookie sheets. Flatten cookies to ¼-inch thickness with a flat-bottomed glass dipped in flour.
• **Bake** at 350° for 12 minutes or until cookies begin to brown around edges. Remove to wire racks to cool. **Yield:** 6 dozen.

Sandra Russell
Gainesville, Florida

CHOCOLATE-RAISIN OATMEAL COOKIES

1¼ cups butter or margarine, softened
¾ cup firmly packed brown sugar
½ cup sugar
1 large egg
1 teaspoon vanilla extract
3 cups quick-cooking oats, uncooked
1½ cups all-purpose flour
1 teaspoon baking soda
1 teaspoon salt
1 teaspoon ground cinnamon
¼ teaspoon ground nutmeg
2 (7-ounce) packages chocolate-covered raisins (2 cups)

• **Beat** butter at medium speed with an electric mixer until creamy; gradually add sugars, beating well. Add egg and vanilla, beating until blended.
• **Combine** oats and next 5 ingredients; gradually add to butter mixture, beating at low speed until blended. Stir in chocolate-covered raisins.
• **Drop** dough by rounded tablespoonfuls onto ungreased cookie sheets.
• **Bake** at 350° for 12 minutes or until browned. Let cookies cool on cookie sheets 10 minutes; remove to wire racks to cool completely. **Yield:** 4 dozen.

Note: For smaller cookies, drop dough by rounded teaspoonfuls, and bake 10 minutes. **Yield:** 7 dozen.

Sharron D. Wright
Austell, Georgia

JUNE

HATS OFF TO SUMMER ENTERTAINING

Dress up isn't just for little girls – it inspired this ladies luncheon. Rediscover vintage hats, hatboxes, and gloves from your grandmother's attic, and use them to create an unforgettable garden party.

SUMMER LUNCHEON MENU
Serves Six

Summery Chicken Salad
Honey Angel Biscuits With Honey Butter
Pink Lemonade
Cute-as-a-Button Cherry Pound Cake

You'll appreciate this luncheon menu for its ease of preparation, low cost, high flavor, and unique appeal.

Summer hats from antique shops and thrift stores embellish tables swagged with tulle and filled with flowers. A hatbox doubles as the container for the centerpiece.

Crystallized lemons and limes made simply from brushing the citrus with egg whites and rolling in sugar complement the festive display. Send your guests home with a party favor of crystallized lemons and limes. Simply tie up several in clear wrap with a rose and a ribbon. (Note: Use the fruit for decoration only.)

Just over two hours of total cooking time is all you'll need to get it ready. (See our decorating hints on the next page.) And afterward you can devote yourself to other important things, like enjoying the party. What an inviting thought.

SUMMERY CHICKEN SALAD
(pictured on page 150)

6   cups chopped cooked
    chicken
1¼ cups sliced celery
1   (8-ounce) can pineapple tidbits,
    drained
1¼ cups reduced-fat mayonnaise
    or salad dressing
2½ tablespoons dry white
    wine
¾   teaspoon salt
¾   teaspoon curry powder
2   Red Delicious apples, thinly
    sliced
1   cantaloupe, thinly sliced
½   pound green grapes
1   pint strawberries
1   cup blackberries
Lettuce leaves
¼   cup chopped walnuts,
    toasted
Garnish: celery leaves

• **Combine** first 3 ingredients in a large bowl; set aside.
• **Combine** mayonnaise and next 3 ingredients. Add to chicken mixture, tossing to coat. Cover and chill 1 to 2 hours.
• **Arrange** apples and next 4 ingredients on a lettuce-lined platter; top with chicken mixture. Sprinkle with toasted walnuts. Garnish, if desired. **Yield:** 6 servings.

Mrs. Wallace Cupit
Seminole, Florida

HONEY ANGEL BISCUITS
(pictured on page 150)

1   package active dry yeast
2   tablespoons warm water
    (105° to 115°)
5   cups all-purpose flour
1   tablespoon baking
    powder
1   teaspoon baking soda
1   teaspoon salt
1   cup shortening
2   cups buttermilk
3   tablespoons honey
Honey Butter

• **Combine** yeast and warm water in a 1-cup liquid measuring cup; let stand 5 minutes.
• **Combine** flour, baking powder, baking soda, and salt in a large bowl; cut in shortening with pastry blender until mixture is crumbly.
• **Combine** yeast mixture, buttermilk, and honey, and add to dry ingredients, stirring just until dry ingredients are moistened.
• **Turn** dough out onto a lightly floured surface, and knead dough 1 minute.
• **Roll** dough to ½-inch thickness. Cut with a 2-inch round cutter, and place on ungreased baking sheets.
• **Bake** at 400° for 10 minutes or until golden. **Yield:** 4 dozen.

Note: You can store unbaked dough in the refrigerator in an airtight container up to 1 week.

Ruth Shirley
Dallas, Texas

Honey Butter

¼ cup honey
½ cup butter or margarine,
    softened

● **Combine** honey and butter in a small bowl, stirring mixture until blended. **Yield:** ⅔ cup.

CUTE-AS-A-BUTTON CHERRY POUND CAKE
(pictured on page 151)

Though this pound cake takes about 2 hours to bake, the results are well worth the effort.

1 cup butter or margarine,
    softened
½ cup shortening
3 cups sugar
6 large eggs
1 (6-ounce) jar red maraschino
    cherries, drained and
    chopped
½ teaspoon almond extract
½ teaspoon vanilla extract
3¾ cups all-purpose flour
¼ teaspoon salt
¾ cup milk
Cream Cheese Frosting
Garnish: 1 (4-ounce) package
    melt-away mints

● **Beat** butter and shortening at medium speed with an electric mixer about 2 minutes or until soft and creamy. Gradually add sugar, beating 5 to 7 minutes. Add eggs, one at a time, beating just until yellow disappears. Stir in cherries and flavorings.
● **Combine** flour and salt; add to the butter mixture alternately with milk, beginning and ending with the flour mixture. Mix at low speed just until blended after each addition. Pour batter into a greased and floured 10-inch tube pan.
● **Bake** at 300° for 1 hour and 45 minutes to 2 hours or until a wooden pick inserted in center comes out clean. Cool in pan on a wire rack 10 minutes; remove from pan, and cool completely on wire rack.

And as you put on your favorite hat, don't forget to load your camera. You'll want to remember your time of dress up.

■ Whatever your special occasion is this season – a wedding, a bridal party, or just a visit with your favorite friends – these ideas will help make your party special. If you don't own old hats and gloves, flea markets and vintage thrift shops are great sources for these wonderful accessories.

■ To emphasize the theme of your party, invite each guest to wear her favorite hat – preferably an old one.

■ For the party, layer two 60-inch-round tables with table skirts made from white sheets sewn together. A pink-and-white gingham overlay adds a soft, feminine touch of color. Swag white tulle around each table, and attach it with florist pins.

■ At each swag, pin a hat to the layered cloths. Use hats from fancy to casual – blending the styles adds to the authenticity and feel of the party.

■ For centerpieces, stack old hatboxes on one table and top them with two hats, a pair of long gloves, and a strand of pearls. A pretty cake stand, a candy dish, and silver pieces complete the table. On the other table, line an old hatbox with a plastic bag and plastic tray. Place florist foam directly onto the plastic tray and secure the foam blocks with waterproof florist tape. Arrange a variety of fresh roses mixed with stock and mums for a touch of color and the look of summertime.

● **Frost** top and sides of cake with Cream Cheese Frosting. Garnish, if desired. **Yield:** 1 (10-inch) cake.

Note: For melt-away mints, we used Smooth 'n Melty Petite Mints by Guittard Chocolate Company.

Cream Cheese Frosting

1 (8-ounce) package cream cheese,
    softened
½ cup butter, softened
1 (16-ounce) package powdered
    sugar, sifted
1 teaspoon vanilla extract

● **Combine** cream cheese and butter, beating until smooth. Add sugar and vanilla; beat until light and fluffy. **Yield:** 3 cups.

Carolyn McDaniel
York, South Carolina

FINGER FOODS:
THE BALANCING ACT

The calendar is packed with weddings, showers, and graduations this time of year. And you're probably going to attend, or host, a few parties where you'll encounter the dreaded finger-food dilemma. How do you gracefully get through one of these eat-on-your-feet events? Business and social etiquette consultant Kay Long Jordan of Winston-Salem, North Carolina, has tips for both sides of the table.

GUEST'S GUIDELINES
■ There's a way to hold both your plate and glass in one hand, leaving the other free for eating and greeting. With the right hand, put your napkin between the pinky and ring finger of your left hand, the plate between the ring finger and middle finger, and the glass atop the plate, holding it with your index finger and thumb. (The lighter weight the glass and plate, the easier this is.)

■ Remember the food is usually meant to be hors d'oeuvres, not a large meal. Take small quantities and you will have less to juggle.

■ After each bite, wipe your fingers on the napkin you are holding under the plate. Then you will be ready to shake hands at a moment's notice.

■ When dips and spreads are served, put them on your plate and move away from the serving table. Don't hover over the table, repeatedly dipping into the bowl.

■ Don't put used plates back on the serving table. Look for waste receptacles, empty tables meant for plate disposal, or someone who has been assigned to cleanup duties.

HOST'S HINTS
■ When planning your menu, keep foods simple and bite size for easy eating.

■ Avoid thin sauces or dips that may drip on party clothes or carpeting.

■ Offer wooden picks for picking up appetizers.

■ Provide some extra napkins with finger foods.

■ Give guests an obvious place for disposing of used dishware.

■ For home parties, set out coasters and wicker lap trays around the living room.

GET A GRIP ON THE MATTER
More practical than pretty, a plastic drink holder (not the car-window type) clipped to your plate will make party eating even easier. It grips a plate, and a stemmed glass slips into a ring, safely suspending your drink to the side. They're less than $1 each and can be ordered in large quantities from Drink Mate International, Inc., in Kissimmee, Florida. Telephone 1-800-929-9363 for information.

BEVERAGES FOR
A CROWD

Your guests will linger around the punch bowl when you serve these cold thirst quenchers. We've included beverages casual enough for paper cups and dressy enough to serve from crystal punch bowls. And as a bonus, all of these refreshers are adaptable to serve any size gathering.

For a thick, creamy drink, try the Mocha Punch; the sherbet punches are great for a refreshing icy froth.

PINEAPPLE-GIN PUNCH

1 (12-ounce) can frozen orange
    juice concentrate, thawed and
    undiluted
1½ quarts ginger ale, chilled
1 cup gin
1 quart pineapple sherbet
Ice Ring (optional)

● **Combine** first 3 ingredients in a large punch bowl. Add sherbet by large spoonfuls, stirring gently. Place Ice Ring in punch, or serve over ice. **Yield:** 3 quarts.

Ice Ring

6 cups water
Fresh mint sprigs

● **Boil** water 1 minute; let cool to room temperature.
● **Pour** 3 cups cooled water into a 6-cup ring mold; freeze.
● **Arrange** mint sprigs in mold as desired. Slowly add enough remaining water to fill mold, and freeze.
● **Let** ring mold stand at room temperature 5 minutes or until loosened to unmold.

Debby G. Milburn
Painter, Virginia

CALYPSO PRESBYTERIAN CHURCH WOMEN'S LIME PUNCH

Calypso Presbyterian Church in Calypso, North Carolina, is described as a "little church that Southern life centers around." Their favorite punch recipe is a real crowd-pleaser.

1 (3-ounce) package lime-flavored gelatin
2 cups sugar
2 cups boiling water
2 cups lemon juice
2 (46-ounce) cans pineapple juice
1 (12-ounce) can frozen orange juice concentrate, thawed and undiluted
½ teaspoon green liquid food coloring
1 (2-liter) bottle ginger ale, chilled

• **Combine** first 3 ingredients in a 1½-gallon container, stirring until sugar dissolves.
• **Add** lemon juice and next 3 ingredients, stirring until blended. Cover and chill.
• **Pour** mixture into a large punch bowl; gently stir in ginger ale. **Yield:** 1½ gallons.

Carolyn Kornegay
Gray, Tennessee

MOCHA PUNCH

This drink is so thick and rich it could almost be dessert.

1 (2-ounce) jar instant coffee granules
2 cups boiling water
1 cup sugar
1 gallon milk
½ gallon chocolate ice cream, softened
½ gallon vanilla ice cream, softened
2 cups whipping cream, whipped

• **Combine** coffee granules and boiling water, stirring until coffee dissolves. Add sugar, stirring until sugar dissolves. Cover and chill.

• **Combine** coffee mixture and milk in a large punch bowl; gently stir in ice creams. Spoon whipped cream on top. **Yield:** about 2½ gallons.

Carolyn Kornegay
Gray, Tennessee

RASPBERRY SHERBET PUNCH

2 (12-ounce) cans frozen pink lemonade concentrate, thawed and undiluted
½ gallon raspberry sherbet, softened
2 (2-liter) bottles ginger ale or raspberry ginger ale, chilled

• **Combine** lemonade concentrate and sherbet in a punch bowl; stir in ginger ale, breaking up sherbet. Serve immediately. **Yield:** 1½ gallons.

Drucie Eaddy
Abbeville, South Carolina

PINEAPPLE SHERBET PUNCH

½ gallon pineapple sherbet, softened
1 (1-liter) bottle ginger ale or raspberry ginger ale, chilled
Garnish: fresh raspberries

• **Place** sherbet in a large punch bowl; add ginger ale, stirring with a wire whisk to blend. Garnish, if desired. **Yield:** 2½ quarts.

Helen Dosier
Sparta, North Carolina

SPARKLING APPLE JUICE

This is a light, crisp drink that's perfect for children's parties.

½ cup apple juice
½ cup ginger ale, chilled

• **Combine** apple juice and ginger ale. **Yield:** 1 cup.

CORDIALLY YOURS

....

Fruits in liqueurs are a gourmet's delight. Liqueurs are pricey if purchased in specialty foods catalogs, but you can take advantage of this season's fresh berries and make your own. Get yourself, and the fruit, in the spirit for less than $20. To double the fun for half the price, pick your own berries.

These bottled jewels make a gorgeous counter display, but during the heat of summer we suggest you store them in the refrigerator. You can purchase decorative jars at Pier 1 Imports, Waccamaw, or kitchen shops. They make great gifts that sweeten any relationship.

SWEETENED PRESERVED LEMONS

6 cups water
4 to 5 large lemons, stem ends removed
½ vanilla bean
1¼ cups vodka
1 cup sugar

• **Bring** water to a boil in a large saucepan; add lemons, and return to a boil. Boil 1 minute; drain and pat lemons dry.
• **Cut** lemons into quarters lengthwise, cutting to ½ inch of stem end, leaving quarters attached.
• **Pack** lemons into a 1-quart widemouthed jar; add ½ vanilla bean.
• **Combine** vodka and sugar in a saucepan, and cook over low heat, stirring until sugar dissolves (do not boil).
• **Pour** over lemons, adding additional vodka to cover lemons, if necessary. Cover and store in refrigerator 2 to 4 weeks or longer.
• **Use** lemon peel to flavor desserts, muffins, or sauces. Use liquid as a liqueur or to sweeten beverages or fresh fruit. **Yield:** 1 quart.

SPIRITED RASPBERRIES

(pictured on page 145)

2 cups fresh raspberries
½ cup superfine sugar
¾ cup vodka or brandy

• **Place** berries in a 1-pint wide-mouthed jar; add sugar. Add enough vodka to cover fruit. Cover and store in a cool, dry place at least 1 week. Serve over cheesecake, Belgian waffles, or ice cream. **Yield:** 2 cups.

Note: Recipe may be doubled to fill a 1-quart jar.

Madelyn Buggs
Birmingham, Alabama

BLUEBERRY CORDIAL

(pictured on page 145)

Blueberry lovers can indulge their passion year-round, using fresh or frozen berries.

1 cup sugar
3 cups fresh or frozen blueberries
1⅔ cups vodka

• **Combine** all ingredients in a 1-quart widemouthed jar. Cover tightly, and shake vigorously. Let stand in a cool place 2 months.
• **Pour** mixture through a wire-mesh strainer into a decorative jar, discarding berries. Serve as a cordial, or mix with an equal amount of club soda, and serve over ice. **Yield:** 2½ cups.

RUMTOPF

(pictured on page 145)

In time, the colors of the fruits may become less vivid as their flavors intensify.

2 cups fresh blueberries
2 cups fresh raspberries
2 cups fresh peach slices
2 cups fresh cherries, pitted
1 cup sugar
2¼ cups spiced rum

• **Layer** fruit in 4 (1-pint) wide-mouthed jars. Pour ¼ cup sugar into each jar. Add enough rum to completely cover fruit. Cover jars with plastic wrap; pierce wrap to allow air to escape (do not seal jars). Store in refrigerator up to 4 months. Serve over pound cake or ice cream. **Yield:** 4 pints.

Note: Amount of rum may vary with size of fruit or shape of decorative jar. Cork seals provide adequate ventilation for fruit also.

Madelyn Buggs
Birmingham, Alabama

ORANGES IN GRAND MARNIER

(pictured on page 145)

The oranges will maintain their sunny appearance for months, if you can resist them that long.

3 to 4 oranges, sliced
1 cup sugar
½ cup water
½ cup Grand Marnier

• **Pack** orange slices into a 1-quart jar. Set aside.
• **Combine** sugar and water in a saucepan; bring to a boil over medium heat, stirring constantly. Boil 1 minute; remove from heat.
• **Stir** in liqueur, and pour over orange slices. Cover tightly, and store in refrigerator up to 2 months. Serve over pound cake or ice cream. **Yield:** 1 quart.

GIVE THEM A WORLDLY SEND-OFF

....

Whether your friends are island-bound on a dream cruise or your child is graduating from college, this menu of international favorites is your passport to success. All of these items can be made ahead and/or frozen – a time-saver for the host.

MEXICAN CROSTINI

To make ahead, mix the spread and toast the bread a day in advance. Just before the party starts, reheat the spread in a slow cooker or fondue pot; surround it with toppings so everyone can make their own crostini. (Crostini means "little crust" in Italian.)

1 French baguette
1 (16-ounce) can refried beans
½ (1¼-ounce) package taco seasoning mix
Shredded Cheddar cheese
Sliced ripe olives
Chopped green onions
Chopped tomatoes
Chopped jalapeño peppers

• **Slice** baguette into 30 (¼- to ½-inch thick) slices, and place slices on a baking sheet.
• **Bake** at 350° for 6 to 8 minutes or until lightly browned, turning once.
• **Combine** beans and taco seasoning mix in a small saucepan. Cook over medium heat until thoroughly heated. Transfer bean mixture to a fondue pot or microwave-safe baking dish.
• **Spread** evenly on bread slices. Top with remaining ingredients, as desired. Serve immediately. **Yield:** 2½ dozen.

Ronda Carman
Houston, Texas

ALABAMA FUDGE-PECAN CHEWIES

Make these treats up to two days before serving, or bake them ahead and freeze. Store them in the freezer up to three months.

¼ cup butter or margarine
1 (14-ounce) can sweetened
    condensed milk
2 cups (12 ounces) semisweet
    chocolate morsels
1 teaspoon vanilla
    extract
1 cup all-purpose flour
½ cup chopped pecans
60 pecan halves

• **Combine** first 3 ingredients in a heavy saucepan; cook over medium-low heat, stirring constantly, until chocolate and butter melt. Remove from heat.
• **Stir** in vanilla, flour, and chopped pecans. Drop by teaspoonfuls onto ungreased cookie sheets. Press a pecan half into the center of each cookie.
• **Bake** at 350° for 7 minutes. (Do not overbake.) Remove cookies to wire racks to cool. **Yield:** 5 dozen.

Jane Boswell
Birmingham, Alabama

TROPICAL DATE-BANANA LOAVES

This recipe produces two loaves that can be made ahead and frozen up to three months.

¾ cup shortening
1½ cups firmly packed brown
    sugar
4 large eggs
1¼ cups mashed ripe banana
    (4 medium)
2 teaspoons vanilla extract
2 cups all-purpose flour
1½ teaspoons baking soda
1 teaspoon salt
1 cup chopped dates
1 cup chopped pecans
1 cup quick-cooking oats,
    uncooked

• **Beat** shortening at medium speed with an electric mixer until fluffy; gradually add brown sugar, beating well. Add eggs, one at a time, beating after each addition. Set aside.
• **Combine** banana and vanilla. Set mixture aside.
• **Combine** flour, soda, and salt; add to shortening mixture alternately with banana mixture, beginning and ending with flour mixture. Stir in dates, pecans, and oats. Spoon batter into 2 greased and floured 8½- x 4½- x 3-inch loafpans.
• **Bake** at 350° for 50 to 55 minutes or until a wooden pick inserted in center comes out clean; shield edges with strips of aluminum foil after 35 minutes to prevent excessive browning.
• **Cool** in pans on wire racks 10 minutes; remove from pans, and cool completely on wire racks. Serve with fresh fruit and pineapple-flavored cream cheese, if desired. **Yield:** 2 loaves.

SLICES OF SUMMER

....

Melons are a lot like tomatoes. In January you'd give anything for a good one. But come summer, they're so plentiful you don't know what to do with them all. Enjoy a daiquiri, chill a salad, put up some jam, bake a pie, or mix some salsa. And take advantage of the season's bounty now.

WATERMELON DAIQUIRI
(pictured on page 185)

4 cups peeled, seeded, and cubed
    watermelon
½ cup light rum
¼ cup fresh lime juice
¼ cup orange-flavored liqueur
Ice cubes

• **Freeze** watermelon in a shallow pan at least 6 hours.
• **Combine** frozen watermelon, rum, lime juice, and liqueur in container of an electric blender; process until smooth, stopping once to scrape down sides.
• **Add** enough ice to bring mixture to 5-cup level; process until smooth. Repeat procedure, if necessary, until mixture measures 5 cups. **Yield:** 5 cups.

Shirley Draper
Winter Park, Florida

CANTALOUPE-PEACH JAM

4 cups peeled, seeded, and
    chopped cantaloupe (about
    1 large)
4 cups peeled, seeded, and
    chopped peaches (about
    4 medium)
6 cups sugar
¼ cup lemon juice
1 teaspoon grated lemon rind

• **Combine** cantaloupe and peaches in a Dutch oven; cook over medium heat, stirring constantly, 15 minutes or until there is enough liquid to prevent fruit from sticking.
• **Add** sugar and lemon juice, stirring well. Bring to a boil, stirring constantly. Reduce heat, and simmer 30 minutes or until thickened.
• **Add** lemon rind, and cook 3 additional minutes, stirring constantly. Remove from heat; skim off foam.
• **Pour** hot jam into hot, sterilized jars, filling to ¼ inch from top. Remove air bubbles; wipe jar rims. Cover at once with metal lids, and screw on bands.
• **Process** in boiling-water bath 5 minutes. **Yield:** 6 half pints.

Janie Wallace
Seguin, Texas

GRILLED MELON SALAD WITH ORANGE-RASPBERRY VINAIGRETTE

½ cup orange marmalade
2 tablespoons lemon juice
2 tablespoons soy sauce
2 teaspoons grated fresh ginger
½ cantaloupe, peeled, seeded, and cut into 1-inch cubes
½ honeydew melon, peeled, seeded, and cut into 1-inch cubes
2 cups fresh strawberries, halved
1 cup fresh raspberries
Orange-Raspberry Vinaigrette
Lettuce leaves

• **Combine** first 4 ingredients in a large bowl; add cantaloupe and honeydew, tossing gently. Arrange melon in a grill basket, or thread on skewers.
• **Cook,** covered with grill lid, over hot coals (400° to 500°) 2 to 3 minutes on each side. Remove melon to a large bowl; cover and chill.
• **Combine** chilled melon, strawberries, and raspberries. Drizzle with Orange-Raspberry Vinaigrette, and toss gently. Serve in a lettuce-lined bowl. **Yield:** 4 servings.

Orange-Raspberry Vinaigrette

½ cup orange marmalade
¼ cup raspberry vinegar
2 tablespoons seeded, finely chopped jalapeño pepper
2 tablespoons finely chopped fresh cilantro

• **Combine** all ingredients in a small bowl. **Yield:** 1 cup.

HOT MELON SALSA

1 cup peeled, seeded, and cubed honeydew melon
1 cup peeled, seeded, and cubed cantaloupe
1 cup peeled, seeded, and cubed watermelon
1 red jalapeño pepper, seeded and finely chopped
1 green jalapeño pepper, seeded and finely chopped
2 tablespoons fresh lime juice
¼ cup finely chopped fresh basil

• **Combine** all ingredients, mixing well. Cover and chill at least 3 hours. **Yield:** 3 cups.

WATERMELON PIE

2 cups peeled and chopped watermelon rind
1 cup sugar
2 teaspoons all-purpose flour
1 teaspoon ground cinnamon
¼ teaspoon ground nutmeg
¼ teaspoon ground cloves
⅛ teaspoon salt
3 tablespoons cider vinegar
½ cup raisins
½ cup chopped pecans
1 (15-ounce) package refrigerated piecrusts

• **Place** rind in a small saucepan; add water to cover. Bring to a boil; cover, reduce heat, and simmer 15 to 20 minutes or until translucent and tender. Remove from heat; drain.
• **Combine** rind, sugar, and next 8 ingredients, stirring well; set aside.
• **Fit** 1 piecrust in a 9-inch pieplate according to package directions. Pour rind mixture into piecrust. Top with remaining piecrust; fold edges under, and crimp. Cut small slits in top piecrust with a sharp knife.
• **Bake** at 350° for 45 to 50 minutes or until golden, shielding edges of pie with strips of aluminum foil after 25 minutes to prevent excessive browning. Cool on a wire rack. **Yield:** one 9-inch pie.

Edith Stone
Greenville, Texas

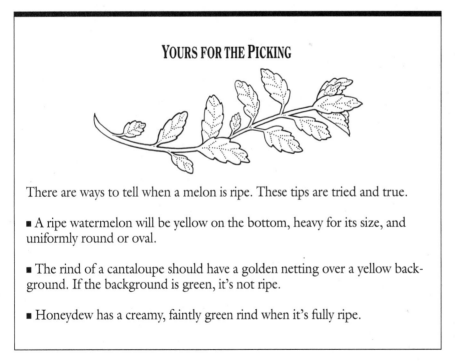

YOURS FOR THE PICKING

There are ways to tell when a melon is ripe. These tips are tried and true.

■ A ripe watermelon will be yellow on the bottom, heavy for its size, and uniformly round or oval.

■ The rind of a cantaloupe should have a golden netting over a yellow background. If the background is green, it's not ripe.

■ Honeydew has a creamy, faintly green rind when it's fully ripe.

Right: Choose assorted jars and decanters to add style and character to your fruits in liqueurs. (Recipes begin on page 141.)

Left: *Flank Steak-and-Spinach Pinwheels served with Zesty Black-Eyed Pea Relish and Toasted Rice and Pasta keep you from running in circles to prepare a special meal. (Recipes begin on page 56.)*

Far left: *A menu of (clockwise from top right) Jeweled Congealed Fresh Fruit, Fresh Mint Tea, Party Tarts, Creamy Ham-and-Chicken Lasagna, and rolls with Garlic Butter is a first-rate choice for a newcomer in the kitchen. (Recipes begin on page 88.)*

Above: *Mesquite-Ginger Beef With Fresh Fruit Relish (recipe, page 158) showcases the prize-winning flavor combination of mesquite-flavored barbecue seasoning, tropical mango, and succulent pineapple.*

Right: *Chicken Tostadas (recipe, page 122) are a flat-out winner when racing against the clock.*

Far right: *Enjoy a picture-perfect summer gathering with beautifully presented Thai Chicken Salad with Peanut Ginger Dressing and Beef Vinaigrette Salad (recipes, page 177).*

Below: *Salmon Bake With Pecan-Crunch Coating (recipe, page 209) casts a sweet, nutty flavor that's ready in no time.*

Above: *Cream cheese frosting dotted with pastel mints makes Cute-As-A-Button Cherry Pound Cake (recipe, page 139) a showstopper.* Left: *For a heavenly luncheon serve Summery Chicken Salad and Honey Angel Biscuits with Honey Butter (recipes, page 138).*

Suit yourself to a tee when choosing from the variety of flavors in (clockwise from top) Lemon Tea Tingler with Lemonade Cubes, Rasp-Berry Good Tea with Berry-Good Cubes, Pink Sangría Tea with Lemon-Mint Cubes, Tropical Tea-ser with Florida Cubes, and Lemon Tea Tingler with Cranberry Cubes. (Recipes begin on page 200.)

THE BIG GRILL: CHICKEN SANDWICHES

....

Spice up your next Saturday afternoon with these jazzy chicken sandwiches. They cook quickly on either the grill or the cooktop. So whether you're hankering for Italian or yearning for tangy island spices, you'll savor these twists on the traditional chicken sandwich. They're sure to satisfy.

HAM 'N' CHEESE CHICKEN SANDWICH

4 skinned and boned chicken
   breast halves
¼ teaspoon seasoned salt
½ teaspoon dried parsley flakes
½ cup teriyaki sauce
4 slices honey ham, folded in half
4 slices Swiss or Monterey Jack
   cheese, folded in half
4 sandwich buns
Dijon or honey mustard
Lettuce leaves

• **Flatten** each piece of chicken slightly, using a meat mallet or rolling pin.
• **Sprinkle** chicken with salt and parsley flakes; place in a shallow dish.
• **Pour** teriyaki sauce over chicken, turning to coat. Cover chicken, and chill 1 hour.
• **Drain** chicken. Place a folded ham slice and a folded cheese slice on each chicken breast; fold breast in half, and secure with a wooden pick.
• **Cook** chicken, covered with grill lid, over medium-hot coals (350° to 400°) 10 to 15 minutes or until chicken is done, turning once.
• **Remove** wooden picks, and place chicken on bottom half of each bun with mustard and lettuce; cover with tops of buns. **Yield:** 4 servings.

Susan Page
Tampa, Florida

JAMAICAN CHICKEN SANDWICH
(pictured on page 111)

1 (20-ounce) can pineapple slices,
   undrained
¼ cup dark rum or pineapple juice
1 tablespoon chili powder
1 tablespoon molasses
¼ teaspoon hot sauce
4 skinned and boned chicken
   breast halves
4 sesame seed sandwich buns,
   toasted
Red Cabbage Slaw
Lettuce leaves
¼ cup flaked coconut, toasted
   (optional)
Red cabbage leaves
Garnish: green onions

• **Drain** pineapple, reserving 2 tablespoons juice for Red Cabbage Slaw and, if desired, ¼ cup juice for basting mixture; set aside.
• **Combine** rum or ¼ cup reserved pineapple juice, chili powder, molasses, and hot sauce; set basting mixture aside.
• **Cook** pineapple and chicken, covered with grill lid, over medium-hot coals (350° to 400°)15 to 20 minutes or until done, basting often.
• **Place** Red Cabbage Slaw on bottom half of each bun; top each with chicken, leaf lettuce, and 2 pineapple slices. Sprinkle with coconut, if desired. Cover with tops of buns. Serve each sandwich on a red cabbage leaf, and garnish, if desired. **Yield:** 4 servings.

Red Cabbage Slaw

1 cup finely shredded red
   cabbage
2 green onions, finely chopped
2 tablespoons reserved pineapple
   juice
2 teaspoons canola or
   vegetable oil
1 teaspoon sesame oil

• **Combine** all ingredients.
• **Cover** and chill. Serve with a slotted spoon. **Yield:** 1 cup.

Sandi Pichon
Slidell, Louisiana

ITALIAN CHICKEN-MOZZARELLA MELT

4 skinned and boned chicken
   breast halves
2 tablespoons olive oil
¼ teaspoon salt
½ teaspoon dried oregano,
   divided
1 cup pizza sauce
½ teaspoon dried basil
4 French rolls, halved and
   toasted
1 small zucchini, shredded
¼ cup (2 ounces) shredded
   mozzarella cheese
¼ cup grated Parmesan cheese

• **Brush** each piece of chicken with olive oil; sprinkle with salt and ¼ teaspoon oregano.
• **Cook** chicken in a grilling skillet or lightly greased nonstick skillet over medium-high heat about 4 minutes on each side or until done. Set chicken aside.
• **Combine** pizza sauce, basil, and remaining ¼ teaspoon oregano in skillet; cook over medium-high heat until thoroughly heated.
• **Remove** from heat; add chicken, and keep warm.
• **Place** rolls on a baking sheet; spread sauce evenly on bottom half of each roll; top evenly with chicken, zucchini, and cheeses.
• **Broil** 3 inches from heat (with electric oven door partially opened) 2 to 3 minutes or until cheese melts. Cover with tops of rolls. **Yield:** 4 servings.

Shirley M. Draper
Winter Park, Florida

Down by the River

Once crab season rolls around, Janet and Butch Kemp

of Easton, Maryland, find time and reason to organize large,

often spontaneous, gatherings of family and friends to reap

the benefits of the Atlantic blue crab's seasonal migration

to the tidal waters of the Miles River. The river's gentle lapping

provides an easy cadence for the evening's festivities.

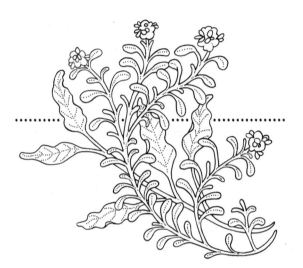

The Kemps' crab feasts are a celebration of Maryland's best. "We serve all the things that are most plentiful: crab, vegetables from our garden, and fresh berries and melons for dessert," says Janet. "Friends and family members each bring a favorite dish or crab specialty to add to the table of summertime dishes. Everyone traps their own crabs and brings them, still alive, to the party for steaming. Even the children like to participate."

The Kemps' feast includes everything from Janet's Hot Crabmeat Dip to her mother-in-law Ann Kemp's traditional Spoonbread. Ever popular Crab Imperial and several varieties of crab cakes add to the celebration.

"It's an easy, relaxed way of enjoying the land, the season, and our friends and family," Butch says. "And it leaves us with lots of wonderful memories."

HOT CRABMEAT DIP

Serve crackers, slices of French bread, or fresh vegetables alongside this rich, creamy appetizer.

3 (8-ounce) packages cream cheese
1 small onion, grated
⅔ cup mayonnaise or salad
   dressing
½ teaspoon garlic powder
½ teaspoon salt
½ teaspoon pepper
¼ cup dry white wine or dry
   vermouth
2 teaspoons prepared mustard
2 teaspoons prepared horseradish
1 pound fresh lump crabmeat,
   drained
2 tablespoons chopped fresh chives
2 tablespoons chopped fresh
   parsley

• **Combine** first 9 ingredients in a saucepan; cook, stirring constantly, over medium heat until cream cheese melts.
• **Stir** in crabmeat and remaining ingredients. Transfer to a chafing dish, and keep warm. **Yield:** 6 cups.

Janet Kemp
Easton, Maryland

FRIED SOFT-SHELL CRABS

Atlantic blue crabs that have shed their hard shells to grow new larger ones are known as softshells. Available from April through September, these crabs are considered a delicacy. When fried to a golden crispness, they do not need to be peeled before eaten.

3 large eggs
½ teaspoon ground black
   pepper
12 soft-shell crabs, cleaned
1½ cups cornmeal
1 cup all-purpose flour
2 teaspoons baking powder
¾ teaspoon salt
½ teaspoon ground black
   pepper
½ teaspoon garlic powder
⅛ teaspoon ground red pepper
Vegetable oil

• **Combine** eggs and ½ teaspoon black pepper in a large shallow dish, stirring to combine. Add crabs, turning to coat. Let stand 10 minutes.
• **Combine** cornmeal and next 6 ingredients. Remove crabs from egg mixture, and dredge in cornmeal mixture. Let stand 5 minutes; dredge in cornmeal mixture again.
• **Pour** oil to depth of ½ inch into an electric skillet or large heavy skillet; heat to 375°. Fry crabs 2 minutes on each side or until browned. Drain on paper towels; serve immediately. **Yield:** 1 dozen.

Note: Sprinkle fried crabs with seafood seasoning, if desired.

Bruce Robson
Salisbury, Maryland

CHESAPEAKE BAY CRAB CAKES

1 large egg
4 saltine crackers, crushed
1½ teaspoons dried parsley flakes
¾ teaspoon Old Bay seasoning
½ teaspoon Worcestershire sauce
3 or 4 drops of hot sauce
⅛ teaspoon freshly ground pepper
3 tablespoons mayonnaise or salad dressing
1 pound lump crabmeat, drained
3 tablespoons mayonnaise or salad dressing
½ teaspoon Old Bay seasoning
Paprika
Tartar Sauce

● **Combine** first 8 ingredients; stir in crabmeat.
● **Shape** into 6 (3-inch) patties. Place on a lightly greased baking sheet.
● **Combine** 3 tablespoons mayonnaise and ½ teaspoon Old Bay seasoning; spread evenly on crab cakes. Sprinkle with paprika.
● **Bake** at 350° for 20 minutes or until lightly golden. (Do not overbake.) Serve with Tartar Sauce. **Yield:** 6 crab cakes.

Tartar Sauce

1 cup mayonnaise or salad dressing
1 teaspoon Dijon mustard
1½ tablespoons finely chopped fresh parsley
1½ tablespoons chopped capers
1 hard-cooked egg, finely chopped
1 tablespoon sweet pickle relish
1 tablespoon chopped fresh chives

● **Combine** all ingredients; cover and chill. **Yield:** 1 cup.

Susan Smith
Easton, Maryland

"Summer's longer days give us more chances to get together with friends. And, with the river at our front door, we often plan our parties around the water. Everyone loves to gather at the boathouse."

— *Butch Kemp*

Blue crabs find their way from the deeper ocean waters to the shallow waters of Maryland, the southeastern seaboard, Florida, and the Gulf Coast. From June through September, fish markets peddle their catch to eager folks waiting to partake of the crustaceans' sweet meat.

If you're landlocked, don't despair. We found fresh crab available via overnight shipment from the following sources:

Captain's Ketch, Easton, Maryland; 1-800-254-7177.
Higgins Crab House, St. Michaels, Maryland; (410) 745-5056 or fax (410) 745-5628.
Obrycki's, Baltimore, Maryland; 1-800-742-1741 or (410) 732-8862 (in the Baltimore area).

Note: All crab is shipped steamed and chilled, ready to reheat by steaming.

CRAB IMPERIAL

Fresh lump crabmeat joins a rich, sherried white sauce in this classic Maryland entrée.

3 tablespoons butter or margarine
2 tablespoons chopped onion
2 tablespoons chopped green pepper
2 tablespoons all-purpose flour
½ cup milk
1 pound fresh lump crabmeat, drained
½ teaspoon Old Bay seasoning
¼ teaspoon ground black pepper
¼ cup mayonnaise or salad dressing
1 tablespoon dry sherry
¼ teaspoon Worcestershire sauce
Paprika

● **Melt** butter in a large skillet over medium-high heat; add onion and green pepper, and cook, stirring constantly, until vegetables are tender.
● **Combine** flour and milk, stirring well. Add to vegetable mixture, and cook about 2 minutes or until thickened, stirring often.
● **Add** crabmeat and next 5 ingredients. Spoon into a greased 2-quart baking dish or individual baking shells. Sprinkle with paprika.
● **Bake** at 350° for 20 to 25 minutes or until bubbly. **Yield:** 6 servings.

Kim Balderson
Trappe, Maryland

SWEET CORN SALSA

This stir-together mixture works equally well as a relish with grilled fish or chicken or as an appetizer with chips.

2   cups fresh whole kernel white
     corn
2   large tomatoes, diced
1   large jalapeño pepper, seeded
     and diced
3   green onions, sliced
½   cup finely chopped purple
     onion
⅓   cup chopped fresh
     parsley
¼   cup finely chopped sweet red
     pepper
1   (4½-ounce) can chopped
     green chiles, undrained
½   cup olive oil
⅓   cup red wine vinegar
2   tablespoons lemon juice
½   teaspoon ground cumin
¼   teaspoon salt
¼   teaspoon pepper
¼   teaspoon hot sauce

• **Combine** all ingredients, and toss gently. Cover and chill at least 2 hours or overnight. **Yield:** 5 cups.

SPOONBREAD

1   quart milk
1   cup yellow cornmeal
1   cup butter or margarine,
     melted
2   tablespoons sugar
1   teaspoon salt
4   large eggs, separated

• **Place** milk in top of a double boiler; bring water to a boil over medium heat. Cook until milk is hot. Gradually add cornmeal, stirring constantly with a whisk.
• **Cook,** stirring constantly, 7 minutes or until mixture is thickened. Remove from heat; stir in butter, sugar, and salt. Set aside.
• **Beat** egg yolks lightly in a large bowl until thick and pale. Gradually stir about one-fourth of hot mixture into yolks; add to remaining hot mixture, stirring constantly.
• **Beat** egg whites at high speed with an electric mixer until soft peaks form; fold into cornmeal mixture.
• **Pour** into a lightly greased 2-quart baking dish; place in a 13- x 9- x 2-inch baking pan. Add water to pan to depth of 1 inch.
• **Bake** at 325° for 1 hour or until set. **Yield:** 8 servings.

Ann Kemp
Easton, Maryland

FROM OUR KITCHEN TO YOURS

. . . .

If Eve had presented Adam with a crab instead of an apple, all of human history might have changed. Imagine Adam's consternation – "You want me to eat *that*?"

History doesn't tell us who ate the first crab, but you can bet they made fools of themselves doing it. After all, properly consuming this irascible crustacean demands considerable insight – the sort needed to operate one of those universal shower controls without severely scalding yourself. If you've mastered the latter, you can accomplish the former. Just heed the following steps.

Step 1: *Make sure that the crab is dead* by either steaming, poaching, or harpooning. The importance of this cannot be overstated. Attempting to eat a live crab will greatly annoy him. Remember, he has sharp claws, and you only have a brain. In a fair fight, claws beat brain tissue hands down.

Step 2: Turn the crab over on his back. Notice the leverlike appendage that fits into a slot on his belly. This is known as the apron or "tail flap." Pry this up and pull it off.

Step 3: Turn the crab right side up and rip off the top shell. Discard it.

Step 4: Here is where the fun really starts. Look inside the crab for the feathery, grayish white gills, often colorfully referred to as "dead man's fingers." Don't eat them, no matter how tasty they sound.

Step 5: Note the yellowish gunk between where the gills used to be. This is fat, also known as "mustard." Some folks consider it a great delicacy. Best get rid of it. Then remove the crab's stomach or "sand bag." Why call it a sand bag? Because if you knew what was really inside it, you'd lose your stomach for this whole operation.

Step 6: Twist off the claws and legs. Then grasp the remaining body on each side and snap it in half. Use a nutcracker or mallet to crack the shells of the claws and body parts, exposing the meat. Cultured folk use dainty cocktail forks to genteelly pick out the meat. The other 99.9% of us use our fingers, which smell like seasoning for two days afterward.

FINAL Step: Gleefully consume the two ounces of crabmeat it took you 15 minutes to expose. The calories provided and the energy expended are exactly equal. This means you can literally eat crabs forever – you'll never get fat and you'll never leave the table. And you'll never have to clean up.

A DELIGHTFUL MIX-UP

What a joy it is to mingle sauces, seasonings, chicken or beef, vegetables, and rice in one dish. With our stir-fry recipes you can create colorful and flavorful meals fast. You'll find that many of the ingredients for these recipes are ones you probably have on hand. And because they're quick to prepare, dinner's ready chop-chop – in about 15 minutes. Fast enough? You bet, especially when you discover how delicious they are.

PEANUTTY BEEF STIR-FRY

1¼ pounds lean boneless top
    sirloin steak
3 tablespoons reduced-sodium soy
    sauce
2 to 3 tablespoons brown sugar
2 tablespoons creamy peanut
    butter
2 teaspoons lemon juice
½ teaspoon garlic powder
¼ teaspoon dried crushed red
    pepper
¼ teaspoon ground black pepper
2 teaspoons sesame or vegetable oil
1 medium-size sweet red pepper,
    seeded and cut into 1-inch
    pieces
4 green onions, cut into 1-inch
    pieces
Hot cooked rice
Garnish: chopped peanuts

• **Trim** fat from steak, and slice steak diagonally across grain into ⅛-inch strips; set aside.
• **Combine** soy sauce and next 6 ingredients, stirring with a whisk until blended; set aside.
• **Pour** oil around top of a preheated nonstick wok or large skillet, coating sides; heat at medium-high (375°) 1 minute. Add steak strips; cook, stirring constantly, 2 minutes. Add sweet red pepper and green onions; cook 2 minutes, stirring constantly. Stir in soy sauce mixture; cover and cook 3 minutes or until thoroughly heated. Serve over rice. Garnish, if desired. **Yield:** 4 servings.

CHICKEN AND SNOW PEA STIR-FRY

¾ cup chicken broth
¼ cup soy sauce
2 tablespoons cornstarch
1 tablespoon peanut or vegetable
    oil
2 skinned and boned chicken
    breast halves, cut into ¼-inch
    strips
1½ cups sliced celery
¼ pound fresh snow pea pods
4 large mushrooms, sliced
3 green onions, sliced
½ cup slivered almonds, toasted
Hot cooked rice

• **Combine** first 3 ingredients in a small bowl; set aside.
• **Pour** oil around top of a preheated nonstick wok or large skillet, coating sides; heat at medium-high (375°) 1 minute. Add chicken; cook, stirring constantly, 4 minutes or until chicken is almost done.
• **Add** celery and next 3 ingredients, and cook, stirring constantly, 3 to 4 minutes or until vegetables are tender and chicken is done. Stir in almonds.
• **Stir** in broth mixture, and cook, stirring constantly, until mixture thickens and boils. Boil 1 minute, stirring constantly. Serve over rice. **Yield:** 2 servings.

Mrs. Lee Good
Wheeling, West Virginia

CONVENIENT VEGETABLE STIR-FRY

Convenience products offer the fastest and, with this recipe, the tastiest way to stir-fry.

1 (4½-ounce) package boil-in-bag
    brown and wild rice mix
3 tablespoons cashew halves
1 tablespoon peanut or vegetable
    oil
1 (16-ounce) package frozen
    broccoli, carrots, water
    chestnuts, and red peppers
1½ tablespoons cornstarch
¾ teaspoon chicken-flavored
    bouillon granules
½ teaspoon garlic powder
⅛ teaspoon ground ginger
¾ cup water
1½ tablespoons soy sauce

• **Prepare** rice according to package directions; keep warm.
• **Cook** cashews in oil in a large skillet over medium-high heat, stirring constantly, until lightly browned; remove from skillet, and set aside.
• **Add** vegetables to skillet, and cook, stirring constantly, 6 to 8 minutes or until tender.
• **Combine** cornstarch and next 3 ingredients; stir in water and soy sauce. Add to vegetables in skillet, and cook, stirring constantly, 4 minutes or until thickened and bubbly. Stir in cashews, and serve immediately over cooked rice mix. **Yield:** 2 to 3 servings.

WINNING WAYS OF SOUTHERN COOKS

······················

It all started when Bessie Burk won the National Catfish Recipe Contest in 1980. Her daughter, Mary Louise Lever, joined her in the winner's circle in 1987 with an entry in the national Old El Paso Contest. And to date, these two Rome, Georgia, residents have won more than 40 local, state, and national first prizes. Bessie set the winning pace early. But in the past seven years, Mary Louise has taken the lead with some 30 first-place awards. Here's a sampling of their winners.

BURK'S FARM-RAISED CATFISH FRY

6 (¾- to 1-pound) farm-raised
   catfish fillets
1 cup buttermilk
1½ to 2 tablespoons salt
1 tablespoon pepper
1½ cups self-rising cornmeal
½ cup self-rising flour
1½ to 2 quarts peanut oil

• **Make** shallow diagonal cuts 2 inches apart in thickest portion of sides of fish. Place in a large, shallow dish.
• **Combine** buttermilk, salt, and pepper; pour over fish. Cover and marinate in refrigerator at least 8 hours, turning fish fillets occasionally.
• **Remove** fish from marinade, discarding marinade.
• **Combine** cornmeal and flour. Dredge fish in cornmeal mixture, coating completely.
• **Pour** peanut oil to depth of 1½ inches into a large deep skillet; heat oil to 370°. Fry fish, two at a time, about 6 minutes or until golden. Drain well on paper towels. Repeat procedure with remaining fish. Serve immediately. **Yield:** 6 servings.

Bessie Burk
Rome, Georgia

CHICKEN LASAGNA FLORENTINE

6 lasagna noodles, uncooked
1 (10-ounce) package frozen
   chopped spinach, thawed
2 cups chopped cooked
   chicken
2 cups (8 ounces) shredded
   Cheddar cheese
⅓ cup finely chopped
   onion
¼ to ½ teaspoon freshly ground
   nutmeg
1 tablespoon cornstarch
½ teaspoon salt
¼ teaspoon pepper
1 tablespoon soy sauce
1 (10¾-ounce) can cream of
   mushroom soup, undiluted
1 (8-ounce) carton sour
   cream
1 (4.5-ounce) jar sliced
   mushrooms, drained
⅓ cup mayonnaise or salad
   dressing
1 cup (4 ounces) freshly grated
   Parmesan cheese
Butter-Pecan Topping

• **Cook** noodles according to package directions; drain and set aside.
• **Drain** spinach well, pressing between layers of paper towels.
• **Combine** spinach, chicken, and next 11 ingredients in a large bowl; stir well.
• **Arrange** 2 noodles in a lightly greased 11- x 7- x 1½-inch baking dish. Spread half of chicken mixture over noodles. Repeat procedure with remaining noodles and chicken mixture. Sprinkle with Parmesan cheese and Butter-Pecan Topping.
• **Cover** and bake at 350° for 55 to 60 minutes or until hot and bubbly. Let stand 15 minutes before cutting. **Yield:** 8 servings.

Butter-Pecan Topping

2 tablespoons butter or
   margarine
1 cup chopped pecans

• **Melt** butter in a skillet over medium heat; add pecans, and cook 3 minutes. Cool completely. **Yield:** 1 cup.

MESQUITE-GINGER BEEF WITH FRESH FRUIT RELISH
(pictured on page 147)

3 tablespoons balsamic vinegar
2 teaspoons ground red pepper
2 teaspoons mesquite-flavored
   barbecue seasoning
2 teaspoons brown sugar
2 teaspoons minced fresh ginger
2 cloves garlic, minced
3 tablespoons sesame oil
4 (1¼-inch-thick) beef tenderloin
   steaks (4 to 6 ounces each)
1 tablespoon canola oil
Fresh Fruit Relish
Garnish: watercress sprigs

• **Combine** first 7 ingredients in a shallow dish or heavy-duty, zip-top plastic bag; add steaks. Cover or seal, and chill 1½ hours, turning steaks occasionally.
• **Remove** steaks from marinade, discarding marinade.
• **Pour** canola oil into a heavy nonstick skillet; place over medium heat until hot. Add steaks, and cook 4 to 6 minutes on each side or to desired degree of doneness. Serve with Fresh Fruit Relish. Garnish, if desired. **Yield:** 4 servings.

Fresh Fruit Relish

1 cup peeled, finely chopped
   mango
½ cup finely chopped fresh
   pineapple
¼ cup chopped sweet red pepper
¼ cup finely chopped green pepper
3 tablespoons thinly sliced green
   onions
3 tablespoons chopped fresh
   watercress
¼ teaspoon dry mustard
2 teaspoons balsamic vinegar
2 teaspoons fresh lime juice

• **Combine** all ingredients; cover and chill. Serve with a slotted spoon. **Yield:** 2 cups.

Mary Louise Lever
Rome, Georgia

MAJORCAN MUSHROOM TAPAS

This appetizer won the $12,000, 16-day trip to Spain in the 1994 Bays English Muffin Contest.

⅓ cup finely chopped shallots
1 teaspoon minced garlic
1 to 2 tablespoons olive oil
¾ pound mixed fresh mushrooms, thinly sliced *
2 tablespoons dry sherry or Madeira wine
½ teaspoon salt
1 tablespoon finely chopped fresh thyme or 1 teaspoon dried thyme
5 English muffins, split and lightly toasted
12 ounces mascarpone or cream cheese, softened
Almond-Garlic Streusel
Garnish: fresh thyme

• **Cook** shallot and garlic in oil over medium-high heat, stirring constantly, until tender. Add mushrooms, sherry, and salt; cook, stirring constantly, 10 to 12 minutes or until mushrooms are tender. Stir in thyme, and cook until most of liquid evaporates.
• **Spread** muffins with cheese; top evenly with mushroom mixture. Place muffins on a baking sheet.
• **Bake** at 350° for 5 minutes or until thoroughly heated. Remove from oven, and spoon Almond-Garlic Streusel over mushroom mixture. Garnish, if desired. **Yield:** 10 appetizer servings.

* Substitute button, cremini, oyster, and/or shiitake mushrooms for mixed fresh mushrooms.

Almond-Garlic Streusel

1 English muffin
2½ teaspoons olive oil
3 cloves garlic, minced
¼ teaspoon freshly ground black pepper
¼ cup chopped slivered almonds

• **Place** muffin in container of an electric blender; process until fine crumbs.
• **Combine** crumbs, olive oil, and remaining ingredients in a large skillet; cook over medium-high heat 3 to 5 minutes or until crumbs and almonds are golden. Spread on a paper plate or paper towel to cool. **Yield:** 1 cup.

SHREDS OF GARDEN GOODNESS

....

Let a grater turn that heap of zucchini biding time in your kitchen into a bounty of colorful, versatile dishes. Consider these recipes a "grate" way to feast on freshness.

SWEET ZUCCHINI RELISH

10 cups grated zucchini (about 5 pounds)
4 cups chopped onion
¼ cup salt
5 cups sugar
2¼ cups white vinegar (5% acidity)
1 tablespoon celery seeds
1 tablespoon ground turmeric
1 tablespoon pepper

• **Combine** first 3 ingredients in a large bowl. Cover and chill at least 8 hours.
• **Transfer** zucchini to a colander; rinse under cold running water. Drain zucchini well, and press between layers of paper towels.
• **Combine** zucchini mixture, sugar, and remaining ingredients in a Dutch oven. Bring to a boil over medium-high heat; reduce heat to medium, and simmer 30 minutes, stirring often.
• **Pack** hot mixture into hot jars, filling to ½ inch from top. Remove air bubbles; wipe jar rims. Cover at once with metal lids, and screw on bands.
• **Process** in boiling-water bath 15 minutes. **Yield:** 9 half pints.

Marge Killmon
Annandale, Virginia

MOCK CRAB CAKES

2 cups grated zucchini (about 2 large)
2 large eggs, lightly beaten
1 cup fine, dry breadcrumbs
3 green onions, chopped
2 to 3 teaspoons Old Bay seasoning
1 teaspoon mayonnaise or salad dressing
Vegetable oil
Tartar sauce (optional)

• **Drain** zucchini well, pressing between layers of paper towels.
• **Combine** zucchini and next 5 ingredients in a large bowl. Divide mixture into 8 portions, shaping each into a patty. (Mixture will be soft.)
• **Pour** oil to depth of ½ inch into a large heavy skillet. Fry patties in hot oil over medium-high heat 2 minutes on each side. Drain on paper towels; serve with tartar sauce, if desired. **Yield:** 8 cakes.

Betty Brooks
Martinsburg, West Virginia

ZUCCHINI

....

Don't let its green color fool you. Zucchini is a summer squash. Although it's available year-round in most grocery stores, it's at the peak of freshness in late spring.

■ When selecting zucchini, choose firm ones that are small with tender skins, free of blemishes, and vibrant in color.

■ You can store zucchini in a heavy-duty, zip-top plastic bag in the refrigerator up to five days.

■ Just before cooking, wash zucchini and trim the ends; peeling isn't required.

ZUCCHINI-PINEAPPLE CAKE

"This is my daughter's annual request for her birthday cake. We love to have guests guess the secret ingredient – zucchini!" – Judith Randall

2 cups grated zucchini (about 2 large)
3 large eggs
1½ cups sugar
1 tablespoon vanilla extract
1 cup vegetable oil
3 cups all-purpose flour
1 teaspoon baking soda
½ teaspoon baking powder
¼ teaspoon salt
1 teaspoon ground cinnamon
1 cup chopped pecans
½ cup raisins
1 (15¼-ounce) can crushed pineapple, drained
Pineapple-Cream Cheese Frosting

• **Drain** zucchini well, pressing between layers of paper towels. Set aside.
• **Beat** eggs at medium speed with an electric mixer until thick and pale. Gradually add sugar, vanilla, and oil, beating well. Stir in zucchini.
• **Combine** flour and next 4 ingredients; gradually stir into zucchini mixture. Stir in pecans, raisins, and pineapple. Pour into 3 greased and floured 8-inch round cakepans.
• **Bake** at 325° for 35 minutes or until a wooden pick inserted in center comes out clean. Cool in pans on wire racks 10 minutes; remove from pans, and cool completely on wire racks.
• **Spread** Pineapple-Cream Cheese Frosting between layers and on top of cake. (The frosting is soft, and recipe works best if sides of cake are left unfrosted.) Cover and chill. **Yield:** one 3-layer cake.

Pineapple-Cream Cheese Frosting

1 (8-ounce) can crushed pineapple, undrained
1 (8-ounce) package cream cheese, softened
¼ cup butter or margarine, softened
1 (16-ounce) package powdered sugar, sifted

• **Place** pineapple in a wire-mesh strainer; press with back of spoon against the sides of the strainer to squeeze out liquid. Set pineapple aside, and discard liquid.
• **Beat** cream cheese and butter at medium speed with an electric mixer until fluffy; gradually stir in powdered sugar and pineapple. (Frosting will be soft and may be refrigerated 1 hour before spreading over cake.) **Yield:** 3 cups.

Judith Randall
Port Charlotte, Florida

OPEN A CAN OF PROMISES

....

Remember when you whacked the can of refrigerated biscuits over the edge of your kitchen counter to get them to open? Then pop! White, doughy biscuits – unbaked promises – peeped from inside a cardboard can. But that's not just a memory – that's tonight's dinner and tomorrow's brunch.

Toss those biscuits with zippy salsa or fold them around cream cheese. Add a fruit glaze or sprinkle them with nuts. Enhancing the basic biscuit certainly works for busy cooks.

NUTTY ORANGE COFFEE CAKE

¾ cup sugar
½ cup chopped pecans
2 teaspoons grated orange rind
½ (8-ounce) package reduced-fat cream cheese
2 (11-ounce) cans refrigerated buttermilk biscuits
½ cup butter or margarine, melted
1 cup sifted powdered sugar
2 tablespoons fresh orange juice

• **Combine** first 3 ingredients in a small bowl; set aside.
• **Place** about 1 teaspoon cream cheese on half of each biscuit; fold biscuit over cheese, pressing edges to seal.
• **Dip** biscuits in melted butter, and dredge in sugar mixture; place, curved side down, in a lightly greased 12-cup Bundt pan, spacing evenly. Drizzle any remaining butter over biscuits; sprinkle with any remaining sugar mixture.
• **Bake** at 350° for 40 minutes or until done. Immediately invert onto a serving plate.
• **Combine** powdered sugar and orange juice, stirring well; drizzle over warm coffee cake. Serve immediately. **Yield:** one 10-inch coffee cake.

Barbara Kennedy
Fort Pierce, Florida

LEMON-CHEESE PARTY BITES

1 (10-ounce) can refrigerated flaky buttermilk biscuits
1 (5-ounce) can refrigerated flaky buttermilk biscuits
1 (8-ounce) package cream cheese
¾ cup sifted powdered sugar
1½ tablespoons lemon juice

• **Separate** each biscuit into 3 or 4 layers.
• **Cut** cream cheese into 48 cubes. Wrap each cube with a biscuit layer, pinching edges to seal; place on lightly greased baking sheets.
• **Bake** at 400° for 8 to 10 minutes or until bites are golden; remove to wire racks to cool.
• **Combine** sugar and lemon juice; drizzle over bites. **Yield:** 4 dozen.

Note: You can bake any remaining biscuits according to package directions, if desired.

Mildred Bickley
Bristol, Virginia

MEXICAN FIESTA SPOON BISCUITS

1 (17.3-ounce) can large
   refrigerated buttermilk
   biscuits
1 (10.8-ounce) can large
   refrigerated buttermilk
   biscuits
1 (16-ounce) jar chunky salsa
2 cups (8 ounces) shredded
   Monterey Jack cheese
1 small green pepper, seeded and
   chopped
½ cup sliced green onions
1 (2¼-ounce) can sliced ripe
   olives, drained

• **Cut** each biscuit into 8 pieces.
• **Combine** biscuits and salsa, tossing gently to coat. Spoon mixture into a lightly greased 13- x 9- x 2-inch baking dish. Top with cheese and remaining ingredients.
• **Bake** at 350° for 45 minutes or until edges are golden and center is set; let stand 15 minutes. Cut into squares, and serve with soup or salad. **Yield:** 15 servings.

La Juan Coward
Jasper, Texas

HERBED BISCUIT RING

3 tablespoons butter or margarine,
   softened
1 teaspoon lemon juice
½ teaspoon celery seeds
¼ teaspoon dried thyme,
   crushed
¼ teaspoon paprika
⅛ teaspoon rubbed sage (optional)
1 (11-ounce) can refrigerated
   buttermilk biscuits

• **Combine** first 6 ingredients; spread over biscuits.
• **Arrange** biscuits in a circle in an 8-inch round cakepan, overlapping edges.
• **Bake** at 400° for 12 to 15 minutes or until golden. Serve immediately. **Yield:** 10 servings.

Marie Davis
Charlotte, North Carolina

LIGHT NIGHT OUT

If you think a low-fat restaurant meal has to be a plain baked potato and a plate of lettuce, stop torturing yourself. A light dinner out doesn't have to be boring, and these recipes prove it.

■ **Chefs' Café** is a small restaurant tacked onto a motel on the south side of Buckhead in Atlanta. Chef Georges Martin and owner Michael Tuohy serve what they call fresh, seasonal American cuisine.

The menu takes advantage of fresh produce, highlighting the foods of the Mediterranean.

If you're watching salt or fat, let your server know. Georges will alter any of his dishes to comply with your requests.

GRILLED PORK TENDERLOIN WITH APPLES, CELERY, AND POTATOES

6 small new potatoes (10 ounces)
⅓ cup chopped purple onion
Vegetable cooking spray
2 Granny Smith apples, cored and
   chopped
⅓ cup dry white wine
2 (10-ounce) pork tenderloins,
   trimmed
¼ teaspoon salt
¼ teaspoon freshly ground pepper
1 shallot, finely chopped
1 tablespoon olive oil
2 stalks celery, thinly sliced
1 tablespoon chopped fresh
   rosemary
⅔ cup white wine vinegar
2 tablespoons sugar
1 tablespoon chopped fresh
   parsley

• **Bake** potatoes at 350° for 20 minutes or until tender; cool. Cut potatoes into quarters; set aside.
• **Cook** onion in a saucepan coated with cooking spray over medium heat until tender. Add apple and wine; bring to a boil. Reduce heat, and simmer 10 minutes. Remove from heat, and set aside.
• **Sprinkle** pork with salt and pepper.
• **Cook** pork, covered with grill lid, over medium-hot coals (350° to 400°) about 20 minutes or until meat thermometer inserted in thickest part registers 170°, turning once.
• **Cook** shallot in olive oil in a large nonstick skillet over medium-high heat, stirring constantly, until lightly browned. Stir in potato, apple mixture, celery, and rosemary. Cook 1 minute or until mixture is thoroughly heated. Place on serving plates, top with sliced pork, and keep warm.
• **Add** vinegar and sugar to skillet, stirring to dissolve sugar and scraping any particles that cling to bottom. Cook 3 to 5 minutes or until reduced by half.
• **Drizzle** over sliced pork and apple; sprinkle with chopped parsley. **Yield:** 4 servings.

Chefs' Café
Atlanta, Georgia

♥ Per serving: Calories 446 (41% from fat)
Fat 20.1g (6g saturated) Cholesterol 101mg
Sodium 255mg Carbohydrate 32.5g
Fiber 4.2g Protein 32.2g

MARINATED GRILLED VEGETABLES

Don't let the long ingredient list discourage you from making this delicious recipe. It's simply a variety of vegetables marinated in a vinaigrette dressing and then grilled.

½ cup balsamic vinegar
¼ cup extra virgin olive oil
2 tablespoons dry white wine
1 tablespoon finely chopped shallot
½ tablespoon minced garlic
½ tablespoon freshly ground black pepper
1 teaspoon kosher salt
4 new potatoes, unpeeled
4 Roma tomatoes, cut in half lengthwise
3 small zucchini, cut in half lengthwise
2 ears yellow corn, cut into 3-inch pieces
2 purple onions, cut into ¾-inch slices
2 portabello mushrooms, quartered
1 pound fresh asparagus, trimmed
1 small eggplant, cut lengthwise into 1-inch slices
1 sweet red pepper, quartered
1 sweet yellow pepper, quartered
1 tablespoon chopped fresh chives
1 tablespoon chopped fresh rosemary
1 tablespoon chopped fresh parsley

• **Combine** first 7 ingredients in a large bowl; set aside.
• **Cook** potatoes in boiling water 5 minutes; drain. Cut potatoes in half.
• **Add** potato, tomato, and next 8 ingredients to vinegar mixture; toss gently to coat. Let stand about 1 hour, tossing occasionally.
• **Remove** vegetables from marinade; reserving marinade.
• **Cook** vegetables, covered with grill lid, over medium-hot coals (350° to 400°) 12 to 14 minutes, turning once.

Remove vegetables from grill as they are done.
• **Drizzle** remaining marinade over cooked vegetables, and arrange on serving plates.
• **Combine** chopped chives, rosemary, and parsley; sprinkle over vegetables. **Yield:** 8 servings.

*Chefs' Café
Atlanta, Georgia*

♥ Per serving: Calories 218 (29% from fat) Fat 7.7g (1.1g saturated) Cholesterol 0mg Sodium 312mg Carbohydrate 36g Fiber 6.1g Protein 6.1g

■ Anne Quatrano and Clifford Harrison of Atlanta's **Bacchanalia** have learned to add a touch of Southern flavor to unexpected dishes. They feature their version of New American cuisine on menus that change weekly.

SESAME-CRUSTED SALMON WITH GINGER VINAIGRETTE

You've got to try this – it's the highest-rated salmon recipe we've ever published. Look for the footlong seedless English cucumbers sealed in plastic wrap in the produce section.

1 large English cucumber, peeled and coarsely chopped
½ cup rice wine vinegar
⅛ teaspoon salt
2 tablespoons sugar
¼ cup water
¼ cup low-sodium soy sauce
2 tablespoons rice wine vinegar
1 tablespoon honey
1 teaspoon hot sauce
½ teaspoon ground coriander
½ teaspoon dark sesame oil
4 (4-ounce) salmon fillets
1 tablespoon sesame seeds, toasted
1 large English cucumber, thinly sliced
Ginger Vinaigrette
Garnish: fresh mint sprigs

• **Position** knife blade in food processor bowl; add chopped English cucumber. Process until smooth, stopping once to scrape down sides.
• **Line** a large wire-mesh strainer with cheesecloth or a coffee filter; pour cucumber mixture through strainer into a bowl, discarding pulp.
• **Stir** ½ cup vinegar and salt into cucumber liquid; set aside.
• **Combine** sugar and water in a small saucepan; cook over medium heat until mixture boils, stirring often. Remove from heat, and stir into cucumber liquid mixture; set aside.
• **Combine** soy sauce and next 5 ingredients in a small bowl; brush over salmon. Place salmon in a lightly greased 13- x 9- x 2-inch pan; sprinkle with sesame seeds.
• **Bake** fillets at 450° for 10 to 12 minutes or until fish flakes when tested with a fork.
• **Arrange** salmon fillets and sliced cucumber evenly in 4 pasta bowls. Spoon cucumber liquid mixture evenly into each dish. Drizzle with a small amount of Ginger Vinaigrette. Garnish, if desired. **Yield:** 4 servings.

♥ Per serving: Calories 395 (52% from fat) Fat 23.1g (3.8g saturated) Cholesterol 63mg Sodium 744mg Carbohydrate 23.6g Fiber 0.8g Protein 24.7g

Ginger Vinaigrette

1 (1½-inch-long) piece fresh ginger, peeled
1 clove garlic
2 tablespoons rice wine vinegar
1 tablespoon low-sodium soy sauce
1 tablespoon honey
⅛ teaspoon dried crushed red pepper
¼ cup peanut oil
½ teaspoon dark sesame oil

• **Position** knife blade in food processor bowl; add ginger and garlic. Process until smooth, stopping once to scrape down sides.
• **Add** vinegar and next 3 ingredients; process 30 seconds. Slowly pour peanut oil and sesame oil through food

chute with processor running, blending just until smooth. **Yield:** ½ cup.

Bacchanalia
Atlanta, Georgia

♥ Per ¼-cup serving: Calories 147 (84% from fat)
Fat 14g (2.4g saturated) Cholesterol 0mg
Sodium 122mg Carbohydrate 5.6g
Fiber 0.1g Protein 0.3g

PINK GRAPEFRUIT AND TARRAGON SORBET

Serve this herbal refresher before the entrée when you are entertaining formally or as a light dessert for a casual dinner.

2 cups sugar
1 cup water
2 (8-inch) sprigs fresh tarragon, coarsely chopped
4 cups pink grapefruit juice

• **Combine** sugar and water in a heavy saucepan; cook over medium heat, stirring constantly, until sugar dissolves. Add tarragon, and bring to a boil. Remove from heat; stir in grapefruit juice. Cover and chill at least 2 hours.
• **Pour** mixture through a wire-mesh strainer into an 8-inch square pan, discarding tarragon.
• **Freeze** until firm, stirring occasionally with a wire whisk.
• **Let** stand at room temperature about 5 minutes before serving. **Yield:** 6½ cups.

Bacchanalia
Atlanta, Georgia

♥ Per ½-cup serving: Calories 149 (0% from fat)
Fat 0g (0g saturated) Cholesterol 0mg
Sodium 1mg Carbohydrate 37.7g
Fiber 0g Protein 0.4g

■ **Luna Notte's** strip-mall location in the historic Alamo Heights area of San Antonio makes it an ideal spot for people-watching. And Chef Scott Boone and his staff at the Italian restaurant provide you with ample entertainment in the exhibition kitchen.

RISOTTO PRIMAVERA
(pictured on page 111)

Short-grained, high-starch Arborio rice is essential when making risotto. The finished dish should be al dente: *tender, yet firm to the bite.*

¼ cup julienne-sliced carrot
4½ cups reduced-sodium, fat-free chicken broth
2 tablespoons butter, divided
1 shallot, finely chopped
1 clove garlic, minced
1¼ cups Arborio rice
¼ teaspoon salt
¼ teaspoon pepper
¼ cup thinly sliced purple onion
¼ cup thinly sliced zucchini
¼ cup thinly sliced yellow squash
¼ cup arugula
2 tablespoons chopped fresh basil
2 tablespoons chopped fresh oregano
3 tablespoons chopped walnuts, toasted
⅓ cup crumbled blue cheese
Garnish: fresh oregano

• **Cover** carrot with boiling water, and boil 1 minute. Drain; rinse with cold water. Set aside.
• **Cook** broth in a saucepan over medium heat until thoroughly heated.
• **Melt** 1 tablespoon butter in a large skillet over medium-high heat; add chopped shallot and garlic, and cook 2 minutes, stirring constantly.
• **Add** rice, and cook 5 minutes or until translucent. Reduce heat to medium.
• **Add** warm chicken broth, ½ cup at a time, stirring constantly, allowing liquid to absorb between additions. Stir in salt and pepper. Set aside.
• **Melt** remaining 1 tablespoon butter in a skillet over medium-high heat; add onion, and cook until lightly browned.
• **Add** carrot, zucchini, and yellow

squash; cook, stirring constantly, about 5 minutes or until tender. Add arugula, and cook 1 minute.
• **Stir** vegetable mixture into rice mixture. Stir in basil and oregano. Sprinkle with chopped walnuts and crumbled blue cheese; garnish, if desired. Serve immediately. **Yield:** 3 cups.

Luna Notte
San Antonio, Texas

♥ Per ½-cup serving: Calories 263 (33% from fat)
Fat 9.4g (4.5g saturated) Cholesterol 20mg
Sodium 277mg Carbohydrate 36.2g
Fiber 1.2g Protein 6.3g

POLENTA'S NOT SO POSH

Polenta is finding its way onto more and more restaurant menus these days, but it's really nothing new. Southerners know this traditional Italian dish better as "cornmeal mush."

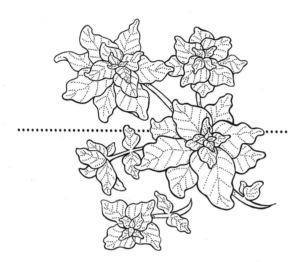

Because we all have less time for home cooking these days, fashionable eateries are offering down-home basics all dressed up. Fresh rosemary and garlic now add zip to basic roasted chicken, pesto perks up plain mashed potatoes, and polenta is appearing in more shapes and flavors than you can imagine.

Here we share some of *our* favorite ideas on flavoring, shaping, reheating, and topping our Basic Polenta recipe. They're sure to get you headed back into the kitchen.

BASIC POLENTA
(pictured on page 74)

Technically, polenta is a coarser grind of cornmeal and is available in some grocery stores, but plain old yellow cornmeal will do nicely.

3½ cups water or milk *
¾ teaspoon salt
1 cup yellow cornmeal

• **Bring** water and salt to a boil over high heat in a heavy saucepan. Gradually add cornmeal, stirring constantly with a wire whisk. Reduce heat, and simmer, whisking often, 10 minutes or until thick and creamy. **Yield:** 3½ cups.

* Substitute 1 (14½-ounce) can ready-to-serve chicken broth and 1¼ cups water for the 3½ cups water or milk. Omit salt.

STIR IN FLAVOR

Choose any of these additions to add flavor to Basic Polenta.

■ Cook 1 to 2 cloves of minced garlic in 2 tablespoons of butter or margarine, and stir into polenta with 2 tablespoons of whipping cream.

■ Add ½ cup toasted, chopped pecans and ¼ cup finely chopped fresh parsley.

■ Stir in ½ cup grated fresh Parmesan cheese.

■ Add ½ cup (2 ounces) shredded mozzarella cheese.

■ Add 1 to 1½ teaspoons dried sage, crushed.

■ Add 1 to 1½ teaspoons dried rosemary, crushed.

■ Add 1 to 1½ teaspoons dried Italian seasoning.

GET IN SHAPE

■ You can serve polenta **soft,** immediately after cooking, as you would grits. Add more liquid, if necessary, and spoon polenta onto serving plates.

■ To make **rectangles,** spoon cooked polenta into a plastic wrap-lined 8½- x 4½- x 3-inch loafpan, smoothing with a spatula. Cover and chill polenta 8 hours. Remove from pan, peel off the plastic wrap, and cut polenta into ½-inch-thick slices. Pan-fry, bake, or broil.

■ For **circles, squares,** or **triangles,** spoon cooked polenta into a lightly greased 11- x 7- x 1½-inch dish. Cover and chill 8 hours. Invert dish, and tap bottom until polenta releases. Remove dish, and cut polenta into shapes with a knife or cookie cutters. Pan-fry, bake, or broil.

HEAT THINGS UP

■ To **pan-fry,** melt butter or margarine in a large skillet; add polenta shapes, and cook 5 minutes on each side or until lightly browned. (Do not crowd skillet or polenta will be difficult to turn.)

■ To **bake,** place shaped polenta on a lightly greased baking sheet. Bake at 425° for 7 minutes or until thoroughly heated and lightly browned.

■ To **broil,** place shaped polenta on a lightly greased baking sheet, and broil 5½ inches from heat (with electric oven door partially opened) 7 minutes or until thoroughly heated and lightly browned.

TOP IT OFF

■ Whether you spoon polenta onto the plate or cut it into elaborate shapes, you'll enjoy what these toppers do for polenta.

SAUSAGE AND PEPPERS
(pictured on page 74)

½ pound Italian link sausage, cut in ¼-inch slices
1 small sweet red pepper, sliced
1 small green pepper, sliced
1 small purple onion, sliced
1 (14½-ounce) can Italian tomatoes, undrained and chopped
½ teaspoon dried Italian seasoning
Freshly grated Parmesan cheese

● **Cook** sausage slices in skillet over medium heat 5 minutes or until browned. Add sliced peppers and onion, and cook 5 minutes or until tender. Drain.
● **Add** tomatoes and Italian seasoning to sausage mixture; cook until thoroughly heated. Spoon mixture over polenta; sprinkle with Parmesan cheese. **Yield:** 2 to 3 servings.

TOMATO, BASIL, AND CHEESE
(pictured on page 74)

Roma tomatoes, thinly sliced
Shredded mozzarella cheese
Chopped fresh basil

● **Layer** tomato slices and shredded mozzarella on polenta shapes; place on a lightly greased baking sheet. Sprinkle with basil.
● **Broil** 5½ inches from heat (with electric oven door partially opened) 4 minutes or until cheese melts. Serve immediately.

EGGS AND CHEESE
(pictured on page 74)

Poached eggs
Shredded Cheddar cheese

● **Place** eggs on polenta, and top with cheese. Serve immediately.

GARLIC AND MUSHROOMS
(pictured on page 74)

½ pound fresh mushrooms, sliced
2 cloves garlic, minced
2 tablespoons butter or margarine

● **Cook** mushrooms and garlic in butter in a skillet over medium heat until tender, stirring often. Spoon over polenta. **Yield:** 1¼ cups.

PEANUTS, POPCORN, AND . . .

. . . .

Forget the major leagues. You don't have to be a pro on the field or in the kitchen to enjoy these snacks. These recipes are so easy, even rookies will have home-run success.

So crank up the VCR and watch your favorite baseball movie with friends, or invite your Little Leaguer's team over for a party.

CARAMEL CRUNCH

12 cups popped popcorn (about ½ cup unpopped)
1 (3-ounce) can chow mein noodles
1 cup dry-roasted peanuts
½ cup raisins
1½ cups firmly packed brown sugar
¾ cup butter or margarine
¾ cup light corn syrup
1 teaspoon ground cinnamon
½ teaspoon baking soda

● **Combine** first 4 ingredients in a lightly greased roasting pan, and set aside.
● **Combine** brown sugar and next 3 ingredients in a large saucepan; cook over medium heat, stirring constantly, 5 minutes or until mixture boils. Remove mixture from heat, and stir in soda (mixture will bubble).
● **Pour** brown sugar mixture over popcorn mixture; stir with a lightly greased long-handled spoon to coat.
● **Bake** at 250° for 1 hour, stirring every 15 minutes. Remove from oven, and immediately pour onto wax paper, breaking apart large clumps as they cool. Store in airtight containers. **Yield:** 4 quarts.

Ann Niedens
Kure Beach, North Carolina

CHILI POPCORN

3 tablespoons butter or margarine, melted
1½ teaspoons chili powder
½ teaspoon salt
½ teaspoon garlic powder
½ teaspoon paprika
12 cups popped popcorn (about ½ cup unpopped)

● Combine first 5 ingredients; drizzle over warm popcorn, stirring to coat. Yield: 3 quarts.

Dorothy Grant
Pensacola, Florida

POP CULTURE

Popcorn is a special variety of dried corn that pops when heated because of the natural moisture trapped inside the hull. When the corn's heated, the moisture evaporates causing immense pressure. When the pressure becomes too great, the hull bursts open, and the kernel's starchy contents explode outward, expanding in volume while turning the kernel inside out.

For our recipes for "Peanuts, Popcorn, and. . ." beginning on page 165, use an air popper, microwave, or skillet.

Our favorite new find is the Presto PowerPop – a microwave popper available at retail and variety stores. It uses any kind of popcorn kernel, so there's no need to buy specially packaged bags. You can use the scantest amount of fat, too. Add pizzazz to your popcorn with herbs and spices such as dried oregano leaves or chili powder added to the oil in which the corn will be popped. Stir in the corn kernels, coating them well; then pop as usual.

WHAT'S FOR SUPPER?

MIX AND MATCH

....

The lazy days of summer are here. Torn between not wanting to slave over a hot cooktop all day and craving fresh produce that's at its peak? Here's the answer to the problem – three simple recipes that are either easily prepared on the cooktop or baked only a short time in the oven. Pair one of these delicious side dishes with your favorite grilled entrée for a perfect warm-weather combination.

These days are meant for enjoyment . . . and so are your meals.

THREE-GRAIN RICE

Orzo looks like short-grain rice, but it's actually pasta. This versatile ingredient can be substituted for rice in most recipes.

⅔ cup orzo, uncooked
2 tablespoons vegetable oil
2 (14½-ounce) cans ready-to-serve chicken broth
½ cup water
⅔ cup wild rice, uncooked
¾ cup long-grain rice, uncooked
1 bay leaf
1 tablespoon chopped fresh thyme or 1 teaspoon dried thyme
1 tablespoon chopped fresh sage or 1 teaspoon rubbed sage
1 teaspoon salt
¼ teaspoon ground white pepper

● Cook orzo in oil in a 3-quart saucepan over medium-high heat, stirring often, until lightly browned. Remove orzo from saucepan, and set aside.
● Add chicken broth, water, and wild rice to saucepan; bring to a boil over medium heat. Cover, reduce heat, and simmer 10 minutes.
● Stir in orzo, long-grain rice, and remaining ingredients. Return to a boil; cover, reduce heat, and simmer 40 minutes or until moisture is absorbed and rice is tender. Remove from heat, and let stand 10 minutes. Remove and discard bay leaf. Yield: 8 servings.

Edie Light
Lynchburg, Virginia

CASHEW CASSEROLE

Serve a fresh spinach salad with this casserole. To complete this meal, offer sherbet for dessert.

1 stalk celery, sliced
1 large carrot, scraped and shredded
1 medium onion, chopped
1 cup sliced fresh mushrooms
Vegetable cooking spray
1 cup cashew nuts, coarsely chopped
1 (8-ounce) can sliced water chestnuts, drained
1 (10¾-ounce) can cream of mushroom soup, undiluted
1¼ cups water
⅛ teaspoon pepper
1 (5-ounce) can chow mein noodles, divided

● Cook first 4 ingredients in a large nonstick skillet coated with cooking spray, stirring constantly until vegetables are tender.
● Add cashews and next 4 ingredients, stirring until blended. Stir in 1 cup chow mein noodles.
● Spoon into 5 (1½-cup) lightly greased casseroles. Sprinkle with remaining noodles.
● Bake at 350° for 20 minutes. Yield: 5 servings.

Note: If you prefer, bake the casserole mixture in a lightly greased 2-quart casserole for 30 minutes. Yield: 6 servings.

Patsy Bell Hobson
Liberty, Missouri

CREAMY PASTA PRIMAVERA

Team colorful, garden-fresh produce like broccoli and carrots with the convenience of salad dressing and frozen snow peas for this quick, refreshing summer dish.

10 ounces fettuccine
2 cups fresh broccoli flowerets
1½ cups thinly sliced carrot
1 (16-ounce) bottle Ranch-style
    salad dressing
1 (6-ounce) package frozen snow
    pea pods, thawed
2 to 3 teaspoons freshly ground
    pepper
¼ cup grated Parmesan
    cheese
2 tablespoons chopped fresh
    parsley

• **Cook** pasta according to package directions, adding broccoli and carrot slices during last 5 minutes of cooking time. Drain.
• **Cook** salad dressing in a large skillet over medium heat until thoroughly heated.
• **Add** noodle mixture, snow peas, and pepper to skillet; toss to coat. Remove from heat; sprinkle with cheese and parsley. Serve immediately. **Yield:** 8 side-dish or 4 main-dish servings.

Lilann Taylor
Savannah, Georgia

PUDDING IS CHILD'S PLAY

. . . .

What comes in a tiny box and turns into wacky fun for kids? Pudding!

Finger painting with pudding is just one of the activities that starts with pudding made from a mix. Kids love it and adults know it's easy to make. So if you're short on time and looking for fun, try one of these kid-approved recipes.

FINGER PAINTING NEVER TASTED SO GOOD

Wear old clothes when you paint with pudding. Afterward, throw away the painting because dried pudding pictures attract ants.

1 (5.1-ounce) package vanilla
    instant pudding mix
2 cups milk
Liquid or paste food coloring
Heavy paper

• **Prepare** pudding according to package directions, using 2 cups milk.
• **Divide** pudding into small bowls; add food coloring to achieve colors.
• **Spread** paper on table or play surface, and let children finger paint, using pudding as paint. **Yield:** 2 cups pudding paint.

BODACIOUS PEANUT PARFAIT

Some kids might prefer this pudding dessert instead of cake and ice cream.

10 peanut-shaped peanut butter
    sandwich cookies, divided
1 (3-ounce) package vanilla
    pudding mix
¼ cup smooth peanut butter
¾ cup fudge sauce

• **Crush** 6 cookies; set aside.
• **Prepare** pudding according to package directions. Remove from heat; add peanut butter, stirring until smooth.
• **Layer** half of pudding evenly into 4 parfait glasses; add half of crushed cookies and half of fudge sauce. Repeat layers with remaining pudding, crushed cookies, and fudge sauce. Arrange a whole cookie on side of each glass. Cover and chill until ready to serve. **Yield:** 4 servings.

A MARTIAN VISIT

. . . .

Has your daughter been feeding the dog without prompting? Does your son consistently make his bed? Are the kids bringing home good grades from school? If so, give them a space-age compliment to remember. It requires only a little preplanning and your most noteworthy theatrical performance.

You and the kids return home. A computer readout is attached to your front door. It says, "Dear Earth Children, as part of my mission to discover your planet's best-behaved kids, I referred to our intergalactic computer system. Your names and photographs repeatedly surfaced as A-#1. For your outstanding behavior, please accept a gift from our Big Green Dessert Machine. Follow the moon rocks to the crater filled with moon rock dust. Add 2 cups of cold cow's milk, and stir for 2 minutes. It will magically turn into cosmic ooze – a favorite food of our Martian children. May Mars' green goodness stay with you forever!"

You open the door and before you is indeed the first of many moon rocks (assorted sizes of crumpled pieces of aluminum foil). The kids follow them to the kitchen and find the crater (a stainless-steel mixing bowl with more aluminum foil crumpled around the outside) filled with a mysterious powder (one 3.9-ounce package of pistachio instant pudding mix). The kids measure 2 cups of milk, and add it to the powder. They stir just as ordered. Whoa! It turns green instantly. And tastes out of this world.

Vacations of sand, sun, and fun are just around the corner – here's a pudding dessert that supplies almost as much fun as being there. Beth Hartley developed this recipe as an alternative to the popular "dirt dessert."

1 (3.4-ounce) package vanilla instant pudding mix
Blue liquid food coloring
1½ cups vanilla wafer crumbs
Shark-shaped chewy candy
Vanilla and chocolate bite-size, bear-shaped graham crackers
Roll-shaped chewy candy
Large marshmallows
Small paper cocktail umbrellas

• **Prepare** pudding according to package directions, adding a few drops of food coloring with milk.
• **Arrange** crumbs in a 9-inch pieplate or shallow dish to resemble a shoreline. Spoon pudding next to crumbs to resemble water.
• **Arrange** shark candies in pudding.
• **Place** a graham cracker bear in center of each roll-shaped candy to resemble floats; arrange in pudding or on crumbs.
• **Place** marshmallows in crumbs, and stick umbrellas in marshmallows. Cover and chill until ready to serve. **Yield:** 4 servings.

Note: For roll-shaped chewy candy, we used GummiSavers.

Beth Hartley
Birmingham, Alabama

SAY HELLO TO DESSERT

This recipe didn't cut it – or at least we couldn't.
The Hello Dolly Dessert slices kept falling apart. But everyone kept sneaking second pieces of the crumbles.
Although the dessert melts in your mouth when warm, it needs to cool completely before cutting. Each slice can then be warmed for a few seconds in the microwave before serving.
The result – perfect slices.

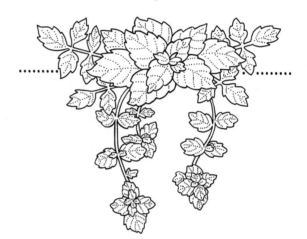

HELLO DOLLY DESSERT

2 cups graham cracker crumbs
¼ cup sugar
2 tablespoons ground cinnamon
½ cup butter or margarine, melted
2½ cups chopped pecans
2 cups (12-ounces) semisweet chocolate morsels
2 (6-ounce) packages white chocolate, finely chopped
1 (14-ounce) package flaked coconut
1 (14-ounce) can sweetened condensed milk

• **Combine** first 3 ingredients; stir in butter. Press into bottom and 1 inch up sides of a 10-inch springform pan.
• **Layer** with chopped pecans, chocolate morsels, white chocolate, and coconut; press down firmly. Pour condensed milk evenly over coconut.
• **Bake** at 350° for 40 to 45 minutes. Cool 10 minutes on a wire rack. Run a knife around edge to release sides; remove sides of pan. Cool completely on wire rack. Slice and reheat before serving. **Yield:** 12 to 15 servings.
Concho Confetti Cafe and Catering
San Angelo, Texas

Note: For white chocolate, we used Nestle's Baking Bars and Baker's Premium White Chocolate. We tried white chocolate morsels, but the layers didn't stay together.

JULY

TOMATOES– NATURE'S CRIMSON DECLARATION OF SUMMER

For "tomatophiles" nothing quite matches the taste of a sun-warmed tomato plucked off the vine and eaten out of hand. We stack it on sandwiches, slice it into salads, stir it into sauces, and savor it in relishes. And we praise its essential attributes: rich flavor, cooking versatility, and broad compatibility with other ingredients.

GREEK CHICKEN BREASTS

¼ cup all-purpose flour
1 tablespoon dried oregano
4 skinned and boned chicken breast halves
3 tablespoons olive oil
⅓ cup dry white wine
⅓ cup chicken broth
2 medium-size ripe tomatoes, peeled and chopped
3 tablespoons sliced ripe olives
2 tablespoons capers
2 tablespoons crumbled feta cheese

• **Combine** flour and oregano in a shallow dish; dredge chicken breasts in flour mixture.
• **Heat** olive oil in a large skillet over medium heat; add chicken breasts, and cook 10 minutes, turning once.
• **Add** wine and broth; simmer 10 to 15 minutes. Add chopped tomato, olives, and capers; cook until thoroughly heated.
• **Spoon** into serving dish; sprinkle with feta cheese. **Yield:** 4 servings.

TOMATO-EGGPLANT BISCUIT CAKES

1 medium eggplant
1¼ teaspoons salt, divided
1 (17.3-ounce) can refrigerated large flaky biscuits
3 tablespoons olive oil
¾ cup whipping cream
½ teaspoon sugar
3 tablespoons balsamic vinegar
2 tablespoons finely chopped fresh basil
5 large ripe tomatoes, peeled, seeded, and coarsely chopped

• **Cut** eggplant into 8 (½-inch-thick) slices; sprinkle with 1 teaspoon salt. Let stand on paper towels 20 minutes; pat slices dry.
• **Prepare** biscuits according to package directions; set aside.
• **Heat** oil in a skillet over medium-high heat until hot; cook eggplant 3 to 4 minutes, turning once. Drain well on paper towels; set aside.
• **Beat** whipping cream at medium speed with an electric mixer until soft peaks form; add sugar, and gradually add vinegar, beating until stiff peaks form. Fold in basil and remaining ¼ teaspoon salt.
• **Split** biscuits. Place an eggplant slice on bottom half of each biscuit; top with chopped tomato. Dollop with whipped cream mixture; cover with biscuit tops. **Yield:** 8 servings.

Haden Ridlehoover
Birmingham, Alabama

FRESH TOMATO TART

½ (15-ounce) package refrigerated piecrusts
2 cups (8 ounces) shredded mozzarella cheese
3 tablespoons chopped fresh basil, divided
3 medium-size ripe tomatoes, peeled and cut into ½-inch slices
1½ tablespoons olive oil
¼ teaspoon salt
¼ teaspoon pepper

• **Fit** piecrust into a 10-inch tart pan according to package directions; trim any excess pastry along edges. Generously prick bottom and sides of pastry with a fork.
• **Bake** at 400° for 5 minutes.
• **Sprinkle** cheese evenly into pastry shell, and top with 2 tablespoons basil. Arrange tomato slices on top; brush with oil, and sprinkle with salt and pepper. Place on a baking sheet; place baking sheet on lower rack of oven.
• **Bake** at 400° for 35 to 40 minutes. Remove from oven; sprinkle with remaining 1 tablespoon basil. Let stand 5 minutes before serving. **Yield:** 8 to 10 servings.

Baiba Wilson
Jackson, Mississippi

TOMATO-ZUCCHINI GRATIN

3 medium zucchini, thinly sliced
4 medium-size ripe tomatoes,
   peeled and thinly sliced
¾ cup grated Parmesan cheese,
   divided
2 cloves garlic, minced
1 teaspoon dried thyme
¼ teaspoon salt
¼ teaspoon pepper
2 tablespoons olive oil

● **Arrange** half of zucchini slices in bottom of an ungreased 8-inch square baking dish; top with half of tomato slices. Sprinkle with ¼ cup cheese.
● **Top** with remaining zucchini and tomato. Sprinkle garlic, thyme, salt, and pepper over tomato; drizzle with olive oil. Sprinkle remaining ½ cup Parmesan cheese over top.
● **Bake** at 400° for 20 to 25 minutes. Serve with a slotted spoon. **Yield:** 6 servings.

Patti Trippeer
Germantown, Tennessee

HOT TOMATO GRITS

2 slices bacon, chopped
2 (14½-ounce) cans ready-to-serve
   chicken broth
½ teaspoon salt
1 cup quick-cooking grits
2 large ripe tomatoes, peeled and
   chopped
2 tablespoons canned chopped
   green chiles
1 cup (4 ounces) shredded
   Cheddar cheese

● **Cook** bacon in a large heavy saucepan until crisp, reserving drippings in pan. Gradually add broth and salt; bring to a boil.
● **Stir** in grits, tomato, and chiles; return to a boil, stirring often. Reduce heat, and simmer 15 to 20 minutes, stirring often.
● **Stir** in cheese; cover and let stand 5 minutes or until cheese melts. **Yield:** 6 servings.

Lucy S. Wheaton
Birmingham, Alabama

FRIED GREEN TOMATOES

4 large green tomatoes (about
   2 pounds)
¼ cup sugar
¾ cup all-purpose flour
1 teaspoon salt
⅛ teaspoon pepper
3 tablespoons bacon drippings
6 tablespoons vegetable oil

● **Remove** and discard a thin slice from tops and bottoms of tomatoes; cut tomatoes into ¼-inch-thick slices.
● **Layer** tomato slices in a small deep dish, sprinkling each layer with sugar; let stand 1 hour. Drain tomato slices, reserving sugar liquid.
● **Combine** flour, salt, and pepper in a shallow dish; dredge tomato slices in mixture.
● **Heat** 1 tablespoon bacon drippings and 2 tablespoons oil in a large cast-iron skillet over medium-high heat until hot; add about one-third of tomato slices. Cook 2 to 3 minutes on each side or until golden. Drain on paper towels. Repeat procedure twice with remaining tomato slices, bacon drippings, and oil.
● **Drain** off pan drippings, reserving 1 tablespoon in skillet. Stir reserved sugar liquid until sugar dissolves. Add to drippings in skillet; bring to a boil.
● **Cook** over medium heat, stirring constantly, 1 minute or until slightly thickened. Place fried tomatoes on a serving platter, and drizzle with sugar mixture. Serve immediately. **Yield:** 4 to 6 servings.

Rose W. Roberson
Ocala, Florida

TOMATO-BASIL-MOZZARELLA SALAD
(pictured on page 187)

3 large ripe tomatoes, cut into
   ½-inch-thick slices (about
   1½ pounds)
8 ounces fresh mozzarella cheese,
   cut into ¼-inch-thick
   slices
8 to 12 fresh basil leaves
1½ tablespoons olive oil
1½ tablespoons lemon juice
¼ teaspoon salt
¼ teaspoon freshly ground
   pepper
Garnish: fresh basil sprig

● **Arrange** tomato slices, cheese, and basil alternately on a large serving plate, overlapping edges.
● **Combine** olive oil and lemon juice; brush over top. Sprinkle with salt and pepper; cover and chill. Garnish, if desired. **Yield:** 4 to 6 servings.

Sadie Elwood
Birmingham, Alabama

> *The tomato has many suitors in the herb garden – thyme, oregano, and dill all pair perfectly with "big red." But no herb marries more beautifully with the tomato than basil, a flavor match made in heaven.*

OVEN-BAKED TOMATO APPETIZERS

1 French baguette
12 Roma tomatoes (1¼ pounds)
2 to 3 teaspoons olive oil
½ teaspoon sugar
½ teaspoon salt
1 teaspoon dried thyme
½ cup crumbled feta cheese

• **Cut** 24 (½-inch) slices from baguette; place on a baking sheet. Bake at 400° for 8 minutes; cool.
• **Cut** tomatoes in half lengthwise; scoop out seeds and pulp, and reserve for another use. Place tomato halves, cut side up, on a rack in a broiler pan; brush lightly with olive oil. Sprinkle evenly with sugar, salt, and thyme.
• **Bake** at 350° for 30 minutes. Place tomato halves, cut side up, on bread; sprinkle with cheese. Serve immediately. **Yield:** 2 dozen.

Jim Griffith
Guntersville, Alabama

SPICY TOMATO GRAVY

2 tablespoons olive oil
2 cloves garlic, minced
4 green onions, finely chopped (white part only)
3 large ripe tomatoes, peeled, seeded, and finely chopped
½ cup whipping cream
¼ teaspoon salt
¼ teaspoon ground red pepper
½ teaspoon dried thyme

• **Heat** oil in a skillet over medium heat until hot; add garlic and green onions. Cook 5 minutes, stirring constantly.
• **Add** chopped tomato; reduce heat, and simmer 2 to 3 minutes, stirring constantly. Stir in whipping cream and remaining ingredients; simmer, stirring constantly, until slightly thickened. Serve over chicken, fish, or pasta. **Yield:** 2 cups.

Mary Isenberg
St. George Island, Florida

GREEN TOMATO SANDWICH SPREAD

3 large green tomatoes, quartered (1¼ pounds)
1 medium onion, coarsely chopped
1 large green pepper, seeded and coarsely chopped
1½ teaspoons salt
¾ cup sugar
½ cup white vinegar
2 tablespoons all-purpose flour
½ cup salad dressing or mayonnaise
2½ tablespoons prepared mustard
¼ cup chopped pimiento-stuffed olives

• **Position** knife blade in food processor bowl; add first 3 ingredients. Process until finely chopped (do not puree), stopping once to scrape down sides.
• **Combine** tomato mixture and salt in a large nonaluminum saucepan; cover and let stand 2 to 3 hours.
• **Drain** tomato mixture, discarding liquid. Return mixture to saucepan, and stir in sugar and vinegar; bring to a boil. Reduce heat, and simmer, 10 minutes, stirring occasionally.
• **Combine** ½ cup tomato mixture and flour, stirring well, and return to remaining tomato mixture in saucepan; cook, stirring constantly, 5 minutes or until thickened. Remove from heat.
• **Stir** in salad dressing and remaining ingredients; cool. Serve on hot dogs or hamburgers or as a relish with meats and vegetables. **Yield:** 3¼ cups.

Drexel Mills
Pontotoc, Mississippi

FLOYD'S FAVORITE TOMATO SANDWICH

1 large ripe tomato, peeled
1 large onion
16 slices sandwich bread
3 tablespoons mayonnaise
1 tablespoon mustard
Salt and pepper

• **Cut** tomato and onion into 8 (¼-inch-thick) slices each. Layer tomato and onion slices in a shallow dish; cover and chill 8 hours.
• **Cut** bread slices into circles the size of the tomato slices. Combine mayonnaise and mustard; spread on one side of each bread round. Discard onion slices; place tomato slices on 8 bread rounds. Sprinkle lightly with salt and pepper. Top with remaining bread rounds. Cover; chill up to 2 days. **Yield:** 8 sandwiches.

John Floyd
Trussville, Alabama

THE TOMATO SANDWICH

The quintessential tomato sandwich? White bread, *very* ripe tomato, mayo, salt, pepper, and a *sink*. You must eat over a sink as that tomato juice drips down your arms. Our staff suggested these tomato sandwich enhancements.

- A hint of dill
- Pimiento cheese
- Potato chips for crunch
- Thinly sliced cucumber
- Roasted garlic
- Cream cheese and ripe olives
- Peanut butter (peanut butter?)
- Sprouts and crazy salt
- Greek peppers and feta cheese
- Chopped parsley, garlic salt, a squeeze of lemon
- Lettuce
- Celery seeds
- Mozzarella cheese and fresh basil leaves
- Raw onions and dill pickles
- Mustard
- Chopped green pepper
- Grilled onions
- Dijon mustard, Havarti cheese, and red leaf lettuce

White bread won hands down (and dripping) as the bread of choice. But when "To toast or not to toast?" was posed, opinions were strong – and about even.

Summer Suppers.

A MIDSUMMER NIGHT'S THEME:
CASUAL YET ELEGANT

We've gathered an armload of ideas for taking advantage of this time of year:

just-picked fruits and vegetables, sunny days and starry nights, family and friends.

Enjoy this simple, make-ahead menu, made elegant by serving in a garden.

PARTY IN THE GARDEN
Serves Eight

Caribbean Punch
Pesto-Spiced Nuts   Cheese Wafers
Blackened 'n' Peppered Steak
Warm Vegetable Salad
Monkey Bread
Planter's Punch Dessert

CARIBBEAN PUNCH

3 cups water
1 to 1½ cups sugar
1 (12-ounce) can frozen orange
    juice concentrate, thawed and
    undiluted
1 (6-ounce) can frozen lemonade
    concentrate, thawed and
    undiluted
½ cup pineapple juice
1½ cups mashed ripe banana
    (about 3 medium)
2 cups light rum (optional)
3 (12-ounce) cans ginger ale

● **Combine** water and sugar in a large saucepan; bring mixture to a boil, stirring until sugar dissolves. Set sugar mixture aside.
● **Combine** orange juice concentrate and next 3 ingredients in container of an electric blender; process until smooth, stopping once to scrape down sides.
● **Combine** sugar mixture and orange juice mixture in a large plastic container. Add rum, if desired, and ginger ale, stirring well. Cover and freeze.
● **Remove** from freezer, and let stand at room temperature 30 minutes before serving. **Yield:** about 3½ quarts.

Joy L. Garcia
Bartlett, Tennessee

PESTO-SPICED NUTS

2 cups pecan halves
2 cups slivered almonds
3 tablespoons olive oil
1 (0.5-ounce) envelope pesto
    sauce mix

● **Combine** pecans and almonds; set aside.
● **Combine** oil and pesto mix, stirring well. Pour over nuts; stir until evenly coated. Spread evenly in a 15- x 10- x 1-inch jellyroll pan.
● **Bake** at 350° for 13 to 15 minutes or until toasted, stirring every 5 minutes. Remove from oven; cool on paper towels. **Yield:** 4 cups.

CHEESE WAFERS

½ cup butter or margarine, softened
1½ cups (6 ounces) shredded sharp Cheddar cheese
1 cup all-purpose flour
Dash of salt
Dash of paprika
1½ cups corn flakes cereal, crushed
½ cup finely chopped almonds

• **Position** knife blade in food processor bowl; add butter and cheese. Process until blended. Add flour, salt, and paprika; process until mixture forms a ball, stopping often to scrape down sides. Add crushed cereal and almonds; pulse 4 times.
• **Shape** dough into ½-inch balls. Place balls about 2 inches apart on ungreased baking sheets. Flatten each ball in a crisscross pattern with a fork dipped in flour.
• **Bake** at 350° for 15 minutes or until lightly browned. Remove to wire racks to cool. **Yield:** 4½ dozen.

Valerie Stutsman
Norfolk, Virginia

BLACKENED 'N' PEPPERED STEAK

This recipe generates plenty of pepper-scented smoke, so you may want to cook outdoors. We seared the steaks in an iron skillet over a propane cooker (like one used for a fish fry; you can purchase one at a hardware store). You can also prepare the steaks with the fan on in a well-ventilated kitchen.

4 (1½-inch-thick) New York strip steaks
¾ cup whole black peppercorns, crushed
¼ cup olive oil
¼ cup butter or margarine
1 cup chopped green onions
3 cups dry red wine
1 (3½-ounce) jar capers, drained

• **Trim** all visible fat from steaks; cut steaks in half crosswise. Dredge in peppercorns, coating all sides of steaks. Set aside.
• **Pour** olive oil in a large cast-iron skillet, and place on burner of a propane cooker. Heat until hot, following manufacturer's instructions. Brown steaks on each edge in skillet. Cook 4 minutes on each side or until meat thermometer inserted in steak registers 160° (medium). Remove steaks to serving plate, and keep warm. Discard drippings.
• **Melt** butter in skillet; add green onions, and cook 1 minute, stirring constantly. Add wine and capers; cook until liquid is reduced to 1½ cups. Serve with steak. **Yield:** 8 servings.

Note: Do not leave skillet unattended. Hot oil and wine can ignite. If mixture ignites, immediately cover skillet with a large lid to extinguish flames, and reduce heat.

Dave Christy
Pine Mountain, Georgia

WARM VEGETABLE SALAD

½ pound carrots, scraped and cut into 1-inch pieces
1 cup water
½ pound yellow squash, sliced
½ pound zucchini, sliced
¼ cup olive oil
1 clove garlic, minced
2 to 3 tablespoons chopped fresh basil
½ teaspoon salt
½ teaspoon freshly ground pepper
⅛ teaspoon sugar
2 tablespoons red wine vinegar
1 pint cherry tomatoes
Lettuce leaves

• **Combine** carrot and water in a large saucepan. Bring to a boil; cover and cook 5 minutes.
• **Add** yellow squash and zucchini; cover and cook 3 minutes or until vegetables are crisp-tender. Drain and keep warm.
• **Combine** olive oil and next 5 ingredients in a small saucepan; cook over low heat 4 minutes. Stir in vinegar.
• **Pour** olive oil mixture over vegetables; add cherry tomatoes, and toss gently. Serve immediately on lettuce leaves. **Yield:** 8 servings.

Birgitt Lopez
Dallas, Texas

MONKEY BREAD

2 packages active dry yeast
1 cup warm water (105° to 115°)
2 large eggs, lightly beaten
1 cup vegetable oil
6 cups all-purpose flour
⅔ cup sugar
1 tablespoon salt
1 cup boiling water
½ cup butter or margarine, melted

• **Combine** yeast and warm water in a 2-cup liquid measuring cup; let stand 5 minutes.
• **Combine** yeast mixture, eggs, and next 4 ingredients in a large bowl, stirring until smooth.
• **Add** boiling water slowly to mixture, stirring until blended. Cover and chill at least 8 hours.
• **Punch** dough down; divide in half. Turn one portion out onto a heavily floured surface, and knead 3 or 4 times. Roll to ¼-inch thickness; cut into 4- x 1½-inch strips.
• **Brush** strips with half of melted butter, and layer, overlapping, in a greased Bundt or 10-inch tube pan. Repeat procedure with remaining dough and butter in another greased Bundt or tube pan. Cover and let rise in a warm place (85°), free from drafts, 1½ hours or until dough is doubled in bulk.
• **Bake** at 350° for 30 to 35 minutes or until golden. **Yield:** 2 loaves.

PLANTER'S PUNCH DESSERT

¾ cup butter or margarine
1 (18.25-ounce) package yellow cake mix
1 (20-ounce) can crushed pineapple, drained
1 (26-ounce) jar refrigerated mango spears, drained and chopped
½ cup dark rum, divided
1 (14-ounce) can sweetened condensed milk
1 (8-ounce) package cream cheese, softened
2 large eggs
1 cup chopped pecans
2 cups whipping cream, whipped

• **Cut** butter into cake mix with pastry blender until mixture is crumbly. Set 1½ cups mixture aside; press remainder into a buttered 13- x 9- x 2-inch baking dish.
• **Layer** pineapple and mango over pastry; drizzle ¼ cup rum over top.
• **Combine** remaining ¼ cup rum, sweetened condensed milk, cream cheese, and eggs; beat at medium speed with an electric mixer until smooth. Pour over dessert; sprinkle evenly with reserved crumb mixture, and top with pecans.
• **Bake** at 350° for 50 to 55 minutes or until set and lightly browned. Cool on a wire rack. Cover and chill 8 hours; pipe or dollop with whipped cream. **Yield:** 15 servings.

Gail S. Moreman
Dadeville, Alabama

A TASTE OF SOUTHERN ELEGANCE

· ·

Irene Smith of Covington, Georgia, introduced her English visitors to the South with a party at Dixie Manor, a 14-room mansion built in 1838. Enjoy a taste of comfortable elegance with her easy-to-prepare banquet with the accent on Southern.

SOUTHERN HOSPITALITY FEAST
Serves Eight

Herbed Gazpacho
Chicken à la Russell
Wild Rice Casserole
Sour Cream Corn Muffins
Peach Fluff

HERBED GAZPACHO

1 (46-ounce) can spicy-hot tomato vegetable juice
1 (16-ounce) can Italian-style tomatoes, undrained
1 (10½-ounce) can condensed beef broth
2 tomatoes, seeded and chopped
1 cucumber, seeded and chopped
1 green pepper, seeded and chopped
3 green onions, chopped
2 tablespoons chopped fresh basil
2 tablespoons chopped fresh oregano
2 cloves garlic, minced
2 tablespoons white wine vinegar
1 tablespoon Worcestershire sauce
½ teaspoon salt
1 teaspoon pepper

• **Combine** all ingredients; cover and chill 2 hours. **Yield:** 12 cups.

CHICKEN À LA RUSSELL

The easy béarnaise sauce drizzled over the top of this dish ties the ingredients together nicely.

1 pound ground pork sausage with sage
¾ cup all-purpose flour
1 teaspoon dried thyme
1 teaspoon salt
1 teaspoon crushed black pepper
8 skinned and boned chicken breast halves
⅓ cup vegetable oil
2 (0.9-ounce) envelopes béarnaise sauce mix
1 (14-ounce) can artichoke hearts, drained and halved
⅓ cup chopped pecans
Garnishes: pecan halves, fresh sage sprigs
Wild Rice Casserole (see recipe on page 176)

• **Brown** sausage in a large skillet, stirring until it crumbles. Drain sausage, and set aside. Discard drippings from skillet.
• **Combine** flour, thyme, salt, and pepper; dredge chicken in flour mixture.
• **Heat** oil in skillet over medium heat.
• **Add** chicken to skillet, and brown on both sides. Drain chicken, and set aside.
• **Prepare** béarnaise sauce according to package reduced-calorie directions; keep warm.
• **Spread** sausage in a lightly greased 11- x 7- x 1½ -inch baking dish. Top with chicken, artichokes, béarnaise sauce, and chopped pecans.
• **Bake** at 325° for 20 minutes or until thoroughly heated. Garnish, if desired. Serve with Wild Rice Casserole. **Yield:** 8 servings.

WILD RICE CASSEROLE

2 (6-ounce) packages long-grain-
    and-wild rice mix
1 (8-ounce) jar process cheese
    spread
1 (8-ounce) can sliced water
    chestnuts, drained
1 (6-ounce) jar sliced mushrooms,
    drained
1 (2-ounce) jar diced pimiento,
    drained
1 (2.8-ounce) can French fried
    onions, crushed

• **Cook** rice mix according to package
directions.
• **Stir** in cheese spread and next 3 ingredients. Spoon into a lightly greased
11- x 7- x 1½-inch baking dish.
• **Cover** and bake at 325° for 20 minutes; uncover and sprinkle with
crushed onions.
• **Bake,** uncovered, 10 additional minutes. **Yield:** 8 servings.

SOUR CREAM CORN MUFFINS

1 cup self-rising yellow cornmeal
    mix
½ teaspoon salt
¼ cup vegetable oil
1 (8.5-ounce) can cream-style corn
1 (8-ounce) carton sour cream *
2 large eggs, lightly beaten

• **Combine** all ingredients, stirring
until smooth. Spoon into a greased
muffin pan, filling two-thirds full.
• **Bake** at 400° for 25 minutes or until
golden. Remove from pan, and serve
immediately. **Yield:** 1 dozen.

* You can substitute 1 (8-ounce) carton nonfat sour cream for regular sour
cream.

PEACH FLUFF

2 (3-ounce) packages peach-
    flavored gelatin
1 (8-ounce) can crushed pineapple,
    undrained
2 cups buttermilk
1 (8-ounce) container frozen
    whipped topping, thawed
Vegetable cooking spray
4 cups sliced fresh peaches (about
    3 large)
¼ cup peach schnapps
Lettuce leaves
Garnish: fresh mint

• **Combine** gelatin and pineapple in a
medium saucepan over low heat, stirring until gelatin dissolves. Remove
from heat, and stir in buttermilk and
whipped topping.
• **Pour** mixture into an 8-cup ring
mold lightly coated with cooking spray.
Cover and chill 1 hour or until firm.
• **Combine** peaches and schnapps;
cover and chill 1 hour.
• **Unmold** salad onto a lettuce-lined
serving tray. Arrange peaches in center
and around sides of mold, using a slotted spoon. Garnish, if desired. **Yield:** 8
to 10 servings.

EASY WEEKEND ENTERTAINING

....

The weekend stretches out before you
and a houseful of guests. With this plan,
you can handle it and live to tell about
it, too.

Get everyone involved. To avoid
tripping over too many cooks, hand
out specific assignments on Friday.
You'll need fire starters and grill cooks,
fruit and vegetable slicers, breakfast
chefs for Saturday and Sunday, and
cleanup crews after each meal. Let the
kids help, too. Keep beverages in tubs

and coolers outside to eliminate traffic
to the refrigerator.
Now, round up your guests and get
set to party. It's the weekend!

WEEKEND MENUS

FRIDAY SUPPER
Cold Cuts and Chips
Cheesy Garlic-Stuffed Bread
Caliente Marinated Olives
Beer and Mineral Water

SATURDAY BREAKFAST
Pancakes or
Make-Your-Own Omelets
Assorted Bagels

SATURDAY LUNCH
Food From a Deli

SATURDAY SUPPER
Thai Chicken Salad
Beef Vinaigrette Salad
Fresh Fruit Tray
Assorted Sandwich Rolls
Honey-Vanilla Ice Cream
Double Chocolate
Chunk-Almond Cookies
Iced Tea and Soft Drinks

SUNDAY BREAKFAST
Cereals   Pastries
Fresh Fruit

KIDS MENU
Pigs in a Blanket
Bugs in a Rug
Polka Dot Punch

CHEESY GARLIC-STUFFED BREAD

1 (8-ounce) package cream cheese,
    softened
1 cup (4 ounces) shredded Swiss
    cheese
1 cup fresh parsley
2 to 4 cloves garlic
1 (20-ounce) large round loaf
    bread

- **Position** knife blade in food processor bowl; add first 4 ingredients. Process until smooth, stopping once to scrape down sides of bowl; set aside.
- **Slice** off top half of bread loaf; set top aside. Hollow out bottom half of bread loaf, leaving a 1-inch shell. Set shell aside.
- **Cut** inside bread pieces into 1-inch cubes; place on a large baking sheet.
- **Bake** at 350° for 12 minutes or until lightly browned.
- **Spoon** cheese mixture into center of bread shell, and replace the bread top. Wrap filled bread in heavy-duty aluminum foil, and place on a baking sheet.
- **Bake** at 350° for 30 minutes or until filled bread is thoroughly heated. Serve with toasted bread cubes. **Yield:** about 8 servings.

Sue-Sue Hartstern
Louisville, Kentucky

CALIENTE MARINATED OLIVES

This spicy appetizer makes a great take-home favor for your guests.

2 (3-ounce) jars pimiento-stuffed olives, drained
2 (3-ounce) jars almond-stuffed olives, drained
4 cloves garlic, minced
2 tablespoons dried crushed red pepper
2 teaspoons dried cumin
½ cup water
1 tablespoon olive oil
3 tablespoons chopped fresh cilantro

- **Combine** first 7 ingredients in a saucepan; bring to a boil over medium heat. Reduce heat, and simmer 5 minutes. Remove from heat; cool.
- **Stir** in chopped cilantro. Cover and chill at least 8 hours or up to 1 week. **Yield:** 2½ cups.

Nan Jacobs
Birmingham, Alabama

THAI CHICKEN SALAD
(pictured on page 149)

4 skinned and boned chicken breast halves
Peanut-Ginger Dressing
3 ounces vermicelli, uncooked
4 cups torn romaine lettuce
2 cups thinly sliced Chinese cabbage
2 medium carrots, coarsely shredded
1 medium cucumber, thinly sliced
1 large sweet red pepper, cut into strips
¼ cup chopped fresh cilantro
Chopped peanuts (optional)
Sliced cucumber (optional)

- **Grill** chicken, without grill lid, over medium coals (300° to 350°) 15 to 20 minutes, turning once. Cut into thin strips. Combine chicken and 3 tablespoons Peanut-Ginger Dressing, tossing to coat; cover and chill 8 hours.
- **Cook** vermicelli according to package directions; drain.
- **Combine** vermicelli and 3 tablespoons Peanut-Ginger Dressing, tossing to coat. Cover and chill 8 hours.
- **Combine** romaine and next 5 ingredients, tossing well; arrange on a serving platter. Top with vermicelli and chicken; sprinkle salad with peanuts, if desired. Arrange cucumber slices around vermicelli, if desired. Serve salad with remaining Peanut-Ginger Dressing. **Yield:** 6 servings.

Peanut-Ginger Dressing

½ cup rice wine vinegar
2 cloves garlic
⅓ cup creamy peanut butter
¼ cup lime juice
¼ cup chopped fresh cilantro
2 tablespoons apple cider vinegar
1 tablespoon honey
1 tablespoon molasses
1 tablespoon hot sauce
2 teaspoons peeled, grated gingerroot
2 teaspoons soy sauce

- **Combine** all ingredients in container of an electric blender; process until smooth. **Yield:** 1½ cups.

Cindie Hackney
Longview, Texas

BEEF VINAIGRETTE SALAD
(pictured on page 149)

2 cups olive oil
⅔ cup balsamic vinegar
½ teaspoon garlic salt
1 teaspoon freshly ground pepper
1½ tablespoons sugar
1 (1-pound) flank steak
2 cups torn romaine lettuce
2 cups torn leaf lettuce
2 cups torn red-tipped leaf lettuce
2 cups chopped bok choy
2 tomatoes, cut into wedges
1 cup sliced radishes
4 green onions, cut into thin strips

- **Combine** first 5 ingredients in container of an electric blender; process until smooth.
- **Place** flank steak in a shallow dish or large heavy-duty, zip-top plastic bag; pour 1 cup dressing over steak. Cover or seal, and chill 3 hours, turning steak occasionally. Chill remaining vinaigrette dressing.
- **Remove** steak from marinade, discarding marinade. Cook, without grill lid, over hot coals (400° to 500°) 7 minutes on each side or until a meat thermometer inserted in steak registers 150°. Remove from heat; let steak cool at least 10 minutes.
- **Cut** steak diagonally into thin slices.
- **Toss** lettuces and bok choy together, and place on a large platter. Arrange steak and remaining vegetables over top. Cover and chill; serve with remaining vinaigrette dressing. **Yield:** 4 servings.

Note: You can substitute thinly sliced, cooked, deli roast beef for flank steak. Marinate in vinaigrette dressing as directed, and drain; arrange over salad.

Ethel Comer
Huntingtown, Maryland

HONEY-VANILLA ICE CREAM

Put the kids in charge of dessert. They'll have as much fun freezing the ice cream as eating it.

6 large eggs, lightly beaten
1 quart milk
1 cup honey
1 quart whipping cream
2 tablespoons vanilla extract

• **Combine** first 3 ingredients in a large saucepan.
• **Cook** over low heat, stirring constantly, 25 to 30 minutes or until mixture thickens and coats a spoon; cool. Stir in whipping cream and vanilla.
• **Cover** and chill at least 8 hours. Pour into a 5-quart, hand-turned or electric ice cream freezer. Freeze according to manufacturer's instructions. **Yield:** about 1 gallon.

Cheryl Welch
Jackson, Mississippi

DOUBLE CHOCOLATE CHUNK-ALMOND COOKIES

These freeze well, so you can make them weeks ahead.

1 cup butter or margarine, softened
1½ cups sugar
2 large eggs
1 teaspoon vanilla extract
2 cups all-purpose flour
⅔ cup cocoa
¾ teaspoon baking soda
¼ teaspoon salt
1 (12-ounce) package semisweet chocolate chunks
½ cup coarsely chopped almonds

• **Beat** butter in a large mixing bowl at medium speed with an electric mixer until creamy; gradually add sugar, beating mixture well. Add eggs, one at a time, beating until blended after each addition. Add vanilla, beating well.

• **Combine** flour, cocoa, baking soda, and salt; gradually add to butter mixture, beating at low speed until blended. Stir in chocolate chunks and almonds.
• **Drop** by rounded teaspoonfuls onto ungreased cookie sheets.
• **Bake** at 350° for 10 to 12 minutes. (Cookies will look soft.) Let cool on cookie sheets 2 minutes; remove to wire racks to cool completely. **Yield:** 6 dozen.

Delana Smith
Homewood, Alabama

PIGS IN A BLANKET

Remember these? Short on ingredients, long on fun. Kids still love them – for snacks or for supper.

1 (10-ounce) can refrigerated biscuits
10 slices American cheese
10 hot dogs
10 wooden picks

• **Flatten** each biscuit on a lightly floured surface with your hands or a rolling pin.

• **Place** 1 cheese slice on each biscuit; top each with a hot dog. Roll up, and secure with a wooden pick. Place on a lightly greased baking sheet.
• **Bake** at 375° for 10 minutes or until browned. **Yield:** 10 servings.

BUGS IN A RUG

This slightly sweet treat is light enough to serve as a midmorning snack.

1 (8-ounce) package reduced-fat cream cheese, softened
⅓ cup sifted powdered sugar
½ teaspoon ground cinnamon
½ teaspoon vanilla extract
¼ cup raisins
6 slices whole wheat or white bread, crusts removed, or 6 (6-inch) flour tortillas

• **Combine** first 4 ingredients, stirring until mixture is smooth; stir in raisins.
• **Spread** about 3 tablespoons mixture evenly on each slice of bread or tortilla; roll up. Wrap each roll separately in plastic wrap, twisting ends to seal.
• **Chill** 1 hour or until firm. **Yield:** 6 servings.

FUN FOOD FOR THE KIDS

If Bugs in a Rug and Pigs in a Blanket sound like culinary child's play, try our kid-pleasing punch.

Polka Dot Punch: Freeze pineapple juice, orange juice, and cranberry juice cocktail in separate ice cube trays. For each serving, pour chilled lemon-lime carbonated beverage over 3 or 4 assorted juice cubes.

FRESH FROM THE GARDEN

....

Collard greens, turnip greens, and beets are always good as solo dishes, but they are fantastic as a team. And the often-overlooked rutabaga has an essential place on this plate. The taste of creamy Rutabaga Whip makes cutting through the large tough root worth the trouble. Whether the vegetables come from your own garden or from the nearest farmers market, this summer's abundance is worth taking a new look.

SKILLET OKRA

Grill the fresh ears of corn, and don't omit the fatback for the full flavor of this summer dish.

3 ears fresh corn
¼ pound fatback
1 large onion, finely chopped
2 pounds fresh okra, sliced
6 medium tomatoes, peeled and chopped
½ teaspoon pepper

• **Cook** corn, covered with grill lid, over medium-hot coals (350° to 400°) about 15 minutes or until tender, turning often. Cool.
• **Cut** corn from cobs; set aside.
• **Make** shallow cuts in fatback, cutting to, but not through, rind. Cook fatback in a large cast-iron skillet over medium-high heat 4 to 5 minutes, turning often.
• **Add** onion, and cook about 3 minutes, stirring constantly.
• **Stir** in corn, okra, tomato, and pepper. Cover, reduce heat, and simmer 20 to 25 minutes or until vegetables are tender, stirring occasionally. Remove and discard fatback. **Yield:** 8 to 10 servings.

BEETS 'N' GREENS

1½ pounds smoked ham hocks
8 cups water
¼ pound chopped country ham
1 (3½-pound) bunch collard greens, trimmed and chopped (about 16 cups)
1 (3½-pound) bunch turnip greens, trimmed and chopped (about 12 cups)
4 medium-size fresh beets, peeled and sliced
½ teaspoon sugar
½ teaspoon liquid from hot peppers in vinegar
¼ teaspoon salt
¼ teaspoon pepper

• **Place** ham hocks in a large Dutch oven; add water, and bring to a boil over high heat. Cover, reduce heat, and simmer 30 minutes. Remove and discard ham hocks.
• **Add** chopped ham to liquid; cook 5 minutes.
• **Add** collards, and cook 15 minutes.
• **Add** turnip greens and remaining ingredients; cook 15 minutes or until vegetables are tender, stirring occasionally. **Yield:** 6 to 8 servings.

RUTABAGA WHIP

Mellow, earthy rutabagas join potatoes and become deliciously rich and fluffy. Even those who think they don't like rutabagas will like this.

2 pounds rutabagas, peeled and chopped
6 cups water
2 pounds baking potatoes, peeled and chopped
¼ cup butter or margarine, softened
½ cup whipping cream
1 teaspoon salt
½ teaspoon pepper

• **Combine** rutabagas and water in a large Dutch oven; bring to a boil, and cook 15 minutes. Add potato, and cook 15 minutes or until vegetables are tender; drain.
• **Combine** vegetables, butter, and remaining ingredients in a large mixing bowl; beat at medium speed with an electric mixer until fluffy. **Yield:** 6 to 8 servings.

THE BEST SIDES OF SUMMER

....

Keeping summertime on an even keel can be as simple as browsing through our terrific side-dish recipes. Try one and you'll see how lucky you can get.

ZUCCHINI CRISPIES

2 tablespoons mayonnaise or salad dressing
2 tablespoons finely chopped green onions
1 tablespoon Dijon mustard
¼ teaspoon dried marjoram
¼ teaspoon dried thyme
2 medium zucchini
¼ cup soft breadcrumbs
½ teaspoon paprika
Butter-flavored cooking spray

• **Combine** first 5 ingredients; set aside.
• **Cut** each zucchini crosswise into 12 slices; spread a small amount of mayonnaise mixture on one side of each slice.
• **Combine** breadcrumbs and paprika; dredge mayonnaise-coated side of zucchini in breadcrumb mixture, and coat with cooking spray. Place on a baking sheet coated with cooking spray.
• **Bake** at 450° for 5 minutes or until browned. Serve immediately. **Yield:** 4 servings.

Edith Askins
Greenville, Texas

SQUASH AND TOMATO BAKE

2 pounds yellow squash, sliced
1 cup water
2 (14½-ounce) cans stewed
   tomatoes
1 tablespoon all-purpose flour
2 teaspoons sugar
1 teaspoon salt
1 teaspoon paprika
½ teaspoon garlic powder
⅛ teaspoon pepper
⅛ teaspoon dried basil
2 cups (8 ounces) shredded
   mozzarella cheese
½ cup grated Parmesan cheese

• **Combine** squash and water in a large saucepan. Bring to a boil; cover, reduce heat, and simmer 10 minutes or until squash is tender, stirring occasionally. Remove from heat; drain.
• **Drain** tomatoes, reserving ¼ cup liquid. Combine tomatoes, liquid, flour, and next 6 ingredients in a saucepan. Bring to a boil; reduce heat, and simmer 5 minutes. Remove from heat.
• **Place** half of squash in a lightly greased shallow 2-quart casserole; pour one-fourth of tomato mixture over squash. Top with 1 cup shredded mozzarella cheese and one-fourth of tomato mixture.
• **Repeat** layers with remaining squash, tomato mixture, and mozzarella cheese. Sprinkle with Parmesan cheese.
• **Bake** at 350° for 30 minutes. Remove from heat, and let stand 10 minutes before serving. **Yield:** 6 to 8 servings.

Note: Parmesan cheese may be sprinkled over casserole during last 5 minutes of baking time, if desired. (Top will not be crusty.)

Kay Castleman Cooper
Madison, Alabama

BREADED TOMATOES

2 tablespoons butter or margarine,
   divided
2 tablespoons all-purpose
   flour
1 cup milk
⅛ teaspoon salt
1 (16-ounce) can whole tomatoes,
   undrained and chopped
2 tablespoons sugar
2 slices white bread, torn into
   1-inch pieces

• **Melt** 1 tablespoon butter in a heavy saucepan over low heat; add flour, stirring until smooth. Cook 1 minute. Gradually add milk; cook over medium heat, stirring constantly, until sauce is thickened and bubbly. Stir in salt. Set aside.
• **Combine** tomatoes, sugar, and remaining 1 tablespoon butter in a small saucepan; bring to a boil. Gradually stir into sauce.
• **Cook** over medium heat, stirring constantly, until mixture is thickened and bubbly. Stir in bread pieces. **Yield:** 4 servings.

Louise Floyd
Selma, Alabama

GRILLED STUFFED ONIONS

1½ cups herb-seasoned stuffing
   mix
1 cup (4 ounces) shredded sharp
   Cheddar cheese
1 teaspoon poultry seasoning
⅓ cup butter or margarine,
   melted
⅓ cup hot water
6 medium-size sweet onions
Vegetable cooking spray
Garnish: fresh oregano

• **Combine** first 5 ingredients, stirring until well blended; set aside.
• **Cut** each onion into 3 horizontal slices. Spread 2 tablespoons stuffing mixture between slices, and reassemble onions. Place each onion on a 12-inch-

square piece of heavy-duty aluminum foil coated with cooking spray; bring opposite corners together and twist foil to seal.
• **Cook,** covered with grill lid, over medium-hot coals (350° to 400°) 25 minutes or until onions are tender. Garnish, if desired. **Yield:** 6 servings.

Note: For an alternative, cover and bake onions, unwrapped, in a lightly greased 11- x 7- x 1½-inch baking dish at 350° for 1 hour or until tender.

Margaret Johns
Tarpon Springs, Florida

MUSHROOM-MACARONI CASSEROLE

2 quarts water
1 teaspoon salt
1 (8-ounce) package elbow
   macaroni, uncooked
1 (10¾-ounce) can cream of
   mushroom soup, undiluted
1 cup mayonnaise
2 cups (8 ounces) shredded sharp
   Cheddar cheese
1 (4-ounce) can sliced mushrooms,
   drained
1 (2-ounce) jar diced pimiento,
   drained (optional)
¾ cup crushed round buttery
   crackers (about 15 crackers)
1 tablespoon butter or margarine,
   melted

• **Bring** water and salt to a boil in a large Dutch oven; stir in macaroni. Return to a rapid boil, and cook 8 to 10 minutes or until tender; drain. Rinse with cold water; drain.
• **Combine** macaroni, soup, and next 3 ingredients; add pimiento, if desired. Spoon into a lightly greased 2-quart casserole. Combine cracker crumbs and butter; sprinkle evenly over macaroni mixture.
• **Bake** at 300° for 30 minutes or until mixture is thoroughly heated. **Yield:** 6 to 8 servings.

Melba Edwards-Johnson
Sunset Beach, North Carolina

LEMON-GARLIC PASTA

2 tablespoons butter or
  margarine
2 tablespoons olive oil
4 to 5 cloves garlic, minced
¼ cup lemon juice
¼ teaspoon salt
½ to 1 teaspoon pepper
8 ounces thin spaghetti,
  cooked
⅓ cup chopped fresh parsley

• **Melt** butter in a large skillet over medium-high heat; add olive oil and minced garlic. Cook 1 minute, stirring constantly. Add lemon juice, salt, and pepper.
• **Bring** to a boil; pour mixture over pasta. Add parsley; toss gently. Serve immediately. **Yield:** 4 servings.

Nina Page Winkler
Orlando, Florida

BUTTERCRUST CORN PIE WITH FRESH TOMATO SALSA

Serve this as an entrée when you're planning a vegetable supper.

1¼ cups finely crushed saltine
  crackers
¼ cup grated Parmesan cheese
½ cup butter or margarine,
  melted
1¼ cups milk, divided
2 cups fresh or frozen corn
½ to 1 teaspoon onion salt
¼ teaspoon ground white
  pepper
1 teaspoon sugar (optional)
2 tablespoons all-purpose flour
¼ cup chopped ripe olives
½ cup sliced green onions
2 large eggs, lightly beaten
Paprika
Fresh Tomato Salsa

• **Combine** first 3 ingredients, stirring well; reserve 2 tablespoons.
• **Press** remaining cracker mixture into bottom and up sides of a 9-inch pieplate. Set aside.

• **Combine** 1 cup milk, corn, salt, pepper, and sugar, if desired, in a large saucepan; bring to a boil over medium heat. Reduce heat, and simmer mixture 3 minutes.
• **Combine** flour and remaining ¼ cup milk, stirring until smooth. Gradually add flour mixture to corn mixture, stirring constantly. Cook 1 minute, stirring constantly. (Mixture will be thick.) Remove from heat.
• **Stir** in olives and green onions. Gradually stir about one-fourth of hot mixture into eggs; add to remaining hot mixture, stirring constantly.
• **Spoon** into prepared pieplate; sprinkle with reserved crumb mixture and paprika.
• **Bake** at 400° for 20 minutes or until filling sets. Cut pie into wedges, and serve with Fresh Tomato Salsa. **Yield:** 6 servings.

Fresh Tomato Salsa

2 cups peeled, chopped tomatoes
1 jalapeño pepper, seeded and
  finely chopped or
  1 (4½-ounce) can chopped
  green chiles, drained
½ cup thinly sliced green
  onions
2 tablespoons lemon juice
½ teaspoon salt
½ teaspoon dried oregano
⅛ teaspoon pepper

• **Combine** all ingredients, stirring well. Cover and chill at least 3 hours. **Yield:** about 2 cups.

Linda Magers
Clemmons, North Carolina

GREEN RICE CASSEROLE

1¼ cups (5 ounces) shredded
  Monterey Jack or Swiss
  cheese, divided
1 cup ricotta cheese
1 cup mayonnaise or salad
  dressing
½ teaspoon garlic salt
¼ teaspoon pepper
3 cups cooked rice
1 (10-ounce) package frozen
  chopped broccoli, thawed
  and drained
1 cup frozen English peas,
  thawed
¼ cup sliced green onions
  (optional)

• **Combine** 1 cup Monterey Jack cheese and next 4 ingredients in a large bowl; stir in rice, broccoli, peas, and green onions, if desired.
• **Spoon** rice mixture into a lightly greased 2-quart casserole.
• **Bake**, uncovered, at 375° for 20 minutes. Sprinkle casserole with remaining ¼ cup Monterey Jack cheese, and bake 5 additional minutes. **Yield:** 8 servings.

PARMESAN POTATO WEDGES

⅔ cup grated Parmesan cheese
2 tablespoons Italian-seasoned
  breadcrumbs
2 large baking potatoes
2 egg whites, lightly beaten
¼ teaspoon salt
⅛ teaspoon pepper
Vegetable cooking spray

• **Combine** Parmesan cheese and breadcrumbs; set aside.
• **Scrub** potatoes, and pat dry; cut each into 8 wedges.
• **Brush** cut sides with egg white; sprinkle with salt and pepper, and coat with cheese mixture. Place potato wedges on a baking sheet coated with cooking spray.
• **Bake** at 425° for 30 to 35 minutes or until tender. **Yield:** 4 servings.

PEPPERY POTATO CASSEROLE

8 large potatoes, unpeeled (about 5 pounds)
¼ cup butter or margarine
1 green pepper, seeded and chopped
1½ tablespoons all-purpose flour
1½ cups milk
1 (6-ounce) package process cheese food with garlic flavor
1 (6-ounce) package process cheese food with jalapeño pepper
¼ to ½ teaspoon salt
¼ to ½ teaspoon pepper

• **Combine** potatoes and water to cover in a Dutch oven; bring to a boil over medium-high heat. Cover, reduce heat, and simmer 25 minutes or until tender; drain and cool.
• **Melt** butter in Dutch oven over medium-high heat; add chopped pepper, and cook, stirring constantly, 5 minutes or until tender. Remove pepper, reserving drippings in pan; set aside.
• **Add** flour to drippings, stirring until smooth. Cook 1 minute, stirring constantly. Gradually add milk, and cook over medium heat, stirring constantly, until mixture thickens and bubbles.
• **Stir** in cheeses, and cook, stirring constantly, until cheeses melt. Remove mixture from heat.
• **Peel** potatoes, and cut into thin slices. Layer potato in a lightly greased 13- x 9- x 2-inch baking dish, sprinkling each layer with salt, pepper, and chopped green pepper.
• **Spoon** cheese mixture over potato. Bake at 375° for 30 minutes or until thoroughly heated. **Yield:** 8 to 10 servings.

Dianna Jolly
Harrison, Arkansas

NOTABLE TOTABLES

....

Summer heat and travel make "What can I bring?" a challenge to even the best of cooks. To help, we've picked a sampling of foods and offered hints on how to make them easily portable.

PICNIC SHRIMP SALAD

An ice chest is a must for carrying this salad. Place the cold shrimp mixture, lettuce leaves, tomato wedges, egg wedges, and Parmesan cheese in separate containers, and assemble the salad just before serving.

3 cups water
1 pound unpeeled medium-size fresh shrimp
1 (8-ounce) package elbow macaroni
1 green pepper, chopped
½ cup olive oil
¼ cup white wine vinegar
½ cup chopped onion
¼ cup sweet salad cube pickles
1 tablespoon chopped fresh parsley
1 tablespoon chopped fresh basil or 1 teaspoon dried basil
½ teaspoon salt
½ teaspoon sugar
½ teaspoon pepper
Lettuce leaves
2 medium tomatoes, cut into wedges
4 hard-cooked eggs, cut into wedges
½ cup freshly grated Parmesan cheese
Paprika

• **Bring** water to a boil; add shrimp, and cook 3 to 5 minutes or until shrimp turn pink. Drain well; rinse with cold water.
• **Peel** shrimp, and devein, if desired; cover and chill.
• **Cook** macaroni according to package directions; drain. Rinse with cold water; drain. Set aside.
• **Combine** shrimp, macaroni, and green pepper in a large bowl; chill.
• **Combine** olive oil and next 8 ingredients; stir with a wire whisk until sugar dissolves. Pour over shrimp mixture; toss gently to coat. Cover and chill at least 2 hours.
• **Spoon** mixture onto a lettuce-lined platter; arrange tomato and egg wedges around edges. Sprinkle with Parmesan cheese and paprika. Serve immediately. **Yield:** 4 servings.

Leslie Coles Walker
Chesapeake, Virginia

BOURBON BAKED BEANS

If you can't keep baked beans hot until they're served, chill and reheat just before mealtime.

4 (16-ounce) cans Boston baked beans
1 (16-ounce) can crushed pineapple, drained
1 (12-ounce) jar chili sauce
½ cup strong brewed coffee
½ cup bourbon
¼ cup firmly packed brown sugar
1 tablespoon molasses
¾ teaspoon dry mustard

• **Combine** all ingredients in an electric slow cooker. Cover and cook on high 2 hours; uncover and cook to desired consistency. Serve with a slotted spoon. **Yield:** 10 to 12 servings.

Note: To make strong coffee, dissolve 1 teaspoon instant coffee granules in ½ cup hot water.

La Juan Coward
Jasper, Texas

CAESAR RAVIOLI SALAD

Pack the ravioli mixture and lettuce separately in a cooler. Assemble just before serving.

1 (9-ounce) package refrigerated
    light cheese ravioli, uncooked
2 cups cherry tomato halves
1 medium cucumber, thinly
    sliced
½ cup chopped purple onion
¼ cup sliced ripe olives
¼ cup freshly grated Parmesan
    cheese
½ teaspoon freshly ground pepper
¾ cup reduced-calorie Caesar salad
    dressing
4 cups shredded romaine lettuce

● **Cook** ravioli according to package directions; drain. Rinse with cold water; drain.
● **Combine** ravioli, tomato halves, and next 6 ingredients. Cover and chill. Serve over lettuce. **Yield:** 4 servings.

CHILLING THOUGHTS

■ Remember the two-hour rule: Meats, poultry, seafood, eggs, and milk (and foods that contain these ingredients) should not be left at room temperature for more than two hours.

■ A cooler with ice or ice packs works best to keep foods cold.

■ Special insulated containers keep cold foods cold and hot foods hot. If you don't have a container designed for hot foods, surround the dish with layers of crumpled newspaper. This will keep foods hot for a short time.

■ If hot foods can't be kept hot, chill and reheat on site.

BUTTERMILK SAUCE

Transport this sauce chilled in an ice chest. Reheat and serve over angel food cake, ice cream, or fresh fruit.

1 cup sugar
½ cup butter or margarine
½ cup buttermilk
1 tablespoon light corn syrup
2 teaspoons vanilla extract
½ teaspoon baking soda
Toasted sliced almonds (optional)

● **Combine** first 6 ingredients in a heavy saucepan.
● **Bring** to a boil over medium heat, stirring constantly. Serve warm over fresh fruit, cake, or ice cream. Sprinkle with toasted almonds, if desired. **Yield:** 1¾ cups.

Cindy Hinton
Franklin, Tennessee

FAST ALFRESCO

. . . .

Grab a blanket and go. It's a beautiful day for a picnic. But if you do all the cooking and packing you'll still be in the kitchen when the sun sets. So don't cook.

    Throw a blanket in the car, stop at the supermarket, and you'll be ready for a carefree picnic. Use our menu suggestions and tips for inspiration as you cruise the supermarket aisles for your impromptu outing.

CITY BREAKFAST

Make open-faced salmon sandwiches: Spread cream cheese on a bagel; add some chopped onion from the salad bar and a few capers. Top it off with sliced smoked salmon. Muffins, jam, and fresh fruit complete the breakfast.

SANDWICH PICNIC

Give your usual deli selections a twist. Instead of mayonnaise or mustard, try pesto from a jar or soft garlic cheese spread. Substitute roasted red peppers from a jar for sliced tomatoes on your sandwich. Buy alfalfa sprouts instead of lettuce. Mix a few oil-packed sun-dried tomatoes, seedless grapes, or pecan pieces into deli chicken salad. Salad bar vegetables with dip, potato salad, and coleslaw round out the meal.

PICNIC À LA DELI

For a beach picnic, choose shrimp and pasta salads, breadsticks, several cheeses, olives, and French baguettes.

POSH PAIRINGS

Choose a variety of cheeses like sharp Cheddar, creamy Brie or Camembert, and mild Swiss or Monterey Jack. Buy a loaf of crusty bread and crackers. Add fresh apple and pear slices, grapes, and a bottle of dry white wine.

PICNIC AT THE PARTHENON

Create a Greek feast with feta cheese, olives, stuffed grape leaves from a jar, and pita or French bread.

A PICNIC TO CELEBRATE

Champagne and anything.

TEX-MEX PICNIC

Buy commercial salsa and guacamole. Serve them with tortilla chips and salad bar vegetables for dipping. Add hot pepper cheese on crackers for extra fire.

ALFRESCO ANTIPASTO

Pick up several kinds of deli meats and cheeses and salad bar items like cherry tomatoes, sliced green peppers, and pickled vegetables. Add a bottle of Italian dressing and a loaf of Italian bread, and you're ready to check out.

COUNTRY BREAKFAST

Stop by the drive-through for a bag of ham biscuits, juice, and coffee. Drive into the country, and enjoy nature's awakening.

SPORTSMAN'S SPECIAL

Fishermen, hunters, and hikers are experts at creating a no-fuss meal on a cracker. Try bologna, Vienna sausages, cheese, sardines, pickled wieners, or cheese spread.

A NOT-SO-FANCY SPREAD

Choose these lighthearted foods for an instant picnic: a watermelon, Moon Pies and RC Colas, fried chicken from the drive-through, or peanut butter and jelly sandwiches.

PICNIC PANACHE

....

Those adorable picnic-basket ensembles you see in posh catalogs are enticing, but have you noticed the prices? Before you reach for the telephone and a credit card, grab a flashlight and head to your attic instead. Your artfully arranged discoveries will look great by the light of day.

Old suitcases you traveled with in the sixties can now be fondly labeled as "vintage." And those bright plates you might never use in your dining room bring whimsy to a "table" under the trees. Load your table setting into your "vintage luggage," securing plates with straps and elastic compartments. Cushion breakables with napkins and a tablecloth. When you arrive at the perfect spot, unpack and use the suitcase for extra serving space.

Plastic bags and containers are practical, but not pretty. Old tin canisters carry the meal with more character than plastic containers and bags (which are concealed inside the tins), and inexpensive cloth napkins and ribbon splash color onto your setting.

While rummaging in the attic, you might even discover an old end table small enough to fit in your car trunk, or you can bring along a patio end table. If your find isn't fashionable on its own, throw a square tablecloth or large fabric scrap over it.

You can have a picnic centerpiece for peanuts . . . and with peanuts. Snip a few blooms from your yard and insert them into florist vials filled with water; then steady them in small, clean flowerpots holding edible treats like peanuts or candies.

PICNIC TIPS

....

■ Let the occasion determine how you'll serve your fare. If it's a romantic picnic for two, pack crystal glasses wrapped in cloth napkins and a tablecloth. For an outing with the kids, throw a package of paper plates and cups in the grocery cart.

■ Bring necessary utensils for your menu from home: serving bowls, sharp knife, corkscrew, can opener.

■ If you haven't noticed the disposable dinnerware at the supermarket lately, you're in for a surprise. You'll find everything from basic white paper plates to printed plates with matching tablecloths and cups.

■ If you've got a long way to drive from the supermarket to the picnic site, take along a cooler and buy ice at the store.

■ Don't forget drinks. Depending on the theme of your menu, choose bottled water, soft drinks, tea, juice, beer, or wine.

■ Before you leave, think about every element. You don't want to find yourself trying to relax at the lake, wondering how you're going to open the canned pâté.

■ Appetites tend to soar outdoors. Buy enough food for everyone to have large portions.

■ Take a mayonnaise jar filled with water for flowers you legally pick at the picnic site.

■ Playing fetch with Fido can be great fun at a picnic. But if you're bringing your dog, don't forget dog food, water, and a water bowl. A hungry dog is not a happy dog.

■ Take along a trash bag or use grocery sacks for easy cleanup. A roll of paper towels will come in handy, too.

Watermelon Daiquiri (recipe, page 143) is as cool and refreshing as a wedge of watermelon.

Above: *Serve Mexican Cornbread Salad (recipe, page 210), and you'll have time left over for a siesta.*

Right: *Tomato-Basil-Mozzarella Salad (recipe, page 171) is perfect for a hot-weather meal.*

Left: *A tomato sandwich is a simple summer delight. See our serving suggestions on page 172.*

Tropical Gazpacho (recipe, page 204) stars as a sweet, light finale for a warm summer evening.

HERBAL LIGHT

The challenge of healthy cooking is to remove most of the fat, but preserve all the flavor. Nobody said it was going to be easy. Fresh herbs are our answer to the frustrated cook. They infuse distinctive flavor into these recipes, deliciously compensating for fat deficits.

STEAMED ORANGE ROUGHY WITH HERBS

This unbelievably simple recipe has so much flavor you won't need to reach for the salt shaker.

½ cup fresh parsley sprigs
½ cup fresh chives
½ cup fresh thyme sprigs
½ cup rosemary sprigs
2 (8-ounce) orange roughy
    fillets
Fresh lemon slices

• **Arrange** half of herbs in bottom of a steaming basket. Top with fillets and remaining herbs.
• **Cover** and steam fillets 7 minutes or until fish flakes easily when tested with a fork. Serve with fresh lemon slices. **Yield:** 4 servings.

Note: Any mild-flavored fish can be substituted in this recipe. Try cod, grouper, snapper, or farm-raised catfish. And don't limit yourself to the herbs we suggest; use any fresh herb you have available.

♥ Per serving: Calories 79 (10% from fat)
Fat 0.8g (0g saturated) Cholesterol 23mg
Sodium 72mg Carbohydrate 0g
Fiber 0g Protein 16.7g

ASIAN PESTO PASTA

Fish sauce is a flavorful extract of anchovies. It's sometimes labeled nam pla *or* nuoc nam. *Look for it in the Oriental foods section of your supermarket.*

½ cup condensed chicken broth,
    undiluted
2 tablespoons reduced-sodium soy
    sauce
2 tablespoons fish sauce
1 tablespoon grated fresh ginger
1 jalapeño pepper, seeded and
    chopped
¼ cup finely chopped fresh basil
¼ cup finely chopped fresh
    cilantro
¼ cup finely chopped fresh mint
    leaves
12 ounces linguine, cooked
    without salt or fat

• **Combine** first 8 ingredients; pour over linguine, and toss gently. Serve immediately. **Yield:** 6 servings.
Adelyne Smith
Dunnville, Kentucky

♥ Per serving: Calories 234 (4% from fat)
Fat 0.9g (0.1g saturated) Cholesterol 0mg
Sodium 272mg Carbohydrate 46.7g
Fiber 1.5g Protein 8g

FIT FOR LIFE

Twenty years ago, Lois Phillips of Trussville, Alabama, decided she couldn't go on gaining a pound a year if she wanted to be as slim at 60 as she was at 40. Her daughter Robin Burns of Springville, Alabama, agreed, and they've been a team ever since. Here are their tips for staying fit.

■ If you're just starting to exercise, try walking at least 30 minutes four times a week. This eases you into increased activity and is key to keeping the pounds off. Work up to more strenuous exercise.

■ It's never too late to start exercising. Lois began running at 40. Last year, at 60, she ran a marathon.

■ Take your lunch from home so you don't have to struggle with the dilemma of finding a low-fat option at a restaurant. But if take-out is the only way out, don't feel guilty about enjoying a burger or taco. Just make sure it's the exception, not the rule. If your fast-food fling sends you over your fat allotment for the day, eat low-fat meals the next day and get in some extra exercise.

■ You don't have to have meat every day. But when you do have it, make vegetables, grains, or pasta the center of the meal.

■ Give in once in a while without feeling guilty. Use Robin's 20% indulgence rule for good measure: Eat low-fat foods 80% of the time and indulge in your weaknesses just 20% of the time.

GREEK GRILLED ZUCCHINI WITH FETA

6 medium zucchini (2 pounds)
½ teaspoon salt
2 teaspoons olive oil
2 tablespoons red wine vinegar
2 tablespoons olive oil
2 tablespoons chopped fresh dill
2 tablespoons chopped fresh mint
1 tablespoon finely chopped shallot
¼ teaspoon pepper
½ cup crumbled feta cheese
Garnish: fresh mint sprigs

• Cut zucchini into spears, and place in a colander; sprinkle with salt. Let stand 15 minutes. Rinse with cold water, and pat dry.
• Drizzle 2 teaspoons olive oil over zucchini; toss gently. Arrange in a grill basket.
• Cook zucchini, covered with grill lid, over medium-hot coals (350° to 400°) 1 to 2 minutes on each side or until tender.
• Combine vinegar and next 5 ingredients in a jar; cover jar tightly, and shake vigorously.
• Arrange zucchini on a serving platter; drizzle with dressing, and sprinkle with feta cheese. Garnish, if desired. **Yield:** 8 servings.

Mary Pappas
Richmond, Virginia

♥ Per serving: Calories 76 (69% from fat)
Fat 6.2g (1.7g saturated) Cholesterol 6mg
Sodium 156mg Carbohydrate 4g
Fiber 0.6g Protein 2.3g

BLUEBERRY CHUTNEY

Ginger and garlic make this chutney a pungent accompaniment with chicken, turkey, lamb, or pork.

4 cups fresh or frozen blueberries
1 large onion, finely chopped
2 tablespoons minced fresh ginger
2 tablespoons minced garlic
¼ cup sugar
¼ cup raisins
¼ cup white wine vinegar
2 tablespoons curry powder
½ teaspoon salt
¼ cup chopped fresh mint

• Combine first 9 ingredients in a non-aluminum saucepan; bring to a boil over medium heat, stirring occasionally. Reduce heat, and cook 25 to 30 minutes or until onion becomes tender and mixture is thickened, stirring often. Remove from heat, and cool.
• Stir in mint. Cover and store in refrigerator up to 5 days. **Yield:** 3 cups.

Mildred Bickley
Bristol, Virginia

♥ Per 2 tablespoons: Calories 32 (5% from fat)
Fat 0.2g (0g saturated) Cholesterol 0mg
Sodium 51mg Carbohydrate 8g
Fiber 1.5g Protein 0.4g

ROSEMARY FOCACCIA

1 package active dry yeast
1¼ cups warm water (105° to 115°)
3½ cups all-purpose flour, divided
1 teaspoon salt, divided
¼ cup butter, melted
½ cup chopped fresh rosemary, divided
Vegetable cooking spray
2 tablespoons olive oil
4 cloves garlic, minced

• Combine yeast and warm water in a 2-cup liquid measuring cup; let stand 5 minutes.
• Combine yeast mixture, 2 cups flour, and ½ teaspoon salt in a large bowl, stirring well.
• Cover and let rise in a warm place (85°), free from drafts, 1 hour or until dough is doubled in bulk.
• Punch dough down, and stir in remaining flour, butter, and ¼ cup chopped rosemary.
• Turn dough out onto a lightly floured surface, and knead 10 minutes.
• Divide dough into thirds; roll each portion into a 9-inch circle on baking sheets coated with cooking spray.
• Brush dough evenly with olive oil; sprinkle evenly with remaining ¼ cup rosemary, ½ teaspoon salt, and garlic. Prick dough generously with a fork.
• Bake at 400° for 20 minutes. **Yield:** 12 servings.

Suzanne Engelmann
Jupiter, Florida

♥ Per serving: Calories 202 (33% from fat)
Fat 7.3g (2.8g saturated) Cholesterol 10mg
Sodium 236mg Carbohydrate 29.8g
Fiber 1.6g Protein 4.2g

FRUITED HERB VINEGARS

Peach-Mint Vinegar: Combine 2 peeled, chopped peaches, ¼ cup chopped fresh mint leaves, 2 tablespoons honey, and 1½ cups white wine vinegar in a jar. Cover and let stand at room temperature 2 weeks. Pour through a wire-mesh strainer into a container; discard solids. **Yield:** 1½ cups.

Leslie Genszler
Roswell, Georgia

Mango-Cilantro Vinegar: Substitute 2 peeled, chopped mangoes for peaches and ¼ cup chopped fresh cilantro for mint. Prepare vinegar as directed for recipe at left. **Yield:** 1½ cups.

Raspberry-Thyme Vinegar: Substitute 1 cup fresh raspberries for peaches and ¼ cup fresh thyme leaves for mint. Prepare vinegar as directed for recipe at left. **Yield:** 1 cup.

CATCH A WAVE

....

When the heat's on to cook a fast meal, consider enlisting the help of that nifty-looking appliance now doubling as your kitchen's breadbox: the microwave. Not only will you enjoy rediscovering how fast it is to cook with one, but you'll also keep your kitchen cool in the process.

All of these recipes can be ready – from start to finish – in less than 15 minutes. Now that's *fast*. And, as a bonus, you'll be putting what's become an expensive coffee warmer back into reputable action.

These recipes were tested using both 600-watt and 700-watt microwave ovens. For 1,000-watt ovens, cooking times will be about 1 to 2 minutes less.

CHEESY BROCCOLI CASSEROLE

1   medium onion, finely chopped
⅔   cup milk
3   large eggs
¼   cup all-purpose flour
1   teaspoon dried Italian
     seasoning
½   teaspoon salt
¼   teaspoon pepper
1   (10-ounce) package frozen
     chopped broccoli, thawed and
     drained
1   cup (4 ounces) shredded
     Cheddar cheese
½   cup cottage cheese

• **Place** onion in a lightly greased 1½-quart baking dish; microwave at HIGH 1 minute or until translucent.
• **Combine** milk and next 8 ingredients, stirring with a whisk; pour over onion.
• **Microwave** at MEDIUM-HIGH (70% power) 10 to 12 minutes, giving dish a half-turn and stirring at 4-minute intervals. **Yield:** 4 servings.

Evelyn Dauphin
Natchez, Mississippi

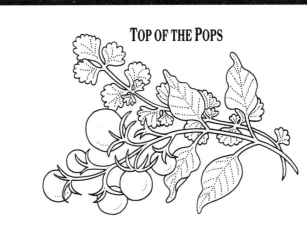

TOP OF THE POPS

Your microwave is great, but it doesn't always work magic on everything that goes in it. That's because not everything *can* go in it. There are limits. Here's our Top 10 list of things that "pop" in the microwave (with tips on how you can avoid the mess).

10. Eggs – Always remove the egg's shell and pierce the yolk once or twice before cooking; otherwise the internal pressure can build and the egg will explode (and possibly ruin your microwave).

9. Bacon – Cover with paper towels to absorb grease splatter. As for the popping noise, we can't help you there.

8. Chicken Livers – Pierce before cooking (to release internal pressure) or you'll open the door to a fine mess.

7. Whole Potatoes – Pierce several times with a fork before cooking. Otherwise the explosion will stick in your microwave – and your memory.

6. Whole Tomatoes – Pierce several times before cooking or "burst of goodness" will take on new meaning.

5. Butter – When melting butter, tightly cover the dish with plastic wrap to avoid high-impact splatters.

4. Spaghetti Sauce – Cover the container with plastic wrap unless you enjoy cleaning your microwave.

3. Cheese-Filled Wieners – Wrap in paper towels, and pierce them before cooking.

2. Popcorn – Sure, but this is the kinda "pop" we like.

And the No. 1 thing that goes "pop" in your microwave . . .

1. Metal – Oh, boy, we've got a whole category devoted to this one. Read on.

ARC DE TRIOMPHE

Putting metal in your microwave is a big no-no. Microwaving metal creates arcing, a luminous discharge of electric current (that's sparking to you and me).

To prevent arching, avoid cooking with aluminum foil, metal or metallic-trimmed dishware, and avoid placing meat thermometers in the microwave. If you should see sparks flashing in the unit, stop the oven immediately; it could severely damage the microwave *and* your dishware.

Tip: Never microwave antiques, especially lead crystal. They're not oven-tempered or heatproof, and you may end up destroying a beautiful dish.

EASY TURKEY SCALOPPINE

1 tablespoon butter or
   margarine
2 teaspoons lemon juice
1 large egg, lightly beaten
¼ cup Italian-seasoned
   breadcrumbs
2 tablespoons grated Parmesan
   cheese
½ teaspoon dried basil
⅛ teaspoon garlic salt
⅛ teaspoon ground black
   pepper
⅛ teaspoon ground red
   pepper
4 slices fresh turkey breast
   cutlets (about ½ pound)
⅓ cup pasta sauce

• Place butter in a microwave-safe
bowl, and microwave at MEDIUM
(50% power) 1 minute or until butter
melts. Add lemon juice and egg, stirring well.
• Combine breadcrumbs and next 5
ingredients in a shallow dish.
• Dip turkey in egg mixture, and
dredge in breadcrumb mixture; place
in a lightly greased 8-inch square baking dish.
• Microwave at HIGH 4 minutes, giving dish a half-turn after 2 minutes.
Spoon pasta sauce evenly over turkey.
Yield: 2 servings.

SEAFOOD-STUFFED POTATOES

2 (9-ounce) baking potatoes
½ pound crab-flavored seafood
   product
1 cup ricotta cheese
½ cup chopped green onions
½ cup chopped sweet red
   pepper
⅓ cup sour cream
1 teaspoon Old Bay seasoning
¼ teaspoon salt
⅛ teaspoon pepper
½ teaspoon lemon juice
Garnishes: sliced green onions,
   paprika

• Scrub potatoes; prick several times
with a fork.

• Place potatoes 1 inch apart on
microwave-safe rack or paper towels.
• Microwave at HIGH 8 minutes or
until done, turning and rearranging
after 4 minutes. Let stand 2 minutes.
• Cut potatoes in half lengthwise.
Scoop out pulp, leaving a ¼-inch shell
intact.
• Mash pulp; stir in pulp, seafood
product, and next 8 ingredients. Spoon
into shells; place on a microwave-safe
plate. Microwave at HIGH 2 minutes.
Garnish, if desired. Yield: 4 servings.

Judi Grigoraci
Charleston, West Virginia

SIZZLING KABOBS

....

Impress your grill-side audience with
easy-to-prepare kabobs sizzling with
goodness. Stars of the show include
tomatoes, sweet red and yellow peppers, green peppers, mushrooms,
chicken, lamb, and even meatballs
(they're fabulous).

Tip: If you plan to use wooden
skewers, soak them in water for at least
an hour before using them so they
won't burn.

MEATBALL KABOBS

1½ pounds ground chuck
1 cup regular oats
1 large egg, lightly beaten
1 teaspoon curry powder
1 teaspoon Worcestershire sauce
1 (4¾-ounce) jar pimiento-stuffed
   olives, drained
16 cherry tomatoes
2 medium-size green peppers,
   seeded and cut into
   fourths
8 new potatoes, cooked
8 mushrooms
¼ cup barbecue sauce
Vegetable cooking spray
Barbecue sauce

• Combine first 5 ingredients; divide
mixture into 24 portions. Shape each
portion into a ball around an olive.
• Alternate meatballs, tomatoes, green
pepper, potatoes, and mushrooms on
six 14-inch skewers. Brush with ¼ cup
barbecue sauce.
• Coat food rack with cooking spray;
place on grill over medium-hot coals
(350° to 400°). Place kabobs on rack.
• Cook, covered with grill lid, 10 minutes or to desired degree of doneness,
turning once. Serve with additional
barbecue sauce. Yield: 4 to 6 servings.

Peggy Huffstetler
Lebanon, Tennessee

LAMB KABOBS

1 cup olive oil
2 tablespoons fresh lemon juice
2 tablespoons chopped fresh
   parsley
½ tablespoon salt
2 teaspoons dried oregano
1 teaspoon pepper
4 cloves garlic, minced
3 bay leaves
1 (3-pound) boneless leg of lamb,
   cut into 2-inch cubes
3 medium onions, cut into
   fourths
3 sweet red peppers, seeded and
   cut into fourths
2 tomatoes, cut into fourths
10 fresh mushrooms
3 tablespoons fresh lemon
   juice
3 tablespoons olive oil
Hot cooked saffron rice or
   couscous

• Combine first 8 ingredients in a large
shallow dish or heavy-duty, zip-top
plastic bag. Add lamb, stirring to coat.
Cover or seal, and store in the refrigerator at least 8 hours.
• Remove lamb from marinade, discarding marinade.
• Alternate lamb cubes, onion, sweet
red pepper, tomato, and mushrooms
on seven 14-inch skewers.
• Combine 3 tablespoons lemon juice
and 3 tablespoons olive oil; brush on
kabobs.

• **Cook,** covered with grill lid, over medium-hot coals (350° to 400°) 10 minutes or to desired degree of doneness, turning once. Serve with rice or couscous. **Yield:** 7 servings.

Sue-Sue Hartstern
Louisville, Kentucky

ORIENTAL CHICKEN KABOBS

1½ pounds skinned and boned chicken breast halves, cut into 1-inch cubes
¼ teaspoon salt
¼ teaspoon pepper
1 medium-size sweet yellow pepper, seeded and cut into 1-inch pieces
1 medium-size sweet red pepper, seeded and cut into 1-inch pieces
1 (15-ounce) jar baby corn, drained and cut in half
⅓ cup hoisin or teriyaki sauce
⅓ cup honey
1 clove garlic, pressed
½ teaspoon minced gingerroot

• **Sprinkle** chicken evenly with salt and pepper.
• **Alternate** chicken, pepper pieces, and corn on eight 14-inch skewers.
• **Combine** hoisin sauce and next 3 ingredients; brush on kabobs.
• **Cook,** covered with grill lid, over medium-hot coals (350° to 400°) 12 minutes, turning and basting with sauce mixture. **Yield:** 4 servings.

SUMMERY SQUASH-AND-PEPPER KABOBS

2 small yellow squash, cut into 1-inch slices
2 small sweet red peppers, seeded and cut into 1-inch pieces
2 small green peppers, seeded and cut into 1-inch pieces
2 small zucchini, cut into ½-inch slices
1 (8-ounce) bottle reduced-fat Italian salad dressing
2 tablespoons grated Parmesan cheese
½ teaspoon ground red pepper

• **Combine** all ingredients in a large heavy-duty, zip-top plastic bag, stirring to coat; seal. Let stand at room temperature 1 hour, turning occasionally.
• **Remove** vegetables from marinade, reserving marinade.
• **Alternate** vegetables on eight 12-inch skewers, leaving ½-inch space between vegetables.
• **Cook,** covered with grill lid, over medium-hot coals (350° to 400°) 10 to 12 minutes or until vegetables are tender, turning once and brushing often with reserved marinade. **Yield:** 4 servings.

WHAT'S FOR SUPPER?

KING RANCH CHICKEN

....

How do you improve on an already classic dish like King Ranch Chicken? Pamala Hanlin of Hilton Head Island, South Carolina, set out on just this mission. She decided to try to give the casserole more zip and make the preparation easy and quick.

By baking the chicken breasts, Pamala eliminated some time while adding flavor. Sautéing the onion and green pepper also gave extra taste. Stirring in a few convenience products came next, and finally the assembly into the casserole dish was a breeze.

Her results – King Ranch Chicken at its best! Mission accomplished.

KING RANCH CHICKEN

4 skinned and boned chicken breast halves
¼ teaspoon salt
¼ teaspoon pepper
2 tablespoons butter or margarine
1 green pepper, chopped
1 medium onion, chopped
2 (10-ounce) cans diced tomatoes with green chiles, undrained
1 (10¾-ounce) can cream of mushroom soup, undiluted
1 (10¾-ounce) can cream of chicken soup, undiluted
12 (6-inch) corn tortillas, cut into quarters
2 cups (8 ounces) shredded Cheddar cheese

• **Sprinkle** chicken with salt and pepper; place in a 13- x 9- x 2-inch baking dish. Bake at 325° for 20 minutes or until done; cool. Coarsely chop chicken, and set aside.
• **Melt** butter in a large skillet over medium heat. Add chopped pepper and onion, and cook, stirring mixture constantly, until vegetables are crisp-tender. Remove from heat, and stir in chicken, tomatoes with green chiles, and soups.
• **Place** one-third of tortilla quarters in bottom of a lightly greased 13- x 9- x 2-inch baking dish; top with one-third chicken mixture, and sprinkle evenly with ⅔ cup shredded Cheddar cheese. Repeat layers twice, reserving remaining ⅔ cup cheese.
• **Bake** at 325° for 35 minutes; sprinkle with reserved Cheddar cheese, and bake 5 additional minutes. Let stand 5 minutes before serving. **Yield:** 6 to 8 servings.

Pamala Hanlin
Hilton Head Island, South Carolina

FROM OUR KITCHEN TO YOURS

....

Backyard grills are sizzling this time of year. Enticing aromas float through the air, tempting you to fire up the coals also. There's no denying that grilling is an easy way to cook an entrée. But some may have difficulty determining when the meat is done – sometimes it's charred on the outside yet raw on the inside. Other times the boneless chicken breast halves are shoe-leather tough. To help novices master grilling skills, here's an explanation of grilling methods, along with a cooking timetable.

SIZZLING STYLE: DIRECT VS. INDIRECT

Meats that cook in 30 minutes or less – such as steaks, chops, kabobs, and hamburgers – use the **direct grilling method.** Place food on the grill rack directly over hot coals or lava rocks, and cook, with or without grill lid, turning food once halfway through the grilling time.

Large cuts of meat (beef tenderloin, chicken quarters, pork roasts) require the slow, even cooking of the **indirect grilling method.** When using a gas grill, light one burner, and place the food over a disposable aluminum foil drip pan on the opposite side, away

GROUND RULES FOR GRILLING MEAT

MEAT	COOKING TIME	METHOD	INSTRUCTIONS
BEEF			
Ground beef patties	8 to 12 minutes	Direct	Cook, without grill lid, until no longer pink.
Steaks (1 to 1½ inches thick)	8 to 12 minutes	Direct	Cook, without grill lid, to at least 145°.
Steaks (2 inches thick)	8 to 10 minutes	Direct	Cook, covered with grill lid, to at least 145°.
Tenderloin	30 to 45 minutes	Indirect	Cook, covered with grill lid, to at least 145°.
Brisket (6 pounds)	3 to 4 hours	Indirect	Cook, covered with grill lid, to at least 145°.
FISH			
Whole fish (per inch of thickness)	10 to 12 minutes	Direct	Cook, covered with grill lid.
Fish fillets (per inch of thickness)	10 minutes	Direct	Cook, without grill lid.
LAMB			
Chops or steaks (1 inch thick)	10 to 12 minutes	Direct	Cook, without grill lid, to at least 150°.
Leg of lamb (boneless or butterflied)	40 to 50 minutes	Indirect	Cook, covered with grill lid, to at least 150°.
PORK			
Pork chops (½ inch thick)	7 to 11 minutes	Direct	Cook, covered with grill lid, to 160°.
Pork chops (¾ inch thick)	10 to 12 minutes	Direct	Cook, covered with grill lid, to 160°.
Pork chops (1½ inches thick)	16 to 22 minutes	Direct	Cook, covered with grill lid, to 160°.
Kabobs (1-inch cubes)	9 to 13 minutes	Direct	Cook, covered with grill lid, to 160°.
Pork Tenderloin (½ to 1½ pounds)	16 to 21 minutes	Direct	Cook, covered with grill lid, to 160°.
Ribs	1½ to 2 hours	Indirect	Cook, covered with grill lid, to 160°.
Boston-butt roast (6 pounds)	3 to 4 hours	Indirect	Cook, covered with grill lid, to 160°.
POULTRY			
Chicken (whole, halves, quarters, and thighs)	50 to 60 minutes	Indirect	Cook, covered with grill lid, to 180°.
Chicken (bone-in breasts)	30 minutes	Indirect	Cook, covered with grill lid, to 170°.
Chicken (boneless breasts)	10 to 12 minutes	Direct	Cook, without grill lid.
Turkey (bone-in breast, cut lengthwise in half)	45 minutes	Indirect	Cook, covered with grill lid, to 170°.

from the heat source. When using a charcoal grill, arrange hot coals at the sides of the grill or around a drip pan, making sure the drip pan is slightly larger than the food. Place meat over the drip pan, and close the lid. With the lid closed, the heat warms the grill like an oven, ensuring faster cooking and juicier meats. Turning the food isn't necessary, unless you're basting with a sauce. To maintain the correct temperature, only lift the lid to add coals as necessary.

HOT OFF THE GRILL

For the chart at left, meat was grilled over medium-hot coals (350° to 400°). These times indicate the degree of doneness to which meat should be cooked and whether or not the grill was covered with the lid. Insert a thermometer into the fleshy part of the meat to take its temperature; meats without temperature readings can be judged for desired degree of doneness by cutting into the meat with a knife and fork.

PEACHES: A BUSHEL AND A PECK

. . . .

How many times have you stopped at a roadside produce stand and debated about buying a whole bushel of peaches? After baking a few pies and cobblers, what are you going to do with the rest of them?

Here are a few answers, featuring everything from salsa to ice cream. And with a little effort now, you can enjoy a "fresh" peach pie any time of year. What could be nicer than delivering a taste of summer to a friend next winter?

While the peaches are at their peak, stock your freezer with Fresh Peach Pie Filling. It's made in a matter of minutes and stored in the freezer. When

you're ready for peach pie, place the filling in a prepared crust, and bake.

FRESH PEACH SALSA

2 large peaches, peeled and chopped
1 jalapeño pepper, seeded and finely chopped
1 tablespoon fresh lime juice
2 to 3 teaspoons chopped fresh cilantro

•**Combine** all ingredients in a small bowl. Serve with ham, pork, or chicken. **Yield:** 1½ cups.

Marc Porter
Birmingham, Alabama

FRESH PEACH PIE FILLING

5 cups peeled, sliced fresh peaches
1½ teaspoons lemon juice
1 cup sugar
¼ cup all-purpose flour
½ teaspoon ground cinnamon
2 tablespoons butter, melted

• **Place** peaches in a medium bowl; sprinkle with lemon juice, tossing gently. Set aside.
• **Combine** sugar, flour, and cinnamon; sprinkle over peaches. Toss gently, and set aside.
• **Line** a 9-inch pieplate with heavy-duty plastic wrap, allowing edges to extend over sides 6 to 8 inches.
• **Spoon** filling into pieplate, and drizzle with butter; fold edges of plastic wrap over top, and seal securely.
• **Freeze** until firm.
• **Remove** filling from pieplate, and wrap in aluminum foil. Label and freeze filling up to a year. **Yield:** enough for one 9-inch pie.

Fresh Peach Pie: Fit 1 crust from 1 (15-ounce) package refrigerated piecrusts into a 9-inch pieplate according to package directions. Unwrap frozen pie filling, and place filling into pastry shell. Roll remaining piecrust on a lightly floured surface to press out fold

lines; place over peach mixture. Fold edges under, and crimp. Cut slits in top crust for steam to escape. Bake at 425° for 15 minutes; cover edges with foil to prevent excessive browning, and bake 25 to 30 minutes or until golden. Cool on a wire rack. **Yield:** one 9-inch pie.

Note: You can bake Fresh Peach Pie Filling in pastry shell immediately. Bake as directed, reducing second baking time to 20 to 25 minutes.

Sandra Enwright
Winter Park, Florida

FRESH PEACH ICE CREAM

4 to 6 cups sliced fresh peaches (1¾ to 2 pounds)
3 cups sugar, divided
⅓ cup all-purpose flour
Dash of salt
4 cups milk
2 (12-ounce) cans evaporated milk
6 large eggs, lightly beaten
1½ tablespoons vanilla extract
1 teaspoon almond extract

• **Combine** peaches and ¾ cup sugar in container of an electric blender or food processor. Process just until finely chopped. Set aside.
• **Combine** remaining 2¼ cups sugar, flour, and salt in a Dutch oven. Stir in milk, evaporated milk, and eggs.
• **Cook** over medium heat, stirring constantly, 10 minutes or until slightly thickened. Cool.
• **Stir** in peaches and flavorings.
• **Pour** mixture into freezer container of a 5-quart hand-turned or electric freezer. Freeze according to manufacturer's instructions. Pack freezer with additional ice and rock salt, and let stand 1 hour. **Yield:** 13 cups.

Linda Myers
Muskogee, Oklahoma

PEACHES AND CREAM

1½ cups all-purpose flour
2 tablespoons sugar
½ teaspoon baking powder
½ teaspoon salt
½ cup butter or margarine
4 to 6 peaches, peeled and halved
1 cup sugar
1 teaspoon ground cinnamon
2 egg yolks
1 cup whipping cream
Vanilla ice cream

• **Combine** first 4 ingredients; cut in butter with pastry blender until mixture is crumbly. Press flour mixture into bottom and 1 inch up sides of an 8-inch square pan.
• **Arrange** peaches, cut side down, over crust. Combine 1 cup sugar and cinnamon; sprinkle over peaches.
• **Bake** at 400° for 15 minutes.
• **Combine** egg yolks and whipping cream; pour over peaches.
• **Bake** 30 additional minutes. Serve warm with vanilla ice cream. **Yield:** 6 servings.

Note: To make individual servings, press flour mixture into six 6-ounce soufflé dishes. Reduce peaches to 3, and place a peach half in each dish. Reduce sugar to ¾ cup; combine sugar and 1 teaspoon cinnamon, and sprinkle over peaches. Bake as directed, topping with egg yolk mixture after 15 minutes. **Yield:** 6 servings.

Ann E. Ludwig
Chattanooga, Tennessee

LAYERED PEACH DESSERT

¼ cup sugar
3 cups chopped fresh peaches
1½ cups all-purpose flour
¼ cup firmly packed brown sugar
½ cup chopped pecans
½ cup butter or margarine, melted
1 (8-ounce) package cream cheese, softened
1¾ cups sifted powdered sugar
1 (8-ounce) container frozen whipped topping, thawed
¼ to ½ teaspoon almond extract

• **Sprinkle** sugar over chopped peaches; stir gently, and let stand 30 minutes.
• **Combine** flour, brown sugar, and pecans in a medium bowl; stir in butter. Press into bottom of a 13- x 9- x 2-inch baking dish.
• **Bake** at 350° for 18 to 20 minutes. Cool crust on a wire rack.
• **Combine** cream cheese and powdered sugar; beat at medium speed with an electric mixer until fluffy. Fold in whipped topping and almond extract.
• **Drain** peaches, discarding liquid. Fold peaches into cream cheese mixture. Spoon over crust, spreading evenly.
• **Cover** and chill 3 to 4 hours. **Yield:** 15 servings.

Linda Walton
Fort Valley, Georgia

EGGPLANT FOR EVERYONE

....

One of the most beautiful vegetables in the produce section, eggplant invites you to pick it up, look it over, and place it in your shopping cart. But its good looks are no match for its flavor personality, and we've got the recipes to prove it.

EGGPLANT CAKES

1 (1½-pound) eggplant, peeled and cubed
½ cup all-purpose flour
½ teaspoon baking powder
1 large egg, lightly beaten
¼ cup grated Parmesan cheese
1 tablespoon butter or margarine, melted
½ teaspoon garlic salt
¼ teaspoon dried thyme
½ cup vegetable oil

• **Cook** eggplant in boiling water to cover 15 minutes; drain well. Mash slightly.
• **Combine** eggplant, flour, and next 6 ingredients.
• **Pour** oil into a large skillet; place over medium heat until hot. Drop eggplant mixture by tablespoonfuls into oil; cook until golden, turning once. **Yield:** 6 to 8 servings.

Note: To bake as a casserole, place eggplant mixture in a lightly greased 1-quart casserole, and bake at 350° for 30 minutes.

Sunny Tiedemann
Bartlesville, Oklahoma

EGGPLANT-AND-OYSTER LOUISIANE

4 slices bacon
3 (1-pound) eggplants, peeled and cubed
1 medium onion, chopped
1 large green pepper, chopped
3 stalks celery, chopped
4 green onions, chopped
6 cloves garlic, minced
¾ cup Italian-seasoned breadcrumbs
1½ tablespoons grated Parmesan cheese
½ teaspoon Creole seasoning
1 tablespoon butter or margarine
2 (12-ounce) containers fresh Standard oysters, drained

• **Cook** bacon in a large skillet until crisp; remove bacon, reserving drippings in skillet. Crumble bacon, and set aside.
• **Add** eggplant and next 5 ingredients to bacon drippings; cover and cook over medium heat 20 minutes, stirring occasionally. Remove mixture from heat; stir in breadcrumbs, cheese, and Creole seasoning. Set aside.
• **Melt** butter in a large skillet over medium heat; add oysters, and cook, stirring constantly, just until edges curl (about 5 minutes). Drain well.
• **Spread** half of eggplant mixture in a lightly greased 13- x 9- x 2-inch baking

dish; top with oysters. Spread remaining eggplant mixture over oysters. Bake, uncovered, at 400° for 20 minutes. Sprinkle with bacon. **Yield: 6 servings.**

Dorothy Trick
Baton Rouge, Louisiana

FREEZER EGGPLANT-SAUSAGE-PASTA CASSEROLE

1 (16-ounce) package penne pasta, uncooked
2 pounds reduced-fat Italian-style turkey sausage
Vegetable cooking spray
2 (¾-pound) eggplants, peeled and cut into ½-inch cubes
1 cup chopped onion
2 cloves garlic, minced
2 teaspoons paprika
1 (28-ounce) can crushed tomatoes, undrained
1 (6-ounce) can tomato paste
1 tablespoon dried Italian seasoning
1 teaspoon dried basil
¾ teaspoon salt
½ teaspoon dried crushed red pepper
1 (15-ounce) container nonfat ricotta cheese
3 cups (12 ounces) shredded part-skim mozzarella cheese, divided

• **Line** 2 (11- x 7- x 1½-inch) baking dishes with aluminum foil. Set aside.
• **Cook** pasta according to package directions, omitting salt and fat; drain and set aside.
• **Brown** sausage in a large nonstick skillet coated with cooking spray, stirring until it crumbles. Drain and pat dry with paper towels. Return sausage to skillet. Add eggplant, onion, and garlic.
• **Cook** mixture 8 minutes or until eggplant is tender. Stir in paprika; cook 1 minute.
• **Stir** in tomatoes and next 5 ingredients. Bring to a boil; reduce heat, and simmer 20 minutes, stirring occasionally. Stir in pasta. Remove from heat, and cool.

• **Spoon** half of eggplant mixture evenly into prepared dishes. Top each evenly with ricotta cheese, and sprinkle each with ¾ cup mozzarella cheese. Spread remaining eggplant mixture evenly over each casserole; freeze just until firm.
• **Remove** casseroles from baking dishes; wrap in heavy-duty aluminum foil or seal in heavy-duty, zip-top plastic bags. Freeze up to 6 months.
• **Place** unwrapped frozen casseroles in 11- x 7- x 1½-inch baking dishes coated with cooking spray. Thaw in refrigerator 24 hours.
• **Bake** at 350° for 45 minutes or until bubbly. Sprinkle each evenly with remaining ¾ cup mozzarella cheese, and bake 5 additional minutes. **Yield: 6 servings per casserole.**

Note: You can assemble casseroles in baking dishes coated with cooking spray, and bake immediately at 350° for 30 minutes. Sprinkle with remaining cheese, and bake 5 additional minutes.

Jeanne S. Hotaling
Augusta, Georgia

♥ Per serving: Calories 399 (26% from fat)
Fat 11.5g (1.2g saturated) Cholesterol 41.2mg
Sodium 833mg Carbohydrate 43.8g
Fiber 3.1g Protein 30.2g

EGGPLANT PARMIGIANA

2 large eggs
½ cup grated Parmesan cheese, divided
¼ cup milk
1 tablespoon chopped fresh parsley
½ teaspoon garlic powder
¼ teaspoon salt
¼ teaspoon pepper
1 cup all-purpose flour
1 (1½-pound) eggplant, peeled and cut into ½-inch slices
⅓ to ½ cup vegetable oil
1 (14-ounce) jar spaghetti sauce
2 cups (8 ounces) shredded mozzarella cheese
Hot cooked spaghetti

• **Combine** eggs, 2 tablespoons Parmesan cheese, milk, and next 4 ingredients in a shallow bowl, stirring well; set aside.
• **Place** flour in a shallow dish. Dredge eggplant slices in flour, shaking off excess; dip in egg mixture.
• **Pour** oil in a large skillet; place over medium-high heat until hot.
• **Fry** eggplant slices in hot oil until golden on each side. Drain on paper towels.
• **Arrange** half of eggplant slices in a lightly greased 11- x 7- x 1½-inch baking dish. Pour half of spaghetti sauce over eggplant, and sprinkle with half of remaining Parmesan cheese. Repeat procedure with remaining eggplant, sauce, and Parmesan cheese.
• **Bake** at 350° for 25 minutes. Sprinkle with mozzarella cheese; bake 10 to 15 additional minutes or until cheese melts. Serve over spaghetti. **Yield: 6 servings.**

Retta D. Warriner
Camden, South Carolina

EGGPLANT INFORMATION

Eggplants are either male or female. Look at the blossom end – if it's indented, it's a female; if it's smooth, it's a male. Males have fewer seeds, which sometimes taste bitter.

To remove most of the bitterness, slice eggplant, and sprinkle with salt; let stand 30 minutes. Rinse and pat dry with paper towels.

Select eggplants that are firm, unblemished, and heavy for their size. Use them within one to two days of purchase, or place them in a plastic bag and store them in the refrigerator up to five days.

GRILLED EGGPLANT APPETIZER

2 (1-pound) eggplants, peeled and
   cut into ½-inch slices
½ teaspoon salt
½ cup coarsely chopped fresh
   basil
2 cloves garlic, minced
1 tablespoon olive oil
Vegetable cooking spray
¼ teaspoon ground red pepper
1 (22-inch) French baguette, cut
   into ½-inch slices
4 Roma tomatoes, each cut into
   10 slices
⅓ cup freshly grated Parmesan
   cheese

• **Sprinkle** eggplant with salt, and let stand 30 minutes.
• **Combine** basil, garlic, and olive oil; set aside.
• **Rinse** eggplant slices, and pat dry.
• **Coat** food rack with vegetable cooking spray; place rack on grill over medium coals (300° to 350°). Place eggplant slices on rack in a single layer.
• **Cook,** without grill lid, 8 to 10 minutes on each side. Place half of eggplant slices in an airtight container, and sprinkle with basil mixture; top with remaining eggplant slices. Cover and chill in an airtight container 8 hours.
• **Position** knife blade in food processor bowl; add eggplant mixture and red pepper. Process until smooth, stopping once to scrape down sides.
• **Spread** about 1½ teaspoons eggplant mixture on each of 40 baguette slices, and top each with a tomato slice. Sprinkle evenly with cheese.
• **Broil** 5½ inches from heat (with electric oven door partially opened) 2 to 3 minutes or until cheese melts. Serve immediately. **Yield:** 40 appetizers.

♥ Per serving: Calories 41 (17% from fat)
Fat 0.8g (0.2g saturated) Cholesterol 1mg
Sodium 99mg Carbohydrate 7.1g
Fiber 0.6g Protein 1.4g

CONSUMING KUDZU

....

This time of year in the South, kudzu jokes and festivals spring up as quickly as the vine. However, the persistent plant that devours trees and covers fields is spreading in another direction. Kudzu is creeping into the kitchen.

The roots, flowers, and young leaves are edible. Try the tender leaves in recipes that call for spinach. Fragrant blossoms, the vine's hidden treasure, make a terrific jelly. Use kudzu root powder as a cornstarch replacement and a coating for frying. And deep-fried leaves are much like potato chips.

The leaves and flowers are yours for the price of an afternoon walk. Harvest in areas where no spraying has been done to control growth. Kudzu root powder, also called kuzu, and capsules are sold at health-food stores.

KUDZU BLOSSOM JELLY

Spoon over cream cheese, or melt and serve over waffles and ice cream.

4 cups kudzu blossoms
4 cups boiling water
1 tablespoon lemon juice
1 (1¾-ounce) package powdered
   pectin
5 cups sugar

• **Wash** kudzu blossoms with cold water, and place in a large bowl. Pour 4 cups boiling water over blossoms; cover and chill at least 8 hours.
• **Pour** blossoms and liquid through a colander into a Dutch oven, discarding blossoms.
• **Add** lemon juice and pectin; bring to a full rolling boil over high heat, stirring constantly.
• **Stir** in sugar; return to a full rolling boil, and boil 1 minute, stirring constantly. Remove from heat; skim off foam with a metal spoon.
• **Quickly** pour jelly into hot, sterilized jars, filling to ¼ inch from top. Wipe

jar rims. Cover at once with metal lids, and screw on bands.
• **Process** in boiling-water bath 5 minutes. Cool on wire racks. **Yield:** 6 half-pints.

Note: Blossom liquid is gray until lemon juice is added.

APPLE CIDER

The kudzu powder gives a silky smooth texture without a starchy taste.

1½ teaspoons kudzu powder
6¼ cups apple cider, divided
4 (3-inch) sticks cinnamon
12 whole cloves
1 teaspoon grated orange rind

• **Combine** kudzu powder and ¼ cup apple cider, stirring well; set kudzu powder mixture aside.
• **Combine** remaining 6 cups apple cider and next 3 ingredients in a Dutch oven; bring apple cider mixture to a boil. Reduce heat; simmer 15 minutes.
• **Pour** apple cider mixture through a wire-mesh strainer into a bowl, discarding spices. Return liquid to Dutch oven, and bring to a boil.
• **Add** kudzu powder mixture, stirring constantly. Reduce heat, and simmer, stirring constantly, 1 minute or until mixture is translucent. Serve hot. **Yield:** 6 cups.

Diane Hoots
Warner Robins, Georgia

Kudzu Fried Chicken: Dredge chicken breast strips in kudzu powder; dip in lightly beaten egg, and dredge strips in dry Italian-seasoned breadcrumbs. Deep fry in hot oil (350°) for 3 to 5 minutes or until golden. Drain on paper towels. Serve immediately. (May also be used to fry fresh sliced okra.)

AUGUST

MIND YOUR TEAS & CUBES

The profusion of flavored teas on supermarket shelves is the inspiration to mix and mingle the South's favorite beverage with fruit juices, ginger ale, and sparkling waters. Beat the heat with our zippy teas paired with fruit-flavored ice cubes. The results are delicious – and much more exciting than pouring a bottled concoction.

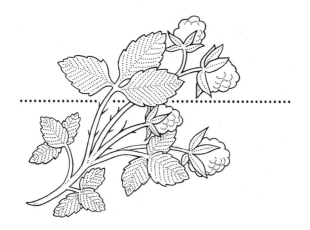

Mix and match our make-your-own fruit-flavored ice cubes on the opposite page with these teas or try them in your favorite beverage. They're easy to make and won't dilute a drink like regular ice cubes will. Instead, these colorful cubes trigger a little meltdown and add some zing to these cooling beverages.

RASP-BERRY GOOD TEA
(pictured on page 152)

2 cups boiling water
4 raspberry zinger herb tea bags
3 tablespoons sugar
2 cups ginger ale, chilled *

• **Pour** boiling water over tea bags; cover and steep 5 minutes.
• **Remove** tea bags from water, squeezing gently. Stir in sugar, and let tea mixture cool.
• **Stir** in ginger ale. Pour over flavored cubes. **Yield:** 4 cups.

* Substitute 2 cups reduced-calorie ginger ale for regular.

LEMON TEA TINGLER
(pictured on page 152)

7 cups boiling water
12 regular-size tea bags
½ cup sugar
1 (6-ounce) can frozen lemonade concentrate, thawed and undiluted
1 cup club soda, chilled

• **Pour** boiling water over tea bags; cover and steep 5 minutes.
• **Remove** tea bags from water, squeezing gently. Stir in sugar; cool.
• **Stir** in lemonade concentrate and club soda. Pour over flavored cubes. **Yield:** 8½ cups.

Elizabeth R. Drawdy
Spindale, North Carolina

PINK SANGRÍA TEA
(pictured on page 152)

2 cups boiling water
4 orange herb tea bags
3 tablespoons sugar
2 cups cranberry juice cocktail
1 cup dry white wine

• **Pour** boiling water over tea bags; cover and steep 5 minutes.
• **Remove** tea bags from water, squeezing gently. Stir in sugar; cool.
• **Stir** in juice cocktail and wine. Pour over flavored cubes. **Yield:** 5 cups.

TROPICAL TEA-SER
(pictured on page 152)

2 cups boiling water
5 orange-mango zinger tea bags
1 cup sugar
2 cups pineapple juice

• **Pour** boiling water over tea bags; cover and steep 5 minutes.
• **Remove** tea bags from water, squeezing gently. Stir in sugar; cool.
• **Stir** in pineapple juice. Pour over flavored cubes. **Yield:** 4½ cups.

They're so pretty, you won't need a garnish.

Here's how you can add pizzazz to your punch or a twist to your tea. Just put whole raspberries, lemon slices or wedges, mint sprigs, strawberry slices, or even edible flowers such as pansies and violets into some ice cube trays, top them off with your favorite beverage, and freeze.

CUBE IT!

■ To make ice cubes that won't dilute your drink as they melt, choose a flavored beverage that's either part of the recipe or blends with its flavor.

■ If you prefer crystal-clear ice cubes, first boil water, and then cool it to room temperature before pouring into ice cube trays and freezing. Bottled spring water will also give you clear cubes.

■ Use muffin pans, madeleine pans, or miniature Bundt pans to make extra large or decoratively shaped ice cubes for punch.

■ Make ice cubes for a party ahead of time, and store them in plastic bags in the freezer. Count on 350 cubes for 50 people or about seven cubes per person.

Lemon-Mint Cubes: (Pictured on page 152) Place a small mint sprig and lemon slice wedge in each section of ice cube trays; add bottled water. Freeze until firm.

Berry-Good Cubes: (Pictured on page 152) Place a fresh whole raspberry or strawberry slice in each section of ice cube trays; add ginger ale. Freeze until firm.

Florida Cubes: (Pictured on page 152) Pour orange juice into ice cube trays; freeze until firm.

Cranberry Cubes: (Pictured on page 152) Pour cranberry juice cocktail into ice cube trays; freeze until firm.

Lemonade Cubes: (Pictured on page 152) Pour lemonade into ice cube trays; freeze until firm.

CROWNING TOUCHES

A lemon slice perched on the rim of a glass lets guests know they're worth this extra effort. Try these garnishing ideas to let them feel even more special.

■ Slip a fresh mint sprig inside a lemon slice, and place it onto the rim of the glass.

■ Cut wedges from limes or oranges instead of lemons.

■ Using a citrus stripper, cut a strip of orange peel. Curl it and place it atop the drink.

■ Moisten the rims of glasses and dip in colored sugar. You can find colored sugar at large grocery stores, or you can make your own with food coloring and granulated sugar. (Combine food coloring and sugar in a jar; cover and shake vigorously.)

■ Some garnishes can serve double-duty as stirrers, like decorative straws or long cinnamon sticks. Or you can thread fruit such as pineapple chunks, maraschino cherries, and lemon slices onto wooden skewers to make colorful stirrers that you can nibble on afterwards.

LOW-CAL TROPICAL

We can't do anything about the heat and humidity of August, but these easy, low-fat recipes will bring a breath of fresh air to the dinner table.

GRILLED CHICKEN SALAD WITH RASPBERRY DRESSING

4 (4-ounce) skinned and boned chicken breast halves
Raspberry Dressing
4 mangoes, peeled and finely chopped
¼ cup chopped fresh basil
1 red jalapeño pepper, seeded and finely chopped
1 green jalapeño pepper, seeded and finely chopped
8 cups mixed salad greens

• **Place** chicken in a shallow dish or large heavy-duty, zip-top plastic bag; add ¼ cup Raspberry Dressing. Cover or seal and chill 2 hours, turning occasionally. Cover and chill remaining dressing.
• **Combine** chopped mango and next 3 ingredients; add 3 tablespoons Raspberry Dressing, stirring gently to coat. Cover and chill.
• **Remove** chicken from marinade, discarding marinade.
• **Cook** chicken, covered with grill lid, over medium-hot coals (350° to 400°) 5 minutes on each side or until done. Remove from grill, and cut chicken into thin strips.

• **Combine** salad greens and remaining Raspberry Dressing, tossing well; arrange on 4 individual plates. Place chicken strips on greens; serve with mango mixture. **Yield:** 4 servings.

❤ Per serving: Calories 355 (15% from fat)
Fat 6.2g (1g saturated) Cholesterol 70mg
Sodium 177mg Carbohydrate 49.9g
Fiber 20.6g Protein 28.4g

Raspberry Dressing

¼ cup lime juice
3 tablespoons seedless raspberry jam
2 tablespoons hot pepper jelly
1 tablespoon vegetable oil
1 clove garlic, minced
¼ teaspoon salt
¼ teaspoon dry mustard
¼ teaspoon freshly ground pepper

• **Combine** all ingredients in container of an electric blender; process until smooth. Cover and chill. **Yield:** ¾ cup.

❤ Per 3 tablespoons: Calories 94 (33% from fat)
Fat 3.5g (0g saturated) Cholesterol 0mg
Sodium 150mg Carbohydrate 15.8g
Fiber 0.1g Protein 0.3g

CARIBBEAN BANANA FISH

These ingredients may seem bizarre for a fish recipe, but the result is surprisingly delicious.

¼ teaspoon coriander seeds
¼ teaspoon lemon pepper
¼ teaspoon ground nutmeg
¼ teaspoon ground allspice
¼ teaspoon salt
¼ teaspoon pepper
Vegetable cooking spray
4 (4-ounce) red snapper fillets, skinned
¼ cup all-purpose flour
2 bananas, peeled and sliced
4 small green onions, chopped
¼ cup sweetened coconut milk
¼ cup rum

• **Crush** coriander seeds, using a mortar and pestle; add lemon pepper and next 4 ingredients, stirring well. Set aside.
• **Coat** a large nonstick skillet with cooking spray, and place over medium heat until hot.
• **Dredge** snapper fillets in flour, and arrange in hot skillet. Sprinkle half of spice mixture over fillets, and cook over medium-high heat until lightly browned. Turn fillets; sprinkle with remaining spice mixture, and cook until browned.
• **Place** banana slices over fillets, and sprinkle with chopped green onions. Add coconut milk, and cook until fish flakes easily when tested with a fork.
• **Add** rum to skillet; cover and let stand 5 minutes. **Yield:** 4 servings.

Teresa Smith
Miami, Florida

❤ Per serving: Calories 286 (25% from fat)
Fat 7.1g (3.8g saturated) Cholesterol 42mg
Sodium 224mg Carbohydrate 21.9g
Fiber 2.4g Protein 25.3g

OKRA, CORN, AND TOMATOES

Helen Goggans adds corn – a staple of Caribbean cuisine – to her version of stewed okra and tomatoes.

4 ears fresh corn
Vegetable cooking spray
1 medium onion, chopped
1 small green pepper, seeded and chopped
3 large tomatoes, peeled and chopped
1 teaspoon sugar
¾ teaspoon salt
¼ teaspoon pepper
¼ teaspoon hot sauce
½ pound small fresh okra pods

● **Cut** corn off cobs; set aside, and discard cobs.
● **Coat** a large skillet with cooking spray, and place over medium-high heat until hot. Add onion and green pepper; cook, stirring constantly, until tender.
● **Stir** in corn, tomato, and next 4 ingredients; arrange okra on top of corn mixture. Cover, reduce heat to low, and cook 20 to 25 minutes or until okra is tender. **Yield:** 6 cups.

Helen Goggans
Kingsland, Arkansas

♥ Per 1 cup: Calories 101 (12% from fat)
Fat 1.5g (0.2g saturated) Cholesterol 0mg
Sodium 312mg Carbohydrate 21.8g
Fiber 3.7g Protein 3.3g

A FAT-FREE TOAST TO THE TROPICS

■ Try sweet potatoes and plantains crisped in the microwave.

Sweet Potato Chips: Combine 1 tablespoon chili powder and ½ teaspoon salt. Cut 1 sweet potato into very thin slices. Place one-half of slices in a single layer on a microwave-safe rack. Sprinkle lightly with chili powder mixture. Microwave at HIGH 5½ to 7 minutes, giving rack a half-turn after 3 minutes. Cool chips on a wire rack. Repeat with remaining slices and chili powder mixture. **Yield:** 3 cups.

Plantain Chips: Substitute 1 plantain, peeled, for sweet potato in recipe above. Proceed as directed, microwaving at HIGH 3½ to 5 minutes or until crisp, giving rack a half-turn after 2 minutes. **Yield:** 1⅓ cups.

■ Extracts give these fat-free drinks flavor without added calories.

Caribbean Cooler: Combine 1 papaya, peeled, seeded, and coarsely chopped; 1 (12-ounce) can evaporated skimmed milk, chilled; 1 (12-ounce) can ginger ale, chilled; ¼ cup lemon juice; ¼ cup lime juice; and ½ teaspoon coconut extract in container of an electric blender. Process until mixture is smooth. Add enough ice to bring to 5-cup level. Process until smooth. **Yield:** 5 cups (120 calories per cup).

Dottie B. Miller
Jonesborough, Tennessee

Piña Coladas: Combine 1 (12-ounce) can evaporated skimmed milk; 1 (8-ounce) can pineapple chunks, undrained; ½ cup frozen pineapple-orange juice concentrate, undiluted; 1 large banana, peeled and sliced; ½ teaspoon rum extract; and ½ teaspoon coconut extract in an electric blender. Add enough ice to measure 5 cups. Process until smooth. **Yield:** 5 cups (100 calories per cup).

Sherida Eddlemun
Memphis, Tennessee

BLACK-EYED PEA SALAD

The curry dressing can be served on the side or stirred into the salad.

1 (15.8-ounce) can black-eyed peas, drained and rinsed
½ cup sliced green onions
½ cup chopped sweet yellow pepper
1 clove garlic, minced
1¼ teaspoons grated lemon rind
¼ teaspoon freshly ground black pepper
2 tablespoons lemon juice
½ cup plain low-fat yogurt
1 tablespoon pineapple juice
1¼ teaspoons curry powder
¼ teaspoon salt
⅛ teaspoon freshly ground black pepper
2 tablespoons dry-roasted cashews

● **Combine** first 7 ingredients; cover and chill at least 1 hour.
● **Combine** yogurt and next 4 ingredients, stirring until smooth. Cover and chill at least 1 hour. Serve with dressing, and sprinkle with cashews. **Yield:** 4 servings.

Carole Record
Huntsville, Alabama

♥ Per serving: Calories 156 (20% from fat)
Fat 3.5g (0.7g saturated) Cholesterol 2mg
Sodium 389mg Carbohydrate 23.4g
Fiber 5.2g Protein 8.9g

PAPAYA SEED DRESSING

When preparing fresh papayas, don't throw away the seeds. Their peppery flavor adds mysterious pungency to this salad dressing.

1 tablespoon cornstarch
1 (7.1-ounce) can papaya nectar
½ cup sugar
½ teaspoon salt
½ teaspoon dry mustard
½ cup white wine vinegar
2 tablespoons chopped onion
3 tablespoons fresh papaya seeds
     (about 1 papaya)

• **Combine** cornstarch and papaya nectar in a small saucepan, stirring well; cook over medium heat, stirring constantly, until mixture thickens and boils. Boil 1 minute, stirring constantly. Remove from heat; cool.
• **Combine** sugar and next 5 ingredients in container of an electric blender, and process until papaya seeds resemble coarsely ground pepper. Stir into nectar mixture; cover and chill at least 2 hours. Serve over mixed fruit. **Yield:** 2 cups.

♥ Per tablespoon: Calories 18 (1% from fat)
Fat 0g (0g saturated) Cholesterol 0mg
Sodium 37mg Carbohydrate 4.5g
Fiber 0g Protein 0g

TROPICAL GAZPACHO

(pictured on page 188)

Top each bowl of gazpacho with a small scoop of fruit-flavored sorbet for extra refreshment.

2 papayas, peeled, seeded, and
     chopped
2 mangoes, peeled, seeded, and
     chopped
2 kiwifruits, peeled and chopped
2 teaspoons grated lime rind
3 tablespoons lime juice
¼ to ½ teaspoon ground
     cardamom
1 teaspoon vanilla extract
3 (8-ounce) bottles papaya nectar
Garnish: carambola slices

• **Combine** all ingredients except carambola slices in a large bowl; cover mixture and chill. Garnish, if desired. **Yield:** 5 cups.

♥ Per 1 cup: Calories 189 (4% from fat)
Fat 0.8g (0g saturated) Cholesterol 0mg
Sodium 11mg Carbohydrate 47.2g
Fiber 3.9g Protein 1.7g

TROPICAL TRIFLE

1 (3-ounce) package vanilla
     pudding mix
2 cups skim milk
1 (16-ounce) package fat-free
     pound cake
½ cup orange juice
1 (10-ounce) package frozen
     sliced strawberries, thawed
     and undrained
1 (20-ounce) can crushed
     unsweetened pineapple,
     undrained
2 bananas, peeled and sliced
1 (8-ounce) container reduced-fat
     frozen whipped topping,
     thawed
¼ cup flaked coconut,
     toasted

• **Combine** pudding mix and skim milk in a large saucepan; bring to a boil over medium heat, stirring constantly. Remove from heat, and cool.
• **Cut** pound cake into 10 slices; cut each slice into 6 cubes.
• **Place** half of cake cubes in bottom of a 2½-quart trifle bowl. Sprinkle with half of orange juice.
• **Spoon** half of strawberries with juice over cake cubes; spread with half of pudding.
• **Combine** undrained pineapple and banana slices, stirring to coat. Drain fruit, discarding liquid.
• **Spoon** half of fruit mixture over pudding; spread half of whipped topping over top. Repeat layers, ending with whipped topping. Sprinkle with toasted coconut.
• **Cover** with plastic wrap, and chill at least 6 hours. **Yield:** 12 servings.

Linda Myers
Muskogee, Oklahoma

♥ Per serving: Calories 258 (11% from fat)
Fat 3.2g (0.5g saturated) Cholesterol 13mg
Sodium 280mg Carbohydrate 53.3g
Fiber 1.2g Protein 4g

COOKING IN AUSTIN

....

Wheeling your grocery cart around the 60,000-square-foot Austin (Texas) Central Market, you're likely to work up quite an appetite. Of course you could have lunch in the cafe. But you might instead don an apron and learn to concoct some superb dishes at the Central Market's Cooking School.

Executive Chef Ron Brannon shares a few of his favorite recipes, along with two by other Texas cooks. For more information on the **Austin Central Market Cooking School,** call (512) 206-1014.

SHRIMP WITH GIN AND GINGER

1½ pounds unpeeled large fresh shrimp (about 28)
3 tablespoons butter or margarine
2 cloves garlic, minced
2 tablespoons minced fresh ginger
⅓ cup gin
2 small carrots, cut into thin strips
2 small stalks celery, cut into thin strips
1 leek, cut into thin strips
4 fresh snow pea pods, cut into thin strips
¼ teaspoon salt
½ cup whipping cream

• **Peel** shrimp, and devein, if desired. Set aside.
• **Melt** butter in a skillet over medium heat; add shrimp, and cook, stirring constantly, until shrimp turn pink (about 2 to 3 minutes). Remove shrimp, reserving drippings in skillet; keep warm.
• **Cook** garlic and ginger in reserved drippings over medium heat 1 minute, stirring constantly.

• **Add** gin, stirring to loosen browned particles that cling to bottom. Stir in carrot and next 5 ingredients; cook over medium heat 5 minutes.
• **Stir** in shrimp; serve immediately. **Yield:** 4 servings.

Kathy Ruiz
Houston, Texas

BONELESS PORK CHOPS WITH ANCHO CREAM SAUCE
(pictured on page 222)

4 (½-inch-thick) boneless pork loin chops
¼ teaspoon salt
¼ teaspoon pepper
4 slices bacon
Vegetable cooking spray
¼ cup Ancho Base
¾ cup whipping cream

• **Sprinkle** pork chops with salt and pepper. Wrap 1 slice bacon around each pork chop; secure with wooden picks, if desired.
• **Coat** food rack with cooking spray; place on grill over medium coals (300° to 350°). Place pork chops on rack, and cook, covered with grill lid, 8 minutes on each side or until done.
• **Combine** ¼ cup Ancho Base and whipping cream in a saucepan, stirring with a wire whisk until smooth. Bring to a boil over medium heat, whisking constantly. Reduce heat, and simmer, whisking constantly, 5 minutes or until thickened.
• **Spoon** Ancho Cream Sauce onto plates; top each with a pork chop. Serve immediately. **Yield:** 4 servings.

Ancho Base

3 dried ancho chile peppers
4 ounces dried tomatoes
3 tablespoons minced garlic
½ cup chopped onion
4 beef-flavored bouillon cubes
1 tablespoon dried oregano
1 tablespoon brown sugar
2 tablespoons Worcestershire sauce
¼ cup tomato paste
1½ cups water

• **Combine** all ingredients in a saucepan. Bring to a boil over medium heat; reduce heat, and simmer 10 minutes, stirring occasionally. Let cool 15 minutes.
• **Position** knife blade in food processor bowl; add pepper mixture. Process until smooth, stopping often to scrape down sides. Cover and chill up to 1 week or freeze up to 3 months. **Yield:** 2¼ cups.

MEGA MARKET

Austin's Central Market is to grocery shopping what Walt Disney World is to amusement parks. There's something to intrigue everyone.

The produce section offers a bountiful display of fruits and vegetables, including a large cart full of unusual miniature varieties for children to purchase. (Proceeds go to local charities.) When we visited, 25 varieties of apples lined one wall, along with many less familiar items.

In addition to fresh flowers, the florist shop sells dried petals by the scoop for blend-your-own potpourri. Did you say cheese? You'll find 500 varieties at Central Market. The meatcase is stocked with everything from Certified Angus beef to wild boar prosciutto. And the buttery wafts from the international bakery are enough to make even a Frenchman drool.

For more information on Central Market, call (512) 206-1000.

CHICKEN ENCHILADAS WITH TOMATILLO SAUCE

1 (6½-ounce) package 6-inch corn
   tortillas
3½ cups chopped cooked chicken
3 cups (12 ounces) shredded
   Monterey Jack cheese
Tomatillo Sauce

• **Wrap** tortillas in aluminum foil; bake at 325° for 15 minutes or until thoroughly heated.
• **Place** about ⅓ cup chicken and ¼ cup cheese down center of each tortilla; roll up, and place, seam side down, in a 13- x 9- x 2-inch baking dish. Repeat procedure with each tortilla. Top with 2 cups Tomatillo Sauce. Sprinkle with remaining 1 cup Monterey Jack cheese.
• **Bake** at 350° for 15 to 20 minutes. **Yield:** 4 to 5 servings.

Tomatillo Sauce

1 pound fresh tomatillos
2 cups water
1 chicken-flavored bouillon cube
¼ cup finely chopped onion
12 to 15 cloves garlic, minced
¼ cup finely chopped cilantro
1 tablespoon finely chopped
   jalapeño pepper
1 tablespoon finely chopped
   commercial roasted sweet red
   pepper
1½ tablespoons brown sugar
2 tablespoons lime juice
¼ teaspoon salt

• **Remove** and discard tomatillo husks, and wash tomatillos.
• **Combine** tomatillos and next 3 ingredients in a saucepan. Bring to a boil over medium heat; reduce heat, and simmer 50 minutes or until thickened.
• **Add** garlic and remaining ingredients; cool. **Yield:** 3 cups.

Note: Serve remaining Tomatillo Sauce over grilled chicken or fish or hot cooked pasta.

AVOCADO-TOMATILLO SAUCE

1 pound fresh tomatillos
2 to 3 cloves garlic
2 tablespoons olive oil
3½ cups loosely packed fresh
   parsley
2½ cups loosely packed fresh
   cilantro
3 cups loosely packed fresh
   spinach
2 avocados, peeled and seeded
1 (4½-ounce) can green chiles,
   drained
2 tablespoons fresh lime juice
   (about 2 limes)
½ teaspoon salt

• **Remove** and discard tomatillo husks; wash tomatillos. Place in a saucepan, and cook in water to cover over medium heat 5 minutes. Remove from heat; cover and let stand 15 minutes. Drain and set aside.
• **Position** knife blade in food processor bowl; add garlic and olive oil. Process until smooth, stopping occasionally to scrape down sides. Remove mixture; set aside.
• **Add** tomatillos, parsley, and next 6 ingredients to processor bowl; process until smooth, stopping occasionally to scrape down sides.
• **Add** garlic mixture slowly through food chute with processor running; process until smooth. Serve on pasta or grilled chicken or as a dip with corn chips. **Yield:** 4½ cups.

Elouise Cooper
Houston, Texas

PAPAYA VINAIGRETTE DRESSING

1 ripe papaya, peeled and
   seeded
4 to 5 cloves garlic
2 tablespoons sugar
2 tablespoons chopped onion
½ teaspoon salt
¼ to ½ teaspoon pepper
½ cup sherry wine vinegar or
   white wine vinegar
½ cup club soda
½ cup olive oil

• **Position** knife blade in food processor bowl; add first 8 ingredients. Process until smooth, stopping occasionally to scrape down sides.
• **Pour** olive oil gradually through food chute with processor running; process until smooth. Serve over fresh spinach. **Yield:** 2 cups.

A TASTE OF RED HOT SUCCESS

....

Call her the "Pepper Lady." "*I am,* you know," Jean Andrews of Austin coyly insists in her best Texas drawl. "The name is my registered trademark."

Commend her devotion to peppers, and you've won a friend, one whose blush is as red as the fiery chiltepín pepper she girlishly plucks off a nearby plate. Without hesitation, she plops the edible bomb into her mouth. Onlookers gasp. "I scare people doing that," she snickers.

With such spice for life driving her, Jean is rightly recognized worldwide as "Our Lady of the Chiles." As an artist, naturalist, certified home economist, teacher, world traveler, Ph.D. scholar, and author of nine books on everything from seashells to bluebonnets, she says it was only natural that she'd be fascinated by peppers' colors, shapes, textures, histories, flavors, heat levels, medicinal values, and "pugnacious personalities."

Jean has written and illustrated two books on peppers. "I started out painting them, but then I wanted to find out more," she says. "That's when I realized there wasn't much published. That did it. I was off and running." Twenty years of groundbreaking research followed.

Her most recent project is *Red Hot Peppers: A Cookbook for the Not So Faint of Heart* (Macmillan Publishing Company, 1993). The James Beard and

Julia Child awards-nominated book offers pepper history and illustrations, along with recipes contributed by Jean and friends she's met during her years of research. Chef Mark Miller, owner of Coyote Cafe/Red Sage, author of *The Great Chile Book,* and recipe contributor, says it's "the definitive book on the fascinating story of chiles."

But it was Jean's first book, *Peppers: The Domesticated Capsicums* (University of Texas Press, 1984; revised version), that placed her atop the pepper pedestal. Its scholarly approach focused on pepper history, taxonomy, and genetics, with 32 reproductions of Jean's pepper paintings and a few recipes thrown in just for good measure.

"I was into peppers before being into peppers was so hot," muses Jean. She now delights in the country's newfound desire to devour everything from mild-to-blazing salsas (see Biting the Bullet at right) to fiery habañeros. "Few, if any, had ever *heard* of a habañero until I told 'em about it. And they think *that's* hot," she laughs. "Wait till they try an ají rocoto."

Jean credits her interest in good food and fine peppers to her relationship to "a long line of Southern women known for their cooking skills." During the years before *Peppers,* "My guests would have been surprised to know that a little chiltepín was in almost everything they ate," she says. "I've always believed in taking the dull edge off."

Her latest book features flavorful pepper-inspired recipes not only from Jean and Miller, but also from other chefs, writers, and a host of others, from Santa Fe to Pakistan.

TABASCO STEAK

1 (5-pound) sirloin tip roast or sirloin butt beefsteak (3½ inches thick)
2 (2-ounce) bottles Tabasco® hot sauce
½ cup butter or margarine
2 to 4 cloves garlic, crushed
Garnishes: fresh serrano and Tabasco chile peppers

● **Place** roast in a large heavy-duty, zip-top plastic bag. Add hot sauce. Seal and chill 8 to 48 hours, turning occasionally.
● **Remove** roast from marinade, discarding marinade.
● **Cook,** covered with grill lid, over medium-hot coals (350° to 400°) about 40 minutes or to desired degree of doneness, turning roast occasionally.
● **Combine** butter and garlic in a small saucepan; cook over medium heat until butter melts. Slice roast, and brush slices with butter mixture. Garnish, if desired. **Yield:** 12 to 15 servings.

Note: For hotter steak, use 2 (5-ounce) bottles hot sauce, and cut slits in roast; insert 7 pickled serrano chile peppers in slits. Cover; chill at least 8 hours. For milder steak, use 1 (2-ounce) bottle hot sauce; chill no more than 8 hours. For a Tabasco bloom garnish, slice 1 serrano chile pepper lengthwise, downward from the stem, into 9 strips. After folding strips back, insert 3 fresh Tabasco peppers.

George O. Jackson
Red Hot Peppers (*Macmillan*)

ROASTED SERRANO SALSA

6 serrano chile peppers
1 pound plum tomatoes, finely chopped
2 tablespoons finely chopped purple onion
¼ cup fresh orange juice
2 tablespoons finely chopped sweet yellow pepper
2 tablespoons finely chopped fresh cilantro
1 tablespoon rice vinegar
½ teaspoon salt
½ teaspoon sugar
Garnishes: fresh cilantro sprigs, purple onion wedge

● **Cook** serrano peppers in a cast-iron skillet on high heat about 10 minutes or until blackened, turning occasionally. Cool. Peel peppers, if desired, and finely chop.
● **Combine** serrano peppers, tomato, and next 7 ingredients in a bowl; cover

and chill 1 hour. Garnish, if desired. **Yield:** 2 cups.

Note: For hotter salsa, use 7 or 8 serrano peppers. For milder salsa, use 2 or 3 serrano peppers.

Mark Miller
Red Hot Peppers (*Macmillan*)

BITING THE BULLET

....

After a tongue-blistering taste-testing of 12 of the hottest salsas we could find thanks to the Albuquerque mail-order company Salsa Express, here's our take on the ones rating an 11 on a scale of 1 to 10.

■ **Salsa Del Diablo,** Stonewall Chili Pepper Co., Stonewall, Texas; 16 ounces. Don't let the sweet, fresh flavor fool ya. "It's pureed napalm," said one tester.

■ **Dave's Insanity Salsa,** Dave's Gourmet, San Francisco; 12 ounces. Perfect name. "Smells like hot, tastes like pain," noted another. "We have seen the afterlife," she said.

■ **Salsa Habañero,** Stonewall Chili Pepper Co., Stonewall, Texas; 9 ounces. We had to let this little monster breathe after we opened it. The label says, "Warning: Salsa Habañero is extremely hot! Keep away from children, pets, eyes, and other sensitive parts of the body." Hmmm.

One benefit? All the salsas contain no fat and only 5 to 10 calories per tablespoon. (But we *dare* anyone to gain weight with this stuff.)

How to order? For a Salsa Express catalog, call 1-800-437-2572.

CHEESE GRITS WITH GREEN CHILES

6 cups water
1½ cups quick-cooking grits, uncooked
2 teaspoons salt
1 teaspoon paprika
1 teaspoon ground red pepper
3 large eggs
4 cups (16 ounces) shredded sharp Cheddar cheese
1 (4.5-ounce) can chopped green chiles, undrained
Garnish: sweet red pepper curls

• **Bring** water to a boil in a saucepan; stir in grits and salt. Return mixture to a boil; cover, reduce heat, and simmer 10 minutes or until thickened, stirring frequently. Stir in paprika and ground red pepper.
• **Beat** eggs in a large bowl. Gradually stir about one-fourth of hot grits mixture into eggs; add to remaining hot grits, stirring constantly.
• **Stir** in cheese and chiles; pour into a lightly greased 11- x 7- x 1½-inch baking dish.
• **Bake** at 325° for 45 minutes or until set. Serve immediately, or spoon grits into 10 lightly greased (6-ounce) custard cups, and cool. Invert cooled grits onto a greased baking sheet; remove custard cups.
• **Bake** grits at 300° for 5 minutes or until thoroughly heated. **Yield:** 8 to 10 servings.

Note: For grits with more fire, substitute 5 pickled jalapeño peppers, unseeded and chopped, for the chopped green chiles. For milder grits, use ½ (4.5-ounce) can chopped green chiles.
Jean Andrews
Red Hot Peppers (*Macmillan*)

FROM OUR KITCHEN TO YOURS

HOT TIPS

Undoubtedly, "A Taste of Red Hot Success" on page 206 has you fired up about chile peppers. Before you rush to the kitchen in the heat of the moment, you might want to collect your thoughts – along with a few of ours – on these often powerful, sometimes painful, but always delightful weapons of southwestern cooking.

■ **Rule No. 1:** There really are no rules on how your taste buds will react to peppers. So, experiment carefully, and know your limits.

■ If you lose control and exceed your limits, skip the water or beer that may be in front of you and run to the fridge for a glass of milk or a bite of ice cream instead. In a restaurant? Hope for a kids' menu that offers milk and a speedy waiter, or grab the last nibbles from the breadbasket in the middle of the table. Still no luck? Have patience: Time will heal all wounds.

■ Be sure to wear rubber gloves when working with peppers. It doesn't hurt while you're seeding and slicing them, but the pain sure kicks in later. This is true for dried chiles as well.

Regular rubber cleaning gloves are too thick and cumbersome for such small, detailed work. Use thinner, surgical or disposable plastic gloves found at some grocery stores, hardware stores, or large discount chains.

■ Much of a chile pepper's heat comes from the seeds and veins (or membranes). Removing them won't completely debilitate the fire, but it will weaken it.

GRATE IDEAS

■ To easily remove lemon or orange rind from the fine teeth of a grater, place a piece of heavy-duty plastic wrap stretched tautly over the fine teeth before grating. (We found Reynolds Wrap works best.) The force of the lemon or orange sticks the plastic wrap to the grater while the teeth go after the rind.

When finished, lift the plastic wrap off the grater, and the rind oh-so-neatly comes up with it. (Don't try this with off-brand, thin plastic wraps unless you like lots of extra fiber with your rind.)

■ Tired of your food processor steel blade chopping pecans unevenly (from big chunks to a powdery mush)? Try the shredder/grater disc instead. (We found that the coarse grater worked best, but the fine one would be good when a recipe calls for ground nuts.)

■ Here's a solution to cutting in the butter without a pastry blender (a set of semicircular blades with a handle that you rock back and forth in the biscuit bowl to work butter into flour).

Unwrap a stick of cold butter only down to the line measuring the exact amount you need. Holding the stick by the still-wrapped portion, pull the butter repeatedly across an ordinary grater, and then toss the flour and bits of butter together with a fork.

REEL IN A FRESH CATCH

....

Seafood is perfect for summer dining: It's light and simple to prepare and has endless flavor possibilities. What's more, you'll be out of a hot kitchen in no time.

SHRIMP SCAMPI

1 pound unpeeled medium-size fresh shrimp
8 ounces angel hair pasta, uncooked
½ cup butter or margarine
4 cloves garlic, minced
⅓ cup dry white wine
¼ teaspoon freshly ground pepper
¾ cup grated Romano cheese
1 tablespoon chopped fresh parsley

● **Peel** shrimp, and devein, if desired; set aside.
● **Cook** pasta according to package directions; drain, place on a large serving platter, and set aside.
● **Melt** butter in a large skillet over medium heat. Add garlic and shrimp, and cook, stirring constantly, 3 to 5 minutes or until shrimp turn pink; add wine and pepper. Bring to a boil; cook 30 seconds, stirring constantly.
● **Pour** shrimp mixture over pasta; sprinkle with cheese and parsley, and toss gently. Serve immediately. **Yield:** 4 servings.

Bunny Campbell
Gainesville, Florida

EASY CRAB BAKE

1 large egg, lightly beaten
¾ cup mayonnaise
2 tablespoons lemon juice
1½ teaspoons hot sauce
¼ teaspoon salt
1 pound fresh crabmeat, drained and flaked
¼ cup fine, dry breadcrumbs
1 tablespoon butter or margarine, melted
Garnishes: fresh parsley sprigs, lemon wedges

● **Combine** first 5 ingredients in a bowl; fold in crabmeat. Spoon mixture evenly into 4 lightly greased shell-shaped baking dishes or 6-ounce ramekins.
● **Combine** breadcrumbs and melted butter; sprinkle mixture evenly over crabmeat mixture.
● **Bake** at 325° for 25 to 30 minutes. Garnish, if desired. **Yield:** 4 servings.

Nora Henshaw
Okemah, Oklahoma

FISH IN CAPER SAUCE

4 medium tomatoes, peeled and chopped
1 medium onion, chopped
1 teaspoon dried oregano
1 teaspoon dried basil
¼ teaspoon garlic powder
1 to 2 tablespoons capers
1½ teaspoons dry sherry (optional)
1¾ pounds orange roughy fillets

● **Combine** first 5 ingredients in a large skillet; cook over medium heat 5 minutes or until onion is tender. Add capers and, if desired, sherry; cook 1 to 2 minutes. Remove mixture from skillet; set aside.
● **Add** fish to skillet; top with vegetable mixture.
● **Cover** and cook 10 to 12 minutes or until fish flakes easily when tested with a fork. **Yield:** 4 to 6 servings.

Sara Hitchcock Beck
Montgomery, Alabama

SALMON BAKE WITH PECAN-CRUNCH COATING
(pictured on page 148)

This Pecan-Crunch Coating also works well on firm fish like grouper and amberjack.

4 (4- to 6-ounce) salmon fillets
⅛ teaspoon salt
⅛ teaspoon pepper
2 tablespoons Dijon mustard
2 tablespoons butter or margarine, melted
1½ tablespoons honey
¼ cup soft breadcrumbs
¼ cup finely chopped pecans
2 teaspoons chopped fresh parsley
Garnishes: fresh parsley sprigs, lemon slices

● **Sprinkle** salmon with salt and pepper. Place fillets, skin side down, in a lightly greased 13- x 9- x 2-inch pan.
● **Combine** mustard, butter, and honey; brush on fillets.
● **Combine** breadcrumbs, pecans, and chopped parsley; spoon mixture evenly on top of each fillet.
● **Bake** fillets at 450° for 10 minutes or until fish flakes easily when tested with a fork. Garnish, if desired. **Yield:** 4 servings.

Helen H. Maurer
Christmas, Florida

TESTING FISH FOR DONENESS

....

To test a fish fillet for doneness, use a fork to prod the fillet at its thickest point (preferably from underneath so the outer appearance remains intact). If the fillet flakes easily and has opaque, milky-white juices, then it's properly cooked. If the fillet is translucent and has watery juices, it's not done; if it's dry and easily falls apart, it's overdone.

WEEKDAY SOLUTIONS

....

It's a relief to figure out what to serve your family for supper. Here's a bonus: four good ideas. Starting Monday, serve one of these entrées each night. On Friday, pull out the leftovers and declare "TGIF!"

ARTICHOKE AND SHRIMP LINGUINE

8 ounces linguine, uncooked
1 pound unpeeled medium-size fresh shrimp
¼ cup olive oil
3 cloves garlic, minced
½ teaspoon dried crushed red pepper
1 (14-ounce) can artichoke hearts, drained and quartered
½ cup ripe olives, sliced
¼ cup fresh lemon juice
⅛ teaspoon salt
⅛ teaspoon pepper
½ cup grated Parmesan cheese

• **Cook** linguine according to package directions; drain and keep warm.
• **Peel** shrimp, and devein, if desired.
• **Heat** oil in a skillet over medium-high heat; add shrimp, garlic, and red pepper, and cook, stirring constantly, 5 minutes or until shrimp turn pink.
• **Stir** in artichoke hearts and next 4 ingredients. Add to pasta, and sprinkle with cheese. **Yield:** 3 to 4 servings.

Ann Winniford
Dallas, Texas

HAMBURGER CASSEROLE

1 cup uncooked brown rice
1½ pounds lean ground beef
½ small onion, chopped
1 cup chopped celery
2 tablespoons chopped green pepper
1 (10¾-ounce) can cream of chicken soup, undiluted
1 (10¾-ounce) can cream of mushroom soup, undiluted
½ teaspoon garlic salt
½ teaspoon pepper
2 tablespoons butter or margarine
1 (4-ounce) can sliced mushrooms, drained
1 (2-ounce) package slivered almonds

• **Prepare** rice according to package directions; set aside.
• **Brown** ground beef and next 3 ingredients in a large skillet, stirring until beef crumbles; drain.
• **Combine** ground beef mixture, rice, chicken soup, and next 3 ingredients in a large bowl; spoon into a lightly greased 13- x 9- x 2-inch baking dish.
• **Bake** at 325° for 1 hour.
• **Melt** butter in a small skillet over medium-high heat; add mushrooms and almonds, and cook until almonds are lightly browned. Sprinkle over casserole; serve immediately. **Yield:** 6 to 8 servings.

Cindy Kendrick
Leawood, Kansas

CHICKEN PARMESAN

6 skinned and boned chicken breast halves
1 large egg, lightly beaten
¼ cup water
½ cup Italian-seasoned breadcrumbs
½ cup grated Parmesan cheese
3 tablespoons butter or margarine
1 (30-ounce) jar spaghetti sauce
Hot cooked egg noodles
1 cup (4 ounces) shredded mozzarella cheese
2 teaspoons grated Parmesan cheese

• **Place** each chicken breast half between two sheets of heavy-duty plastic wrap, and flatten each to ¼-inch thickness, using a meat mallet or rolling pin.
• **Combine** egg and water in a bowl. Combine breadcrumbs and Parmesan cheese in a separate bowl. Dip chicken in egg mixture; dredge in breadcrumb mixture.
• **Melt** butter in a large skillet over medium heat; add half of chicken, and cook, turning once, until browned. Repeat procedure.
• **Return** chicken to skillet; add spaghetti sauce. Cover and simmer 10 minutes. Place noodles on platter. Spoon chicken and sauce over noodles; sprinkle with mozzarella and Parmesan cheeses. Cover and let stand until cheese melts. **Yield:** 6 servings.

Kimberly D. Newcomb
Augusta, Georgia

MEXICAN CORNBREAD SALAD
(pictured on page 187)

1 (6-ounce) package Mexican cornbread mix
1 (4½-ounce) can chopped green chiles, undrained
Dash of ground sage
1 (1-ounce) package Ranch-style salad dressing mix
1 (8-ounce) carton reduced-fat sour cream
1 cup reduced-fat mayonnaise
2 (16-ounce) cans pinto beans, drained
1 cup chopped green pepper
2 (15¼-ounce) cans whole kernel corn, drained
3 large tomatoes, chopped
10 slices bacon, cooked and crumbled
1 (8-ounce) package shredded reduced-fat Cheddar cheese
1 cup sliced green onions
Lettuce leaves
Tomato wedges (optional)

• **Prepare** cornbread mix according to package directions, adding green chiles and sage; cool.

- **Combine** salad dressing mix, sour cream, and mayonnaise; set aside.
- **Crumble** half of cornbread into a bowl. Top with half each of beans, sour cream mixture, green pepper, and next 5 ingredients. Repeat layers.
- **Cover** and chill 2 hours. Serve in individual lettuce-lined bowls, and top with tomato wedges, if desired. **Yield:** 8 servings.

Anne Ringer
Warner Robins, Georgia

FEAST WITHOUT MEAT

....

These main dishes are every bit as satisfying as meat-laden entrées. Whether you're looking for a cooktop supper solution that's quick or a make-ahead brunch idea for visitors, these three recipes are guaranteed to charm even the staunchest meat lover.

PASTA WITH GREENS

Toasted pine nuts add satisfying crunch to this meatless entrée.

1 (8-ounce) package fettuccine, uncooked
1 (16-ounce) package frozen collards or other greens
2 to 3 cloves garlic, minced
3 tablespoons olive oil
½ teaspoon salt
¼ teaspoon freshly ground pepper
½ cup freshly grated Parmesan cheese
1 (1¾-ounce) jar pine nuts, toasted
Garnishes: freshly grated Parmesan cheese, toasted pine nuts

- **Cook** pasta according to package directions; drain and set aside.

- **Cook** greens according to package directions; drain and set aside.
- **Cook** garlic in olive oil in a large skillet over medium-high heat until tender but not brown. Add greens, salt, and pepper; cook until heated.
- **Combine** pasta, greens, ½ cup Parmesan cheese, and 1 jar pine nuts in a large serving bowl. Garnish, if desired. **Yield:** 2 main-dish or 4 side-dish servings.

Melinda Clement
Kingsville, Texas

MUSHROOM CASSEROLE

¼ cup butter or margarine
1½ pounds fresh mushrooms, sliced *
1 large onion, chopped
½ cup chopped celery
½ cup chopped green pepper
½ cup mayonnaise or salad dressing
8 slices white bread, cut into 1-inch pieces
2 large eggs, lightly beaten
1½ cups milk
1 (10¾-ounce) can cream of mushroom soup, undiluted
1 cup freshly grated Romano cheese

- **Melt** butter in a large skillet or Dutch oven. Add mushrooms and next 3 ingredients, and cook over medium heat, stirring constantly, until tender; drain well. Stir in mayonnaise.
- **Place** half of bread evenly into a lightly greased 13- x 9- x 2-inch baking dish. Spoon mushroom mixture evenly over bread. Top with remaining bread.
- **Combine** eggs and milk; pour over bread. Cover and chill at least 8 hours.
- **Pour** soup over casserole; top with Romano cheese.
- **Bake** at 350° for 1 hour or until heated and bubbly. **Yield:** 6 servings.

* You can substitute gourmet mushrooms like shiitake, cremini, and portabello. Portabello mushrooms should be chopped.

Yvonne M. Greer
Mauldin, South Carolina

VEGETABLE LASAGNA

Sunny Tiedemann serves any leftover slices of this garden-fresh favorite chilled. "It's even better the second day," she says.

10 lasagna noodles, uncooked
2 cups sliced fresh mushrooms
1 cup grated carrot (about 1 large)
½ cup chopped onion
1 tablespoon olive oil
1 (15-ounce) can tomato sauce
1 (12-ounce) can tomato paste
1 (4¼-ounce) can chopped ripe olives, drained
1 (4½-ounce) can chopped green chiles, undrained
1½ teaspoons dried oregano
2 cups cottage cheese
1 (10-ounce) package frozen chopped spinach, thawed and well drained
4 cups (16 ounces) shredded Monterey Jack cheese
1 (3-ounce) package refrigerated shredded Parmesan cheese

- **Cook** noodles according to package directions. Drain and set aside.
- **Cook** mushrooms, carrot, and onion in olive oil over medium-high heat, stirring constantly, until tender. Stir in tomato sauce and next 4 ingredients.
- **Place** half of lasagna noodles in a greased 13- x 9- x 2-inch baking dish or pan. Layer with half each of cottage cheese, spinach, tomato sauce mixture, Monterey Jack cheese, and Parmesan cheese. Repeat layers.
- **Bake** at 375° for 45 minutes or until bubbly. Let stand 10 minutes before serving. **Yield:** 8 servings.

Sunny Tiedemann
Bartlesville, Oklahoma

PANTRY SHAPE-UP

Bend, reach, stretch, and lift. Shift, push, and pull. No, this isn't an aerobics class, it's the pantry shuffle. Do you do this dance every time you cook? A well-stocked pantry is no luxury if you can't find the goodies you've got. Let's get organized. These recipes and tips will help.

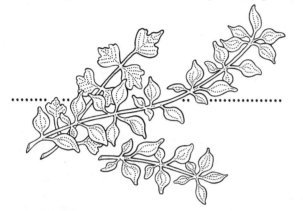

CLAM LINGUINE

½ pound linguine, uncooked
2 tablespoons butter
1 clove garlic, minced
2 tablespoons all-purpose flour
1 teaspoon dried oregano
2 (10-ounce) cans whole clams, undrained
½ cup dry white wine
¼ cup whipping cream
¼ cup grated Parmesan cheese
Garnish: fresh oregano sprigs

• **Cook** linguine according to package directions; drain and keep warm.
• **Melt** butter in a large skillet over medium heat; add garlic, and cook 1 minute, stirring constantly. Add flour and oregano; cook 1 minute, stirring constantly.
• **Stir** in clams and wine; cook, stirring constantly, 8 minutes or until reduced slightly. Remove from heat.
• **Stir** in whipping cream, and cook mixture over low heat until thoroughly heated.
• **Spoon** over linguine; sprinkle with cheese. Garnish, if desired. **Yield:** 4 servings.

LIGHT LASAGNA

4 ounces lasagna noodles, uncooked
½ pound lean ground beef
1 clove garlic, pressed
½ teaspoon dried parsley flakes
½ teaspoon dried basil
1 (14½-ounce) can tomatoes, undrained and chopped
1 (6-ounce) can tomato paste
2 egg whites
1 (12-ounce) container 1% fat cottage cheese
¼ teaspoon pepper
¼ cup fat-free grated Parmesan cheese
1½ cups (6 ounces) shredded part-skim mozzarella cheese
1 (4.2-ounce) can sliced mushrooms, drained

• **Cook** lasagna noodles according to package directions; drain noodles, and set aside.
• **Brown** ground beef in a large non-stick skillet, stirring until it crumbles. Drain and pat dry with paper towels. Return beef to skillet.
• **Stir** in garlic and next 4 ingredients; simmer 10 to 15 minutes or until thick, stirring occasionally.
• **Combine** egg whites and next 3 ingredients; set aside.
• **Spread** about ½ cup meat mixture in bottom of a greased 8-inch square baking dish. Place half of noodles over meat mixture, trimming noodles to fit.
• **Spread** half of cottage cheese mixture over noodles; top with half of mozzarella. Layer with half of mushrooms, and spread half of remaining meat mixture over mushrooms.
• **Repeat** layers, beginning with noodles and ending with meat mixture.
• **Cover** with aluminum foil, and bake at 350° for 45 minutes or until bubbly. Let stand 10 minutes before serving. **Yield:** 4 servings.

Note: Cover unbaked lasagna with plastic wrap, and chill 8 hours. Remove plastic wrap, and cover with aluminum foil; bake as directed.

Bill Jackson
Alpine, Alabama

❤ Per serving: Calories 521 (31% from fat)
Fat 17.9g (8.9g saturated) Cholesterol 65mg
Sodium 1000mg Carbohydrate 44.5g
Fiber 1.8g Protein 45.5g

FIVE-INGREDIENT CHILI

2 pounds ground chuck
1 medium onion, chopped
4 (16-ounce) cans chili-hot beans, undrained
2 (1¾-ounce) packages chili seasoning mix
1 (46-ounce) can tomato juice

• **Cook** ground chuck and onion in a Dutch oven, stirring until meat crumbles; drain. Stir in beans and remaining ingredients.
• **Bring** mixture to a boil; reduce heat, and simmer 2 hours, stirring occasionally. **Yield:** 3½ quarts.

Judy Tynes
Summerville, South Carolina

TAMALE SOUP

1 pound ground beef
1 medium onion, chopped
1 green pepper, seeded and
    chopped
1 (14¼-ounce) can stewed
    tomatoes, undrained
2 (16-ounce) cans pinto beans,
    undrained
1 (15-ounce) can creamed corn
1 (10¾-ounce) can condensed beef
    broth, undiluted
2 (15-ounce) cans tamales,
    drained and cut into 1-inch
    pieces

● **Cook** ground beef, chopped onion, and pepper in a Dutch oven until ground beef is browned, stirring until meat crumbles.
● **Add** stewed tomatoes and next 3 ingredients; simmer 1 hour.
● **Stir** in tamale pieces, and serve immediately. **Yield:** 3 quarts.

Carol Barclay
Portland, Texas

MACARONI, CHEESE, AND TOMATOES

For a Southwestern flavor, use tomatoes with green chiles. Italian-style stewed tomatoes will add the flavors of onion, green pepper, celery, and herbs.

2 cups elbow macaroni,
    uncooked
1 (14½-ounce) can tomatoes,
    undrained
⅔ cup water
1 (8-ounce) package Cheddar
    cheese, cubed
½ teaspoon salt
¼ teaspoon pepper
2 to 3 tablespoons sugar
1 (6-ounce) package Cheddar
    cheese slices

● **Cook** macaroni according to package directions; drain.
● **Place** tomatoes in a 2-quart casserole dish; mash. Stir in macaroni, water, and next 4 ingredients; arrange cheese slices on top.

● **Bake** at 375° for 30 minutes or until bubbly. Let stand 5 minutes before serving. **Yield:** 6 servings.

Leslie Coles Walker
Chesapeake, Virginia

MY FAVORITE PASTA

4 ounces spinach linguine,
    uncooked
1 cup whipping cream
1 cup chicken broth
½ cup freshly grated Parmesan
    cheese
½ cup frozen English peas
3 slices bacon, cooked and
    crumbled

● **Cook** linguine according to package directions; drain and keep warm.
● **Combine** whipping cream and chicken broth in a saucepan; bring to a boil. Reduce heat, and simmer 25 minutes or until thickened and reduced to 1 cup. Remove mixture from heat.
● **Add** cheese, peas, and bacon, stirring until cheese melts. Toss with linguine; serve immediately. **Yield:** 2 servings.

Note: Whipping cream and chicken broth may be simmered longer for a thicker sauce. Peeled cooked shrimp or chopped cooked chicken may be added with the cheese, peas, and bacon for a heartier dish.

Nora Henshaw
Okemah, Oklahoma

ROSEMARY CANNELLINI BEANS

2 (15-ounce) cans cannellini beans,
    drained *
⅓ cup chicken broth
4 cloves garlic, pressed
1 tablespoon chopped fresh or
    1 teaspoon dried rosemary
⅛ teaspoon salt
¼ teaspoon freshly ground
    pepper

● **Combine** all ingredients in a medium saucepan.

● **Cook** over medium heat 5 minutes or until thoroughly heated, stirring occasionally. Drain, if necessary. **Yield:** 4 servings.

* Substitute 2 (15-ounce) cans Great Northern beans for cannellini.

TAKE STOCK

If the pantry shuffle is cramping your creative cooking style, get organized. These helpful hints will get you started.

■ Buy the right size. Bulk packages are no bargain if they outlast their freshness and appeal.

■ Group ingredients for favorite recipes together.

■ Store pantry items so you can see everything. This saves time and money – no searching and no costly duplications. Check into getting tiered racks – they're definitely worth the investment.

■ Store herbs and spices in alphabetical order; you'll know at a glance what you have and what's missing.

■ Post a board to record "low on/out of" items so you won't be surprised in the middle of a recipe.

■ Give family members the rules of the new arrangement.
    1. Put it back where you found it – every time!
    2. If you use it all, then add it to the "out of" list.

CORN SALAD

2 (11-ounce) cans white shoepeg
  corn, drained
1 green pepper, seeded and
  chopped
½ cup chopped purple onion
½ cup sour cream
1 tablespoon mayonnaise or salad
  dressing
1 tablespoon white vinegar
¼ teaspoon celery salt
⅛ teaspoon salt
⅛ teaspoon pepper

• **Combine** all ingredients, stirring
well. Cover and chill at least 3 hours.
Serve with a slotted spoon. **Yield:** 6
to 8 servings.

Michelle Clark
Columbus, Georgia

CHEWY PEANUT BUTTER MACAROONS

1 (14-ounce) can sweetened
  condensed milk
½ cup creamy peanut butter
3 cups flaked coconut

• **Combine** all ingredients. Drop by
rounded teaspoonfuls onto lightly
greased cookie sheets.
• **Bake** at 325° for 12 to 15 minutes.
Cool. Store in an airtight container up
to 3 weeks or freeze up to 3 months.
Yield: about 5 dozen.

Joy Garcia
Bartlett, Tennessee

WINNING SNACKS

....

Whether you're off to the courts for a
game of tennis or the beach for a
round of volleyball, keep your snacks
healthful. All of these can be made
ahead, even enjoyed for several days
after. And they're easy to tote with you.

BIG BATCH MOIST BRAN MUFFINS

*This make-ahead batter can be stored
in the refrigerator and baked as
needed. Ingredients also can be easily
cut in half to make a smaller batch.*

3 cups sugar
1 cup vegetable oil
4 large eggs
1 tablespoon plus 2 teaspoons
  baking soda
1 tablespoon plus 1 teaspoon
  ground cinnamon
2 teaspoons salt
1 (17-ounce) can fruit cocktail,
  undrained
5 cups all-purpose flour
1 quart buttermilk
1 (15-ounce) package wheat bran
  flakes cereal with raisins

• **Combine** all ingredients in a large
mixing bowl; beat at medium speed
with an electric mixer 2 minutes.
Spoon batter into lightly greased muffin pans, filling two-thirds full.
• **Bake** at 400° for 16 to 18 minutes or
until muffins are done. Remove
muffins from pans immediately. **Yield:**
about 4½ dozen.

Note: Batter may be covered tightly
and stored in refrigerator up to 3
weeks. Do not stir before using. For
cereal we used raisin bran.

Linda Janca
Mount Mourne, North Carolina

COCONUT MUFFINS

2 cups all-purpose flour
1 cup sugar
2 teaspoons baking powder
½ cup frozen coconut, thawed
2 large eggs, lightly beaten
½ cup butter or margarine, melted
1 (8-ounce) carton plain low-fat
  yogurt
¼ teaspoon coconut extract

• **Combine** first 4 ingredients in a large
bowl; make a well in center of mixture.
• **Combine** eggs and next 3 ingredients; add to dry ingredients, stirring

just until moistened. Spoon into lightly
greased or paper-lined muffin pans, filling three-fourths full.
• **Bake** at 375° for 25 minutes. Remove
from pans immediately. **Yield:** 1
dozen.

Carol Joffrion
Shreveport, Louisiana

GRANOLA BARS

2 cups granola cereal with raisins
¼ cup firmly packed brown sugar
¼ cup sunflower kernels
1 large egg, lightly beaten
1 teaspoon vanilla extract

• **Combine** all ingredients. Press evenly
into a well-greased 8-inch square baking pan.
• **Bake** at 350° for 18 to 20 minutes.
Cool in pan on a wire rack 5 minutes,
and cut into bars. Store in an airtight
container. **Yield:** 1 dozen.

Note: For cereal we used Low-Fat
Granola With Raisins.

Trenda Leigh
Richmond, Virginia

ORANGE-ALMOND SNACK BALLS

2 cups graham cracker crumbs
⅔ cup sifted powdered sugar
⅓ cup currants or raisins
¼ cup instant nonfat dry milk
  powder
¼ cup finely chopped almonds,
  toasted
½ cup unsweetened orange juice
¼ cup light corn syrup
¾ teaspoon grated orange rind
2 tablespoons powdered sugar

• **Combine** first 5 ingredients in a
medium bowl; set aside.
• **Combine** orange juice, corn syrup,
and orange rind; stir into crumb mixture. Cover and chill 1 hour.
• **Shape** mixture into 1-inch balls; roll
in 2 tablespoons powdered sugar. Store
in an airtight container. **Yield:** 2
dozen.

ONE OF A KIND ★★★ Southern Living HALL OF FAME

Junior League members of Mobile, Alabama, took the name of their cookbook from the way they view the Port City, that is, *One of a Kind*. The menu section that introduces the book offers a good sampling of the city's history and customs. The league focuses its charitable work in the area of education. We know you'll welcome these additions from the Mobile area to your recipe collection.

....

SHERRY CHEESE PÂTÉ

2 (3-ounce) packages cream cheese, softened
1 cup (4 ounces) shredded sharp Cheddar cheese
¼ cup dry sherry
½ teaspoon curry powder
⅓ cup chutney
2 green onions, thinly sliced

• **Combine** first 4 ingredients; shape into a 5-inch circle on a serving plate, and chill. Just before serving, spread chutney over cheese, and sprinkle with green onions. Serve with assorted crackers. **Yield:** 12 servings.

VIC'S OVEN SHRIMP

1 pound butter
1 pound margarine
4 lemons, thinly sliced
¾ cup Worcestershire sauce
¼ cup pepper
2 teaspoons salt
1 teaspoon dried rosemary
1 teaspoon hot sauce
10 pounds unpeeled medium-size fresh shrimp

• **Combine** first 8 ingredients in a large saucepan; bring to a boil. Remove from heat.
• **Place** shrimp in a large roasting pan. Pour butter mixture over shrimp, stirring to coat.

• **Bake** at 400° for 20 to 25 minutes, stirring occasionally. Serve with French bread. **Yield:** 12 servings.

SQUASH SOUFFLÉ

1 pound yellow squash, chopped
1 medium onion, chopped
¼ cup butter or margarine
2 cups (8 ounces) shredded Cheddar cheese, divided
2 cups round buttery cracker crumbs, divided
¼ cup milk
¼ teaspoon salt
¼ teaspoon pepper
3 large eggs, lightly beaten

• **Cook** squash and onion in boiling water to cover 5 minutes or until tender; drain and mash.
• **Add** butter, 1¾ cups cheese, 1¾ cups cracker crumbs, milk, salt, and pepper. Stir in eggs.
• **Spoon** mixture into a lightly greased 2-quart casserole. Sprinkle with remaining ¼ cup cheese and cracker crumbs.
• **Bake** at 350° for 45 minutes. **Yield:** 6 servings.

FRIED APRICOT PIES

1 (6-ounce) package dried apricot halves, chopped
1¼ cups water
½ cup sugar
½ teaspoon ground cinnamon
½ teaspoon ground nutmeg
1 tablespoon lemon or orange juice
1 (15-ounce) package refrigerated piecrusts
Vegetable oil
Powdered sugar

• **Combine** apricot and water in a small saucepan; bring to a boil. Cover, reduce heat, and simmer 20 minutes or until apricot is tender. Drain, if necessary.
• **Mash** apricot. Stir in sugar, cinnamon, nutmeg, and lemon juice; set mixture aside.
• **Unfold** 1 piecrust, and press out fold lines. Roll piecrust to ⅛-inch thickness on a lightly floured surface. Cut into 5 (5-inch) circles; stack circles between wax paper. Repeat procedure with remaining piecrust.
• **Spoon** 2 tablespoons apricot mixture on half of each circle. Moisten edges with water; fold dough over apricot mixture, pressing edges to seal. Crimp edges with a fork.
• **Pour** oil to depth of 1 inch into a large heavy skillet. Fry pies in hot oil (375°) about 2 minutes or until golden, turning once. Drain well on paper towels. Sprinkle with powdered sugar. **Yield:** 10 pies.

COOL OFF WITH CUCUMBERS

Genuinely fresh, unwaxed cucumbers arrive at produce stands just in time to cool you off during the season's hottest days. But if you're like some, neither you nor the cucumbers will be cool for long. This summer, we've searched for cucumber recipes that require little or no cooking, so you and your kitchen can remain a few degrees below the boiling point.

CUCUMBER MOUSSE WITH DILL SAUCE

2 envelopes unflavored gelatin
3 tablespoons cold water
1 cup boiling water
2 large cucumbers, cut in half
1 cup small-curd cottage cheese
½ cup whipping cream
1 (8-ounce) carton sour cream
3 tablespoons chopped fresh dill
2 tablespoons chopped green onions
1 tablespoon chopped parsley
½ teaspoon salt
¼ teaspoon ground white pepper
Lettuce leaves
Dill Sauce
Cucumber slices

• **Sprinkle** gelatin over 3 tablespoons cold water; stir and let stand 1 minute. Add 1 cup boiling water; stir until gelatin dissolves. Set aside.
• **Peel** and seed 3 cucumber halves; thinly slice remaining cucumber half, and set aside.
• **Position** knife blade in food processor bowl, and add peeled and seeded cucumber. Pulse 2 or 3 times or until cucumber is finely chopped.
• **Add** cottage cheese and whipping cream; process 20 seconds, stopping once to scrape down sides. Pour gelatin gradually through food chute with processor running.
• **Combine** sour cream and next 5 ingredients in a large bowl; stir in cucumber mixture. Spoon into lightly oiled individual molds, and chill until firm.
• **Arrange** lettuce leaves on salad plates. Unmold onto prepared plates; top with Dill Sauce. Top with cucumber slices. **Yield:** 9 servings.

Dill Sauce

1 (8-ounce) carton sour cream
2 to 3 tablespoons milk
2 tablespoons fresh lemon juice
2 teaspoons chopped fresh dill
½ teaspoon chopped fresh parsley

• **Combine** all ingredients in a small bowl. **Yield:** 1 cup.

Lynne Teal Weeks
Columbus, Georgia

SMOKED SALMON AND CUCUMBER TARTLETS
(pictured on page 221)

1 cup cottage cheese
½ cup finely chopped, peeled, and seeded cucumber
⅓ pound smoked salmon
1 (8-ounce) package cream cheese, softened
3 tablespoons pepper vodka
2 tablespoons lemon juice
1 tablespoon Dijon mustard
2 teaspoons prepared horseradish
2 tablespoons capers, rinsed and drained
⅛ teaspoon freshly ground pepper
2 tablespoons chopped fresh dill
Phyllo Tartlet Shells
Garnishes: cucumber wedges, capers, fresh dill sprigs

• **Place** cottage cheese in a wire-mesh strainer lined with 2 layers of cheesecloth. Place strainer over a medium bowl; cover and chill 8 hours.
• **Drain** chopped cucumber well, patting between layers of paper towels. Set cucumber aside.
• **Position** knife blade in food processor bowl; add cottage cheese, salmon, and next 5 ingredients. Process until smooth, stopping once to scrape down sides. Stir in drained cucumber, capers, pepper, and chopped dill; cover and chill.
• **Spoon** into Phyllo Tartlet Shells; garnish, if desired. **Yield:** 4 dozen tartlets.

Phyllo Tartlet Shells

8 sheets frozen phyllo pastry, thawed
Butter-flavored cooking spray

• **Place** 1 sheet of phyllo on a flat surface (keep remaining phyllo covered with a slightly damp towel). Lightly spray phyllo with cooking spray. Repeat procedure with 3 more sheets of phyllo and cooking spray. Cut phyllo into 24 (3-inch) squares, using kitchen shears or a sharp knife.

• **Coat** miniature (1¾-inch) muffin pans with cooking spray; place one square of layered phyllo into each muffin cup, pressing gently in center to form a pastry shell. Repeat procedure with remaining 4 sheets of phyllo and butter-flavored cooking spray.

• **Bake** shells at 350° for 8 minutes or until golden. Carefully remove from pans; let cool on wire racks. **Yield:** 4 dozen.

♥ To reduce fat and calories, substitute 1% low-fat cottage cheese and nonfat cream cheese for the regular versions.

Note: Store unfilled shells in airtight containers up to 4 days. Fill just before serving.

Ray Overton
Alpharetta, Georgia

CAN-DO TOMATOES

....

For a change try our *flavored* canned tomatoes. We've added fresh herbs, garlic, and peppers before canning to make products similar to (but better than) some of the commercially canned tomatoes.

Do some planning before you start canning. Look at our list; then select those that go well in recipes you use. Or experiment with a new flavor.

CANNED FLAVORED TOMATOES

To can tomatoes without flavorings, fill each jar with tomatoes to ½ inch from top, and proceed with canning instructions.

8 pounds fresh tomatoes
Lemon juice
Salt (optional)

• **Dip** tomatoes in boiling water 30 to 60 seconds or until skins split. Dip in cold water; remove and discard skins and stem ends. Cut into quarters.

• **Place** 12 quarters in a large Dutch oven. Bring to a boil, crushing tomatoes with back of a spoon. Gradually add remaining tomatoes, stirring constantly. Bring to a boil, and simmer 5 minutes.

• **Add** 1 tablespoon lemon juice to each hot jar. Add ½ teaspoon salt to each jar, if desired. Add hot tomatoes, filling to 1 inch from top. Add desired flavorings, stirring so the ingredients are mixed thoroughly. Remove air bubbles with a rubber spatula; wipe jar rims. Cover at once with metal lids, and screw on bands.

• **Process** in boiling-water bath 35 minutes. **Yield:** 6 pints.

Mediterranean flavor: Add 1 tablespoon chopped fresh thyme and 1 tablespoon chopped fresh rosemary per pint of tomatoes.

Italian flavor: Add 1 tablespoon chopped fresh basil and 1 tablespoon chopped fresh oregano per pint.

Greek flavor: Add 1 teaspoon dried fennel and 1 teaspoon chopped fresh lemon mint or mint per pint.

Garden-fresh flavor: Add 1 tablespoon chopped fresh chives and 1 clove garlic per pint.

Mexican flavor: Add 2 teaspoons chopped fresh cilantro and 1 sliced jalapeño pepper per pint. (Seed pepper, if desired.) Cilantro and jalapeño pepper must be thoroughly mixed with crushed tomatoes.

Savory flavor: Add 1 tablespoon chopped fresh savory per pint.

CAN IT BE SAFE?

The tradition of food preservation continues in many homes, but the recipes used in grandmother's kitchen must be updated. The USDA's revised food safety guidelines for canning ensure that the food you preserve is safe. Follow our tips for safety and quality.

■ Use only standard canning jars and lids for home canning; leftover food jars aren't safe to use.

■ The amount of headspace to leave in the jar after filling varies with type of canning. The space between the inside of the lid and the top of the food is mandatory for the expansion of food as it processes and forms a vacuum in the cooled jars. Check your recipe for specifics.

■ Canned goods must be processed in a boiling-water bath or a pressure canner. The open-kettle method (placing cooked food in jars and sealing without processing) is NOT a safe practice for any home-canned food.

■ Use the boiling-water bath method for high-acid foods like fruit, tomatoes, and pickles. This method doesn't require as much time or the use of a pressure canner. The boiling-water bath processes jars of food at 212°, destroying microorganisms that cause spoilage and food poisoning.

■ Make sure lids have sealed properly before storing home-canned food. When sealed, you should feel a downward curve to the lid.

■ Label all your canned products, listing the name of the recipe and date it was prepared. Store in a cool, dry place.

FRENCH BREAD FIX-UPS

. . . .

Bread alone is just bread. But thick, crusty French bread with butter, herbs, and cheese is an *event*.

Here we've transformed loaves into appetizers and snacks – even a container for dip.

DILLY GARLIC BREAD

½ cup butter or margarine, softened
2 cloves garlic, pressed
¼ cup finely chopped fresh dill
1 (16-ounce) loaf French bread, cut in half horizontally
¼ cup grated Parmesan cheese

● **Combine** first 3 ingredients; spread mixture evenly on cut sides of bread. Sprinkle with Parmesan cheese. Place on a baking sheet.
● **Bake** at 375° for 8 minutes or until golden. Slice bread crosswise into 1-inch slices, and serve immediately. **Yield:** 1 loaf.

Joy Knight Allard
San Antonio, Texas

GARLIC BREAD

The addition of cheese and herbs perks up this familiar favorite.

½ cup butter or margarine, softened
¼ cup grated Parmesan cheese
2 cloves garlic, pressed
¼ teaspoon dried marjoram
¼ teaspoon dried oregano
1 (16-ounce) loaf French bread, cut into 1-inch slices

● **Combine** first 5 ingredients, and spread between bread slices.

● **Reassemble** loaf, and wrap in heavy-duty aluminum foil; place on a baking sheet.
● **Bake** at 350° for 20 minutes. Open foil, and bake 5 additional minutes or until crisp and golden. Slice crosswise into 1-inch slices. Serve immediately. **Yield:** 1 loaf.

Jane Krebs
Fernandina Beach, Florida

CHEESY FRENCH BREAD

1 (8-ounce) package shredded Mexican blend cheese
¾ cup mayonnaise or salad dressing
1½ teaspoons dried parsley flakes
⅛ teaspoon garlic powder
1 (16-ounce) loaf French bread, cut in half horizontally

● **Combine** cheese, mayonnaise, parsley, and garlic powder, stirring well. Spread evenly on cut sides of bread; place on a baking sheet.
● **Bake** at 350° for 15 to 20 minutes or until cheese is melted and bread is lightly browned. Slice crosswise into 1-inch slices. Serve immediately. **Yield:** 1 loaf.

Lisa Lock
Fort Worth, Texas

TENNESSEE SIN

With a name like this, it's got to be good. The bread loaf is the container for a rich cheesy ham dip.

2 (16-ounce) loaves French bread
1 (8-ounce) package cream cheese, softened
1 (8-ounce) carton sour cream
2 cups (8 ounces) shredded Cheddar cheese
½ cup chopped cooked ham
⅓ cup chopped green onions
⅓ cup chopped green pepper
¼ teaspoon Worcestershire sauce
Paprika

● **Slice** off top fourth of 1 bread loaf. Hollow out bottom section leaving a 1-inch shell.
● **Cut** bread top, inside pieces, and remaining bread loaf into 1-inch cubes; place bread shell and cubes on a large baking sheet.
● **Bake** at 350° for 12 minutes or until lightly browned.
● **Beat** cream cheese at medium speed with an electric mixer until smooth; add sour cream, beating until creamy.
● **Stir** in Cheddar cheese and next 4 ingredients. Spoon into bread shell, wrap in heavy-duty aluminum foil, and place on a baking sheet.
● **Bake** at 350° for 30 minutes; unwrap and place on a serving platter. Sprinkle with paprika, and serve with toasted bread cubes. **Yield:** 1 loaf.

Christina Gray
Hohenwald, Tennessee

PANE CUNSADO
(Sicilian for "Fixed Bread ")

Associate Art Director Leonard Loria shares this taste from his childhood. "It has lots of olive oil slathered on with lots and lots of cheese."

1 (16-ounce) loaf French bread, cut in half horizontally
3 tablespoons olive oil
¼ teaspoon freshly ground pepper
1 (5-ounce) package Romano cheese, grated

● **Brush** cut sides of bread with olive oil. Sprinkle bottom half with pepper and cheese.
● **Reassemble** loaf, and wrap in heavy-duty aluminum foil; place on a baking sheet.
● **Bake** at 350° for 25 minutes. Slice crosswise into 1-inch slices. Serve immediately. **Yield:** 1 loaf.

Leonard Loria
Birmingham, Alabama

Yogurt: The Key Ingredient

What's for dessert? Make it with yogurt. It's low in fat, sodium, and cholesterol, and it gets high marks for its health benefits.

So, the next time you need a dessert, try these rich-tasting, low-fat winners that use yogurt, proving that you can satisfy your sweet tooth without sacrificing your waistline.

ALL SEASONS LEMON TRIFLE

1 (14½-ounce) package angel food cake mix *
1 (14-ounce) can low-fat sweetened condensed milk
2 teaspoons grated lemon rind
⅓ cup fresh lemon juice
1 (8-ounce) carton lemon nonfat yogurt
1 (8-ounce) container reduced-fat frozen whipped topping, thawed and divided
1 cup sliced fresh strawberries
1 cup fresh blueberries or blackberries
1 cup fresh raspberries
½ cup flaked coconut, lightly toasted

● **Prepare** cake according to package directions; bake in a 10-inch tube pan. Invert pan; cool completely.
● **Cut** cake into bite-size pieces, and set aside.

● **Combine** condensed milk and next 3 ingredients. Fold in 2 cups whipped topping, and set aside.
● **Place** one-third of cake pieces in bottom of a 4-quart trifle bowl; top with one-third of lemon mixture. Top with strawberries. Repeat layers twice, using remaining cake pieces, lemon mixture, blueberries, and raspberries, ending with raspberries.
● **Spread** remaining whipped topping over raspberries; sprinkle with toasted coconut.
● **Cover** and chill 8 hours. **Yield:** 16 to 18 servings.

* Substitute 1 (16-ounce) angel food cake for cake mix. Cut cake into bite-size pieces, and proceed as directed.

Della Schultz
Mobile, Alabama

♥ Per serving: Calories 216 (17% from fat)
Fat 4g (2.5g saturated) Cholesterol 4.1mg
Sodium 264mg Carbohydrate 40.7g
Fiber 1.7g Protein 5g

LEMON DELIGHT CHEESECAKE
(pictured on page 224)

1 cup graham cracker crumbs
3 tablespoons sugar
2 tablespoons margarine, melted
3 (8-ounce) packages fat-free cream cheese, softened
¾ cup sugar
2 tablespoons all-purpose flour
3 tablespoons lemon juice
¾ cup egg substitute
1 (8-ounce) carton lemon nonfat yogurt
Garnishes: lemon slices, fresh mint sprigs

● **Combine** first 3 ingredients; firmly press into bottom of a 9-inch springform pan.
● **Combine** cream cheese, ¾ cup sugar, and flour; beat at medium speed with an electric mixer until fluffy. Gradually add lemon juice and egg substitute, beating well. Add yogurt, beating well; pour into prepared pan. Cover loosely with aluminum foil.
● **Bake** at 350° for 1 hour or until set. Remove from oven, and immediately run a knife around sides of cheesecake to loosen. Cool completely in pan on a wire rack. Cover and chill at least 8 hours.
● **Remove** sides of pan. Garnish, if desired. **Yield:** 6 servings.

Note: For a crisper crust, bake crust at 350° for 6 to 8 minutes.

Lynette Granade
Mobile, Alabama

♥ Per serving: Calories 402 (15% from fat)
Fat 6.6g (1.3g saturated) Cholesterol 22mg
Sodium 894mg Carbohydrate 58.4g
Fiber 0.1g Protein 22.6g

MAKE-AHEAD CHOCOLATE-MINT CAKE ROLL

(pictured on page 224)

1 (8-ounce) carton plain low-fat yogurt
Vegetable cooking spray
2 large eggs
1 egg white
¾ cup sugar
¼ cup water
1 cup sifted cake flour
3 tablespoons cocoa
1 teaspoon baking powder
⅛ teaspoon salt
1 to 2 tablespoons powdered sugar
½ cup sour cream
1 tablespoon mint-flavored liqueur
1 (12-ounce) container reduced-fat frozen whipped topping, thawed

• **Spread** yogurt on several layers of paper towels; let stand 1 hour.
• **Line** a 15- x 10- x 1-inch jellyroll pan with wax paper; coat with cooking spray, and set aside.
• **Beat** eggs and egg white at high speed with an electric mixer 3 minutes or until thick and pale. Gradually add sugar, 1 tablespoon at a time, beating well after each addition. Add water, beating until blended.
• **Combine** flour and next 3 ingredients; gradually add to egg mixture, beating at low speed just until blended after each addition. Spread evenly in prepared pan.
• **Bake** at 350° for 8 to 10 minutes or until cake springs back when lightly touched in center.
• **Sift** 1 to 2 tablespoons powdered sugar in a 15- x 10-inch rectangle on a cloth towel. When cake is done, immediately loosen from sides of pan, and turn out onto prepared towel. Peel off wax paper. Starting at narrow end, roll up cake and towel together; place, seam side down, on a wire rack. Cool completely.
• **Combine** drained yogurt, sour cream, and liqueur; beat at medium speed with an electric mixer until light and fluffy. Remove 1 cup whipped topping; cover and chill. Fold remaining whipped topping into yogurt mixture. Cover and chill at least 1 hour.

• **Unroll** cake; spread with yogurt mixture. Reroll cake without towel; place, seam side down, on a baking sheet. Cover and freeze at least 2 hours. Thaw cake in refrigerator, and dollop with reserved whipped topping. **Yield:** 10 servings.

Kate L. Settles
Point Clear, Alabama

❤ Per serving: Calories 250 (33% from fat)
Fat 9.1g (6.6g saturated) Cholesterol 51mg
Sodium 133mg Carbohydrate 36.4g
Fiber 0g Protein 5.3g

DE-LIGHT-FUL DESSERT

(pictured on page 224)

1 (14.5-ounce) package angel food cake mix
1 (8-ounce) package reduced-fat cream cheese, softened
1 (8-ounce) carton plain nonfat yogurt, divided
½ cup sifted powdered sugar
¼ cup aspartame sweetener (about 45 packets)
1 (1.2-ounce) package fat-free, sugar-free vanilla instant pudding mix
1¾ cups skim milk
1 (12-ounce) container reduced-fat frozen whipped topping, thawed and divided
1 (20-ounce) can crushed pineapple packed in its own juice, drained and divided
Garnishes: pineapple slices, mint sprigs

• **Prepare** cake mix according to package directions; spoon batter evenly into 5 ungreased 8-inch round cakepans, spreading to edges.
• **Bake** at 350° for 15 minutes. Immediately invert pans onto wire racks; cool completely.
• **Loosen** cakes from sides of pans using a narrow metal spatula; remove from pans. Set aside 3 cake layers; reserve remaining 2 cake layers for another use.
• **Beat** cream cheese at medium speed with an electric mixer until smooth. Add ½ cup yogurt, powdered sugar, and sweetener, beating until smooth; set aside.
• **Combine** pudding mix and milk in a mixing bowl; beat with a wire whisk or at low speed with an electric mixer 2 minutes. Let mixture stand 5 minutes to thicken. Stir in remaining ½ cup yogurt.
• **Fold** 1 cup whipped topping into pudding mixture; set aside.
• **Spoon** ¼ cup pineapple into a 3-quart trifle bowl; place 1 cake layer in bowl. Top with ⅔ cup cream cheese mixture, one-third of remaining pineapple, 1⅓ cups pudding mixture, and 1 cup whipped topping. Repeat layers twice with remaining ingredients, ending with whipped topping. Garnish, if desired.
• **Cover** and chill at least 2 hours. **Yield:** 12 servings.

Alice Gunthorpe
Semmes, Alabama

❤ Per serving: Calories 317 (20% from fat)
Fat 7.1g (5.7g saturated) Cholesterol 12mg
Sodium 490mg Carbohydrate 57.1g
Fiber 0.4g Protein 8.5g

YOGURT TIPS

■ To make thickened yogurt for sauces and desserts, spoon yogurt onto several layers of heavy-duty paper towels; spread to ½-inch thickness. Cover with additional paper towels, and let stand 5 minutes. Using a rubber spatula, scrape yogurt into a bowl; cover and chill. An 8-ounce carton of low-fat yogurt yields ¼ cup drained yogurt.

■ Reduce calories in salad dressing and dips by substituting plain yogurt for mayonnaise or sour cream.

■ If yogurt is added to a mixture that is at room temperature or warm, yogurt should be at room temperature to prevent separation.

Smoked Salmon and Cucumber Tartlets (recipe, page 216) combine make-ahead ease with sophisticated taste.

Above: *No need to meet in St. Louis for this specialty dish. St. Louis Toasted Ravioli (recipe, page 117) can be a specialty in your kitchen, too.* Left: *Dried ancho chile peppers provide the punch in Boneless Pork Chops With Ancho Cream Sauce (recipe, page 205).*

Yogurt is the secret ingredient keeping Lemon Delight Cheesecake, Make-Ahead Chocolate-Mint Cake Roll, and De-Light-Ful Dessert mysteriously light and delicious. (Recipes begin on page 219.)

SEPTEMBER

FOOD OF OUR NATIVE FATHERS

The rich tradition of American Indian foods continues today. We celebrate the cuisine with simple rustic dishes similar to native compositions, but updated with aromatic seasonings.

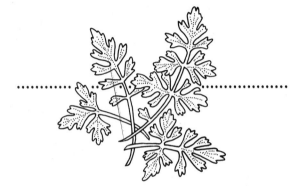

RED CHILI STEW

1½ pounds lean beef chuck roast, cut into 1-inch cubes
2 cups water
3 tablespoons ground red chile
1 teaspoon salt
1 teaspoon ground oregano
1 clove garlic, pressed
3 large tomatoes, chopped

• **Combine** beef and water in a Dutch oven; bring to a boil over medium-high heat. Cover, reduce heat, and simmer 45 minutes or until tender, stirring occasionally.
• **Stir** in ground chile and remaining ingredients; cook 30 additional minutes. **Yield:** 4 cups.

Rose Trujillo
Nambe Pueblo, New Mexico

POSOLE
(Poh-SOH-leh)

2 cups white, yellow, or blue posole corn (dried hominy)
12 cups water, divided
½ pound boneless fresh pork, cut into ½-inch cubes
3 to 4 tablespoons ground red chile
¼ cup chopped onion
2 cloves garlic, pressed
2 teaspoons salt
2 teaspoons ground oregano

• **Soak** posole in 6 cups water at least 2 hours; drain.
• **Combine** posole and remaining 6 cups water in a Dutch oven; bring to a boil over medium heat. Cover, reduce heat, and simmer 30 minutes.
• **Add** pork and remaining ingredients; return to a boil. Cover, reduce heat, and simmer 4 hours or until posole is tender and pork shreds easily, adding additional water as necessary, stirring occasionally. **Yield:** 8 cups.

Margie Garcia
Santa Fe, New Mexico

STEWED ANASAZI BEANS WITH MUSHROOMS

2 cups dried Anasazi beans *
6 cups beef broth
½ cup chopped onion
3 fresh basil leaves, chopped
2 cloves garlic, minced
2 bay leaves
2 sprigs fresh thyme
2 jalapeño peppers, finely chopped
1 tablespoon tomato preserves
1 teaspoon chopped fresh chervil
1 teaspoon salt
1 teaspoon mesquite-flavored barbecue seasoning
4 scallions, chopped
1½ cups chopped mushrooms
1 tablespoon vegetable oil

• **Sort** and wash beans; soak in water to cover 8 hours. Drain.
• **Combine** beans and next 11 ingredients in a Dutch oven; bring to a boil over medium heat. Cover, reduce heat, and simmer 1 hour or until beans are tender.
• **Cook** scallions and mushrooms in oil over medium-high heat, stirring constantly, until tender. Stir into bean mixture; return to a boil. Reduce heat, and simmer 15 minutes. Remove and discard bay leaves. **Yield:** 6 cups.

* Substitute 2 cups dried pinto beans.

THE HUNT IS ON

If you have difficulty locating the posole corn, Anasazi beans, or ground red chile found in these recipes or want to try other native foods, you can order them by mail. For a catalog from one source we found most helpful, write to:

Trujillo Family Farms
Route 1, Box 125
Santa Fe, NM 87501
(505) 455-3495

SAUTÉED CHAYOTE SQUASH WITH CILANTRO

1 (¾-pound) chayote squash, cut into wedges
2 tablespoons hot red chili oil
1 teaspoon coarsely chopped fresh cilantro
1 clove garlic, pressed
¼ teaspoon salt
1 cup bean sprouts

• **Cook** squash in oil in a skillet over medium-high heat, turning often, 10 minutes or until tender. Add cilantro, garlic, and salt; cook 2 minutes. Add sprouts, and serve immediately. **Yield:** 2 to 3 servings.

Siegfried Eisenberger
Broadmoor Hotel
Colorado Springs, Colorado

PUMPKIN-CORN SOUP WITH GINGER-LIME CREAM

3 cups fresh or frozen corn kernels
1½ cups water
2 cloves garlic, minced
¾ teaspoon salt
½ to ¾ teaspoon ground white pepper
3 to 3½ cups chicken broth
3 cups cooked, mashed pumpkin *
Ginger-Lime Cream
Garnish: lime zest

• **Combine** corn and water; cook, covered, over medium-high heat 10 minutes or until tender. Pour into container of a food processor; process 2 minutes or until smooth. Pour mixture through a wire-mesh strainer into a bowl, discarding pulp.
• **Combine** corn mixture, garlic, salt, pepper, and 3 cups chicken broth in a Dutch oven; bring to a boil over medium-high heat. Reduce heat to low; stir in pumpkin. Simmer 10 minutes, adding additional chicken broth as necessary, stirring constantly.
• **Spoon** into individual bowls, and dollop with Ginger-Lime Cream. Garnish, if desired. **Yield:** 8 cups.

* Substitute 3 cups canned pumpkin.

These creature comforts have sustained lives for centuries and continue to bring us pleasurable tastes.

By the time Christopher Columbus landed in the Western Hemisphere, he found its inhabitants already thriving on vegetables like corn and beans. Many other foods originated in the Americas, including peppers, tomatoes, potatoes, pumpkins, melons, cherries, cranberries, blueberries, peanuts, walnuts, piñon nuts (pine nuts), chestnuts, sunflower seeds, and maple sugar. Wild game and birds, fish, shellfish, and honey were also plentiful.

Today we enjoy these same foods, but with a modern flair that involves experimenting with local herbs and foreign spices. And that's exactly what chefs and cookbook authors are doing with traditional American Indian foods.

You can create your own showcase with our recipes, many drawn from American Indians who share their rich food heritage.

Ginger-Lime Cream

¼ cup fresh lime juice
1 tablespoon grated fresh ginger
1½ teaspoons grated lime rind
½ cup whipping cream

• **Combine** lime juice and ginger in a small saucepan; cook over medium heat 2 minutes. Remove from heat; pour through a wire-mesh strainer into a small bowl, discarding pulp.

• **Add** lime rind and whipping cream to juice mixture; beat at medium speed with an electric mixer until soft peaks form. **Yield:** 1 cup.

Lois Ellen Frank,
Native American Cooking:
Foods of the Southwest
Indian Nations
(Clarkson Potter Publishers, 1991)

PUEBLO INDIAN COOKIES

2 cups butter or margarine, softened
2¾ cups sugar, divided
2 large eggs
6 cups all-purpose flour
1 tablespoon baking powder
2 teaspoons anise seeds, crushed
¾ teaspoon salt
½ cup milk
1½ teaspoons ground cinnamon

• **Beat** butter at medium speed with an electric mixer until creamy; gradually add 2½ cups sugar, beating mixture well. Add eggs, one at a time, beating after each addition.
• **Combine** flour and next 3 ingredients; add to butter mixture alternately with milk, beginning and ending with flour mixture.
• **Divide** dough in half; roll each half to ¼-inch thickness on a well-floured surface. Cut with a 2½-inch daisy or round cutter, and place on lightly greased cookie sheets.
• **Combine** remaining ¼ cup sugar and cinnamon; sprinkle over cookies.
• **Bake** at 350° for 12 to 15 minutes. **Yield:** about 8 dozen.

Note: Look for anise seeds in the spice section of grocery stores.

Gloria Trujillo
Santa Fe, New Mexico

CHEFS' WHISK-AND-TELL SECRETS

....

In their restaurants, these top regional chefs wow diners with involved recipes, but what do these Southern culinary artists create at home? Simply delicious dishes that you can make as well. Each has just five to 10 ingredients and is ready for your kitchen.

SUNDAY CHICKEN

1 large lemon
1 (3-pound) broiler-fryer
1 tablespoon olive oil
1 tablespoon Creole seasoning
1 tablespoon chopped fresh or dried rosemary

• **Cut** lemon in half, and squeeze juice over chicken. Put lemon halves in cavity of chicken. Brush oil on chicken, and sprinkle with Creole seasoning and rosemary.
• **Bake** at 400° for 45 minutes to an hour or until a meat thermometer inserted in thigh registers 180°, basting occasionally with pan drippings. **Yield:** 4 servings.

Emeril Lagasse
Emeril's
New Orleans, Louisiana

HAM-MUSHROOM-STUFFED ARTICHOKES

2 medium-size fresh artichokes
Lemon wedge
1½ tablespoons fresh lemon juice
1 cup sliced fresh mushrooms
1 teaspoon olive or vegetable oil
3 ounces smoked ham, cut into strips (about ½ cup strips)
2 tablespoons dry vermouth or chicken broth
¼ cup whipping cream
2 tablespoons chopped fresh chives
½ cup (2 ounces) shredded Swiss cheese

• **Hold** artichokes by stems, and wash by plunging up and down in cold water. Cut off stem end, and trim about ½ inch from top of each artichoke. Remove any loose bottom leaves. With kitchen scissors, trim one-fourth off top of each outer leaf, and rub top and edges of leaves with lemon wedge to prevent discoloring.
• **Place** artichokes in a large nonaluminum Dutch oven; cover with water, and add lemon juice.

• **Bring** to a boil; cover, reduce heat, and simmer 35 minutes or until lower leaves pull out easily. Drain; place in a baking pan.
• **Cook** mushrooms in oil in a large skillet over medium-high heat 3 minutes, stirring often. Add ham, and cook 3 minutes, stirring often. Add vermouth and whipping cream; cook 3 minutes. Remove from heat; stir in chives and cheese.
• **Spoon** mixture into and over artichokes. Broil 5½ inches from heat (with electric oven door partially opened) 3 minutes or until golden. Serve immediately. **Yield:** 2 servings.

José Guiterrez
Chez Phillipe
Memphis, Tennessee

LATE-NIGHT PASTA CHEZ FRANK
(pictured on page 260)

6 cloves garlic, pressed
2 tablespoons olive oil
4 jalapeño peppers or other chile peppers, seeded and minced
8 plum tomatoes, chopped
½ teaspoon salt
⅓ to ½ cup chopped fresh basil
1 (8-ounce) package spaghettini or vermicelli, cooked
Freshly grated Parmesan cheese
Garnish: fresh basil sprigs

• **Cook** garlic in oil in a large nonstick skillet over medium heat, stirring constantly, 1 to 2 minutes or until golden. Add pepper, and cook 1 minute, stirring constantly.
• **Add** tomato and salt; cook 3 minutes or until thoroughly heated. Stir in chopped basil. Serve immediately over pasta, and sprinkle with Parmesan cheese. Garnish, if desired. **Yield:** 2 or 3 servings.

Frank Stitt
Highlands Bar & Grill
Birmingham, Alabama

HERBED CHERRY TOMATOES OVER PASTA

4 cups cherry tomatoes, cut
   in half
⅓ cup balsamic vinegar
½ cup olive oil
¼ cup chopped fresh basil
12 ounces bow tie pasta, cooked

• **Combine** first 4 ingredients. Serve over pasta. **Yield:** 4 to 6 servings.

Note: You can add ½ pound fresh lump crabmeat to tomato mixture just before serving.

Ben Barker
Magnolia Grill
Durham, North Carolina

FRESH VEGETABLE SKILLET DINNER

2 tablespoons butter or margarine
1 large onion, sliced
2 medium-size yellow squash,
   sliced (about ½ pound)
1 large sweet red or green pepper,
   seeded and sliced
2 large tomatoes, cut into
   wedges
¼ teaspoon salt
¼ teaspoon freshly ground black
   pepper
3 cups packed fresh spinach
1 cup (4 ounces) shredded
   Monterey Jack cheese

• **Melt** butter in a large skillet over medium-high heat; add onion, and cook 5 minutes, stirring often. Add squash and red or green pepper; cook 3 to 5 minutes, stirring often.
• **Add** tomato, salt, and pepper; cover, reduce heat, and simmer 5 to 10 minutes. Place spinach over mixture; cover and cook over low heat 3 additional minutes.
• **Add** cheese; cover and cook 2 minutes or until spinach wilts and cheese melts. Serve immediately. **Yield:** 2 or 3 servings.

Mark Abernathy
Juanita's
Little Rock, Arkansas

SUMMER ZUCCHINI SALAD

8 medium zucchini, cut into thin
   strips (about 3 pounds)
1 tablespoon minced garlic
¼ cup olive oil
2 tablespoons finely chopped fresh
   basil
2 tablespoons finely chopped fresh
   mint
½ teaspoon salt
¼ cup chopped pecans,
   toasted

• **Cook** zucchini and garlic in oil in a large skillet over medium-high heat, stirring constantly, 3 minutes or until tender. Remove from skillet; cool.
• **Combine** zucchini mixture, basil, and remaining ingredients in a bowl, stirring gently. Serve at room temperature or chill, if desired. **Yield:** 8 servings.

Elizabeth Terry
Elizabeth on 37th
Savannah, Georgia

SWEET ONION TARTS

½ (15-ounce) package refrigerated
   piecrusts
4 cups thinly sliced sweet onion
   (about 1¼ pounds)
2 tablespoons butter or margarine
1½ teaspoons fresh thyme or
   ½ teaspoon dried thyme
2½ tablespoons whipping cream
1 egg yolk
Dash of salt (optional)
Dash of pepper (optional)
2 tablespoons crumbled goat
   cheese (optional)
Garnish: fresh thyme sprigs

• **Unfold** piecrust, and press out fold lines with a rolling pin on a lightly floured surface. Cut 2 (5½-inch) circles out of piecrust; fit circles into 2 (5-inch) round tart pans with removable bottoms. Place pans on a baking sheet. Prick bottom and sides of crusts with a fork.
• **Bake** at 450° for 8 minutes; remove to wire racks to cool.
• **Cook** sliced onion in butter in a large heavy skillet over medium heat 30 minutes or until onion is tender, stirring often. Stir in thyme; remove skillet from heat.
• **Combine** whipping cream, egg yolk, and if desired, salt and pepper; stir into onion. Pour mixture into prepared crusts.
• **Bake** at 350° for 20 to 30 minutes or until golden, sprinkling with goat cheese after 15 minutes, if desired. Garnish, if desired. **Yield:** 2 tarts.

Note: You can double the recipe, but onion mixture will take longer to brown and become tender.

Louis Osteen
Louis's Charleston Grill
Charleston, South Carolina

OVEN-ROASTED VEGETABLE CHOWDER

1½ pounds red potatoes, cut into
   ½-inch cubes
2 large carrots, scraped and cut
   into ½-inch cubes
1 large onion, coarsely chopped
6 plum tomatoes, quartered
   lengthwise
3 (14½-ounce) cans ready-to-serve
   chicken broth
Dash of salt (optional)
Dash of pepper (optional)

• **Combine** potato and carrot in a lightly greased aluminum foil-lined 13- x 9- x 2-inch pan. Bake at 375° for 15 minutes.
• **Stir** in onion. Place tomato at one end of pan, keeping separate from potato mixture. Bake 1 hour, stirring every 15 minutes.
• **Remove** from oven. Coarsely chop tomato; set aside.
• **Bring** broth to a boil in a large saucepan; add potato mixture. Reduce heat, and simmer 10 to 15 minutes.
• **Stir** in tomato; if desired, add salt and pepper. Serve immediately. **Yield:** about 7 cups.

Marcel Desaulniers
Trellis Restaurant
Williamsburg, Virginia

Seasoned With A Southern Accent

When Susan Mack and her husband, Andy Armstrong of Atlanta, packed their bags for a monthlong tour of France, they never expected to return home wearing souvenirs of the trip on their waistlines. The weight gain on that vacation spurred Susan's initial interest in low-fat cooking, but the real wake-up call came a few years later when she discovered her cholesterol level was approaching 300.

Susan and Andy immediately launched a new lifestyle. Exercise became a daily routine. They adopted the fresh, simple cooking style of the Mediterranean: abundant grains and breads, vegetables, legumes, olive oil, fruits, and very little red meat.

"The people of the region are inspiring," Susan says. "I've tried to tap into their way of eating to reproduce the same robust good health and joy of living for myself."

Try these delicious Mediterranean-influenced recipes Susan shared with us, and you'll agree that low-fat foods can taste great without a lot of fuss.

GRILLED SWORDFISH WITH CAPER SAUCE
(pictured on page 259)

½ cup dry white wine
5 cloves garlic, minced
2 teaspoons chopped fresh
   rosemary, divided
¼ teaspoon salt
¼ teaspoon pepper
4 (4-ounce) swordfish steaks
Vegetable cooking spray
⅓ cup lemon juice
3 tablespoons Basil-Infused
   Olive Oil or Lemon-Infused
   Olive Oil (see recipes,
   page 231)
1 tablespoon capers
3 tablespoons fine, dry
   breadcrumbs
Garnish: fresh rosemary sprigs

• **Combine** wine, garlic, and 1 teaspoon chopped rosemary in an 8-inch square dish.
• **Sprinkle** salt and pepper over fish; place in dish, turning to coat. Cover and chill at least 1 hour. Remove fish from marinade, discarding marinade.

• **Coat** food rack with cooking spray; place on grill over hot coals (400° to 500°). Cook fish, covered with grill lid, 4 to 5 minutes on each side.
• **Combine** remaining 1 teaspoon chopped rosemary, lemon juice, and next 3 ingredients. Spoon over fish. Garnish, if desired, and serve immediately. **Yield:** 4 servings.

Note: You can substitute extra virgin olive oil for infused oil.

❤ Per serving: Calories 271 (52% from fat)
Fat 15.1g (2.7g saturated) Cholesterol 44mg
Sodium 461mg Carbohydrate 7.5g
Fiber 0.4g Protein 23.6g

CAESAR SALAD PASTA

Add chopped cooked chicken to turn this dish into a hearty one-dish meal.

8 ounces linguine, cooked without
   salt or fat
Vegetable cooking spray
2 tablespoons olive oil, divided
2 tablespoons minced garlic
3 anchovy fillets, finely chopped
¾ cup seasoned croutons,
   divided
⅓ cup grated Parmesan cheese,
   divided
4 cups sliced romaine lettuce
2 teaspoons grated lemon rind

• **Coat** a nonstick skillet with cooking spray, and place over medium heat until hot. Add 1 tablespoon olive oil, garlic, and anchovies. Cook 2 minutes, stirring constantly.
• **Add** half of croutons and 3 tablespoons cheese; stir well. Add lettuce; cook, stirring constantly, 2 to 3 minutes or until lettuce wilts. Add linguine and lemon rind, tossing to combine.
• **Transfer** to a serving bowl; top with remaining croutons and cheese. Drizzle with remaining 1 tablespoon oil. Serve immediately. **Yield:** 4 servings.

❤ Per serving: Calories 345 (29% from fat)
Fat 11g (2.5g saturated) Cholesterol 5mg
Sodium 272mg Carbohydrate 48.5g
Fiber 2.5g Protein 12.6g

MOROCCAN GRILLED CHICKEN SALAD

½ cup plain nonfat yogurt
3 tablespoons Moroccan Spice Rub (see recipe in box)
6 (5-ounce) boned chicken breast halves
Vegetable cooking spray
10 cups mixed salad greens
Vinaigrette Dressing

• **Combine** yogurt and Moroccan Spice Rub, stirring well. Lift skin of chicken breast halves; spread one-half yogurt mixture under skin. Replace skin; spread remaining yogurt mixture over chicken. Cover and chill.
• **Coat** grill rack with cooking spray; place on grill over hot coals (400° to 500°).
• **Cook** chicken, skin side down, covered with grill lid, over hot coals about 4 minutes. Turn chicken; cook about 2 additional minutes or until done.
• **Remove** and discard skin from chicken; cut chicken into thin strips.
• **Arrange** salad greens evenly on six individual serving plates; top with chicken strips, and drizzle with Vinaigrette Dressing. Serve immediately. **Yield:** 6 servings.

Vinaigrette Dressing

Vinaigrette Dressing has 81 calories and 9 fat grams per tablespoon.

⅓ cup olive oil
2 tablespoons red wine vinegar
1 tablespoon balsamic vinegar
1 teaspoon Dijon mustard
Dash of curry powder

• **Combine** all ingredients in a jar; cover tightly, and shake vigorously. **Yield:** ½ cup.

♥ Per serving: Calories 287 (52% from fat) Fat 16.5g (2.6g saturated) Cholesterol 71mg Sodium 547mg Carbohydrate 5.7g Fiber 1.2g Protein 28.4g

INFUSED WITH FLAVOR

Susan Mack of Atlanta uses infused oils in the sauce on her Grilled Swordfish and for making salad dressings and marinades. Flavored oils are available in many supermarkets and specialty foods stores. If you can't find them in your area, here's how to make Lemon-Infused Olive Oil and Basil-Infused Olive Oil.

Lemon-Infused Olive Oil: Cut the rind from 2 lemons, reserving lemon sections for another use. Combine rind and 1 cup olive oil in a heavy saucepan; bring to a boil. Reduce heat to low; simmer 15 minutes. Remove from heat, and cool. Pour oil mixture through a wire-mesh strainer into a jar, discarding peel. Cover and store in refrigerator up to 2 weeks. **Yield:** 1 cup.

Basil-Infused Olive Oil: Combine 1 cup fresh basil leaves and 1 cup olive oil in a heavy saucepan; bring to a boil. Reduce heat to low, and simmer 15 minutes. Remove from heat, and cool. Pour oil mixture through a wire-mesh strainer into a jar, discarding basil leaves. Cover and store in refrigerator up to 2 weeks. **Yield:** 1 cup.

Note: Let oils return to room temperature before using. Clouding from refrigeration is normal.

RUB IT IN

"If it can be cooked, I rub this spice mix on it," Susan says. She uses it in her Moroccan Grilled Chicken Salad, as well as with vegetables, pasta, fish, potatoes, pork, lamb, shrimp, and turkey. It also makes a great seasoning for anything that's grilled.

MOROCCAN SPICE RUB

Fenugreek is an aromatic Mediterranean plant belonging to the pea family. The seeds from the pods are slightly bitter. They're roasted and ground, and then used as a flavoring in curries.

¼ cup paprika
1 tablespoon kosher salt
1 tablespoon sweet red pepper flakes
2 teaspoons instant minced onion
1 teaspoon cracked peppercorns
1 teaspoon ground ginger
1 teaspoon ground cardamom
1 teaspoon ground cumin
1 teaspoon fenugreek
Dash of ground cloves
Dash of ground cinnamon
Dash of ground allspice

• **Combine** all ingredients in a skillet, and cook mixture over medium-high heat, stirring constantly, 3 to 5 minutes or until spices are roasted and darker. Let cool.
• **Position** knife blade in food processor bowl, and add spice mixture. Process 2 to 3 minutes. Store spice rub in a sealed container in a cool, dark place up to 3 months. **Yield:** ½ cup.

RICE WITH TOMATOES AND BASIL

This easy dish can be served cold as a salad or hot as a side dish. Drizzle with balsamic vinegar for even more flavor.

3 cups cooked rice (cooked without salt or fat)
1 cup coarsely chopped tomato
2 tablespoons coarsely chopped fresh basil
½ teaspoon salt

• **Combine** all ingredients, tossing gently. **Yield:** 4 servings.

♥ Per serving: Calories 164 (3% from fat)
Fat 0.5g (0g saturated) Cholesterol 0mg
Sodium 750mg Carbohydrate 35.5g
Fiber 0.6g Protein 3.6g

EXPERT ADVICE

"I will not put low-fat food on the table unless it tastes wonderful," Susan Mack says. Try her tricks.

■ Use enough fat that you don't suffer. You won't last long when eating only fat-free foods. Use olive oil and butter judiciously to add richness.

■ Try to be adventurous with flavor. Buy or bake breads made with whole grains or flavored with vegetables. Add flavored oils, fresh vegetables, or herbs to rice. Before cooking meat, chicken, or fish, rub them with spices or herbs.

■ Eat lots of grains. Barley, couscous, orzo, and flavored pastas make meals interesting.

■ Don't buy processed foods. You'll save money and maximize nutrition. Quality produce, flavored vinegars, and salsas add diversity to dinner.

MICROWAVE RATATOUILLE

(pictured on page 259)

Pair this colorful side dish with Grilled Swordfish With Caper Sauce (page 230), and make quick work of dinner.

3 cups chopped unpeeled eggplant
2 cups chopped yellow squash
2 cups chopped zucchini
1 sweet red pepper, seeded and chopped
1 sweet yellow pepper, seeded and chopped
Vegetable cooking spray
1 medium onion, chopped
4 cloves garlic, minced
1½ cups spaghetti sauce
¼ cup coarsely chopped fresh Italian parsley
1 teaspoon dried oregano
1 teaspoon dried thyme
1 tablespoon finely chopped fresh basil

• **Place** eggplant in a 9-inch pieplate; cover with a paper towel, and microwave at HIGH 4 minutes. Transfer to a large bowl. Repeat procedure with squash, zucchini, and peppers. Set vegetable mixture aside.
• **Coat** a very large skillet or Dutch oven with cooking spray; place over medium heat until hot. Add onion and garlic, and cook, stirring constantly, until tender.
• **Stir** in vegetable mixture, spaghetti sauce, and next 3 ingredients. Cook 4 minutes, stirring occasionally. Stir in basil. **Yield:** 6 servings.

♥ Per serving: Calories 97 (32% from fat)
Fat 3.9g (0.1g saturated) Cholesterol 0mg
Sodium 272mg Carbohydrate 15.4g
Fiber 2g Protein 2.9g

FRESH FRUIT WITH MINT-BALSAMIC TEA

Serve this versatile compote on lettuce leaves as a salad, in a large bowl for a brunch or breakfast buffet, or in individual dishes as a dessert.

1½ cups water
¼ cup sugar
1 regular-size tea bag
½ cup loosely packed fresh mint sprigs
1 tablespoon balsamic vinegar
2 cups cubed fresh pineapple
1 cup cubed honeydew
1 cup cubed cantaloupe
1 cup orange sections
1 cup fresh blueberries

• **Combine** water and sugar in a heavy saucepan; bring to a boil. Add tea bag and mint; remove from heat, and let steep 5 minutes. Remove tea bag; stir in balsamic vinegar, and let stand 5 minutes.
• **Pour** mixture through a wire-mesh strainer into a large bowl, discarding mint. Add fruit, stirring gently to coat. Cover mixture, and chill at least 1 hour. **Yield:** 5 cups.

♥ Per serving: Calories 158 (4% from fat)
Fat 0.7g (0.1g saturated) Cholesterol 0mg
Sodium 11mg Carbohydrate 40.1g
Fiber 5.7g Protein 1.4g

COUSCOUS WITH MIXED FRUIT

1 cup ready-to-serve reduced-sodium, fat-free chicken broth
½ cup unsweetened apple juice
½ cup chopped dried fruit mix
½ cup peeled and chopped cooking apple
¼ teaspoon salt
1 cup couscous, uncooked

• **Combine** first 4 ingredients in a large nonaluminum saucepan; let stand 15 minutes.
• **Add** salt, and bring mixture to a boil over medium heat. Stir in couscous; cover and remove from heat. Let stand

5 to 7 minutes or until liquid is absorbed. Fluff mixture with a fork. **Yield:** 4 servings.

♥ Per serving: Calories 288 (0% from fat)
Fat 0g (0g saturated) Cholesterol 0mg
Sodium 162mg Carbohydrate 64.4g
Fiber 3.9g Protein 6.5g

EAT YOUR GREENS

....

Collards are a country classic – a staple of true Southern cuisine. Today, we cook them faster and serve them in new and different ways. If you've only eaten them "cooked down" and sprinkled with vinegar with green peppers, then you're in for a treat with Grits and Greens, and Parmesan-Collards Casserole.

Fresh collards are inexpensive and available much of the year. Select crisp, dark green leaves. Remove and discard the stems and any discolored spots; wash the leaves in lots of cold water. Roughly chop the leaves to reduce the cooking time.

Try these recipes for a fresh taste of this down-home basic.

COLLARD GREENS

5 to 6 pounds fresh collard greens
1 (10½-ounce) can condensed
    chicken broth, undiluted
⅔ cup water
½ cup chopped onion
1½ tablespoons bacon drippings
1 teaspoon seasoned salt
¼ teaspoon sugar
½ teaspoon freshly ground pepper

• **Remove** and discard stems and any discolored spots from greens. Wash greens thoroughly, drain, and coarsely chop. Place in a large Dutch oven; add broth and remaining ingredients.

• **Bring** to a boil over medium-high heat. Cover, reduce heat, and simmer 1 hour or until tender. Serve with commercial vinegar with green peppers. **Yield:** 6 to 8 servings.

Carol Barclay
Portland, Texas

GRITS AND GREENS

If you don't have stone-ground grits on hand or can't find them at your grocery store, substitute regular grits.

1 cup whipping cream
4 cups chicken broth, divided
1 cup stone-ground grits
¼ to ½ cup milk
1 pound fresh collard greens
¼ cup butter or margarine
1 to 1½ cups freshly grated
    Parmesan cheese
¼ to ½ teaspoon freshly ground
    pepper
Garnish: chopped cooked bacon or
    cubed cooked ham

• **Combine** whipping cream and 3 cups chicken broth in a large saucepan. Bring mixture to a boil, and gradually stir in grits.

• **Cook** over medium heat until mixture returns to a boil; cover, reduce heat, and simmer 25 to 30 minutes, stirring often. Gradually add milk, if necessary, for desired consistency.

• **Remove** and discard stems and any discolored spots from greens. Wash greens thoroughly, drain, and cut into ½-inch strips.

• **Combine** greens and remaining 1 cup chicken broth in a large skillet; bring to a boil. Cover, reduce heat, and simmer 5 minutes or until greens are tender. Drain and plunge into ice water to stop the cooking process. Drain well on paper towels.

• **Add** butter, cheese, and pepper to grits, stirring until butter and cheese melt. Stir in greens.

• **Cook,** stirring constantly, until thoroughly heated. Garnish, if desired. **Yield:** 6 to 8 servings.

Marion Sullivan
Charleston, South Carolina

PARMESAN-COLLARDS CASSEROLE

1½ pounds fresh collard greens *
¼ cup water
¼ cup dry white wine
1 teaspoon sugar
1½ cups milk
½ cup canned condensed chicken
    broth, undiluted
¼ cup all-purpose flour
¾ cup freshly grated Parmesan
    cheese, divided
½ (8-ounce) package reduced-fat
    cream cheese, cubed
¼ teaspoon salt
½ teaspoon freshly ground pepper
3 tablespoons fine, dry
    breadcrumbs

• **Remove** and discard stems and any discolored spots from greens. Wash greens thoroughly, drain, and cut into 1-inch strips; set aside.

• **Combine** water, wine, and sugar in a large skillet or Dutch oven; bring to a boil. Gradually add greens, stirring after each addition until leaves wilt. Cover and cook 10 minutes or until tender, stirring occasionally. Drain and set aside.

• **Combine** milk, chicken broth, and flour in a large saucepan, stirring with a wire whisk until smooth. Cook over medium heat, stirring constantly, until thickened. Add ½ cup Parmesan cheese, cream cheese, salt, and pepper, stirring until cheese melts. Stir in prepared greens.

• **Spoon** into a lightly greased 2-quart baking dish. Sprinkle with breadcrumbs and remaining ¼ cup Parmesan cheese.

• **Bake** at 350° for 25 minutes or until casserole is thoroughly heated. **Yield:** 6 servings.

* Substitute 3 (10-ounce) packages frozen collards, thawed and drained.

STEWED TOMATOES AND GREENS

3 (14.5-ounce) cans whole
   tomatoes, undrained
1 small onion, finely chopped
⅓ cup sugar
2 tablespoons butter or margarine
¼ teaspoon salt
½ teaspoon pepper
3 tablespoons apple cider vinegar
Hot cooked collard greens

• **Drain** tomatoes, reserving ½ cup liquid. Chop tomatoes.
• **Combine** chopped tomato, reserved tomato liquid, onion, and next 5 ingredients in a nonaluminum saucepan; bring to a boil. Reduce heat, and simmer 45 minutes, stirring occasionally. Serve over collard greens. **Yield:** 6 servings.

Rita Helton
Birmingham, Alabama

MESS O' GREENS

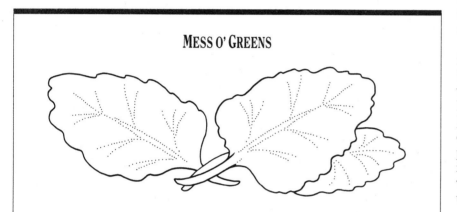

Collards are versatile. Here we share a few facts and ideas we've learned.

■ Raw collards will yield approximately one-fourth the original amount when cooked.

■ Collards are said to be sweetest when they've been kissed by frost. They're quite tender and will require less cooking time.

■ Add a splash of white wine or a dash of sugar to sweeten the collards and add character to the pot liquor.

■ Toss a whole pecan, shell and all, in the pot with collards to soften the strong cooking odors.

■ Cooked collards are very low in calories – approximately 30 calories per cup. These greens are also a good source of calcium, vitamin A, phosphorus, and ascorbic acid.

■ Cook collards long and slow for a mass of soft, mellow leaves. Or simmer the leaves in a seasoned broth for 15 to 30 minutes for a crisp-tender texture.

■ Blanch and chop collard greens to use for stuffing ham or other pork cuts. Or combine with ground meat or cheese in a calzone – a stuffed pizza that resembles a large turnover.

■ Experiment with collards. Try them with bacon, blue cheese, goat cheese, Italian salad dressing, sweet relish, or chowchow. Pair greens with sour cream for a baked potato topping or stuff into mushrooms and sprinkle with Parmesan cheese.

■ Convinced of their therapeutic powers, Julius Caesar is rumored to have eaten a plateful of collards after a heavy meal to ward off indigestion (from Bert Greene's *Greene on Greens*).

IN PURSUIT OF PERFECT FRIED CHICKEN

....

Without fried chicken, a picnic is just a meal with ants; a family reunion only a series of endless hugs; and a church covered-dish supper – well, the very thought of this omission leaves the spirit wanting.

An occasional rendezvous with the frying pan won't kill you – and it can be downright fun. Our day with foods writer and historian John Egerton of Nashville, Tennessee, proved that. John's book *Southern Food* (University of North Carolina Press, Chapel Hill, paperback) has provided history and inspiration to our staff for years. So it was only natural to invite him to join us. Here's what we gleaned from him.

■ A cast-iron skillet is ideal, but an electric skillet or a stainless steel frying pan will do the job. The chicken cooks more evenly, browns to a prettier color, and is much more crispy when fried in a cast-iron skillet because the oil's temperature remains more constant.

■ A fresh chicken is best. Some stores fool us with frozen birds that are thawed before they're sold. Get to know your butcher, and ask for help.

■ Vegetable oil with ¼ cup bacon drippings is our fat of choice.

■ In an effort to keep the kitchen somewhat clean, we opted for the oil in our cast-iron skillet to be three-fourths the height of the chicken – usually 2 inches deep.

■ The chicken absorbed less oil (we measured how much oil was left in the skillet after each batch) when it was soaked in buttermilk or salt water in the refrigerator 8 hours. Salt water offered the best results for us; buttermilk ran a close second.

■ Seasoning the chicken offers more room for variation than any other step. We dredged the chicken in a combination of flour, salt, and pepper. Dipping in beaten egg before flouring left the chicken clumpy, and it absorbed much more oil. We tried batters with herb seasonings, but the flavor didn't come through.

■ Add the chicken to the skillet when the oil reaches 360°. Then keep the oil sizzling at 300° to 325° for the remainder of the frying. Use a candy thermometer to test the oil's temperature.

■ Cover the cast-iron skillet after adding the chicken. Covering helps to eliminate spatters, and it didn't make our chicken soggy.

"The whole objective is to get the right color and outside texture and cook the chicken through in about 30 minutes," John says. "Take the chicken out of the pan when it's brown enough to suit your taste."

And when we did take it out of the pan, we drained it on paper towels, let it cool, and sampled it gustily.

OUR BEST SOUTHERN FRIED CHICKEN

3   quarts water
1   tablespoon salt
1   (2- to 2½-pound) broiler-fryer, cut up
1   teaspoon salt
1   teaspoon pepper
1   cup all-purpose flour
2   cups vegetable oil
¼   cup bacon drippings

• Combine water and 1 tablespoon salt in a large bowl; add chicken. Cover and chill 8 hours.
• Drain chicken; rinse with cold water, and pat dry.
• Combine 1 teaspoon salt and pepper; sprinkle half of mixture over all sides of chicken.
• Combine remaining mixture and flour in a large heavy-duty, zip-top plastic bag.

• Place 2 pieces of chicken in bag; seal. Shake to coat completely. Remove chicken, and repeat procedure with remaining pieces.
• Combine vegetable oil and bacon drippings in a 12-inch cast-iron skillet or chicken fryer; heat to 360°.
• Add chicken, a few pieces at a time, skin side down. Cover and cook 6 minutes; uncover and cook 9 additional minutes.
• Turn chicken pieces; cover and cook 6 additional minutes. Uncover and cook 5 to 9 additional minutes, turning pieces during the last 3 minutes for even browning, if necessary.
• Drain chicken on a paper towel-lined plate placed over a large bowl of hot water. Yield: 4 servings.

Note: For best results, keep the oil temperature between 300° to 325°. Also, substitute 2 cups buttermilk for the saltwater solution used to soak the chicken pieces. Proceed as directed.

John Egerton
Nashville, Tennessee

FRIED CHICKEN GRAVY

1   recipe Our Best Southern Fried Chicken
¼   cup all-purpose flour
2   cups milk or water
½   teaspoon salt
¼   teaspoon pepper

• Fry chicken according to recipe directions.
• Pour off pan drippings, reserving ¼ cup drippings in skillet.
• Place skillet over medium heat. Add flour to drippings, stirring constantly, until browned.
• Add milk gradually; cook, stirring constantly, until thickened and bubbly (about 3 to 5 minutes).
• Stir in salt and pepper. Serve immediately. Yield: 1⅔ cups.

Note: Warm the milk to help prevent lumping.

HOW TO CUT UP CHICKEN WITH A PULLEY BONE

....

Cutting up a chicken, using a sharp knife to get at the joints and kitchen shears to trim the rest, saves money – and many argue that it's a better product altogether.

But cutting up your own chicken may leave some new cooks harried. Here's a quick lesson.

1. First remove the legs by cutting at the joints with a sharp knife.

2. Crack the back thigh joint, finding the joint with your fingers. Cut straight through to remove thigh; repeat on the other side. Use kitchen shears to trim extra skin and fat.

3. Stretch out wings and cut into the joints, removing the wings.

4. Cut down the back from the tail end to the neck end. Clip along the ribs with kitchen shears. You'll now have a large breast section.

5. Press your fingers on the neck end of the breasts; the pulley bone (or wishbone) connects to these two plump muscles. You can feel its V-shape breastbone with your fingers. Cut straight down from the top of the breast to the cutting board, cutting between the ribs and pulley bone and separating the pulley bone from the rest of the breast. Your piece will be shaped like a plump "V." Be careful not to crack the bone while you're feeling around for it.

Tip: If you don't cut up your own chicken, you'll find pieces packaged with the pulley bone cut out.

OVEN-FRIED CHICKEN

If you want to eat crispy chicken on a frequent basis, we recommend this oven-fried version. The secret is baking the chicken at a high temperature, ensuring that almost-fried crispness.

1 quart water
1 teaspoon salt
6 chicken drumsticks
4 bone-in chicken breast halves, skinned
½ cup nonfat buttermilk
3 cups corn flake crumbs
2 to 3 teaspoons Creole seasoning
2 teaspoons dried Italian seasoning
½ teaspoon garlic powder
⅛ teaspoon freshly ground black pepper
⅛ teaspoon ground red pepper (optional)
Vegetable cooking spray

• **Combine** water and salt in a large bowl; add chicken. Cover and chill 8 hours.
• **Drain** chicken; rinse with cold water, and pat dry. Place chicken in a shallow dish; pour buttermilk over chicken, turning pieces to coat.
• **Combine** corn flake crumbs and next 4 ingredients in a large heavy-duty, zip-top plastic bag. Add red pepper, if desired. Place 2 pieces chicken in bag; seal. Shake to coat completely. Remove chicken, and repeat procedure with remaining pieces.
• **Place** coated chicken, bone side down, in a 15- x 10- x 1-inch jellyroll pan coated with cooking spray, and spray chicken with cooking spray. Place pan on lowest rack in oven.
• **Bake** at 400° for 45 minutes (do not turn). **Yield:** 6 to 8 servings.

♥ Per Serving:
Breast meat:
Calories 281 Fat 3.6g Cholesterol 68mg
Drumstick meat:
Calories 176 Fat 3.6g Cholesterol 48mg

RIBS, RIBS, RIBS

....

Gnaw the bones, sop up every bit of sauce, and lick your fingers. That's barbecue at its best. Try these sweet and tangy or hot and spicy sauces at your next rib fest, and get ready for the raves to roll in.

BARBECUED SPARERIBS

These spareribs from Evelyn Milam have a tangy sweetness. The recipe was a gift from a friend. Here the ribs are precooked on a cooktop and then grilled. "They can also be baked in the oven the old-timey way if the weather is bad or you don't have a grill," Evelyn advises.

4 pounds pork spareribs
½ cup chopped onion
2 cloves garlic, pressed
1½ cups ketchup
¾ cup honey
¼ cup water
2 tablespoons apple cider vinegar
2 tablespoons steak sauce
1 tablespoon prepared mustard
½ teaspoon salt
½ teaspoon pepper

• **Cut** ribs into serving-size pieces, and place in a stockpot; add water to cover. Bring to a boil; cover, reduce heat, and simmer 30 minutes. Drain.
• **Combine** onion and next 9 ingredients in a saucepan; cook over medium heat 5 minutes. Reserve 1½ cups ketchup mixture.
• **Cook** ribs, without grill lid, over medium-hot coals (350° to 400°) 15 minutes, and baste with remaining ketchup mixture. Cook 25 to 40 additional minutes, turning and basting occasionally. Serve with reserved 1½ cups ketchup mixture. **Yield:** 6 servings.

Note: For steak sauce, we used A-1.
Evelyn Milam
Knoxville, Tennessee

ADAMS' RIBS

Adams' Ribs is the hot and spicy product of a marriage. Anne-Marie Adams's Cajun background is the source of the spicy heat. Oscar Adams's commitment to the best equipment and a perfectly built fire contributes the smoky tenderness. A spice rub and two adapted sauces yield a taste and texture that give the ribs their signature.

2 tablespoons pepper
1 tablespoon garlic powder
1 tablespoon Creole seasoning
1 tablespoon Worcestershire sauce
8 pounds pork spareribs
Hickory wood chunks
Grill Basting Sauce
The Sauce

• **Combine** pepper, garlic powder, seasoning, and Worcestershire sauce; rub on all sides of ribs.
• **Soak** wood chunks in water to cover 30 minutes.
• **Prepare** charcoal fire in grill; drain wood chunks, and place on coals.
• **Cook** ribs, covered with grill lid, over medium coals (300° to 350°) about 3 hours, turning ribs after 1 hour and basting with Grill Basting Sauce after 2 hours. Turn once more after basting. Serve with The Sauce. **Yield:** 10 to 12 servings.

Grill Basting Sauce

¼ cup firmly packed brown sugar
¼ cup Worcestershire sauce
¼ cup prepared mustard
¾ cup ketchup
2 tablespoons ground black pepper
2 tablespoons dried crushed red pepper
2¾ cups red wine vinegar
1¾ cups water
¾ cup dry white wine
2 to 4 tablespoons salt

• **Combine** all ingredients in a saucepan; cook over medium heat 1 hour. **Yield:** 6 cups.

The Sauce

1 tablespoon butter or margarine
1 medium onion, finely chopped
½ tablespoon minced garlic
1 cup ketchup
½ cup white vinegar
¼ cup fresh lemon juice
¼ cup steak seasoning
2 tablespoons brown sugar
1 tablespoon Cajun seasoning
2 tablespoons liquid smoke

• **Melt** butter in a large skillet over medium-high heat; add onion, and cook, stirring constantly, until tender. Add garlic and remaining ingredients; reduce heat, and simmer about 15 minutes. **Yield:** 2½ cups.

Note: For steak seasoning, we used Dale's. For Creole seasoning, we used Zatarain's. For Cajun seasoning, we used Luzianne.

Oscar and Anne-Marie Adams
Birmingham, Alabama

BARBECUED COUNTRY-STYLE RIBS

Thanks to Mildred Bickley of Bristol, Virginia, we have Rollin Johnson's recipe for ribs. He served these at family gatherings for decades.

1 small onion, finely chopped
1 cup finely chopped celery
1½ tablespoons bacon drippings
1 (15-ounce) can tomato sauce
¾ cup honey
½ cup water
¼ cup dry red wine
2 tablespoons lemon juice
2 tablespoons Worcestershire sauce
1 teaspoon salt
½ teaspoon pepper
¼ teaspoon garlic powder
1 cup water
2 tablespoons white vinegar
4 pounds boneless country-style pork ribs *

• **Cook** onion and celery in bacon drippings in a large saucepan over medium-high heat, stirring constantly, until tender. Add tomato sauce and next 8 ingredients. Bring mixture to a boil; reduce heat, and simmer 1 hour, stirring occasionally. Reserve 1½ cups tomato sauce mixture.
• **Combine** water and vinegar in a spray bottle.
• **Cut** ribs apart; cook, covered with grill lid, over medium coals (300° to 350°) 1 to 1½ hours, spraying with vinegar solution and turning ribs occasionally. Baste with remaining 1 cup tomato sauce mixture after 30 minutes. Serve with reserved 1½ cups tomato sauce mixture. **Yield:** 8 servings.

* You can substitute 4 pounds bone-in country-style pork ribs. Cook as directed. **Yield:** 6 servings.

Rollin Johnson
Bristol, Virginia

A FAMILY COOKOUT

....

Cookouts need not be complicated events. Follow these simple steps to a barbecue that's easy enough for a weeknight, yet lively enough for a Labor Day celebration.

COOKOUT MENU
Serves Four

Quick Fiesta Dip
Marinated Flank Steak
Pasta-Vegetable Salad
Raspberry Milk Shakes

THE NIGHT BEFORE
■ Marinate steak and make the salad.

WHEN YOU'RE READY TO COOK
■ Fire up the grill.
■ Prepare the dip, and serve it with chips while the grill heats up.
■ Grill the steak.
■ After supper, prepare the milk shakes.

QUICK FIESTA DIP

1 (12-ounce) jar chunky salsa or picante sauce
1 cup (4 ounces) shredded Monterey Jack cheese

• **Pour** salsa into a 9-inch pieplate. Cover tightly with heavy-duty plastic wrap; fold back a small edge of wrap to allow steam to escape.
• **Microwave** at HIGH 2 to 4 minutes or until bubbly. Uncover; sprinkle with cheese, and cover tightly with wrap. Let stand 5 minutes or until cheese melts. Serve with tortilla or corn chips. **Yield:** 1½ cups.

MARINATED FLANK STEAK

1 cup vegetable oil
½ cup soy sauce
⅓ cup red wine vinegar
¼ cup lemon juice
3 tablespoons Worcestershire sauce
2 tablespoons Dijon mustard
1 teaspoon freshly ground pepper
1 large onion, sliced
1 clove garlic, minced
2 (1-pound) flank steaks

• **Combine** first 9 ingredients in a shallow dish or a large heavy-duty, zip-top plastic bag; add steaks. Cover or seal, and store in refrigerator 8 to 12 hours, turning occasionally.
• **Remove** steaks and onion slices from marinade, discarding marinade. Wrap onion in heavy-duty aluminum foil.
• **Cook** steaks and onion slices, covered with grill lid, over medium-hot coals (350° to 400°) about 15 minutes or to desired degree of doneness, turning occasionally.
• **Cut** steaks diagonally across grain into thin strips; serve with onion slices. **Yield:** 4 to 6 servings.

Karen Dibble
Dallas, Texas

PASTA-VEGETABLE SALAD

6 ounces tricolor rotini pasta, uncooked (about 3 cups)
1 pound fresh broccoli, cut into flowerets
3 stalks celery, sliced
1 bunch radishes, sliced
1 (8-ounce) can sliced water chestnuts, drained
1 (2¼-ounce) can sliced ripe olives, drained
1 (0.6-ounce) envelope zesty Italian-style salad dressing mix
2 tablespoons chopped fresh oregano
½ cup crumbled feta cheese

• **Prepare** pasta according to package directions; drain. Rinse with cold water; drain.
• **Combine** pasta, broccoli, and next 4 ingredients in a bowl; set aside.
• **Prepare** dressing mix according to package directions; stir in oregano. Pour over pasta mixture, stirring to coat. Sprinkle with cheese. Cover and chill at least 6 hours. **Yield:** 8 to 10 servings.

Gayle Gardner
Owensboro, Kentucky

RASPBERRY MILK SHAKES

1 (10-ounce) package frozen raspberries
½ cup milk
1 quart vanilla ice cream

• **Combine** frozen raspberries and milk in container of an electric blender; process until smooth. Add ice cream, and process until mixture is smooth. **Yield:** 5 cups.

Janie Wallace
Seguin, Texas

TOAST TO TOUCHDOWN

....

Kick off your football party with gallons of thirst quenchers. Cold or hot, alcoholic or not, these beverages complement any appetizer buffet. If your team is winning, you'll need lots of punch. And if your team is losing, you'll need even more.

HOT CIDER PUNCH

1 (2½-inch) stick cinnamon
5 whole cloves
10 whole allspice
2 cups orange juice
8 cups apple cider
¾ cup lemon juice
¼ cup honey
1½ teaspoons butter or margarine

• **Tie** cinnamon stick, cloves, and allspice in a cheesecloth bag.
• **Combine** spice bag, orange juice, and remaining ingredients in a large saucepan or Dutch oven; bring to a boil. Reduce heat, and simmer 1 hour; remove and discard spice bag. **Yield:** 2 quarts.

Katharine Reinke
Baltimore, Maryland

CRANBERRY SANGRIA

Get the full-bodied flavor of the original with just four ingredients.

1 (48-ounce) bottle cranberry juice cocktail
3 cups port wine
1 orange, thinly sliced
1 lemon, thinly sliced

• **Combine** all ingredients; cover and chill at least 3 hours. **Yield:** 2½ quarts.

Agnes L. Stone
Ocala, Florida

SOUTHERN FRUIT PUNCH

1 (750-milliliter) bottle sweet bourbon, chilled
¾ cup lemon juice, chilled
1 (12-ounce) can frozen pineapple-orange juice concentrate, thawed and undiluted
1 (2-liter) bottle lemon-lime carbonated beverage, chilled
1 orange, thinly sliced

• **Combine** first 3 ingredients in a large punch bowl, stirring until juice concentrate dissolves.
• **Stir** in carbonated beverage; add orange slices, and serve. **Yield:** 1 gallon.

Note: For sweet bourbon, we used Southern Comfort.

Jan Aaron
Shalimar, Florida

GRAPEFRUIT DRINK

Add 1½ to 2 cups gin or vodka to get this drink in the spirit of the season.

¾ cup sugar
2 cups water
1 cup grapefruit juice
½ cup chopped grapefruit sections
¼ cup maraschino cherries, halved
2 to 3 tablespoons lemon juice
2 cups sparkling mineral water, chilled

• **Combine** sugar and water in a medium saucepan; bring to a boil, stirring until sugar dissolves. Remove from heat; cool.
• **Combine** sugar mixture, grapefruit juice, and next 3 ingredients. Cover and chill at least 2 hours.
• **Stir** in mineral water just before serving. **Yield:** 1½ quarts.

Jane N. Noe
Sandia, Texas

MIXED FRUIT PUNCH

To spike this fruited combo, add 5 to 6 cups of light rum.

1 (46-ounce) can pineapple
  juice
1 cup fresh orange juice
⅔ cup fresh lemon juice
1½ tablespoons fresh lime juice
1 cup sugar
½ cup loosely packed fresh mint
  leaves
1 (2-liter) bottle ginger ale,
  chilled
1 (1-liter) bottle club soda,
  chilled
1 cup fresh strawberries, quartered
1 lemon, thinly sliced
1 lime, thinly sliced
Ice ring (optional)

• **Combine** first 6 ingredients, stirring until sugar dissolves. Cover and chill at least 4 hours.
• **Pour** mixture through a wire-mesh strainer into a large punch bowl, discarding mint leaves. Stir in ginger ale and next 4 ingredients. Add ice ring, if desired. **Yield:** 5½ quarts.

Molly Ellis
Clarksville, Tennessee

APPETIZERS THAT SCORE BIG

....

At home – in the company of good friends watching a long-awaited televised football matchup – you relax, refreshments in hand.

There's only one catch: You can't keep your eyes off the party appetizers. They're spicy, cheesy, creamy, crunchy, easy to prepare, and delicious. Honestly, we didn't mean for these munchies to be distracting. But rest assured, you and your guests will find each to be a pleasant diversion.

SPICY BUFFALO WINGS

2½ to 3 pounds chicken wings
¾ cup butter or margarine
½ cup hot sauce
1 (1-ounce) envelope dry onion
  soup mix
1 to 3 teaspoons ground red
  pepper
1 (8-ounce) bottle blue cheese
  salad dressing

• **Cut** off and discard wingtips; cut wings in half at joint. Place chicken on a lightly greased rack of a broiler pan; set aside.
• **Melt** butter in a small saucepan; add hot sauce, soup mix, and red pepper. Brush chicken with butter mixture.
• **Bake** at 375° for 30 minutes. Remove from oven; turn chicken and brush with remaining butter mixture. Bake 10 to 15 additional minutes or until tender. Serve warm with salad dressing. **Yield:** about 3 dozen.

Sandy San Jose
Richmond, Texas

TURKEY SAUSAGE TURNOVERS

½ pound ground turkey sausage
½ cup finely chopped onion
1 tablespoon all-purpose
  flour
1 tablespoon dry sherry
1 (15-ounce) package refrigerated
  piecrusts
1 egg yolk
1 tablespoon water
Paprika
Sour cream

• **Cook** sausage and onion in a large skillet over high heat, stirring until sausage crumbles. Remove from heat. Stir in flour and sherry; cool.
• **Unfold** refrigerated piecrusts; roll each to ⅛-inch thickness on a lightly floured surface. Cut with a 3-inch round cutter. Place 1 teaspoon sausage mixture on half of each pastry circle. Moisten edges of pastry circles with water, and fold circles in half. Press edges with a fork to seal, and place pastries on baking sheets.

• **Combine** egg yolk and water; brush over pastries. Cut 3 small slits in top of each pastry.
• **Bake** at 400° for 12 to 14 minutes, and sprinkle with paprika. Serve warm with sour cream. **Yield:** 2½ dozen.

Note: Turnovers may be frozen in an airtight container after baking. To serve, bake frozen turnovers at 350° for 5 to 8 minutes.

BAKED ARTICHOKE DIP

1 (14-ounce) can artichoke hearts,
  chopped and drained
¾ cup mayonnaise or salad
  dressing
1 cup grated Parmesan cheese
1 clove garlic, minced
¼ teaspoon Worcestershire sauce
2 or 3 drops of hot sauce

• **Combine** all ingredients; spoon into a lightly greased 1-quart casserole.
• **Bake** at 350° for 20 minutes or until bubbly. Serve with melba toast rounds. **Yield:** 2 cups.

Linda Lefler
Roxboro, North Carolina

CHEESY BARBECUE POPCORN

2 tablespoons butter or margarine,
  melted
½ teaspoon chili powder
½ teaspoon garlic salt
¼ teaspoon onion powder
8 cups popped popcorn
¼ cup grated Parmesan
  cheese

• **Combine** first 4 ingredients; pour mixture over popcorn, stirring to coat. Sprinkle with cheese, stirring well. **Yield:** 8 cups.

Anna Rucker
Norfolk, Virginia

BACON-JALAPEÑO-TOMATO QUESADILLAS

2　tablespoons butter or margarine, softened
6　(8-inch) flour tortillas
4　cups (16 ounces) shredded Monterey Jack cheese
12　slices bacon, cooked and crumbled
1　small tomato, peeled, seeded, and chopped
4　pickled jalapeño peppers, finely chopped
1　teaspoon ground cumin
Garnish: fresh cilantro sprigs
Salsa

• **Spread** butter on one side of each tortilla. Place tortillas, buttered side up, on ungreased baking sheets.
• **Bake** at 400° for 3 minutes or until lightly browned. (Tortillas may be baked up to 2 hours ahead.)
• **Combine** cheese and next 4 ingredients; sprinkle evenly over tortillas.
• **Bake** at 400° for 5 minutes or until cheese is bubbly. Cut each tortilla into fourths; garnish, if desired. Serve with salsa. **Yield:** 2 dozen.

SAVORY SOUTHERN PECANS

¼　cup unsalted butter
1½　teaspoons ground cumin
¼　teaspoon ground red pepper
3　cups pecan halves
2　tablespoons sugar
1　teaspoon salt

• **Melt** butter in a large saucepan; add cumin and red pepper, and cook mixture 1 minute. Remove pan from heat; add pecans, sugar, and salt, stirring gently to coat.
• **Spread** pecans in a single layer in a 15- x 10- x 1-inch jellyroll pan.
• **Bake** at 300° for 20 minutes, stirring occasionally. Serve warm or at room temperature. Store in an airtight container up to 5 days. **Yield:** 3 cups.
Marion Hall
Knoxville, Tennessee

PEPPERS APLENTY

Cost puts limits on sweet red and yellow peppers for most of the year, so a frugal and creative cook budgets for one or two as a garnish. However, the end of summer in the South brings an abundance of these colorful peppers to both backyard gardens and grocery stores. Try this selection of recipes when the peppers are affordable.

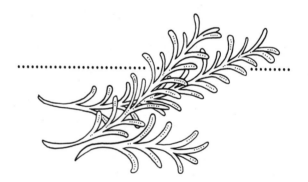

BELL PEPPER-CHEESE CHOWDER

⅓　cup butter or margarine
1　cup chopped sweet red pepper
1　cup chopped sweet yellow pepper
½　cup chopped carrot
½　cup sliced celery
½　cup chopped onion
2　cloves garlic, minced
½　cup all-purpose flour
1　quart half-and-half
2　(10½-ounce) cans condensed chicken broth, undiluted
1　(12-ounce) can beer
½　teaspoon dry mustard
¼　teaspoon dried rosemary, crushed
¼　teaspoon salt
¼　teaspoon ground red pepper
½　teaspoon freshly ground black pepper
2　cups (8 ounces) shredded sharp Cheddar cheese
Garnishes: fresh rosemary sprig, finely chopped sweet red and yellow pepper

• **Melt** butter in a large Dutch oven over medium-high heat. Add chopped pepper and next 4 ingredients. Cook, stirring constantly, 5 minutes or until tender.
• **Add** flour, stirring constantly. Cook 1 minute, stirring constantly. Gradually add half-and-half, chicken broth, and beer; cook, stirring constantly, until thickened and bubbly.
• **Stir** in mustard and next 4 ingredients; gradually add cheese, stirring until cheese melts. Garnish, if desired, and serve immediately. **Yield:** 11 cups.
Elizabeth A. Crawley
New Orleans, Louisiana

ROASTED RED BELL PEPPER BREAD

Serve this flavorful bread with soup, toast it for a snack, or slice it for sandwiches.

1 package active dry yeast
1 teaspoon sugar
1⅓ cups warm water (105° to 115°)
2 tablespoons olive oil
3½ to 4½ cups bread flour, divided
1½ teaspoons salt
1 tablespoon cracked pepper
1 cup (4 ounces) shredded provolone cheese
1 cup grated Parmesan cheese
2 roasted sweet red peppers, seeded and chopped (see box)
2 tablespoons chopped fresh rosemary

● **Combine** first 3 ingredients in a 2-cup liquid measuring cup; let stand 5 minutes. Stir in olive oil. Set aside.

● **Combine** 3½ cups flour and next 6 ingredients in a large bowl; gradually add yeast mixture, stirring until blended.

● **Turn** dough out onto a well-floured surface, and knead until smooth and elastic (approximately 10 minutes), adding remaining 1 cup flour as needed to prevent sticking. Place dough in a well-greased bowl, turning to grease top.

● **Cover** and let rise in a warm place (85°), free from drafts, 1 hour or until doubled in bulk.

● **Punch** dough down, and divide in half; shape each portion into a 12-inch loaf. Place loaves on a lightly greased large baking sheet. Let rise in a warm place (85°), free from drafts, 45 minutes or until doubled in bulk.

● **Bake** at 450° for 25 minutes or until loaves sound hollow when tapped, covering with aluminum foil after 15 minutes to prevent excessive browning. Remove from baking sheet immediately; cool on wire racks. **Yield:** 2 loaves.

Rublelene Singleton
Scotts Hill, Tennessee

ROASTED PEPPER PRIMER

If you're choosing peppers for color, select sweet red or yellow ones because they retain their rich color. When cooked, green peppers turn a dull shade. Peppers mellow and sweeten during roasting. Use them to add flavor to pizzas, soups, pastas, and salads.

To freeze roasted peppers, cut them into strips, and place in a single layer on a baking sheet sprayed with cooking spray. Freeze; remove from baking sheet, and place in a heavy-duty, zip-top plastic bag. Return to the freezer. Then you can use only as many peppers as you need.

Try any of these methods for roasting peppers.

Gas Cooktop Method: Spear the stem end of a pepper with a long-handled fork. Hold the pepper above the flame of a gas cooktop, turning it until the skin blackens. Place in a heavy-duty, zip-top plastic bag; seal and let stand 10 minutes to loosen skin. Peel pepper, and remove and discard core and seeds. This works well when you need one pepper.

Seeded Method: Cut peppers in half lengthwise. Remove and discard core and seeds; make additional cuts at the ends until they lie flat. Place the pepper halves, skin side up, on a baking sheet, and bake at 500° for 5 to 10 minutes or until blackened. Place peppers in a heavy-duty, zip-top plastic bag; seal and let stand 10 minutes to loosen skins. Peel peppers. This method is more work in the beginning, but you don't have the hassle of removing seeds later.

Broiler Method: Place whole peppers on a baking sheet, and broil 5½ inches from heat (with electric oven door partially opened) about 5 minutes on each side or until blackened. Place peppers in a heavy-duty, zip-top plastic bag; seal and let stand 10 minutes to loosen skins. Peel peppers; remove and discard seeds. This is the quickest way when you have a lot of peppers to roast.

Lazy Cook's Method: Place whole peppers on a baking sheet, and bake at 500° for 20 minutes or until blackened. There's no need to turn the peppers with this method, but it takes a few minutes longer.

ROASTED BELL PEPPERS IN OLIVE OIL

An overnight soaking in vinegar raises the acidity of these roasted peppers so they will store longer. Because the finished peppers have a mildly acidic flavor, use them in recipes that welcome a little tartness. Add them to pasta and potato salads, antipasto trays, or sandwiches. Layered in a decorative jar tied with a ribbon, they make a savory hostess gift.

12 roasted sweet red peppers
    (see box on page 241)
12 roasted sweet yellow peppers
    (see box on page 241)
1 tablespoon salt
4 cups white vinegar
2 to 3 cups extra virgin olive oil

• **Cut** peppers along one side, and press to flatten. Place in a large shallow dish.
• **Combine** salt and vinegar; pour over peppers. Cover and store in the refrigerator at least 8 hours or overnight.
• **Drain** peppers; pat dry with paper towels. Pack into sterilized jars, alternating red and yellow peppers. Pour oil into jars, filling to ½ inch from top. Carefully insert a knife between peppers and jar to remove any air bubbles. Cover at once with metal lids, and screw on bands. Store in the refrigerator up to 3 months. **Yield:** 4 half-pints.

Note: Olive oil will solidify and turn cloudy when refrigerated and return to a clear liquid at room temperature.

Megen McCully
Knoxville, Tennessee

RED BELL PEPPER JAM

6 sweet red peppers, seeded and
    finely chopped
1½ teaspoons salt
1½ cups sugar
1 cup white vinegar

• **Combine** peppers and salt; let stand 3 to 4 hours. Rinse with water; drain.

• **Combine** peppers, sugar, and vinegar in a Dutch oven; bring to a boil over medium heat, stirring constantly. Reduce heat, and simmer 35 minutes or until mixture forms a light syrup, stirring occasionally.
• **Pack** hot mixture into hot jars, filling to ½ inch from top. Carefully insert a knife between peppers and jar to remove air bubbles, and wipe jar rims. Cover at once with metal lids, and screw on bands.
• **Process** in boiling-water bath 10 minutes. Serve with cream cheese and crackers, chicken, or pork. Store in refrigerator after opening. **Yield:** 2 half-pints.

Ione B. Chapman
Huntsville, Alabama

ROASTED RED BELL PEPPER BUTTER

1 cup butter, softened
¼ teaspoon salt
¼ teaspoon ground red pepper
½ teaspoon grated lemon rind
1 large roasted sweet red pepper,
    seeded and chopped (see box
    on page 241)

• **Position** knife blade in food processor bowl; add first 4 ingredients. Process until smooth, stopping once to scrape down sides.
• **Add** sweet red pepper; pulse 3 or 4 times. **Yield:** 1⅓ cups.

WHAT'S FOR SUPPER?

BBQ ASAP

....

Just say the word *barbecue* and your mouth begins to water. This wonderfully spicy dish is delicious just about anywhere, anytime.

To always have it on hand when the mood strikes, keep a supply of Individual Barbecued Beef Loaves in your freezer. They're ready to cook whenever a craving for 'cue hits.

One recipe will make six individual loaves. If you like lots of sauce on your barbecue, double the first four ingredients.

With Peggy Brown's recipe, barbecue is ready and waiting in six little loaves for a no-fuss supper. Just couple it with french fries or coleslaw, and satisfy your craving.

INDIVIDUAL BARBECUED BEEF LOAVES

½ cup ketchup
⅓ cup cider vinegar
3 tablespoons brown sugar
1 teaspoon beef-flavored bouillon
    granules
1½ pounds lean ground beef
1 cup fine, dry breadcrumbs
2 tablespoons finely chopped
    onion
½ teaspoon salt
¼ teaspoon pepper
1 cup evaporated milk

• **Combine** ketchup, vinegar, brown sugar, and bouillon granules in a saucepan; cook over medium heat, stirring constantly, until bouillon granules dissolve. Set barbecue sauce aside.
• **Combine** lean ground beef and bread crumbs, onion, salt, pepper, and milk, stirring until mixture is thoroughly blended.
• **Shape** mixture into 6 loaves; place loaves in a lightly greased 11- x 7- x 1½-inch baking dish. Spoon barbecue sauce over loaves.
• **Bake** at 350° for 45 minutes. Serve immediately. **Yield:** 6 servings.

Peggy C. Brown
Winston-Salem, North Carolina

THE TEXAS EXPERIENCE

The marketing slogan for *The Texas Experience* is, "There is no experience like a Texas experience. And everyone should have one!" The slogan seems to have served the Richardson Woman's Club well, as the book has sold nearly 85,000 copies since it was published in 1982.

....

The ever-growing popularity of the Southwest and the double testing of the recipes contribute to the success of this book. More than $125,000 has been raised for ongoing scholarships and endowment funds, the YWCA, American Heart Association, and a local theater and arts association.

GAZPACHO DIP
(pictured on page 258)

3 large tomatoes, chopped
3 firm avocados, chopped
4 green onions, thinly sliced
1 (4-ounce) can chopped ripe olives, undrained
1 (4.5-ounce) can chopped green chiles, undrained
3 tablespoons vegetable oil
1½ tablespoons apple cider vinegar
1 teaspoon salt
1 teaspoon garlic salt
¼ teaspoon pepper

● **Combine** the first 5 ingredients in a large bowl.
● **Combine** oil and next 4 ingredients; drizzle over tomato mixture, and toss gently.
● **Chill** up to 4 hours. Serve with tortilla chips. **Yield:** 5 cups.

Note: To serve dip as a flavorful salad, spoon evenly over shredded lettuce, and top with shredded cheese and sour cream.

WILD TUNA SALAD

1 (6-ounce) package long-grain-and-wild rice mix
½ cup mayonnaise
¼ cup sour cream
½ cup finely chopped celery
2 tablespoons finely chopped onion
1 (12-ounce) can solid white tuna in spring water, drained and flaked
1 cup salted cashews
Lettuce leaves
Alfalfa sprouts (optional)

● **Cook** rice according to package directions; chill completely.
● **Add** mayonnaise and next 5 ingredients, stirring well. Serve on lettuce leaves with alfalfa sprouts, if desired. **Yield:** 6 servings.

LUCY'S APRICOT PRALINE TORTE

1 (16-ounce) loaf pound cake
1 cup apricot preserves
Praline Buttercream
Sifted powdered sugar

● **Cut** cake loaf horizontally into 3 layers.
● **Melt** preserves in a saucepan over low heat. Spread half of preserves over bottom layer of cake. Spread half of Praline Buttercream over preserves, and place second layer of cake on buttercream. Repeat procedure with remaining preserves and buttercream; top with remaining layer of cake. Sprinkle lightly with powdered sugar. **Yield:** 10 to 12 servings.

Praline Buttercream

½ cup unsalted butter, softened
2½ cups sifted powdered sugar
2 to 3 tablespoons whipping cream
½ cup Praline Powder
1 teaspoon vanilla extract

● **Beat** butter at medium speed with an electric mixer until creamy; gradually add sugar, beating mixture well. Beat in whipping cream, and fold in Praline Powder and vanilla. **Yield:** 2 cups.

Praline Powder

2 tablespoons butter
¼ cup sugar
¾ cup almonds, chopped and toasted

● **Cook** butter and sugar in a small saucepan over medium heat until sugar melts and turns a light caramel color (mixture will separate), stirring occasionally. Remove from heat; stir in almonds.
● **Pour** onto a greased aluminum foil-lined baking sheet, and cool. Break into chunks.
● **Position** knife blade in food processor bowl; add chunks of praline mixture. Process until finely crushed. **Yield:** 1 cup.

SNACKS COOL FOR AFTER SCHOOL

Kids aren't that different from grown-ups. After a hard day shuffling papers, erasing mistakes, and making the grade, the first thing all of us want to do when we get home is *eat*. But to kids, those hours before supper can seem like an eternity.

These snacks are a welcome rescue. Just add a little supervision by an older sibling, babysitter, or an adult friend, and these munchies will be as fun to prepare as they are to eat. (And if eaten in moderation, they won't spoil supper appetites.)

PIZZA BITES

½ cup grated Parmesan cheese
1 cup (4 ounces) shredded pizza-blend cheese *
1 (10-ounce) can refrigerated flaky biscuits
1 (3½-ounce) package pepperoni slices

• **Combine** cheeses; set aside.
• **Separate** each biscuit in half horizontally. Roll each half into a 3-inch circle on a lightly floured surface.
• **Place** 2 pepperoni slices and 1 tablespoon cheese mixture on one side of each circle. Moisten edges with water; fold biscuit in half, pressing edges with a fork to seal. Place on an ungreased baking sheet.

• **Bake** at 400° for 10 to 12 minutes or until lightly browned, and serve warm. **Yield:** 20 appetizers.

* Substitute ½ cup shredded Cheddar cheese and ½ cup shredded mozzarella cheese.

Betty Sue Adams
Fort Payne, Alabama

ORANGE-BANANA WHIP

2 bananas
2 cups orange juice
2 ice cubes

• **Peel** and slice bananas, and freeze until firm.
• **Combine** frozen banana slices, orange juice, and ice cubes in container of an electric blender; process until smooth, stopping once to scrape down sides. **Yield:** 4 cups.

Leanne McMullen
Natchez, Mississippi

CINNAMON STICKS

1 (11-ounce) can refrigerated soft breadsticks
¼ cup butter or margarine, melted
2 tablespoons honey
½ cup sugar
1½ teaspoons ground cinnamon

• **Unroll** dough; separate into strips. Cut strips in half crosswise.
• **Bake** dough according to package directions.
• **Combine** butter and honey; brush on breadsticks while still warm.
• **Combine** sugar and cinnamon in a large zip-top plastic bag; add 3 breadsticks, and shake vigorously to coat. Repeat procedure with remaining breadsticks; serve immediately. **Yield:** 16 appetizers.

Note: For smaller appetizers, cut strips crosswise into 3 pieces.

Keith D. McNeil
Dallas, Texas

PLAY IT SAFE IN THE KITCHEN

It's never too early to teach your kids or grandkids about kitchen safety. Share these tips with them before beginning after-school snack preparations.

■ Before using any electric or gas appliance, make sure there's an adult around to help with it.

■ Always use thick, dry pot holders to handle hot pans. Thin or wet ones won't provide enough heat insulation.

■ Always turn the sharp edge of a knife away from you while chopping foods.

■ Immediately wipe up any spills to keep floors from becoming slippery.

CHOCOLATE COOKIE ICE CREAM

1 (16-ounce) package cream-filled
   chocolate sandwich cookies,
   coarsely crumbled
   (42 cookies)
½ gallon vanilla ice cream,
   softened
1 (8-ounce) container frozen
   whipped topping, thawed

• **Combine** all ingredients, stirring
until blended; cover and freeze. **Yield:**
10 cups.

Janice M. France
Louisville, Kentucky

START WITH BISCUIT MIX

....

It may already be on your shelf. If not,
you can find it with the flour at your
grocery store. It's so unassuming, you
might not think of it as versatile and
speedy – but it is. So bring out the biscuit mix, and see how easy it is to whip
up one of these recipes for dinner
tonight. There's a lot of good food in
that box.

CHICKEN DUMPLING PIE

3 cups chopped cooked chicken
   or turkey
2 (10¾-ounce) cans cream of
   chicken soup, undiluted
1 (10½-ounce) can condensed
   chicken broth, undiluted
1 (15-ounce) can mixed
   vegetables, drained
½ teaspoon poultry seasoning
2 cups biscuit mix
1 (8-ounce) carton sour cream
1 cup milk

• **Combine** first 5 ingredients in a large
bowl, stirring well; pour chicken mixture into a lightly greased 13- x 9- x 2-
inch baking dish.
• **Combine** biscuit mix, sour cream,
and milk in a medium bowl; spoon
over chicken mixture.
• **Bake** at 350° for 50 to 60 minutes or
until topping is golden. **Yield:** 6 to 8
servings.

Lilann Taylor
Savannah, Georgia

DILLY CHEESE MUFFINS

3 cups biscuit mix
1½ cups (12 ounces) shredded
   Swiss cheese
1 tablespoon sugar
1 large egg
1¼ cups milk
1 tablespoon vegetable oil
1 tablespoon chopped fresh
   dill
½ teaspoon dry mustard
Vegetable cooking spray

• **Combine** first 3 ingredients in a large
bowl, and make a well in center of
mixture.
• **Combine** egg, milk, oil, dill, and
mustard in a bowl, stirring well; add to
dry ingredients, stirring just until
moistened.
• **Place** paper baking cups in muffin
pans, and coat with cooking spray;
spoon batter into cups.
• **Bake** at 350° for 25 to 28 minutes.
Remove muffins from pans immediately; let cool on wire racks. **Yield:** 1½
dozen.

Kathy Jones
Montreal, Missouri

QUICK ROLLS

2¼ cups biscuit mix, divided
1 (8-ounce) carton sour
   cream
½ cup butter, melted

• **Combine** 2 cups biscuit mix, sour
cream, and butter, stirring well.
• **Sprinkle** remaining ¼ cup biscuit
mix on a flat surface. Drop dough by
level tablespoonfuls onto biscuit mix,
and roll into balls. Place 3 balls into
each of 12 greased muffin cups.
• **Bake** at 350° for 15 to 20 minutes or
until rolls are golden. **Yield:** 1 dozen.

Carolyn W. Olah
Crawfordville, Florida

PEANUT BLOSSOM COOKIES

1 (14-ounce) can sweetened
   condensed milk
¾ cup creamy peanut butter
1 teaspoon vanilla extract
2 cups biscuit mix
⅓ cup sugar
1 (9-ounce) package milk
   chocolate kisses, unwrapped

• **Combine** sweetened condensed milk
and peanut butter, stirring until
smooth; stir in vanilla. Add biscuit mix,
stirring well.
• **Shape** dough into 1-inch balls; roll in
sugar, and place on ungreased cookie
sheets. Make an indention in center of
each ball of dough with thumb or
spoon handle.
• **Bake** at 375° for 8 to 10 minutes or
until lightly browned. Remove cookies
from oven, and press a chocolate kiss in
center of each cookie. Remove to wire
racks to cool completely. **Yield:** 4
dozen.

Ann Elsie Schmetzer
Madisonville, Kentucky

FROM OUR KITCHEN TO YOURS

HOLY SMOKE!

We tested some high-temperature recipes for roasting pork and whole chickens. Cranking the oven up to 500° for the first 15 minutes of cooking really seals in the flavor and moisture. Then drop the temperature to 325° for pork and 425° or 450° for chicken to finish the cooking process.

But a word of caution: Be sure not to use a glass baking dish. And open the window and temporarily disconnect the smoke detector. We never had a flare-up in the oven, but the visibility plummeted to four feet in our kitchens. When tasting the heavenly flavor, we deemed the cloud of holy smoke worth the trouble.

NO MORE TEARS

Unless you just need an excuse for a good cry, you'll want to try this milder method for chopping onions. It seems the culprit – sulfuric compounds – lies in the root end, or bottom, of the onion.

If you can avoid cutting off the root end before chopping up the onion, the sulfuric compounds are less likely to escape and wander into your eyes.

Place the onion, root end down, on a cutting board. Slice at ¼-inch intervals almost to the bottom of, but not through, the root end of the onion. Roll the onion over on its side, and – starting at the top end of the onion – slice again at ¼-inch intervals, stopping just before the root end.

Chilling the onion for 20 to 30 minutes before chopping it should also slow the flow of those tear-producing compounds. For a no-smell, no-tell finish, rub your hands with lemon juice.

PIE IN OUR FACE

Look in just about any cookbook, and the old rules of piecrusts are there:
1. Use as little water as possible.
2. Be sure it's ice cold water.
3. *Never* overhandle the dough. Break these tenets and you're sure to be punished with a tough or soggy pastry. Or so we thought.

But Eloise Pope of Milton, West Virginia, wrote a letter so compelling that we had to take a good look at our own advice. Sure, we had done piecrusts in the food processor, ever heeding the warning to just pulse a few times, lest our pastry quickly became unforgivingly "overworked." But her advice was much more renegade than a runaway food processor.

Not a little ice water, but ¼ cup of *boiling* water, *whipped* into shortening. She told us her recipe is so easy, you can't fail. "It can be played with, patched, or rerolled, and you still come out with a delicious, flaky crust," she boasted. Eloise is 81 and makes a dozen (sometimes two dozen) pies a week. At that rate, she certainly has more experience than all of us, so we tried her recipe.

In went the boiling water. And not only did we whip the ingredients with a fork as Eloise suggested, we also used a wire whisk, and then even an electric mixer. That pastry refused to get tough, and we lost count of the flaky layers.

READ 'EM AND DON'T WEEP

Eloise also sent advice for keeping meringues from "weeping" (forming tiny golden beads on the surface). She beats **3 egg whites** with an electric mixer for 2 minutes, gradually adding ⅓ **cup sugar**. Then she adds the key ingredient,

1 heaping teaspoon meringue powder, and beats 1½ minutes or until stiff.

After baking we chilled the pie overnight. There were only one or two beads the next day. When we tasted the meringue alone, it had a slightly chalky, but not offensive, texture. In a bite of pie we didn't notice the chalkiness. (Find meringue powder at crafts shops and crafts sections of some discount stores.)

WATER-WHIPPED BAKED PASTRY SHELL

¾ cup shortening
1 tablespoon milk
¼ cup boiling water
2 cups all-purpose flour
1 teaspoon salt

- **Place** first 3 ingredients in a small, deep mixing bowl; beat at medium speed with an electric mixer until light and fluffy, and liquid is incorporated into mixture.
- **Add** flour and salt; beat at lowest speed until dry ingredients are moistened. Divide dough in half; shape each portion into a ball. Wrap in plastic wrap; chill at least 4 hours.
- **Remove** one dough portion from refrigerator. Place between 2 (12-inch-long) pieces of wax paper. Roll into a 12-inch circle. Carefully peel one piece of wax paper from dough; invert dough into a 9-inch pieplate.
- **Remove** remaining wax paper carefully; fit dough in pieplate, and flute edges. Prick bottom and sides of pastry with a fork. Repeat procedure with remaining dough, if desired. (Dough may be stored in the refrigerator up to 1 week.)
- **Bake** pastry at 350° for 18 minutes or until lightly browned. Cool. **Yield:** two 9-inch pastry shells.

Eloise Pope
Milton, West Virginia

OCTOBER

FABULOUS FRUITCAKE

Even if you lack a fondness for fruitcake, you'll find recipes here

to quiet your criticism. And we've even thought of what to do with

all the leftovers. So get started on your holiday baking now.

With just one bite of any of these fruit-filled delights, you'll taste

why this jeweled dessert is such a Southern tradition.

GRANDMOTHER'S FRUITCAKE

Bake a bit of history. Grandmother's Fruitcake has been in Catherine Maddux's family for 150 years.

4 cups all-purpose flour, divided
1 pound chopped dates
1 pound candied citron
1 pound chopped pecans
1 pound dried figs, coarsely chopped
1 (15-ounce) package raisins
1 (10-ounce) package currants
1 cup butter or margarine, softened
2 cups sugar
12 large eggs, lightly beaten
1 cup milk
¾ cup light corn syrup
2 teaspoons baking soda
2 teaspoons ground nutmeg
2 teaspoons ground cinnamon
2 teaspoons ground allspice
1 teaspoon baking powder
1 cup brandy
30 pecan halves (optional)
Brandy
6 red candied cherry halves (optional)

● **Make** a liner for a 10-inch tube pan by drawing an 18-inch circle on brown paper (not recycled). Cut out circle; set pan in center, and draw around base of pan and inside tube. Remove pan, and fold circle into eighths, with lines on the outside.
● **Cut** off pointed tip of triangle along line. Unfold paper; cut along folds to the outside line. Place liner in pan; grease and set aside. Repeat procedure for second pan.
● **Combine** ½ cup flour, dates, and next 5 ingredients in a large bowl, tossing gently to coat. Set aside.
● **Beat** butter at medium speed with an electric mixer until creamy; gradually add sugar, beating mixture well. Add eggs, beating until blended after each addition. Add milk and corn syrup, mixing well.
● **Combine** remaining 3½ cups flour, baking soda, and next 4 ingredients; add to butter mixture alternately with 1 cup brandy, beginning and ending with flour mixture. Mix at low speed after each addition until blended. Pour over fruit mixture; stir well. Spoon batter into prepared pans. Place pecan halves in flower designs on top of batter, if desired.

● **Bake** at 350° for 1 hour or until a wooden pick inserted in center comes out clean. Remove from oven; cool completely in pans on wire racks.
● **Remove** cakes from pans; peel paper from cakes. Wrap in brandy-soaked cheesecloth; store in airtight containers in a cool place. Pour a small amount of brandy over cakes each week for at least one month. Before serving, place cherry halves in center of pecan flowers, if desired. **Yield:** 2 (5-pound) cakes.

Catherine Maddux
Memphis, Tennessee

CAKE MIX FRUIT CAKE

1 pound chopped dates
2 cups chopped pecans
½ pound candied pineapple, chopped
½ pound red and green candied cherries, cut in half
¼ cup all-purpose flour
1 (18.25-ounce) package yellow cake mix
1 cup applesauce
4 large eggs, lightly beaten
2 teaspoons lemon extract
2 teaspoons orange extract

● **Grease** 2 (9- x 5- x 3-inch) loafpans, and line with wax paper. Set aside. Combine first 5 ingredients, tossing gently to coat. Set aside.
● **Combine** cake mix and next 4 ingredients; beat at medium speed with an electric mixer until blended. Stir fruit mixture into batter. Spoon into prepared pans.
● **Bake** at 275° for 2 hours and 45 minutes or until a wooden pick inserted in center comes out clean. Cool in pans on wire racks 10 minutes; remove from pans, and cool completely on wire racks. **Yield:** 2 (2-pound) loaves.

Rhonda Johnson
Maiden, North Carolina

JILL'S FRUITCAKE

4 cups all-purpose flour, divided
1½ cups pecan halves, divided
1 cup chopped almonds
1 cup chopped pecans
1 cup chopped dates
1 pound fruitcake mix
½ pound red and green candied
    cherries
1 teaspoon baking powder
½ teaspoon salt
1 tablespoon ground cinnamon
1 tablespoon ground cloves
1 tablespoon ground allspice
1 tablespoon freshly grated
    nutmeg
¾ cup butter, softened
2 cups sugar
5 large eggs
1 teaspoon vanilla extract
Brandy

• **Line** 6 (5- x 3- x 2-inch) loafpans with parchment paper; set aside.
• **Combine** ½ cup flour, 1 cup pecan halves, almonds, and next 4 ingredients, tossing gently to coat. Set aside.
• **Combine** remaining 3½ cups flour, baking powder, and next 5 ingredients; set aside.
• **Beat** butter at medium speed with an electric mixer until creamy; gradually add sugar, beating well. Add eggs, one at a time, beating until blended after each addition.
• **Add** vanilla, beating well. Gradually add flour mixture, mixing well.
• **Stir** fruit mixture into batter; stir in remaining ½ cup pecan halves. Spoon batter evenly into pans; smooth tops with back of a wet spoon.
• **Bake** at 325° for 20 minutes; decrease temperature to 300°, and bake 40 additional minutes or until cake springs back when lightly touched. Cool in pans on wire racks 20 minutes; remove from pans, and cool completely on wire racks.
• **Peel** paper from cakes; wrap cakes in brandy-soaked cheesecloth. Store in airtight containers in a cool place.
• **Pour** a small amount of brandy over cakes each week for 4 weeks; then each month. **Yield:** 6 (¾-pound) loaves.

Jill Ryan
Austin, Texas

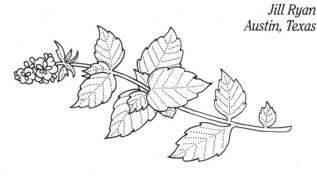

"I'm still eating fruitcake I made in 1987. If you make a lot at once, you'll only have to go to the trouble of making it every 10 years."

Jill Ryan
Austin, Texas

All joking aside, fruitcake is serious business for a lot of Southerners. Just ask Jill Ryan, dedicated fruitcake connoisseur. "Fruitcake must be put on a regular feeding schedule," she advises. She wraps her cakes in brandy-soaked cheesecloth. "I saturate the cheesecloth with brandy every day for the first month, then every month for the next six months. It gets booze-logged and no bacteria is going to grow in there."

She doesn't even taste her fruitcake in less than six months. "A couple of years – at least – is better." Jill is more patient than most, though. We thought her fruitcake, recipe at left, was perfectly moist after only one month.

NO-BAKE FRUITCAKE

For gifts, cut each loaf lengthwise into fourths. Wrap in plastic wrap; then in decorative paper. Tie ends with ribbon.

1 (16-ounce) package round
    buttery crackers
1 (7-ounce) can flaked coconut
1 cup chopped walnuts, toasted
4 cups chopped pecans, toasted
1 pound candied pineapple,
    chopped
1 pound red and green candied
    cherries
1 (15-ounce) package golden
    raisins
1 (12-ounce) can evaporated milk
1 pound large marshmallows

• **Line** 3 (9- x 5- x 3-inch) loafpans with heavy-duty plastic wrap; set aside.

Place 1 stack crackers in a gallon-size heavy-duty, zip-top plastic bag; finely crush crackers, using a meat mallet or rolling pin. Place cracker crumbs in a large bowl. Repeat procedure with remaining crackers.
• **Add** coconut and next 5 ingredients to crumbs, tossing gently to coat.
• **Combine** evaporated milk and marshmallows in a heavy saucepan; cook over medium heat, stirring constantly, until marshmallows melt. Pour over fruit mixture, and stir well. Spoon mixture evenly into prepared pans, pressing firmly.
• **Cover** and store in refrigerator 3 days. Remove from pans; wrap in heavy-duty plastic wrap, and then aluminum foil. Store in the refrigerator. **Yield:** 3 (2½-pound) cakes.

Lois Edwards
Sparta, North Carolina

CHOCOLATE FRUITCAKES

*You'll still be jogging in January
to get this addictive dessert
off your waistline.*

1 cup butter or margarine
6 (1-ounce) squares semisweet
     chocolate
1¼ cups sugar
3 large eggs
1 cup all-purpose flour
¼ teaspoon salt
1 cup red candied cherries, cut in
     half
1 cup green candied pineapple, cut
     into ½-inch wedges
¾ cup walnut halves
¾ cup pecan halves
Garnishes: red candied cherries,
     smilax leaves

● **Melt** butter and chocolate in a heavy saucepan over low heat, stirring often. Remove from heat, and cool about 15 minutes.
● **Stir** in sugar. Add eggs, one at a time, stirring well after each addition. Add flour and salt, stirring until blended. Stir in cherries and next 3 ingredients. Spoon mixture into 4 greased and floured 5- x 3- x 2-inch loafpans.
● **Bake** at 350° for 35 minutes or until a wooden pick inserted in center comes out clean. Cool in pans on wire racks 10 minutes; remove from pans, and cool on wire racks.
● **Seal** cakes in heavy-duty plastic wrap; chill 8 hours before cutting. Garnish, if desired. **Yield:** 4 (12-ounce loaves).

Note: To make a less rich chocolate fruitcake, reduce butter to ½ cup and chocolate to 4 (1-ounce) squares.
*Leslie Coles Walker
Chesapeake, Virginia*

FRUITCAKE-STUFFED PORK LOIN

*Fruitcake breaks tradition
as a delicious stuffing for this
elegant entrée.*

⅓ cup chopped onion
1 clove garlic, minced
1 tablespoon olive oil
3 cups crumbled fruitcake
1 (5-pound) rolled boneless pork
     loin roast
¼ teaspoon salt
¼ teaspoon pepper
2 tablespoons dried thyme, divided
1 cup apple juice
1 cup chicken broth
¼ cup bourbon
¼ cup honey
2 tablespoons butter or margarine
2 tablespoons all-purpose
     flour
2 tablespoons bourbon
¼ cup whipping cream
Garnishes: fresh grapes, kumquats,
     thyme sprigs, canned
     crabapples

● **Cook** onion and garlic in olive oil in a skillet over medium-high heat, stirring constantly, until tender. Remove skillet from heat; add fruitcake, and stir well.
● **Remove** pork loin from elastic net. (There should be 2 pieces.) Trim excess fat. Make a cut lengthwise down the center of each piece, cutting to, but not through, bottom. Starting from center cut of each piece, slice horizontally toward one side, stopping ½ inch from edge. Repeat on opposite side. Unfold each piece of meat so that it lies flat.
● **Flatten** to ½-inch thickness, using a meat mallet or rolling pin.
● **Sprinkle** salt, pepper, and 1 tablespoon thyme evenly over pork. Sprinkle fruitcake mixture over pork.
● **Roll** each loin half, jellyroll fashion, starting with long side. Secure with string, and place, seam side down, in a shallow roasting pan.
● **Pour** apple juice and chicken broth around rolled pork loins in pan.
● **Combine** ¼ cup bourbon and honey. Brush lightly over rolled pork loins. Sprinkle with remaining tablespoon thyme.

● **Bake** at 350° for 50 minutes or until meat thermometer inserted in thickest portion registers 160°, basting with bourbon mixture at 20-minute intervals. Remove pork loins from pan, reserving pan drippings, and keep pork warm.
● **Pour** pan drippings into a saucepan; bring to a boil, and cook 10 to 15 minutes until mixture is reduced to 1 cup. Set aside.
● **Melt** butter in a heavy saucepan over low heat; add flour, stirring until smooth. Cook 1 minute, stirring constantly. Gradually add reduced drippings and 2 tablespoons bourbon; cook over medium heat, stirring constantly, until mixture thickens and boils. Remove from heat; stir in whipping cream. Garnish, if desired. Serve with sliced pork. **Yield:** 10 servings.

AUTUMN IN A JAR

....

Canning is not only a delightful way to preserve the season's bounty but also a family tradition.

NANNIE'S CHOWCHOW

5½ pounds green tomatoes, cored
     and chopped
2¼ pounds onions, chopped
2 pounds green peppers, seeded
     and chopped
1 pound sweet red peppers, seeded
     and chopped
1 (5-pound) head cabbage,
     shredded
½ cup salt
1 quart water
1½ quarts white vinegar
     (5% acidity)
1½ cups sugar
½ cup mustard seeds
2 tablespoons celery seeds
1 tablespoon whole allspice

- **Combine** first 5 ingredients in a large nonmetallic container. Combine salt and water, stirring until dissolved; pour over vegetables. Cover and chill at least 8 hours.
- **Drain** vegetables; discard liquid.
- **Combine** vinegar and next 4 ingredients in a stockpot; add vegetables to pan. Bring mixture to a boil over medium heat; reduce heat, and simmer 10 minutes.
- **Pack** hot mixture into hot jars, filling to ½ inch from top. Remove air bubbles; wipe jar rims. Cover at once with metal lids, and screw on bands.
- **Process** in boiling-water bath 10 minutes. **Yield:** 12 pints.

PEAR CHUTNEY

1 pound onions, quartered
9 cloves garlic
5 pounds firm pears, peeled, cored, and chopped
1 quart white vinegar (5% acidity)
6 cups sugar
1 (24-ounce) package raisins
½ teaspoon dry mustard
1½ cups chopped crystallized ginger
½ teaspoon ground ginger
3 tablespoons mustard seeds

- **Position** knife blade in food processor bowl; add half of onion quarters and garlic. Pulse 4 or 5 times or until onion quarters are chopped. Transfer to a Dutch oven; repeat procedure with remaining onion quarters and garlic.
- **Add** chopped pears and vinegar to onion mixture; bring to a boil. Reduce heat, and simmer 20 to 25 minutes or until chopped pears are tender.
- **Add** sugar, stirring until dissolved; cook over medium heat 10 minutes, stirring occasionally. Add raisins and mustard; cook 20 minutes.
- **Add** crystallized ginger, ground ginger, and mustard seeds; cook over medium heat 10 minutes or until mixture thickens.
- **Pour** hot mixture into hot jars, filling to ½ inch from top. Remove air

bubbles, and wipe jar rims. Cover jars at once with metal lids, and screw on bands.
- **Process** in boiling-water bath 10 minutes. **Yield:** 7 pints.

Jean Graham
Wilmington, North Carolina

SPICED APPLE JELLY

4 pounds cooking apples
2 cups water
1½ cups apple cider vinegar
2 (3-inch) sticks cinnamon
2 teaspoons whole cloves
3 cups sugar

- **Remove** stem and blossom ends from apples. Cut apples into large slices. (Do not peel or core.)
- **Combine** apple slices, 2 cups water, and next 3 ingredients in a Dutch oven, and bring to a boil. Cover, reduce heat, and simmer 25 minutes or until apple slices are tender. Cool slightly.
- **Pour** apple mixture through a jelly bag or a colander lined with four layers of cheesecloth into a bowl, reserving apple liquid in bowl. (Do not press or squeeze mixture through bag or colander.) Add water to apple liquid to equal 4 cups.
- **Combine** apple liquid and sugar in a large saucepan; bring to a boil over medium heat, stirring until sugar dissolves. Boil 30 to 35 minutes or until thermometer registers 220° and jelly mixture sheets from a spoon. Remove from heat, and skim off foam with a metal spoon.
- **Pour** jelly into hot, sterilized jars quickly, filling to ¼ inch from top; wipe jar rims. Cover at once with metal lids, and screw on bands.
- **Process** in boiling-water bath 5 minutes; cool. **Yield:** 3 half-pints.

Anna Robinson
Oak Ridge, Tennessee

APPLE PIE FILLING IN A JAR

2 quarts cold water
¼ cup ascorbic-citric powder
10 pounds cooking apples
2 quarts water
5½ cups sugar
1½ cups ClearJel *
1 tablespoon ground cinnamon
1 teaspoon ground nutmeg
2½ cups water
5 cups apple juice
¾ cup lemon juice

- **Combine** 2 quarts cold water and ascorbic-citric powder in a large bowl.
- **Peel,** core, and cut apples into ½-inch slices; immediately add slices to ascorbic mixture.
- **Bring** 2 quarts water to a boil in a large Dutch oven. Remove 6 cups apple slices from ascorbic mixture, and add to Dutch oven; return to a boil. Boil 1 minute. Remove apple from boiling water; keep warm. Repeat procedure 3 times with remaining apple slices; keep warm. Discard ascorbic mixture.
- **Combine** sugar and next 3 ingredients in a Dutch oven; gradually stir in 2½ cups water and apple juice.
- **Cook** over medium-high heat, stirring constantly, until mixture thickens and boils. Add lemon juice, and boil 1 minute, stirring constantly. Add apple slices, stirring to coat.
- **Pack** hot fruit into hot jars, filling to 1 inch from top. Remove air bubbles; wipe jar rims. Cover at once with metal lids, and screw on bands.
- **Process** in boiling-water bath 25 minutes. **Yield:** 6 quarts (enough for 6 double-crust pies).

* ClearJel is available from Sweet Celebrations, Inc.; 1-800-328-6722.

Note: For ascorbic-citric powder, we used Fruit-Fresh.

Elizabeth Andress
Athens, Georgia

DO YOURSELF A FLAVOR

If light meals at your house mean a dinner with little taste, then give these recipes a try. When you start with vibrant flavors and add minimal fat, dinner doesn't have to be a compromise.

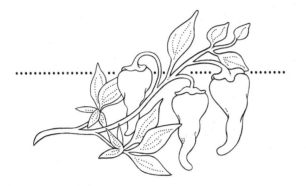

GRILLED TURKEY BREAST WITH CRANBERRY SALSA
(pictured on page 1)

1 (6-pound) turkey breast
1 cup cranberry juice cocktail
¼ cup orange juice
¼ cup olive oil
1 teaspoon salt
1 teaspoon pepper
¼ cup chopped fresh cilantro
3 cups frozen cranberries
½ cup honey
2 tablespoons fresh lime juice
½ cup coarsely chopped purple onion
2 jalapeño peppers, seeded and coarsely chopped
½ cup coarsely chopped dried apricot halves
½ cup fresh cilantro leaves
2 large oranges, peeled, seeded, and coarsely chopped

• **Remove** and discard skin and breast bone from turkey breast, separating breast halves; place turkey in a large heavy-duty, zip-top plastic bag.
• **Combine** cranberry juice cocktail and next 5 ingredients in a jar; cover tightly, and shake vigorously. Reserve ½ cup marinade, and chill. Pour remaining marinade over turkey. Seal bag, and chill 8 hours, turning occasionally.

• **Position** knife blade in food processor bowl; add cranberries and next 7 ingredients. Pulse until chopped, stopping once to scrape down sides (do not overprocess). Transfer cranberry mixture to a serving bowl; chill.
• **Remove** turkey from marinade, discarding marinade.
• **Cook** turkey, covered with grill lid, over medium-hot coals (350° to 400°), about 15 minutes on each side or until a meat thermometer inserted in thickest portion registers 170°, basting occasionally with reserved marinade. Let stand 10 minutes before slicing. Serve with cranberry mixture. **Yield:** 8 servings.

Julie Downey
Houston, Texas

♥ Per serving: Calories 322 (16% from fat)
Fat 5.6g (1.1g saturated) Cholesterol 79mg
Sodium 240mg Carbohydrate 36.5g
Fiber 2.8g Protein 32.2g

TROUT FILLETS WITH CAPERS

If you're watching your sodium intake, capers are not for you. But their pungency adds loads of flavor and no fat.

½ cup all-purpose flour
¼ teaspoon salt
½ teaspoon pepper
1 teaspoon paprika
4 (6-ounce) trout fillets
1 tablespoon olive oil
¼ cup fresh lemon juice
¼ cup capers, undrained

• **Combine** first 4 ingredients in a shallow dish; dredge fillets in mixture.
• **Pour** olive oil in a large nonstick skillet; place over medium heat. Add fillets, and cook 3 minutes; turn fillets, and cook 1 additional minute. Add lemon juice and capers; cover and remove from heat. Let stand 3 to 5 minutes or until fish flakes easily when tested with a fork.
• **Transfer** fillets to a serving platter; spoon sauce over fillets, and serve immediately. **Yield:** 4 servings.

Carrie Easley
Dallas, Texas

♥ Per serving: Calories 297 (29% from fat)
Fat 9.4g (1.6g saturated) Cholesterol 97mg
Sodium 863mg Carbohydrate 14.3g
Fiber 0.6g Protein 37.2g

PASTA WITH PEANUT SAUCE

8 ounces spaghetti, uncooked
12 green onions
3 yellow squash
1 sweet red pepper
1 tablespoon dark sesame oil
1 tablespoon minced garlic
¼ cup creamy peanut butter
¼ cup reduced-sodium soy sauce
3 tablespoons lime juice
1 tablespoon sugar
1 teaspoon dried crushed red pepper

• **Cook** spaghetti according to package directions, omitting salt and fat; drain and keep warm.

• **Cut** white portion of green onions into 2-inch pieces; reserve green tops for another use. Cut squash in half lengthwise; cut halves into slices. Remove and discard seeds from sweet red pepper, and cut sweet red pepper into thin strips.

• **Cook** vegetables in a saucepan in boiling water to cover 3 minutes; drain vegetables, and set aside.

• **Pour** oil into a large skillet; place over medium heat until hot. Add minced garlic, and cook 1 minute, stirring constantly. Add peanut butter, stirring until smooth. Stir in soy sauce and next 3 ingredients.

• **Add** vegetables to skillet, and toss gently to coat; remove vegetables from skillet with a slotted spoon.

• **Add** spaghetti to sauce in skillet, tossing to coat; transfer to a serving platter, and top with vegetables. Serve immediately. **Yield:** 4 servings.

Bruce Messer
Middlesboro, Kentucky

❤ Per serving: Calories 400 (28% from fat)
Fat 13g (2g saturated) Cholesterol 0mg
Sodium 577mg Carbohydrate 59.3g
Fiber 5.3g Protein 14.8g

GRILLED FENNEL AND RADICCHIO WITH ORANGE VINAIGRETTE

4 bulbs fennel
1 head radicchio, separated into
    leaves
½ cup orange juice
¼ cup orange marmalade
2 tablespoons olive oil
1 tablespoon white wine
    vinegar
2 cloves garlic, minced
½ teaspoon salt
¼ teaspoon freshly ground
    pepper
Garnish: fennel sprigs

• **Cut** fennel bulbs vertically into ½-inch slices. Cook in boiling water to cover 3 minutes; drain. Combine fennel and radicchio in a large bowl; set aside.

• **Combine** orange juice and next 6 ingredients in a jar. Cover tightly, and shake vigorously. Chill ¼ cup vinaigrette; pour remaining vinaigrette over fennel and radicchio, tossing gently to coat. Let fennel mixture stand 15 minutes; drain.

• **Cook** fennel, covered with grill lid, over medium-hot coals (350° to 400°) 15 minutes, turning once. Add radicchio, and cook fennel and radicchio, covered with grill lid, 2 minutes or until crisp-tender. Toss fennel and radicchio with reserved vinaigrette, and serve immediately. **Yield:** 4 servings.

Note: Don't core the fennel before grilling. The core will hold the slices of fennel together so they won't fall through the grill rack.

❤ Per serving: Calories 213 (29% from fat)
Fat 7.4g (0.9g saturated) Cholesterol 0mg
Sodium 441mg Carbohydrate 37.2g
Fiber 2.4g Protein 4.2g

LIGHT 'N' EASY IDEAS

···

RECIPES TO RELISH

Shannon Ritchie of Birmingham sent us her onion relish recipe to spice up meat or fish. We made a bourbon version, too.

Purple Onion Relish: Cook 3 large, chopped purple onions in 1 tablespoon olive oil in a skillet over medium-high heat 15 minutes. Add ½ cup firmly packed brown sugar, and cook 20 minutes or until caramelized. Add 1 cup dry red wine, and cook until almost dry. Stir in 1 tablespoon balsamic vinegar and 1 teaspoon beef-flavored bouillon granules; cook just until dissolved. **Yield:** 2 cups.

Chicken With Bourbon-Purple Onion Relish: Sprinkle 4 skinned and boned chicken breast halves with salt and pepper. Cook chicken in 2 teaspoons olive oil in a large skillet over medium-high heat; remove and keep warm. Pour ¼ cup bourbon into skillet, and cook until reduced to 1 tablespoon. Stir in 1 cup prepared Purple Onion Relish (see recipe); pour over chicken. **Yield:** 4 servings.

KEEPING A CHECK ON CHOLESTEROL

Charlotte Tower's husband, Ben, constantly battles high cholesterol. Before the Huntsville, Alabama, couple married, Charlotte had always watched her weight, but now she's adapted her cooking to lower cholesterol, too. Try her tips for keeping weight off and cholesterol in check.

■ When you make a casserole, cut the amount of meat in half, and replace it with more of the rice, pasta, or vegetables in the recipe. You get just as much flavor, and you cut fat, cholesterol, and calories.

■ Remember: There are more ways to cook chicken than to fry it. Marinate skinless chicken breasts in a little oil, citrus juice, and wine, and then bake or grill them.

■ Because canola oil is less saturated than other oils, make it the one you use most of the time. Also, use egg substitute or egg whites.

PEPPERY GREENS WITH RASPBERRY DRESSING

A sweet raspberry dressing counterbalances the sharp flavors of watercress and arugula.

¼ cup cranberry-raspberry juice drink
¼ cup seedless raspberry jam
3 tablespoons raspberry vinegar
2 tablespoons olive oil
½ teaspoon salt
⅛ teaspoon freshly ground pepper
3 cups watercress leaves
1½ cups arugula
¼ cup freshly shredded Parmesan cheese

● **Combine** first 6 ingredients in a jar; cover tightly, and shake vigorously.
● **Combine** watercress and arugula in a serving bowl; add raspberry dressing, tossing gently to coat. Sprinkle with cheese; serve immediately. **Yield: 4 servings.**

♥ Per serving: Calories 140 (54% from fat) Fat 8.4g (1.9g saturated) Cholesterol 4mg Sodium 400mg Carbohydrate 13.5g Fiber 0.7g Protein 2.9g

PERFECT BAKED PAELLA

....

Ask 100 cooks how to make paella and you'll get 100 different answers. A classic Spanish dish named after the special two-handled pan in which it's traditionally prepared and served, paella always starts with saffron-flavored rice simmered with your choice of meats, seafood, and vegetables. In this version, paella bakes in the oven for a no-hassle dinner to serve eight.

PAELLA CASSEROLE

½ pound chorizo or Italian link sausage, sliced
1 (2½- to 3-pound) broiler-fryer, cut up
1 medium onion, chopped
1 medium-size green pepper, seeded and chopped
1 medium-size sweet red pepper, seeded and chopped
2 cloves garlic, minced
2 medium tomatoes, chopped
1 (10-ounce) package yellow saffron rice mix, uncooked
3½ cups water
1 pound unpeeled medium-size fresh shrimp
1 (10-ounce) package frozen English peas, thawed

● **Brown** sausage in a large Dutch oven over medium heat. Remove sausage, reserving drippings in Dutch oven; set sausage aside.
● **Add** chicken pieces to reserved drippings, and cook until browned, turning once. Remove chicken, reserving drippings in Dutch oven; set chicken aside.
● **Cook** onion, pepper, and garlic in drippings. Cook, stirring constantly, until tender. Stir in tomato.
● **Add** rice mix and 3½ cups water; bring to a boil. Stir in sausage.
● **Spoon** mixture into a lightly greased 4-quart paella pan or baking dish. Arrange chicken pieces on top.
● **Cover** casserole, and bake at 375° for 30 minutes.
● **Peel** shrimp, and devein, if desired; set aside.
● **Remove** casserole from oven; top with shrimp and peas. Cover and bake at 375° for 30 additional minutes or until chicken is done. **Yield: 8 servings.**
Barbara Dryden
Pollock, Louisiana

CASSEROLES FOR ANY OCCASION

....

Casserole cookery has always been popular in the South. You can serve these dishes to guests, as well as make them for your family. And they're easy to transport to parties or give to friends. Our delicious versions feature chicken, sausage, and ground beef as main ingredients.

SIMPLY GOOD CHICKEN CASSEROLE

1 (3-pound) broiler-fryer
1 quart water
1 teaspoon salt
1 teaspoon pepper
1 (10¾-ounce) can cream of chicken soup, undiluted
1 (10¾-ounce) can cream of celery soup, undiluted
1 (8-ounce) carton sour cream
½ teaspoon pepper
½ (16-ounce) package oval-shaped buttery crackers, crushed (2 stacks)
¼ cup butter or margarine, melted

● **Combine** first 4 ingredients in a large Dutch oven; bring to a boil. Cover, reduce heat, and simmer 1 hour or until tender. Remove chicken, and cool slightly.
● **Skin** and bone chicken; cut chicken into bite-size pieces. Combine chicken, chicken soup, and next 3 ingredients, stirring well.
● **Place** half of crushed crackers in a lightly greased 11- x 7- x 1½-inch baking dish; spoon chicken mixture over crackers. Top with remaining crackers, and drizzle with butter.
● **Bake** at 325° for 35 minutes or until lightly browned. **Yield:** 6 to 8 servings.

❤ To reduce fat and calories, substitute 6 skinned chicken breast halves, reduced-fat cream of chicken and cream of celery soups, reduced-fat sour cream, and reduced-fat buttery crackers. Reduce butter to 2 tablespoons, and coat dish and top of casserole with butter-flavored cooking spray.

Note: You can add ½ teaspoon salt for flavor, if desired.

Jane Harber
Decatur, Georgia

SAUSAGE-AND-NOODLE CASSEROLE

1 (8-ounce) package medium egg noodles, uncooked
1 (16-ounce) package mild ground pork sausage
1 (10¾-ounce) can cream of chicken soup, undiluted
1 (8-ounce) carton sour cream
½ cup crumbled blue cheese
1 (4½-ounce) jar sliced mushrooms, drained
1 (2-ounce) jar diced pimiento, drained
2 tablespoons finely chopped green pepper
½ cup soft breadcrumbs
1 tablespoon butter or margarine, melted

● **Cook** noodles according to package directions; drain and set aside.
● **Brown** sausage in a large nonstick skillet, stirring until it crumbles; drain and set aside.
● **Combine** soup, sour cream, and blue cheese in a large saucepan; cook over medium heat, stirring constantly, until cheese melts.
● **Add** noodles, sausage, mushrooms, pimiento, and green pepper, tossing to coat. Spoon mixture into a lightly greased 11- x 7- x 1½-inch baking dish.
● **Combine** breadcrumbs and butter; sprinkle over casserole.
● **Bake** at 350° for 30 minutes. **Yield:** 6 servings.

Claudia Barnes
Birmingham, Alabama

CHEESEBURGER CASSEROLE

1 pound lean ground beef
½ teaspoon salt
½ teaspoon pepper
¼ cup chopped onion
¼ cup chopped green pepper
1 (8-ounce) can tomato sauce
4 slices process American cheese
1 (6-ounce) can refrigerated biscuits

● **Brown** ground beef in a large skillet over medium heat, stirring until it crumbles; drain. Return beef to skillet. Stir in salt and next 3 ingredients; cook 1 minute. Add tomato sauce; reduce heat, and simmer 15 minutes.
● **Spoon** into an 8-inch square baking dish; top with cheese.
● **Flatten** biscuits into 3½-inch circles, and place over cheese.
● **Bake** at 350° for 20 to 25 minutes or until biscuits are golden. **Yield:** 3 to 4 servings.

Judith Jones
Chinquapin, North Carolina

WHAT CAN I BRING?

Has your schedule left you no time to cook for that special occasion – a family gathering, potluck supper, or homebound friend? Here're some suggestions to help.

■ Make a salad using assorted fruit or greens from the grocery salad bar, or buy a deli salad and transfer it to your own serving dish.

■ Go in with several people to buy a ham or smoked turkey.

■ Pick up fried chicken or barbecue and buns.

■ Purchase a special dessert from a local bakery.

DINNER IN A PIECRUST

....

Want to serve your family nutritious and flavorful meals? You can, even when your busy schedule doesn't leave time to prepare a traditional meat-and-three-vegetable dinner. All you really need is one of these all-in-one-dish recipes. So, gather all your dinner ingredients under one crust, and get ready for a terrific meal.

HAM-AND-CHEESE PIE

1 (8-ounce) can refrigerated crescent rolls
1½ cups finely chopped ham
1 (8-ounce) package Monterey Jack cheese, cubed
2 tablespoons grated Parmesan cheese
2 tablespoons finely chopped onion
2 large eggs, lightly beaten

• **Unroll** crescent rolls, and separate into 8 triangles. Fit 5 triangles into a 9-inch pieplate, pressing edges together to seal.
• **Combine** chopped ham and next 4 ingredients; spoon into pieplate.
• **Cut** remaining 3 triangles into thin strips; arrange over mixture.
• **Bake** on lower oven rack at 325° for 1 hour. Let stand 5 minutes before serving. **Yield:** 6 servings.

Kathy Miller
Olney, Maryland

CONTINENTAL MEAT PIE

¾ pound ground chuck
¾ pound ground pork
1 large egg
1 teaspoon dried Italian seasoning
3 tablespoons all-purpose flour
3 tablespoons vegetable oil
½ pound Italian hot link sausage, cut into ½-inch slices (optional)
3 cups water
1 (1⅝-ounce) package dry spaghetti sauce mix
1 (6-ounce) can tomato paste
1 pound carrots, scraped
1½ pounds small zucchini
1 (16-ounce) jar whole white onions, drained
½ (15-ounce) package refrigerated piecrusts
1 large egg, lightly beaten

• **Combine** first 4 ingredients; shape into 2-inch balls, and roll in flour.
• **Pour** oil in a large skillet, and place over medium-high heat until hot. Add meatballs, and cook until browned, stirring occasionally. Add sausage, if desired, and cook until browned; drain well.
• **Add** water, sauce mix, and tomato paste to meatball mixture, stirring well; cook over low heat 15 minutes.
• **Cut** carrots and zucchini into 1-inch pieces; place in a saucepan, and cover with water. Bring to a boil over medium heat; cover, reduce heat, and simmer 10 minutes or until tender. Drain well; spoon vegetables into a 13- x 9- x 2-inch baking dish. Add meatball mixture and onions.
• **Roll** piecrust into a 14- x 10-inch rectangle on a lightly floured surface; cut lengthwise into 9 strips. Place 3 pastry strips lengthwise over meatball mixture; weave 3 pastry strips crosswise over meatball mixture. Cover rim of dish with remaining 3 pastry strips, pressing to seal. Brush pastry strips with beaten egg.
• **Bake** at 425° for 30 minutes or until golden. **Yield:** 6 servings.

Mrs. Michael Dryden
Pollock, Louisiana

CHICKEN POT PIE

¼ cup butter or margarine
¼ cup all-purpose flour
1½ cups chicken broth
1½ cups half-and-half
¾ teaspoon salt
½ teaspoon freshly ground pepper
2 tablespoons butter or margarine
1 (8-ounce) package sliced fresh mushrooms
1 small onion, chopped
3 stalks celery, sliced
3½ cups chopped cooked chicken
2 hard-cooked eggs, chopped
1 (15-ounce) package refrigerated piecrusts

• **Melt** ¼ cup butter in a heavy saucepan over low heat; add flour, stirring until mixture is smooth. Cook 1 minute, stirring constantly. Gradually add chicken broth and half-and-half; cook over medium heat, stirring constantly, until thickened and bubbly. Stir in salt and pepper; set sauce aside.
• **Melt** 2 tablespoons butter in a skillet over medium-high heat; add mushrooms, onion, and celery, and cook, stirring constantly, until tender. Drain. Stir vegetable mixture, chicken, and eggs into sauce.
• **Fit** 1 piecrust into a 9-inch deep-dish pieplate according to package directions. Spoon filling evenly into crust; top with remaining piecrust. Trim off excess pastry. Fold edges under, and flute. Cut slits in top.
• **Bake** at 375° for 30 to 40 minutes or until golden, covering edges with strips of aluminum foil after 20 minutes to prevent excessive browning. **Yield:** 6 servings.

Angie Williams
Montgomery, Alabama

Farm-fresh flavor is made quick and easy with Hash Brown Bake (recipe, page 281). A crust made from frozen shredded potatoes nestles a savory filling of eggs, ham, Cheddar cheese, and green pepper.

Tex-Mex flavored Gazpacho Dip (recipe, page 243) does double-duty. Scoop it up with crunchy tortilla chips, or serve it on shredded lettuce as a salad.

Salmon in Parchment (recipe, page 311) takes only minutes to make and won't leave you wrapped up in the kitchen.

Mediterranean-inspired Grilled Swordfish With Caper Sauce (recipe, page 230) and Microwave Ratatouille (recipe, page 232) team up to make a heart-healthy meal.

Chef Frank Stitt whips up Late-Night Pasta Chez Frank (recipe, page 228) after a long day at Highlands Bar & Grill in Birmingham.

More Cluck, Less Buck

....

The next time you automatically reach for those boneless chicken breasts, give the broiler-fryers a second glance. Yep, that price tag says just $2 or $3 . . . for the *whole* bird. That's the way we cook them, so forget the hassle of cutting a raw chicken into parts.

FORTY-CLOVES-OF-GARLIC CHICKEN

So much garlic sounds excessive, but it's fantastic. And true garlic lovers will welcome the rich gravy that tops this piquant chicken.

1 (2½- to 3-pound) broiler-fryer
40 cloves garlic, unpeeled
½ cup dry white wine
½ to ⅔ cup chicken broth, divided
½ cup whipping cream
¼ teaspoon salt
⅛ teaspoon pepper

• **Place** chicken, breast side up, on a rack in a shallow roasting pan. Place 5 garlic cloves in cavity, and arrange remaining garlic cloves around chicken.
• **Bake** at 375° for 20 minutes.
• **Pour** wine over chicken, and bake 40 minutes or until done, basting occasionally with pan juices.
• **Remove** chicken from pan, reserving garlic and pan drippings; keep chicken warm. Remove garlic cloves, and set aside.
• **Remove** and discard fat from pan drippings; add enough broth to drippings to measure ½ cup.
• **Combine** drippings mixture and whipping cream in a small saucepan. Cook over medium-high heat 2 to 3 minutes, stirring occasionally.
• **Squeeze** pulp from garlic cloves into container of an electric blender or food processor. Add 2 tablespoons broth;

process until smooth, stopping once to scrape down sides. Stir garlic mixture, salt, and pepper into hot drippings mixture. Serve chicken with garlic mixture immediately. **Yield:** 4 servings.

Mrs. Harland J. Stone
Ocala, Florida

CREOLE CHICKEN

This dish is great for a fall leaf-raking day. It cooks for a total of three hours, requiring you to occasionally take a break from raking to add ingredients to the pot and stir.

1 (3½-pound) broiler-fryer
2 quarts water
1 teaspoon salt
1 tablespoon butter or margarine
1 medium onion, chopped
2 cloves garlic, minced
2 (16-ounce) cans whole tomatoes, undrained and chopped
2 teaspoons curry powder
2 teaspoons dried thyme
¼ teaspoon salt
Dash of ground red pepper
1 cup currants
8 ounces blanched almonds, toasted
Hot cooked rice

• **Combine** first 3 ingredients in a large Dutch oven; bring to a boil. Cover, reduce heat, and simmer 1 hour or until tender.
• **Remove** chicken, reserving 1 cup liquid; let chicken cool. Skin, bone, and cut chicken into large chunks. Cover and chill reserved liquid and chicken.
• **Melt** butter in a large skillet over medium-high heat; add onion and garlic, and cook, stirring constantly, until crisp-tender. Add tomatoes and next 4 ingredients; cover and cook over low heat 1 hour, stirring occasionally.
• **Add** currants, almonds, and chicken; cover and cook over low heat 1 hour, adding reserved liquid as necessary to prevent sticking. Serve over rice. **Yield:** 6 servings.

John Feagin
Birmingham, Alabama

ROAST CHICKEN WITH RICE

1 (2½- to 3-pound) broiler-fryer
2 tablespoons light corn syrup
½ teaspoon grated orange rind
1 tablespoon orange juice
⅛ teaspoon ground ginger
1 (16-ounce) can ready-to-serve, reduced-sodium, fat-free chicken broth *
1 (6.25-ounce) package quick-cooking long-grain-and-wild rice mix, uncooked
1 tablespoon dried onion flakes
1 (3-ounce) can sliced mushrooms, drained

• **Place** chicken, breast side up, in a lightly greased roasting pan. Bake at 375° for 1 hour.
• **Combine** corn syrup and next 3 ingredients; brush half of corn syrup mixture over chicken, reserving remaining mixture. Bake 10 additional minutes or until done; brush with remaining corn syrup mixture. Keep chicken warm.
• **Combine** chicken broth, rice mix (including seasoning packet), and onion flakes; cook according to package directions. Remove from heat, and stir in mushrooms.
• **Place** rice on a serving platter; top with chicken. **Yield:** 4 servings.

* You can substitute regular canned chicken broth, but the flavor may be too salty.

Marie Davis
Charlotte, North Carolina

Hash Things Out

....

Don't you just love the crispy browned edges of the meat and vegetables in hash? Well, here's your chance to enjoy it without waiting for leftovers.

TURKEY HASH

1 tablespoon butter or margarine
1 large potato, peeled and cubed
1 green pepper, chopped
1 cup chopped onion
Rubbed sage
Ground red pepper
2 cups chopped cooked turkey
1 (8-ounce) jar turkey gravy
1 (6-ounce) package cornbread
    stuffing mix

• **Melt** butter in a nonstick skillet over medium heat; add potato, green pepper, and onion. Sprinkle with sage and red pepper to taste. Top with half of turkey, gravy, and stuffing mix; repeat layers.
• **Cover,** reduce heat, and cook 35 to 50 minutes or until vegetables are tender. **Yield:** 6 servings.

Rublelene Singleton
Scotts Hill, Tennessee

AUSTRIAN HASH WITH CABBAGE SALAD

6 cups shredded cabbage
½ cup commercial red wine
    vinegar and oil salad dressing
1 (1½-pound) eye-of-round roast
2 pounds potatoes, peeled and cut
    into ¼-inch cubes
4 slices bacon
1 large onion, chopped
2 tablespoons caraway seeds
2 tablespoons dried parsley
    flakes
¾ teaspoon salt
½ teaspoon pepper
½ cup beef broth

• **Combine** cabbage and salad dressing, tossing to coat. Cover and chill.
• **Cut** roast into 1-inch-thick slices; place in a large saucepan. Cover roast with water; bring to a boil. Cover, reduce heat, and simmer 30 minutes; drain and cool. Cut roast into ¼-inch cubes; set aside.
• **Cook** potato in boiling water to cover 8 to 10 minutes or until tender; drain and set aside.
• **Cook** bacon in a large skillet until crisp; remove bacon, reserving 2 tablespoons drippings in skillet. Crumble bacon, and set aside.
• **Cook** onion in bacon drippings over medium-high heat, stirring constantly, until tender. Add beef, potato, caraway seeds, and next 3 ingredients.
• **Cook** over medium-high heat, stirring frequently until potato is lightly browned. Add broth, and cook until liquid is absorbed. Serve with cabbage mixture; sprinkle with crumbled bacon. **Yield:** 6 servings.

Bob and Susan Page
Tampa, Florida

CORNED BEEF HASH

2¾ pounds potatoes
2 tablespoons butter or margarine
1 medium onion, finely chopped
1 small green pepper, finely
    chopped
1 pound corned beef, cut into
    ¼-inch cubes
½ teaspoon salt
¼ teaspoon pepper
⅛ teaspoon ground nutmeg

• **Cook** potatoes in boiling water to cover 15 minutes or until tender; drain and cool slightly. Peel potatoes, and cut into ¼-inch cubes. Set aside.
• **Melt** butter in a large skillet over medium-high heat; add onion and green pepper, and cook, stirring constantly, until tender.
• **Add** potato, corned beef, and remaining ingredients; cook until heated and potato is lightly browned, stirring occasionally. **Yield:** 4 servings.

Wilda Jackson
Birmingham, Alabama

VEGETABLE HASH

2 large potatoes, about 1¼ pounds
¼ cup chicken broth
1 cup chopped sweet red pepper
1 cup chopped green pepper
1 cup chopped onion
1 cup fresh corn kernels
Olive oil-flavored cooking spray
1 teaspoon dried thyme
1 teaspoon dried tarragon
½ teaspoon salt
¼ teaspoon pepper
¼ cup chopped fresh parsley
Garnishes: fresh thyme sprigs, fresh
    spinach leaves

• **Cook** potatoes in boiling water to cover 15 to 20 minutes or until tender; drain and cool slightly. Peel potatoes, and cut into ¼-inch cubes. Place in a large bowl, and set aside.
• **Combine** broth and next 3 ingredients in a nonstick skillet; bring to a boil. Reduce heat, and cook 5 minutes, stirring occasionally. Add corn; cook 1 minute. Add to potato in bowl; toss gently. Wipe out skillet.
• **Coat** skillet with cooking spray. Add potato mixture, and spread evenly in skillet.
• **Cook** over medium heat, without stirring, 5 to 7 minutes or until bottom layer of potato turns golden.
• **Add** thyme and next 3 ingredients, tossing to coat; spray with additional cooking spray.
• **Cook** 3 minutes. Sprinkle with 3 tablespoons parsley; toss gently. Sprinkle with remaining parsley. Serve warm; garnish, if desired. **Yield:** 6 servings.

LaJuan Coward
Jasper, Texas

SOUTHERN COMFORT FOOD

Go back to the warmth of mother's love and simpler times with meat loaf, macaroni and cheese, and peach cobbler. That's Southern food that satisfies two hungers – the physical and the emotional. After all, a dose of comforting food can be the best medicine.

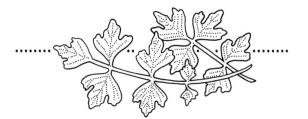

TENNESSEE HAM

1 (16- to 18-pound) whole
　　smoked, fully cooked,
　　bone-in ham
2 cups water
2 tablespoons powdered sugar
Dried Lady Apple Slices
Fresh cranberries
¼ cup apple jelly, melted

• **Place** ham in a stockpot; add water to cover. Bring to a boil; cover, reduce heat, and simmer 30 minutes. Carefully remove ham from stockpot, and place, fat side up, on a rack in a roasting pan.
• **Remove** skin from ham, and trim fat to ¼-inch thickness; make shallow cuts in fat in a diamond pattern. Add 2 cups water to roasting pan.
• **Cover** and bake at 325° for 2½ hours or until meat thermometer registers 140°. Uncover and sprinkle with powdered sugar. Bake at 375° for 10 additional minutes.
• **Arrange** Dried Lady Apple Slices over ham, securing center of slices with wooden picks. Bake at 325° for 5 additional minutes.
• **Press** cranberries onto picks in ham; brush ham and apple slices with melted jelly.
• **Bake** at 325° for 5 minutes. **Yield:** 25 to 30 servings.

Dried Lady Apple Slices

3 to 5 Lady apples, unpeeled *
3 tablespoons lemon juice
2 cups water
½ teaspoon salt

• **Cut** apples into ⅛-inch slices (do not core).
• **Combine** lemon juice and water; pour over apples, stirring to coat well. Drain. Sprinkle both sides of apple slices with salt, and place on wire racks.
• **Bake** on racks at 200° for 3½ to 4 hours; turn oven off, and let stand in oven at least 8 hours. **Yield:** about 2 dozen.

* You can substitute small Red Delicious apples.

BEEF ROAST WITH BURGUNDY GRAVY

1 (4½- to 5-pound) sirloin tip
　　roast
1 teaspoon salt
1¼ teaspoons pepper, divided
½ cup warm water
⅓ cup all-purpose flour
1 cup ready-to-serve beef broth
½ cup dry red wine

• **Preheat** oven to 500°.
• **Rub** roast with salt and 1 teaspoon pepper. Place on a rack in a shallow roasting pan. Place in oven; immediately reduce temperature to 325°.
• **Bake** at 325° for 1 hour and 10 minutes or until a meat thermometer registers 150°.
• **Remove** roast and rack from pan; keep roast warm. Remove fat from drippings; reserve ¼ cup fat.
• **Add** warm water to remaining drippings in pan; stir to loosen browned particles that cling to bottom. Strain mixture, reserving ¾ cup drippings; discard solids.
• **Heat** reserved ¼ cup fat in a small skillet; add flour, stirring until smooth. Cook 1 minute, stirring constantly. Gradually add reserved ¾ cup drippings, beef broth, and wine; cook over medium heat, stirring constantly, until thickened. Stir in remaining ¼ teaspoon pepper. Serve with sliced roast. **Yield:** 10 to 12 servings.

Mike Singleton
Memphis, Tennessee

CHICKEN AND GRITS

2 (14½-ounce) cans ready-to-serve
　　chicken broth
1 cup quick-cooking grits,
　　uncooked
1 (8-ounce) jar process cheese
　　spread
3 large eggs, lightly beaten
2 cups chopped cooked chicken
½ teaspoon poultry seasoning

• **Bring** broth to a boil in a large saucepan over medium-high heat; stir in grits. Cover, reduce heat, and simmer 5 minutes; stir occasionally.
• **Add** cheese and remaining ingredients; stirring well. Pour into a greased 11- x 7- x 1½-inch baking dish.
• **Bake** at 375° for 30 minutes. **Yield:** 4 to 6 servings.

Mrs. Harland J. Stone
Ocala, Florida

MEAT LOAF WITH CHUNKY TOMATO SAUCE

1 pound ground chuck
1 medium onion, chopped
1 medium-size green pepper, chopped
2 cloves garlic, minced
¾ cup quick-cooking oats, uncooked
½ cup ketchup
2 large eggs, lightly beaten
1 tablespoon steak sauce
¼ teaspoon salt
¼ teaspoon seasoned salt
¼ teaspoon pepper
Chunky Tomato Sauce

• **Combine** all ingredients except Chunky Tomato Sauce; press mixture into a 9- x 5- x 3-inch loafpan, or shape into a loaf and place on a rack in a broiler pan.
• **Bake** at 350° for 50 to 60 minutes or until done. Serve with Chunky Tomato Sauce. **Yield:** 4 servings.

Chunky Tomato Sauce

1 (14½-ounce) can diced tomatoes, undrained
1 (5½-ounce) can spicy vegetable juice
½ cup chopped celery
½ cup chopped green pepper
½ cup chopped onion
½ teaspoon garlic powder
1 teaspoon dried basil
1 teaspoon dried marjoram
1 teaspoon dried oregano
1 teaspoon dried parsley flakes

• **Combine** all ingredients in a large saucepan; bring to a boil. Reduce heat, and simmer 15 minutes, stirring occasionally. **Yield:** 2 cups.

Kathy Rogers
Carey, North Carolina

MACARONI AND CHEESE SOUP

1 cup elbow macaroni, uncooked
¼ cup butter or margarine
½ cup finely chopped carrot
½ cup finely chopped celery
1 small onion, finely chopped
4 cups milk
1½ cups (6 ounces) shredded process American cheese
2 tablespoons chicken-flavored bouillon granules
½ teaspoon ground white pepper
2 tablespoons cornstarch
2 tablespoons water
1 (8-ounce) can whole kernel corn, drained
½ cup frozen English peas

• **Cook** macaroni according to package directions, omitting salt; drain well. Rinse macaroni with cold water; drain and set aside.
• **Melt** butter in a large skillet over medium-high heat; add carrot, celery, and onion, and cook, stirring constantly, 5 to 7 minutes or until tender. Remove vegetable mixture from heat; set aside.
• **Combine** milk and cheese in a heavy Dutch oven, and cook over medium heat until cheese melts, stirring mixture often. Stir in bouillon granules and pepper.
• **Combine** cornstarch and water in a small bowl, stirring well; stir into milk mixture. Cook over medium heat, stirring constantly, until mixture thickens and comes to a boil. Boil 1 minute, stirring constantly.
• **Stir** in macaroni, vegetable mixture, corn, and peas; cook over low heat, stirring constantly, until thoroughly heated. **Yield:** 8 cups.

W. N. Cottrell II
New Orleans, Louisiana

PEACH COBBLER

1 (15-ounce) package refrigerated piecrusts
1 teaspoon all-purpose flour
4 cups frozen sliced peaches
½ cup sugar
½ teaspoon ground cinnamon
¼ cup cornstarch
½ cup water
2 tablespoons butter or margarine, melted
1 large egg
2 tablespoons milk
1 tablespoon sugar

• **Roll** 1 piecrust into a 12-inch circle. Sprinkle flour over surface. Place crust, floured side down, in a 9½-inch quiche dish. Place peaches in crust.
• **Combine** ½ cup sugar, cinnamon, and cornstarch; sprinkle over peaches, and drizzle with water and butter.
• **Unfold** remaining piecrust, and roll on a lightly floured surface into a 12-inch circle; place over peaches. Fold edges under, and flute.
• **Cut** 6 (1-inch) slits in top of piecrust with a sharp knife.
• **Combine** egg and milk, stirring well; brush over top piecrust, and sprinkle evenly with 1 tablespoon sugar. Place on a baking sheet.
• **Bake** at 350° for 1 hour or until golden. **Yield:** 8 servings.

EARTHY DELIGHTS

....

Sticker shock may well be your first reaction to shiitake mushrooms. But indulge yourself in one of these recipes, and your palate will thank you.

Shiitake (shee-TAH-kee) mushrooms have a strong, woodsy flavor and a meaty texture. Just a few of the dark brown caps can make an ordinary meal extraordinary.

Here's all it takes to buy, store, and prepare shiitakes.

■ Look for shiitakes with dry caps. Those with a slick surface are past their prime. Store in the refrigerator in a paper bag up to three days.

■ To clean shiitakes, wipe them with a damp paper towel or give them a quick rinse under running water. Shiitakes absorb water like a sponge, and the water dilutes their flavor.

■ Shiitake stems are tough and chewy, even after cooking. Discard them or add them to a stockpot.

■ You can substitute white mushrooms for shiitakes, but the results won't be nearly as flavorful.

FILET MIGNONS WITH SHIITAKE MADEIRA SAUCE

½ pound fresh shiitake
   mushrooms
1 tablespoon olive oil
2 cloves garlic, minced
1 teaspoon dried thyme
½ teaspoon freshly ground pepper
4 (5-ounce) beef tenderloin steaks
   (1 inch thick)
2 shallots, finely chopped
2 cloves garlic, minced
1 cup Madeira wine
½ cup condensed beef broth,
   undiluted
¼ cup whipping cream

• **Remove** stems from mushrooms, discard stems. Cut mushroom caps into thin slices; set aside.
• **Combine** oil and next 3 ingredients in a bowl; coat steaks with mixture.
• **Place** a large nonstick skillet over medium-high heat until hot; add steaks. Cook 10 to 15 minutes or until a meat thermometer registers 160° (medium) or to desired degree of doneness, turning once. Remove steaks from skillet, reserving drippings in skillet. Keep steaks warm.
• **Cook** shallot and garlic in drippings, stirring constantly, until tender.
• **Add** Madeira; bring to a boil. Reduce heat, and simmer 10 minutes or until reduced to ½ cup.

• **Add** broth and mushrooms; cook 3 minutes or until tender, stirring occasionally. Remove from heat.
• **Stir** in whipping cream; pour over steaks, and serve immediately. **Yield:** 4 servings.

Frances Butler
Decatur, Georgia

GRILLED SHIITAKES

The simple ingredients of this recipe belie its fabulous flavor.

1 pound large fresh shiitake
   mushrooms
½ cup butter or margarine, melted
4 cloves garlic, minced
¼ cup chopped fresh parsley
½ teaspoon freshly ground pepper
¼ teaspoon salt

• **Remove** stems from mushrooms; discard. Combine butter and next 4 ingredients; spread evenly on both sides of mushroom caps.
• **Cook**, without grill lid, over medium-hot coals (350° to 400°) 8 minutes, turning once. **Yield:** 4 servings.
Dale Glennon
Florence, Alabama

CREAM OF SHIITAKE SOUP

½ pound fresh shiitake
   mushrooms
¼ cup butter or margarine
2 cups chopped onion
3 tablespoons all-purpose flour
2 (14½-ounce) cans ready-to-serve
   chicken broth
2 cups whipping cream
¼ teaspoon pepper
¼ teaspoon ground nutmeg

• **Remove** stems from mushrooms; discard. Finely chop mushroom caps.
• **Melt** butter in a saucepan over medium-high heat; add chopped mushroom caps and onion, and cook, stirring constantly, until tender.
• **Add** flour; cook 1 minute, stirring constantly. Gradually add broth; cook,

stirring constantly, until thickened. Remove from heat.
• **Stir** in whipping cream, pepper, and nutmeg. **Yield:** 7 cups.

Jean Hartgroves
Charlestown, West Virginia

GOLDEN CHEESE-SHIITAKE OMELET

2 ounces large shiitake mushrooms
2 tablespoons butter, divided
1 small onion, finely chopped
⅔ cup cottage cheese
4 large eggs, lightly beaten
¼ teaspoon salt
¼ teaspoon freshly ground pepper

• **Remove** stems from mushrooms; discard. Cut mushroom caps into thin slices.
• **Melt** 1 tablespoon butter in a nonstick skillet over medium-high heat; add mushrooms and onion, and cook, stirring constantly, until tender. Transfer to a bowl, and stir in cottage cheese. Wipe out skillet.
• **Combine** eggs, salt, and pepper; beat lightly with a fork.
• **Melt** remaining 1 tablespoon butter, rotating pan to coat bottom evenly. Add egg mixture. As mixture starts to cook, gently lift edges with a spatula, and tilt pan so uncooked portion flows underneath.
• **Spoon** mushroom mixture onto omelet; fold in half, and transfer to a serving plate. **Yield:** 2 servings.
Mariet Van den Munckhof Vedder
Dublin, Georgia

TOP CHOPS

New Orleanians recently picked not shrimp or crawfish but pork chops as their favorite entrée at two white-tablecloth eateries. The chefs shared their recipes, and we made a few substitutions and shortcuts to bring a taste of the Big Easy to your kitchen.

PECAN-BREADED PORK CHOPS WITH BEER SAUCE

Want a romantic dinner overlooking the mighty Mississippi? Bella Luna is the spot. Chef Horst Pfeifer uses a local product – Abita beer – to give pork chops a Louisiana twist. If you can't find it in your area, use another dark beer.

2 slices white bread
1 teaspoon dry mustard
1 teaspoon celery salt
¼ teaspoon pepper
1 cup pecan pieces
6 (¾-inch-thick) bone-in pork loin chops
¾ cup all-purpose flour
2 large eggs, lightly beaten
¼ cup milk
3 tablespoons butter or margarine
Beer Sauce

• **Position** knife blade in food processor bowl; add first 4 ingredients. Process 30 seconds or until bread is in fine crumbs. Add pecan pieces, and process until finely chopped; place pecan mixture in a shallow dish.
• **Dredge** chops in flour, shaking off excess. Combine eggs and milk in a shallow bowl. Dip chops in egg mixture and then in pecan mixture, coating all sides and shaking off excess.
• **Melt** butter in a large nonstick skillet over medium-high heat; add chops, and cook 2 minutes on each side or until browned. Remove chops to a baking sheet.
• **Bake** at 350° for 10 to 15 minutes. Serve immediately with Beer Sauce. **Yield:** 6 servings.

Beer Sauce

1 cup chopped onion
1 tablespoon caraway seeds
1 clove garlic, minced
1 tablespoon vegetable oil
1 (12-ounce) bottle Abita or other dark beer
1 (10½-ounce) can condensed beef consommé, undiluted
¼ teaspoon pepper
1½ tablespoons cornstarch
1½ tablespoons water

• **Cook** first 3 ingredients in oil in a large skillet over medium heat, stirring constantly, until tender.
• **Add** beer, beef consommé, and pepper. Bring mixture to a boil; reduce heat, and simmer 15 minutes.
• **Combine** cornstarch and water, stirring until smooth; add to beer mixture.
• **Cook** over medium heat, stirring constantly, until mixture thickens and boils. Boil 1 minute, stirring constantly. **Yield:** 2 cups.

TAMARIND-GLAZED PORK CHOPS WITH GREEN MOLE SAUCE

The ingredients for this recipe from Emeril Lagasse at Emeril's are many, but most are processed into a seasoning paste and a sauce. (His recipe uses tamarind, but it's hard to find. So we used apricots, dates, and lemon juice.)

2½ tablespoons Southwest Seasoning, divided
⅛ teaspoon pepper
⅓ cup cane syrup or molasses
2 tablespoons ketchup
2 tablespoons water
2 teaspoons lemon juice
6 dried apricot halves
2 pitted dates
1 clove garlic
6 (1-inch-thick) boneless pork loin chops
1 tablespoon olive oil
Green Mole Sauce
Garnish: fresh cilantro

• **Position** knife blade in food processor bowl; add 1 tablespoon Southwest Seasoning, pepper, and next 7 ingredients. Process until smooth; set aside.
• **Coat** chops with remaining Southwest Seasoning. Cook in oil in a skillet over medium-high heat 2 minutes on each side or until browned. Remove to an aluminum foil-lined baking sheet; brush with syrup mixture.
• **Broil** 5½ inches from heat (with electric oven door partially opened) 15 minutes, turning and basting chops every 5 minutes. Serve with Green Mole Sauce. Garnish, if desired. **Yield:** 6 servings.

Southwest Seasoning

2 tablespoons chili powder
2 tablespoons paprika
1 tablespoon salt
1 tablespoon garlic powder
1 tablespoon ground coriander
2 teaspoons ground cumin
2 teaspoons ground red pepper
1 teaspoon dried oregano
1 teaspoon ground black pepper

• **Combine** all ingredients; store in an airtight container. **Yield:** ½ cup.

Green Mole Sauce

1 poblano pepper
3 dried apricot halves
1 pitted date
1 cup pistachio nuts, pine nuts, or pumpkin seeds
1 tablespoon cane syrup or molasses
1 teaspoon chili powder
1 teaspoon ground cumin
¼ teaspoon salt
1 teaspoon white vinegar
1 teaspoon lemon juice
1 tablespoon olive oil
¾ cup chicken broth
½ cup whipping cream

• **Place** chile pepper on an ungreased baking sheet. Broil 5½ inches from heat (with electric oven door partially opened) about 5 minutes on each side or until pepper looks blistered. Cool.
• **Peel** chile pepper; remove and discard membranes and seeds.
• **Position** knife blade in food processor bowl; add chile pepper, apricot halves, and next 9 ingredients. Process until smooth.
• **Combine** pepper mixture, broth, and whipping cream in a medium saucepan. Bring mixture to a boil; reduce heat, and simmer 2 minutes, stirring constantly. **Yield:** 1 cup.

BEYOND PEPPERONI

....

Would you like a little roux and Creole seasoning on your pizza? How about country ham and turnip greens? Or black beans and cilantro? These recipes experiment with ingredients beyond plain pepperoni. (We included that, too, so don't get nervous.)

You don't even have to make your own crust. Several kinds are ready and waiting at your supermarket. Our favorite is Mama Mary's two 12-inch crusts, found in the refrigerator section. (Or try the nonrefrigerated Boboli crusts or the refrigerated canned kind you shape yourself.)

PESTO SAUCE

Lemon juice keeps the basil from turning too dark and brightens the flavor of this pesto.

2 cloves garlic
½ cup walnuts, toasted
2 cups loosely packed fresh basil leaves
½ cup olive oil
¾ cup freshly grated Parmesan or Romano cheese
¼ teaspoon salt
2 teaspoons lemon juice
1 teaspoon hot water

• **Position** knife blade in food processor bowl; add first 3 ingredients. Process until smooth, stopping once to scrape down sides.
• **Pour** oil through food chute with processor running. Add cheese and remaining ingredients; process until smooth, stopping once to scrape down sides. **Yield:** 1 cup.

BLAZING SUNSET PIZZA

⅔ cup Pesto Sauce (see recipe)
1 (12-inch) refrigerated pizza crust
2 plum tomatoes, sliced
½ sweet red pepper, seeded and thinly sliced
½ sweet yellow pepper, seeded and thinly sliced
½ sweet orange pepper, seeded and thinly sliced
1 cup (4 ounces) shredded colby-Monterey Jack cheese blend
Garnish: fresh basil sprig

• **Spread** Pesto Sauce over crust; top with tomato and next 4 ingredients.
• **Bake** at 425° for 10 minutes or until bubbly. Garnish, if desired. **Yield:** one 12-inch pizza.

TRADITIONAL PIZZA SAUCE

1 (14½-ounce) can pasta-style tomatoes, undrained
1 (8-ounce) can tomato sauce
1 clove garlic, pressed
½ teaspoon dried oregano
⅛ teaspoon garlic salt
⅛ teaspoon pepper

• **Combine** all ingredients in a medium saucepan. Bring to a boil, stirring constantly. Reduce heat, and simmer, uncovered, 5 minutes, stirring often. **Yield:** about 2 cups.

THE KING HENRY PIZZA

If he were alive today, Henry VIII no doubt would have the well-known drumstick in one hand and a slice of this meaty pizza in the other.

1¼ cups Traditional Pizza Sauce (see recipe)
1 (12-inch) refrigerated pizza crust
½ pound ground pork sausage, cooked and drained
½ (3.5-ounce) package sliced pepperoni
8 slices bacon, cooked and crumbled
1 (8-ounce) package shredded four-cheese blend

• **Spread** Traditional Pizza Sauce over pizza crust, and top evenly with remaining ingredients.
• **Bake** at 425° for 10 minutes or until bubbly. **Yield:** one 12-inch pizza.

ROASTED GARLIC SAUCE

That's two heads of garlic, not cloves. The flavor mellows with roasting.

2 heads garlic, unpeeled
1 teaspoon olive oil
1½ tablespoons butter or margarine
1½ tablespoons all-purpose flour
⅔ cup chicken broth

• **Place** garlic on a piece of aluminum foil, and drizzle with olive oil. Fold edges together to seal.
• **Bake** at 425° for 30 minutes; cool.
• **Melt** butter in a heavy saucepan over medium-high heat. Cut top off each garlic head, and squeeze cooked garlic into pan. (Garlic will be soft and sticky.)
• **Add** flour, and cook, stirring constantly with a wire whisk, 1 minute or until lightly browned.
• **Add** chicken broth. Cook, stirring constantly, until mixture is thick and bubbly. **Yield:** ⅔ cup.

PUT-'EM-TO-WORK PIZZA PARTY

Instead of asking friends over and making one of these pizzas for them, just invite them to a pizza party. Before they arrive, set out the crusts and toppings. Hand everyone an apron as they arrive and tell them to fix dinner.

This really isn't as obnoxious as it sounds. It turns dinner into a lively, fun evening. Everyone loves getting into the action; they get to eat what they want and skip the ingredients they don't like. Because you can bake only a pizza or two at a time, people just eat when theirs is ready – mingling and checking out the other pizzas.

The only problem is, you're such a relaxed hostess, your friends may figure out that you're the one who's being entertained.

SOUTHWEST DELUXE PIZZA

This one takes more time than the others, but it's worth it.

3 skinned and boned chicken breast halves
1 teaspoon cumin
½ teaspoon salt
2 tablespoons butter or margarine
Juice of 1 lime
4 poblano peppers
1 (12-inch) refrigerated pizza crust
⅔ cup Roasted Garlic Sauce (see recipe)
½ cup canned black beans, rinsed and drained
1 medium purple onion, thinly sliced and separated into rings
½ cup chopped fresh cilantro, divided
1½ cups (6 ounces) shredded Monterey Jack cheese with peppers

• **Sprinkle** chicken with cumin and salt. Melt butter in a skillet over medium heat; add chicken, and cook 10 minutes or until tender. Cut into 1-inch pieces, and pour lime juice over chicken. Set chicken aside.
• **Place** peppers on an aluminum foil-lined baking sheet. Broil 5½ inches from heat (with electric oven door partially opened) 5 minutes on each side or until peppers look blistered.
• **Place** peppers in a heavy-duty, zip-top plastic bag; seal and let stand 10 minutes. Peel peppers; remove and discard cores, membranes, and seeds. Chop peppers, and set aside.
• **Bake** pizza crust at 425° for 10 minutes. Spread Roasted Garlic Sauce over pizza crust; top with chicken, chopped pepper, black beans, onion, ¼ cup cilantro, and cheese.
• **Bake** at 425° for 15 minutes or until bubbly. Serve with remaining ¼ cup cilantro. **Yield:** one 12-inch pizza.

THE BEST OF THE BAYOU PIZZA

The garlic sauce is actually a classic white roux.

1 pound unpeeled large fresh shrimp
½ cup chopped green pepper
½ cup chopped onion
½ cup chopped celery
2 teaspoons Creole seasoning
1 tablespoon olive oil
⅔ cup Roasted Garlic Sauce (see recipe)
1 (12-inch) refrigerated pizza crust
1 cup (4 ounces) shredded mozzarella cheese
¼ cup freshly grated Parmesan cheese

• **Peel** shrimp, and devein, if desired.
• **Cook** shrimp and next 4 ingredients in oil in a large skillet over medium-high heat, stirring constantly, 3 to 5 minutes or until shrimp turn pink.
• **Spread** Roasted Garlic Sauce over pizza crust; top with shrimp mixture. Sprinkle with cheeses.
• **Bake** at 425° for 10 minutes or until bubbly. **Yield:** one 12-inch pizza.

Note: We used Tony Chachere's More Spice, Less Salt Creole Seasoning.

SOUTHERN CLASSIC PIZZA

Traditional ingredients of a meat-and-three add homecooked flavor.

¼ pound thinly sliced country ham
⅔ cup Roasted Garlic Sauce (see recipe)
1 (12-inch) refrigerated pizza crust
1 (10-ounce) package frozen chopped turnip greens or spinach, cooked and drained well
1 cup (4 ounces) shredded mozzarella cheese
½ cup freshly grated Parmesan cheese

• **Cook** ham according to package directions, and cut into thin strips.

- **Spread** Roasted Garlic Sauce over pizza crust; top with ham, turnip greens, and remaining ingredients.
- **Bake** at 425° for 10 minutes or until bubbly. **Yield:** one 12-inch pizza.

A PLEASING RISOTTO

Dallas restaurant **Mi Piaci**, an Italian phrase meaning "you are pleasing to me," offers one of the creamiest risottos we've had. Tomato-Basil Risotto takes less than 20 minutes to prepare.

TOMATO-BASIL RISOTTO
(Risotto Pomodoro Al Fresco e Basilico)

8 cups chicken broth
¼ cup butter, divided
¼ cup chopped onion
3 cups chopped plum tomatoes
    (about 6 tomatoes)
2 cups Arborio rice
¼ cup chopped fresh basil
¼ cup grated Parmesan cheese
¼ teaspoon salt
¼ teaspoon pepper

- **Cook** broth in a saucepan over medium heat until hot.
- **Melt** 2 tablespoons butter in a large Dutch oven over medium-high heat; add onion, and cook 2 minutes, stirring constantly.
- **Add** tomato; cook 2 minutes, stirring constantly. Add rice; cook 5 minutes. Reduce heat to medium.
- **Add** broth, ½ cup at a time, stirring constantly; allow rice to absorb liquid before adding more broth.
- **Stir** in remaining 2 tablespoons butter, chopped basil, and remaining ingredients. **Yield:** 5 cups.

Chef Mark Morrow
Mi Piaci Ristorante Italiano
Dallas, Texas

FREEZER-EASY POTATOES

....

Frozen potatoes are more than just plain French fries. They're hash browns, dinner fries, shoestring fries, and even mashed potatoes. Pull a bag from the freezer, and start up a meal.

POTATO-BACON FRITTATA

3 tablespoons butter or margarine
2 cups frozen potatoes with
    onions and peppers
6 large eggs
2 tablespoons milk
¼ teaspoon salt
¼ teaspoon pepper
1 cup (4 ounces) shredded
    Cheddar cheese
6 slices bacon, cooked and
    crumbled
Garnish: diced fresh tomato or
    picante sauce

- **Melt** butter in a 10-inch nonstick skillet over medium heat; add frozen potatoes, and cook 10 minutes or until browned.
- **Combine** eggs and next 3 ingredients, stirring with a wire whisk; pour over potatoes. As mixture starts to cook, gently lift edges of frittata with a spatula, and tilt pan so uncooked portion flows underneath. If center remains uncooked, carefully turn frittata over, and cook 5 minutes or until center is done.
- **Place** frittata on serving platter, and sprinkle with shredded cheese. Cover with aluminum foil, and let stand 5 minutes.
- **Sprinkle** with crumbled bacon; garnish, if desired. Serve immediately. **Yield:** 6 servings.

Note: For potatoes, we used Potatoes O'Brien.

Judi Grigoraci
Charleston, West Virginia

POTATO-CHEESE PUFF

1 (22-ounce) package frozen
    mashed potatoes
½ teaspoon salt (optional)
2 cups (8 ounces) shredded
    Cheddar cheese
1 cup whipping cream, whipped

- **Prepare** potato according to package directions; stir in salt, if desired. Spread potato in a lightly greased 2-quart shallow baking dish.
- **Combine** cheese and whipped cream, stirring gently; spread mixture over potatoes.
- **Bake** at 350° for 25 minutes or until lightly browned. **Yield:** 6 to 8 servings.

Note: You can bake Potato-Cheese Puff in 12 (6-ounce) custard cups at 325° for 15 minutes or until puffs are lightly browned.

Shirley Awood Glaab
Hattiesburg, Mississippi

POTATO-ONION PATTIES

3 cups frozen shredded potatoes
½ cup finely chopped onion
1 large egg, lightly beaten
2 teaspoons all-purpose flour
½ teaspoon seasoned salt
¼ teaspoon pepper
2 tablespoons vegetable oil

- **Thaw** potatoes on paper towels.
- **Combine** potato, onion, and next 4 ingredients in a large bowl, stirring well. Shape mixture into 4 patties (patties will be loose).
- **Fry** patties in hot oil in a large skillet over medium-high heat 3 to 4 minutes on each side or until golden. Remove from skillet, and drain on paper towels. Serve warm. **Yield:** 4 servings.

Clara Watkins
Garden Ridge, Texas

HEADS UP

....

Wheel through the produce section of the supermarket to the mounds of red and green cabbages. Choose a head that's heavy for its size with firmly packed, crisp leaves. Store it in the refrigerator, tightly wrapped, up to one week. With these recipes, you can enjoy cabbage raw or cooked, plain or fancy.

QUICK COOKED CABBAGE

2 slices bacon, cut into 1-inch pieces
¼ cup chopped onion
1¼ pounds cabbage, sliced
1 teaspoon dried parsley flakes
¾ teaspoon salt
¼ teaspoon dried basil
¼ teaspoon dried oregano
¼ teaspoon dried marjoram
¼ teaspoon ground black pepper
Dash of ground red pepper

• Cook bacon in a large skillet over medium heat until crisp; remove bacon, reserving drippings in skillet. Crumble bacon, and set aside.
• Cook chopped onion in reserved drippings over medium heat about 2 minutes, stirring often.
• Add cabbage and next 7 ingredients; cook 1 minute, stirring constantly. Cover and cook about 3 minutes. Sprinkle with crumbled bacon. Yield: 6 servings.

Sharon McClatchey
Muskogee, Oklahoma

FRIED CABBAGE ROLLS

12 cabbage leaves
½ pound lean ground beef
¾ cup finely chopped cooked ham
4 slices bacon, cut into ½-inch pieces
1 (4-ounce) can chopped olives, drained
¼ teaspoon salt
¼ teaspoon pepper
⅛ teaspoon ground nutmeg
1 large egg, lightly beaten
1 cup fine, dry breadcrumbs
Vegetable oil

• Cook cabbage leaves in boiling water to cover 5 minutes; drain well, and let cool.
• Brown ground beef in a large skillet, stirring until it crumbles; remove from skillet, and drain.
• Combine ham and bacon in skillet; cook until bacon is crisp. Drain.
• Combine beef, ham, bacon, olives, and next 3 ingredients in a large bowl, stirring well.
• Place about ¼ cup meat mixture in center of each leaf; fold left and right sides over mixture, and roll up, beginning at bottom. Secure each with a wooden pick.
• Dip cabbage rolls in egg; dredge in breadcrumbs.
• Pour oil to depth of 1 inch into a large skillet. Fry cabbage rolls in hot oil, a few at a time, until golden, turning once. Drain on paper towels; serve immediately. Yield: 6 servings.

Edith Askins
Greenville, Texas

SPANISH CABBAGE RELISH

4 cups coarsely chopped cabbage
1 cup chopped onion
1 cup coarsely chopped celery
1 small green pepper, seeded and chopped
1 (14-ounce) bottle hot ketchup
½ cup apple cider vinegar
¼ cup vegetable oil
1 teaspoon salt
½ teaspoon pepper

• Combine all ingredients in a Dutch oven; bring to a boil over high heat, stirring often.
• Reduce heat, cover, and simmer 10 minutes, stirring occasionally. Serve warm or cold with hot dogs or black-eyed peas. Yield: 4 cups.

Ann Winniford
Dallas, Texas

BLUE CHEESE COLESLAW

For crisp slaw, first soak the shredded cabbage in ice water for an hour. Then drain the cabbage, pat dry, and store in the refrigerator in a plastic bag until ready to use.

3 tablespoons apple cider vinegar
2 tablespoons finely chopped onion
1 tablespoon sugar
¾ teaspoon celery seeds
¼ teaspoon salt
⅛ teaspoon dry mustard
¼ teaspoon pepper
1 clove garlic, minced
¼ cup vegetable oil
1 pound cabbage, finely shredded
1 (4-ounce) package crumbled blue cheese

• Combine first 8 ingredients in a small bowl; add oil in a slow, steady stream, stirring constantly with a wire whisk until mixture is blended. Cover and chill at least 1 hour.
• Combine cabbage and blue cheese; cover and chill 1 hour.
• Drizzle vinegar mixture over cabbage mixture; toss gently, and serve immediately. Yield: 6 servings.

Janie Baur
Spring, Texas

COMMON SCENTS

· · · · · · · · · · · · · · · · · · · ·

As surely as frosty nights promise wool sweaters and hot chocolate, this time of year entices us to the kitchen. You'll have fun trying these classic favorites that smell as delicious as they taste. The aromas will make it hard to wait till dinner.

BETTER-THAN-POTPOURRI BREW

Although this mixture smells great, it's not for consumption.

6 cups water
Peel from 1 apple
Rind from 1 lemon
Rind from 1 orange
1 (1-inch) piece fresh ginger, peeled and quartered
3 (2-inch) sticks cinnamon
16 whole cloves
1 teaspoon whole allspice
2 teaspoons pickling spice

● **Bring** all ingredients to a boil in a Dutch oven over high heat. Reduce heat, and simmer. Gradually add more water as the liquid evaporates.

Janie Landis
Marietta, Georgia

ORANGE BAKED APPLES WITH COOKIE CRUMBS

6 medium cooking apples (about 2¼ pounds)
¼ cup unsweetened apple juice
1 tablespoon lemon juice
1 (4-inch) stick cinnamon, broken in half
⅓ cup orange marmalade
6 small gingersnaps, crushed

● **Core** apples, starting at stem end, to, but not through, opposite end. Peel top third of each apple.

● **Place** apples in an 11- x 7- x 1½-inch baking dish; add apple juice, lemon juice, and cinnamon stick to baking dish. Cover.
● **Bake** at 350° for 30 minutes. Uncover and spoon marmalade into center of each apple; sprinkle with crushed gingersnaps. Bake 10 minutes or until apples are tender. **Yield:** 6 servings.

Beth Workman
Greensboro, North Carolina

OLD-FASHIONED BREAD PUDDING WITH BOURBON CUSTARD SAUCE

⅓ cup butter or margarine, melted
24 slices dry white bread with crust, cut into ½-inch cubes
¾ cup raisins
½ cup chopped pecans
3 large eggs, lightly beaten
1½ cups sugar
3 cups milk
1 teaspoon ground cinnamon
1 teaspoon apple pie spice
1 teaspoon vanilla extract
Bourbon Custard Sauce

● **Pour** butter into a 13- x 9- x 2-inch baking pan; add bread cubes, and sprinkle with raisins and pecans. Set aside.
● **Combine** eggs and sugar; stir in milk and next 3 ingredients. Pour over bread mixture.
● **Bake** at 350° for 45 minutes or until golden. Let cool completely. Serve with Bourbon Custard Sauce. **Yield:** 15 servings.

Bourbon Custard Sauce

1 cup butter
1½ cups sugar
2 large eggs, lightly beaten
¼ cup bourbon

● **Combine** butter and sugar in a saucepan. Cook over low heat, stirring constantly, 20 minutes.
● **Add** ½ cup of hot mixture gradually to beaten eggs, stirring constantly. Add to remaining hot mixture, stirring constantly. Cook sauce, stirring constantly, until thickened and temperature reaches 160°. Cool; stir in bourbon. **Yield:** 2¼ cups.

Mrs. J. A. Allard
San Antonio, Texas

MAKE SCENTS OF THE SPICE RACK

■ Did you know cinnamon sticks are actually the curled up bark from a tropical evergreen tree? Cinnamon is also ground from the bark. The sticks easily flavor simmering liquids and beverages, while the ground version is best for baked goods.

■ What's the difference between ground and whole spices? Most ground spices are simply powdered versions of their original forms.

Recipes generally specify which form of the spice is preferred. Freshly grated nutmeg has more intense flavor than commercially ground nutmeg. You can grate the whole spice with a nutmeg grater or grinder.

■ Fooled you! Most people think allspice is a blend of cinnamon, nutmeg, and cloves. It's actually a berry from a tropical evergreen, although it tastes like "all spices."

THESE COOKIES TAKE THE CAKE

....

Marie Davis of Charlotte, North Carolina, is quick to divulge the inspiration for her deliciously varied cookies made from cake mixes: "Kids – when they're hungry – you've got to think fast."

Marie, a longtime recipe contributor, has made these and similar varieties for almost 15 years. She began when her daughter, Jacqui, was in grade school and her husband, Jack, was a volunteer football coach who'd bring home hungry players. "A cake mix has everything you need," Marie says. "All you have to do is add whatever you'd like – nuts, chips, fruit – to make your cookies extra special. And," she adds, "it's a great way to have three to four dozen cookies in a half hour."

APRICOT-ALMOND SQUARES

1 (18.25-ounce) package yellow
   cake mix with pudding
½ cup butter or margarine, melted
½ cup finely chopped almonds
1⅓ cups apricot preserves, divided
1 (8-ounce) package cream cheese,
   softened
¼ cup sugar
2 tablespoons all-purpose flour
⅛ teaspoon salt
1 large egg
1 teaspoon vanilla extract
½ cup flaked coconut

• **Combine** cake mix and butter in a large bowl, and beat at low speed with an electric mixer until mixture is crumbly. Stir in almonds. Reserve 1 cup crumb mixture.
• **Press** remaining crumb mixture into a lightly greased 13- x 9- x 2-inch baking pan. Carefully spread 1 cup preserves over crumb mixture, leaving a ¼-inch border.
• **Beat** cream cheese at medium speed with an electric mixer until smooth;

add remaining ⅓ cup preserves, sugar, and next 4 ingredients, beating well. Carefully spread cream cheese mixture over top of preserves.
• **Combine** 1 cup reserved crumb mixture and coconut; sprinkle over cream cheese mixture.
• **Bake** at 350° for 30 minutes or until golden and center is set. Cool completely in pan on a wire rack.
• **Cut** into squares. Cover and store in refrigerator. **Yield:** 3 dozen.

ORANGE CRINKLES

To celebrate Halloween, add pumpkin faces to these bright-orange cookies, using brown decorating frosting and assorted candies.

1 (18.25-ounce) package orange
   cake mix
½ cup vegetable oil
2 large eggs
2 teaspoons grated orange rind

• **Combine** all ingredients, stirring mixture well.
• **Drop** dough by rounded teaspoonfuls 2 inches apart onto ungreased cookie sheets.
• **Bake** at 350° for 12 minutes or until lightly browned. Cool on cookie sheets 1 minute; remove to wire racks to cool completely. **Yield:** 3 dozen.

LEMON CRISPS

1 (18.25-ounce) package lemon
   cake mix with pudding
1 cup crisp rice cereal
½ cup butter or margarine, melted
1 large egg

• **Combine** all ingredients, stirring mixture well.
• **Shape** dough into 1-inch balls; place about 2 inches apart on ungreased cookie sheets.
• **Bake** at 350° for 9 minutes or until edges are golden. Cool on cookie sheets 1 minute; remove to wire racks to cool completely. **Yield:** 4 dozen.

POLKA DOTS

1 (21.2-ounce) package fudge
   brownie mix
½ cup vegetable oil
2 large eggs
1 cup white chocolate morsels or
   vanilla-milk chocolate morsels

• **Combine** first 3 ingredients, stirring well. Stir in morsels.
• **Drop** dough by rounded teaspoonfuls about 2 inches apart onto ungreased cookie sheets.
• **Bake** at 350° for 10 minutes. Cool cookies on cookie sheets 2 minutes; remove to wire racks to cool completely. **Yield:** 4 dozen.

DOUBLE-CHOCOLATE COOKIES

1 (18.25-ounce) package devil's
   food cake mix with pudding
½ cup vegetable oil
2 large eggs
1 cup (6 ounces) semisweet
   chocolate morsels

• **Combine** first 3 ingredients, and beat at medium speed with an electric mixer until blended. Stir in chocolate morsels.
• **Drop** dough by rounded teaspoonfuls about 2 inches apart onto ungreased cookie sheets.
• **Bake** at 350° for 10 minutes. Cool cookies on cookie sheets 5 minutes; remove to wire racks to cool completely. **Yield:** 3 dozen.

SCARE UP A HALLOWEEN PARTY

······················

It's late in the evening when this scare arrives: "Oh, yeah," your daughter says nonchalantly, "I need some Halloween cookies or something for tomorrow's school party. I gotta have 'em in the morning."

Well, you've come to the right place. We've discovered that a dash to your pantry, combined with some no-fuss decorating, will have these Halloween treats put to bed in no time.

FRUITY WITCHES' BREW

12 cups cranberry-raspberry juice drink
4½ cups orange juice
2 cups pineapple juice
2 cups fresh lime juice

• **Combine** all ingredients in a large container; cover and chill.
• **Pour** juice mixture into a punch bowl. Serve over crushed ice. **Yield:** 5 quarts.

Lela Coggins
Brevard, North Carolina

DIVINITY GHOSTS

1 (7.2-ounce) package fluffy white frosting mix
⅓ cup light corn syrup
1 teaspoon vanilla extract
½ cup boiling water
1 (16-ounce) package powdered sugar, sifted
Semisweet chocolate mini-morsels
Semisweet chocolate morsels

• **Combine** first 4 ingredients in a large mixing bowl; beat at high speed with an electric mixer until stiff peaks form. Gradually add powdered sugar, beating at very low speed. (Mixture may be too stiff for some mixers; beat by hand, if necessary.)
• **Spoon** into a decorating bag fitted with a large round tip, or a heavy-duty, zip-top plastic bag. (Snip a tiny hole in one corner of bag.)
• **Pipe** ghost shapes onto wax paper-lined cookie sheets; smooth surface with a wet finger. Press 2 chocolate mini-morsels and 1 chocolate morsel in candy to resemble eyes and a mouth.
• **Let** stand 2 to 3 hours or until candy feels firm. Carefully turn candy over, and let stand 12 hours or until dry. Store in airtight containers. **Yield:** about 5 dozen.

Note: For testing, we used Betty Crocker Fluffy White Frosting mix.

Wade DeNero
Davie, Florida

JACK-O'-LANTERN COOKIES

2 (20-ounce) packages refrigerated sugar cookie dough
1 (16-ounce) container white ready-to-spread frosting
Orange paste food coloring
1 (4¼-ounce) tube green decorating frosting
1 (4¼-ounce) tube brown decorating frosting
Black licorice candy, milk chocolate kisses, assorted Halloween candy

• **Roll** packages of cookie dough to ⅛-inch thickness on a lightly floured surface; cut with pumpkin-shaped cutter dipped in flour. Place cookies on greased cookie sheets.
• **Bake** at 350° for 7 minutes or until lightly browned. Cool on cookie sheets 1 minute; remove cookies to wire racks to cool completely.
• **Combine** white frosting and a small amount of food coloring, stirring until evenly colored; spread over each cookie. Decorate cookies with decorating frostings and candies, as desired. **Yield:** 20 (5-inch) cookies or about 6 dozen (2¾-inch) cookies.

Evelyn Dauphin
Natchez, Mississippi

SPOOKY EYES

You can use commercial cookie dough if you're short on time, but these peanut butter cookies are worth the effort.

¼ cup shortening
¼ cup butter or margarine, softened
½ cup sugar
½ cup firmly packed brown sugar
1 large egg
½ cup creamy peanut butter
¼ teaspoon vanilla extract
1½ cups all-purpose flour
1 teaspoon baking soda
¼ teaspoon salt
4¼-ounce tubes assorted colors decorating frosting
1 (0.75-ounce) tube red writing gel

• **Beat** shortening and butter at medium speed with an electric mixer until fluffy; gradually add sugars, beating well. Add egg, beating well. Stir in peanut butter and vanilla.
• **Combine** flour, baking soda, and salt; add to peanut butter mixture, stirring well. Cover and chill 2 to 3 hours.
• **Roll** dough to ¼-inch thickness on a heavily floured surface; cut with a 2½-inch eye-shaped cutter or sharp knife. Place on lightly greased cookie sheets.
• **Bake** at 350° for 10 to 12 minutes; remove to wire racks to cool.
• **Decorate** with assorted decorating frostings and writing gel, as desired. **Yield:** 2 dozen.

Carrie Treichel
Johnson City, Tennessee

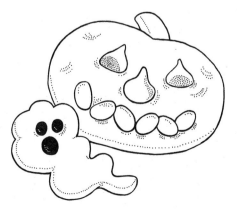

SWAMP STICKS

Here's a healthy, fun-to-eat alternative to sweet Halloween treats.

1 (2-pound) package carrots, scraped
1 (15½-ounce) container creamy vegetable dip
4 drops of green liquid food coloring

• **Cut** carrots lengthwise into thin strips. Gather carrot strips into a bundle; secure with a rubber band. Set bundle aside.
• **Combine** vegetable dip and food coloring, stirring well; spoon onto plate. Place carrot strip bundle upright in middle of plate. Tie raffia around bundle to conceal rubber band. **Yield:** 18 appetizer servings.

MONSTER MOUTHS

Monster Mouths will make your kids smile.

5 medium-size Red Delicious apples
¼ cup orange juice
1 cup creamy peanut butter
1 (10½-ounce) package miniature marshmallows

• **Core** and cut each apple into 14 (¼-inch) wedges. Brush each wedge with orange juice, and spread 1 side of each wedge evenly with peanut butter.
• **Press** 4 marshmallows into peanut butter on half of wedges; top with remaining wedges, peanut butter side down. **Yield:** 35 servings.

Shellie Smith
Oklahoma City, Oklahoma

FROM OUR KITCHEN TO YOURS

Try these kitchen time-savers that will help you with everything from spills to cooking up culinary thrills – fast.

SMART TARTS

You might love to eat cute little tarts at parties, but you probably hate to make them. Lining the miniature muffin pans with ready-made piecrust is easy; spooning the filling into each hole without dripping it all over the pan is not. Neither is scrubbing off the baked-on goop later.

Try this. Mix the filling in a large measuring cup or spouted bowl, and pour the filling instead of spooning it. Wipe the spout occasionally with a paper towel. If your filling has pecans or chocolate chips, don't stir them in and hope they pour out evenly. Instead, hold chunky ingredients out of the mixture. Place them in the pastry with your fingers; then pour the liquid filling over them.

A WELCOME OIL SLICK

The next time you bake muffins or stir together a salad dressing that calls for both oil and honey or corn syrup, try this clever tip from reader Fay Brewer of Atlanta. If you measure the oil first and then measure the honey or corn syrup in the same oily spoon or cup, you'll be surprised at how easily the sticky ingredient slides out.

SOUPER SAVERS

Can't toss out even the smallest amount of leftovers? Then team with the master of disguise – the blender – and you're on your way to a nice bowl of soup. Pull a can or two of chicken broth from your pantry, blend with one or more of your fridge finds, and sprinkle in some dried herbs or spices. Add a little lemon or lime juice for bright flavor or cream for richness; then heat and eat.

GRILL SKILL

Love grilled vegetables, but tired of seeing them fall through the rack to a fiery death? Good news: Discover the grill wok. This open-faced tray has dime-size holes that let smoky flavor through and keep the vegetables in. You can close the grill lid and even stir.

Look for grill woks or grill toppers in the housewares section of stores. Or order one from Chef's Catalog at 1-800-338-3232. A large grill topper (item number 3564) and a round grill topper (item number 4239) are available for $14.99 each. A grill combo set with a wok and topper (item number 3824) is available for $19.99. (Shipping is not included.)

NOVEMBER

GRAB A CUP AND A CONVERSATION

Chatting over coffee is back in style, and cafes and shops across the country keep pots brewing from sunup to long after sundown. Now, with our easy version, you can enjoy a coffee bar at home. Choose from our instant coffee mixes or use your favorite. And enjoy our coffee-loaded desserts.

COFFEE BLENDS

Make-ahead tip: Quickly stir together these blends, and store in airtight containers at room temperature for several months. The directions for all of them are the same, so that's where we start.

● **Combine** all ingredients for each blend in container of an electric blender; process until smooth, stopping once to scrape down sides, if necessary. For each serving, spoon 2 tablespoons coffee blend of your choice into an 8-ounce cup of boiling water.

Vienna Blend

½ cup instant coffee granules
⅔ cup sugar
⅔ cup powdered nondairy coffee creamer
½ teaspoon ground cinnamon

● **Yield:** 1⅔ cups.

Orange Blend

½ cup instant coffee granules
¾ cup sugar
1 cup powdered nondairy coffee creamer
½ teaspoon dried orange peel

● **Yield:** 2 cups.

Mocha Blend

½ cup instant coffee granules
¾ cup sugar
1 cup powdered nondairy coffee creamer
2 tablespoons cocoa

● **Yield:** 2 cups.

*Michelle Ettenger
Alpharetta, Georgia*

COFFEE NAPOLEONS

Make-ahead tip: Bake pastry, and store in an airtight container for a day or two. Make filling and chocolate sauce the day before, and chill. Assemble just before serving.

1 (3.4-ounce) package chocolate pudding and pie filling mix (not instant)
1 cup milk
2 teaspoons instant coffee granules
1 (8-ounce) package cream cheese, cut into pieces and softened
½ cup whipping cream, whipped
1 (17¼-ounce) package frozen puff pastry sheets, thawed
¼ cup whipping cream
2 teaspoons instant coffee granules
6 (1-ounce) squares semisweet chocolate, chopped
1 tablespoon powdered sugar

● **Combine** pudding mix and milk in a saucepan, stirring well; stir in 2 teaspoons coffee granules. Bring to a boil over medium heat, stirring constantly; remove from heat. Stir in cream cheese; cool completely.
● **Fold** whipped cream into pudding mixture; cover and chill.
● **Unfold** 1 pastry sheet on a lightly floured baking sheet. Roll into a 12-inch square. Cut into 2 (12- x 6-inch) rectangles. Cut each rectangle into 6 (6- x 2-inch) strips. Prick each strip several times with a fork. Place another baking sheet directly on pastry strips (to prevent overpuffing).
● **Bake** at 425° for 10 minutes. Remove top baking sheet; bake 5 additional minutes or until golden. Cool on wire racks. Repeat with remaining pastry.
● **Combine** ¼ cup whipping cream, 2 teaspoons coffee granules, and chocolate in a heavy saucepan; cook over low heat, stirring constantly, until chocolate melts. Cool slightly; spoon into a heavy-duty, zip-top plastic bag, and snip a tiny hole in one corner of bag. Drizzle over 12 pastry strips.
● **Pipe** or spoon filling evenly on remaining 12 pastry strips; top with chocolate-drizzled strips. Sprinkle with powdered sugar, and serve immediately. **Yield:** 12 servings.

CHOCOLATE CHIFFON CAKE WITH COFFEE BUTTERCREAM

Make-ahead tip: Bake and freeze the cake layers up to three months ahead. Assemble a few hours before serving.

6 (1-ounce) squares bittersweet
    chocolate, chopped
¾ cup water
1 cup butter, softened
2 cups sugar
4 large eggs
2 teaspoons vanilla extract
2½ cups sifted cake flour
2 teaspoons baking soda
⅛ teaspoon salt
1½ cups sour cream
Coffee Buttercream
Chocolate-covered coffee beans

● **Combine** chocolate and water in a heavy saucepan; cook over low heat, stirring constantly, until melted.
● **Beat** butter at medium speed with an electric mixer until creamy; gradually add sugar, beating well. Add eggs, one at a time, beating after each addition. Add chocolate mixture and vanilla; beat 1 minute or just until combined.
● **Combine** flour, soda, and salt; add to chocolate mixture alternately with sour cream, beginning and ending with flour mixture. Mix at low speed just until blended after each addition. Pour batter into 3 greased and floured 9-inch round cakepans.
● **Bake** at 350° for 25 to 30 minutes or until a wooden pick inserted in center comes out clean. Cool in pans on wire racks 10 minutes; remove from pans, and cool completely on wire racks.
● **Spread** Coffee Buttercream between layers and on top and sides of cake. Arrange coffee beans on top of cake. **Yield:** 1 (3-layer) cake.

Coffee Buttercream

3 tablespoons water
4 to 5 tablespoons instant coffee
    granules
1 cup butter, softened
6 cups sifted powdered sugar

● **Combine** water and coffee granules, stirring until coffee dissolves.

● **Beat** butter at medium speed with an electric mixer; gradually add sugar and coffee mixture, beating until blended. **Yield:** 2½ cups.

Susan Curtin
Birmingham, Alabama

DIPPED CHOCOLATE-ALMOND SPOONS

4 (1-ounce) squares semisweet or
    sweet dark chocolate,
    chopped
1½ tablespoons whipping
    cream
⅛ teaspoon almond extract
20 stainless, silver, or disposable
    plastic spoons *
2 (2-ounce) squares vanilla-
    flavored candy coating,
    melted

● **Combine** semisweet or sweet dark chocolate and whipping cream in a 1-cup liquid measuring cup. Microwave at MEDIUM (50% power) 1 minute or until chocolate melts, stirring after 30 seconds. Stir in almond extract.
● **Dip** each spoon in melted chocolate, covering bowl of spoon and ¼ inch up handle; allow excess to drip off. Place spoons on wax paper-lined baking sheet; freeze 15 minutes or until set.
● **Place** candy coating in a heavy-duty, zip-top plastic bag. Microwave at MEDIUM (50% power) 1 minute to melt. Snip a tiny hole in one corner of bag, and drizzle coating over chilled spoons. Leave on wax paper, and store in refrigerator until serving. **Yield:** 20 spoons.

* Substitute long cinnamon sticks for spoons.

MIDNIGHT DELIGHTS

Make-ahead tip: Bake and freeze up to three months. Dollop with whipped cream mixture before serving.

⅔ cup boiling water
2 teaspoons instant coffee granules
1¾ cups all-purpose flour
⅓ cup cocoa
¼ cup sugar
Dash of salt
¾ cup butter, cut into small pieces
2 cups (12 ounces) semisweet chocolate morsels, melted
⅔ cup sugar
2 tablespoons butter, melted
2 tablespoons milk
2 teaspoons coffee-flavored liqueur or strong brewed coffee
2 large eggs
½ cup chopped pecans or walnuts
½ cup whipping cream
1 tablespoon powdered sugar

• **Combine** water and coffee granules, stirring well; let cool. Reserve 2 teaspoons.
• **Combine** flour and next 3 ingredients; cut in butter with pastry blender (or 2 knives) until crumbly. Sprinkle remaining coffee mixture, 1 tablespoon at a time, evenly over flour mixture, and stir with a fork until dry ingredients are moistened.
• **Turn** dough out onto a lightly floured surface, and knead 2 or 3 times. Wrap in wax paper, and chill at least 1 hour.
• **Shape** dough into ¾-inch balls; press into lightly greased miniature (1¾-inch) muffin pans, using a tart tamper or back of a spoon. Cover and chill slightly.
• **Combine** melted chocolate and next 4 ingredients, stirring until smooth; stir in eggs and chopped pecans. Spoon 1 rounded teaspoonful of mixture into each tart shell.
• **Bake** at 350° for 20 minutes. Cool in pans on wire racks 15 minutes; remove from pans, and cool completely on wire racks.
• **Combine** reserved 2 teaspoons coffee mixture, whipping cream, and powdered sugar; beat at medium speed with an electric mixer until soft peaks form. Pipe or dollop a small amount onto each tart just before serving. **Yield:** 4 dozen.

Yetta J. Burrell
Valdosta, Georgia

COFFEE NUGGETS

Make-ahead tip: Bake and freeze cookies up to three months in advance, or store in an airtight container at room temperature a couple of days before serving.

2 tablespoons instant coffee granules
1 cup butter or margarine, softened
⅓ cup sifted powdered sugar
2 teaspoons vanilla extract
2 cups all-purpose flour
1 cup finely chopped pecans
Sifted powdered sugar

• **Crush** coffee granules into a fine powder, using a mortar and pestle or back of a spoon; set coffee powder aside.
• **Beat** butter at medium speed with an electric mixer until creamy; gradually add ⅓ cup powdered sugar, beating well. Add coffee powder, vanilla, flour, and pecans, mixing until blended. Cover and chill at least 1 hour.
• **Shape** dough into 1-inch balls; place on ungreased cookie sheets.
• **Bake** at 350° for 12 minutes or until lightly browned. Transfer to wire racks; cool 10 minutes. Roll in powdered sugar; cool completely on wire racks. Roll in powdered sugar again, if desired. **Yield:** 3½ dozen.

Katharine Reinke
Baltimore, Maryland

BREWING BASICS

If you prefer fresh brewed coffee, follow these guidelines for a perfect cup every time.

■ Remove any residual coffee oils by cleaning and rinsing your coffeemaker with hot water before each use.

■ Start coffee with fresh, cold water. Water high in minerals or chlorine or treated with chemical softeners won't make as flavorful coffee. Use bottled water if you don't like the way your water tastes.

■ When possible, buy coffee beans and grind them just before use.

(Grinders for home kitchens are available at department stores, and gourmet coffee and kitchen shops.) Store the beans in an airtight container in the refrigerator for two to three weeks, or in the freezer for two to three months.

■ Grind the beans (either at home or in the grocery store's grinder) as directed for your coffeemaker. If the grind is too coarse or too fine you won't get the best flavor.

■ Use about two level tablespoons (one standard coffee measure) for each six ounces of water. Adjust the amount of coffee to your taste.

HOLIDAY DINNERS.

COMPANY'S COOKING

When Liz Lorber of Atlanta throws a party for 12, she'd rather run a three-ring circus than cook.

And that's just what she does. She plans a menu, types the recipes, buys groceries, does some

preliminary chopping, prepares an appetizer, sets up a bar, creates several workstations in her kitchen,

gives a mini cooking lesson – and then lets her *guests* do the cooking.

MENU FOR A WHITE-APRON AFFAIR
Serves 12

White Bean Spread   Assorted Vegetables and Crackers
Seafood Risotto
Winter Salad
Assorted Bakery Breads
Pears With Orange-Caramel Sauce   Fennel Ice Cream

"As long as you're organized, anyone can do this," Liz says. "Just a word of caution though – don't assign yourself to a task. Your job will be to pinpoint potential disasters and to fix them before they go too wrong."

Guests don't have to be experts, as you'll see from reading the quotes before each recipe. It's certain there will be a few mishaps, but this is a party for friends, not gourmets.

Use Liz's menu or one of your own. But be sure to read her Secrets to Success on page 280 before you start. She's a seasoned professional at *not* cooking.

WHITE BEAN SPREAD

"If you don't like garlic – leave now." – Liz Lorber

2 (2-ounce) cans anchovies, drained and chopped
9 cloves garlic, minced
⅓ cup chopped fresh rosemary
2 tablespoons olive oil
4 (15-ounce) cans cannellini beans, drained *
⅓ cup lemon juice
¾ teaspoon salt
¾ teaspoon ground white pepper
1 teaspoon olive oil (optional)

• **Cook** first 3 ingredients in 2 tablespoons olive oil in a small skillet over medium heat 2 to 3 minutes, stirring constantly. Remove from heat; set aside.

• **Position** knife blade in food processor bowl; add beans. Process until smooth, stopping once to scrape down sides. Add anchovy mixture, lemon juice, salt, and pepper; process until smooth.

• **Spoon** into a serving bowl; brush top with 1 teaspoon olive oil, if desired, and swirl bean mixture with a knife. Serve with fresh vegetables and crackers. **Yield:** 4 cups.

* Substitute 4 (15-ounce) cans Great Northern beans, drained.

Note: Recipe halves easily.

SEAFOOD RISOTTO

(pictured on page 293)

"There's no squid for the risotto."
– Denise Cauthen

"Henry! Run down to the freezer in the basement." – Liz Lorber

1 pound unpeeled medium-size
   fresh shrimp
½ pound fresh sea scallops
1 pound fresh squid *
1 pound fresh unshelled mussels
1 pound fresh unshelled clams
6 cloves garlic, minced
¼ cup olive oil
½ cup dry white wine
¼ cup lemon juice
4 sprigs fresh thyme, finely
   chopped
4 sprigs fresh oregano, finely
   chopped
Risotto
Lettuce leaves
2½ tablespoons Gremolata
½ teaspoon finely ground sea salt
½ teaspoon freshly ground
   pepper

• **Peel** shrimp, and devein, if desired; set aside. Cut sea scallops in half crosswise; set aside.
• **Rinse** squid under cold water. Cut into ½-inch slices, and set aside.
• **Remove** "beards" from mussels. Scrub mussels and clams with a brush to remove grit; set aside.
• **Cook** garlic in olive oil in a large skillet over medium heat 2 to 3 minutes, stirring constantly. Add shrimp and scallops; cook, stirring constantly, 2 to 3 minutes or just until shrimp turn pink. Remove shrimp and scallops with a slotted spoon; set aside.
• **Cook** squid in skillet over medium heat 2 to 3 minutes, stirring constantly; remove with a slotted spoon, and set aside.
• **Add** mussels, clams, wine, and next 3 ingredients to skillet. Bring to a boil over high heat. Cover and cook, shaking pan frequently, 3 to 5 minutes or until shells open. Remove and discard unopened shells.

• **Add** shrimp, scallops, and squid. Cook over medium heat until thoroughly heated.
• **Remove** seafood with a slotted spoon, reserving liquid. Stir liquid into cooked Risotto. Place Risotto on a lettuce-lined serving plate, and top with seafood mixture. Sprinkle with 2½ tablespoons Gremolata, salt, and pepper; serve immediately. **Yield:** 12 servings.

* Substitute 1 pound sea scallops or shrimp.

Risotto

⅓ cup olive oil
¼ cup butter or margarine
1 large onion, chopped
4 cups Arborio rice (short grain),
   uncooked
1 cup dry white wine
2 pounds Roma tomatoes,
   peeled, seeded, and
   chopped
8 cups chicken broth, heated
2½ tablespoons Gremolata

• **Heat** olive oil and butter in a Dutch oven over medium heat. Add onion; cook 2 to 3 minutes, stirring constantly. Add rice, stirring to coat well. Stir in wine, and cook until wine is absorbed. Stir in tomato; cook 2 minutes, stirring constantly. Reduce heat to medium-low.
• **Add** about 1 cup hot chicken broth; cook, stirring constantly, until liquid is absorbed. Repeat procedure, using remaining chicken broth, 1 cup at a time allowing liquid to be absorbed after each addition, stirring constantly. (This process will take about an hour.)
• **Stir** Gremolata into rice mixture. **Yield:** 12 servings.

Gremolata

6 cloves garlic, minced
½ cup finely chopped fresh
   flat-leaf parsley
¼ cup grated lemon rind

• **Combine** all ingredients in a small bowl. **Yield:** ⅓ cup.

WINTER SALAD

"Oops. There's not enough salad dressing for these greens." – Linda Gunshor

"Oh, let's just add some oil and vinegar to what we've got." – Liz Lorber

2 heads fresh fennel
12 cups mixed salad greens
2 heads radicchio, torn into
   bite-size pieces
Balsamic Dressing
Lettuce leaves

• **Rinse** fennel thoroughly. Trim and discard bulb bases. Trim stalks from the bulb; discard hard outside stalks and leaves. Cut bulbs lengthwise into ⅛-inch slices; set aside.
• **Combine** salad greens and radicchio; drizzle with Balsamic Dressing, and toss gently. Spoon onto a lettuce-lined serving plate. Top with sliced fennel. Serve immediately. **Yield:** 12 servings.

SECRETS TO SUCCESS

■ Be sure to plan a simple menu.

■ Include enough guests to make an interesting evening, but not enough to crowd your kitchen.

■ Decide how many people will be assigned to prepare each recipe. When dividing up, make sure guests don't cook with the person they came with.

■ Allow 30 minutes before the cooking begins to let the guests get acquainted.

Balsamic Dressing

¾ cup olive oil
¼ cup balsamic vinegar
1 shallot, finely chopped
¼ teaspoon salt
¼ teaspoon freshly ground
   pepper

● **Combine** all ingredients in a jar. Close tightly, and shake vigorously. **Yield:** 1 cup.

PEARS WITH ORANGE-CARAMEL SAUCE

"This sauce looks curdled. Is this stuff going to work?" – Bette Cromwell

"Here, Mother – stir with a whisk." – Liz Lorber

10 medium-size ripe pears
¾ cup orange juice, divided
1½ cups unsalted butter
1 cup sugar
¼ cup water
2 tablespoons grated orange
   rind
2 tablespoons pear liqueur *
Fennel Ice Cream

● **Peel** and core pears; cut each into 6 wedges. Place in a large bowl; drizzle with ¼ cup orange juice, and toss gently to coat. Set aside.
● **Melt** butter in a large heavy skillet over medium heat. Add sugar, and cook, stirring constantly, until sugar dissolves. Add pear wedges, and cook about 10 minutes or until syrup thickens and pear wedges are tender, stirring mixture often. (Do not overcook pear mixture.)
● **Remove** pear wedges with a slotted spoon; set aside. Continue cooking 10 minutes or until mixture is a light caramel color, stirring often. (Mixture will look curdled.)
● **Add** ¼ cup water, remaining ½ cup orange juice, orange rind, and liqueur, stirring with a wire whisk until mixture is smooth.

● **Return** pear wedges to skillet, and cook 1 minute or until thoroughly heated. Serve immediately with Fennel Ice Cream. **Yield:** 12 to 14 servings.

* For testing, we used Poire William pear liqueur.

FENNEL ICE CREAM

"What's that burning smell?"
– Stephen Boyd

"Nothing." (It was the ice cream.) – Jeff Gunshor

2½ cups whipping cream
2 cups milk
¾ cup sugar
2 tablespoons fennel seeds
8 egg yolks

● **Combine** first 4 ingredients in a heavy saucepan; bring mixture to a boil over medium-high heat, stirring occasionally. Reduce heat, and simmer 5 minutes.
● **Beat** egg yolks with a wire whisk until thick and pale. Gradually stir about one-fourth of hot mixture into yolks; add to remaining hot mixture, stirring constantly.
● **Pour** hot mixture through a wire-mesh strainer into a bowl, discarding fennel seeds. Cool slightly; place plastic wrap directly on surface of mixture. Chill until mixture is completely cooled.
● **Pour** mixture into freezer container of a 1-gallon hand-turned or electric freezer. Freeze according to manufacturer's instructions.
● **Pack** freezer with additional ice and rock salt, and let stand 1 hour before serving. **Yield:** 6 cups.

Note: To make ahead, store ice cream in an airtight container in freezer. Let stand at room temperature 10 minutes before serving.

BREAKFAST MADE BEAUTIFUL

....

For holiday breakfast gatherings large or small, fried eggs, bacon, and buttered toast just won't cut it. That's everyday stuff. But our recipes make your morning meal out-of-the-ordinary.

HASH BROWN BAKE
(pictured on page 257)

3 cups frozen shredded potatoes
⅓ cup butter or margarine, melted
1 cup finely chopped cooked ham
1 cup (4 ounces) shredded
   Cheddar cheese
¼ cup finely chopped green pepper
2 large eggs, beaten
½ cup milk
½ teaspoon salt
¼ teaspoon pepper

● **Thaw** potato between layers of paper towels to remove excess moisture. Press potato into bottom and up sides of an ungreased 9-inch pieplate; drizzle with butter.
● **Bake** at 425° for 25 minutes or until lightly browned; cool on a wire rack 10 minutes.
● **Combine** ham, cheese, and green pepper; spoon into potato shell. Combine eggs and next 3 ingredients, stirring well; pour over ham mixture.
● **Bake** at 350° for 25 to 30 minutes or until set; let stand 10 minutes before serving. **Yield:** 6 to 8 servings.

Note: Hash Brown Bake may be assembled, omitting egg mixture, and stored in refrigerator 8 hours. Let stand at room temperature 30 minutes. Combine eggs, milk, salt, and pepper; pour over ham mixture. Bake at 350° for 25 to 30 minutes.

Bernadette Colvin
Houston, Texas

CHRISTMAS MORNING STRATA

1 pound ground pork sausage
2 teaspoons prepared mustard
6 slices white sandwich bread, crusts removed
2 cups (8 ounces) shredded Swiss cheese
1½ cups milk
3 large eggs, lightly beaten
½ teaspoon Worcestershire sauce
⅛ teaspoon salt
⅛ teaspoon pepper
⅛ teaspoon ground nutmeg

• **Brown** sausage in a skillet over medium heat, stirring until it crumbles; drain well. Stir in mustard.
• **Fit** bread into a greased 11- x 7- x 1½-inch baking dish; top with sausage mixture and cheese.
• **Combine** milk and next 5 ingredients; pour over bread mixture. Cover and chill 8 hours.
• **Bake,** uncovered, at 350° for 50 minutes or until set. **Yield:** 6 servings.

Karen Belle
Lovettsville, Virginia

MACADAMIA NUT FRENCH TOAST

4 large eggs, lightly beaten
¼ cup sugar
¼ teaspoon ground nutmeg
⅔ cup orange juice
⅓ cup milk
½ teaspoon vanilla extract
1 (16-ounce) loaf Italian bread, cut into 1-inch slices
⅔ cup butter or margarine, melted
½ cup macadamia nuts, chopped and toasted
Garnishes: powdered sugar, ground nutmeg

• **Combine** first 6 ingredients in a bowl, stirring well.
• **Fit** bread slices in a single layer into a lightly greased 13- x 9- x 2-inch baking dish. Pour egg mixture over bread slices; cover and chill at least 8 hours, turning bread once.

• **Pour** butter in a 15- x 10- x 1-inch jellyroll pan; place bread slices in a single layer in pan.
• **Bake** at 400° for 10 minutes; sprinkle with nuts. Bake 10 additional minutes. Garnish, if desired. Serve immediately with maple syrup. **Yield:** 6 servings.

Michelle Ettenger
Alpharetta, Georgia

GINGERBREAD PANCAKES

1½ cups all-purpose flour
1½ tablespoons baking powder
1½ teaspoons cocoa
½ teaspoon ground ginger
½ teaspoon ground cloves
½ teaspoon ground cinnamon
2½ tablespoons ground pecans or hazelnuts
3 egg whites, lightly beaten
1½ cups skim milk
2½ tablespoons molasses
2½ teaspoons vegetable oil

• **Combine** first 7 ingredients in a medium bowl; make a well in center of mixture.
• **Combine** egg whites and next 3 ingredients; add to dry ingredients, stirring just until moistened.
• **Spoon** about 2 tablespoons batter for each pancake onto a moderately hot, lightly greased griddle. Cook pancakes until tops are covered with bubbles and edges look cooked; turn and cook other side.
• **Top** with assorted chopped fruit, and serve with maple syrup or honey, if desired. **Yield:** 18 (3-inch) pancakes.

Martin L. Walker
Lynchburg, Virginia

PUMPKIN WAFFLES

2¼ cups all-purpose flour
¼ cup firmly packed brown sugar
4 teaspoons baking powder
1½ teaspoons ground cinnamon
1 teaspoon ground allspice
½ teaspoon salt
½ teaspoon ground ginger
4 large eggs, separated
2 cups milk
1 cup mashed cooked pumpkin
¼ cup butter or margarine, melted

• **Combine** first 7 ingredients in a large bowl. Combine egg yolks, milk, and pumpkin; add to flour mixture, stirring just until moistened. Stir in melted butter. Set waffle batter aside.
• **Beat** egg whites at high speed with an electric mixer until soft peaks form; gently fold into batter.
• **Bake** in a preheated, oiled waffle iron until crisp. Serve with butter, maple syrup, and toasted pecans. **Yield:** 24 (4-inch) waffles.

Virginia Tompkins
Lubbock, Texas

CHRISTMAS MORNING GAME PLAN

If you're like most people, the last thing you want to do on Christmas morning is cook. So . . .

■ Set the table the night before.

■ The pancakes, waffles and scones from this story will taste freshest if made Christmas morning, but you can get a head start. Measure dry ingredients the night before.

■ Make Hash Brown Bake, Christmas Morning Strata, or Macadamia Nut French Toast the night before; chill. Bake it Christmas morning.

CRANBERRY SCONES

"A pretty basket filled with tea and Cranberry Scones makes a great gift during the holidays. My friends find it so nice to have something other than sweets to eat on rushed mornings." – Mary Bonney

2½ cups all-purpose flour
½ cup sugar
2 teaspoons baking powder
½ teaspoon salt
½ teaspoon ground cloves
¼ cup butter or margarine
1 cup whipping cream
¾ cup fresh or frozen cranberries, coarsely chopped

● **Combine** first 5 ingredients; cut in butter with pastry blender until mixture is crumbly.
● **Reserve** 1 tablespoon whipping cream; add remaining whipping cream and cranberries to flour mixture, stirring just until moistened.
● **Turn** dough out onto a lightly floured surface; knead 5 or 6 times. Shape into an 8-inch circle. Cut into 8 wedges, and place on a lightly greased baking sheet. Prick wedges with a fork 3 or 4 times, and brush with reserved 1 tablespoon whipping cream.
● **Bake** at 425° for 18 minutes or until lightly browned. Serve warm with whipped cream, if desired. **Yield:** 8 servings.

Mary Bonney
Sterling, Virginia

GREAT BEGINNINGS

....

Finger foods, appetizers, or pickups – whatever you call them, we all agree: They're delicious beginnings (and even full meals) at holiday get-togethers. So why not follow our suggested menu and throw an appetizer party to celebrate the season? Some recipes yield more servings than others, but all are suited to doubling or dividing.

APPETIZER MENU
Serves 12 to 15

Red Wine-Marinated Flank Steak
Commercial Biscuits
Ham-Pineapple Nibbles
Caraway-Cheese Crisps
Spinach-Artichoke-Tomato Puffs
Creamy Dried Tomato Hummus
Assorted Vegetables and Crackers

RED WINE-MARINATED FLANK STEAK

"I've had this Red Wine-Marinated Flank Steak recipe for so long – I think it actually came from my mother. I serve it probably twice a month, either in biscuits for a party or sliced as a main dish for the family." – Mildred Bickley

1 cup reduced-calorie Italian salad dressing
⅔ cup soy sauce
⅔ cup dry red wine
1 lemon, thinly sliced
⅓ cup sliced green onions
1 teaspoon dry mustard
¼ teaspoon lemon-pepper seasoning
2 cloves garlic, minced
2 (1½-pound) flank steaks

● **Combine** first 8 ingredients in a large shallow dish or heavy-duty zip-top plastic bag; add steaks, turning to coat. Cover dish, or seal bag; chill 8 to 12 hours, turning steaks occasionally.
● **Remove** steaks from marinade, discarding marinade. Place on a lightly greased rack in a broiler pan.
● **Broil** 3 inches from heat (with electric oven door partially opened) 7 to 10 minutes on each side or to desired degree of doneness. Thinly slice steaks diagonally across grain; serve with biscuits and coarse-grained Dijon mustard. **Yield:** 24 appetizer servings.

Mildred Bickley
Bristol, Virginia

HAM-PINEAPPLE NIBBLES

1 large egg, lightly beaten
1 (8¼-ounce) can crushed pineapple, drained
¼ cup soft breadcrumbs
2 green onions, sliced
¼ teaspoon rubbed sage
1½ cups ground cooked ham
½ cup (2 ounces) shredded mozzarella cheese
3 (8-ounce) cans refrigerated crescent rolls

● **Combine** first 7 ingredients in a large bowl; set aside.
● **Separate** each package of rolls into 4 rectangles, pressing perforations to seal. Roll each rectangle into an 8- x 4-inch rectangle; cut each crosswise into thirds.
● **Place** about 1 tablespoon ham mixture in center of each third of dough. Fold dough over ham mixture, pressing edges to seal; crimp with a fork. Place on ungreased baking sheets.
● **Bake** at 375° for 10 minutes or until golden. **Yield:** 3 dozen.

Ellie Wells
Lakeland, Florida

CARAWAY-CHEESE CRISPS

1 cup butter or margarine,
   softened
2 cups (8 ounces) shredded sharp
   Cheddar cheese
2 cups all-purpose flour
1 teaspoon ground red pepper
¼ teaspoon salt
1 cup finely chopped pecans
2 teaspoons caraway seeds

• **Beat** butter at medium speed with an electric mixer; gradually add cheese, beating well.
• **Combine** flour, red pepper, and salt; gradually add to cheese mixture, mixing after each addition. Add pecans and caraway seeds, mixing until thoroughly blended.
• **Shape** dough into ¾-inch balls. Place on ungreased baking sheets; flatten each dough ball with a fork dipped in flour.
• **Bake** at 350° for 15 minutes or until lightly browned around edges. Remove to wire racks to cool. Store in an airtight container. **Yield:** 5 dozen.

Note: Caraway-Cheese Crisps may be frozen up to three months in an airtight container. Thaw at room temperature just before serving.

Betty Joyce Mills
Birmingham, Alabama

SPINACH-ARTICHOKE-TOMATO PUFFS

1 (10-ounce) package frozen
   chopped spinach, thawed
1 (14-ounce) can artichoke hearts,
   drained
1 (8-ounce) jar marinated dried
   tomatoes, drained
1 (3-ounce) package goat cheese
¼ teaspoon salt
¼ teaspoon pepper
1½ (17¼-ounce) packages frozen
   puff pastry, thawed

• **Drain** spinach well, pressing between layers of paper towels.

• **Position** knife blade in food processor bowl; add spinach, artichoke hearts, and tomato. Pulse 5 times or until mixture is chopped, stopping often to scrape down sides. Add goat cheese, salt, and pepper; process until blended. Set spinach mixture aside.
• **Roll** 1 pastry sheet into a 15- x 12-inch rectangle on a surface sprinkled lightly with cornmeal. Cut into 3-inch squares.
• **Spoon** about 1 tablespoon spinach mixture in center of each square. Fold all corners toward center, slightly overlapping edges.
• **Grease** baking sheets, and sprinkle with cornmeal. Place filled pastries on prepared baking sheets. Repeat procedure with remaining puff pastry and spinach mixture.
• **Bake** at 400° for 12 to 15 minutes. Serve immediately. **Yield:** 5 dozen.

Jim Napolitano
Nashville, Tennessee

CREAMY DRIED TOMATO HUMMUS

1 (15-ounce) can chick-peas,
   rinsed and drained
1 cup oil-packed dried tomatoes,
   drained
1 clove garlic, chopped
½ cup mayonnaise or salad
   dressing
¼ cup freshly grated Parmesan
   cheese
2 tablespoons lemon juice
¼ teaspoon dried basil
⅛ teaspoon ground red pepper
Garnish: chopped dried tomatoes

• **Position** knife blade in food processor bowl; add first 8 ingredients. Process until smooth, stopping once to scrape down sides. Garnish, if desired. Serve with fresh vegetables and crackers. **Yield:** 2 cups.

Note: Chick-peas are also called garbanzo beans. Find them in the Mexican foods section at your grocery store.

Krista Becker
Nashville, Tennessee

TRY LAMB THIS SEASON

....

Most like the chance to make our mark as great cooks, so test your talents with lamb this holiday season.

HAZELNUT-CRUSTED RACK OF LAMB WITH CHERRY-WINE SAUCE
(pictured on page 295)

"I have always enjoyed lamb at restaurants, so I decided to give rack of lamb a try. Happily, assembling the recipe was easy. When the delicious aroma wafted through the kitchen, I felt great about my choice. We now have a new Christmas tradition." – Lynda Maksin

2 (8-rib) lamb rib roasts (2¾ to 3
   pounds each), trimmed
3 to 4 tablespoons coarse-grained
   Dijon mustard
⅓ cup fine, dry breadcrumbs
⅓ cup finely chopped hazelnuts
¼ cup finely chopped fresh
   parsley
1 teaspoon dried thyme
½ teaspoon freshly ground pepper
¼ teaspoon salt
Cherry-Wine Sauce

• **Place** lamb roasts in a roasting pan, fat side out and ribs crisscrossed. Spread mustard over roasts. Combine breadcrumbs and next 5 ingredients; pat over roasts. Insert meat thermometer into thickest portion of lamb, making sure it does not touch fat or bone.
• **Bake** at 400° for 10 minutes. Shield exposed bones with strips of aluminum foil to prevent excessive browning. Reduce heat to 375°; bake 30 additional minutes or until meat thermometer registers 145°. Remove from oven, cover loosely with foil, and let stand 5

minutes or until meat thermometer registers 150° (medium-rare). Serve with Cherry-Wine Sauce. **Yield:** 5 to 8 servings.

Cherry-Wine Sauce

⅔ cup dry red wine
⅓ cup beef broth
3 tablespoons honey
½ teaspoon dried thyme
¼ teaspoon salt
¼ teaspoon dry mustard
2 teaspoons cornstarch
2 tablespoons balsamic vinegar
1 (16½-ounce) can pitted dark cherries, drained

● **Combine** first 6 ingredients in a heavy saucepan; bring to a boil. Boil 5 minutes.
● **Combine** cornstarch and vinegar, stirring well; add to wine mixture. Bring to a boil over medium-high heat; boil 1 minute. Stir in cherries. **Yield:** 1½ cups.

Lynda Maksin
Farmington, Missouri

TEMPERATURE TALK

The American Lamb Council recommends using a meat thermometer when cooking large cuts of lamb. For an accurate reading, insert a meat thermometer into the thickest portion before roasting, taking care not to touch bone or fat.

Remove the lamb from the oven when it registers 5 degrees lower than the desired degree of doneness. Allow it to stand in a warm place 10 minutes. During this time, the internal temperature will rise. For medium-rare lamb cook it to 145° and let the roast stand until it reaches 150° before serving.

LEG OF LAMB

1 teaspoon salt
1 teaspoon dried mint flakes
½ teaspoon ground red pepper
1 (9-pound) leg of lamb
2 medium onions, chopped
3 cups dry white wine
½ cup olive oil
½ cup Dijon mustard
3 cloves garlic, chopped
2 tablespoons Worcestershire sauce

● **Combine** first 3 ingredients; sprinkle over lamb. Place chopped onion in center of a roasting pan; place lamb on top of onion.
● **Combine** wine and next 4 ingredients; pour mixture over lamb. Insert meat thermometer into thickest portion of lamb, making sure it does not touch fat or bone.
● **Bake** at 325° for 1 hour and 45 minutes or until meat thermometer registers 160°, basting lamb every 30 minutes. Let stand 10 minutes. **Yield:** 10 servings.

Marilyn Mertz
San Angelo, Texas

DIJON-ROSEMARY LAMB CHOPS

¼ cup Dijon mustard
8 lamb chops (4 pounds)
1 tablespoon dried rosemary, crushed
All-purpose flour
2 tablespoons olive oil
1 cup dry white wine, divided
½ cup whipping cream
Salt and pepper

● **Spread** mustard over lamb chops; sprinkle evenly with rosemary. Dredge chops in flour, shaking off excess flour.
● **Pour** oil in a large skillet; place over medium-high heat until hot. Add chops, and cook until browned, turning once. Reduce heat to medium; cover and cook 10 minutes.

● **Turn** chops over, and add ¼ cup dry white wine. Cook 10 additional minutes or to desired degree of doneness. Remove from skillet, and keep warm.
● **Add** remaining ¾ cup wine to pan drippings, stirring to loosen browned particles that cling to bottom.
● **Cook** 10 minutes or until liquid is reduced to about 1 cup, stirring occasionally. Add whipping cream; simmer 2 minutes. Season with salt and pepper to taste. Serve sauce with lamb chops. **Yield:** 4 servings.

Chef J. R. Contway
Bentwood Country Club
San Angelo, Texas

ROLLED LAMB ROAST

1 clove garlic, sliced
1 tablespoon chopped fresh parsley
1 teaspoon salt
½ teaspoon pepper
½ teaspoon chopped fresh thyme
1 (5-pound) lamb shoulder, boned
3 tablespoons olive oil
2 tomatoes, chopped
2 onions, chopped
1 green pepper, chopped
2 bay leaves
½ cup Madeira wine
8 small turnips, peeled

● **Combine** first 5 ingredients; sprinkle over lamb. Top with half of chopped vegetables. Roll roast, starting at the shortest end; tie securely.
● **Pour** oil in a large Dutch oven; place over medium-high heat until hot. Brown lamb in oil about 20 minutes. Add tomato, onion, and green pepper; stir in bay leaves, wine, and turnips.
● **Cover** and bake at 325° for 2 hours and 15 minutes or until tender. Remove and discard bay leaves. **Yield:** 10 servings.

Irma Seidensticker
Comfort, Texas

WINE AND DINE

....

With all the fanfare Beaujolais Nouveau (boh-zhoh-LAY NEW-voh) gets when it's released every year on the third Thursday in November, you'd think it was a fine vintage wine. It's not. This inexpensive, fruity red wine produced in the Beaujolais region of France reaches peak flavor in November and December, and should be enjoyed by Easter.

Don't spend a lot of time thinking about what to serve it *with* or what to serve it *in*. Beaujolais Nouveau is a smooth, go-with-anything wine you can savor in a water glass or a goblet. Just chill it 20 minutes before serving.

NOUVEAU MENU
Serves Four

Parmesan-Coated Brie
Crackers or French Bread
Mediterranean Shrimp and Pasta
Butter Pecan Mousse

PARMESAN-COATED BRIE

1 large egg, lightly beaten
1 tablespoon water
½ cup Italian-seasoned breadcrumbs
¼ cup freshly grated Parmesan cheese
1 (15-ounce) mini Brie with herbs
¼ cup vegetable oil
Garnish: fresh rosemary sprigs

• **Combine** egg and water in a shallow dish; set aside.
• **Combine** breadcrumbs and Parmesan cheese in a shallow dish; set aside.
• **Dip** Brie into egg mixture, turning to coat all sides. Place Brie in breadcrumb mixture, turning to coat. Repeat procedure.

• **Chill** at least 1 hour.
• **Cook** Brie in hot oil in a heavy skillet over medium heat 2 minutes on each side or until golden. Garnish, if desired. Serve with crackers or French bread. **Yield:** 4 to 6 servings.

Sue-Sue Hartstern
Louisville, Kentucky

MEDITERRANEAN SHRIMP AND PASTA

1 pound unpeeled medium-size fresh shrimp
8 ounces linguine, uncooked
5 green onions, sliced
3 cloves garlic, minced
2 tablespoons olive oil
1 (12-ounce) jar marinated artichoke hearts, undrained
6 Roma tomatoes, chopped
1 cup sliced mushrooms
¼ cup dry white wine
2 teaspoons dried Italian seasoning
¼ teaspoon dried rosemary, crushed
¼ teaspoon salt
¼ teaspoon pepper
Freshly grated Parmesan cheese

• **Peel** shrimp, and devein, if desired; set aside.
• **Cook** linguine according to package directions; drain and keep warm.
• **Cook** green onions and garlic in oil in a large skillet over medium-high heat, stirring constantly, until tender. Stir in artichokes and next 7 ingredients.
• **Bring** to a boil; reduce heat, and simmer 5 minutes.
• **Add** shrimp; cook 3 minutes or until shrimp turn pink, stirring occasionally. Serve over pasta, and sprinkle with cheese. **Yield:** 4 servings.

Amanda Broome Jarvis
Durham, North Carolina

BUTTER PECAN MOUSSE

¾ cup pecan pieces
1 tablespoon butter or margarine, melted
2 (8-ounce) packages cream cheese, softened
¼ cup sugar
¼ cup firmly packed brown sugar
½ teaspoon vanilla extract
1 cup whipping cream, whipped
Garnish: toasted pecan pieces

• **Combine** pecans and butter, stirring well; spread on a baking sheet.
• **Bake** at 350° for 5 minutes or until toasted; cool. Finely chop, and set aside.
• **Beat** cream cheese at medium speed with an electric mixer until smooth. Add sugars and vanilla, beating well. Stir in ¾ cup toasted pecans.
• **Gently** fold whipped cream into pecan mixture; spoon or pipe into serving dishes. Garnish, if desired. **Yield:** 4 to 6 servings.

Gay McClelland
Atlanta, Georgia

TEN YEARS LATER, TEN TIMES EASIER

....

What were we thinking 10 years ago when one of our *Holiday Dinners* menus featured *13* recipes? The turkey entrée took at least four hours to make and the menu suggested four vegetables and three desserts.

A lot of us have come to our senses in the last decade (though we're always happy to dine with those die-hard traditionalists who revel in preparing a dozen or more dishes). Here our updated menu focuses on ease and enjoyment for both the cook and the guests.

HOLIDAY DINNERS

DINNER OF THE DECADE
Serves Eight

Lemonade-Bourbon Punch
Gazpacho-Stuffed Endive
Apricot-Mushroom Stuffed
Pork Chops
Green Beans With
Caramelized Onions
Roasted Garlic Mashed Potatoes
Apple Dumplings With
Maple-Cider Sauce

LEMONADE-BOURBON PUNCH

*"Punch is just part of the holidays
for me. Served in a big cut-glass bowl,
it can be part of your centerpiece
for the buffet table. I make two batches
and leave the bourbon out of one
so the children can have their own
festive drink." – Molly Ellis*

2 (6-ounce) cans frozen lemonade
    concentrate, thawed and
    undiluted
1¾ cups orange juice, chilled
¾ cup lemon juice, chilled
1 (2-liter) bottle lemon-lime
    carbonated beverage,
    chilled
1 quart club soda, chilled
1 pint bourbon, chilled

• **Combine** first 3 ingredients in a
punch bowl, stirring well. Slowly add
lemon-lime beverage and remaining ingredients, stirring well. Serve punch
over ice, if desired. **Yield:** 18 cups.
Molly Ellis
Clarksville, Tennessee

GAZPACHO-STUFFED ENDIVE

6 green onions, sliced
2 cloves garlic, minced
2 tablespoons capers
⅓ cup olive oil
2 tablespoons white wine vinegar
½ teaspoon salt
½ teaspoon freshly ground pepper
1⅓ pounds plum tomatoes
1 cucumber, peeled and seeded
½ sweet red pepper
½ avocado, peeled and seeded
¼ cup fresh basil leaves
2 ounces mozzarella cheese
4 to 5 heads Belgian endive

• **Combine** first 7 ingredients in a large
bowl. Finely chop tomatoes and next 4
ingredients; add to green onion mixture. Cut cheese into small cubes; add
to vegetable mixture. Cover and chill at
least 2 hours.
• **Separate** endive into leaves; spoon
vegetable mixture into leaves, using a
slotted spoon. **Yield:** 8 servings.

APRICOT-MUSHROOM STUFFED
PORK CHOPS

*Ask your butcher to cut pockets
in the pork chops – it's one less thing
you'll have to worry about.*

4 tablespoons butter or margarine,
    divided
1 (8-ounce) package sliced fresh
    mushrooms
⅓ cup chopped onion
⅓ cup chopped celery
1 cup soft breadcrumbs
½ cup dried apricot halves,
    chopped
½ cup chopped fresh parsley
½ teaspoon rubbed sage
8 (1-inch-thick) center-cut pork
    loin chops, cut with pockets
2 teaspoons salt
1 teaspoon freshly ground
    pepper
1 cup dry white wine
1½ tablespoons cornstarch
2 tablespoons water

• **Melt** 2 tablespoons butter in a large
skillet over medium-high heat; add
mushrooms, onion, and celery, and
cook, stirring constantly, 5 minutes or
until tender. Stir in breadcrumbs and
next 3 ingredients; remove from heat.
• **Sprinkle** both sides and pocket of
each pork chop with salt and pepper.
Spoon vegetable mixture evenly into
pockets, and secure with wooden picks.
• **Melt** remaining 2 tablespoons butter
in skillet; add chops, and cook until
browned, turning once. Place chops in
a lightly greased roasting pan or large
shallow baking dish; add white wine.
• **Cover** and bake at 350° for 45 minutes or until done. Remove chops from
pan, and discard wooden picks; keep
chops warm.
• **Remove** and discard fat from pan
drippings; place 1½ cups drippings in a
small saucepan.
• **Combine** cornstarch and water, stirring until smooth; stir into reserved
drippings.
• **Cook** over medium heat, stirring
constantly, until mixture thickens and
boils. Boil 1 minute, stirring constantly.
Remove from heat; serve with chops.
Yield: 8 servings.
Margret Stewart
Murfreesboro, Tennessee

FACE-LIFT FOR THE NINETIES

■ Guests won't miss the turkey
when they taste upscale
Apricot-Mushroom Stuffed
Pork Chops.

■ Dress up plain mashed potatoes
with roasted garlic, and ordinary
green beans with caramelized pearl
onions.

■ Apple Dumplings With Maple-
Cider Sauce offer more flair than
the apple strudel we included in
our menu 10 years ago.

GREEN BEANS WITH CARAMELIZED ONIONS

2 pounds fresh green beans *
1 pound pearl onions
¼ cup butter or margarine
¼ cup firmly packed brown sugar

• **Arrange** beans in a steamer basket over boiling water. Cover and steam 15 minutes; set aside.
• **Place** onions in boiling water 3 minutes; drain and rinse with cold water. Cut off root end of each onion, and peel onions.
• **Arrange** onions in steamer basket over boiling water. Cover and steam 5 minutes; set onions aside.
• **Melt** butter in a large heavy skillet over medium heat; add sugar, and cook, stirring constantly, until bubbly. Add onions; cook 3 minutes, stirring constantly. Add beans; cook, stirring constantly, until thoroughly heated. **Yield:** 8 servings.

* Substitute 2 pounds fresh brussels sprouts.

Sue P. Wilson
Etowah, North Carolina

ROASTED GARLIC MASHED POTATOES

4 heads garlic
1 tablespoon olive oil
4 pounds baking potatoes, peeled and cut into 1-inch pieces
½ cup butter or margarine
1 cup milk
1½ teaspoons salt
½ teaspoon pepper

• **Place** garlic on a square of aluminum foil; drizzle with oil, and wrap in foil.
• **Bake** at 425° for 30 minutes; remove from oven, and set aside.
• **Cook** potato in boiling water to cover 15 to 20 minutes or until tender; drain and transfer to a mixing bowl. Add butter and next 3 ingredients; beat at medium speed with an electric mixer until fluffy (do not overbeat).

• **Cut** off pointed ends of garlic; squeeze pulp from garlic cloves, and stir into mashed potato mixture. **Yield:** 8 servings.

Adelyne Smith
Dunnville, Kentucky

APPLE DUMPLINGS WITH MAPLE-CIDER SAUCE
(pictured on page 300)

3 cups all-purpose flour
1 teaspoon salt
¾ cup butter or margarine, chilled and cut into pieces
5 tablespoons shortening
½ cup apple cider, chilled
8 large Granny Smith apples
½ cup firmly packed brown sugar
½ cup currants
½ cup chopped walnuts
⅓ cup butter or margarine, softened
1 large egg
1 tablespoon water
4 (3-inch) sticks cinnamon, broken in half
Maple-Cider Sauce

• **Combine** flour and salt; cut in butter and shortening with pastry blender until mixture is crumbly. Sprinkle cider, 1 tablespoon at a time, evenly over surface; stir with a fork until dry ingredients are moistened. Shape into 2 (½-inch-thick) squares; cover and chill.
• **Core** each apple, leaving ½ inch intact on bottom. Peel top two-thirds of each apple; set apples aside.
• **Combine** sugar, currants, and walnuts; stir in softened butter, blending well. Spoon evenly into each apple.
• **Roll** pastry squares to ⅛-inch thickness on a floured surface; cut each square into 4 (7-inch) squares.
• **Press** 1 pastry square around each apple; remove excess pastry from bottom so apple will sit level. Reroll pastry scraps, if desired, and cut into leaf shapes.
• **Combine** egg and water, beating lightly with a fork. Brush over apples, and attach leaf shapes, if desired.

• **Place** a cinnamon stick half in top of each apple to resemble a stem. Place apples in a lightly greased 15- x 10- x 1-inch jellyroll pan.
• **Bake** at 375° for 40 minutes. Pour Maple-Cider Sauce over apples; bake 15 additional minutes or until apples are tender. Place apples on a serving plate; spoon sauce around apples. **Yield:** 8 servings.

Note: Serve maple whipped cream with the apples. To make it, combine 1 cup whipping cream and 3 tablespoons maple syrup in a medium bowl, and beat at high speed with an electric mixer until soft peaks form.

Maple-Cider Sauce

2 teaspoons cornstarch
1½ cups apple cider
⅔ cup maple syrup
¼ cup firmly packed brown sugar
¼ cup fresh lemon juice

• **Combine** cornstarch and cider in a saucepan, stirring until smooth; add maple syrup and remaining ingredients. Bring to a boil over medium-high heat; boil 1 minute. **Yield:** 2 cups.

Mildred Bickley
Bristol, Virginia

DRESSED FOR SUCCESS

Stuffing versus dressing: There *is* a difference: Stuffing is what's baked inside the bird or roast; dressing is what's baked alongside it.

These delicately seasoned bread and rice dishes passed down through generations are dear to our holiday tables. You'll find a variety of recipes to serve as dressings (in casseroles) or stuffings (yields given in cup measures).

APPLE-WALNUT STUFFING
(pictured on page 294)

⅓ cup butter or margarine
1 large onion, finely chopped
2 stalks celery, finely chopped
1 cup chopped red cooking apple
1 cup chopped green cooking
   apple
2 cups white bread cubes, toasted
1 cup chopped walnuts
2 tablespoons dried whole-leaf
   sage
½ teaspoon dried rosemary
½ teaspoon dried thyme
1 large egg, beaten
½ cup milk
½ teaspoon salt
¼ teaspoon pepper

● **Melt** butter in a small skillet over medium-high heat; add onion and celery, and cook, stirring constantly, until tender.
● **Combine** apple, bread cubes, and next 4 ingredients in a large bowl; stir in vegetable mixture, egg, and remaining ingredients. Spoon mixture into a lightly greased 11- x 7- x 1½-inch baking dish.
● **Bake** at 350° for 30 minutes. **Yield:** 6 servings (4½ cups).

Crown Pork Roast With Apple-Walnut Stuffing: (Pictured on page 294) Purchase a well-trimmed (12-rib) crown pork roast (about 7 pounds), and season it with salt and pepper. Fold a piece of aluminum foil into an 8-inch square; place on rack in roasting pan. Place roast, bone ends up, on foil-lined rack. Bake at 325° for 1 hour. Cut a piece of foil long enough to fit around ribs. Wrap foil around ribs, and fold over tips of ribs. Spoon Apple-Walnut Stuffing into center of roast, and cover with additional foil. Insert a meat thermometer into roast without touching fat or bone. Bake at 325° for 1½ hours or until meat thermometer registers 160°. Remove foil from roast, and let stand 15 minutes before serving. **Yield:** 12 servings.

Susie Smith
Springville, Alabama

CREOLE DRESSING

"This Creole Dressing recipe was handed down to my sisters and me from our mother, who was from New Orleans. Every time we make it, we think of our family and home. It's nice that the tradition carries on." – Glenda LaRocca

1 (16-ounce) container chicken
   livers, drained
1 (10-ounce) container fresh
   oysters, undrained
½ (16-ounce) loaf day-old French
   bread, crumbled
½ cup butter or margarine
2 bunches green onions, chopped
2 large onions, chopped
4 cloves garlic, minced
5 stalks celery, chopped
1 cup chopped fresh parsley
½ pound ground beef, cooked
   and drained
½ pound ground pork, cooked
   and drained
1 teaspoon rubbed sage
1 teaspoon ground thyme
½ teaspoon pepper
2 tablespoons Creole seasoning

● **Chop** chicken livers, and cook in boiling water until tender. Drain and set aside.
● **Drain** oysters, reserving liquid; coarsely chop oysters. Pour reserved liquid over bread; set aside.
● **Melt** butter in a large skillet over medium-high heat; add green onions and next 4 ingredients, and cook, stirring constantly, until vegetables are tender. Add chopped chicken livers, oysters, bread mixture, beef, and remaining ingredients; reduce heat, and simmer about 15 minutes. Spoon into a 13- x 9- x 2-inch baking dish.
● **Bake** at 350° for 30 minutes or until thoroughly heated. **Yield:** 10 servings (10 cups).

Glenda LaRocca
Houston, Texas

SAUSAGE-CORNBREAD DRESSING

1 pound ground pork sausage
2 medium onions, chopped
4 stalks celery, chopped
6 cups crumbled cornbread
3 cups white bread cubes, toasted
2 teaspoons rubbed sage
¼ teaspoon salt (optional)
1 teaspoon pepper
4 cups turkey broth
2 large eggs, lightly beaten

● **Combine** sausage, onion, and celery in a large skillet; cook over medium heat, stirring until sausage crumbles. Drain well.
● **Combine** cornbread and next 4 ingredients in a large bowl; stir in sausage mixture. Add broth and eggs, stirring well. Spoon into a lightly greased 13- x 9- x 2-inch baking dish.
● **Bake** at 350° for 45 minutes or until browned. **Yield:** 10 to 12 servings (9 cups).

Marjorie Henson
Benton, Kentucky

STUFFING TIPS:
TO YOUR HEALTH

■ Loosely stuff turkey just before roasting. Harmful bacteria can multiply in the stuffing and cause food poisoning, even when the stuffed bird is refrigerated a short time.

■ Count on ½ cup stuffing per pound for turkeys up to 10 pounds; if heavier, use ¾ cup per pound.

■ More questions? Call the Butterball Turkey Talk-Line at 1-800-323-4848 (holiday season only); Reynolds Company's Turkey Information Line at 1-800-745-4000; or USDA Meat and Poultry Hotline at 1-800-535-4555.

RICE STUFFING

1½ cups long-grain rice, uncooked
2½ cups chopped onion
1½ cups chopped green onion tops
1½ cups chopped celery and leaves
½ cup chopped sweet red pepper
¼ cup bacon drippings
1 teaspoon seasoned salt
1 teaspoon celery seeds
½ teaspoon salt
½ teaspoon pepper
1 tablespoon Worcestershire sauce
¼ cup chopped fresh parsley

● **Cook** rice according to package directions; set aside.
● **Cook** onion, green onion tops, celery, and red pepper in bacon drippings in a large skillet over medium-high heat, stirring constantly, until mixture is tender. Stir in seasoned salt and next 4 ingredients.
● **Combine** rice, vegetable mixture, and parsley in a serving bowl, tossing gently to combine; serve immediately, or use for stuffing. **Yield:** 8 to 10 servings (8½ cups).

Freddie Lee Gee
Natchez, Mississippi

SQUASH DRESSING

2 (6-ounce) packages Mexican
    cornbread mix
2 pounds yellow squash, sliced
2 cups water
½ cup butter or margarine
1 cup chopped onion
1 cup chopped celery
½ cup chopped green pepper
½ cup sliced green onions
1 (10¾-ounce) can cream of
    chicken soup, undiluted
2 cups milk
½ teaspoon salt
¼ teaspoon pepper

● **Bake** cornbread according to package directions; cool on a wire rack. Crumble and set aside.
● **Combine** squash and water in a large saucepan, and bring to a boil. Cover,

reduce heat, and simmer 8 minutes or until squash is tender; drain and set aside.
● **Melt** butter in a large heavy skillet over medium-high heat; add onion and next 3 ingredients, and cook, stirring constantly, until tender.
● **Combine** cornbread, squash, onion mixture, soup, and remaining ingredients; spoon into a lightly greased 11- x 7- x 1½-inch baking dish.
● **Bake** at 350° for 40 minutes or until thoroughly heated. **Yield:** 8 to 10 servings (10 cups).

Anita James
Natchitoches, Louisiana

SWEET ON SWEET POTATOES

....

Rich and rustic sweet potatoes are almost delectable enough to qualify as an underground fruit.

These marquise-shaped roots sweeten in repose. Buy them fresh up to one month before using, and store them in a dark, cool, dry place.

George Washington Carver is said to have created 500 recipes using the sweet potato. If he were at our holiday table, we'd love to serve him a few new dishes to add to his list.

SWEET POTATO BUTTER

1 large sweet potato
1 teaspoon grated orange
    rind
⅔ cup orange juice
½ teaspoon ground cinnamon
¼ teaspoon ground nutmeg
2 tablespoons white vinegar

● **Pierce** sweet potato several times with a fork; place on a microwave-safe plate.

● **Microwave** at HIGH 6 minutes or until tender; cool to touch. Peel sweet potato, and mash.
● **Combine** sweet potato, orange rind, and remaining ingredients in a large microwave-safe bowl.
● **Microwave,** uncovered, at HIGH 10 minutes, stirring at 3-minute intervals. **Yield:** 1¼ cups.

Pat Worthy
Boaz, Alabama

STACKED SWEET POTATO BLUES

4 (3-ounce) packages cream cheese,
    softened
1 (4-ounce) package crumbled
    blue cheese
3 large sweet potatoes
¼ cup butter or margarine
1 tablespoon olive oil

● **Beat** cheeses at medium speed with an electric mixer 1 minute; set aside.
● **Peel** sweet potatoes, and cut into 18 (½-inch-thick) slices; cover with plastic wrap, and set aside.
● **Cut** remaining potato pieces into ⅛-inch-thick slices; cut into very thin strips, using a vegetable peeler.
● **Combine** butter and oil in a large nonstick skillet; place over medium-high heat until hot. Add potato strips, and cook 3 to 5 minutes or until crisp; remove strips with slotted spoon, and drain on paper towels.
● **Add** sweet potato slices to skillet; cook over low heat 15 minutes or until tender, turning once.
● **Place** a sweet potato slice on an individual serving plate; pipe or dollop about 1 tablespoon cheese mixture on slice. Repeat layers twice, ending with cheese mixture. Sprinkle with sweet potato strips. Repeat procedure with remaining potato slices, cheese mixture, and potato strips.
● **Serve** with mixed green salad or baby green beans, if desired. **Yield:** 6 servings.

SWEET POTATO-EGGNOG CASSEROLE

"I like to be creative in the kitchen – open the refrigerator door and improvise with what's there. One Thanksgiving, I found a little eggnog on the shelf and added it to my sweet potatoes. I've been making them that way ever since. Sometimes experimenting brings great surprises. I've seldom put together anything that was inedible." – Mary G. Swift

5 pounds large sweet potatoes
½ cup golden raisins
¼ cup brandy
⅔ cup refrigerated eggnog
3 tablespoons butter or margarine, melted
2 tablespoons sugar
⅛ teaspoon salt
Oatmeal Cookie Topping

• **Cook** sweet potatoes in water to cover in a large Dutch oven 40 minutes or until tender; drain and cool to touch. Peel sweet potatoes, and mash.
• **Combine** raisins and brandy; let stand 30 minutes. Drain.
• **Combine** mashed sweet potato, eggnog, and next 3 ingredients; reserve 2 cups sweet potato mixture. Stir raisins into remaining sweet potato mixture, and spoon into a lightly greased 2-quart baking dish. Sprinkle top with Oatmeal Cookie Topping.
• **Pipe** or dollop reserved 2 cups sweet potato mixture around edge of casserole. Bake at 350° for 20 minutes or until thoroughly heated. **Yield:** 6 to 8 servings.

Oatmeal Cookie Topping

2 (2-inch) oatmeal cookies, crumbled
2 tablespoons dark brown sugar
2 tablespoons chopped pecans, toasted

• **Combine** ingredients in a small bowl. **Yield:** ½ cup.

Mary G. Swift
New Orleans, Louisiana

SWEET POTATO PEAKS

2 cups mashed cooked sweet potato, cooled
3 tablespoons butter or margarine, softened
⅓ cup crushed corn flakes cereal
⅔ cup sugar
½ teaspoon ground cinnamon
1 cup finely chopped pecans
1 (15¼-ounce) can unsweetened sliced pineapple, drained
2 tablespoons butter or margarine
2 tablespoons honey
1 teaspoon water

• **Combine** first 5 ingredients, stirring until blended; shape into 8 cones. Coat cones with pecans; cover and chill at least 4 hours.
• **Arrange** pineapple slices in a single layer in a lightly greased 11- x 7- x 1½-inch baking dish; place cones upright on pineapple rings. Set aside.
• **Combine** 2 tablespoons butter, honey, and water in a small saucepan; bring to a boil over medium heat, stirring constantly. Cook 1½ to 2 minutes, or until thickened, stirring often; set honey mixture aside.
• **Bake** sweet potato cones, uncovered, at 350° for 30 minutes, spooning honey mixture over sweet potato cones during last 10 minutes of baking. **Yield:** 8 servings.

Gwen Louer
Roswell, Georgia

SWEET POTATO FLAN
(pictured on page 298)

2 medium sweet potatoes (1¾ pounds) *
¾ cup sugar
2 (14-ounce) cans sweetened condensed milk
2 cups milk
10 large eggs
1 teaspoon ground cinnamon
½ teaspoon ground allspice
¼ teaspoon ground cloves
1 teaspoon vanilla extract
Garnish: toasted coconut

• **Pierce** sweet potatoes several times with a fork; place on a baking sheet.
• **Bake** at 375° for 1 hour or until done; cool to touch. Peel sweet potatoes, and mash. Set aside 1 cup sweet potato; reserve any remaining sweet potato for another use.
• **Sprinkle** sugar in a 10-inch round cakepan; place over medium heat and cook, shaking pan constantly, until sugar melts and turns a light golden brown. Remove from heat; set aside. (Mixture may crack slightly as it cools.)
• **Combine** ½ cup sweet potato, 1 can sweetened condensed milk, and half of next 6 ingredients in container of an electric blender; process until smooth, stopping once to scrape down sides. Pour mixture into a large bowl.
• **Repeat** procedure; add to bowl, stirring well with a wire whisk.
• **Pour** mixture over caramelized sugar in cakepan; cover with aluminum foil, and place cakepan in a larger shallow pan. Add hot water to larger pan to depth of ½ inch.
• **Bake** at 325° for 1 hour and 15 minutes or until a knife inserted in center comes out clean. Remove pan from water, and uncover; cool on a wire rack 30 minutes.
• **Cover** and chill at least 8 hours.
• **Run** a knife around edge of flan to loosen; invert onto a serving plate, and garnish, if desired. **Yield:** 1 (10-inch) flan.

* Substitute 1 cup canned mashed sweet potatoes.

W. N. Cottrell
New Orleans, Louisiana

ON A ROLL

....

You'll earn the title "Master Roll Baker" with these delicious recipes. From traditional to timesaving, these rolls are perfect for even the novice cook. The aroma of these rolls baking will quickly summon hungry diners.

BUTTER CRESCENT ROLLS

"I've been baking these rolls for six years, and they're perfect for any occasion. My children like them smaller, so I make them in two sizes."
– Marlene Compston

2 packages active dry yeast
¾ cup warm water (105° to 115°)
½ cup sugar
½ cup butter, melted
2 large eggs, lightly beaten
1½ teaspoons salt
4 cups all-purpose flour, divided
¼ cup butter, softened

• **Combine** yeast and warm water in a 2-cup liquid measuring cup; let stand 5 minutes.
• **Combine** yeast mixture, sugar, and next 3 ingredients in a large bowl; add 2 cups flour, stirring well. Gradually stir in remaining flour to make a soft dough.
• **Turn** dough out onto a well-floured surface, and knead 3 or 4 times. Place in a well-greased bowl, turning to grease top.
• **Cover** and let rise in a warm place (85°), free from drafts, 1 hour or until doubled in bulk.
• **Punch** dough down, and divide into thirds; shape each portion into a ball. Roll each ball into a 12-inch circle on a lightly floured surface; spread with softened butter. Cut each circle into 12 wedges. Roll up each wedge, starting with wide end; place rolls, point side down, on greased baking sheets.
• **Cover** and let rise in a warm place (85°), free from drafts, 20 minutes or until doubled in bulk.
• **Bake** at 375° for 12 minutes or until golden. Brush the rolls with additional melted butter, if desired. **Yield:** 3 dozen.

Marlene Compston
Owasso, Oklahoma

ONION-AND-SESAME ROLLS

Start with convenience products and whip these up in under 30 minutes.

1½ tablespoons grated Parmesan cheese
1 tablespoon instant minced onion
½ teaspoon garlic powder
1 (8-ounce) can refrigerated crescent rolls
2 tablespoons Italian salad dressing
1 tablespoon sesame seeds

• **Combine** first 3 ingredients; set cheese mixture aside.
• **Unroll** crescent rolls, and separate into two rectangles; press perforations to seal. Sprinkle cheese mixture over rectangles, leaving a ½-inch border. Roll up each rectangle, jellyroll fashion, starting with short side; pinch seams to seal. Cut each roll into 5 (1-inch-thick) slices, and place on an ungreased baking sheet. Brush rolls with salad dressing, and sprinkle with sesame seeds.
• **Bake** at 375° for 15 minutes or until lightly browned; serve immediately. **Yield:** 10 rolls.

Kira F. Giffin
Houston, Texas

ROLL-SHAPING TECHNIQUES

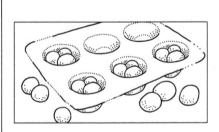

Cloverleaf Rolls: Lightly grease muffin pans. Shape dough into 1-inch balls; place 3 dough balls in each muffin cup. Cover and let rise until doubled in bulk. Bake as directed.

S Rolls: Divide dough in several small portions. Roll each portion into a 9-inch rope about ¾ to 1 inch thick. Place on greased baking sheets; curl ends in opposite directions, forming an S shape. Cover and let rise until doubled in bulk. Bake as directed.

Bow Ties: Roll dough into several long ropes about ½ inch in diameter. Cut ropes into 8-inch strips. Carefully tie each dough strip into a knot. Place bow ties on a lightly greased baking sheet. Cover and let rise until doubled in bulk. Bake as directed.

A bountiful spread of Seafood Risotto (recipe, page 280), bakery breads, and fresh fruit, makes feeding your holiday guests simple.

Above: *Savor the flavors of autumn with succulently tender Hazelnut-Crusted Rack of Lamb With Cherry-Wine Sauce (recipe, page 284).*

Far left: *Dressed for the holidays, Crown Pork Roast With Apple-Walnut Stuffing (recipe, page 289) garnished with kale and apple slices, would make an elegant centerpiece for any buffet.*

Left: *An old-time family favorite, Holiday Cranberry Salad (recipe, page 301) is chock-full of cranberries, celery, and walnuts.*

Nannie's Cornbread Dressing, gravy, Roast Turkey With Herbs, and Brandied Cranberries are essential dishes for a traditional Thanksgiving meal. (Recipes begin on page 305.)

Above: *Enjoy some down-home cooking with Turnip Greens, Aunt Glennie's Pear Relish, Peach Ketchup, and your favorite baked country ham. (Recipes begin on page 305.)*

Right: *Move the sweet potato from side dish to center stage with Sweet Potato Flan (recipe, page 291), a dessert that's sure to be the star of any meal.*

Add traditional holiday flavor to your table by creating a Pastry Cornucopia from commercial puff pastry – it's easier to assemble than it appears. Filled with hearty Make-Ahead Yeast Rolls stuffed with ham, it's sure to be a hit (recipes, page 307).

Bourbon-soaked raisins, sweet apples, and toasted pecans peek through a crown of piecrust holly leaves, making Apple-Bourbon Pie (recipe, page 302) a scrumptious holiday treasure. Inset: *Cinnamon sticks make clever stems for Apple Dumplings With Maple-Cider Sauce (recipe, page 288), a special dish your guests will wish for year after year.*

HOLIDAY GREENERY

······················

Salads can be a beautiful tumble of textures, flavors, and colors. For a mouth-watering salad course, combine crunch with something soft, accent tangy ingredients with sweet ones, and *never* overdress.

Toasted nuts and chunks of cheese add depth, while crisp greens and lively dressings yield a palate-pleasing product with real eye appeal.

GREENS AND GRAPEFRUIT SALAD

8 cups torn mixed salad
    greens
2 heads radicchio, separated
    into leaves
2 heads Belgian endive, separated
    into leaves
1 medium-size purple onion,
    thinly sliced (optional)
2 tablespoons chopped fresh
    basil
2 pink grapefruit, peeled and
    sectioned
Dijon Vinaigrette
¼ cup pine nuts, toasted

• **Combine** first 6 ingredients in a large bowl; drizzle with ¾ cup Dijon Vinaigrette. Sprinkle with pine nuts. Serve with remaining vinaigrette. **Yield:** 10 servings.

Dijon Vinaigrette

½ cup red wine vinegar
¼ cup Dijon mustard
2 tablespoons sugar (optional)
2 tablespoons lime juice
¼ teaspoon salt
¼ teaspoon freshly ground
    pepper
¾ cup olive oil

• **Combine** first 6 ingredients in container of an electric blender; process until smooth, stopping once to scrape down sides. Add oil in a slow, steady stream with blender running. **Yield:** 1½ cups.

Barbara Sherrer
Bay City, Texas

MIXED GREENS WITH PARMESAN WALNUTS

"Experiment with flavors when you make salad by using lots of different greens. Wild watercress has become one of my favorite salad ingredients."
– Rublelene Singleton

2 tablespoons butter or
    margarine
¼ teaspoon hickory salt
1½ cups chopped walnuts
3 tablespoons freshly grated
    Parmesan cheese
1 medium head iceberg lettuce,
    torn
1 medium head leaf lettuce,
    torn
½ bunch curly endive, torn
½ bunch watercress, torn
½ pound fresh spinach, torn
½ cup vinegar-and-oil salad
    dressing

• **Combine** butter and salt in a 8-inch square pan.
• **Bake** at 350° for 2 to 3 minutes or until butter melts. Stir in walnuts, and bake 5 minutes. Sprinkle with cheese, tossing to coat; bake 4 to 5 minutes or until cheese is lightly browned. Cool completely.
• **Combine** iceberg lettuce and next 5 ingredients; toss gently to coat. Top mixture with walnuts, and serve. **Yield:** 12 servings.

Rublelene Singleton
Scotts Hill, Tennessee

CRANBERRY OPTIONS

······················

Cranberries turn simple, everyday food into festive holiday meals, so why not accent your celebrations in new ways with these versatile red berries?

HOLIDAY CRANBERRY SALAD
(pictured on page 295)

2 cups fresh or frozen cranberries,
    thawed
1 cup sugar
1 (3-ounce) package lemon-
    flavored gelatin
1 cup boiling water
1 cup chopped celery
1 cup chopped walnuts,
    toasted
Lettuce leaves
Garnishes: lemon slices, celery
    leaves, cranberries

• **Position** knife blade in food processor bowl; add cranberries. Process 30 seconds or until chopped.
• **Combine** cranberries and sugar in a large bowl; let stand 1 hour or until sugar dissolves.
• **Combine** gelatin and boiling water in a large bowl; stir 2 minutes or until gelatin dissolves. Chill until the consistency of unbeaten egg white.
• **Stir** cranberry mixture, celery, and walnuts into gelatin mixture. Pour into a lightly oiled 4-cup mold. Cover and chill until firm.
• **Unmold** salad onto a lettuce-lined plate. Garnish, if desired. **Yield:** 6 to 8 servings.

Sunny Tiedemann
Bartlesville, Oklahoma

FROZEN CRANBERRY RELISH

Susan Stamberg discovered that her mother-in-law's old "family" recipe, Mama Stamberg's Frozen Cranberry Relish, was really a creation of foods writer Craig Claiborne. "I'm delighted to share the recipe for Mama Stamberg's Frozen Cranberry Relish – the relish that sounds terrible, but tastes terrific." – Susan Stamberg

2 cups fresh cranberries
1 small onion, cut into fourths
½ cup sugar
¾ cup sour cream
2 tablespoons prepared
    horseradish

• **Position** knife blade in food processor bowl; add cranberries and onion. Process 10 seconds, stopping once to scrape down sides of bowl. Pulse 3 or 4 times or until finely chopped, but not smooth.
• **Combine** cranberry mixture, sugar, sour cream, and horseradish in a medium bowl. Spoon into an 8-inch square pan. Cover and freeze until firm.
• **Remove** from freezer, and break into chunks about 1 hour before serving. Store any remaining relish in freezer. **Yield:** 3 cups.

Susan Stamberg
Washington, D.C.

CRANBERRY CRAVINGS

■ Most of the cranberry crop comes to market during November and December. Consider freezing fresh cranberries to satisfy cravings throughout the year.

CLASSIC ENDINGS

....

No matter how you begin planning your dinner menu, have a grand finale. And for the sweet certainty of scrumptious, lasting impressions, serve one of these classic desserts.

APPLE-BOURBON PIE
(pictured on page 300)

"I started making desserts when I was 10 years old. My first was a yellow cake from a baking powder recipe booklet. My uncle wants that cake each year for our reunion. Now, my recipe inspiration comes from travels to bed-and-breakfast and country inns." – Eugenia W. Bell

½ cup raisins
½ cup bourbon
3 pounds cooking apples
¾ cup sugar
2 tablespoons all-purpose
    flour
1 teaspoon ground cinnamon
¼ teaspoon salt
⅛ teaspoon ground nutmeg
½ cup chopped pecans or walnuts,
    toasted
1 (15-ounce) package refrigerated
    piecrusts
2 teaspoons apricot preserves,
    melted
1 tablespoon buttermilk
1 tablespoon sugar

• **Combine** raisins and bourbon, and let soak at least 2 hours.
• **Peel** apples, and cut into ½-inch slices; arrange apple slices in a steamer basket over boiling water. Cover and steam 10 minutes or until apple slices are tender.
• **Combine** ¾ cup sugar and next 4 ingredients in a large bowl; add apple slices, raisin mixture, and pecans, stirring to combine.

• **Fit** 1 piecrust into a 9-inch pieplate according to package directions; brush preserves over piecrust. Spoon apple mixture into piecrust.
• **Roll** remaining piecrust to press out fold lines; cut with a 3-inch leaf-shaped cutter. Mark veins on leaves with a pastry wheel or sharp knife. Arrange pastry leaves over apple mixture; brush leaves with buttermilk, and sprinkle pie with sugar.
• **Bake** at 450° on lower rack of oven 15 minutes. Shield edges of pie with strips of aluminum foil to prevent excessive browning. Bake at 350° for 30 to 35 additional minutes. **Yield:** 1 (9-inch) pie.

Eugenia W. Bell
Lexington, Kentucky

KENTUCKY MINCEMEAT PIE

1 (23-ounce) can mincemeat pie
    filling
1 (8-ounce) can crushed pineapple,
    drained
2 cups sliced cooking apples
1 (15-ounce) package refrigerated
    piecrusts
1 tablespoon sugar

• **Combine** first 3 ingredients in a large bowl; set aside.
• **Fit** 1 piecrust into a 9-inch pieplate according to package directions. Spoon mincemeat mixture into piecrust.
• **Roll** remaining piecrust to press out fold lines; cut with a 3-inch leaf-shaped cutter. Mark veins on leaves with a pastry wheel or sharp knife. Arrange pastry leaves over mincemeat mixture; sprinkle pie with sugar.
• **Bake** at 425° for 30 to 32 minutes or until golden. Shield edges of pie with strips of aluminum foil after 12 minutes to prevent excessive browning. **Yield:** 1 (9-inch) pie.

Betty Lee Long
Chapel Hill, North Carolina

HOLIDAY DINNERS

WHITE CHOCOLATE CHESS TART

½ (15-ounce) package refrigerated piecrusts
1 (4-ounce) white chocolate bar, chopped
½ cup buttermilk
3 large eggs, lightly beaten
1 tablespoon vanilla extract
1¼ cups sugar
Pinch of salt
3 tablespoons all-purpose flour
1 tablespoon cornmeal

• Fit 1 piecrust into a 9-inch tart pan with removable bottom according to package directions; trim edges. Line pastry with aluminum foil, and fill with pie weights or dried beans.
• Bake at 450° for 8 minutes. Remove weights and foil; bake 3 to 4 additional minutes. Cool piecrust on a wire rack.
• Combine chocolate and buttermilk in a small saucepan; cook over low heat, stirring constantly, until chocolate melts and mixture is smooth. Cool 15 minutes.
• Combine eggs and vanilla in a bowl; gradually stir in chocolate mixture.
• Combine sugar and next 3 ingredients; gradually add to chocolate mixture, stirring until blended. Pour mixture into piecrust.
• Bake at 325° for 50 minutes or until a knife inserted in center comes out clean. Cool on a wire rack. **Yield:** 1 (9-inch) tart.

FLAN DE QUESO

½ cup sugar
1 (14-ounce) can sweetened condensed milk
1 (8-ounce) package cream cheese, cubed and softened
4 large eggs
3 slices white bread, torn
1 cup water
⅔ cup evaporated milk
3 tablespoons butter or margarine, melted
1 teaspoon vanilla extract

• Sprinkle sugar in a 9-inch round cakepan; place over medium heat. Shake pan occasionally until sugar melts and turns a light golden brown; cool. (Caramelized sugar may crack slightly as it cools.)
• Combine condensed milk and next 7 ingredients in container of an electric blender; process until smooth, stopping once to scrape down sides. Pour over caramelized sugar.
• Place cakepan in a larger shallow pan. Add hot water to larger pan to depth of 1 inch.
• Bake, uncovered, at 350° for 55 minutes or until a knife inserted in center of flan comes out clean.
• Remove cakepan from water; cool on a wire rack at least 30 minutes.
• Run a knife around edge of flan to loosen; invert flan onto a serving plate. Cool. **Yield:** 6 servings.

Note: You can also caramelize sugar on a gas cooktop, stirring to speed caramelization.

Myrna M. Ruiz
Marietta, Georgia

ITALIAN RICOTTA CHEESECAKE
(pictured on page 333)

¾ cup all-purpose flour
2 tablespoons sugar
⅛ teaspoon salt
⅓ cup butter or margarine, softened
2½ cups ricotta cheese
½ cup sugar
3 tablespoons all-purpose flour
3 large eggs
1 teaspoon grated orange rind
1 teaspoon vanilla extract
¼ teaspoon salt
2 tablespoons golden raisins
2 tablespoons finely chopped candied citron
2 tablespoons chopped almonds
Garnishes: orange sections, orange rind strips

• Combine first 3 ingredients in a small bowl; cut in butter with pastry blender until mixture is crumbly. Press mixture into a 9-inch springform pan.
• Bake at 475° for 5 minutes. Cool on a wire rack.
• Combine ricotta cheese, ½ cup sugar, and 3 tablespoons flour; beat at medium speed with an electric mixer until smooth. Add eggs and next 3 ingredients; beat 4 minutes. Stir in raisins, citron, and almonds, and spoon over crust.
• Bake at 350° for 1 hour to 1 hour and 15 minutes or until center is set.
• Run a knife around edge of cheesecake to loosen; cool in pan on a wire rack. Cover and chill at least 8 hours. Carefully remove sides of pan just before serving. Garnish, if desired. **Yield:** 12 to 16 servings.

Michelle King
Duluth, Georgia

BETTY'S HOLIDAY CREAM

½ gallon vanilla ice cream, softened
1 (16-ounce) container frozen whipped topping, thawed
1 (27-ounce) jar mincemeat
2 tablespoons cream sherry (optional)

• Combine all ingredients in a large bowl, stirring until blended. Spoon mixture into miniature foil muffin cups; cover and freeze until firm. **Yield:** 20 dozen.

Note: Cream may also be frozen in parfait glasses. **Yield:** 3 quarts.

Betty Snyder
Milledgeville, Georgia

SPECIAL DELIVERY

....

Eddy McGee of Elkin, North Carolina, says, "I'm different than most letter carriers. I bake for the folks on my route." For those who aren't, we'll deliver some of Eddy's sweets to you.

CREAM CHEESE POUND CAKE

This cake won the highest mark a recipe can receive in our Test Kitchens – a 3.

1½ cups butter, softened
1 (8-ounce) package cream cheese, softened
3 cups sugar
6 large eggs
1½ teaspoons vanilla extract
3 cups all-purpose flour
⅛ teaspoon salt

● **Beat** butter and cream cheese at medium speed with an electric mixer 2 minutes or until mixture is creamy. Gradually add sugar, beating 5 to 7 minutes. Add eggs, one at a time, beating just until yellow disappears. Add vanilla, mixing well.
● **Combine** flour and salt; gradually add to butter mixture, beating at low speed just until blended after each addition. Pour batter into a greased and floured 10-inch tube pan.
● **Fill** a 2-cup, ovenproof measuring cup with water, and place in oven with tube pan.
● **Bake** at 300° for 1 hour and 30 minutes or until a wooden pick inserted in center of cake comes out clean. Cool in pan on a wire rack 10 to 15 minutes; remove from pan, and cool completely on wire rack. **Yield:** 1 (10-inch) cake.

MORAVIAN SUGAR CAKE

2 packages active dry yeast
½ teaspoon sugar
½ cup warm water (105° to 115°)
1 cup butter or margarine, melted and divided
¾ cup water
½ cup sugar
¼ cup instant potato flakes
2 tablespoons instant nonfat dry milk powder
½ teaspoon salt
2 large eggs
3 cups all-purpose flour
1 cup firmly packed brown sugar
1 teaspoon ground cinnamon

● **Combine** first 3 ingredients in a large bowl; let stand 5 minutes.
● **Add** ½ cup melted butter, ¾ cup water, and next 5 ingredients. Add 1 cup flour; beat at low speed with an electric mixer 2 minutes. Stir in remaining 2 cups flour to make a soft dough.
● **Cover** and let rise in a warm place (85°), free from drafts, 45 minutes or until doubled in bulk.
● **Punch** dough down; spread in a greased 15- x 10- x 1-inch jellyroll pan. Cover and let rise in a warm place (85°), free from drafts, 30 minutes.
● **Make** shallow indentations in dough at 1-inch intervals, using the handle of a wooden spoon. Drizzle with remaining ½ cup butter.
● **Combine** brown sugar and cinnamon; sprinkle over dough.
● **Bake** at 375° for 12 to 15 minutes. Cut into squares. **Yield:** 15 servings.

SECRETS TO SUCCESS

....

What makes the holidays so special are the people involved. That's why personalized gifts from your kitchen make the season more meaningful. Try these wrapping and packaging tips from letter carrier Eddy McGee for sending edible holiday treats.

■ Wrap cookies or cakes in plastic wrap or aluminum foil, and then pack snugly in a sturdy container. Colorful holiday tins and boxes are available in stores.

■ Fill each food container as full as practical, padding the top with crushed wax paper to prevent shaking and breakage.

■ If you'd like to personalize your package, don't settle for the same tin your fruitcake came in or that old Christmas wrapping paper. Consider using the sports pages of your newspaper for your favorite sports fan or sheet music for the music lover in your family. You may even want to try your hand at custom-printing your own paper by using rubber stamps, sponges, or stencils on brown parcel paper.

■ Be sure to cushion containers with crumpled newspaper or foam "peanuts" within a larger box for careful shipping.

■ Seal packing box with shipping tape, and cover the address label with transparent tape for protection. Be sure to label the package perishable to encourage careful handling.

THANKSGIVING, SOUTHERN STYLE

Carole Miller Radford's eyes twinkle when she speaks of her family and the food legacy that has become a part of her life in Lincolnton, Georgia. Carole's grandmother and her 12 children – now known as "the twelve" – created a strong heritage of food. And Buddy, Carole's husband, adds recipes from his family that date back to Civil War times.

A GEORGIA FAMILY'S THANKSGIVING FEAST
Serves 8 to 10

Homemade Relish Tray
Roast Turkey With Herbs   Commercial Gravy
Aunt Glennie's Pear Relish   Peach Ketchup
Nannie's Cornbread Dressing   Steamed Rice
Nannie's Candied Sweet Potatoes
Turnip Greens
Brandied Cranberries
Make-Ahead Yeast Rolls in Pastry Cornucopia
Betty's Butternut Pound Cake With Caramel Sauce

With such history, Carole came to mind when we researched Southern Thanksgivings. She takes a practical approach to holiday food. "The more you can do ahead of time, the better off you are," she says. "If you can take shortcuts, by all means, do it!"

When it comes to the holiday feast, Carole believes "the more, the better." She sometimes adds a country ham and a marinated vegetable salad to this menu. Most recipes serve 8 to 10. All items served together will feed more.

ROAST TURKEY WITH HERBS
(pictured on page 296)

1 (14-pound) turkey
½ cup fresh rosemary sprigs
½ cup fresh sage leaves
1 cooking apple, cut into quarters
1 stalk celery, cut in half
1 onion, cut in half
½ cup butter or margarine, melted

• **Remove** giblets and neck from turkey; reserve for other uses. Rinse turkey with cold water; pat dry.
• **Loosen** skin from turkey breast without totally detaching skin; carefully place rosemary and sage under skin. Replace skin.
• **Place** apple quarters, celery, and onion into neck cavity of turkey. Place turkey, breast side up, on a rack in a shallow roasting pan; brush entire bird with melted butter. Loosely cover turkey with heavy-duty aluminum foil.
• **Bake** at 325° until meat thermometer registers 180° (about 3½ to 4½ hours). (To prevent overcooking turkey, begin checking for doneness after 3 hours.) Remove turkey from roasting pan, and let stand 15 minutes before carving. Serve with gravy. **Yield:** 12 servings.

AUNT GLENNIE'S PEAR RELISH
(pictured on page 298)

This highly rated relish calls for a peck (12½ pounds) of pears. We used Bosc pears for testing.

12½ pounds pears, peeled and cored
8 jalapeño peppers, seeded
6 sweet red peppers, seeded and quartered
6 green peppers, seeded and quartered
6 medium onions, quartered
1 tablespoon salt
1 tablespoon celery seeds
5 cups sugar
5 cups white vinegar (5% acidity)

• **Position** knife blade in food processor bowl; add pears, a few at a time. Pulse 2 or 3 times or until pears are chopped. Transfer chopped pears to a large Dutch oven. Repeat procedure until all pears, peppers, and onions are chopped.
• **Add** salt and remaining ingredients to Dutch oven, stirring well. Bring to a boil over medium heat; reduce heat, and simmer 30 minutes, stirring mixture occasionally.
• **Spoon** hot relish into hot jars, filling to ½ inch from top. Remove air bubbles; wipe jar rims. Cover at once with metal lids, and screw on bands.
• **Process** in boiling-water bath 20 minutes. **Yield:** 14 pints.

PEACH KETCHUP

(pictured on page 298)

1 (16-ounce) can sliced peaches in heavy syrup, undrained
½ cup finely chopped onion
½ cup white vinegar
¼ teaspoon salt
½ teaspoon ground cinnamon
¼ teaspoon ground cloves
¼ teaspoon ground allspice
¼ teaspoon ground red pepper

• **Drain** peaches, reserving syrup in a small saucepan; set peaches aside.
• **Cook** syrup over medium heat 5 to 7 minutes or until reduced to ½ cup, stirring occasionally. Add peaches, onion, and remaining ingredients; bring to a boil. Reduce heat, and simmer. Cook 45 to 50 minutes or until thickened, stirring often; cool.
• **Position** knife blade in food processor bowl; add peach mixture. Process until mixture is smooth, stopping once to scrape down sides. Transfer to a serving bowl; cover and chill at least 8 hours. Serve with poultry or pork. **Yield:** about 1¼ cups.

NANNIE'S CORNBREAD DRESSING

(pictured on page 297)

This recipe comes from Carole's grandmother. It's a light color; some might mistake it for a potato casserole – until they take the first tantalizing bite.

2 cups self-rising flour
1 cup self-rising white cornmeal
2 cups buttermilk
3 large eggs
½ cup butter or margarine, melted
Vegetable cooking spray
1 cup chopped celery
1 to 2 medium onions, chopped
1 jalapeño pepper, seeded and chopped
¼ teaspoon pepper
2 to 3 cups chicken broth
Paprika
Garnish: celery leaves

• **Combine** flour and cornmeal in a large bowl; make a well in center of mixture.
• **Combine** buttermilk, eggs, and butter, stirring well, and add to dry ingredients, stirring mixture just until moistened.
• **Place** a 9-inch square pan in a 400° oven for 5 minutes or until hot. Remove pan from oven; coat with cooking spray. Spoon batter into hot pan.
• **Bake** at 400° for 25 minutes or until lightly browned. Cool in pan on a wire rack, and crumble cornbread into a large bowl.
• **Add** celery, onion, jalapeño pepper, and pepper, stirring well. Stir in enough chicken broth to make a moist, thick mixture.
• **Spoon** cornbread mixture into an 11- x 7- x 1½-inch baking dish coated with cooking spray.
• **Bake** at 350° for 20 minutes or until lightly browned. Sprinkle with paprika; garnish, if desired. **Yield:** 8 servings.

NANNIE'S CANDIED SWEET POTATOES

6 large sweet potatoes (about 4 pounds)
1 lemon
1 orange
¾ cup butter or margarine, melted
2 cups sugar
½ cup orange juice
2 teaspoons ground cinnamon
1 teaspoon vanilla extract (optional)

• **Peel** potatoes; cut potatoes, lemon, and orange into ¼-inch slices.
• **Place** potato slices in a lightly greased 11- x 7- x 1½-inch baking dish; arrange lemon and orange slices over potato.
• **Combine** melted butter, sugar, orange juice, and cinnamon; stir in vanilla, if desired. Pour mixture over potato mixture; cover with plastic wrap, and let stand 1 hour.
• **Bake**, uncovered, at 350° for 1½ hours, basting often with pan juices. **Yield:** 8 to 10 servings.

TURNIP GREENS

(pictured on page 298)

These greens add a Southern accent to your Thanksgiving table.

2 quarts water
2 teaspoons salt
1 ham hock
6 pounds fresh turnip greens, trimmed and rinsed *
½ cup sugar
1 tablespoon hot sauce
1 tablespoon dry white wine

• **Combine** first 3 ingredients in a stockpot, and bring mixture to a boil. Cover, reduce heat, and simmer 20 minutes.
• **Add** greens, a few at a time, to stockpot; add sugar, hot sauce, and wine. Cover and cook over medium heat 40 minutes or until greens are tender; drain. **Yield:** 6 to 8 servings.

* You can substitute 3 (10-ounce) packages frozen chopped turnip greens, thawed.

BRANDIED CRANBERRIES

(pictured on page 297)

Using brandy for the liquid in this cranberry relish recipe creates a bold new flavor for a traditional favorite.

3 (12-ounce) packages fresh or frozen cranberries, thawed
3 cups sugar
½ cup brandy
Garnish: fresh thyme sprigs

• **Place** cranberries in a single layer in two lightly greased 15- x 10- x 1-inch jellyroll pans; pour sugar over cranberries. Cover tightly with aluminum foil.
• **Bake** at 350° for 1 hour.
• **Spoon** cranberries into a large serving bowl; gently stir in brandy. Cool.
• **Serve** cranberries chilled or at room temperature. Garnish, if desired. Store cranberries in refrigerator up to 1 week. **Yield:** 5 cups.

MAKE-AHEAD YEAST ROLLS

(pictured on page 299)

Carole says this recipe "turns out the same way, no matter what mood you're in or what the weather is." We didn't even need to butter the tops. The baked rolls freeze well.

2 packages active dry yeast
1¼ cups warm water, divided
    (105° to 115°)
4½ to 5 cups all-purpose flour,
    divided
3 large eggs, lightly beaten
½ cup shortening, melted
½ cup sugar
2 teaspoons salt

• **Combine** yeast and ¼ cup warm water in a 2-cup liquid measuring cup; let stand 5 minutes.
• **Combine** yeast mixture, remaining 1 cup water, 2 cups flour, eggs, and next 3 ingredients in a large bowl; beat with a wooden spoon 2 minutes. Gradually stir in enough remaining flour to make a soft dough.
• **Cover** and let rise in a warm place (85°), free from drafts, 1 hour.
• **Punch** dough down; cover and chill at least 8 hours.
• **Punch** dough down; turn dough out onto a floured surface, and knead 3 or 4 times. Divide dough in half; shape each portion into 16 (2-inch) balls. Place balls in two lightly greased 9-inch square pans.
• **Cover** and let rise in a warm place (85°), free from drafts, 1½ hours or until doubled in bulk.
• **Bake** at 375° for 12 minutes or until golden. **Yield:** 32 rolls.

Note: This is an excellent, supple dough. You can make these rolls into a variety of shapes. Your yield will vary depending on how you shape the rolls.

PASTRY CORNUCOPIA STEP-BY-STEP

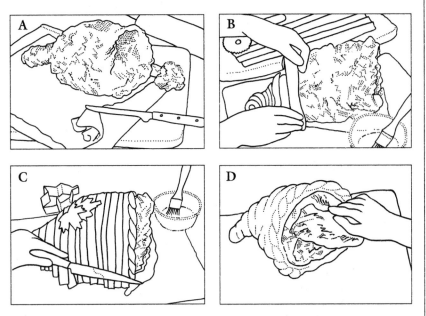

PASTRY CORNUCOPIA

(pictured on page 299)

Vegetable cooking spray
1 (17¼-ounce) package frozen
    puff pastry sheets, thawed
1 large egg
2 teaspoons water
Garnish: fresh thyme sprigs

• **Crumple** 12 (12-inch) pieces heavy-duty aluminum foil into balls; place balls onto a 20-inch piece of foil. Pull two sides of foil over balls, and fold together to seal. Shape packet to resemble a 12-inch-long cornucopia. Coat lightly with cooking spray; set aside.
• **Roll** 1 pastry sheet on a lightly floured surface into a 14- x 12-inch rectangle. Place form on pastry; trim pastry ½ inch larger than bottom of form. (See A.) Place pastry base and form on a greased baking sheet. (Or place on a foil-lined baking sheet coated with cooking spray.) Cut remaining pastry into 1-inch strips. Set aside 1 strip and scraps for decorations.
• **Roll** remaining pastry sheet into a 14- x 12-inch rectangle, and cut into 12 (14- x 1-inch) strips. (Keep pastry strips covered with a damp towel to prevent drying out.)
• **Combine** egg and water, beating lightly with a fork.
• **Brush** pastry strips, one at a time, with egg mixture. Starting at small end, completely cover form with pastry strips, overlapping strips ¼ inch and pressing ends onto pastry base. (See B. Do not cover opening.) Trim excess dough from around bottom of base.
• **Cut** pastry strip reserved for decoration in half lengthwise; twist pieces together to form a rope, and place on edge of pastry around opening. Cut remaining pastry scraps into decorative shapes, and attach to pastry with egg mixture. (See C.) Brush entire pastry cornucopia with egg mixture.
• **Bake** at 425° for 10 minutes; reduce heat to 350°, and bake 15 minutes or until golden. Cool completely.
• **Remove** foil form very carefully. (See D.) Fill cornucopia with rolls or cookies, and use as a centerpiece. Garnish, if desired. **Yield:** 1 cornucopia.

Note: Store cornucopia, loosely covered, in a cool, dry place. Do not store in refrigerator after baking.

BETTY'S BUTTERNUT POUND CAKE WITH CARAMEL SAUCE

This mouth-watering combo comes from Carole's sister, Betty Wilkins of Prosperity, South Carolina.

1 cup butter or margarine, softened
½ cup shortening
3 cups sugar
5 large eggs
1 (5-ounce) can evaporated milk
3¼ cups all-purpose flour
¼ teaspoon salt
2 tablespoons vanilla, butter, and nut flavoring
Caramel Sauce

• **Beat** butter and shortening at medium speed with an electric mixer about 2 minutes or until creamy. Gradually add sugar, and beat 5 to 7 minutes. Add eggs, one at a time, beating just until yellow disappears.
• **Add** enough water to evaporated milk to measure 1 cup.
• **Combine** flour and salt; add to butter mixture alternately with milk mixture, beginning and ending with flour mixture. Mix at low speed just until blended after each addition. Stir in flavoring. Pour into a greased and floured 10-inch tube pan.
• **Bake** at 325° for 1 hour and 25 minutes or until a wooden pick inserted in center of cake comes out clean. Cool in pan on a wire rack 10 to 15 minutes; remove from pan, and cool completely on wire rack. Serve with warm Caramel Sauce. **Yield:** one (10-inch) cake.

Note: Cake may be baked in 2 (8½- x 4½- x 3-inch) loaf pans at 325° for 1 hour and 15 minutes.

Caramel Sauce

1 cup firmly packed brown sugar
1 cup whipping cream
1 cup half-and-half
3 tablespoons butter or margarine

• **Combine** all ingredients in a heavy saucepan; cook over low heat 45 minutes or until thickened, stirring occasionally. **Yield:** about 2 cups.

WHAT'S FOR SUPPER?

CALM IN THE KITCHEN

....

During the busy holiday season, simple things seem more precious than ever – especially in the kitchen. These easy recipes deliver mighty big tastes with only a moderate amount of effort.

ALL-STAR PIZZA CALZONES

These calzones may be frozen. Prepare as directed; bake at 300° for 15 minutes or until lightly browned. Let cool. Freeze in airtight containers. Bake on a greased baking sheet at 300° for 40 minutes or until golden.

1½ (32-ounce) packages frozen bread dough
1 pound ground pork sausage, cooked and drained
½ pound ground baked ham
½ pound ground salami
1 cup (4 ounces) shredded Swiss cheese
1 cup (4 ounces) shredded mozzarella cheese
1 cup (4 ounces) shredded provolone cheese
2 cups (8 ounces) shredded mild Cheddar cheese
¼ cup chopped ripe olives
1 cup chopped onion
3 jalapeño peppers, seeded and chopped
3 tablespoons butter or margarine, melted

• **Allow** dough to rise according to package directions.
• **Combine** sausage and next 9 ingredients, stirring well.
• **Roll** 1 loaf of dough into a 9- x 11-inch rectangle on a lightly floured surface. Place 3½ cups sausage mixture on one short side of dough; fold dough over sausage mixture, and pinch edges to seal. Place on a lightly greased baking sheet, and brush with 1 tablespoon

butter. Repeat with remaining dough, sausage mixture, and butter.
• **Bake** at 300° for 30 minutes or until golden. Let stand 5 minutes; slice each into 3 or 4 portions with an electric knife, and serve warm. **Yield:** 9 to 12 servings.

Monica Pierce
Covington, Louisiana

HAM STRATA

1 tablespoon butter or margarine
1 cup chopped celery
⅓ cup chopped green pepper
2 tablespoons chopped onion
2 cups chopped cooked ham *
¼ cup mayonnaise or salad dressing, divided
12 slices white bread, crusts removed
1 (6-ounce) package sharp Cheddar cheese slices
4 large eggs
3 cups milk
¾ teaspoon salt
¼ teaspoon pepper
Garnishes: sour cream, fresh parsley sprigs

• **Melt** butter in a large skillet over medium-high heat. Add celery, green pepper, and onion; cook, stirring constantly, until tender. Remove from heat; stir in ham. Cool.
• **Spread** 1 teaspoon mayonnaise on each bread slice. Arrange 6 bread slices, mayonnaise side up, in a lightly greased 13- x 9- x 2-inch baking dish. Spoon ham mixture over bread slices. Top with cheese and remaining bread, mayonnaise side down.
• **Combine** eggs and next 3 ingredients, stirring well; pour over bread slices. Cover and chill at least 8 hours. Remove from refrigerator 30 minutes before baking.
• **Bake** at 300° for 1½ hours. Garnish, if desired. Serve immediately. **Yield:** 6 servings.

* You can substitute 2 cups chopped cooked chicken or turkey.

Tonya Vann
Birmingham, Alabama

PARTY POTPOURRI

If you like to entertain, *Party Potpourri* is a must for your cookbook collection.

Published by the Junior League of Memphis, the book features ideas on themed parties, brunches,

coffees, luncheons, receptions, casual and formal entertaining, and children's parties.

The Junior League has contributed more than $2.5 million to charitable projects and numerous educational and support services.

DOVE AU VIN

1 cup all-purpose flour
1 teaspoon salt
1 teaspoon pepper
12 doves, dressed
⅓ cup butter or margarine
1 cup chopped celery
1 cup chopped onion
1 small green pepper, chopped
1 (10½-ounce) can beef consommé
½ cup dry red wine
Hot cooked noodles or rice

• **Combine** first 3 ingredients in a large heavy-duty, zip-top plastic bag. Add doves, a few at a time; seal and shake to coat.
• **Melt** butter in a large nonstick skillet over medium-high heat; add doves, and cook until browned, turning once.
• **Place** doves in a lightly greased 13- x 9- x 2-inch baking dish. Sprinkle celery, onion, and green pepper evenly over doves; add consommé. Cover with aluminum foil.
• **Bake** at 350° for 1½ hours. Pour wine over doves; cover and bake 30 additional minutes. Serve with noodles or rice. **Yield:** 6 servings.

BLACK BEANS AND RICE

1 pound dried black beans
10 cups water
1 large green pepper, cut in half
⅓ cup vegetable oil
1 large onion, chopped
4 cloves garlic, minced
1 medium-size green pepper, chopped
2 teaspoons salt
⅛ teaspoon dried oregano, crushed
⅛ teaspoon pepper
1 bay leaf
2 teaspoons sugar
2 tablespoons white vinegar
2 tablespoons dry white wine
2 tablespoons olive oil (optional)
Hot cooked rice

• **Sort** and wash beans; place in a Dutch oven. Add water and pepper halves; bring to a boil. Reduce heat, and simmer 45 minutes. Remove from heat; cover and chill 8 hours.
• **Pour** oil into a skillet; place over medium-high heat. Add onion, garlic, and chopped green pepper; cook, stirring constantly, until tender. Remove from heat; set aside.
• **Cook** beans over medium heat 1 hour, stirring often. Remove and discard green pepper halves. Place 1 cup cooked beans in container of an electric blender; process until smooth. Stir bean puree, onion mixture, salt, and next 6 ingredients into remaining cooked beans; simmer 50 minutes or until tender, adding additional water if needed, stirring occasionally. Stir in olive oil, if desired. Remove and discard bay leaf. Serve over rice. **Yield:** 6 servings.

NED'S EGGPLANT STICKS

3 medium eggplants (3 pounds)
1 cup Italian-seasoned breadcrumbs
1 teaspoon salt
1 teaspoon pepper
3 large eggs
¼ cup milk
Vegetable oil

• **Peel** eggplant, and cut into 3- x ½-inch sticks. Place in ice water 30 minutes; drain and set aside.
• **Combine** Italian-seasoned breadcrumbs, salt, and pepper.
• **Combine** eggs and milk, beating with a fork until blended. Dip eggplant sticks in milk mixture, and dredge in breadcrumb mixture; cover and chill 30 minutes.
• **Pour** oil to depth of 1 inch into a large skillet; heat to 350°. Fry eggplant sticks, 10 to 12 at a time, 2 minutes or until golden, turning once. Drain on paper towels. Repeat procedure with remaining eggplant sticks. Serve with salsa, if desired. **Yield:** 10 to 12 appetizer servings.

WRAP AND ROLL

Foreign cuisines are known for the mystique of their wrapped foods. Part of the fun of eating Italian calzones, Mexican enchiladas, and French dishes *en papillote* is the element of surprise in that first bite. Unwrap one of these low-fat packages, and discover a world of wonderful flavor inside.

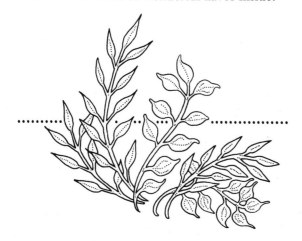

SHRIMP ENCHILADAS IN TOMATILLO SAUCE

Commercial green chile sauce makes a spicy substitution for the tomatillo sauce in this recipe.

1 pound unpeeled large fresh shrimp
1 large onion, finely chopped
2 teaspoons olive oil
1 tablespoon all-purpose flour
1½ cups reduced-sodium, fat-free chicken broth
1 (12-ounce) can tomatillo sauce
1 teaspoon ground cumin
½ teaspoon dried oregano
8 corn tortillas
1½ cups (6 ounces) shredded reduced-fat Monterey Jack cheese
½ cup nonfat sour cream

• **Peel** shrimp, and devein, if desired. Set shrimp aside.
• **Cook** onion in oil in a large nonstick skillet over medium-high heat, stirring constantly, until tender. Add flour, stirring until smooth; cook 1 minute.
• **Stir** in chicken broth and next 3 ingredients; cook 15 minutes or until thickened.
• **Add** shrimp; cook 5 minutes or until shrimp turn pink. Remove from heat, and cool slightly.
• **Dip** corn tortillas in shrimp mixture; place on a flat surface. Place 3 or 4 shrimp in center of each tortilla, using a slotted spoon; sprinkle each with about 1 tablespoon cheese, and roll tightly.
• **Place** tortillas, seam side down, in a lightly greased 11- x 7- x 1½-inch baking dish. Pour remaining shrimp mixture over top, and sprinkle with remaining cheese.
• **Cover** and bake at 350° for 15 minutes. Uncover and bake 10 minutes or until cheese melts. Serve with sour cream. **Yield:** 4 servings.

Karl Harvey
Baton Rouge, Louisiana

♥ Per serving: Calories 360 (33% from fat)
Fat 13.3g (5.4g saturated) Cholesterol 114mg
Sodium 438mg Carbohydrate 30.6g
Fiber 2.7g Protein 29.8g

SPINACH-AND-CHEESE CALZONES

½ cup chopped onion
1 tablespoon garlic powder
½ teaspoon salt
1 (10-ounce) package frozen chopped spinach, thawed and well drained
½ (6-ounce) package Canadian bacon, chopped
1 teaspoon dried Italian seasoning
1 (15-ounce) carton fat-free ricotta cheese
1 cup (4 ounces) shredded reduced-fat mozzarella cheese
¼ cup freshly grated Parmesan cheese
1 (16-ounce) loaf frozen bread dough, thawed
Vegetable cooking spray
1 (27½-ounce) jar light pasta sauce

• **Combine** first 5 ingredients in a large skillet; cook over medium-high heat, stirring constantly, until bacon is browned. Remove from heat.
• **Combine** Italian seasoning and next 3 ingredients; stir into spinach mixture.
• **Divide** dough into 8 portions; roll each portion into a 6-inch circle on a lightly floured surface.
• **Spoon** about ½ cup spinach mixture onto each circle; lightly brush edges of dough with water. Fold in half, pressing edges to seal. Place calzones on a baking sheet coated with cooking spray; coat tops with cooking spray.
• **Bake** at 375° for 15 to 20 minutes or until golden. Serve with warm pasta sauce. **Yield:** 8 servings.

Shannon Gaudin
Shreveport, Louisiana

♥ Per serving: Calories 312 (19% from fat)
Fat 6.8g (1.2g saturated) Cholesterol 18mg
Sodium 816mg Carbohydrate 42.1g
Fiber 1.4g Protein 22.2g

SALMON IN PARCHMENT

(pictured on page 258)

Serve this dish with rice or couscous to soak up the flavorful wine and citrus cooking liquid.

⅓ cup white wine
⅓ cup lime juice
2 tablespoons chopped fresh
   dill
6 (4-ounce) salmon steaks
4 carrots
2 leeks
1 sweet red pepper
Vegetable cooking spray
½ teaspoon salt
¼ teaspoon pepper
6 slices lime
12 fresh dill sprigs, divided

• **Combine** first 3 ingredients in a shallow dish; add salmon. Cover and chill 30 minutes.
• **Slice** carrots diagonally; thinly slice white part of leeks, and separate into rings. Thinly slice red pepper.
• **Combine** carrot, leek, and red pepper in a saucepan; add water to pan to depth of 1 inch. Bring to a boil; boil 1 minute. Drain vegetables, and plunge into ice water to stop the cooking process; drain.
• **Cut** 6 (18- x 12-inch) pieces of parchment paper; fold each piece in half to make a 12- x 9-inch rectangle (see box below). Trim into half heart-shaped pieces. Coat one side of each piece of parchment with cooking spray; arrange three-fourths of vegetable mixture evenly on coated sides of parchment, leaving a 1-inch border.
• **Remove** salmon from marinade, reserving marinade. Place fish over vegetables; sprinkle with salt and pepper. Top each with a lime slice. Place remaining vegetables on fish; top each with 1 dill sprig.
• **Bring** opposite sides of parchment together; fold edges over twice to seal, and fold pointed ends underneath packet. Place on baking sheets.
• **Bake** at 425° for 10 to 12 minutes. Cut opening in packets; top with remaining dill sprigs. **Yield:** 6 servings.

Patricia A. Chapman
Huntsville, Alabama

♥ Per serving: Calories 225 (34% from fat)
Fat 8.5g (1.3g saturated) Cholesterol 62mg
Sodium 273mg Carbohydrate 13g
Fiber 2.3g Protein 23.8g

PAPER ROUTE

If you're planning to make the recipe above for company, practice your packaging skills by wrapping an unopened can of tuna – you'll be a pro by the night of the party. You won't believe how easy these dramatic bundles are to wrap.

Make the parchment packages the same way you make heart-shaped valentines. Cut the paper into an 18- x 12-inch rectangle; fold it in half lengthwise, and trim the rectangle into a heart-shaped design.

To seal the package, begin folding the edges together at the top of the heart. Double each fold to ensure a tight seal, and continue folding to the pointed end of the heart. Fold the pointed end underneath, and bake.

FAST DISHES FOR BUSY DAYS

On the day before Thanksgiving or Christmas, the only creature stirring is *you*. There's a mountain of salads, side dishes, and desserts – *and*, of course, that colossal turkey, ham, or roast – to be prepped for the next day's feast. Give yourself a break during the holidays with these easy-to-prepare meals.

CHEESE ENCHILADAS

2 (10-ounce) cans enchilada
   sauce, divided
1 (12-ounce) container reduced-fat
   cottage cheese
1 (8-ounce) carton reduced-fat
   sour cream
1 (4.5-ounce) can chopped green
   chiles, undrained
¼ teaspoon salt
8 (8-inch) flour tortillas
1 cup (4 ounces) shredded
   reduced-fat Monterey Jack
   cheese
1 (2¼-ounce) can sliced ripe
   olives, drained
1 cup (4 ounces) shredded
   reduced-fat Cheddar
   cheese
Garnishes: sour cream, sliced ripe
   olives, cilantro sprigs

• **Spread** ¾ cup enchilada sauce evenly in a lightly greased 13- x 9- x 2-inch baking dish.
• **Combine** cottage cheese and next 3 ingredients; spoon about ⅓ cup mixture down center of each tortilla. Sprinkle evenly with Monterey Jack cheese; roll up, and place, seam side down, in dish. Top evenly with remaining enchilada sauce; sprinkle with olives.
• **Cover** and bake at 350° for 25 minutes. Uncover and sprinkle with Cheddar cheese; garnish, if desired. **Yield:** 4 servings.

TURKEY AND PEPPERS IN CORNBREAD CRUST

2 cups chopped cooked turkey
1 (7-ounce) jar roasted sweet red peppers, drained and sliced
1 (4.5-ounce) can chopped green chiles, undrained
1 (10¾-ounce) can cream of chicken soup, undiluted
½ cup sour cream
¼ cup milk
1 teaspoon chili powder
1 (11.5-ounce) can refrigerated cornbread twists

• **Combine** first 7 ingredients. Spoon into a lightly greased 8-inch square baking dish; set aside.
• **Prepare** cornbread twists according to package directions, but do not bake. Place over turkey mixture. Cover loosely with aluminum foil.
• **Bake** at 375° for 30 minutes. Uncover and bake 10 additional minutes or until cornbread is golden. **Yield:** 4 to 6 servings.

Beppy Hassey
Montgomery, Alabama

WEEKNIGHT SPAGHETTI PIE

6 ounces spaghetti or vermicelli, uncooked
2 teaspoons dried basil, divided
1 clove garlic, pressed
¼ cup butter or margarine, melted
½ cup grated Parmesan cheese
1 large egg, lightly beaten
1 cup ricotta cheese
1 pound lean ground beef
½ cup chopped onion
1 (15-ounce) can tomato sauce
1 (6-ounce) can tomato paste
1 teaspoon dried oregano
1 cup sliced mushrooms
¼ cup white wine (optional)
6 ounces sliced mozzarella cheese

• **Cook** spaghetti according to package directions; drain.
• **Combine** spaghetti, 1 teaspoon basil, garlic, and next 3 ingredients. Press mixture into a lightly greased 10-inch pieplate.

• **Spread** ricotta cheese over spaghetti mixture.
• **Cook** ground beef and chopped onion over medium-high heat in a large skillet, stirring until meat crumbles; drain well.
• **Add** remaining 1 teaspoon basil, tomato sauce, and next 3 ingredients to beef mixture; stir in wine, if desired. Cook 5 minutes or until thoroughly heated. Spoon ground beef mixture over ricotta cheese.
• **Bake** at 350° for 25 minutes. Remove from oven, and top with cheese slices. Bake 5 additional minutes or until cheese melts. **Yield:** 6 servings.

Rachel Adair Gilbert
Tulsa, Oklahoma

THESE RECIPES CUT THE MUSTARD

....

You're not at the mercy of gourmet food companies for custom mustards. These five simple recipes start with dry and prepared mustards and are ready in less than 15 minutes. That's a lot of homemade flavor on short notice.

REALLY HOT MUSTARD

There are at least three kinds of dry mustard at the grocery store: mild, hot, and Coleman's – a mixture of the first two. We used Coleman's in this recipe.

¼ cup dry mustard
2 to 3 teaspoons hot sauce
2 tablespoons milk
1 clove garlic, pressed
¼ teaspoon ground red pepper
⅛ teaspoon salt

• **Combine** all ingredients, stirring well. **Yield:** ¼ cup.

Note: Recipe may be doubled.

JALAPEÑO MUSTARD

"Prepared mustard" is the classic yellow mustard most often used at ballpark concession stands. Spread this dressed-up version on hot dogs, hamburgers, and sandwiches.

2 cups prepared mustard
1 small onion, finely chopped
1 to 2 jalapeño peppers, seeded and minced
Dash of salt
1 tablespoon white vinegar
Garnish: minced jalapeño pepper

• **Combine** first 5 ingredients, stirring well. Garnish, if desired. **Yield:** 2 cups.

Jean Cole
Lafayette, Alabama

PEPPERED HONEY MUSTARD

This mustard is excellent with chicken or mixed into a homemade vinaigrette salad dressing.

¾ cup Dijon mustard
¼ cup honey
1 tablespoon cracked pepper
⅛ teaspoon salt
Garnish: cracked pepper

• **Combine** first 4 ingredients in a small serving bowl, stirring well. Garnish, if desired. **Yield:** 1 cup.

SWEET CIDER MUSTARD

Teri Schmid serves this mustard as a dip for pretzels.

½ cup sugar
¼ cup dry mustard
Dash of salt
1 large egg
⅓ cup apple cider vinegar

• **Combine** all ingredients in container of an electric blender; process 20 seconds or until smooth, stopping once to scrape down sides. Pour mixture into a heavy saucepan.

• **Cook** over medium heat, stirring constantly, 5 minutes or until mixture is thickened; cool completely. **Yield:** about 1 cup.

Teri Schmid
Marietta, Georgia

RASPBERRY MUSTARD

This recipe calls for a few more ingredients than the others, but the results are worth it.

½ cup fresh raspberries
¼ cup chopped onion
1 clove garlic
¼ cup dry mustard
2 teaspoons sugar
½ teaspoon pepper
¼ teaspoon salt
½ cup raspberry wine vinegar
1 teaspoon lemon juice
Garnish: whole fresh raspberry

• **Combine** all ingredients except garnish in container of an electric blender; process until smooth, stopping once to scrape down sides. Pour mixture into a small saucepan.
• **Cook** over medium heat 10 minutes or until thickened; cool. Garnish, if desired. Serve on chicken sandwiches or with sausage, cheese, or crackers. **Yield:** 1 cup.

MUSTARD FACTS

There are two kinds of mustard seeds: the milder white (or yellow) mustard seeds and the more pungent brown (or Oriental) seeds. The white seeds are used as the base for American-style prepared mustards, while brown seeds are used in zestier European and Chinese mustards. You'll find the white and brown seeds blended in English mustard, a hot powdered mustard.

USE YOUR NOG IN . . .

. . . .

Traditionally, we know eggnog as a creamy holiday beverage concocted of milk, eggs, sugar, and – oftentimes – a splash of spirits like bourbon or rum. In each of these recipes, however, we discover a generous helping of festive eggnog is a new way to boost flavor.

After the holidays are over, you can freeze any leftover eggnog up to six months. To reuse, thaw in the refrigerator, and stir vigorously before using.

EGGNOG FRENCH TOAST

1½ cups commercial refrigerated eggnog
½ teaspoon freshly grated nutmeg
8 (1-inch-thick) slices French bread
2 tablespoons butter or margarine
Rum Syrup

• **Combine** eggnog and nutmeg in a shallow dish. Place bread slices in dish, turning to coat.
• **Melt** butter in a large skillet. Remove bread slices from eggnog mixture, allowing excess to drain. Cook in skillet 3 minutes on each side or until golden. Serve immediately with Rum Syrup. **Yield:** 4 servings.

Rum Syrup

1 cup pure maple syrup
2 tablespoons butter or margarine
2 tablespoons light rum *

• **Combine** ingredients in a saucepan; cook over low heat until heated, stirring often. **Yield:** 1¼ cups.

* Substitute ½ teaspoon rum extract.
Hugh Montgomery
Birmingham, Alabama

EGGNOG-PECAN POUND CAKE

1 cup butter or margarine, softened
½ cup vegetable oil
3 cups sugar
6 large eggs
3 cups all-purpose flour
1 tablespoon ground mace
1 teaspoon baking powder
1½ cups commercial refrigerated eggnog
1 teaspoon vanilla extract
1 teaspoon lemon extract
2 cups coarsely chopped pecans

• **Beat** butter and oil at medium speed with an electric mixer about 2 minutes. Gradually add sugar, beating at medium speed 5 to 7 minutes. Add eggs, one at a time, beating just until yellow disappears.
• **Combine** flour, mace, and baking powder; add to butter mixture alternately with eggnog, beginning and ending with flour mixture. Mix at low speed just until blended after each addition. Stir in flavorings; fold in pecans. Pour batter into a greased and floured 10-inch tube pan.
• **Bake** at 350° for 1 hour and 15 minutes or until a wooden pick inserted in center of cake comes out clean; cover loosely with aluminum foil after 45 minutes to prevent excessive browning. Cool cake in pan on a wire rack 10 to 15 minutes. Remove from pan, and cool completely on wire rack. **Yield:** 1 (10-inch) cake.

Sharon Griffin Squire
Little Rock, Arkansas

EGGNOG DESSERT

1 quart commercial refrigerated
    eggnog, divided
¼ cup sugar
2 envelopes unflavored gelatin
1 teaspoon rum extract
2 cups whipping cream, whipped
    and divided
Freshly grated nutmeg

• **Combine** 1 cup eggnog and sugar in a heavy saucepan. Sprinkle gelatin over mixture; let stand 1 minute. Cook over low heat, stirring until sugar and gelatin dissolve (about 4 minutes). Stir in rum extract and remaining eggnog.
• **Chill** until consistency of unbeaten egg white.
• **Fold** in half of whipped cream; spoon into individual dishes. Dollop or pipe with remaining whipped cream; sprinkle with nutmeg. **Yield:** 8 servings.

Amanda McNeal
El Paso, Texas

IRISH COFFEE-EGGNOG PUNCH

2 quarts commercial refrigerated
    eggnog
⅓ cup firmly packed brown sugar
3 tablespoons instant coffee
    granules
½ teaspoon ground cinnamon
½ teaspoon ground nutmeg
1 cup Irish whiskey (optional) *
1 quart coffee ice cream, scooped
    into balls
Garnishes: sweetened whipped
    cream, freshly grated nutmeg

• **Combine** first 5 ingredients in a large mixing bowl; beat at low speed with an electric mixer until sugar dissolves. Chill 15 minutes; stir until coffee granules dissolve. Stir in whiskey, if desired.
• **Cover** and chill at least 1 hour. Pour into a punch bowl or individual cups, leaving enough room for ice cream. Spoon in ice cream. Garnish, if desired. **Yield:** about 3 quarts.

* Substitute ½ teaspoon rum extract.
Paula McCollum
Springtown, Texas

FROM OUR KITCHEN TO YOURS

....

BUTTER'S BETTER

Remember when the cutting edge choice was butter or "oleo"? These days there are more options than you can shake a stick of margarine at. Labels touting "butter," "margarine," "vegetable oil spread," "low fat," and "no fat" swim before you in a yellow sea of confusion.

If you're just going to plop a pat onto a baked potato, your choice isn't so crucial. But if you're baking, your decision is indeed a big fat deal.

Our results? Go for the real butter. It makes the prettiest and – even more importantly – the best-tasting cakes and cookies.

FRUITCAKE – THE LAZY WAY

We decided that when we were too busy to bake everything from scratch, we'd grab a phone to order our holiday fruitcakes. Some suppliers are:
■ Cryer Creek Kitchens, Corsicana, Texas; 1-800-468-0088

Beautifully decorated, this dense fruitcake tastes as good as it looks. A 1-pound, 14-ounce round cake costs $16.75, including shipping.

■ Collin Street Bakery, Corsicana, Texas; 1-800-248-3366, Ext. 5

This cake is pure simplicity. It's a combination of pecans and fruit that is held together by an apricot glaze. Prices range from $15.75 for a 1⅞-pound round cake to $37.95 for a 4⅞-pound cake, including shipping.

■ Gethsemani Farms, Trappist, Kentucky

The Trappist monks who make these moist, dark, spicy cakes soak the candied fruits in wine and then infuse the baked cakes with Kentucky bourbon. A 2½-pound round cake costs $19.95 and a 5-pound round cake costs $39.25, including shipping. Fax your order to (502) 549-4124 or write

to Gethsemani Farms, P.O. Box SL, Trappist, KY 40051.

■ Mary of Puddin Hill, Greenville, Texas; 1-800-545-8889

Eating this cake is like eating a moist, chewy fruit-and-nut candy. Both pecan and walnut versions are available. Prices range from $24 for a 1½-pound loaf Walnut Fruitcake to $58 for a 4½-pound round Pecan Fruitcake, including shipping.

■ Southern Supreme, Bear Creek, North Carolina; (910) 581-3141

Their Nutty Fruitcake will remind you of a nut roll with pineapples and cherries. Guaranteed to be eaten by even the most avid fruitcake haters. Prices start at $5.50 for an 8-ounce loaf and go to $32.75 for a 4½-pound round cake, excluding shipping.

A BRUSH WITH GRATENESS

Stretching heavy-duty plastic wrap over a fine-toothed grater before grating citrus rind makes cleanup easy. But here's another "grate" tip: Forget the plastic wrap; sweep the rind from the grater with a pastry brush instead.

KEEPING TROUBLE AT BAY

Don't you love all of those recipes for colossal pots of winter soup that instruct you to simply "remove and discard the bay leaf before serving"? It's a culinary needle-in-a-haystack pursuit.

Here's a suggestion from Floridian Doris Sumner: Insert a wooden pick through each of the bay leaves before adding them to the pot. The wooden picks keep the leaves from lying on the bottom of the stockpot and make them easier targets for your handy ladle.

And as for those few pitiful fragments of bay leaves in every bottle you buy, don't throw them out. Tie several of them in a small piece of cheesecloth.

HOLIDAY HOTLINE

This season, if your cake falls flat and your fudge is as hard as a brick, help is only a call away. Just phone the test kitchens at Land O'Lakes with your baking dilemmas at 1-800-782-9606 from November 1 to December 24, 8 a.m. to 6 p.m. (central time).

DECEMBER

KENTUCKY TRADITIONS

The kitchen at Kentucky's Longfield Farm bursts with anticipation. Sissy Nash and her daughter, Kathy Nash Cary, work side by side preparing treasured recipes for another family holiday gathering.

BLUEGRASS CELEBRATION MENU
Serves Eight

Spinach Puffs
Leg of Lamb With Hunter Sauce or
Roasted Turkey or Baked Country Ham
Tee's Corn Pudding or Kathy's Onion Pudding
Steamed Broccoli   Hollandaise Sauce
Scalloped Oysters
Cranberry Relish
Chocolate Pots de Crème With Orange Meringues or
Coconut-Lemon Cake   Orange Cake

Many traditional favorites still hold a place of honor on this family's menu. Using those as a source of inspiration, Kathy introduces a few new flavor surprises and combinations to each year's recipes.

Here Kathy and Sissy share some of their favorites – both old and new – in this Bluegrass Celebration Menu. Their wish and ours is that you'll find inspiration aplenty to complement your holiday season.

SPINACH PUFFS

Goat cheese and dried tomatoes add flavorful surprises to the traditional spinach casserole.

1¾ cups all-purpose flour
1 teaspoon salt
⅛ teaspoon ground red pepper
1½ cups water
6 tablespoons butter or margarine
1 cup (4 ounces) shredded Cheddar cheese
6 large eggs
Spinach Filling
½ cup freshly grated Parmesan cheese

- **Combine** first 3 ingredients.
- **Combine** water and butter in a large saucepan over medium-high heat; bring to a boil. Stir in flour mixture all at once. Reduce heat, and cook 5 minutes, stirring constantly. (Mixture will pull away from sides of saucepan and form a thin crust on bottom of saucepan.) Remove from heat; cool slightly.
- **Spoon** batter into a large mixing bowl; add Cheddar cheese, beating at medium speed with an electric mixer until well blended. Add eggs, one at a time, beating well after each addition.
- **Shape** dough into 60 (1-inch) balls, and place on lightly greased baking sheets.
- **Bake** at 350° for 45 minutes or until puffed and lightly browned. Transfer to wire racks to cool.
- **Cut** off tops of puffs, and set aside. Spoon Spinach Filling into puffs; replace tops, if desired. Cover and chill.
- **Place** filled puffs on lightly greased baking sheets. Sprinkle with Parmesan cheese.
- **Bake** at 350° for 5 to 10 minutes or until thoroughly heated. Serve immediately. **Yield:** 5 dozen.

Spinach Filling

¼ cup butter or margarine
½ cup all-purpose flour
1 cup milk
1½ cups chicken broth
¾ teaspoon salt
¼ teaspoon pepper
10 dried tomato halves (about ¼ cup)
1 cup boiling water
2 quarts water
¼ pound trimmed spinach leaves
½ cup chopped onion
1 teaspoon olive oil
6 ounces goat cheese, crumbled

- **Melt** butter in a saucepan over medium heat; add flour, stirring with a wire whisk until smooth. Cook 1 minute, stirring constantly. Gradually add milk and broth, stirring until smooth. Cook over medium-high heat 3 to 5 minutes or until thickened and bubbly.

> *"Not a lot has changed since our Christmas Eve celebrations here when I was growing up. I cherish those holiday traditions and want to share them with my children."*

Kathy Nash Cary
chef-owner
Louisville's Lilly's restaurant

While Sissy's pace is measured and sure, each motion almost second nature, Kathy's hands move in a blur of red and green as she creatively garnishes a towering Coconut-Lemon Cake with fresh cranberries and greenery. Nearby bowls of Candied Orange Zest and Orange Glaze stand ready to crown the Nash's traditional Orange Cake.

Kathy and Sissy share a special love of the Bluegrass country and the bounty it provides.

"I wanted my children to experience the same sense of the land that I knew as a child," says Sissy. "Every year we had a garden that always played an important part in our summer. There were tomatoes to can or blackberries to pick. And each fall we made home-made applesauce."

Kathy also credits time she spent with her maternal grand-mother, "Tee," as stimulating her interest in food. "With 13 grandchildren visiting at once, there was always something going on in my grandmother's kitchen. I loved to spend time in Tee's kitchen. I always thought, 'This is the best seat in the house – the most exciting place to be.'"

Now along with son Will and daughter Lilly, Kathy and her husband, Will, host the Nashes in their Louisville home for the family's annual Christmas Eve dinner.

- **Stir** in salt and pepper; remove from heat, and keep warm.
- **Combine** tomato and boiling water; let stand 15 minutes. Drain tomato, and coarsely chop; set aside.
- **Bring** 2 quarts water to a boil. Add spinach, and cook 30 seconds; drain. Rinse with cold water; drain well, pressing between layers of paper towels. Finely chop spinach; set aside.
- **Cook** onion in oil in a large skillet over medium-high heat until tender, stirring constantly. Stir in broth mixture, tomato, and spinach; fold in goat cheese. **Yield:** 4 cups.

LEG OF LAMB WITH HUNTER SAUCE

1 (5-pound) leg of lamb
3 cloves garlic, thinly sliced
3 tablespoons Dijon mustard
1 tablespoon chopped fresh
   rosemary
2 teaspoons cracked pepper
Hunter Sauce

- **Cut** small slits in lamb with a sharp knife; insert garlic slices into slits. Place lamb in a large shallow dish.
- **Combine** mustard, rosemary, and pepper; spread over lamb. Cover and store in refrigerator 1 to 2 days. Remove lamb from refrigerator, and place in a roasting pan; let stand at room temperature 30 minutes.
- **Bake** at 450° for 15 minutes; reduce heat to 350°, and bake 1 additional hour or until meat thermometer inserted in thickest portion registers 145°. Remove from oven; cover loosely with aluminum foil, and let stand 20 minutes or until thermometer registers 150° (medium-rare). Serve with Hunter Sauce. **Yield:** 8 to 10 servings.

Hunter Sauce

½ cup firmly packed brown sugar
½ cup ketchup
¼ cup butter or margarine
¼ cup apple jelly
3 tablespoons lemon juice
1 teaspoon ground cinnamon
½ teaspoon ground allspice
½ teaspoon pepper
¼ teaspoon ground cloves

- **Combine** all ingredients in a medium saucepan; cook over low heat, stirring until smooth. **Yield:** 1⅓ cups.

TEE'S CORN PUDDING

During testing, Sissy's mother's recipe for this classic Southern side dish earned a 3 – our Test Kitchens' highest rating. Kathy's onion version boasts the same creamy richness.

¼ cup sugar
3 tablespoons all-purpose flour
2 teaspoons baking powder
2 teaspoons salt
6 large eggs
2 cups whipping cream
½ cup butter or margarine, melted
6 cups fresh corn kernels *

• **Combine** first 4 ingredients.
• **Beat** eggs with a fork in a large bowl; stir in whipping cream and butter. Gradually add sugar mixture, stirring until smooth; stir in corn. Pour mixture into a lightly greased 13- x 9- x 2-inch baking dish.
• **Bake** at 350° for 45 minutes or until deep golden and mixture is set. Let stand 5 minutes. **Yield:** 8 servings.

* Substitute 6 cups frozen whole kernel or canned shoepeg corn.

Kathy's Onion Pudding: Combine first 4 ingredients as in original recipe. Beat eggs with a fork in a large bowl; stir in whipping cream. Gradually add sugar mixture, stirring until smooth. Substitute 6 cups thinly sliced onion for corn kernels. Combine onion and melted butter in a large skillet over medium heat. Cook 30 to 40 minutes or until onion is caramel colored, stirring often; remove from heat. Add onion to cream mixture, stirring well. Pour into a lightly greased 11- x 7- x 1½-inch baking dish. Bake as directed above, shielding with aluminum foil after 30 minutes to prevent excessive browning.

SCALLOPED OYSTERS

1 quart oysters, undrained
5 cups crushed round buttery crackers, divided
½ teaspoon salt
½ teaspoon ground red pepper
2 teaspoons Worcestershire sauce
2 cups half-and-half
¼ cup unsalted butter, cut into pieces

• **Drain** oysters, reserving 3 tablespoons liquid.
• **Place** half of cracker crumbs in a greased 13- x 9- x 2-inch baking dish. Arrange oysters over crumbs; sprinkle with salt, pepper, and Worcestershire sauce. Top with remaining crumbs; drizzle with reserved oyster liquid and half-and-half. Top with butter.
• **Bake** at 400° for 30 minutes. **Yield:** 8 servings.

CRANBERRY RELISH

2 cups sugar
¾ cup orange juice
4 cups fresh or frozen cranberries
2 teaspoons grated orange rind

• **Combine** sugar and orange juice in a saucepan, stirring well; add cranberries and orange rind. Bring to a boil over medium heat, stirring often.
• **Reduce** heat, and simmer 5 minutes or until cranberry skins pop and mixture thickens. **Yield:** 4 cups.

CHOCOLATE POTS DE CRÈME WITH ORANGE MERINGUES

16 ounces milk chocolate
1½ cups milk
6 egg yolks, lightly beaten
2 to 3 tablespoons bourbon
Garnish: grated milk chocolate
Orange Meringues

• **Combine** 16 ounces chocolate and milk in a heavy saucepan; cook over low heat until chocolate melts, stirring occasionally.
• **Stir** about one-fourth of hot mixture into egg yolks; add to remaining hot mixture, stirring constantly.
• **Cook** over low heat 10 to 15 minutes or until mixture is thickened (do not boil). Remove from heat, and stir in bourbon.
• **Pour** mixture into 6 (4-ounce) custard cups; cool. Cover and chill. Garnish, if desired; serve with Orange Meringues. **Yield:** 6 servings.

Orange Meringues

6 egg whites
½ teaspoon cream of tartar
1 cup sugar
2 teaspoons grated orange rind

• **Beat** egg whites in a large bowl at high speed with an electric mixer until foamy. Add cream of tartar; beat until soft peaks form.
• **Add** sugar, 1 tablespoon at a time, beating until stiff peaks form. Stir in orange rind.
• **Drop** ¼ cup mixture onto a parchment paper-lined baking sheet; spread into a 3-inch circle. Repeat procedure with remaining mixture.
• **Bake** at 200° for 2 hours or until meringues are almost dry. Turn oven off; let cool in oven at least 8 hours.
• **Carefully** remove meringues from parchment paper; store in an airtight container at room temperature up to 2 days or in freezer up to 1 month. **Yield:** 2 dozen.

Note: If meringues become soft or sticky, bake at 200° for 5 minutes. Turn oven off; let meringues cool in oven until dry.

COCONUT-LEMON CAKE
(pictured on front cover and on page 334)

1 cup unsalted butter,
    softened
2 cups sugar
4 large eggs, separated
3 cups all-purpose flour
1 tablespoon baking powder
1 cup milk
1 teaspoon vanilla extract
⅛ teaspoon salt
Lemon Filling
Fluffy White Frosting
1 cup flaked coconut
Garnishes: fresh cranberries,
    seasonal greenery

● **Beat** butter at medium speed with an electric mixer until fluffy; gradually add sugar, beating well. Add egg yolks, one at a time, beating after each addition.
● **Combine** flour and baking powder; add to butter mixture alternately with milk, beginning and ending with flour mixture. Beat at low speed until blended after each addition. Stir in vanilla.
● **Beat** egg whites and salt at high speed with mixer until stiff peaks form. Stir about one-third of egg white into batter; fold in remaining egg white. Spoon batter into three greased and floured 9-inch round cakepans.
● **Bake** at 350° for 18 to 20 minutes or until a wooden pick inserted in center comes out clean. Cool in pans on wire racks 10 minutes; remove from pans, and cool completely on wire racks.
● **Spread** Lemon Filling between layers. Spread Fluffy White Frosting on top and sides of cake. Sprinkle top and sides with coconut; garnish, if desired. **Yield:** 1 (3-layer) cake.

Note: If nonedible greenery is used as a garnish, cut a small circle of heavy-duty plastic wrap and position it in center of cake before arranging greenery and cranberries on top of cake to prevent direct contact with the cake. Remove garnish before serving.

Lemon Filling

1 cup sugar
¼ cup cornstarch
1 cup boiling water
4 egg yolks, lightly beaten
⅓ cup fresh lemon juice
2 tablespoons butter

● **Combine** sugar and cornstarch in a medium saucepan; stir in water. Cook over medium heat, stirring constantly, until sugar and cornstarch dissolve (about 3 minutes). Gradually stir about one-fourth of hot mixture into yolks; add to remaining hot mixture, stirring constantly with a wire whisk. Stir in lemon juice.
● **Cook,** stirring constantly, until mixture is thickened. Remove from heat; stir in butter, and let cool, stirring occasionally. **Yield:** 1⅔ cups.

Fluffy White Frosting

1 cup sugar
1½ cups water
2 tablespoons light corn syrup
4 egg whites
¼ teaspoon cream of tartar

● **Combine** first 3 ingredients in a small heavy saucepan; cook over medium heat, stirring constantly, until clear. Cook, without stirring, until mixture reaches soft ball stage or candy thermometer registers 240°.
● **Beat** egg whites and cream of tartar at high speed with an electric mixer until soft peaks form; slowly add syrup mixture, beating constantly. Beat until stiff peaks form and frosting is desired consistency. **Yield:** 7 cups.

"The kitchen has always been a place of good times. I remember our sitting around the table during holidays making cookies to give our friends or bourbon balls to share with neighbors who stopped by for a visit."

Kathy Nash Cary

Behind the kitchen's frost-etched windowpanes, the air is warm and fragrant with chocolate

and citrus from the morning's baking on this bright, blustery December day.

ORANGE CAKE

(pictured on front cover and on page 335)

Using a 12-cup Bundt pan or 10-inch tube pan streamlines preparation.

½ cup butter, softened
2 cups sugar
7 large eggs, separated
3 cups sifted cake flour
1 tablespoon baking powder
¼ teaspoon salt
½ cup orange juice
½ cup water
1 teaspoon vanilla extract
Orange Glaze
Candied Orange Zest

• **Beat** butter at medium speed with an electric mixer about 2 minutes or until creamy. Gradually add sugar, beating 5 to 7 minutes.
• **Beat** egg yolks lightly; add to butter mixture, beating until well blended.
• **Combine** flour, baking powder, and salt; add to butter mixture alternately with orange juice and water, beginning and ending with flour mixture. Beat at low speed with an electric mixer until blended after each addition. Stir in vanilla.
• **Beat** egg whites at high speed with an electric mixer until foamy; reduce speed to medium, and beat until stiff peaks form. Fold egg white into batter; spoon batter into a greased and floured 12-cup Bundt pan or 10-inch tube pan.
• **Bake** at 350° for 35 to 40 minutes or until a wooden pick inserted in center comes out clean. Immediately place pan on a double layer of damp cloth towels; press towels around sides of pan, and let stand 10 to 15 minutes. Remove cake from pan, and cool completely on a wire rack.
• **Spoon** Orange Glaze over cake; top with Candied Orange Zest. **Yield:** 1 (10-inch) cake.

Orange Glaze

2 large oranges
2 cups sugar
1 tablespoon cornstarch
⅓ cup lemon juice
8 egg yolks, lightly beaten
½ cup butter, softened

• **Squeeze** juice from oranges; pour through a wire-mesh strainer into a 1-cup liquid measuring cup, straining out any seeds. Measure 1 cup juice; reserve remaining orange juice for another use.
• **Combine** sugar and cornstarch in a small saucepan; add lemon juice and 1 cup orange juice, stirring well with a wire whisk. Cook over low heat, stirring until sugar dissolves (about 10 minutes).
• **Stir** about one-fourth of hot mixture into yolks; add to remaining hot mixture, stirring constantly. Cook over low heat, stirring constantly, 10 minutes or until thickened. Remove from heat; add butter, stirring until well blended. Cool; cover and chill. **Yield:** 3½ cups.

Candied Orange Zest

2 large oranges
1 cup water
½ cup sugar
Additional sugar (optional)

• **Remove** zest (orange part only) from oranges, using a zester, being careful not to remove white pith. Cut zest into 2-inch strips.
• **Combine** water and sugar in a small saucepan; cook over medium heat until boiling. Reduce heat to low; stir in zest, and cook mixture 15 to 20 minutes or until candy thermometer registers 220°.
• **Remove** zest strips from syrup with a slotted spoon, and spread on wax paper to cool.
• **Sprinkle** with additional sugar, if desired. **Yield:** 1 cup.

THE 12 DOUGHS OF CHRISTMAS

....

On the first dough of Christmas, our true love came to be . . . *mmm, yes,* the Easy Santa Cookies – a delicious homage to St. Nick. Yet those Pinwheels were festive and scrumptious, too. So were the Christmas Jammies. And the Lollipop Cookies. Well, it's easy to get carried away.

Southern Living reader Ellender Mills of Raleigh, North Carolina, told us how much fun it is to use one basic butter cookie dough, divide it into quarters, add a little peanut butter and frosting here, some peppermint and cinnamon there, to create a delightful variety of recipes. Enter "The 12 Doughs of Christmas," a nod to Ellender and the famous carol.

BASIC BUTTER COOKIE DOUGH

You can make four varieties of cookies from one recipe. To make all 12 types, prepare the recipe three times. (Most mixers are not large enough to accommodate such a heavy volume of dough.)

2 cups butter or margarine, softened
1 cup firmly packed brown sugar
1 cup sugar
2 large eggs
7½ cups all-purpose flour
4 teaspoons baking powder
1 teaspoon salt
¼ cup milk
1 tablespoon vanilla extract

• **Beat** butter at medium speed with an electric mixer until fluffy; gradually add sugars, beating well. Add eggs, one at a time, beating after each addition.
• **Combine** flour, baking powder, and salt; add to butter mixture alternately with milk, beginning and ending with flour mixture. Beat at low speed after each addition until mixture is blended. Stir in vanilla.
• **Divide** dough into 4 equal portions; wrap each portion in plastic wrap to prevent drying out. Chill. Proceed with cookie instructions of choice. **Yield:** 4½ pounds.

Note: This dough may be frozen, but cookies made from thawed dough may be dry. To bake Basic Butter Cookie

Dough cookies, follow the directions for Easy Santa Cookies, omitting decorating ingredients.

Ellender Mills
Raleigh, North Carolina

EASY SANTA COOKIES

¼ Basic Butter Cookie Dough
   recipe (see recipe)
Sugar
1 (4¼-ounce) tube red decorating
   frosting
1 (4¼-ounce) tube white
   decorating frosting
¼ cup (1½ ounces) semisweet
   chocolate morsels
¼ cup red cinnamon candies
30 miniature marshmallows
⅔ cup flaked coconut

● **Shape** Basic Butter Cookie Dough into 1-inch balls, and place on lightly greased cookie sheets. Dip a flat-bottomed glass into sugar, and flatten balls to ¼-inch thickness.
● **Bake** at 350° for 10 minutes or until lightly browned. Remove to wire racks to cool.
● **Spread** red frosting on top portion of cookie to resemble hat; spread white frosting on lower portion of cookie to resemble beard. Attach 2 chocolate morsels and 1 cinnamon candy with a small amount of frosting to resemble eyes and nose. Gently press coconut into white frosting. Press marshmallow onto red frosting to resemble tassel on hat. **Yield:** 2½ dozen.

PINWHEELS

¼ Basic Butter Cookie Dough
   recipe (see recipe)
1 (1-ounce) square unsweetened
   chocolate, melted

● **Divide** Basic Butter Cookie Dough in half. Knead chocolate into 1 portion until well blended.
● **Roll** each portion into a 12- x 9-inch rectangle on wax paper. Invert chocolate dough onto plain dough; peel off wax paper. Press chocolate dough firmly onto plain dough with a rolling pin. Roll up, jellyroll fashion, starting with long side; cover and chill 1 hour or until firm.
● **Cut** dough into ¼-inch slices; place on lightly greased cookie sheets.
● **Bake** at 350° for 10 to 12 minutes or until lightly browned. Remove to wire racks to cool. **Yield:** 3½ dozen.

CHERRY CHOCOLATES

¼ Basic Butter Cookie Dough
   recipe (see recipe)
36 milk chocolate stars
   (4½ ounces)
18 red candied cherries, cut
   in half

● **Press** rounded teaspoonfuls of Basic Butter Cookie Dough around chocolate stars, pinching tops to form peaks. Place cherry halves on peaks.
● **Bake** at 350° for 12 minutes or until firm (cookies will be pale). **Yield:** 3 dozen.

ALMOND BRICKLE TREATS

1 (7.5-ounce) package almond
   brickle chips
¼ Basic Butter Cookie Dough
   recipe (see recipe)
2 cups (12 ounces) semisweet
   chocolate morsels
½ cup chopped pecans

● **Stir** or knead almond brickle into Basic Butter Cookie Dough; press into a lightly greased 15- x 10- x 1-inch jellyroll pan.
● **Bake** at 350° for 14 minutes or until lightly browned.
● **Sprinkle** chocolate morsels on top; cover with aluminum foil, and let stand 10 minutes.
● **Spread** melted morsels evenly over surface; sprinkle with pecans, and press gently into chocolate. Cool completely on a wire rack.
● **Cut** into 2- x 1-inch bars. **Yield:** 6 dozen.

PEANUT BUTTER SHORTBREAD

⅔ cup creamy peanut butter
¼ Basic Butter Cookie Dough
   recipe (see recipe)
36 milk chocolate kisses,
   unwrapped

● **Knead** peanut butter into Basic Butter Cookie Dough until smooth and well blended.
● **Shape** dough into 1-inch balls, and place on lightly greased cookie sheets. Press thumb in center of each ball to make an indentation.
● **Bake** at 350° for 12 minutes or until lightly browned. Immediately press chocolate kiss in center of each cookie. Remove to wire racks to cool. **Yield:** 3 dozen.

SUGARPLUM STICKS

1 cup mixed chopped candied
   fruit
1 cup chopped pecans
¼ Basic Butter Cookie Dough
   recipe (see recipe)
Sifted powdered sugar

● **Knead** candied fruit and pecans into Basic Butter Cookie Dough until well blended.
● **Shape** dough into 2- x ½-inch logs, and place on lightly greased cookie sheets.
● **Bake** at 350° for 12 minutes or until lightly browned. Roll warm cookies in powdered sugar; place on wire racks to cool. **Yield:** about 3 dozen.

CHRISTMAS JAMMIES

¼ Basic Butter Cookie Dough recipe (see recipe on page 320)
¼ cup seedless raspberry jam

• **Roll** Basic Butter Cookie Dough to ⅛-inch thickness on a lightly floured surface. Cut with a 2-inch round cutter, and place on lightly greased baking sheets. Cut center from half of cookies with a 1-inch star-shaped cutter.
• **Bake** at 350° for 8 to 10 minutes or until lightly browned. Remove to wire racks to cool.
• **Spread** ½ teaspoon jam on solid cookies; top with cutout cookies. **Yield:** 2 dozen.

APRICOT COOKIES

⅔ cup apricot preserves, divided
¼ Basic Butter Cookie Dough recipe (see recipe on page 320)
Granulated sugar
1¾ cups sifted powdered sugar
2 tablespoons butter or margarine, softened
½ cup sliced almonds or coconut, toasted

• **Knead** 2 tablespoons preserves into Basic Butter Cookie Dough.
• **Shape** dough into 1-inch balls; place on lightly greased baking sheets. Dip a flat-bottomed glass in granulated sugar; flatten balls to ¼-inch thickness.
• **Bake** at 350° for 10 to 12 minutes or until lightly browned. Remove to wire racks to cool.
• **Combine** remaining preserves, 1¾ cups powdered sugar, and butter in a mixing bowl. Beat at medium speed with an electric mixer until well blended. Spread over cookies; sprinkle with almonds. **Yield:** 2½ dozen.

DATE BARS

1 (8-ounce) package chopped dates
½ cup sugar
½ cup hot water
1 tablespoon lemon juice
¼ Basic Butter Cookie Dough recipe (see recipe on page 320)

• **Combine** first 4 ingredients in a saucepan; bring to a boil over medium heat. Reduce heat, and cook 4 to 5 minutes or until thickened, stirring occasionally. Cool.
• **Press** two-thirds of Basic Butter Cookie Dough into a lightly greased 13- x 9- x 2-inch pan; spread date mixture over dough. Crumble remaining dough over date mixture.
• **Bake** at 350° for 25 minutes or until browned. Cool completely in pan on a wire rack.
• **Cut** into 2- x 1-inch bars. **Yield:** 3 dozen.

LOLLIPOP COOKIES

¼ Basic Butter Cookie Dough recipe (see recipe on page 320)
12 wooden craft sticks
Assorted candies and sprinkles

• **Shape** Basic Butter Cookie Dough into 1½-inch balls; place on greased cookie sheets. Dip a flat-bottomed glass into flour, and flatten balls to ⅜-inch thickness.
• **Insert** a wooden craft stick into each cookie to resemble a lollipop. Decorate with candies or sprinkles as desired.
• **Bake** at 350° for 10 to 12 minutes or until lightly browned. Cool completely on cookie sheets. **Yield:** 1 dozen.

PEPPERMINT COOKIES

⅓ cup crushed hard peppermint candy (about 15 candies)
¼ Basic Butter Cookie Dough recipe (see recipe on page 320)
1 (16-ounce) container white frosting, divided
2 drops of red liquid food coloring
2 to 3 teaspoons water

• **Knead** candy into Basic Butter Cookie Dough until well blended.
• **Roll** dough to ⅛-inch thickness on a lightly floured surface. Cut with a 2½-inch round cutter, and place on lightly greased cookie sheets.
• **Bake** at 350° for 10 to 12 minutes or until lightly browned. Remove to wire racks to cool.
• **Combine** ¼ cup frosting and food coloring, stirring well. Add enough water to mixture to reach drizzling consistency.
• **Spread** cookies with white frosting. Immediately drizzle lines of pink frosting across cookies, and carefully draw a wooden pick across lines to create a pattern. **Yield:** 2½ dozen.

SPICE THINS

½ teaspoon ground ginger
½ teaspoon ground cinnamon
¼ teaspoon ground nutmeg
¼ Basic Butter Cookie Dough recipe (see recipe on page 320)
2 (2-ounce) squares vanilla-flavored candy coating, melted
Ground cinnamon

• **Stir** or knead first 3 ingredients into Basic Butter Cookie Dough.
• **Shape** dough into 1-inch balls, and place on lightly greased cookie sheets. Dip a flat-bottomed glass into flour, and flatten balls to ¼-inch thickness.
• **Bake** at 350° for 10 minutes or until lightly browned. Remove to wire racks to cool.
• **Drizzle** candy coating over cookies; sprinkle with cinnamon. **Yield:** 2½ dozen.

Crème Brûlée

Crème brûlée's reputation as a complicated, hoity-toity French dessert is misleading. It's simple. Crème brûlée (krehm broo-LAY), which means "burnt cream" in French, is simply a custard wearing a brown sugar cap.

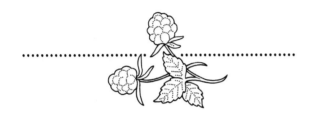

If your grandmother didn't leave you a set of antique silver crème brûlée servers, glass custard cups will work equally well. All baking times are for 5- x 1-inch round individual baking dishes. As a general rule, to use 4-, 6-, or 8-ounce custard cups, bake for an additional 15 to 20 minutes. When the crème brûlée is done, the center will still be slightly liquid and a knife inserted near center will not come out clean. The yield will vary with different size dishes: For 4-ounce cups you'll get 10 servings, for 6-ounce cups you'll get 7 servings, and for 8-ounce cups you'll get 5 servings.

BASIC CRÈME BRÛLÉE

2 cups whipping cream
5 egg yolks
½ cup sugar
1 tablespoon vanilla extract
½ cup firmly packed light brown sugar
Garnishes: fresh raspberries, fresh mint sprigs

• **Combine** first 4 ingredients, stirring with a wire whisk until sugar dissolves and mixture is smooth. Pour evenly into 5 (5- x 1-inch) round individual baking dishes; place dishes in a large roasting pan or a 15- x 10- x 1-inch jellyroll pan. Add hot water to pan to depth of ½ inch.

• **Bake** at 275° for 45 to 50 minutes or until almost set. Cool custards in water in pan on a wire rack. Remove from pan; cover and chill at least 8 hours.
• **Sprinkle** about 1½ tablespoons brown sugar evenly over each custard; place custards in pan.
• **Broil** 5½ inches from heat (with electric oven door partially opened) until sugar melts. Let stand 5 minutes to allow sugar to harden. Garnish, if desired. **Yield:** 5 servings.

Almond Crème Brûlée: Reduce vanilla to 1 teaspoon; add 1 additional egg yolk, 2 tablespoons almond liqueur, and ¼ cup chopped toasted almonds to custard mixture. Proceed as directed in basic recipe, baking 1 hour.

Berry Crème Brûlée: Place 8 to 10 fresh blackberries or raspberries in each baking dish; pour custard mixture over berries. Proceed as directed in basic recipe, baking 45 minutes.

Chocolate Crème Brûlée: Combine 4 (1-ounce) squares semisweet chocolate and ½ cup whipping cream from basic recipe in a small heavy saucepan; cook over low heat, stirring constantly, until chocolate melts. Add remaining 1½ cups whipping cream; reduce vanilla to 1 teaspoon. Proceed as directed in basic recipe, baking 55 minutes. For a Chocolate-Raspberry version, place 8 to 10 fresh raspberries in each baking dish, add custard, and increase baking time to 1 hour and 5 minutes.

Coffee Crème Brûlée: Combine 1½ teaspoons instant coffee granules and ¼ cup whipping cream from basic recipe; cook over medium heat, stirring constantly, about 2 minutes or until coffee dissolves. Add remaining 1¾ cups whipping cream; reduce vanilla to 1 teaspoon. Proceed as directed in basic recipe, baking 45 to 50 minutes.

Double Raspberry Crème Brûlée: Reduce vanilla to 1 teaspoon; add 1 additional egg yolk and 1½ tablespoons raspberry liqueur to custard mixture. Place 8 to 10 fresh raspberries in each baking dish; pour custard mixture over berries. Proceed as directed in basic recipe, baking 55 minutes.

Ginger Crème Brûlée: Reduce vanilla to 1 teaspoon; add 2 tablespoons grated fresh ginger to custard mixture. Proceed as directed in basic recipe, baking 1 hour and 5 minutes.

Orange Crème Brûlée: Reduce vanilla to 1 teaspoon; add 1 additional egg yolk, 2 tablespoons grated orange rind, and 2 tablespoons orange liqueur to custard mixture. Proceed as directed in basic recipe, baking 1 hour.

Peppermint Crème Brûlée: Reduce vanilla to 1 teaspoon; add 1 additional egg yolk and 3 tablespoons peppermint schnapps. Proceed as directed in basic recipe, baking 50 minutes. Substitute 5 hard peppermint candies, crushed, for the brown sugar; broil as directed.

White Chocolate-Macadamia Nut Crème Brûlée: (Pictured on page 336) Combine 4 ounces white chocolate and ½ cup whipping cream from basic recipe in a heavy saucepan; cook over low heat, stirring constantly, until chocolate melts. Add remaining 1½ cups whipping cream; reduce vanilla to 1 teaspoon. Proceed as directed in basic recipe. Place 1 tablespoon chopped macadamia nuts, toasted, in each dish; pour custard over nuts. Bake as directed 1 hour and 10 minutes.

BRÛLÉE BASICS

■ Always bake crème brûlée in a baking dish in a larger pan filled with hot water. This is a water bath. The water creates a cushion from the heat of the oven, allowing the custards to bake slowly without curdling.

■ We found that Dixie Crystals brand brown sugar works best for crème brûlées. It caramelizes evenly to a perfect golden brown.

■ Be careful not to burn yourself. Before you take the water bath out of the oven, remove some of the water with a basting bulb or a long-handled ladle.

■ You can bake the crème brûlées ahead of time, but wait until just a few minutes before serving to caramelize the sugar. The caramelized sugar will begin to liquify if the custards sit for more than an hour.

■ When you broil the brown sugar, get the crème brûlées as close to the heating element as possible. To do this, place an inverted roasting pan on the top shelf of the oven; then place the crème brûlées on a baking sheet on top of the roasting pan.

■ An adventurous alternative to the broiler is a welding torch. Your dinner guests will think you have gone mad, but the torch gives the ultimate glassy crust. Torching is the professional chef's method of choice.

■ Don't waste your money on a salamander – a kitchen gadget sold in gourmet catalogs and used for caramelizing the top of crème brûlées or browning the top of foods. It works like a branding iron to melt the brown sugar. When we tried one, we ended up with burnt – not caramelized – sugar.

■ Crème brûlée is an even more extraordinary dessert if the custard is cold and firm when you crack into the warm caramelized sugar topping. Here's the secret: Place the custards in a roasting pan filled with ice, and then broil them. The ice keeps the custards cold while the sugar melts.

SAVORY CRÈME BRÛLÉES

For these savory brûlées, use the basic recipe on the previous page, but omit the brown sugar topping. Serve them warm from the oven as an appetizer with a mixed green salad or as an accompaniment to steaks, roasts, or chops.

Onion Crème Brûlée: Melt 2 tablespoons butter in a skillet over low heat; add 1 cup coarsely chopped onion, and cook 45 minutes or until caramelized, stirring occasionally. Reduce sugar to 1 tablespoon in basic recipe (page 323), omit vanilla, and add 1 teaspoon salt and caramelized onion to custard mixture. Place mixture in container of an electric blender, and process until smooth. Proceed as directed in basic recipe, baking 50 minutes.

Roasted Garlic Crème Brûlée: Cut off the flat end of 2 garlic heads, and spread apart whole cloves, leaving tight outer covering intact. Trim pointed end so head will sit flat. Place garlic heads, trimmed ends down, on a sheet of aluminum foil. Drizzle with 2 teaspoons olive oil; wrap in aluminum foil. Bake at 350° for 1 hour; cool. Squeeze out pulp from each clove. Reduce sugar to 1 tablespoon in basic recipe (page 323), omit vanilla, and add 1 teaspoon salt and garlic pulp to custard mixture. Place mixture in container of an electric blender, and process until smooth. Proceed as directed in basic recipe, baking 40 minutes.

Roquefort-and-Black Pepper Crème Brûlée: Reduce sugar to 1 tablespoon in basic recipe (page 323), omit vanilla, and add 1 teaspoon salt, ¼ cup Roquefort cheese, and 1 teaspoon freshly ground black pepper to custard mixture. Place mixture in container of an electric blender, and process until smooth. Proceed as directed in basic recipe, baking 45 minutes.

IT'S ALL IN THE GAME

....

Though "Cornish hen" *sounds* English, and with its dignified trussing *looks* English, it's actually as American as iced tea. (We can thank American crossbreeding of Cornish gamecocks and White Rock hens.)

Such a well-bred reputation pays off, especially during the holidays, when the small but plump golden birds decorate holiday platters beautifully. They also keep cooking times short (less than whole chickens), and costs down. Here are a few more bonuses.

■ Each hen, from ¾ to 1½ pounds, is enough for one serving and will hold 1 cup of stuffing.

■ Hens feature all white meat with a slightly gamey flavor, due in part to a diet of fitting holiday flavors: acorns and cranberries.

CRANBERRY-CORNBREAD STUFFED CORNISH HENS

1 (6-ounce) package cornbread stuffing mix
½ cup water
½ cup thinly sliced celery
1 (8-ounce) container soft cream cheese with chives and onions, divided
½ cup fresh or frozen cranberries, halved
¼ cup coarsely chopped pecans
4 (1 to 1½-pound) Cornish hens
1 tablespoon vegetable oil

● **Combine** seasoning packet from stuffing mix, water, and celery in a large saucepan; bring to a boil. Cover, reduce heat, and simmer 5 minutes.
● **Add** ¼ cup cream cheese, stirring until blended. Stir in stuffing mix, cranberries, and pecans. Remove from heat; cover and let stand 5 minutes.

● **Loosen** skin from hens without totally detaching skin; place remaining cream cheese under skin of hens. Lightly spoon stuffing mixture into hens; close opening with skewers. Place hens, breast side up, in a roasting pan; brush with oil.
● **Bake** at 350° for 1 hour or until thermometer inserted in stuffing registers 165°. Remove skewers, and serve. **Yield:** 4 servings.

Betty E. Taylor
Piqua, Ohio

CORNISH HENS À L'ORANGE

1 seedless orange, sliced
6 leaves fresh basil *
2 (1½-pound) Cornish hens, split
1 teaspoon salt
1 teaspoon ground white pepper
2 teaspoons grated orange rind
2 teaspoons dried thyme
¼ cup orange juice concentrate, thawed and undiluted
¾ cup water
1 tablespoon all-purpose flour
2 tablespoons water

● **Arrange** orange slices in a single layer in a lightly greased 11- x 7- x 1½-inch baking dish; top with basil.
● **Sprinkle** hens with salt and pepper; place hens, breast side down, in baking dish. Sprinkle with orange rind and thyme.
● **Bake** at 375° for 40 minutes.
● **Combine** orange juice concentrate and ¾ cup water. Remove hens from oven, and turn hens breast side up; pour juice mixture over hens. Increase heat to 400°, and bake 20 additional minutes. Transfer hens to a serving platter, reserving drippings; keep hens warm. Pour pan drippings into a saucepan, and place over medium heat.
● **Combine** flour and 2 tablespoons water, stirring well; add to pan drippings, stirring constantly. Bring to a boil; boil 1 minute. Serve with hens. **Yield:** 2 servings.

* Substitute 4 teaspoons dried basil.
Georgie O'Neill-Massa
Welaka, Florida

HOW TO PLAY THE GAME

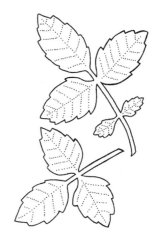

Sure, that whole Cornish hen on your plate looks harmless, but there's one delicate matter. *How do you properly eat the thing without sending it into orbit?*

For the answer, we looked to the country's most formal city – Washington, D.C., and The Protocol School of Washington.

"A Cornish hen," says school director Dorothea Johnson, "is what I put under the category of 'challenging food' – everybody is a little hesitant about eating it."

The protocol, she says, "is that one should not use one's hands to eat the bird. It really should be eaten with a knife and fork, which should be kept as close to the plate as possible to keep the bird secured." She laughs at a humorous memory. "I've seen birds scoot right off the plate because they hadn't been secured."

Most important? "Don't be nervous," she says. "You have to eat it with as much confidence as possible. Otherwise, accidents will happen." The trick for the Cornish-hen-weary, she suggests, is to ask that birds be presented deboned or presplit.

CORNISH HENS TARRAGON

4 (1½-pound) Cornish hens, split
¼ cup olive oil
¼ cup fresh lemon juice
¼ cup soy sauce
¼ cup dry vermouth
2 cloves garlic, crushed
1½ teaspoons salt
½ teaspoon coarsely ground black pepper
3 teaspoons dried tarragon, divided
Vegetable cooking spray

• **Place** hens, breast side down, in a large baking dish or heavy-duty zip-top plastic bag.
• **Combine** oil and next 6 ingredients; pour over hens. Sprinkle with 1½ teaspoons tarragon; cover or seal, and store in refrigerator at least 8 hours.
• **Arrange** hens, breast side up, on a broiler rack coated with cooking spray; place rack in broiler pan. Sprinkle remaining 1½ teaspoons tarragon evenly over hens.
• **Bake** at 350° for 1 hour or until tender. **Yield:** 4 servings.

Lisa Conlon
Crystal River, Florida

CAJUN-FRIED CORNISH HENS

You like fried chicken, right? Why not try Cajun-Fried Cornish Hens? We loved 'em. (It's nice to have a whole bird to yourself.)

3 tablespoons Cajun seasoning
1 teaspoon ground red pepper
4 (1¼-pound) Cornish hens
½ cup Italian salad dressing
1 cup all-purpose flour
1½ gallons vegetable oil

• **Combine** seasoning and pepper; rub over inside and outside of hens.
• **Fill** the injector needle of a bulb baster with salad dressing and squirt under skin of hens. Tie legs together with one end of a 30-inch string.
• **Place** flour in a large plastic bag; add hens, one at a time, and shake to coat thoroughly.

• **Pour** oil to depth of 4 inches into a deep pot of a propane cooker; heat to 350°. Carefully lower hens into hot oil, using string.
• **Fry** 18 to 20 minutes or until meat thermometer inserted in hen registers 180°. Remove hens from oil, and drain on paper towels; remove string. **Yield:** 4 servings.

Denise Boudreaux Schexnayder
Houma, Louisiana

AN ENCHANTED EVENING

....

Indulge in our extravagant menu that is so wonderful you can't afford *not* to try it. Yes, it's expensive – probably as much as you'd spend at a nice restaurant. Because this menu is so special, treat yourselves at least once.

LUXURY DINNER MENU
Serves Two

Mixed Greens With Tarragon Vinaigrette
Crab-Stuffed Lobster Tails
Blue Cheese-Walnut Stuffed Fillets
Chocolate Truffle Mousse With Raspberry Sauce

MIXED GREENS WITH TARRAGON VINAIGRETTE

½ teaspoon sugar
½ teaspoon dried tarragon
¼ teaspoon salt
¼ teaspoon dry mustard
⅛ teaspoon pepper
½ teaspoon minced onion
1 tablespoon tarragon vinegar
1 tablespoon cider vinegar
2 tablespoons olive oil
2 cups mixed salad greens
1 tablespoon pine nuts, toasted

• **Combine** first 9 ingredients in a jar; cover tightly, and shake vigorously. Pour over salad greens; toss gently to coat. Sprinkle with pine nuts. **Yield:** 2 servings.

CRAB-STUFFED LOBSTER TAILS

Have lobsters steamed at your supermarket to save time.

2 quarts water
2 tablespoons salt
2 (1½- to 1¾-pound) live lobsters
½ pound fresh lump crabmeat
1 clove garlic, minced
1 tablespoon chopped fresh parsley
2 tablespoons freshly grated Parmesan cheese
2 tablespoons fine, dry breadcrumbs
¼ teaspoon salt
¼ teaspoon Old Bay seasoning
¼ teaspoon pepper
2 tablespoons butter, melted
1 teaspoon lemon juice
Garlic-Butter Sauce
Garnishes: lemon halves, fresh Italian parsley sprigs

• **Combine** water and 2 tablespoons salt in a large Dutch oven; bring to a boil. Plunge lobsters, head first, into boiling water; return to a boil. Cover, reduce heat, and simmer, 10 minutes; drain and let cool.
• **Break** off large claws and legs. Crack claw and leg shells, using a seafood or nut cracker; remove meat, and set aside. Break off tail. Cut top side of tail shell lengthwise, using kitchen shears. Cut through center of meat and remove vein. Leave meat in shell. Rinse and set aside.
• **Drain** and flake crabmeat, removing any bits of shell. Combine crabmeat and next 9 ingredients; toss gently. Spoon into lobster tail. Place on a baking sheet.
• **Bake** at 400° for 12 minutes or until thoroughly heated. Serve with Garlic-Butter Sauce and claw and leg meat. Garnish, if desired. **Yield:** 2 servings.

Garlic-Butter Sauce

½ cup butter
2 tablespoons whipping cream
2 tablespoons lemon juice
1 clove garlic, minced

● **Melt** butter in a saucepan over low heat; add whipping cream, and cook 1 minute, stirring constantly. Stir in lemon juice and garlic. **Yield:** ⅔ cup.

BLUE CHEESE-WALNUT STUFFED FILLETS

¼ cup crumbled blue cheese
2 tablespoons finely chopped walnuts, toasted
2 teaspoons half-and-half
2 (1-inch-thick) beef tenderloin steaks (6 ounces each)
2 tablespoons butter or margarine
1 clove garlic, minced
3 green onions, finely chopped
⅓ cup Madeira wine

● **Combine** first 3 ingredients. Cut a pocket into side of each steak. Spoon blue cheese mixture evenly into steak pockets. Set aside.
● **Melt** butter in a medium skillet over medium-high heat; add garlic and green onions, and cook, stirring constantly, until tender. Remove garlic mixture, reserving butter in skillet; set garlic mixture aside.
● **Cook** steaks in skillet over medium-high heat 7 minutes on each side or to desired degree of doneness. Remove steaks, reserving drippings in skillet. Add wine to drippings, and cook 1 to 2 minutes or until reduced by half. Stir in garlic mixture; spoon over steaks. **Yield:** 2 servings.

Wanda Sanders Randall
Birmingham, Alabama

CHOCOLATE TRUFFLE MOUSSE WITH RASPBERRY SAUCE

8 (1-ounce) squares semisweet chocolate
¼ cup light corn syrup
¼ cup butter or margarine
2 egg yolks, lightly beaten
1 cup whipping cream, divided
2 tablespoons powdered sugar
½ teaspoon vanilla extract
Garnish: chocolate curls
Raspberry Sauce

● **Combine** first 3 ingredients in a heavy saucepan; cook over low heat, stirring constantly, until chocolate melts.
● **Combine** yolks and ¼ cup whipping cream. Gradually stir about ½ cup chocolate mixture into yolk mixture; add to remaining chocolate mixture, stirring constantly. Cook over medium-low heat 1 minute or until a thermometer registers 160°. Remove from heat; cool to room temperature.
● **Beat** remaining ¾ cup whipping cream until foamy; gradually add powdered sugar, beating until soft peaks form. Stir in vanilla.
● **Stir** ½ cup whipped cream mixture into chocolate mixture; fold in remaining cream mixture. Spoon into 4 stemmed glasses; cover and chill at least 8 hours. Garnish, if desired. Serve with Raspberry Sauce. **Yield:** 4 servings.

Raspberry Sauce

1 (10-ounce) package frozen raspberries, thawed
2 teaspoons cornstarch
⅓ cup light corn syrup

● **Place** raspberries in container of an electric blender; process 1 minute or until smooth, stopping once to scrape down sides. Pour mixture through a wire-mesh strainer into a small saucepan, discarding seeds. Add cornstarch, stirring well; stir in corn syrup.
● **Cook** over medium heat, stirring constantly, until mixture boils. Boil 1 minute, stirring constantly. Remove from heat; cool. **Yield:** 1⅓ cups.

Nancy Williams
Starkville, Mississippi

MERRY MOUSSE

....

For an elegant, easy appetizer showpiece, choose a festive mold and fill it with a rich, airy mousse (French for "froth" or "foam"). Rising above sliced fruit and vegetables, cold cuts, dainty crackers, and hearty breads, these recipes make decorative, delicious centerpieces with little effort and lots of imagination.

Or you could try piping your favorite mousse into sliced vegetables, pita wedges, rolled strips of tenderloin – you name it. Coming up with serving ideas is almost as fun as savoring these recipes.

CRAB MOUSSE

1 envelope unflavored gelatin
¼ cup cold water
2 egg yolks, lightly beaten
1 teaspoon dry mustard
½ teaspoon salt
¼ teaspoon paprika
1 cup milk
2 tablespoons butter or margarine
3 tablespoons lemon juice
1 pound fresh lump crabmeat, drained

● **Sprinkle** gelatin over cold water in a 1-cup liquid measuring cup.
● **Combine** egg yolks and next 6 ingredients in a heavy saucepan; cook over low heat, stirring constantly, until mixture thickens. Add gelatin mixture, stirring until gelatin dissolves; chill until consistency of unbeaten egg white.
● **Flake** crabmeat, removing any bits of shell; gently fold crabmeat into gelatin mixture, and spoon into a lightly oiled 3-cup mold. Cover and chill at least 8 hours. Unmold and serve with crackers. **Yield:** 2⅔ cups.

Ethel Jernegan
Savannah, Georgia

CURRIED CHICKEN MOUSSE

1 envelope unflavored gelatin
1 cup cold water, divided
2 teaspoons chicken-flavored
   bouillon granules
¼ teaspoon salt
¼ teaspoon ground red pepper
1 teaspoon curry powder
2 teaspoons minced onion
1½ cups finely chopped cooked
   chicken
¼ cup finely chopped celery
1 (2-ounce) jar diced pimiento,
   drained
1 tablespoon chopped fresh
   parsley
1 cup whipping cream

• **Sprinkle** gelatin over ½ cup cold water in a saucepan; let stand 1 minute. Cook over low heat, stirring until gelatin dissolves (about 2 minutes).
• **Add** bouillon granules and next 3 ingredients, stirring until granules dissolve; remove from heat. Add remaining ½ cup water and onion, stirring well; chill until consistency of unbeaten egg white.
• **Stir** in chicken and remaining ingredients; spoon into a lightly oiled 4-cup mold. Cover and chill at least 8 hours. Unmold and serve with crackers. **Yield:** 4 cups.

HAM MOUSSE PITAS

1 (8-ounce) package cream cheese,
   softened
½ cup butter or margarine,
   softened
1 tablespoon Dijon mustard
1 tablespoon cognac
¼ cup finely chopped green
   onions
1½ teaspoons salt
1 teaspoon pepper
½ pound ham, finely chopped
1 cup whipping cream,
   whipped
2 (8-ounce) packages miniature
   pita bread rounds
1 (8-ounce) package Swiss cheese
   slices
1 head Bibb lettuce

• **Beat** cream cheese and butter at medium speed with an electric mixer until creamy. Add mustard and next 4 ingredients; beat at low speed just until blended. Fold in ham and whipped cream.
• **Cut** pita rounds in half; cut cheese slices into small triangles. Tear lettuce to fit pita halves.
• **Place** a cheese triangle and lettuce piece in each pita half; pipe or spoon about 1½ tablespoons ham mixture into each pita half. Cover loosely; chill 1 hour or until firm. **Yield:** 2½ dozen.

Barbara Seiler
Saluda, North Carolina

MUSTARD MOUSSE

1 envelope unflavored gelatin
¼ cup cold water
¼ cup dry white wine
2 (8-ounce) cartons sour
   cream
2 cups mayonnaise or salad
   dressing
2 tablespoons prepared
   horseradish
⅓ cup chopped fresh or frozen
   chives
½ cup spicy brown mustard
2 tablespoons dry mustard
2 teaspoons lemon juice
¼ teaspoon ground red pepper
Garnishes: fresh chives, lemon
   rind strip

• **Sprinkle** gelatin over cold water in a small saucepan; let stand 1 minute. Cook over low heat, stirring until gelatin dissolves; stir in wine.
• **Combine** sour cream and next 7 ingredients; add to gelatin mixture, stirring until blended. Spoon mixture into a lightly oiled 6-cup mold; cover and chill at least 8 hours.
• **Unmold** and garnish, if desired. Serve with sliced salami, ripe olives, pimiento-stuffed olives, gherkins, pepperoncini peppers, and assorted breads. **Yield:** 5 cups.

ANGEL WINGS AND SOUTHERN THINGS

....

A tiny halo with wispy ribbon streamers falls from each invitation as it unfolds. It announces an angelic theme with Southern touches – and the beginning of another cherished memory for a circle of Rockwall, Texas, friends.

This time they'll celebrate at Palmer Ragsdale's home with a mother-daughter brunch that creatively joins the traditions of Southern Christmas of the past and the talent of Christmas present.

HEAVENLY MENU
Serves Eight

Spicy Tomato Warm-Up
Starlight Cheese Bites
Angel's Wing Rolls
Curried Fruit Medley
Toasty Southern Pecan Tarts
Boiled Christmas Custard

SPICY TOMATO WARM-UP

1 (46-ounce) can spicy
   vegetable juice
3 beef-flavored bouillon
   cubes
1 tablespoon Worcestershire
   sauce
3 tablespoons lemon juice
⅛ teaspoon pepper
¼ to ½ teaspoon hot
   sauce

• **Combine** all ingredients in a large saucepan; cook over medium heat until bouillon cubes dissolve. Serve warm. **Yield:** 5½ cups.

Note: Recipe may be doubled.

STARLIGHT CHEESE BITES

½ cup butter or margarine,
   softened
2 cups (8 ounces) shredded extra-
   sharp Cheddar cheese
2½ cups all-purpose flour
¾ teaspoon salt
¾ teaspoon ground red pepper
⅓ cup cold water

• **Beat** butter at medium speed with an electric mixer; add cheese, beating until blended.
• **Combine** flour, salt, and red pepper; gradually add to cheese mixture, beating until blended after each addition. Add water, beating until mixture forms a firm dough.
• **Roll** dough to ¼-inch thickness on a lightly floured surface. Cut, using a 1½-inch star-shaped cutter, and place on lightly greased baking sheets.
• **Bake** at 350° for 15 minutes or until golden. Remove from pans, and cool on wire racks. Store in an airtight container. **Yield:** 4½ dozen.

ANGEL'S WING ROLLS

2 (8-ounce) cans refrigerated
   crescent rolls
2 tablespoons poppy seeds
2 tablespoons sesame seeds

• **Unroll** 1 can of rolls, and separate into 2 long rectangles. Press perforations to seal. Using a knife, cut rectangles in half crosswise, forming 4 small rectangles. Cut each rectangle in half, forming 8 squares. Cut each square diagonally to form 4 triangles. Repeat procedure with remaining can rolls.
• **Press** 3 triangles together on a baking sheet to resemble angel body and wings. Roll 1 triangle into a ball; dip into poppy seeds to resemble hair. Press ball against body and wings to resemble head. Sprinkle wings with sesame seeds. Repeat procedure with remaining triangles.
• **Bake** at 375° for 5 minutes or until rolls are golden. Carefully transfer to a serving plate with a wide spatula. **Yield:** 16 rolls.

CURRIED FRUIT MEDLEY

1 (29-ounce) can sliced peaches
2 (15¼-ounce) cans pineapple
   chunks
1 (10-ounce) jar maraschino
   cherries
1 cup firmly packed brown sugar
1 teaspoon curry powder
¼ cup butter or margarine,
   cut into pieces

• **Drain** fruit; place in an 11- x 7- x 1½-inch baking dish.
• **Combine** brown sugar and curry, stirring well; sprinkle over fruit. Dot with butter.
• **Cover** and bake at 350° for 30 minutes or until thoroughly heated. **Yield:** 8 servings.

TOASTY SOUTHERN PECAN TARTS

1 tablespoon butter or margarine
1 cup chopped pecans
⅛ teaspoon salt
1 (15-ounce) package refrigerated
   piecrusts
½ cup butter or margarine
1 cup light corn syrup
1 cup sugar
¼ teaspoon ground cinnamon
3 large eggs, beaten
1 teaspoon vanilla extract
½ teaspoon lemon juice

• **Place** 1 tablespoon butter in a large shallow pan; bake at 350° until melted. Add pecans, stirring to coat; bake 8 to 10 minutes or until toasted, stirring once. Remove from oven, and sprinkle with salt; cool.
• **Roll** 1 piecrust on a lightly floured surface to press out fold lines. Cut into rounds with a 2½-inch round cutter. Fit pastry rounds into miniature 1¾-inch muffin pans; do not trim edges. Repeat procedure with remaining piecrust. Sprinkle toasted pecans evenly into tart shells; set aside.
• **Place** ½ cup butter in a small heavy saucepan; cook over medium heat, stirring constantly, until lightly browned (do not burn). Remove from heat; cool 10 minutes.

• **Add** corn syrup and next 5 ingredients to butter, stirring well; spoon evenly over pecans into tart shells.
• **Bake** at 350° for 35 to 40 minutes or until set. Cool in pans 5 minutes. Remove from pans; cool completely on wire racks. **Yield:** 4½ dozen.

BOILED CHRISTMAS CUSTARD

Palmer's friend, Ann Cain, remembers her grandmother sharing the secret to this recipe: "You have to hold your tongue just right to get the knack of it." Actually, if you remember to stir and keep the heat low, you'll do just fine.

1 quart milk
4 large eggs
¾ cup sugar
2 tablespoons all-purpose flour
2 teaspoons vanilla extract

• **Cook** milk in a heavy nonaluminum (to avoid discoloring) saucepan over medium heat 10 minutes or until hot.
• **Combine** eggs and next 3 ingredients in a small bowl, beating with a wire whisk until blended. Gradually stir 1 cup hot milk into egg mixture; add to remaining hot milk, stirring mixture constantly.
• **Cook** over medium heat, stirring constantly, 6 to 8 minutes or until mixture begins to thicken and thermometer registers 180° (do not boil).
• **Remove** from heat, and pour through a nonaluminum strainer into a bowl, if desired. Place heavy-duty plastic wrap directly on surface of custard (to keep "skin" from forming); chill. **Yield:** 5 cups.

Note: For a spoonable custard, cook mixture, stirring constantly, 9 to 10 minutes or until a thermometer registers 190°. Recipe may be doubled, but mixture will take longer to reach the required temperatures.

Ann Cain
Rockwall, Texas

SEASONS TEACHINGS

Ray Overton of Atlanta admits he was dragged kicking and screaming into the world of low-fat cooking. "It had never occurred to me to try to use less fat in a recipe," Ray says. "But I figured out that low fat is what everyone wants to learn about. It forced me to be more creative with my recipes."

LIGHT HOLIDAY MENU
Serves Eight

Pork Medaillons With Port Wine and Dried Cranberry Sauce
Buttermilk-Basil Mashed Potatoes   **Steamed Green Beans**
Olde English Trifle

MAKE-AHEAD MENU TIPS

■ Roast sweet red pepper; chop onion, shallots, and ginger; grate orange rind; and cut and pound meat for Pork Medaillons With Port Wine and Dried Cranberry Sauce. The best thing about this recipe is that once the sauce is made, the pork cooks in less than 10 minutes.

■ Peel garlic, and chop onion for Buttermilk-Basil Mashed Potatoes.

■ Assemble Olde English Trifle the night before. The day of the party, add the garnishes, if desired.

PORK MEDAILLONS WITH PORT WINE AND DRIED CRANBERRY SAUCE

1 large sweet red pepper
1 teaspoon olive oil
1 medium-size purple onion, finely chopped
2 shallots, finely chopped
2 tablespoons minced fresh ginger
½ cup port wine
⅓ cup balsamic vinegar
2 tablespoons sugar
1 ripe pear, peeled, cored, and chopped
2 teaspoons grated orange rind
½ cup dried cranberries
1 cup ready-to-serve, reduced-sodium, fat-free chicken broth
2 tablespoons fresh thyme leaves
¼ teaspoon ground red pepper
2 (1-pound) pork tenderloins, trimmed
½ teaspoon salt
½ teaspoon freshly ground pepper
Garnish: fresh thyme sprigs

• **Place** sweet red pepper on an aluminum foil-lined baking sheet. Bake at 500° for 20 minutes or until skin looks blistered, turning once.
• **Place** pepper immediately into a heavy-duty, zip-top plastic bag; seal and let stand 10 minutes to loosen skin. Peel pepper; remove and discard seeds. Cut pepper into strips; set aside.
• **Pour** oil into a large skillet; place over medium heat until hot. Add onion and shallot, and cook 10 minutes, stirring often.
• **Add** ginger and next 3 ingredients; bring to a boil. Reduce heat, and simmer 10 minutes or until liquid is reduced by three-fourths, stirring often.
• **Add** pepper strips, pear, and next 5 ingredients; simmer 10 minutes or until pear is tender, stirring occasionally. Remove from heat; keep warm.
• **Cut** each tenderloin into 8 slices. Place each slice between two sheets of heavy-duty plastic wrap; flatten slightly with a rolling pin. Sprinkle each side of slices with salt and pepper; arrange in a single layer on a rack in a broiler pan.
• **Broil** 5½ inches from heat (with electric oven door partially opened) 3 minutes on each side or to desired degree of doneness. Garnish, if desired, and serve with sauce. **Yield:** 8 servings.

❤ Per serving: Calories 254 (32% from fat)
Fat 9g (3g saturated) Cholesterol 66.1mg
Sodium 204mg Carbohydrate 18.3g
Fiber 1.7g Protein 25g

BUTTERMILK-BASIL MASHED POTATOES

3½ pounds baking potatoes, peeled and cut into 1-inch cubes
1 onion, chopped
3 stalks celery, cut in half
12 cloves garlic, peeled
½ teaspoon salt
¾ cup nonfat cottage cheese
½ cup nonfat buttermilk
2 to 4 tablespoons chopped fresh basil
1 teaspoon salt
¼ teaspoon freshly ground pepper

- **Combine** first 5 ingredients in a Dutch oven; add water to cover. Bring to a boil over high heat; reduce heat, and simmer 20 minutes or until potato is tender. Drain; remove and discard celery. Mash potato mixture.
- **Position** knife blade in food processor bowl; add cottage cheese and buttermilk. Process until smooth, stopping once to scrape down sides.
- **Add** cottage cheese mixture to potato mixture; stirring mixture thoroughly until smooth. Stir in basil, 1 teaspoon salt, and pepper.
- **Cook** over low heat until thoroughly heated. Serve immediately. **Yield:** 8 servings.

♥ Per serving: Calories 205 (1% from fat)
Fat 0.3g (0.1g saturated) Cholesterol 2mg
Sodium 639mg Carbohydrate 41.2g
Fiber 3.8g Protein 10.9g

OLDE ENGLISH TRIFLE

3 cups milk
⅔ cup sugar
⅓ cup cornstarch
1 cup nonfat sour cream
1 tablespoon vanilla extract
1 (14-ounce) angel food cake
⅓ cup seedless raspberry preserves
⅓ cup raspberry liqueur
1 kiwifruit, peeled and thinly sliced
1 orange, peeled and sectioned
1 cup sliced strawberries
1 cup raspberries
1 cup blackberries
1 cup halved seedless green grapes
Garnishes: ½ cup raspberries; 2 star fruit, sliced; 2 tablespoons sliced almonds, toasted

- **Combine** first 3 ingredients in a heavy saucepan; cook over medium heat, stirring constantly, until mixture comes to a boil. Boil 1 minute, stirring constantly. Remove from heat, and cool slightly.
- **Stir** in sour cream and vanilla until blended; set aside.
- **Cut** cake into 24 slices; spread preserves over 1 side of each slice. Cut each slice into 4 cubes.
- **Arrange** half of cake cubes, preserves side down, in bottom of a 4-quart trifle bowl; drizzle with half of raspberry liqueur.
- **Arrange** kiwifruit around bottom edge; spoon half of fruits over cake; top with half of sour cream mixture.

Repeat layers with remaining cake and liqueur; add remaining fruits and top with remaining sour cream mixture.
- **Cover** and chill 8 hours. Garnish, if desired. **Yield:** 10 servings.

♥ Per serving: Calories 361 (21% from fat)
Fat 8.2g (5.8g saturated) Cholesterol 10mg
Sodium 358mg Carbohydrate 62.8g
Fiber 4.6g Protein 6.3g

Whether you try just one of his light recipes or serve the entire holiday menu, you'll appreciate Ray's flair for putting great taste into healthy cooking.

■ If you don't have a fat separator, use a heavy-duty, zip-top plastic bag. Pour stock into bag, place bag in a bowl, and chill 10 minutes. Cut a small hole in one corner of bag, and let stock pour out of hole into a bowl. When the fat gets close to bottom of bag, pinch the end, and discard fat in bag.

■ To thicken soup, remove part of the vegetables and broth, puree in a blender or food processor, and stir the mixture back into the soup.

■ Accept the fact that recipes modified to be low-fat are not going to taste the same as the originals. When you take away fat, you lose the silky texture that makes cream sauces and rich desserts so wonderful. A low-fat Alfredo sauce may not be as creamy as a regular version, but think of all the fat and calories you're saving.

■ Replace all the fat in marinade recipes with chicken or vegetable broth, wine, or fruit juice.

■ Just a little Romano, Parmesan, or feta cheese adds tremendous flavor with hardly any fat.

Not a Creature Was Stirring

....

" 'Twas the night before . . ."
  You know the rest.
  "Not a creature was stirring";
  That's the line I like best.
  No baking required to demonstrate skill,
  No time in the kitchen to show your goodwill.
  Wrap in bowls, pans, or pots
  And take a good look,
  None of these recipes require you to cook.

GIFTS THAT MEASURE UP

These kitchen essentials leave no recipe to chance.

1 set measuring cups
1 set measuring spoons
1 instant-read thermometer
1 timer
1 food scale
1 ruler
1 tablecloth

• **Gather** all tools in tablecloth. Bring corners of cloth together, and tie ends.

HOT HANDLERS

1 pair of canning tongs
1 set of trivets
2 oven mitts
2 large pot holders

• **Wrap** all items together in several sheets of red and orange cellophane to resemble flames.

OFF-THE-WALL GADGETS

Each of these tools will become an absolute necessity after just one use.

1 garlic crusher
1 mallet
1 pizza cutter
1 pastry wheel
1 cherry pitter
1 zester
1 apple corer
1 ginger grater
1 nutmeg grater

• **Combine** an assortment of these inexpensive items for a valuable gift.

WINE TASTING

If this is your favorite, be sure to make two. One for your friend and one for you.

3 bottles of wine
1 no-fail corkscrew
2 glasses
1 set vacuum pumps
1 pocket-size wine guide
1 wine cooler

• **Arrange** items in a large basket for your favorite wine connoisseur.

MINIATURE LIQUEUR SAMPLER

Introduce liqueurs to a new cook. For an added touch, include a few of your favorite recipes, using the flavors you've selected.

1 miniature bottle amaretto
1 miniature bottle Grand
    Marnier
1 miniature bottle Kahlúa
1 miniature bottle Irish Cream
1 miniature bottle Chambord
1 miniature bottle Truffles
1 book on cooking with liqueurs

• **Assemble** any combination of the ingredients in a basket with Spanish moss. Add a bow for a festive touch.

GREAT GIFTS

■ Give yourself and a few friends a true gift this holiday season – time. Make a pact. Instead of buying each other gifts, gather for a relaxing evening. Make it a covered-dish supper and let everyone pitch in and help. Ask friends to bring their favorite dish, along with copies of their recipe. Or plan on calling out for pizza – even easier on the hostess. Have guests bring shopping finds for their families, along with paper, ribbon, scissors, and tape. After dinner, turn on some Christmas music, wrap your gifts, and enjoy the company.

■ For a gift almost as precious as time, draw names with your family or friends, and ask each person to buy a child's gift to match the personality of the name drawn: a tiara for the Miss America wannabe or a barrel of monkeys for the humorous one in the group. You'll have lots of laughs opening the gifts. Then simply rewrap, and give them to a local charity for children.

■ Now here's a great holiday gift idea! Give your friends an assortment of frozen appetizers with directions for baking. You can prepare them to the point of baking and divide them among heavy-duty, zip-top plastic bags for several of your closest – and busiest – friends.

■ Don't settle for the same old Christmas tin to wrap the gift from your kitchen. Wrap up homemade cocoa mix in a plastic bag and put it in a Christmas mug. Place freshly baked scones or biscuits in a basket lined with a holiday napkin. And don't forget the family pet. Try wrapping up Fido's favorite doggie biscuits along with a new water dish.

Italian Ricotta Cheesecake (recipe, page 303) sparkles with candied citron, golden raisins, and a hint of orange; it's the grand finale of a holiday meal.

These two holiday cakes are full of sweet surprises. Sneak a peek past the fluffy white frosting and you'll find a creamy lemon filling inside Coconut-Lemon Cake (recipe, page 319). And the tantalizing flavor of orange glaze and candied orange zest add zing to Orange Cake (recipe, page 320).

Make it a white Christmas with White Chocolate-Macadamia Nut Crème Brûlée (recipe, page 323), a two-cup-of-coffee dessert.

Sip Into Something Comfortable

A warm drink makes a cold night cozier. Right after work or just before bedtime, these soothing sippers are a welcome change from coffee and hot tea. And if it's a frosty beverage you crave, try our recipe for a slushy punch to make all at once or just one serving at a time.

SPARKLING CITRUS PUNCH

1 (46-ounce) can pineapple juice
1½ cups orange juice
¾ cup lemon juice
¼ cup lime juice
1¼ cups sugar
2 (2-liter) bottles ginger ale, chilled

● **Combine** first 5 ingredients, stirring until sugar dissolves. Pour into ice cube trays; cover and freeze until firm.
● **Place** 4 juice cubes in each tall glass. Pour 1 cup ginger ale over cubes in each glass; stir until slushy. **Yield:** about 17 servings.

Note: You can freeze juice mixture in an airtight container. Thaw slightly in a punch bowl; add ginger ale, stirring until slushy.

Julia Garmon
Colonial Beach, Virginia

CINNAMON WINTER CIDER

1 (12-ounce) can frozen apple juice concentrate, thawed and undiluted
1 (12-ounce) can frozen cranberry-apple juice concentrate, thawed and undiluted
1 (6-ounce) can frozen lemonade concentrate, thawed and undiluted
9 cups water
5 (3-inch) sticks cinnamon
6 whole cloves
1 teaspoon ground nutmeg
⅓ cup cinnamon schnapps or rum

● **Combine** first 7 ingredients in a Dutch oven; bring to a boil. Cover, reduce heat, and simmer 15 minutes. Remove and discard spices. Stir in schnapps; serve warm. **Yield:** 3 quarts.

Note: You can freeze cider in 1-cup servings before adding schnapps. Thaw and reheat cider; stir in 1 to 1½ teaspoons schnapps per cup cider.

Louise W. Mayer
Richmond, Virginia

MULLED WINE PUNCH

2 cups cranberry juice cocktail
¼ cup sugar
¼ cup firmly packed brown sugar
3 whole cloves
3 whole allspice
1½ cups dry red wine
Garnish: cinnamon sticks

● **Combine** cranberry juice cocktail, sugars, cloves, and allspice in a saucepan; bring to a boil over medium heat, stirring until sugars dissolve.
● **Reduce** heat, and simmer 5 minutes. Remove and discard spices; stir in wine. Garnish, if desired; serve warm. **Yield:** 4 cups.

Pamela Natchus
Chesapeake, Virginia

SPICE UP YOUR HOLIDAYS

When brewed, the spices in Cinnamon Winter Cider and Mulled Wine Punch send a wonderful aroma throughout your house. Here are some tips for keeping their aromatic ingredients fresh and on-hand during the busy season:

■ Buy ground spices in small quantities because they quickly lose potency.

■ Store spices in airtight containers in a cool, dark place for no more than six months. Never store spices near heat, like over the cooktop.

■ Label each spice container with date of purchase so you'll know when to buy fresh.

■ You can intensify the flavor of whole spices, such as whole allspice, by roasting them in a 350° oven for about 10 minutes. Cool completely before using.

A CRAVING FOR CHICKEN AND DUMPLINGS

....

Chicken and Dumplings With Herbed Broth takes a few twists on an old favorite. For instance, we used chicken legs and thighs (they're inexpensive) rather than a whole chicken (some feel intimidated by a whole bird).

We browned the chicken pieces before cooking them in broth for more flavor. We also added herbs to the canned broth.

If you're short on time, try a quick and easy version, using canned chicken, canned broth, and canned biscuits. Even purists will enjoy it.

CHICKEN AND DUMPLINGS WITH HERBED BROTH

1 cup self-rising flour
1 teaspoon pepper
3 pounds chicken legs and thighs
¼ cup vegetable oil
1 medium onion, chopped
2 cloves garlic, minced
1 tablespoon self-rising flour
3 (14½-ounce) cans ready-to-serve chicken broth
2 tablespoons chopped fresh basil or 2 teaspoons dried basil
2 tablespoons chopped fresh thyme or 2 teaspoons dried thyme
1 tablespoon chopped fresh or dried rosemary
½ teaspoon grated lemon rind
2 tablespoons lemon juice
2 cups self-rising flour
1 cup whipping cream
¼ cup reduced-fat sour cream (optional)
Garnish: fresh herbs

• **Combine** 1 cup flour and pepper. Dredge chicken in flour mixture.
• **Heat** oil in a Dutch oven over medium heat; add chicken, and cook until golden, turning once. Add additional oil, if needed. Remove chicken from Dutch oven, reserving drippings in Dutch oven.
• **Cook** onion and garlic in drippings, stirring constantly, until tender.
• **Add** 1 tablespoon flour, and cook 1 minute, stirring constantly; gradually add broth, stirring constantly.
• **Add** basil and next 4 ingredients; bring to a boil. Return chicken to Dutch oven; cover, reduce heat, and simmer 30 minutes.
• **Remove** chicken from Dutch oven, and keep warm.
• **Combine** 2 cups self-rising flour and whipping cream in a large bowl, stirring with a fork (mixture will be dry and crumbly). Gently pat mixture into 2-inch balls, handling dough as little as possible.
• **Bring** broth mixture to a rolling boil; add dumplings. Cover, reduce heat, and simmer, without stirring, 7 to 10 minutes or until dumplings are firm in center.
• **Remove** broth mixture from heat. Stir in sour cream, if desired. Serve dumplings and broth over chicken, and garnish, if desired. **Yield:** 4 servings.

Note: Adding the sour cream makes this broth creamy – like a Hungarian-style dish. The texture is more traditional without the sour cream.

REBUILDING THE REUBEN

....

Most Reuben sandwiches are real jaw stretchers, piled high with corned beef, Swiss cheese, and sauerkraut. Here's a low-profile Reuben with the classic flavors already rolled together.

REUBEN LOAF

2 (12-ounce) cans corned beef, crumbled
2 cups soft breadcrumbs (about 5 slices white bread)
2 large eggs, lightly beaten
2 tablespoons chopped fresh parsley
¼ teaspoon garlic salt
1 (10-ounce) can chopped sauerkraut, drained
1 cup (4 ounces) shredded Swiss cheese
½ teaspoon caraway seeds
3 (1-ounce) slices Swiss cheese, cut in half diagonally

• **Combine** first 5 ingredients in a large bowl. Shape into a 10-inch square on heavy-duty plastic wrap; set aside.
• **Press** sauerkraut between layers of paper towels to remove excess moisture. Combine sauerkraut, shredded cheese, and caraway seeds; spoon down center of meat mixture.
• **Fold** 2 opposite sides of meat mixture over sauerkraut mixture, using plastic wrap to lift, overlapping edges. Press edges and ends to seal. Carefully place loaf in a lightly greased 13- x 9- x 2-inch pan.
• **Bake** at 350° for 45 minutes or until done. Arrange cheese slices on top; bake 5 additional minutes. **Yield:** 8 servings.

Elisabeth Weaver Winstead
Nashville, Tennessee

THE REUBEN'S ORIGIN

The Reuben Sandwich reportedly debuted in Arthur Reuben's New York delicatessen in 1914. Originally made with ham, it was created for actress Annette Seelos. Another version claims that Omaha grocer Reuben Kay made it during a poker game in 1955. It came to national attention when it won a recipe contest.

TACOS MANY WAYS

....

You can satisfy your craving for the spicy flavors of tacos in many ways. Expand your enjoyment beyond ground beef, and include seafood and grilled vegetables in a variety of wrappers.

TACO TASSIES

1 pound ground round
2 tablespoons dry taco seasoning mix
2 tablespoons water
½ cup sour cream
1 tablespoon taco sauce
⅓ cup coarsely crushed tortilla chips
¾ cup (3 ounces) shredded Monterey Jack cheese with peppers
Tortilla chips
Taco sauce
Garnishes: sour cream, fresh cilantro

• **Combine** first 3 ingredients. Divide mixture into 24 equal portions; using a fork, press each portion into a miniature (1¾-inch) muffin cup to form a shell.
• **Combine** sour cream, taco sauce, and crushed tortilla chips; spoon 1 teaspoon mixture into each beef shell.
• **Bake** at 425° for 10 minutes. Sprinkle with cheese, and bake 5 additional minutes. Remove from pans, and serve immediately on tortilla chips with additional taco sauce. Garnish, if desired. **Yield:** 2 dozen.

Judi Grigoraci
Charleston, West Virginia

CHINESE TACO ROLLS

1 pound lean ground beef
1 cup chopped onion
2 cloves garlic, minced
2 cups (8 ounces) shredded sharp Cheddar cheese
1 tablespoon chili powder
1 teaspoon salt
¾ teaspoon pepper
1 (16-ounce) package refrigerated egg roll wrappers
Vegetable oil
Taco sauce

• **Cook** first 3 ingredients in a large skillet over medium-high heat, stirring until beef crumbles; drain. Add cheese and next 3 ingredients, stirring until cheese melts.
• **Spoon** 1 heaping tablespoon beef mixture in center of each egg roll wrapper. Fold bottom edge of wrapper over filling; fold left and right sides over filling. Lightly brush remaining edge with water. Starting at bottom, tightly roll up filled wrapper; gently press to seal. Secure with wooden picks, if desired.
• **Pour** oil to depth of 2 inches in a Dutch oven; heat to 375°. Fry egg rolls, 4 at a time, in hot oil and fry 1 minute on each side or until golden brown; drain on paper towels. Remove wooden picks, if used. Repeat procedure with remaining egg rolls. Serve with taco sauce. **Yield:** 8 servings.

Sandy Guthrie
Lutz, Florida

BARBECUED FISH TACOS

4 (8-inch) flour tortillas
1 pound amberjack or other lean, mild fish fillet
¼ teaspoon salt
¼ teaspoon pepper
¼ cup sweet barbecue sauce
Vegetable cooking spray
Sour cream
Sliced green onions
Lime wedges

• **Wrap** tortillas in aluminum foil.
• **Bake** at 350° for 10 minutes or until thoroughly heated.

• **Sprinkle** fish with salt and pepper; lightly brush each side with barbecue sauce. Place fish in a grill basket coated with cooking spray.
• **Cook,** covered with grill lid, over medium coals (300° to 350°) 5 minutes on each side or until fish flakes easily when tested with a fork. Remove fish from basket, and flake gently with a fork.
• **Spoon** fish evenly down center of tortillas; top with sour cream and green onions. Squeeze lime wedges over tortillas; fold opposite sides over filling. **Yield:** 4 servings.

SHRIMP-AND-PEPPER SOFT TACOS

¾ pound unpeeled medium-size fresh shrimp
2 cloves garlic, minced
1 tablespoon olive oil
½ teaspoon ground cumin
1 large onion, chopped
2 tomatoes, chopped
1 Anaheim chile pepper, seeded and minced
1 jalapeño pepper, seeded and minced
¼ cup chopped fresh cilantro
¼ teaspoon salt
4 (8-inch) flour tortillas
Fresh lime wedges
Shredded Monterey Jack cheese with peppers
Sour cream

• **Peel** shrimp, and devein, if desired.
• **Cook** garlic in oil in a large skillet over medium heat, stirring constantly, until tender; add shrimp and cumin, and cook about 1 minute, stirring constantly. Remove shrimp, and set aside.
• **Add** onion to skillet; cook, stirring constantly, until tender. Add shrimp, tomato, and peppers; cook until thoroughly heated. Remove from heat, and stir in cilantro and salt.
• **Spoon** ¾ cup shrimp mixture in center of each tortilla; squeeze lime wedges over shrimp mixture, and top with cheese and sour cream. Fold tortillas in half. **Yield:** 4 servings.

Julia Hardie Kaczvinsky
Ruston, Louisiana

PIZZA-FLAVORED CHICKEN TACOS

1 pound ground chicken
1 small onion, chopped
1 small green pepper, seeded and chopped
4 ounces fresh mushrooms, sliced
1 clove garlic, minced
1 tablespoon all-purpose flour
½ teaspoon salt
½ teaspoon dried basil
½ teaspoon dried oregano
¼ teaspoon pepper
1 (8-ounce) can tomato sauce
½ cup water
8 taco shells
Toppings: chopped tomato, chopped onion, shredded lettuce, sliced ripe olives, shredded mozzarella cheese, grated Parmesan cheese

• **Brown** ground chicken in a large nonstick skillet over medium-high heat, stirring until it crumbles. Add onion and next 3 ingredients, and cook, stirring constantly, until onion is tender.
• **Add** flour and next 4 ingredients; stir in tomato sauce and water. Bring to a boil, stirring occasionally. Reduce heat, and simmer 15 minutes.
• **Heat** taco shells according to package directions. Spoon chicken mixture evenly into shells. Add desired toppings, and serve. **Yield:** 4 servings.

Anna Rucker
Norfolk, Virginia

BREAKFAST TACOS

4 (8-inch) whole wheat tortillas
½ pound chorizo sausage
8 large eggs, lightly beaten
½ teaspoon salt
½ teaspoon pepper
½ cup (2 ounces) shredded Monterey Jack cheese
Taco sauce

• **Wrap** tortillas in aluminum foil. Bake at 350° for 10 minutes.
• **Remove** sausage from casing.
• **Brown** sausage in a large skillet over medium-high heat, stirring until it crumbles; drain and return to skillet.
• **Add** eggs, salt, and pepper to sausage. Cook, without stirring, until mixture begins to set on bottom. Draw a spatula across bottom of pan to form large curds. Continue cooking until eggs are thickened, but still moist. Do not stir constantly.
• **Spoon** egg mixture evenly down center of tortillas; top each with cheese and taco sauce. Fold opposite sides over filling, and serve immediately with additional taco sauce. **Yield:** 4 servings.

GRILLED PEPPER TACOS

2 green peppers
2 sweet red peppers
2 sweet yellow peppers
2 poblano chile peppers
1 large purple onion
2 to 3 tablespoons pepper oil
8 taco shells
1 (8-ounce) package shredded Mexican blend cheese
2 tomatoes, chopped
1 cup taco sauce
1 (8-ounce) carton reduced-fat sour cream

• **Seed** peppers and cut into 1-inch strips; cut onion into 16 wedges. Combine peppers, onion, and oil, tossing to coat; set aside.
• **Preheat** a grill wok over hot coals (400° to 500°) 5 to 10 minutes. Spread pepper mixture evenly in wok; place on grill, and cook, covered with grill lid, 15 to 20 minutes or until

tender and browned, stirring mixture every 5 minutes.
• **Heat** taco shells according to package directions. Spoon pepper mixture evenly into shells; top with cheese and remaining ingredients. Serve immediately. **Yield:** 8 servings.

Note: For pepper oil, we used Consorzio's Five Pepper Oil. If a grill wok is unavailable, use a grill basket. Cut peppers and onion into fourths for grilling, and then cut grilled vegetables into thin strips.

Darnelle Wesley
Birmingham, Alabama

WHAT'S FOR SUPPER?

PAUSE FOR PASTA

....

Is there a week that goes by at your house without pasta for dinner at least one night? Pasta is so versatile – good hot or cold, as an entrée or side dish. During this month of big meals and fancy entertaining, slow down one night, and pause for pasta.

ZITI WITH SAUSAGE AND BROCCOLI

1 pound Italian link sausage
2 cloves garlic, crushed
½ teaspoon dried crushed red pepper
1 teaspoon olive oil
2 (14.5-ounce) cans diced tomatoes, undrained
8 ounces ziti pasta, uncooked
2 cups broccoli flowerets
½ cup freshly grated Romano or Parmesan cheese

• **Cut** sausage diagonally into ½-inch-thick slices. Cook sausage in a large nonstick skillet over medium-high heat until browned; remove sausage, and set aside. Wipe skillet with paper towels.

• **Cook** garlic and red pepper in oil in skillet, stirring constantly, until lightly browned; add tomatoes, and cook until thoroughly heated. Remove from heat; keep warm.

• **Cook** pasta according to package directions, adding broccoli during last 5 minutes of cooking time. Drain and toss gently with sausage mixture and cheese. Serve immediately. **Yield:** 3 servings.

Candace Reed
Dallas, Texas

SPINACH AND MUSHROOMS WITH BOW TIE PASTA

1 (8-ounce) package sliced fresh mushrooms
1 tablespoon lemon juice
2 tablespoons butter or margarine
3 cloves garlic, crushed
1 cup whipping cream
½ teaspoon salt
¾ teaspoon freshly ground pepper
8 ounces bow tie pasta, uncooked
4 cups fresh spinach, torn
¼ cup freshly grated Parmesan cheese

• **Combine** mushrooms and lemon juice, stirring to coat.

• **Melt** butter in a large skillet over medium-high heat; add garlic, and cook, stirring constantly, 1 to 2 minutes or until tender. Add mushrooms; cook 5 minutes, stirring constantly.

• **Add** whipping cream, and bring to a boil. Stir in salt and pepper; remove from heat.

• **Cook** pasta according to package directions, adding spinach during last minute of cooking time. Drain and toss gently with mushroom mixture.

• **Sprinkle** with Parmesan cheese, and serve immediately. **Yield:** 2 main-dish servings or 4 side-dish servings.

Ronda Carman
Houston, Texas

MEDITERRANEAN PASTA

Liven up dinnertime with the savory flavors of the Mediterranean that highlight this dish.

8 ounces penne pasta, uncooked
⅔ cup crumbled feta cheese, divided
¼ cup freshly grated Parmesan cheese, divided
1 medium purple onion, halved and sliced
2 tablespoons olive oil
1 (14-ounce) can quartered artichoke hearts, rinsed and drained
1 (16-ounce) can crushed tomatoes, undrained
1 (2.25-ounce) can sliced ripe olives, drained
¼ teaspoon salt
½ teaspoon freshly ground pepper

• **Cook** pasta according to package directions; drain. Place pasta in a lightly greased 11- x 7- x 1½-inch baking dish; sprinkle with half each of feta and Parmesan cheeses, and set aside.

• **Cook** onion in oil in a large skillet over medium-high heat, stirring constantly, until tender. Add artichokes and tomatoes; cook 2 to 3 minutes.

• **Add** olives, salt, and pepper; cover, reduce heat, and simmer 10 minutes. Pour over pasta; sprinkle with remaining cheeses.

• **Bake** pasta at 350° for 15 to 20 minutes or until cheese melts. **Yield:** 3 to 4 servings.

Brenda Kalfas
Camp Hill, Pennsylvania

SENSATIONAL SIDES

....

These side dishes perform beautifully with any star attraction – roast beef, chicken, or turkey. They're also easy to prepare and attractive to present. With the holidays (and company) just around the bend, these are sure to win raves.

BROCCOLI WITH STUFFING

2 (10-ounce) packages frozen broccoli spears
1 cup (4 ounces) shredded Cheddar cheese
2 large eggs, lightly beaten
1 (10¾-ounce) can cream of mushroom soup, undiluted
½ cup mayonnaise or salad dressing
½ cup finely chopped onion
¾ cup herb-seasoned stuffing mix
2 tablespoons butter or margarine, melted

• **Cook** broccoli according to package directions; drain.

• **Arrange** broccoli in a lightly greased 11- x 7- x 1½-inch baking dish. Sprinkle with cheese.

• **Combine** eggs and next 3 ingredients; spread over cheese.

• **Combine** stuffing mix and butter; sprinkle over casserole.

• **Bake** casserole at 350° for 30 minutes or until thoroughly heated. **Yield:** 8 servings.

♥ To reduce fat and calories, substitute reduced-fat Cheddar cheese, ½ cup egg substitute, reduced-fat cream of mushroom soup, reduced-fat mayonnaise, and butter-flavored vegetable cooking spray.

Sharon McClatchey
Muskogee, Oklahoma

BALSAMIC-FLAVORED EGGPLANT

2 medium tomatoes, sliced
1 purple onion, sliced and
   separated into rings
1 (6-ounce) can medium pitted
   ripe olives, drained
¾ cup balsamic vinegar
1 medium eggplant
½ teaspoon salt
2 tablespoons olive oil
1 (8-ounce) package firm farmer
   cheese, cut into ½-inch
   cubes

• **Combine** first 3 ingredients in a shallow dish; drizzle with vinegar. Cover and chill 2 hours.
• **Cut** eggplant into 1-inch slices; sprinkle both sides of slices with salt, and drain on paper towels 30 minutes. Pat dry. Brush both sides of slices with oil.
• **Cook,** covered with grill lid, over medium-hot coals (350° to 400°) about 3 minutes on each side or until tender. Remove from heat, and cool.
• **Remove** vegetables from marinade, reserving marinade.
• **Arrange** vegetables and eggplant slices on a serving plate. Sprinkle cheese over vegetables; drizzle with ¼ cup marinade. **Yield:** 6 servings.

Sandy Davis
Emory, Virginia

CAULIFLOWER BAKE

1 large cauliflower, cut into
   flowerets
½ teaspoon salt
3 cups water
¼ cup butter or margarine,
   melted
1 tablespoon sugar
½ teaspoon salt
½ teaspoon pepper
1 cup round buttery cracker
   crumbs
1½ cups (6 ounces) shredded
   Cheddar cheese, divided
1 medium onion, chopped
½ cup chopped green
   pepper
1 (16-ounce) can whole tomatoes,
   undrained and chopped

• **Combine** first 3 ingredients in a large saucepan; bring to a boil. Cover, reduce heat, and cook 5 minutes or until tender; drain. Set aside.
• **Combine** butter and next 4 ingredients in a large bowl; stir in cauliflower, 1 cup cheese, onion, chopped green pepper, and tomatoes. Spoon into three lightly greased 1½-cup individual baking dishes.
• **Bake** at 350° for 20 to 25 minutes. Sprinkle with remaining ½ cup cheese, and bake 5 additional minutes. **Yield:** 6 servings.

Note: You can bake casserole in a 13- x 9- x 2-inch baking dish at 350° for 35 minutes. Add remaining ½ cup cheese, and bake as directed.

Estelle Beavers Gilbert
Charlottesville, Virginia

GARLIC ROASTED POTATOES

3 tablespoons butter or margarine,
   melted
3 tablespoons olive oil
3 to 4 cloves garlic, minced
4 medium-size baking potatoes,
   cut into 1-inch pieces
¼ teaspoon salt
¼ teaspoon pepper
⅓ cup grated Parmesan cheese

• **Combine** first 6 ingredients in a 13- x 9- x 2-inch pan, and toss mixture gently to coat.
• **Bake** at 500° for 25 minutes or until potato is tender, stirring every 10 minutes. Sprinkle with cheese; bake 5 additional minutes. **Yield:** 4 servings.

Ellen W. Benjamin
Stephens City, Virginia

SOUTHERN BOY MAKES GOOD

....

Small-town Southerners, proudly take note: In *Food and Wine* magazine's '95 list of "America's Best New Chefs" (only eight) – right up there with rising culinary stars from New York and San Francisco – shines one from Louisiana. Not New Orleans even, but a couple of hours and a world away, in the tiny bayou town of New Iberia.

It's worth the half-hour drive out of Lafayette to leRosier Country Inn and Restaurant to taste the talent of chef Hallman Woods III.

Like most Southern cooks, Hallman is glad to share his recipes. We left the complicated dazzlers to him, but asked for some of his simplest accompaniments. Try these at home to whet your appetite; then make plans to head to Louisiana for a meal you can't get in the Big Apple.

EGGPLANT RELISH

Hallman keeps a big batch of this in his refrigerator and reheats to serve several ways: just a spoonful as a relish for meats, a larger portion as a side dish, or over pasta for a main dish.

4 medium eggplants (4½
   pounds)
3 medium onions, chopped
⅓ cup olive oil
1 (16-ounce) can tomatoes,
   undrained and chopped
¼ cup chopped fresh parsley
2 tablespoons minced garlic
1 tablespoon sugar
1½ teaspoons dried oregano
1 teaspoon salt
½ teaspoon pepper
¼ cup oyster sauce
1 (8-ounce) can tomato sauce
⅛ teaspoon ground red
   pepper
⅛ teaspoon hot sauce

- **Peel** eggplant; cut into ½-inch cubes.
- **Combine** eggplant cubes and water to cover in a Dutch oven; bring to a boil. Reduce heat, and simmer 10 minutes or until tender. Drain and set aside.
- **Cook** chopped onion in oil in Dutch oven over medium heat 10 minutes, stirring often. Add eggplant and tomatoes; cook over low heat 10 minutes or until liquid is almost evaporated, stirring often.
- **Add** parsley and next 7 ingredients; cook 5 minutes, stirring occasionally. Add red pepper and hot sauce. Serve immediately or cover and chill up to 5 days. **Yield:** 10 cups.

Note: Look for oyster sauce in the Oriental foods section of most grocery stores.

BRAISED RED CABBAGE

Hallman serves this with pork roast and wild game dishes.

1 small onion, chopped
1 clove garlic, minced
½ teaspoon dried thyme
¼ teaspoon celery seeds
2 bay leaves
½ teaspoon grated lemon rind
½ teaspoon salt
¼ teaspoon ground white pepper
2 tablespoons olive oil
1½ quarts water
1 cup red wine vinegar
¼ cup salt
1 small head red cabbage, thinly sliced (8 cups)
2 tablespoons red wine vinegar
¼ cup chicken broth

- **Cook** first 8 ingredients in olive oil in a large skillet over medium-high heat, stirring constantly until onion is tender.
- **Combine** water, 1 cup vinegar, and ¼ cup salt in a large Dutch oven; bring to a boil. Add cabbage, and cook 10 seconds, stirring constantly; drain.

- **Add** cabbage, 2 tablespoons vinegar, and chicken broth to onion mixture; bring to a boil.
- **Cover,** reduce heat, and simmer 15 minutes or until cabbage is crisp-tender. Remove and discard bay leaves. **Yield:** 4 to 6 servings.

FROM OUR KITCHEN TO YOURS

....

BOOKS FROM COOKS

Make your next hostess gift unique – your own cookbook filled with a treasured collection of your favorite recipes and lively party ideas illustrated with colorful lettering and drawings. Just call a copy shop for information on paper types and sizes and plastic binding, then start penning with pizzazz. Tie with a ribbon, wrap with a large dish towel, tuck in an inexpensive kitchen gadget or potholder, and know that this is one cookbook that won't end up in someone's closet.

If you're not that industrious, check bookstores for *Recipes Remembered,* an attractive, hardback scrapbook-to-be for someone in your family or for close friends. You or the recipient can scrawl old treasured recipes under headings like "How I Learned to Cook," "Wedding Memories," and "Birthday Celebrations." Food quotes from Cleopatra, Mark Twain, James Beard, and others complete the 62-page book written by Marcia Adams and published by Clarkson N. Potter, Inc. (1995). If you can't locate the book in your area, you can order it by calling 1-800-733-3000.

SWEETS TO THE SWEET . . .

. . . and desserts to the deserving. For a holiday gift idea from the kitchen, sign someone up for your own "dessert-of-the-month-club." The recipient will have 12 months of sugary surprises to savor.

Following are some tips for sending goodies via the mail.

- Fruitcakes are as heavy as gold bricks and cost a lot to send.

- Wrap fragile cookies individually in wax paper, and then seal them in zip-top plastic bags.

- Send goodies early in the week so they don't sit in the parcel service or post office getting stale on Sunday.

- Be generous with plastic wrap and bags to keep things fresh; then cushion with plenty of bubble wrap and plastic foam peanuts in case the ride is bumpy.

- Send cookies and cakes that can be frozen once they arrive so the recipient doesn't have to gobble a huge quantity at once, unless, of course, he wants to.

- Don't tempt fate by mailing chocolate candy in August.

A-PEELING NEWS

No food snob would be caught without one – a zester. It's an inexpensive kitchen gadget for removing strips of citrus rind. But an average vegetable peeler will work, too. Two hints for easier peeling: Be sure your vegetable peeler is sharp and your limes, lemons, or oranges are firm with thick skin.

YOUR CUP RUNNETH OVER

Next time coleslaw is on the menu, don't just plop it on the plate next to the baked beans. Serve it in cups made from cabbage leaves.

Choose the smallest heads of cabbage you can find; then wash them under hot water, carefully separating several outer leaves. (The hot water will make them pliable and easier to remove from the head without tearing.) Drop the leaves into a bowl of ice water for several minutes, and they'll crisp and curl just enough to hold a serving of coleslaw. No need for neatness; turn the cups on their sides and let the slaw casually spill out.

RECIPE TITLE INDEX

An alphabetical listing of every recipe by exact title

All microwave recipe page numbers are preceded by an "M."

Adams' Ribs, 236
Alabama Fudge-Pecan Chewies, 143
All Seasons Lemon Trifle, 219
All-Star Pizza Calzones, 308
Almond Brickle Treats, 321
Almond Crème Brûlée, 323
Almond-Garlic Streusel, 159
Aloha Shrimp Salad, 46
Amaretto Slush, 90
Ancho Base, 205
Angel's Wing Rolls, 329
Apple-Bourbon Pie, 302
Apple Chimichangas, 43
Apple Cider, 198
Apple Dumplings with Maple-Cider Sauce, 288
Apple-Mushroom Pork Tenderloin, 53
Apple Pie Filling in a Jar, 251
Apple-Walnut Stuffing, 289
Apricot-Almond Squares, 272
Apricot Cookies, 322
Apricot-Mushroom Stuffed Pork Chops, 287
Apricot-Yogurt Tortoni, 124
Artichoke and Shrimp Linguine, 210
Asian Pesto Pasta, 189
Asparagus Stir-Fry, 83
Asparagus with Garlic Cream, 83
Aunt Glennie's Pear Relish, 305
Austrian Hash with Cabbage Salad, 262
Avocado-Tomatillo Sauce, 206

Bacon-Jalapeño-Tomato Quesadillas, 240
Baked Artichoke Dip, 239
Baked Hush Puppies, 108
Baked Mushroom Rice, 84
Baked Pears à la Mode, 129
Baked Trout, 106
Balsamic Dressing, 281
Balsamic-Flavored Eggplant, 342
Barbecued Country-Style Ribs, 237
Barbecued Fish Tacos, 339
Barbecued Spareribs, 236
Basic Butter Cookie Dough, 320
Basic Crème Brûlée, 323
Basic Polenta, 164
Basil-Infused Olive Oil, 231
Bean-and-Hominy Soup, 23
Beef Burgundy, 69
Beef Hash, 24
Beef Roast with Burgundy Gravy, 263
Beef Stock, 17

Beef Vinaigrette Salad, 177
Beer Sauce, 266
Beets 'n' Greens, 179
Bell Pepper-Cheese Chowder, 240
Berry-Citrus Twist, 100
Berry Crème Brûlée, 323
Berry-Good Cubes, 201
Berry Sauce, 103
Berry Shrub, 29
Better-Than-Potpourri Brew, 271
Betty's Butternut Pound Cake with Caramel
   Sauce, 308
Betty's Holiday Cream, 303
Big Batch Moist Bran Muffins, 214
Bird's Nests, 102
Black Bean Chili Marsala, 16
Black Bean Dip, 93
Black Beans and Rice, 309
Black Beans and Yellow Rice, 126
Blackened 'n' Peppered Steak, 174
Black-Eyed Pea Salad, 203
Black-Eyed Pea-Spinach-Stuffed Potatoes, 22
Black, White, and Red All Over Soup, 126
Blazing Sunset Pizza, 267
Blueberry Chutney, 190
Blueberry Cordial, 142
Blueberry Sauce, 135
Blue Cheese Coleslaw, 270
Blue Cheese-Pecan Grapes, 48
Blue Cheese Spread, 79, 92
Blue Cheese-Walnut Stuffed Fillets, 327
Bodacious Chili, 14
Bodacious Peanut Parfait, 167
Boiled Christmas Custard, 329
Boneless Pork Chops with Ancho Cream
   Sauce, 205
Bourbon Baked Beans, 182
Bourbon Custard Sauce, 271
Braised Red Cabbage, 343
Brandied Cranberries, 306
Breaded Tomatoes, 180
Breakfast Tacos, 340
Brie-Mushroom Burgers, 128
Broccoli and Walnut Sauté, 52
Broccoli Salad, 95
Broccoli with Stuffing, 341
Buck's Taters, 72
Bugs in a Rug, 178
Bunny Trail Mix, 101
Burger Boat, 70
Burk's Farm-Raised Catfish Fry, 158

Burned Bourbon with Molasses Sauce, 17
Burnt Sugar Sponge Cake with Berry Sauce, 103
Butter Crescent Rolls, 292
Buttercrust Corn Pie with Fresh Tomato
   Salsa, 181
Buttermilk-Basil Mashed Potatoes, 330
Buttermilk Bread Pudding with Butter-Rum
   Sauce, 134
Buttermilk Fudge, 52
Buttermilk-Lemon Pudding Cake with Blueberry
   Sauce, 135
Buttermilk Sauce, 183
Butternut Squash Soup, 62
Butter Pecan Mousse, 286
Butter-Pecan Topping, 158
Butter-Rum Sauce, 134
Buttery Ham Spread, 93

Caesar Ravioli Salad, 183
Caesar Salad Pasta, 230
Cajun Blackened Filet Mignon, 85
Cajun-Fried Cornish Hens, 326
Cake Mix Fruit Cake, 248
Calabacitas, 130
Caliente Marinated Olives, 177
Calypso Presbyterian Church Women's Lime
   Punch, 141
Candied Orange Zest, 320
Canned Flavored Tomatoes, 217
Cantaloupe-Peach Jam, 143
Caramel Crunch, 165
Caramel Dessert Biscuits, 36
Caramel Fondue, 35
Caramel Ice Cream Dessert, 36
Caramel Sauce, 308
Caraway-Cheese Crisps, 284
Caribbean Banana Fish, 202
Caribbean Cooler, 203
Caribbean Grapes, 48
Caribbean Punch, 173
Carne Guisada Burritos, 43
Carolina Gumbo, 70
Cashew Casserole, 166
Casserole of Black Beans, 27
Casserole Spaghetti, 132
Cauliflower Bake, 342
Cauliflower-English Pea Salad, 66
Celebrity Chicken Breasts, 60
Cheeseburger Casserole, 255
Cheese-Chive Scrambled Eggs, 34

Cheese Enchiladas, 311
Cheese Grits with Green Chiles, 208
Cheese Wafers, 174
Cheesy Barbecue Popcorn, 239
Cheesy Broccoli Casserole, M191
Cheesy Chicken Shortcakes, 98
Cheesy Florentine Bake, 131
Cheesy French Bread, 218
Cheesy Garlic-Stuffed Bread, 176
Cheesy Onion Biscuits, 98
Cherry Chocolates, 321
Cherry-Cola Salad, 94
Cherry-Wine Sauce, 285
Chesapeake Bay Crab Cakes, 155
Chewy Peanut Butter Macaroons, 214
Chicken à la Russell, 175
Chicken and Dumplings with Herbed Broth, 338
Chicken and Grits, 263
Chicken and Rice, 54
Chicken and Snow Pea Stir-Fry, 157
Chicken Dumpling Pie, 245
Chicken Enchiladas with Tomatillo Sauce, 206
Chicken Lasagna Bake, 55
Chicken Lasagna Florentine, 158
Chicken Noodle Salad, 25
Chicken Noodle Soup, 45
Chicken on Egg Bread, 120
Chicken Parmesan, 210
Chicken Pot Pie, 54, 256
Chicken-Squash Casserole, 121
Chicken Stock, 18
Chicken Tostadas, 122
Chicken with Bourbon-Purple Onion Relish, 253
Chili Popcorn, 166
Chili Verde, 14
Chilled Cucumber-Buttermilk Soup, 134
Chinese Taco Rolls, 339
Chocolate Chiffon Cake with Coffee
   Buttercream, 277
Chocolate-Cola Frosting, 56
Chocolate Cookie Ice Cream, 245
Chocolate Crème Brûlée, 323
Chocolate Fruitcakes, 250
Chocolate-Hazelnut Biscotti, 80
Chocolate Plunge, 35
Chocolate Pots de Crème with Orange
   Meringues, 318
Chocolate-Raisin Oatmeal Cookies, 136
Chocolate-Raspberry Bags, 97
Chocolate-Raspberry Shortcake, 99
Chocolate Truffle Mousse with Raspberry
   Sauce, 327
Christmas Jammies, 322
Christmas Morning Strata, 282
Chunky Tomato Sauce, 264
Cinnamon-Apple Sweet Potatoes, M23
Cinnamon Ice Cream, 126
Cinnamon Sticks, 244
Cinnamon Winter Cider, 337
Citrus-Marinated Smoked Shrimp, 114
Clam Linguine, 212
Coconut-Lemon Cake, 319
Coconut Muffins, 214
Coffee Blends, 276
Coffee Buttercream, 277
Coffee Crème Brûlée, 323
Coffee Napoleons, 276
Coffee Nuggets, 278
Collard Greens, 233
Continental Meat Pie, 256
Convenient Hash Browns, 135
Convenient Vegetable Stir-Fry, 157
Cornbread Bowls, 58

Corned Beef Hash, 262
Cornish Hens à l'Orange, 325
Cornish Hens Tarragon, 326
Cornmeal Biscuits, 98
Corn Salad, 214
Country Crab Cakes, 20
Couscous with Mixed Fruit, 232
Cowboy Coffee Cake, 84
Crab Imperial, 155
Crab Louis, 94
Crabmeat Brunch Scramble, 32
Crabmeat-Topped Potatoes, 22
Crab Mousse, 327
Crab-Stuffed Lobster Tails, 326
Cranberry-Cornbread Stuffed Cornish Hens, 325
Cranberry Cubes, 201
Cranberry Relish, 318
Cranberry Sangría, 238
Cranberry Scones, 283
Cream Cheese Frosting, 139
Cream Cheese Pound Cake, 304
Creamed Asparagus on Toast, 61
Creamed Chipped Tuna, 127
Creamed Shrimp on Pecan-Cornmeal
   Rounds, 99
Cream of Roasted Sweet Red Pepper
   Soup, 65
Cream of Shiitake Soup, 265
Creamy Almond Fudge, 51
Creamy Asparagus-and-Chicken Soup, 82
Creamy Dressing, 66
Creamy Dried Tomato Hummus, 284
Creamy Ham-and-Chicken Lasagna, 88
Creamy Mocha Fudge, 51
Creamy Pasta Primavera, 167
Creamy Rice and Squash Casserole, 26
Creole Chicken, 261
Creole Dressing, 289
Crispy Oatmeal-Toffee Lizzies, 136
Crown Pork Roast with Apple-Walnut
   Stuffing, 289
Crunchy Crisp Salad, 28
Cucumber Canapés, 88
Cucumber-Dill Salsa, 107
Cucumber Mousse with Dill Sauce, 216
Cucumber Salsa, 131
Curried Chicken Mousse, 328
Curried Chicken Skillet Dinner, 47
Curried Corn and Sweet Red Peppers, 47
Curried Fruit Medley, 329
Curried Tuna Melts, 46
Curry Mayonnaise, 66
Curry Sauce, 18
Cute-as-a-Button Cherry Pound Cake, 139

Date Bars, 322
De-Light-Ful Dessert, 220
Dijon-Rosemary Lamb Chops, 285
Dijon Vinaigrette, 301
Dill-Cheese-Ham Omelet, 33
Dill Sauce, 216
Dilly Cheese Muffins, 245
Dilly Garlic Bread, 218
Dinglewood Pharmacy's Scrambled Dog, 118
Dipped Chocolate-Almond Spoons, M277
Divinity Ghosts, 273
Double Chocolate Chunk-Almond Cookies, 178
Double-Chocolate Cookies, 272
Double-Good Fudge, M50
Double Raspberry Crème Brûlée, 323
Dove au Vin, 309
Dried Lady Apple Slices, 263

Easter Basket and Eggs, 101
Easy Caramel-Chocolate Sticky
   Buns, 36
Easy Crab Bake, 209
Easy Guacamole, 94
Easy Meat Loaf, 125
Easy Santa Cookies, 321
Easy Shrimp Creole, 68
Easy Turkey Scaloppine, M192
Egg Bread, 121
Eggnog Dessert, 314
Eggnog French Toast, 313
Eggnog-Pecan Pound Cake, 313
Eggplant-and-Oyster Louisiane, 196
Eggplant Cakes, 196
Eggplant Parmesan, 84
Eggplant Parmigiana, 197
Eggplant Relish, 342
Eggs and Cheese, 165
Emerald Isle Stew, 71
English Muffin Bread, M79

Fearrington House Goat Cheese and
   Black-Eyed Pea Salad, 60
Fennel Ice Cream, 281
Fibber McGee Cookies, 72
Filet Mignons with Shiitake Madeira
   Sauce, 265
Finger Painting Never Tasted So
   Good, 167
Fish in Caper Sauce, 209
Fish Stock, 19
Five-Ingredient Chili, 212
Five Pounds of Chocolate Fudge, 51
Flan de Queso, 303
Flank Steak-and-Spinach Pinwheels, 56
Florida Cubes, 201
Flour Tortillas, 44
Floyd's Favorite Tomato Sandwich, 172
Fluffy White Frosting, 319
Forty-Cloves-of-Garlic Chicken, 261
Freezer Eggplant-Sausage-Pasta
   Casserole, 197
French Bread Bowls, 58
French Market Beignets, 80
French Onion Casserole, 26
Fresh Fruit Dip, 94
Fresh Fruit Relish, 158
Fresh Fruit with Mint-Balsamic
   Tea, 232
Fresh Mint Tea, 88
Fresh Peach Ice Cream, 195
Fresh Peach Pie, 195
Fresh Peach Pie Filling, 195
Fresh Peach Salsa, 195
Fresh Salsa, 42
Fresh Tomato Salsa, 181
Fresh Tomato Tart, 170
Fresh Vegetable Skillet Dinner, 229
Fried Apricot Pies, 215
Fried Cabbage Rolls, 270
Fried Chicken Gravy, 235
Fried Green Tomatoes, 171
Fried Soft-Shell Crabs, 154
Fried Stuffed Jalapeño Peppers, 22
Fried Wonton Envelopes, 96
Frozen Cranberry Relish, 302
Frozen Margarita Punch, 91
Fruitcake-Stuffed Pork Loin, 250
Fruity Banana Bread, 78
Fruity Witches' Brew, 273
Fudge Brownie Muffins, M50

Garlic-and-Herb Cheese Grits, 122
Garlic and Mushrooms, 165
Garlic Bread, 218
Garlic Broccoli, 54
Garlic Butter, 89
Garlic-Butter Sauce, 327
Garlicky Pasta with Asparagus, Tomatoes, and
     Shrimp, 82
Garlic-Roasted Potatoes, 87, 342
Garlic Vinaigrette, 65
Gazpacho Dip, 243
Gazpacho-Stuffed Endive, 287
Gifts That Measure Up, 332
Gingerbread Pancakes, 282
Ginger Crème Brûlée, 323
Gingered Fruit Salad, 95
Ginger-Lime Cream, 227
Ginger Vinaigrette, 162
Golden Cheese-Shiitake Omelet, 265
Gold Nugget Chicken, 120
Grandmother's Fruitcake, 248
Granola Bars, 214
Granola Muffins, 78
Grapefruit Drink, 238
Greek Chicken Breasts, 170
Greek Chili, 16
Greek Grilled Zucchini with Feta, 190
Green Bean Slaw, 108
Green Beans with Caramelized
     Onions, 288
Green Mole Sauce, 267
Green Rice Casserole, 181
Greens and Grapefruit Salad, 301
Green Tomato Sandwich Spread, 172
Gremolata, 280
Grill Basting Sauce, 236
Grilled Chicken Salad with Raspberry
     Dressing, 202
Grilled Eggplant Appetizer, 198
Grilled Fennel and Radicchio with Orange
     Vinaigrette, 253
Grilled Fruit with Honey Yogurt, 87
Grilled Lamb with Mango Salsa, 104
Grilled Lamb with Sweet Pepper Relish, 104
Grilled Melon Salad with Orange-Raspberry
     Vinaigrette, 144
Grilled Pepper Tacos, 340
Grilled Pork Tenderloin with Apples,
     Celery, and Potatoes, 161
Grilled Portabello Mushrooms, 123
Grilled Salmon Quesadilla with Cucumber
     Salsa, 131
Grilled Shiitakes, 265
Grilled Stuffed Onions, 180
Grilled Swordfish with Caper Sauce, 230
Grilled Trout, 106
Grilled Turkey Breast with Cranberry
     Salsa, 252
Grits and Greens, 233
Guacamole Dip, 96
Gumbo Potatoes, 22

Ham-and-Cheese Pie, 256
Ham-and-Potato Salad, 94
Ham-and-Turkey Spaghetti, 19
Hamburger-Bean Bake, 121
Hamburger Casserole, 210
Ham Mousse Pitas, 328
Ham-Mushroom-Stuffed Artichokes, 228
Ham 'n' Cheese Chicken Sandwich, 153
Ham-Pineapple Nibbles, 283
Ham Strata, 308

Ham Stroganoff on Cheesy Onion
     Biscuits, 98
Hash Brown Bake, 281
Hazelnut-Crusted Rack of Lamb with
     Cherry-Wine Sauce, 284
Healthy Salad, 133
Heavenly Smoked Brisket, 114
Hello Dolly Dessert, 168
Herbed Biscuit Ring, 161
Herbed Cherry Tomatoes over Pasta, 229
Herbed Gazpacho, 175
Holiday Cranberry Salad, 301
Hollandaise Sauce, 86
Honey Angel Biscuits, 138
Honey Butter, 139
Honeyed Grapes, 47
Honey-Lemon Dressing, 133
Honey-Mustard Pork Tenderloin, 52
Honey-Vanilla Ice Cream, 178
Hot Cider Punch, 238
Hot Crabmeat Dip, 154
Hot Cross Buns, 100
Hot Curried Fruit, 72
Hot Handlers, 332
Hot Melon Salsa, 144
Hot Tomato Grits, 171
Hot Tuna Melts, 126
Hunter Sauce, 317

Ice Ring, 140
Individual Barbecued Beef Loaves, 242
Irish Coffee-Eggnog Punch, 314
Irish Soda Bread, 71
Italian Cheese Breadsticks, 126
Italian Chicken and Artichokes, 68
Italian Chicken-Mozzarella Melt, 153
Italian Ricotta Cheesecake, 303

Jack-o'-Lantern Cookies, 273
Jalapeño Mustard, 312
Jamaican Chicken Sandwich, 153
Jeweled Congealed Fresh Fruit, 89
Jill's Fruitcake, 249

Kathy's Onion Pudding, 318
Kentucky Mincemeat Pie, 302
Key Lime Muffins, 50
Key Lime Pies, 86
King Ranch Chicken, 193
Kudzu Blossom Jelly, 198
Kudzu Fried Chicken, 198

Lamb Kabobs, 192
Late-Night Pasta Chez Frank, 228
Lahvosh Cracker Bread Bowls, 58
Layered Peach Dessert, 196
Leg of Lamb, 285
Leg of Lamb with Hunter Sauce, 317
Lemonade-Bourbon Punch, 287
Lemonade Cubes, 201
Lemon Basting Sauce, 32
Lemon Broccoli, 53
Lemon Butter, 32
Lemon-Cheese Party Bites, 160
Lemon Crisps, 272
Lemon Delight Cheesecake, 219
Lemon Filling, 319
Lemon-Garlic Pasta, 181
Lemon-Herb Grilled Chicken, 87

Lemon-Infused Olive Oil, 231
Lemon-Lime Flank Steak, 55
Lemon Mayonnaise, 32
Lemon-Mint Cubes, 201
Lemon-Mint Sugar, 32
Lemon-Roasted Chicken, 24
Lemon Squeezers, 32
Lemon Tea Tingler, 200
Lemon Vinaigrette, 31
Lemon Vinegar, 31
Lemony Barbecue Sauce, 31
Lemony Tartar Sauce, 32
Lentil Burgers, 123
Light Lasagna, 212
Lima Bean Casserole, 132
Lollipop Cookies, 322
Lucy's Apricot Praline Torte, 243

Macadamia Nut French Toast, 282
Macaroni and Cheese Soup, 264
Macaroni, Cheese, and Tomatoes, 213
Macaroni-Cheese-Beef Casserole, 125
Majorcan Mushroom Tapas, 159
Make-Ahead Chocolate-Mint Cake
     Roll, 220
Make-Ahead Yeast Rolls, 307
Mamma Mia Pasta, 25
Mango-Cilantro Vinegar, 190
Mango Salsa, 104
Manny and Isa's Key Lime Pie, 118
Maple-Cider Sauce, 288
Marble Pound Cake, 29
Marinated Artichoke Hearts, 66
Marinated Artichoke Salad, 66
Marinated Asparagus with Prosciutto, 83
Marinated Bourbon Steak, 91
Marinated Cheese, 21
Marinated Flank Steak, 237
Marinated Grilled Vegetables, 162
Marinated Tomato and Brie Salad, 95
Marinated Vegetable Medley, 91
Meatball Kabobs, 192
Meat Loaf with Chunky Tomato
     Sauce, 264
Mediterranean Pasta, 341
Mediterranean Salad, 132
Mediterranean Shrimp and Pasta, 286
Memmie's Spoonbread, 27
Mesquite-Ginger Beef with Fresh Fruit
     Relish, 158
Mexican Chicken Tortilla Salads, 129
Mexican Cornbread Salad, 210
Mexican Crostini, 142
Mexican Fiesta Spoon Biscuits, 161
Mexican Pinwheels, 21
Mexican Stack-Up, 69
Microwave Portabello Mushrooms, M123
Microwave Ratatouille, M232
Midnight Delights, 278
Miniature Liqueur Sampler, 332
Miniature Orange Éclairs, 92
Mini Swiss Cheese Loaves, 80
Mint Fudge, 50
Mixed Fruit Punch, 239
Mixed Greens with Parmesan Walnuts, 301
Mixed Greens with Tarragon Vinaigrette, 326
Mocha Blend, 276
Mocha Punch, 141
Mock Crab Cakes, 159
Monkey Bread, 174
Monster Mouths, 274
Moravian Sugar Cake, 304

Moroccan Grilled Chicken Salad, 231
Moroccan Spice Rub, 231
Mozzarella Tamale, 70
Mr. Funk of New Orleans, 57
Mulled Wine Punch, 337
Mushroom Casserole, 211
Mushroom-Macaroni Casserole, 180
Mustard Mousse, 328
My Favorite Pasta, 213

Nacho Fondue, 35
Nannie's Candied Sweet Potatoes, 306
Nannie's Chowchow, 250
Nannie's Cornbread Dressing, 306
Ned's Eggplant Sticks, 309
No-Bake Fruitcake, 249
Northern New Mexican Vegetable Quesadilla
    with Roasted Salsa, 130
Now, Thatsa Chili, 16
Nutty Orange Coffee Cake, 160

Oatmeal-Chocolate Morsel Cookies, 46
Oatmeal Cookie Topping, 291
Off-the-Wall Gadgets, 332
Okra, Corn, and Tomatoes, 203
Olde English Trifle, 331
Old-Fashioned Bread Pudding with Bourbon
    Custard Sauce, 271
One-Minute Salsa, 93
Onion-and-Sesame Rolls, 292
Onion Crème Brûlée, 324
Open-Face Eggplant Sandwiches, 124
Orange-Almond Snack Balls, 214
Orange Baked Apples with Cookie
    Crumbs, 271
Orange-Banana Whip, 244
Orange Blend, 276
Orange Butter Cake, 46
Orange-Buttermilk Salad, 134
Orange Cake, 320
Orange Crème Brûlée, 323
Orange Crinkles, 272
Orange Glaze, 320
Orange Meringues, 318
Orange-Pecan Truffles, 92
Orange-Raspberry Vinaigrette, 144
Oranges in Grand Marnier, 142
Orange-Strawberry Shortcake, 100
Orange Vinegar, 31
Oregano Cheese Puffs, 21
Oregano Chicken, 84
Oriental Chicken Kabobs, 193
Our Best Southern Fried Chicken, 235
Out West Chili, 15
Oven-Baked Tomato Appetizers, 172
Oven-Fried Catfish, 106
Oven-Fried Chicken, 236
Oven-Roasted Vegetable Chowder, 229

Paella Casserole, 254
Pane Cunsado (Fixed Bread), 218
Papaya Seed Dressing, 204
Papaya Vinaigrette Dressing, 206
Paprika Chicken, 125
Parmesan-Coated Brie, 286
Parmesan-Collards Casserole, 233
Parmesan Potato Wedges, 181
Parmesan-Zucchini Fries, 129
Party Tarts, 90
Passover Brisket, 102

Pasta-Vegetable Salad, 238
Pasta with Greens, 211
Pasta with Peanut Sauce, 252
Pastry Cornucopia, 307
Peach Cobbler, 264
Peaches and Cream, 196
Peach Fluff, 176
Peach Ketchup, 306
Peach-Mint Vinegar, 190
Peanut Blossom Cookies, 245
Peanut Butter Fudge, 51
Peanut Butter Shortbread, 321
Peanut-Ginger Dressing, 177
Peanutty Beef Stir-Fry, 157
Pear Chutney, 251
Pears with Orange-Caramel Sauce, 281
Pecan-Breaded Pork Chops with Beer
    Sauce, 266
Pecan-Cornmeal Rounds, 99
Peppered Honey Mustard, 312
Peppermint Cookies, 322
Peppermint Crème Brûlée, 323
Peppermint Fondue, 35
Peppery Greens with Raspberry
    Dressing, 254
Peppery Potato Casserole, 182
Pesto Dip, 93
Pesto Sauce, 267
Pesto-Spiced Nuts, 173
Phyllo Bowls, 58
Phyllo Tartlet Shells, 216
Picnic Shrimp Salad, 182
Pigs in a Blanket, 178
Piña Coladas, 203
Piña Colada Slush, 90
Pineapple-Cream Cheese Frosting, 160
Pineapple-Gin Punch, 140
Pineapple Sherbet Punch, 141
Pink Grapefruit and Tarragon
    Sorbet, 163
Pink Sangría Tea, 200
Pinwheels, 321
Pita Bread Salad, 86
Pizza Bites, 244
Pizza-Flavored Chicken Tacos, 340
Plantain Chips, M203
Planter's Punch Dessert, 175
Poached Trout, 106
Polka Dot Punch, 178
Polka Dots, 272
Poppy Seed Cake, 63
Pork Cacciatore, 69
Pork Medaillons with Port Wine and Dried
    Cranberry Sauce, 330
Posole, 226
Potato-Bacon Frittata, 269
Potato-Cheese Puff, 269
Potato-Onion Patties, 269
Potato Sourdough Bread, 77
Potato Sourdough Bread Dough, 77
Potato Sourdough Cinnamon Rolls, 77
Potato Sourdough Rolls, 77
Potato Sourdough Starter, 77
Praline Buttercream, 243
Praline Powder, 243
Pub Fondue, 35
Pueblo Indian Cookies, 228
Puff Pastry Bowls, 58
Pumpkin-Corn Soup with Ginger-Lime
    Cream, 282
Pumpkin Waffles, 282
Punch for a Bunch, 90
Purple Onion Relish, 253

Quiche Casserole, 33
Quick Chicken and Dumplings, 125
Quick Chocolate Cola Cake, 56
Quick Cooked Cabbage, 270
Quick Fiesta Dip, M237
Quick Full-Bodied Stock, 17
Quick Hummus, 93
Quick Rolls, 245
Quick Yeast Rolls, 45

Raisin-Nut Spread, 79
Raspberry Dressing, 202
Rasp-Berry Good Tea, 200
Raspberry Milk Shakes, 238
Raspberry Mustard, 313
Raspberry Sauce, 327
Raspberry Sherbet Punch, 141
Raspberry-Thyme Vinegar, 190
Really Hot Mustard, 312
Red Bell Pepper Jam, 242
Red Cabbage Slaw, 153
Red Chile Sauce, 17
Red Chili Stew, 226
Red Seafood Sauce, 107
Red Wine-Marinated Flank Steak, 283
Reuben Loaf, 338
Rhubarb-Raspberry Pear Pie, 119
Rice Stuffing, 290
Rice with Tomatoes and Basil, 232
Rich Brownies, 84
Risotto, 280
Risotto Primavera, 163
Roast Chicken with Rice, 261
Roasted Bell Peppers in Olive Oil, 242
Roasted Chiles Rellenos, 64
Roasted Garlic Crème Brûlée, 324
Roasted Garlic Mashed Potatoes, 288
Roasted Garlic Sauce, 268
Roasted Onion Salad, 65
Roasted Red Bell Pepper Bread, 241
Roasted Red Bell Pepper Butter, 242
Roasted Salsa, 130
Roasted Serrano Salsa, 207
Roasted Tomatillo Salsa, 64
Roasted Tomato Salsa, 64
Roasted Vegetables, 64
Roast Turkey with Herbs, 305
Rolled Lamb Roast, 285
Roquefort-and-Black Pepper Crème Brûlée, 324
Rosemary-Baked Potatoes, 23
Rosemary Biscuits, 91
Rosemary Cannellini Beans, 213
Rosemary Focaccia, 190
Rosemary-Roasted Potatoes, 20
Rum Syrup, 313
Rumtopf, 142
Rutabaga Whip, 179

Salmon Bake with Pecan-Crunch Coating, 209
Salmon Burgers, 24
Salmon in Parchment, 311
Sausage-and-Bean Dinner, 108
Sausage-and-Noodle Casserole, 255
Sausage and Peppers, 165
Sausage-Cornbread Dressing, 289
Sausage Muffins, 49
Sautéed Chayote Squash with Cilantro, 227
Sautéed Portabello Mushrooms, 123
Savannah Red Rice, 27
Savory Crème Brûlées, 324
Savory Southern Pecans, 240

Scalloped Oysters, 318
Scottish Shortbread, 34
Seafood Risotto, 280
Seafood-Stuffed Potatoes, M192
Sealed with a Quiche, 135
Seared Scallops with Tomato-Mango Salsa, 122
Sesame-Crusted Salmon with Ginger
    Vinaigrette, 162
Sesame Pork Tenderloin, 53
Sesame Shrimp, 92
Sherry Cheese Pâté, 215
Shrimp-and-Pepper Soft Tacos, 339
Shrimp Bisque, 19
Shrimp Enchiladas in Tomatillo Sauce, 310
Shrimp Scampi, 209
Shrimp with Gin and Ginger, 205
Simply Good Chicken Casserole, 255
Skillet Okra, 179
Smoked Salmon, 114
Smoked Salmon and Cucumber Tartlets, 216
Smoky Herb Chicken, 116
Soda Pop Pears, 55
Sour Cream Corn Muffins, 176
Sour Cream Fudge, 52
Southern Classic Pizza, 268
Southern Fruit Punch, 238
Southern Spareribs, 116
Southwest Deluxe Pizza, 268
Southwestern Tuna Melts, 127
Southwestern Veggie Pizza, 126
Southwest Seasoning, 266
Spanish Cabbage Relish, 270
Sparkling Apple Juice, 141
Sparkling Citrus Punch, 337
Sparkling Cranberry Punch, 101
Special Peas, 133
Speedy Blueberry Muffins, 135
Spiced Apple Jelly, 251
Spice Thins, 322
Spicy Buffalo Wings, 239
Spicy Chicken Quesadillas, 42
Spicy Sour Cream Topping, 15
Spicy Tomato Gravy, 172
Spicy Tomato Warm-Up, 328
Spinach-and-Cheese Calzones, 310
Spinach and Mushrooms with Bow Tie
    Pasta, 341
Spinach-Artichoke Bake, 48
Spinach-Artichoke-Tomato Puffs, 284
Spinach Cornbread, 49
Spinach Filling, 316
Spinach Pie with Muenster Crust, 48
Spinach Puffs, 316
Spinach Salad with the Blues, 66
Spinach Squares, 49
Spirited Raspberries, 142
Spooky Eyes, 273
Spoonbread, 156
Squash and Tomato Bake, 180
Squash Dressing, 290
Squash Soufflé, 215

Stacked Sweet Potato Blues, 290
Standing Rib Roast, 28
Starlight Cheese Bites, 329
Starter Food, 77
Steamed Orange Roughy with Herbs, 189
Stewed Anasazi Beans with Mushrooms, 226
Stewed Tomatoes and Greens, 234
St. Louis Toasted Ravioli, 117
Strawberry-Champagne Sorbet, 20
Strawberry-Rhubarb Crisp, 119
Strawberry Spread, 79
Stuffed Shrimp with Hollandaise Sauce, 86
Sugar-and-Spice Hot Chocolate, 34
Sugarplum Sticks, 321
Summery Chicken Salad, 138
Summery Squash-and-Pepper Kabobs, 193
Summer Zucchini Salad, 229
Sunday Chicken, 228
Sunday Egg Casserole, 100
Surprise Pull-Apart Biscuits, 46
Swamp Sticks, 274
Sweet Cider Mustard, 312
Sweet Corn Salsa, 156
Sweetened Preserved Lemons, 141
Sweet Onion Tarts, 229
Sweet Pepper Relish, 104
Sweet Peppery Sausage, 69
Sweet Potato-and-Sausage Soup, 23
Sweet Potato Butter, M290
Sweet Potato Chips, M203
Sweet Potato-Eggnog Casserole, 291
Sweet Potato Flan, 291
Sweet Potato Peaks, 291
Sweet Zucchini Relish, 159
Swiss Chicken, 54
Swiss-Onion Dip, 93
Swiss Vegetable Medley, 26

Tabasco Steak, 207
Taco Tassies, 339
Tamale Soup, 213
Tamarind-Glazed Pork Chops with Green Mole
    Sauce, 266
Tangy Fruit Shake, 129
Tartar Sauce, 107, 155
Tee's Corn Pudding, 318
Tennessee Ham, 263
Tennessee Sin, 218
Texas Firecrackers, 96
Tex-Mex Egg Burritos, 34
Thai Chicken Salad, 177
The Beach, 168
The Best of the Bayou Pizza, 268
The King Henry Pizza, 267
The Sauce, 237
Three-Grain Rice, 166
Toasted Oatmeal Cookies, 136
Toasted Rice and Pasta, 57
Toasty Southern Pecan Tarts, 329
Tomatillo Sauce, 206

Tomato, Basil, and Cheese, 165
Tomato-Basil-Mozzarella Salad, 171
Tomato-Basil Risotto, 269
Tomato-Eggplant Biscuit Cakes, 170
Tomato-Zucchini Gratin, 171
Tortilla Bites, 42
Traditional Pizza Sauce, 267
Tropical Cheese Spread, 46
Tropical Date-Banana Loaves, 143
Tropical Gazpacho, 204
Tropical Tea-Ser, 200
Tropical Trifle, 204
Trout Fillets with Capers, 252
Tuna Burgers, 128
Tuna Nachos, 127
Tuna Tapenade, 127
Turkey and Peppers in Cornbread Crust, 312
Turkey Hash, 262
Turkey Sausage Turnovers, 239
Turkey Taco Salad, 25
Turnip Greens, 306
Tzimmes, 102

Vegetable Hash, 262
Vegetable Lasagna, 211
Vegetables in Wine Sauce Casserole, 133
Vegetarian Sauté, 69
Vic's Oven Shrimp, 215
Vienna Blend, 276
Vinaigrette, 61
Vinaigrette Dressing, 231

Warm Vegetable Salad, 174
Watermelon Daiquiri, 143
Watermelon Pie, 144
Water-Whipped Baked Pastry Shell, 246
Weeknight Spaghetti Pie, 312
Weidmann's Black Bottom Pie, 118
White Bean Spread, 279
White Chocolate Chess Tart, 303
White Chocolate Fudge, 51
White Chocolate-Macadamia Nut Crème
    Brûlée, 323
Wild Rice Casserole, 176
Wild Rice with Grapes, 48
Wild Tuna Salad, 243
Wine Tasting, 332
Winter Salad, 280
Wonton Wrapper Bowls, 58

Yataklete Kilkil, 71
Yummy Coconut Biscuits, 99

Zesty Black-Eyed Pea Relish, 56
Ziti with Sausage and Broccoli, 340
Zucchini Crispies, 179
Zucchini-Pineapple Cake, 160

MONTH-BY-MONTH INDEX

An alphabetical listing within the month of every food article and accompanying recipes

All microwave recipe page numbers are preceded by an "M."

JANUARY

After-Christmas Casserole, 19
Ham-and-Turkey Spaghetti, 19
Appetizers On The Cheesy Side, 21
Fried Stuffed Jalapeño Peppers, 22
Marinated Cheese, 21
Mexican Pinwheels, 21
Oregano Cheese Puffs, 21
Celebrate In A New Light, 20
Country Crab Cakes, 20
Rosemary-Roasted Potatoes, 20
Strawberry-Champagne Sorbet, 20
Delicious Indulgence, 36
Caramel Dessert Biscuits, 36
Caramel Ice Cream Dessert, 36
Easy Caramel-Chocolate Sticky
Buns, 36
**Ever-Changing Chili: Make It Mild
Or Make It Wild, 14**
Black Bean Chili Marsala, 16
Bodacious Chili, 14
Chili Verde, 14
Greek Chili, 16
Now, Thatsa Chili, 16
Out West Chili, 15
From Our Kitchen To Yours, 30
Shortcuts and Time-savers for Everyday
Cooking, 30
High-Yield Stocks, 17
Beef Stock, 17
Burned Bourbon with Molasses
Sauce, 17
Chicken Stock, 18
Curry Sauce, 18
Fish Stock, 19
Quick Full-Bodied Stock, 17
Red Chile Sauce, 17
Shrimp Bisque, 19
Just Dip It!, 35
Caramel Fondue, 35
Chocolate Plunge, 35
Nacho Fondue, 35
Peppermint Fondue, 35
Pub Fondue, 35

Lively Lemons Add Zing, 31
Lemon Basting Sauce, 32
Lemon Butter, 32
Lemon Mayonnaise, 32
Lemon-Mint Sugar, 32
Lemon Squeezers, 32
Lemon Vinegar, 31
Lemony Barbecue Sauce, 31
Lemony Tartar Sauce, 32
Make A Break For It, 32
Cheese-Chive Scrambled Eggs, 34
Crabmeat Brunch Scramble, 32
Dill-Cheese-Ham Omelet, 33
Quiche Casserole, 33
Tex-Mex Egg Burritos, 34
**Old Favorites Made New: Mama's Cooking
Just Got Better, 28**
Berry Shrub, 29
Crunchy Crisp Salad, 28
Marble Pound Cake, 29
Standing Rib Roast, 28
Savannah Style, **27**
Casserole of Black Beans, 27
Memmie's Spoonbread, 27
Savannah Red Rice, 27
Seasonal Sensation, 34
Scottish Shortbread, 34
Sugar-and-Spice Hot Chocolate, 34
Serve These Casseroles On The Side, 26
Creamy Rice and Squash Casserole, 26
French Onion Casserole, 26
Swiss Vegetable Medley, 26
Super Spud Toppers, 22
Black-Eyed Pea-Spinach-Stuffed Potatoes, 22
Cinnamon-Apple Sweet Potatoes, M23
Crabmeat-Topped Potatoes, 22
Gumbo Potatoes, 22
Rosemary-Baked Potatoes, 23
Tighten Your Belt, 23
Bean-and-Hominy Soup, 23
Beef Hash, 24
Chicken Noodle Salad, 25
Lemon-Roasted Chicken, 24
Mamma Mia Pasta, 25
Salmon Burgers, 24
Sweet Potato-and-Sausage Soup, 23
Turkey Taco Salad, 25

FEBRUARY

Bake A Bread Bowl, 58
Cornbread Bowls, 58
French Bread Bowls, 58
Lahvosh Cracker Bread Bowl, 58
Phyllo Bowls, 58
Puff Pastry Bowls, 58
Wonton Wrapper Bowl, 58
Batter Up, 49
Fudge Brownie Muffins, M50
Key Lime Muffins, 50
Sausage Muffins, 49
Breakfast At Brennan's – By The Book, 57
Mr. Funk of New Orleans, 57
Chicken Are It's Chicken, 54
Chicken and Rice, 54
Chicken Lasagna Bake, 55
Chicken Pot Pie, 54
Swiss Chicken, 54
Company Coming? No Problem, 56
Flank Steak-and-Spinach Pinwheels, 56
Toasted Rice and Pasta, 57
Zesty Black-Eyed Pea Relish, 56
Curry In A Hurry, 46
Aloha Shrimp Salad, 46
Curried Chicken Skillet Dinner, 47
Curried Corn and Sweet Red Peppers, 47
Curried Tuna Melts, 46
Flat-Out Winners, 42
Apple Chimichangas, 43
Carne Guisada Burritos, 43
Spicy Chicken Quesadillas, 42
Tortilla Bites, 42
Fools For Fudge, 50
Buttermilk Fudge, 52
Creamy Almond Fudge, 51
Creamy Mocha Fudge, 51
Double-Good Fudge, M50
Five Pounds of Chocolate
Fudge, 51
Mint Fudge, 50
Peanut Butter Fudge, 51
Sour Cream Fudge, 52
White Chocolate Fudge, 51

FEBRUARY
(continued)

Fresh From The Vine, 47
Blue Cheese-Pecan Grapes, 48
Caribbean Grapes, 48
Honeyed Grapes, 47
Wild Rice with Grapes, 48
From Our Kitchen To Yours, 44
Flour Tortillas, 44
Homemade Made Easy, 45
Chicken Noodle Soup, 45
Oatmeal-Chocolate Morsel Cookies, 46
Orange Butter Cake, 46
Quick Yeast Rolls, 45
Surprise Pull-Apart Biscuits, 46
One Meal Three Ways, 52
Apple-Mushroom Pork Tenderloin, 53
Broccoli and Walnut Sauté, 52
Garlic Broccoli, 54
Honey-Mustard Pork Tenderloin, 52
Lemon Broccoli, 53
Sesame Pork Tenderloin, 53
Soda's The Secret, 55
Lemon-Lime Flank Steak, 55
Quick Chocolate Cola Cake, 56
Soda Pop Pears, 55
Spinach On The Side, 48
Spinach-Artichoke Bake, 48
Spinach Cornbread, 49
Spinach Pie with Muenster
Crust, 48
Spinach Squares, 49

MARCH
••••••••••••••••

A Touch O' Irish, 70
Emerald Isle Stew, 71
Irish Soda Bread, 71
Bake It Light, 78
Blue Cheese Spread, 79
Chocolate-Hazelnut Biscotti, 80
English Muffin Bread, M79
Fruity Banana Bread, 78
Granola Muffins, 78
Mini Swiss Cheese Loaves, 80
Raisin-Nut Spread, 79
Strawberry Spread, 79
Beignets For Breakfast, 80
French Market Beignets, 80
Build A Meal, 68
Beef Burgundy, 69
Easy Shrimp Creole, 68
Italian Chicken and Artichokes, 68
Mexican Stack-Up, 69
Pork Cacciatore, 69
Sweet Peppery Sausage, 69
Vegetarian Sauté, 69
Dinner On A Shoestring, 70
Burger Boat, 70
Carolina Gumbo, 70
Mozzarella Tamale, 70
From Our Kitchen To Yours, 67
Discover the Wide Selection of Salad
Greens at the Supermarket, 67
Glorious Goat Cheese, 60
Butternut Squash Soup, 62
Celebrity Chicken Breasts, 60
Creamed Asparagus on Toast, 61

Fearrington House Goat Cheese and
Black-Eyed Pea Salad, 60
Poppy Seed Cake, 63
Out Of Africa, 71
Yataklete Kilkil, 71
Searing Heat, Subtle Flavors, 64
Cream of Roasted Sweet Red Pepper
Soup, 65
Roasted Chiles Rellenos, 64
Roasted Onion Salad, 65
Roasted Tomatillo Salsa, 64
Roasted Tomato Salsa, 64
Roasted Vegetables, 64
Simple Salads Made Sensational, 66
Cauliflower-English Pea Salad, 66
Marinated Artichoke Salad, 66
Spinach Salad with the Blues, 66
Sourdough Made Simple, 77
Potato Sourdough Bread, 77
Potato Sourdough Bread Dough, 77
Potato Sourdough Cinnamon Rolls, 77
Potato Sourdough Rolls, 77
Potato Sourdough Starter, 77
To Market, To Market, 72
Buck's Taters, 72
Fibber McGee Cookies, 72
Hot Curried Fruit, 72

APRIL
••••••••••••••••

A Memorable Passover, 102
Burnt Sugar Sponge Cake with Berry
Sauce, 103
Passover Brisket, 102
Tzimmes, 102
Easter Sunday Brunch, 100
Berry-Citrus Twist, 100
Hot Cross Buns, 100
Sparkling Cranberry Punch, 101
Sunday Egg Casserole, 100
From Our Kitchen To Yours, 105
How to Cook Lamb, 105
Lamb – Texas Style, 104
Grilled Lamb with Mango Salsa, 104
Grilled Lamb with Sweet Pepper
Relish, 104
Low-Fat Catch, 106
Baked Hush Puppies, 108
Baked Trout, 106
Green Bean Slaw, 108
Grilled Trout, 106
Oven-Fried Catfish, 106
Poached Trout, 106
Nontaxing Standbys, 84
Baked Mushroom Rice, 84
Cowboy Coffee Cake, 84
Eggplant Parmesan, 84
Oregano Chicken, 84
Rich Brownies, 84
PB & J For Easter, 101
Bird's Nests, 102
Bunny Trail Mix, 101
Easter Basket and Eggs, 101
Shortcakes Deliciously Layered, 98
Cheesy Chicken Shortcakes, 98
Chocolate-Raspberry Shortcake, 99
Creamed Shrimp on Pecan-Cornmeal
Rounds, 99
Ham Stroganoff on Cheesy Onion
Biscuits, 98

Orange-Strawberry Shortcake, 100
Yummy Coconut Biscuits, 99
Something Good To Talk About, 108
Sausage-and-Bean Dinner, 108

SPRING CELEBRATIONS, 85
Bubble Over, 90
Amaretto Slush, 90
Frozen Margarita Punch, 91
Piña Colada Slush, 90
Punch for a Bunch, 90
Dinner On The Lawn, 85
Cajun Blackened Filet Mignon, 85
Garlic-Roasted Potatoes, 87
Grilled Fruit with Honey Yogurt, 87
Key Lime Pies, 86
Lemon-Herb Grilled Chicken, 87
Pita Bread Salad, 86
Stuffed Shrimp with Hollandaise
Sauce, 86
Easy Things Come In Small Packages, 96
Chocolate-Raspberry Bags, 97
Fried Wonton Envelopes, 96
Texas Firecrackers, 96
Happy Anniversary, 91
Blue Cheese Spread, 92
Marinated Bourbon Steak, 91
Marinated Vegetable Medley, 91
Miniature Orange Éclairs, 92
Orange-Pecan Truffles, 92
Rosemary Biscuits, 91
Sesame Shrimp, 92
Say "I Do" To Great Food, 88
Creamy Ham-and-Chicken Lasagna, 88
Cucumber Canapés, 88
Fresh Mint Tea, 88
Garlic Butter, 89
Jeweled Congealed Fresh Fruit, 89
Party Tarts, 90
Spring's Best Salads, 94
Broccoli Salad, 95
Cherry-Cola Salad, 94
Crab Louis, 94
Gingered Fruit Salad, 95
Ham-and-Potato Salad, 94
Marinated Tomato and Brie Salad, 95
Stir Up Some Fun, 93
Black Bean Dip, 93
Buttery Ham Spread, 93
Easy Guacamole, 94
Fresh Fruit Dip, 94
One-Minute Salsa, 93
Pesto Dip, 93
Quick Hummus, 93
Swiss-Onion Dip, 93

Sweet Stalks Of Spring, 82
Asparagus Stir-Fry, 83
Asparagus with Garlic Cream, 83
Creamy Asparagus-and-Chicken Soup, 82
Garlicky Pasta with Asparagus, Tomatoes,
and Shrimp, 82
Marinated Asparagus with Prosciutto, 83

MAY
••••••••••••••••

An Oatmeal Cookie Sampler, 136
Chocolate-Raisin Oatmeal Cookies, 136
Crispy Oatmeal-Toffee Lizzies, 136
Toasted Oatmeal Cookies, 136

A Taste Of La Paz, 130
  Grilled Salmon Quesadilla with Cucumber
    Salsa, 131
  Northern New Mexican Vegetable
    Quesadilla with Roasted Salsa, 130
Dinner On The Ground, 121
  Chicken-Squash Casserole, 121
  Hamburger-Bean Bake, 121
Dinner's A Done Deal, 128
  Baked Pears à la Mode, 129
  Brie-Mushroom Burgers, 128
  Mexican Chicken Tortilla Salads, 129
  Parmesan-Zucchini Fries, 129
  Tangy Fruit Shake, 129
From Our Kitchen To Yours, 116
  Rites and Wrongs of Using a Smoker, 116
Garden Club Vegetable Favorites, 132
  Healthy Salad, 133
  Lima Bean Casserole, 132
  Special Peas, 133
  Vegetables in Wine Sauce Casserole, 133
Hometown Favorites, 117
  Dinglewood Pharmacy's Scrambled Dog, 118
  Manny and Isa's Key Lime Pie, 118
  St. Louis Toasted Ravioli, 117
  Weidmann's Black Bottom Pie, 118
Hooked On Tuna, 126
  Creamed Chipped Tuna, 127
  Hot Tuna Melts, 126
  Southwestern Tuna Melts, 127
  Tuna Burgers, 128
  Tuna Nachos, 127
  Tuna Tapenade, 127
Light And Lazy, 122
  Apricot-Yogurt Tortoni, 124
  Chicken Tostadas, 122
  Garlic-and-Herb Cheese Grits, 122
  Grilled Portabello Mushrooms, 123
  Lentil Burgers, 123
  Microwave Portabello Mushrooms, M123
  Open-Face Eggplant Sandwiches, 124
  Sautéed Portabello Mushrooms, 123
  Seared Scallops with Tomato-Mango
    Salsa, 122
Menu For Mom, 135
  Convenient Hash Browns, 135
  Sealed with a Quiche, 135
  Speedy Blueberry Muffins, 135
Not-So-Ordinary Spaghetti, 131
  Casserole Spaghetti, 132
  Cheesy Florentine Bake, 131
  Mediterranean Salad, 132
Spring For Rhubarb, 119
  Rhubarb-Raspberry Pear Pie, 119
  Strawberry-Rhubarb Crisp, 119
Start With Buttermilk, 134
  Buttermilk Bread Pudding with Butter-Rum
    Sauce, 134
  Buttermilk-Lemon Pudding Cake with
    Blueberry Sauce, 135
  Chilled Cucumber-Buttermilk Soup, 134
  Orange-Buttermilk Salad, 134
The Nashville Cookbook, 120
  Chicken on Egg Bread, 120
  Gold Nugget Chicken, 120
True Confessions (Of The Food Kind), 125
  Black Beans and Yellow Rice, 126
  Black, White, and Red All Over Soup, 126
  Cinnamon Ice Cream, 126
  Easy Meat Loaf, 125
  Italian Cheese Breadsticks, 126
  Macaroni-Cheese-Beef Casserole, 125
  Paprika Chicken, 125

Quick Chicken and Dumplings, 125
Southwestern Veggie Pizza, 126
When Smoke Gets In Your Eyes, 114
  Citrus-Marinated Smoked Shrimp, 114
  Heavenly Smoked Brisket, 114
  Smoked Salmon, 114
  Smoky Herb Chicken, 116
  Southern Spareribs, 116

JUNE

....

A Delightful Mix-up, 157
  Chicken and Snow Pea Stir-Fry, 157
  Convenient Vegetable Stir-Fry, 157
  Peanutty Beef Stir-Fry, 157
Beverages For A Crowd, 140
  Calypso Presbyterian Church Women's Lime
    Punch, 141
  Mocha Punch, 141
  Pineapple-Gin Punch, 140
  Pineapple Sherbet Punch, 141
  Raspberry Sherbet Punch, 141
  Sparkling Apple Juice, 141
Cordially Yours, 141
  Blueberry Cordial, 142
  Oranges in Grand Marnier, 142
  Rumtopf, 142
  Spirited Raspberries, 142
  Sweetened Preserved Lemons, 141
Down By The River, 154
  Chesapeake Bay Crab Cakes, 155
  Crab Imperial, 155
  Fried Soft-Shell Crabs, 154
  Hot Crabmeat Dip, 154
  Spoonbread, 156
  Sweet Corn Salsa, 156
Finger Foods: The Balancing Act, 140
  Guidelines for Eating Finger Foods
    Gracefully, 140
From Our Kitchen To Yours, 156
  Cracking Crabs Step-by-Step, 156
Give Them A Worldly Send-Off, 142
  Alabama Fudge-Pecan Chewies, 143
  Mexican Crostini, 142
  Tropical Date-Banana Loaves, 143
Hats Off To Summer Entertaining, 138
  Cute-as-a-Button Cherry Pound
    Cake, 139
  Honey Angel Biscuits, 138
  Summery Chicken Salad, 138
Light Night Out, 161
  Grilled Pork Tenderloin with Apples, Celery,
    and Potatoes, 161
  Marinated Grilled Vegetables, 162
  Pink Grapefruit and Tarragon Sorbet, 163
  Risotto Primavera, 163
  Sesame-Crusted Salmon with Ginger
    Vinaigrette, 162
Mix And Match, 166
  Cashew Casserole, 166
  Creamy Pasta Primavera, 167
  Three-Grain Rice, 166
Open A Can Of Promises, 160
  Herbed Biscuit Ring, 161
  Lemon-Cheese Party Bites, 160
  Mexican Fiesta Spoon Biscuits, 161
  Nutty Orange Coffee Cake, 160
Peanuts, Popcorn, And . . . , 165
  Caramel Crunch, 165
  Chili Popcorn, 166

Polenta's Not So Posh, 164
  Basic Polenta, 164
  Eggs and Cheese, 165
  Garlic and Mushrooms, 165
  Sausage and Peppers, 165
  Tomato, Basil, and Cheese, 165
Pudding Is Child's Play, 167
  Bodacious Peanut Parfait, 167
  Finger Painting Never Tasted So Good, 167
  The Beach, 168
Say Hello To Dessert, 168
  Hello Dolly Dessert, 168
Shreds Of Garden Goodness, 159
  Mock Crab Cakes, 159
  Sweet Zucchini Relish, 159
  Zucchini-Pineapple Cake, 160
Slices Of Summer, 143
  Cantaloupe-Peach Jam, 143
  Grilled Melon Salad with Orange-Raspberry
    Vinaigrette, 144
  Hot Melon Salsa, 144
  Watermelon Daiquiri, 143
  Watermelon Pie, 144
The Big Grill: Chicken Sandwiches, 153
  Ham 'n' Cheese Chicken Sandwich, 153
  Italian Chicken-Mozzarella Melt, 153
  Jamaican Chicken Sandwich, 153
Winning Ways Of Southern Cooks, 158
  Burk's Farm-Raised Catfish Fry, 158
  Chicken Lasagna Florentine, 158
  Majorcan Mushroom Tapas, 159
  Mesquite-Ginger Beef with Fresh Fruit
    Relish, 158

JULY

....

Catch A Wave, 191
  Cheesy Broccoli Casserole, M191
  Easy Turkey Scaloppine, M192
  Seafood-Stuffed Potatoes, M192
Consuming Kudzu, 198
  Apple Cider, 198
  Kudzu Blossom Jelly, 198
  Kudzu Fried Chicken, 198
Eggplant For Everyone, 196
  Eggplant-and-Oyster Louisiane, 196
  Eggplant Cakes, 196
  Eggplant Parmigiana, 197
  Freezer Eggplant-Sausage-Pasta
    Casserole, 197
  Grilled Eggplant Appetizer, 198
From Our Kitchen To Yours, 194
  Grilling Methods and Timetable, 194
Herbal Light, 189
  Asian Pesto Pasta, 189
  Blueberry Chutney, 190
  Greek Grilled Zucchini with Feta, 190
  Mango-Cilantro Vinegar, 190
  Peach-Mint Vinegar, 190
  Raspberry-Thyme Vinegar, 190
  Rosemary Focaccia, 190
  Steamed Orange Roughy with
    Herbs, 189
King Ranch Chicken, 193
  King Ranch Chicken, 193
Peaches: A Bushel And A Peck, 195
  Fresh Peach Ice Cream, 195
  Fresh Peach Pie, 195
  Fresh Peach Pie Filling, 195
  Fresh Peach Salsa, 195

JULY

(continued)

Layered Peach Dessert, 196
Peaches and Cream, 196
Sizzling Kabobs, 192
Lamb Kabobs, 192
Meatball Kabobs, 192
Oriental Chicken Kabobs, 193
Summery Squash-and-Pepper
Kabobs, 193

SUMMER SUPPERS, 173
*A Midsummer Night's Theme: Casual Yet
Elegant, 173*
Blackened 'n' Peppered Steak, 174
Caribbean Punch, 173
Cheese Wafers, 174
Monkey Bread, 174
Pesto-Spiced Nuts, 173
Planter's Punch Dessert, 175
Warm Vegetable Salad, 174
A Taste Of Southern Elegance, 175
Chicken à la Russell, 175
Herbed Gazpacho, 175
Peach Fluff, 176
Sour Cream Corn Muffins, 176
Wild Rice Casserole, 176
Easy Weekend Entertaining, 176
Beef Vinaigrette Salad, 177
Bugs in a Rug, 178
Caliente Marinated Olives, 177
Cheesy Garlic-Stuffed Bread, 176
Double Chocolate Chunk-Almond
Cookies, 178
Honey-Vanilla Ice Cream, 178
Pigs in a Blanket, 178
Thai Chicken Salad, 177
Fast Alfresco, 183
Picnic Suggestions for Any
Setting, 183
Fresh From The Garden, 179
Beets 'n' Greens, 179
Rutabaga Whip, 179
Skillet Okra, 179
Notable Totables, 182
Bourbon Baked Beans, 182
Buttermilk Sauce, 183
Caesar Ravioli Salad, 183
Picnic Shrimp Salad, 182
Picnic Panache, 184
Set a Fashionable Picnic Table with
Items on Hand, 184
The Best Sides Of Summer, 179
Breaded Tomatoes, 180
Buttercrust Corn Pie with Fresh
Tomato Salsa, 181
Green Rice Casserole, 181
Grilled Stuffed Onions, 180
Lemon-Garlic Pasta, 181
Mushroom-Macaroni Casserole, 180
Parmesan Potato Wedges, 181
Peppery Potato Casserole, 182
Squash and Tomato Bake, 180
Zucchini Crispies, 179

**Tomatoes – Nature's Crimson Declaration
Of Summer, 170**
Floyd's Favorite Tomato Sandwich, 172
Fresh Tomato Tart, 170
Fried Green Tomatoes, 171
Greek Chicken Breasts, 170

Green Tomato Sandwich Spread, 172
Hot Tomato Grits, 171
Oven-Baked Tomato Appetizers, 172
Spicy Tomato Gravy, 172
Tomato-Basil-Mozzarella Salad, 171
Tomato-Eggplant Biscuit Cakes, 170
Tomato-Zucchini Gratin, 171

AUGUST

················

A Taste Of Red Hot Success, 206
Cheese Grits with Green Chiles, 208
Roasted Serrano Salsa, 207
Tabasco Steak, 207
Can-Do Tomatoes, 217
Canned Flavored Tomatoes, 217
Cooking In Austin, 205
Avocado-Tomatillo Sauce, 206
Boneless Pork Chops with Ancho Cream
Sauce, 205
Chicken Enchiladas with Tomatillo
Sauce, 206
Papaya Vinaigrette Dressing, 206
Shrimp with Gin and Ginger, 205
Cool Off With Cucumbers, 216
Cucumber Mousse with Dill
Sauce, 216
Smoked Salmon and Cucumber
Tartlets, 216
Feast Without Meat, 211
Mushroom Casserole, 211
Pasta with Greens, 211
Vegetable Lasagna, 211
French Bread Fix-ups, 218
Cheesy French Bread, 218
Dilly Garlic Bread, 218
Garlic Bread, 218
Pane Cunsado (Fixed Bread), 218
Tennessee Sin, 218
From Our Kitchen To Yours, 208
Recipe Preparation Tips from Peppers to
Piecrust, 208
Low-Cal Tropical, 202
Black-Eyed Pea Salad, 203
Caribbean Banana Fish, 202
Caribbean Cooler, 203
Grilled Chicken Salad with Raspberry
Dressing, 202
Okra, Corn, and Tomatoes, 203
Papaya Seed Dressing, 204
Piña Coladas, 203
Plantain Chips, M203
Sweet Potato Chips, M203
Tropical Gazpacho, 204
Tropical Trifle, 204
Mind Your Teas & Cubes, 200
Berry-Good Cubes, 201
Cranberry Cubes, 201
Florida Cubes, 201
Lemonade Cubes, 201
Lemon-Mint Cubes, 201
Lemon Tea Tingler, 200
Pink Sangría Tea, 200
Rasp-Berry Good Tea, 200
Tropical Tea-Ser, 200
One Of A Kind, 215
Fried Apricot Pies, 215
Sherry Cheese Pâté, 215
Squash Soufflé, 215
Vic's Oven Shrimp, 215

Pantry Shape-up, 212
Chewy Peanut Butter Macaroons, 214
Clam Linguine, 212
Corn Salad, 214
Five-Ingredient Chili, 212
Light Lasagna, 212
Macaroni, Cheese, and
Tomatoes, 213
My Favorite Pasta, 213
Rosemary Cannellini Beans, 213
Tamale Soup, 213
Reel In A Fresh Catch, 209
Easy Crab Bake, 209
Fish in Caper Sauce, 209
Salmon Bake with Pecan-Crunch
Coating, 209
Shrimp Scampi, 209
Weekday Solutions, 210
Artichoke and Shrimp Linguine, 210
Chicken Parmesan, 210
Hamburger Casserole, 210
Mexican Cornbread Salad, 210
Winning Snacks, 214
Big Batch Moist Bran Muffins, 214
Coconut Muffins, 214
Granola Bars, 214
Orange-Almond Snack Balls, 214
Yogurt: The Key Ingredient, 219
All Seasons Lemon Trifle, 219
De-Light-Ful Dessert, 220
Lemon Delight Cheesecake, 219
Make-Ahead Chocolate-Mint Cake
Roll, 220

SEPTEMBER

················

A Family Cookout, 237
Marinated Flank Steak, 237
Pasta-Vegetable Salad, 238
Quick Fiesta Dip, M237
Raspberry Milk Shakes, 238
Appetizers That Score Big, 239
Bacon-Jalapeño-Tomato Quesadillas, 240
Baked Artichoke Dip, 239
Cheesy Barbecue Popcorn, 239
Savory Southern Pecans, 240
Spicy Buffalo Wings, 239
Turkey Sausage Turnovers, 239
BBQ ASAP, 242
Individual Barbecued Beef Loaves, 242
Chefs' Whisk-And-Tell Secrets, 228
Fresh Vegetable Skillet Dinner, 229
Ham-Mushroom-Stuffed Artichokes, 228
Herbed Cherry Tomatoes over
Pasta, 229
Late-Night Pasta Chez Frank, 228
Oven-Roasted Vegetable Chowder, 229
Summer Zucchini Salad, 229
Sunday Chicken, 228
Sweet Onion Tarts, 229
Eat Your Greens, 233
Collard Greens, 233
Grits and Greens, 233
Parmesan-Collards Casserole, 233
Stewed Tomatoes and Greens, 234
Food Of Our Native Fathers, 226
Posole, 226
Pueblo Indian Cookies, 228
Pumpkin-Corn Soup with Ginger-Lime
Cream, 227

Red Chili Stew, 226
Sautéed Chayote Squash with Cilantro, 227
Stewed Anasazi Beans with
Mushrooms, 226
From Our Kitchen To Yours, 246
Water-Whipped Baked Pastry Shell, 246
In Pursuit Of Perfect Fried Chicken, 234
Fried Chicken Gravy, 235
Our Best Southern Fried Chicken, 235
Oven-Fried Chicken, 236
Peppers Aplenty, 240
Bell Pepper-Cheese Chowder, 240
Red Bell Pepper Jam, 242
Roasted Bell Peppers in Olive Oil, 242
Roasted Red Bell Pepper Bread, 241
Roasted Red Bell Pepper Butter, 242
Ribs, Ribs, Ribs, 236
Adams' Ribs, 236
Barbecued Country-Style Ribs, 237
Barbecued Spareribs, 236
Seasoned With A Southern Accent, 230
Basil-Infused Olive Oil, 231
Caesar Salad Pasta, 230
Couscous with Mixed Fruit, 232
Fresh Fruit with Mint-Balsamic Tea, 232
Grilled Swordfish with Caper Sauce, 230
Lemon-Infused Olive Oil, 231
Microwave Ratatouille, M232
Moroccan Grilled Chicken Salad, 231
Moroccan Spice Rub, 231
Rice with Tomatoes and Basil, 232
Snacks Cool For After School, 244
Chocolate Cookie Ice Cream, 245
Cinnamon Sticks, 244
Orange-Banana Whip, 244
Pizza Bites, 244
Start With Biscuit Mix, 245
Chicken Dumpling Pie, 245
Dilly Cheese Muffins, 245
Peanut Blossom Cookies, 245
Quick Rolls, 245
The Texas Experience, 243
Gazpacho Dip, 243
Lucy's Apricot Praline Torte, 243
Wild Tuna Salad, 243
Toast To Touchdown, 238
Cranberry Sangría, 238
Grapefruit Drink, 238
Hot Cider Punch, 238
Mixed Fruit Punch, 239
Southern Fruit Punch, 238

OCTOBER
....

A Pleasing Risotto, 269
Tomato-Basil Risotto, 269
Autumn In A Jar, 250
Apple Pie Filling in a Jar, 251
Nannie's Chowchow, 250
Pear Chutney, 251
Spiced Apple Jelly, 251
Beyond Pepperoni, 267
Blazing Sunset Pizza, 267
Pesto Sauce, 267
Roasted Garlic Sauce, 268
Southern Classic Pizza, 268
Southwest Deluxe Pizza, 268
The Best of the Bayou Pizza, 268
The King Henry Pizza, 267
Traditional Pizza Sauce, 267

Casseroles For Any Occasion, 255
Cheeseburger Casserole, 255
Sausage-and-Noodle Casserole, 255
Simply Good Chicken Casserole, 255
Common Scents, 271
Better-Than-Potpourri Brew, 271
Old-Fashioned Bread Pudding with
Bourbon Custard Sauce, 271
Orange Baked Apples with Cookie
Crumbs, 271
Dinner In A Piecrust, 256
Chicken Pot Pie, 256
Continental Meat Pie, 256
Ham-and-Cheese Pie, 256
Do Yourself A Flavor, 252
Chicken with Bourbon-Purple Onion
Relish, 253
Grilled Fennel and Radicchio with Orange
Vinaigrette, 253
Grilled Turkey Breast with Cranberry
Salsa, 252
Pasta with Peanut Sauce, 252
Peppery Greens with Raspberry
Dressing, 254
Purple Onion Relish, 253
Trout Fillets with Capers, 252
Earthy Delights, 264
Cream of Shiitake Soup, 265
Filet Mignons with Shiitake Madeira
Sauce, 265
Golden Cheese-Shiitake Omelet, 265
Grilled Shiitakes, 265
Fabulous Fruitcake, 248
Cake Mix Fruit Cake, 248
Chocolate Fruitcakes, 250
Fruitcake-Stuffed Pork Loin, 250
Grandmother's Fruitcake, 248
Jill's Fruitcake, 249
No-Bake Fruitcake, 249
Freezer-Easy Potatoes, 269
Potato-Bacon Frittata, 269
Potato-Cheese Puff, 269
Potato-Onion Patties, 269
From Our Kitchen To Yours, 274
Grilling and Baking Tips, 274
Hash Things Out, 262
Austrian Hash with Cabbage Salad, 262
Corned Beef Hash, 262
Turkey Hash, 262
Vegetable Hash, 262
Heads Up, 270
Blue Cheese Coleslaw, 270
Fried Cabbage Rolls, 270
Quick Cooked Cabbage, 270
Spanish Cabbage Relish, 270
More Cluck, Less Buck, 261
Creole Chicken, 261
Forty-Cloves-of-Garlic Chicken, 261
Roast Chicken with Rice, 261
Perfect Baked Paella, 254
Paella Casserole, 254
Scare Up A Halloween Party, 273
Divinity Ghosts, 273
Fruity Witches' Brew, 273
Jack-o'-Lantern Cookies, 273
Monster Mouths, 274
Spooky Eyes, 273
Swamp Sticks, 274
Southern Comfort Food, 263
Beef Roast with Burgundy Gravy, 263
Chicken and Grits, 263
Macaroni and Cheese Soup, 264
Meat Loaf with Chunky Tomato Sauce, 264

Peach Cobbler, 264
Tennessee Ham, 263
These Cookies Take The Cake, 272
Apricot-Almond Squares, 272
Double-Chocolate Cookies, 272
Lemon Crisps, 272
Orange Crinkles, 272
Polka Dots, 272
Top Chops, 266
Pecan-Breaded Pork Chops with Beer
Sauce, 266
Tamarind-Glazed Pork Chops with Green
Mole Sauce, 266

NOVEMBER
....

Calm In The Kitchen, 308
All-Star Pizza Calzones, 308
Ham Strata, 308
Fast Dishes For Busy Days, 311
Cheese Enchiladas, 311
Turkey and Peppers in Cornbread
Crust, 312
Weeknight Spaghetti Pie, 312
From Our Kitchen To Yours, 314
Various Baking, Cooking, and Kitchen
Helps, 314
Grab A Cup And A Conversation, 276
Chocolate Chiffon Cake with Coffee
Buttercream, 277
Coffee Blends, 276
Coffee Napoleons, 276
Coffee Nuggets, 278
Dipped Chocolate-Almond
Spoons, M277
Midnight Delights, 278

HOLIDAY DINNERS, 279
Breakfast Made Beautiful, 281
Christmas Morning Strata, 282
Cranberry Scones, 283
Gingerbread Pancakes, 282
Hash Brown Bake, 281
Macadamia Nut French Toast, 282
Pumpkin Waffles, 282
Classic Endings, 302
Apple-Bourbon Pie, 302
Betty's Holiday Cream, 303
Flan de Queso, 303
Italian Ricotta Cheesecake, 303
Kentucky Mincemeat Pie, 302
White Chocolate Chess Tart, 303
Company's Cooking, 279
Fennel Ice Cream, 281
Pears with Orange-Caramel
Sauce, 281
Seafood Risotto, 280
White Bean Spread, 279
Winter Salad, 280
Cranberry Options, 301
Frozen Cranberry Relish, 302
Holiday Cranberry Salad, 301
Dressed For Success, 288
Apple-Walnut Stuffing, 289
Creole Dressing, 289
Crown Pork Roast with Apple-Walnut
Stuffing, 289
Rice Stuffing, 290
Sausage-Cornbread Dressing, 289
Squash Dressing, 290

NOVEMBER
(continued)

Great Beginnings, 283
    Caraway-Cheese Crisps, 284
    Creamy Dried Tomato
      Hummus, 284
    Ham-Pineapple Nibbles, 283
    Red Wine-Marinated Flank
      Steak, 283
    Spinach-Artichoke-Tomato
      Puffs, 284
Holiday Greenery, 301
    Greens and Grapefruit Salad, 301
    Mixed Greens with Parmesan
      Walnuts, 301
On A Roll, 292
    Butter Crescent Rolls, 292
    Onion-and-Sesame Rolls, 292
    Roll-shaping Techniques, 292
Special Delivery, 304
    Cream Cheese Pound Cake, 304
    Moravian Sugar Cake, 304
Sweet On Sweet Potatoes, 290
    Stacked Sweet Potato Blues, 290
    Sweet Potato Butter, M290
    Sweet Potato-Eggnog Casserole, 291
    Sweet Potato Flan, 291
    Sweet Potato Peaks, 291
Ten Years Later, Ten Times Easier, 286
    Apple Dumplings with Maple-Cider
      Sauce, 288
    Apricot-Mushroom Stuffed Pork
      Chops, 287
    Gazpacho-Stuffed Endive, 287
    Green Beans with Caramelized
      Onions, 288
    Lemonade-Bourbon Punch, 287
    Roasted Garlic Mashed
      Potatoes, 288
Try Lamb This Season, 284
    Dijon-Rosemary Lamb Chops, 285
    Hazelnut-Crusted Rack of Lamb with
      Cherry-Wine Sauce, 284
    Leg of Lamb, 285
    Rolled Lamb Roast, 285
Wine And Dine, 286
    Butter Pecan Mousse, 286
    Mediterranean Shrimp and
      Pasta, 286
    Parmesan-Coated Brie, 286

Party Potpourri, 309
    Black Beans and Rice, 309
    Dove au Vin, 309
    Ned's Eggplant Sticks, 309
Thanksgiving, Southern Style, 305
    Aunt Glennie's Pear Relish, 305
    Betty's Butternut Pound Cake with Caramel
      Sauce, 308
    Brandied Cranberries, 306
    Make-Ahead Yeast Rolls, 307
    Nannie's Candied Sweet Potatoes, 306

    Nannie's Cornbread Dressing, 306
    Pastry Cornucopia, 307
    Peach Ketchup, 306
    Roast Turkey with Herbs, 305
    Turnip Greens, 306
These Recipes Cut The Mustard, 312
    Jalapeño Mustard, 312
    Peppered Honey Mustard, 312
    Raspberry Mustard, 313
    Really Hot Mustard, 312
    Sweet Cider Mustard, 312
Use Your Nog In . . . , 313
    Eggnog Dessert, 314
    Eggnog French Toast, 313
    Eggnog-Pecan Pound Cake, 313
    Irish Coffee-Eggnog Punch, 314
Wrap And Roll, 310
    Salmon in Parchment, 311
    Shrimp Enchiladas in Tomatillo Sauce, 310
    Spinach-and-Cheese Calzones, 310

DECEMBER

· · · · · · · · · · · · · · · ·

A Craving For Chicken And Dumplings, 338
    Chicken and Dumplings with Herbed
      Broth, 338
An Enchanted Evening, 326
    Blue Cheese-Walnut Stuffed
      Fillets, 327
    Chocolate Truffle Mousse with Raspberry
      Sauce, 327
    Crab-Stuffed Lobster Tails, 326
    Mixed Greens with Tarragon
      Vinaigrette, 326
Angel Wings And Southern
** Things, 328**
    Angel's Wing Rolls, 329
    Boiled Christmas Custard, 329
    Curried Fruit Medley, 329
    Spicy Tomato Warm-up, 328
    Starlight Cheese Bites, 329
    Toasty Southern Pecan Tarts, 329
Crème Brûlée, 323
    Basic Crème Brûlée, 323
    Savory Crème Brûlées, 324
From Our Kitchen To Yours, 343
    Suggestions for Hostess Gifts, 343
It's All In The Game, 325
    Cajun-Fried Cornish Hens, 326
    Cornish Hens à l'Orange, 325
    Cornish Hens Tarragon, 326
    Cranberry-Cornbread Stuffed Cornish
      Hens, 325
Kentucky Traditions, 316
    Chocolate Pots de Crème with Orange
      Meringues, 318
    Coconut-Lemon Cake, 319
    Cranberry Relish, 318
    Kathy's Onion Pudding, 318
    Leg of Lamb with Hunter
      Sauce, 317

    Orange Cake, 320
    Scalloped Oysters, 318
    Spinach Puffs, 316
    Tee's Corn Pudding, 318
Merry Mousse, 327
    Crab Mousse, 327
    Curried Chicken Mousse, 328
    Ham Mousse Pitas, 328
    Mustard Mousse, 328
Not A Creature Was Stirring, 332
    Gifts That Measure Up, 332
    Hot Handlers, 332
    Miniature Liqueur Sampler, 332
    Off-the-Wall Gadgets, 332
    Wine Tasting, 332
Pause For Pasta, 340
    Mediterranean Pasta, 341
    Spinach and Mushrooms with Bow Tie
      Pasta, 341
    Ziti with Sausage and Broccoli, 340
Rebuilding The Reuben, 338
    Reuben Loaf, 338
Seasons Teachings, 330
    Buttermilk-Basil Mashed Potatoes, 330
    Olde English Trifle, 331
    Pork Medaillons with Port Wine and
      Dried Cranberry Sauce, 330
Sensational Sides, 341
    Balsamic-Flavored Eggplant, 342
    Broccoli with Stuffing, 341
    Cauliflower Bake, 342
    Garlic Roasted Potatoes, 342
Sip Into Something Comfortable, 337
    Cinnamon Winter Cider, 337
    Mulled Wine Punch, 337
    Sparkling Citrus Punch, 337
Southern Boy Makes Good, 342
    Braised Red Cabbage, 343
    Eggplant Relish, 342
Tacos Many Ways, 339
    Barbecued Fish Tacos, 339
    Breakfast Tacos, 340
    Chinese Taco Rolls, 339
    Grilled Pepper Tacos, 340
    Pizza-Flavored Chicken
      Tacos, 340
    Shrimp-and-Pepper Soft
      Tacos, 339
    Taco Tassies, 339
The 12 Doughs Of Christmas, 320
    Almond Brickle Treats, 321
    Apricot Cookies, 322
    Basic Butter Cookie
      Dough, 320
    Cherry Chocolates, 321
    Christmas Jammies, 322
    Date Bars, 322
    Easy Santa Cookies, 321
    Lollipop Cookies, 322
    Peanut Butter Shortbread, 321
    Peppermint Cookies, 322
    Pinwheels, 321
    Spice Thins, 322
    Sugarplum Sticks, 321

GENERAL RECIPE INDEX

A listing of every recipe by food category and/or major ingredient

All microwave recipe page numbers are preceded by an "M."

ALMONDS
Desserts
Apricot-Almond Squares, 272
Brickle Treats, Almond, 321
Cookies, Double Chocolate Chunk-Almond, 178
Crème Brûlée, Almond, 323
Fudge, Creamy Almond, 51
Pesto-Spiced Nuts, 173
Snack Balls, Orange-Almond, 214
Spoons, Dipped Chocolate-Almond, M277
Streusel, Almond-Garlic, 159
APPETIZERS. *See also* Pâté.
Asparagus with Garlic Cream, 83
Bacon-Jalapeño-Tomato Quesadillas, 240
Canapés, Cucumber, 88
Cheese
Bites, Lemon-Cheese Party, 160
Brie, Parmesan-Coated, 286
Caraway-Cheese Crisps, 284
Fondue, Nacho, 35
Fondue, Pub, 35
Grapes, Blue Cheese-Pecan, 48
Marinated Cheese, 21
Pinwheels, Mexican, 21
Puffs, Oregano Cheese, 21
Wafers, Cheese, 174
Wonton Envelopes, Fried, 96
Chicken
Quesadillas, Spicy Chicken, 42
Wings, Spicy Buffalo, 239
Chiles Rellenos, Roasted, 64
Cinnamon Sticks, 244
Crème Brûlée, Onion, 324
Crème Brûlée, Roasted Garlic, 324
Crème Brûlée, Roquefort-and-Black Pepper, 324
Crème Brûlées, Savory, 324
Crostini, Mexican, 142
Dips
Artichoke Dip, Baked, 239
Black Bean Dip, 93
Crabmeat Dip, Hot, 154
Fruit Dip, Fresh, 94
Gazpacho Dip, 243
Guacamole Dip, 96
Hummus, Creamy Dried Tomato, 284
Hummus, Quick, 93
Pesto Dip, 93
Quick Fiesta Dip, M237

Swiss-Onion Dip, 93
Tennessee Sin, 218
Eggplant Appetizer, Grilled, 198
Eggplant Sticks, Ned's, 309
Filet Mignon, Cajun Blackened, 85
Firecrackers, Texas, 96
Flank Steak, Red Wine-Marinated, 283
Fondue, Peppermint, 35
Guacamole, Easy, 94
Ham-Pineapple Nibbles, 283
Jalapeño Peppers, Fried Stuffed, 22
Mix, Bunny Trail, 101
Monster Mouths, 274
Mousses
Chicken Mousse, Curried, 328
Crab Mousse, 327
Ham Mousse Pitas, 328
Mustard Mousse, 328
Mushroom Tapas, Majorcan, 159
Nuts, Pesto-Spiced, 173
Olives, Caliente Marinated, 177
Orange-Almond Snack Balls, 214
Pecans, Savory Southern, 240
Pizza Bites, 244
Plantain Chips, M203
Ravioli, St. Louis Toasted, 117
Shrimp
Sesame Shrimp, 92
Smoked Shrimp, Citrus-Marinated, 114
Tortilla Bites, 42
Spinach-Artichoke-Tomato Puffs, 284
Spinach Puffs, 316
Spreads and Fillings
Blue Cheese Spread, 92
Ham Spread, Buttery, 93
Tuna Tapenade, 127
White Bean Spread, 279
Swamp Sticks, 274
Sweet Potato Chips, M203
Tarts, Party, 90
Tomato Appetizers, Oven-Baked, 172
Tuna Nachos, 127
Turkey Sausage Turnovers, 239
APPLES
Beverages
Cider, Apple, 198
Juice, Sparkling Apple, 141
Desserts
Baked Apples with Cookie Crumbs, Orange, 271
Chimichangas, Apple, 43

Dumplings with Maple-Cider Sauce, Apple, 288
Pie, Apple-Bourbon, 302
Dried Lady Apple Slices, 263
Jelly, Spiced Apple, 251
Monster Mouths, 274
Pie Filling in a Jar, Apple, 251
Pork Tenderloin, Apple-Mushroom, 53
Pork Tenderloin with Apples, Celery, and Potatoes, Grilled, 161
Stuffing, Apple-Walnut, 289
Sweet Potatoes, Cinnamon-Apple, M23
APRICOTS
Desserts
Almond Squares, Apricot-, 272
Cookies, Apricot, 322
Pies, Fried Apricot, 215
Torte, Lucy's Apricot Praline, 243
Tortoni, Apricot-Yogurt, 124
Pork Chops, Apricot-Mushroom Stuffed, 287
ARTICHOKES
Appetizers
Dip, Baked Artichoke, 239
Puffs, Spinach-Artichoke-Tomato, 284
Bake, Spinach-Artichoke, 48
Chicken and Artichokes, Italian, 68
Linguine, Artichoke and Shrimp, 210
Marinated Artichoke Hearts, 66
Salad, Marinated Artichoke, 66
Stuffed Artichokes, Ham-Mushroom-, 228
ASPARAGUS
Creamed Asparagus on Toast, 61
Garlic Cream, Asparagus with, 83
Marinated Asparagus with Prosciutto, 83
Pasta with Asparagus, Tomatoes, and Shrimp, Garlicky, 82
Soup, Creamy Asparagus-and-Chicken, 82
Stir-Fry, Asparagus, 83
AVOCADOS
Dip, Gazpacho, 243
Guacamole
Dip, Guacamole, 96
Easy Guacamole, 94
Sauce, Avocado-Tomatillo, 206

BACON
Frittata, Potato-Bacon, 269
Pizza, The King Henry, 267
Quesadillas, Bacon-Jalapeño-Tomato, 240

BANANAS
Breads
Date-Banana Loaves, Tropical, 143
Fruity Banana Bread, 78
Fish, Caribbean Banana, 202
Whip, Orange-Banana, 244
BARBECUE
Beef Loaves, Individual Barbecued, 242
Fish Tacos, Barbecued, 339
Popcorn, Cheesy Barbecue, 239
Ribs
Country-Style Ribs, Barbecued, 237
Spareribs, Barbecued, 236
Sauce, Lemony Barbecue, 31
BEANS
Anasazi Beans with Mushrooms,
Stewed, 226
Baked
Bourbon Baked Beans, 182
Hamburger-Bean Bake, 121
Black
Casserole of Black Beans, 27
Chili Marsala, Black Bean, 16
Dip, Black Bean, 93
Rice, Black Beans and, 309
Yellow Rice, Black Beans and, 126
Cannellini Beans, Rosemary, 213
Crostini, Mexican, 142
Green
Caramelized Onions, Green Beans
with, 288
Slaw, Green Bean, 108
Hummus, Quick, 93
Lima Bean Casserole, 132
Sausage-and-Bean Dinner, 108
Sauté, Vegetarian, 69
Soup, Bean-and-Hominy, 23
Spread, White Bean, 279
BEEF
Brisket, Heavenly Smoked, 114
Brisket, Passover, 102
Burgundy, Beef, 69
Burritos, Carne Guisada, 43
Chili, Bodacious, 14
Chili Marsala, Black Bean, 16
Chili, Out West, 15
Chili Verde, 14
Corned Beef
Hash, Corned Beef, 262
Reuben Loaf, 338
Filet Mignon, Cajun Blackened, 85
Hash, Beef, 24
Hash with Cabbage Salad, Austrian, 262
Roasts
Burgundy Gravy, Beef Roast with, 263
Rib Roast, Standing, 28
Salad, Beef Vinaigrette, 177
Steaks
Blackened 'n' Peppered Steak, 174
Blue Cheese-Walnut Stuffed Fillets, 327
Filet Mignons with Shiitake Madeira
Sauce, 265
Flank Steak-and-Spinach Pinwheels, 56
Flank Steak, Lemon-Lime, 55
Flank Steak, Marinated, 237
Flank Steak, Red Wine-Marinated, 283
Marinated Bourbon Steak, 91
Mesquite-Ginger Beef with Fresh Fruit
Relish, 158
Tabasco Steak, 207
Stews
Emerald Isle Stew, 71
Red Chili Stew, 226

Stir-Fry, Peanutty Beef, 157
Stock, Beef, 17
BEEF, GROUND
Burger Boat, 70
Burgers, Brie-Mushroom, 128
Cabbage Rolls, Fried, 270
Casseroles
Cheeseburger Casserole, 255
Hamburger-Bean Bake, 121
Hamburger Casserole, 210
Lasagna, Light, 212
Macaroni-Cheese-Beef Casserole, 125
Spaghetti, Casserole, 132
Tamale, Mozzarella, 70
Chili
Five-Ingredient Chili, 212
Greek Chili, 16
Now, Thatsa Chili, 16
Gumbo, Carolina, 70
Meatball Kabobs, 192
Meat Loaf
Barbecued Beef Loaves, Individual, 242
Easy Meat Loaf, 125
Tomato Sauce, Meat Loaf with
Chunky, 264
Mexican Stack-Up, 69
Pies
Continental Meat Pie, 256
Spaghetti Pie, Weeknight, 312
Soup, Tamale, 213
Taco Rolls, Chinese, 339
Taco Tassies, 339
BEETS
Greens, Beets 'n', 179
BEVERAGES. *See also* Coffee, Tea.
Alcoholic
Amaretto Slush, 90
Blueberry Cordial, 142
Cider, Cinnamon Winter, 337
Daiquiri, Watermelon, 143
Grapefruit Drink, 238
Liqueur Sampler, Miniature, 332
New Orleans, Mr. Funk of, 57
Piña Coladas, 203
Piña Colada Slush, 90
Punch, Caribbean, 173
Punch, Frozen Margarita, 91
Punch, Irish Coffee-Eggnog, 314
Punch, Lemonade-Bourbon, 287
Punch, Mixed Fruit, 239
Punch, Mulled Wine, 337
Punch, Pineapple-Gin, 140
Punch, Southern Fruit, 238
Sangría, Cranberry, 238
Wine Tasting, 332
Apple Juice, Sparkling, 141
Berry Shrub, 29
Caribbean Cooler, 203
Cider, Apple, 198
Cubes, Berry-Good, 201
Cubes, Cranberry, 201
Cubes, Florida, 201
Cubes, Lemonade, 201
Cubes, Lemon-Mint, 201
Grapefruit Drink, 238
Hot Chocolate, Sugar-and-Spice, 34
Ice Ring, 140
Orange-Banana Whip, 244
Punch. *See also* Beverages/Alcoholic.
Bunch, Punch for a, 90
Cider Punch, Hot, 238
Citrus Punch, Sparkling, 337
Cranberry Punch, Sparkling, 101

Fruity Witches' Brew, 273
Lime Punch, Calypso Presbyterian
Church Women's, 141
Mocha Punch, 141
Pineapple Sherbet Punch, 141
Polka Dot Punch, 178
Raspberry Sherbet Punch, 141
Shakes
Fruit Shake, Tangy, 129
Raspberry Milk Shakes, 238
Spoons, Dipped Chocolate-Almond, M277
Tomato Warm-Up, Spicy, 328
BISCUITS
Caramel Dessert Biscuits, 36
Coconut Biscuits, Yummy, 99
Cornmeal Biscuits, 98
Herbed Biscuit Ring, 161
Honey Angel Biscuits, 138
Onion Biscuits, Cheesy, 98
Pull-Apart Biscuits, Surprise, 46
Rosemary Biscuits, 91
Spoon Biscuits, Mexican Fiesta, 161
Tomato-Eggplant Biscuit Cakes, 170
BLACKBERRIES
Berry Shrub, 29
Crème Brûlée, Berry, 323
BLUEBERRIES
Chutney, Blueberry, 190
Cordial, Blueberry, 142
Muffins, Speedy Blueberry, 135
Sauce, Berry, 103
Sauce, Blueberry, 135
BRAN
Muffins, Big Batch Moist Bran, 214
BREADS. *See also* Biscuits, Cornbreads, French Toast,
Muffins, Rolls and Buns.
Banana Bread, Fruity, 78
Cheese Breadsticks, Italian, 126
Cinnamon Sticks, 244
Date-Banana Loaves, Tropical, 143
Egg Bread, 121
French Bread Bowls, 58
French Bread, Cheesy, 218
Garlic Bread, 218
Garlic Bread, Dilly, 218
Garlic-Stuffed Bread, Cheesy, 176
Irish Soda Bread, 71
Lahvosh Cracker Bread Bowls, 58
Pane Cunsado (Fixed Bread), 218
Pecan-Cornmeal Rounds, 99
Pita Bread Salad, 86
Potato
Sourdough Bread Dough,
Potato, 77
Sourdough Bread, Potato, 77
Sourdough Starter, Potato, 77
Puddings
Buttermilk Bread Pudding with Butter-
Rum Sauce, 134
Old-Fashioned Bread Pudding with
Bourbon Custard Sauce, 271
Scones, Cranberry, 283
Spoonbreads
Memmie's Spoonbread, 27
Spoonbread, 156
Starter Food, 77
Tennessee Sin, 218
Yeast
Beignets, French Market, 80
English Muffin Bread, M79
Focaccia, Rosemary, 190
Monkey Bread, 174
Potato Sourdough Bread, 77

Potato Sourdough Bread Dough, 77
Potato Sourdough Starter, 77
Roasted Red Bell Pepper Bread, 241
Swiss Cheese Loaves, Mini, 80

BROCCOLI
Casseroles
Cheesy Broccoli Casserole, M191
Stuffing, Broccoli with, 341
Garlic Broccoli, 54
Lemon Broccoli, 53
Salad, Broccoli, 95
Sauté, Broccoli and Walnut, 52
Ziti with Sausage and Broccoli, 340

BROWNIES
Muffins, Fudge Brownie, M50
Rich Brownies, 84

BURRITOS
Carne Guisada Burritos, 43
Egg Burritos, Tex-Mex, 34

BUTTER
Garlic Butter, 89
Honey Butter, 139
Lemon Butter, 32
Roasted Red Bell Pepper Butter, 242
Sauce, Butter-Rum, 134
Sauce, Garlic-Butter, 327
Sweet Potato Butter, M290

BUTTERSCOTCH
Trail Mix, Bunny, 101

CABBAGE. *See also* Slaws.
Braised Red Cabbage, 343
Quick Cooked Cabbage, 270
Relish, Spanish Cabbage, 270
Rolls, Fried Cabbage, 270
Salad, Austrian Hash with
Cabbage, 262

CAKES. *See also* Breads, Cheesecakes.
Chocolate
Chiffon Cake with Coffee Buttercream,
Chocolate, 277
Cola Cake, Quick Chocolate, 56
Roll, Make-Ahead Chocolate-Mint
Cake, 220
Shortcake, Chocolate-Raspberry, 99
Coconut-Lemon Cake, 319
Coffee Cakes
Cowboy Coffee Cake, 84
Orange Coffee Cake, Nutty, 160
Fruitcakes
Cake Mix Fruit Cake, 248
Chocolate Fruitcakes, 250
Grandmother's Fruitcake, 248
Jill's Fruitcake, 249
No-Bake Fruitcake, 249
Moravian Sugar Cake, 304
Orange Butter Cake, 46
Orange Cake, 320
Pecan-Cornmeal Rounds, 99
Poppy Seed Cake, 63
Pound
Butternut Pound Cake with Caramel
Sauce, Betty's, 308
Cherry Pound Cake, Cute-as-a-
Button, 139
Cream Cheese Pound Cake, 304
Eggnog-Pecan Pound Cake, 313
Marble Pound Cake, 29
Pudding Cake with Blueberry Sauce,
Buttermilk-Lemon, 135
Shortcake, Orange-Strawberry, 100
Shortcakes, Cheesy Chicken, 98

Sponge Cake with Berry Sauce, Burnt
Sugar, 103
Torte, Lucy's Apricot Praline, 243
Zucchini-Pineapple Cake, 160

CANDIES
Divinity Ghosts, 273
Fudge
Almond Fudge, Creamy, 51
Buttermilk Fudge, 52
Chocolate Fudge, Five Pounds of, 51
Double-Good Fudge, M50
Mint Fudge, 50
Mocha Fudge, Creamy, 51
Peanut Butter Fudge, 51
Sour Cream Fudge, 52
White Chocolate Fudge, 51
Truffles, Orange-Pecan, 92

CARAMEL
Biscuits, Caramel Dessert, 36
Crunch, Caramel, 165
Fondue, Caramel, 35
Ice Cream Dessert, Caramel, 36
Sauce, Caramel, 308
Sauce, Pears with Orange-Caramel, 281
Sticky Buns, Easy Caramel-Chocolate, 36

CARROTS
Swamp Sticks, 274

CASSEROLES
Bean
Black Beans, Casserole of, 27
Lima Bean Casserole, 132
Egg Casserole, Sunday, 100
Eggplant-and-Oyster Louisiane, 196
Eggplant-Sausage-Pasta Casserole,
Freezer, 197
Grits with Green Chiles, Cheese, 208
Lasagna, Creamy Ham-and-Chicken, 88
Meat
Beef Casserole, Macaroni-Cheese-, 125
Cheeseburger Casserole, 255
Hamburger-Bean Bake, 121
Hamburger Casserole, 210
Tamale, Mozzarella, 70
Oysters, Scalloped, 318
Paella Casserole, 254
Pork
Ham Strata, 308
Sausage-and-Noodle Casserole, 255
Strata, Christmas Morning, 282
Poultry
Chicken à la Russell, 175
Chicken and Grits, 263
Chicken and Rice, 54
Chicken Casserole, Simply Good, 255
Chicken, King Ranch, 193
Chicken Lasagna Bake, 55
Chicken-Squash Casserole, 121
Chicken, Swiss, 54
Quiche Casserole, 33
Rice Casserole, Green, 181
Rice, Savannah Red, 27
Spaghetti, Casserole, 132
Vegetable
Broccoli Casserole, Cheesy, M191
Broccoli with Stuffing, 341
Cashew Casserole, 166
Cauliflower Bake, 342
Collards Casserole, Parmesan-, 233
Eggplant Cakes, 196
Eggplant Parmesan, 84
Eggplant Parmigiana, 197
Mushroom Casserole, 211
Mushroom-Macaroni Casserole, 180

Onion Casserole, French, 26
Potato Casserole, Peppery, 182
Spinach-Artichoke Bake, 48
Squash and Tomato Bake, 180
Squash Casserole, Creamy Rice and, 26
Sweet Potato-Eggnog Casserole, 291
Swiss Vegetable Medley, 26
Wine Sauce Casserole, Vegetables in, 133
Wild Rice Casserole, 176

CAULIFLOWER
Bake, Cauliflower, 342
Salad, Cauliflower-English Pea, 66

CELERY
Pork Tenderloin with Apples, Celery, and
Potatoes, Grilled, 161

CHEESE. *See also* Appetizers/Cheese, Cheesecakes.
Breads
Biscuits, Cheesy Onion, 98
Biscuits, Mexican Fiesta Spoon, 161
Biscuits, Surprise Pull-Apart, 46
Breadsticks, Italian Cheese, 126
French Bread, Cheesy, 218
Garlic-Stuffed Bread, Cheesy, 176
Muffins, Dilly Cheese, 245
Pane Cunsado (Fixed Bread), 218
Swiss Cheese Loaves, Mini, 80
Bugs in a Rug, 178
Burgers, Brie-Mushroom, 128
Calzones, Spinach-and-Cheese, 310
Casseroles
Broccoli Casserole, Cheesy, M191
Cheeseburger Casserole, 255
Chicken, Swiss, 54
Collards Casserole, Parmesan-, 233
Eggplant Parmesan, 84
Florentine Bake, Cheesy, 131
Macaroni, Cheese, and Tomatoes, 213
Macaroni-Cheese-Beef Casserole, 125
Parmigiana, Eggplant, 197
Tamale, Mozzarella, 70
Vegetable Medley, Swiss, 26
Chicken Breasts, Celebrity, 60
Chicken-Mozzarella Melt, Italian, 153
Chicken Parmesan, 210
Chiles Rellenos, Roasted, 64
Crème Brûlée, Roquefort-and-Black
Pepper, 324
Desserts
Bites, Starlight Cheese, 329
Cake, Cream Cheese Pound, 304
Cake, Poppy Seed, 63
Frosting, Cream Cheese, 139
Frosting, Pineapple-Cream
Cheese, 160
Dressing, Creamy, 66
Eggs and Cheese, 165
Eggs, Cheese-Chive Scrambled, 34
Enchiladas, Cheese, 311
Fillets, Blue Cheese-Walnut Stuffed, 327
Grits, Garlic-and-Herb Cheese, 122
Grits with Green Chiles, 208
Omelet, Dill-Cheese-Ham, 33
Omelet, Golden Cheese-Shiitake, 265
Pasta, Mamma Mia, 25
Pie, Ham-and-Cheese, 256
Popcorn, Cheesy Barbecue, 239
Salads
Coleslaw, Blue Cheese, 270
Goat Cheese and Black-Eyed Pea Salad,
Fearrington House, 60
Greens with Parmesan Walnuts,
Mixed, 301
Marinated Tomato and Brie Salad, 95

CHEESE
(continued)

Spinach Salad with the Blues, 66
Tomato-Basil-Mozzarella Salad, 171
Sandwich, Ham 'n' Cheese Chicken, 153
Shortcakes, Cheesy Chicken, 98
Soups
Chowder, Bell Pepper-Cheese, 240
Macaroni and Cheese Soup, 264
Spreads
Blue Cheese Spread, 79, 92
Tropical Cheese Spread, 46
Tomato, Basil, and Cheese, 165
Vegetables
Asparagus on Toast, Creamed, 61
Potato-Cheese Puff, 269
Potato Wedges, Parmesan, 181
Spinach Pie with Muenster Crust, 48
Squash and Tomato Bake, 180
Sweet Potato Blues, Stacked, 290
Zucchini Fries, Parmesan-, 129
Zucchini with Feta, Greek Grilled, 190
Wafers, Cheese, 174

CHEESECAKES
Lemon Delight Cheesecake, 219
Ricotta Cheesecake, Italian, 303

CHERRIES
Cake, Cute-as-a-Button Cherry Pound, 139
Chocolates, Cherry, 321
Salad, Cherry-Cola, 94
Sauce, Cherry-Wine, 285

CHICKEN
Artichokes, Italian Chicken and, 68
Bourbon-Purple Onion Relish, Chicken with, 253
Breasts, Celebrity Chicken, 60
Breasts, Greek Chicken, 170
Casseroles
à la Russell, Chicken, 175
Enchiladas with Tomatillo Sauce, Chicken, 206
Good Chicken Casserole, Simply, 255
Grits, Chicken and, 263
King Ranch Chicken, 193
Lasagna Bake, Chicken, 55
Lasagna, Creamy Ham-and-Chicken, 88
Lasagna Florentine, Chicken, 158
Paella Casserole, 254
Rice, Chicken and, 54
Squash Casserole, Chicken-, 121
Swiss Chicken, 54
Creole Chicken, 261
Dinner, Curried Chicken Skillet, 47
Dumplings, Quick Chicken and, 125
Dumplings with Herbed Broth, Chicken and, 338
Egg Bread, Chicken on, 120
Firecrackers, Texas, 96
Fried
Gravy, Fried Chicken, 235
Kudzu Fried Chicken, 198
Oven-Fried Chicken, 236
Southern Fried Chicken, Our Best, 235
Garlic Chicken, Forty-Cloves-of-, 261
Gold Nugget Chicken, 120
Grilled Chicken, Lemon-Herb, 87
Herb Chicken, Smoky, 116
Italian Chicken-Mozzarella Melt, 153
Kabobs, Oriental Chicken, 193
Mousse, Curried Chicken, 328
Oregano Chicken, 84

Paprika Chicken, 125
Parmesan, Chicken, 210
Pie, Chicken Dumpling, 245
Pie, Chicken Pot, 54, 256
Pizza, Southwest Deluxe, 268
Potatoes, Gumbo, 22
Quesadillas, Spicy Chicken, 42
Roast Chicken with Rice, 261
Roasted Chicken, Lemon-, 24
Salads
Crisp Salad, Crunchy, 28
Grilled Chicken Salad, Moroccan, 231
Grilled Chicken Salad with Raspberry Dressing, 202
Noodle Salad, Chicken, 25
Summery Chicken Salad, 138
Thai Chicken Salad, 177
Tortilla Salads, Mexican Chicken, 129
Sandwich, Ham 'n' Cheese Chicken, 153
Sandwich, Jamaican Chicken, 153
Sauce, Curry, 18
Shortcakes, Cheesy Chicken, 98
Soups
Asparagus-and-Chicken Soup, Creamy, 82
Noodle Soup, Chicken, 45
Stock, Chicken, 18
Stir-Fry, Chicken and Snow Pea, 157
Sunday Chicken, 228
Tacos, Pizza-Flavored Chicken, 340
Tostadas, Chicken, 122
Wings, Spicy Buffalo, 239

CHILI
Black Bean Chili Marsala, 16
Bodacious Chili, 14
Dog, Dinglewood Pharmacy's Scrambled, 118
Five-Ingredient Chili, 212
Greek Chili, 16
Now, Thatsa Chili, 16
Out West Chili, 15
Stew, Red Chili, 226
Verde, Chili, 14

CHOCOLATE
Bags, Chocolate-Raspberry, 97
Bars and Cookies
Biscotti, Chocolate-Hazelnut, 80
Cherry Chocolates, 321
Double Chocolate Chunk-Almond Cookies, 178
Double-Chocolate Cookies, 272
Fibber McGee Cookies, 72
Fudge-Pecan Chewies, Alabama, 143
Oatmeal-Chocolate Morsel Cookies, 46
Oatmeal-Toffee Lizzies, Crispy, 136
Peanut Blossom Cookies, 245
Pinwheels, 321
Polka Dots, 272
Raisin Oatmeal Cookies, Chocolate-, 136
Beverages
Hot Chocolate, Sugar-and-Spice, 34
Mocha Blend, 276
Mocha Punch, 141
Cakes and Tortes
Chiffon Cake with Coffee Buttercream, Chocolate, 277
Cola Cake, Quick Chocolate, 56
Fruitcakes, Chocolate, 250
Pound Cake, Marble, 29
Roll, Make-Ahead Chocolate-Mint Cake, 220
Shortcake, Chocolate-Raspberry, 99
Candies
Fudge, Creamy Almond, 51
Fudge, Creamy Mocha, 51

Fudge, Double-Good, M50
Fudge, Five Pounds of Chocolate, 51
Fudge, Mint, 50
Fudge, White Chocolate, 51
Truffles, Orange-Pecan, 92
Crème Brûlée, Chocolate, 323
Crème Brûlée, White Chocolate-Macadamia Nut, 323
Dessert, Hello Dolly, 168
Frosting, Chocolate-Cola, 56
Ice Cream, Chocolate Cookie, 245
Mousse with Raspberry Sauce, Chocolate Truffle, 327
Muffins, Fudge Brownie, M50
Napoleons, Coffee, 276
Parfait, Bodacious Peanut, 167
Pies and Tarts
Midnight Delights, 278
Party Tarts, 90
White Chocolate Chess Tart, 303
Plunge, Chocolate, 35
Pots de Crème with Orange Meringues, Chocolate, 318
Spoons, Dipped Chocolate-Almond, M277
Sticky Buns, Easy Caramel-Chocolate, 36

CHOWDERS. *See also* Gumbo, Soups.
Bell Pepper-Cheese Chowder, 240
Vegetable Chowder, Oven-Roasted, 229

CHRISTMAS
Cookies, Easy Santa, 321
Custard, Boiled Christmas, 329
Jammies, Christmas, 322
Strata, Christmas Morning, 282
Sugarplum Sticks, 321

CHUTNEYS. *See also* Relishes, Toppings.
Blueberry Chutney, 190
Pear Chutney, 251

CLAMS
Linguine, Clam, 212

COCONUT
Biscuits, Yummy Coconut, 99
Cake, Coconut-Lemon, 319
Macaroons, Chewy Peanut Butter, 214
Muffins, Coconut, 214

COFFEE
Beverages
Blends, Coffee, 276
Mocha Blend, 276
Orange Blend, 276
Punch, Irish Coffee-Eggnog, 314
Vienna Blend, 276
Buttercream, Coffee, 277
Crème Brûlée, Coffee, 323
Mocha
Blend, Mocha, 276
Fudge, Creamy Mocha, 51
Punch, Mocha, 141
Napoleons, Coffee, 276
Nuggets, Coffee, 278

COLESLAW. *See* Slaws.

COOKIES. *See also* Brownies.
Apricot Cookies, 322
Bars and Squares
Almond Brickle Treats, 321
Apricot-Almond Squares, 272
Date Bars, 322
Granola Bars, 214
Christmas
Jammies, Christmas, 322
Santa Cookies, Easy, 321
Sugarplum Sticks, 321

Drop
 Chocolate Chunk-Almond Cookies,
  Double, 178
 Chocolate Cookies, Double-, 272
 Chocolate-Raisin Oatmeal Cookies, 136
 Fibber McGee Cookies, 72
 Fudge-Pecan Chewies, Alabama, 143
 Oatmeal-Chocolate Morsel
  Cookies, 46
 Oatmeal Cookies, Toasted, 136
 Orange Crinkles, 272
 Peanut Butter Macaroons,
  Chewy, 214
 Polka Dots, 272
Easter Basket and Eggs, 101
Lemon Crisps, 272
Peanut Blossom Cookies, 245
Peanut Butter Shortbread, 321
Refrigerator
 Biscotti, Chocolate-Hazelnut, 80
 Butter Cookie Dough, Basic, 320
 Cherry Chocolates, 321
 Coffee Nuggets, 278
 Jack-o'-Lantern Cookies, 273
 Lollipop Cookies, 322
 Oatmeal-Toffee Lizzies,
  Crispy, 136
 Spooky Eyes, 273
Rolled
 Cheese Bites, Starlight, 329
 Peppermint Cookies, 322
 Pinwheels, 321
 Pueblo Indian Cookies, 228
Shortbread, Peanut Butter, 321
Shortbread, Scottish, 34
Spice Thins, 322

CORN
Curried Corn and Sweet Red
 Peppers, 47
Okra, Corn, and Tomatoes, 203
Pie with Fresh Tomato Salsa, Buttercrust
 Corn, 181
Posole, 226
Pudding, Tee's Corn, 318
Salad, Corn, 214
Salsa, Sweet Corn, 156
Soup with Ginger-Lime Cream, Pumpkin-
 Corn, 227

CORNBREADS. *See also* Hush Puppies.
Bowls, Cornbread, 58
Cornish Hens, Cranberry-Cornbread
 Stuffed, 325
Crust, Turkey and Peppers in
 Cornbread, 312
Dressings
 Nannie's Cornbread Dressing, 306
 Sausage-Cornbread Dressing, 289
Muffins, Sour Cream Corn, 176
Salad, Mexican Cornbread, 210
Spinach Cornbread, 49

CORNISH HENS
à l'Orange, Cornish Hens, 325
Cajun-Fried Cornish Hens, 326
Stuffed Cornish Hens, Cranberry-
 Cornbread, 325
Tarragon, Cornish Hens, 326

COUSCOUS
Fruit, Couscous with Mixed, 232

CRAB
Appetizers
 Dip, Hot Crabmeat, 154
 Mousse, Crab, 327
Bake, Easy Crab, 209

Brunch Scramble, Crabmeat, 32
Cakes, Chesapeake Bay Crab, 155
Cakes, Country Crab, 20
Cakes, Mock Crab, 159
Fried Soft-Shell Crabs, 154
Imperial, Crab, 155
Lobster Tails, Crab-Stuffed, 326
Louis, Crab, 94
Potatoes, Crabmeat-Topped, 22

CRANBERRIES
Beverages
 Cubes, Cranberry, 201
 New Orleans, Mr. Funk of, 57
 Punch, Sparkling Cranberry, 101
 Sangría, Cranberry, 238
 Tea, Pink Sangría, 200
Brandied Cranberries, 306
Cornish Hens, Cranberry-Cornbread
 Stuffed, 325
Relish, Cranberry, 318
Relish, Frozen Cranberry, 302
Salad, Holiday Cranberry, 301
Sauces
 Dried Cranberry Sauce, Pork Medaillons
  with Port Wine and, 330
 Salsa, Grilled Turkey Breast with
  Cranberry, 252
Scones, Cranberry, 283

CUCUMBERS
Canapés, Cucumber, 88
Gazpacho-Stuffed Endive, 287
Mousse with Dill Sauce,
 Cucumber, 216
Salsa, Cucumber, 131
Salsa, Cucumber-Dill, 107
Soup, Chilled Cucumber-Buttermilk, 134
Tartlets, Smoked Salmon and
 Cucumber, 216

CURRY
Chicken
 Dinner, Curried Chicken
  Skillet, 47
 Mousse, Curried Chicken, 328
Corn and Sweet Red Peppers,
 Curried, 47
Fruit, Hot Curried, 72
Fruit Medley, Curried, 329
Mayonnaise, Curry, 66
Sauce, Curry, 18
Tuna Melts, Curried, 46

CUSTARDS. *See also* Puddings.
Boiled Christmas Custard, 329
Crème Brûlée, Almond, 323
Crème Brûlée, Basic, 323
Crème Brûlée, Berry, 323
Crème Brûlée, Chocolate, 323
Crème Brûlée, Coffee, 323
Crème Brûlée, Double
 Raspberry, 323
Crème Brûlée, Ginger, 323
Crème Brûlée, Onion, 324
Crème Brûlée, Orange, 323
Crème Brûlée, Peppermint, 323
Crème Brûlée, Roasted Garlic, 324
Crème Brûlée, Roquefort-and-Black
 Pepper, 324
Crème Brûlées, Savory, 324
Crème Brûlée, White Chocolate-Macadamia
 Nut, 323
Flans
 de Queso, Flan, 303
 Sweet Potato Flan, 291
Sauce, Bourbon Custard, 271

DATES
Bars, Date, 322
Loaves, Tropical Date-Banana, 143
DESSERTS. *See also* Brownies, Cakes, Candies,
 Cheesecakes, Cookies, Custards, Ice Creams, Mousses,
 Pies and Pastries, Puddings, Sherbets.
Caramel Dessert Biscuits, 36
Caramel Fondue, 35
Chocolate
 Bags, Chocolate-Raspberry, 97
 Hello Dolly Dessert, 168
 Midnight Delights, 278
 Plunge, Chocolate, 35
 Pots de Crème with Orange Meringues,
  Chocolate, 318
De-Light-Ful Dessert, 220
Éclairs, Miniature Orange, 92
Eggnog Dessert, 314
Frozen
 Cream, Betty's Holiday, 303
 Ice Cream Dessert, Caramel, 36
 Tortoni, Apricot-Yogurt, 124
Fruit
 Curried Fruit, Hot, 72
 Gazpacho, Tropical, 204
 Mint-Balsamic Tea, Fresh Fruit with, 232
 Planter's Punch Dessert, 175
 Trifle, Tropical, 204
Peach
 Cream, Peaches and, 196
 Layered Peach Dessert, 196
Pear
 Baked Pears à la Mode, 129
 Orange-Caramel Sauce, Pears with, 281
Sauces
 Berry Sauce, 103
 Blueberry Sauce, 135
 Buttermilk Sauce, 183
 Butter-Rum Sauce, 134
 Caramel Sauce, 308
 Raspberry Sauce, 327
Trifle, All Seasons Lemon, 219
Trifle, Olde English, 331
DRESSINGS. *See also* Salad Dressings, Stuffings.
Cornbread
 Nannie's Cornbread Dressing, 306
 Sausage-Cornbread Dressing, 289
Creole Dressing, 289
Squash Dressing, 290
DUMPLINGS
Apple Dumplings with Maple-Cider
 Sauce, 288
Chicken and Dumplings, Quick, 125
Chicken and Dumplings with Herbed
 Broth, 338

EGGNOG
Cake, Eggnog-Pecan Pound, 313
Casserole, Sweet Potato-Eggnog, 291
Dessert, Eggnog, 314
French Toast, Eggnog, 313
Punch, Irish Coffee-Eggnog, 314
EGGPLANT
Appetizer, Grilled Eggplant, 198
Balsamic-Flavored Eggplant, 342
Biscuit Cakes, Tomato-Eggplant, 170
Cakes, Eggplant, 196
Casseroles
 Eggplant Cakes, 196
 Oyster Louisiane, Eggplant-
  and-, 196
 Parmesan, Eggplant, 84

EGGPLANT

(continued)

Parmigiana, Eggplant, 197
Sausage-Pasta Casserole, Freezer Eggplant-, 197
Relish, Eggplant, 342
Sandwiches, Open-Face Eggplant, 124
Sticks, Ned's Eggplant, 309

EGGS

Burritos, Tex-Mex Egg, 34
Casserole, Sunday Egg, 100
Cheese, Eggs and, 165
Frittata, Potato-Bacon, 269
Omelets
Cheese-Shiitake Omelet, Golden, 265
Dill-Cheese-Ham Omelet, 33
Scrambled
Cheese-Chive Scrambled Eggs, 34
Crabmeat Brunch Scramble, 32

ENCHILADAS

Cheese Enchiladas, 311
Chicken Enchiladas with Tomatillo Sauce, 206
Shrimp Enchiladas in Tomatillo Sauce, 310

FILLINGS

Savory
Spinach Filling, 316
Sweet
Lemon Filling, 319
Peach Pie Filling, Fresh, 195
Praline Buttercream, 243

FISH. *See also* Clams, Crab, Lobster, Oysters, Salmon, Scallops, Seafood, Shrimp, Tuna.
Caper Sauce, Fish in, 209
Caribbean Banana Fish, 202
Catfish
Fry, Burk's Farm-Raised Catfish, 158
Oven-Fried Catfish, 106
Orange Roughy with Herbs, Steamed, 189
Stock, Fish, 19
Swordfish with Caper Sauce, Grilled, 230
Tacos, Barbecued Fish, 339
Trout
Baked Trout, 106
Fillets with Capers, Trout, 252
Grilled Trout, 106
Poached Trout, 106

FRANKFURTERS

Pigs in a Blanket, 178
Scrambled Dog, Dinglewood Pharmacy's, 118

FRENCH TOAST

Eggnog French Toast, 313
Macadamia Nut French Toast, 282

FROM OUR KITCHEN TO YOURS

Bay leaves
removing from soups, 314
Biscuits
cutting dough, 30
Butter, 314
Cakes
cutting, 30
Cookies, 30
crushing, 30
Cheese
shredding, 31 (illustration)
Chicken
cooking, 246

Crab
cracking, 156
Food processor
chopping nuts, 208
Fruitcakes, 314, 343
Garnishes
vegetable, 343
Gifts of food, 343
freezing, 343
mailing, 343
wrapping, 343
Grating citrus rind, 314
Grilling
cooking times, 194 (chart)
direct/indirect cooking methods, 194
equipment, 274
temperature of fire, 195
thermometer, 195
Herbs
amounts to use, 30
Kitchen
gadgets, 343
Kiwifruit
peeling, 31 (illustration)
Lamb
cooking, 105 (chart)
seasoning, 105
storing, 105 (chart)
Leftovers, 30, 274
Lettuce, 67
Marinating, 30
Meringue
preventing weeping, 246
Onions, 30
chopping, 246
grating, 30
Pastas
cooking, 30
reheating, 31
Pecans
chopping, 208
Peppers, 30, 208
working with hot peppers, 208
Piecrust, 246
equipment, 208
mixing, 246
preventing overbrowning, 30
recipe, Water-Whipped Baked Pastry Shell, 246
Pork
cooking, 246
Recipe preparation
cleaning up, 31 (illustration)
doubling recipes, 30
measuring, 274
preparing ingredients, 30, 31 (illustration), 208
Rice
cooking, 30
Salads, 67
Sauces, 30
Smoking (cooking method), 116
adding food, 116
cleaning smoker, 117
filling water pan, 116
maintaining temperature, 116
soaking wood, 116
starting fire, 116
Soups, 274
removing bay leaf, 314
stocks, 30
Stir frying, 30
Tarts, 274

Tomatoes, 30
Tortillas, 44
equipment, 44
how to cook, 44
how to shape, 44
reheating, 44
storing, 44
recipe, Flour Tortillas, 44
Vegetable cooking spray
cleanup, easy, 31
Vegetables, 30
grilling, 274

FROSTINGS. *See also* Fillings, Glaze, Toppings.
Cheese Spread, Tropical, 46
Chocolate-Cola Frosting, 56
Coffee Buttercream, 277
Cream Cheese Frosting, 139
Fluffy White Frosting, 319
Pineapple-Cream Cheese Frosting, 160

FRUIT. *See also* specific types.
Beverages
Brew, Fruity Witches', 273
Punch, Caribbean, 173
Punch for a Bunch, 90
Punch, Mixed Fruit, 239
Punch, Polka Dot, 178
Punch, Southern Fruit, 238
Shake, Tangy Fruit, 129
Tea-Ser, Tropical, 200
Bread, Fruity Banana, 78
Couscous with Mixed Fruit, 232
Curried Fruit, Hot, 72
Desserts. *See also* Fruit/Fruitcakes.
Curried Fruit, Hot, 72
Planter's Punch Dessert, 175
Rumtopf, 142
Sugarplum Sticks, 321
Trifle, Olde English, 331
Dip, Fresh Fruit, 94
Fruitcakes
Cake Mix Fruit Cake, 248
Chocolate Fruitcakes, 250
Grandmother's Fruitcake, 248
Jill's Fruitcake, 249
No-Bake Fruitcake, 249
Grilled Fruit with Honey Yogurt, 87
Medley, Curried Fruit, 329
Mint-Balsamic Tea, Fresh Fruit with, 232
Pork Loin, Fruitcake-Stuffed, 250
Relish, Fresh Fruit, 158
Salads
Berry-Citrus Twist, 100
Chicken Salad, Summery, 138
Congealed Fresh Fruit, Jeweled, 89
Gingered Fruit Salad, 95

GAME

Dove au Vin, 309

GARNISH

Orange Zest, Candied, 320

GIFTS

Gadgets, Off-the-Wall, 332
Gifts That Measure Up, 332
Hot Handlers, 332
Miniature Liqueur Sampler, 332
Wine Tasting, 332

GLAZE. *See also* Frostings, Toppings.
Orange Glaze, 320

GRANOLA

Bars, Granola, 214
Muffins, Granola, 78
Trail Mix, Bunny, 101

GRAPEFRUIT
Drink, Grapefruit, 238
Salad, Greens and Grapefruit, 301
Sorbet, Pink Grapefruit and Tarragon, 163
GRAPES
Blue Cheese-Pecan Grapes, 48
Caribbean Grapes, 48
Honeyed Grapes, 47
Wild Rice with Grapes, 48
GRAVIES. *See also Sauces.*
Burgundy Gravy, Beef Roast with, 263
Chicken Gravy, Fried, 235
Tomato Gravy, Spicy, 172
GREENS
Beets 'n' Greens, 179
Collard Greens, 233
Collards Casserole, Parmesan-, 233
Grits and Greens, 233
Pasta with Greens, 211
Stewed Tomatoes and Greens, 234
Turnip Greens, 306
GRILLED
Beef
Flank Steak, Marinated, 237
Steak, Marinated Bourbon, 91
Steak, Tabasco, 207
Chicken
Lemon-Herb Grilled Chicken, 87
Salad, Moroccan Grilled Chicken, 231
Salad with Raspberry Dressing, Grilled
Chicken, 202
Fennel and Radicchio with Orange
Vinaigrette, Grilled, 253
Fish
Salmon Quesadilla with Cucumber Salsa,
Grilled, 131
Swordfish with Caper Sauce,
Grilled, 230
Trout, Grilled, 106
Fruit with Honey Yogurt, Grilled, 87
Lamb with Mango Salsa, Grilled, 104
Lamb with Sweet Pepper Relish, Grilled, 104
Melon Salad with Orange-Raspberry
Vinaigrette, Grilled, 144
Pork
Ribs, Adams', 236
Ribs, Barbecued Country-Style, 237
Spareribs, Barbecued, 236
Tenderloin with Apples, Celery, and
Potatoes, Grilled Pork, 161
Sandwich, Ham 'n' Cheese Chicken, 153
Tortilla Bites, 42
Turkey Breast with Cranberry Salsa,
Grilled, 252
Vegetables
Eggplant Appetizer, Grilled, 198
Eggplant, Balsamic-Flavored, 342
Marinated Grilled Vegetables, 162
Onions, Grilled Stuffed, 180
Pepper Tacos, Grilled, 340
Portabello Mushrooms, Grilled, 123
Shiitakes, Grilled, 265
Zucchini with Feta, Greek
Grilled, 190
GRITS
Cheese
Garlic-and-Herb Cheese Grits, 122
Green Chiles, Cheese Grits with, 208
Chicken and Grits, 263
Greens, Grits and, 233
Tomato Grits, Hot, 171
GUMBO. *See also Chowders, Soups, Stews.*
Carolina Gumbo, 70

HAM. *See also Pork.*
Appetizers
Mousse Pitas, Ham, 328
Nibbles, Ham-Pineapple, 283
Spread, Buttery Ham, 93
Tennessee Sin, 218
Artichokes, Ham-Mushroom-Stuffed, 228
Biscuits, Surprise Pull-Apart, 46
Casseroles
Lasagna, Creamy Ham-and-Chicken, 88
Quiche Casserole, 33
Spaghetti, Ham-and-Turkey, 19
Strata, Ham, 308
Hash Brown Bake, 281
Omelet, Dill-Cheese-Ham, 33
Pie, Ham-and-Cheese, 256
Pizza, Southern Classic, 268
Salads
Asparagus with Prosciutto, Marinated, 83
Potato Salad, Ham-and-, 94
Sandwiches
Cheese Chicken Sandwich, Ham 'n', 153
Stroganoff on Cheesy Onion Biscuits,
Ham, 98
Tennessee Ham, 263
HOMINY
Soup, Bean-and-Hominy, 23
Soup, Black, White, and Red All Over, 126
HONEY
Biscuits, Honey Angel, 138
Butter, Honey, 139
Dressing, Honey-Lemon, 133
Grapes, Honeyed, 47
Ice Cream, Honey-Vanilla, 178
Mustard, Peppered Honey, 312
Pork Tenderloin, Honey-Mustard, 52
HORS D'OEUVRES. *See Appetizers.*
HOT DOGS. *See Frankfurters.*
HUSH PUPPIES
Baked Hush Puppies, 108

ICE CREAMS. *See also Sherbets.*
Caramel Ice Cream Dessert, 36
Chocolate Cookie Ice Cream, 245
Cinnamon Ice Cream, 126
Fennel Ice Cream, 281
Honey-Vanilla Ice Cream, 178
Peach Ice Cream, Fresh, 195
Sorbets
Pink Grapefruit and Tarragon
Sorbet, 163
Strawberry-Champagne Sorbet, 20

JAMS AND JELLIES
Apple Jelly, Spiced, 251
Cantaloupe-Peach Jam, 143
Kudzu Blossom Jelly, 198
Red Bell Pepper Jam, 242

KABOBS
Chicken Kabobs, Oriental, 193
Lamb Kabobs, 192
Meatball Kabobs, 192
Squash-and-Pepper Kabobs, Summery, 193

LAMB
Chops, Dijon-Rosemary Lamb, 285
Grilled Lamb with Sweet Pepper Relish, 104
Kabobs, Lamb, 192

Leg of Lamb
Grilled Lamb with Mango Salsa, 104
Hunter Sauce, Leg of Lamb
with, 317
Leg of Lamb, 285
Rack of Lamb with Cherry-Wine Sauce,
Hazelnut-Crusted, 284
Roast, Rolled Lamb, 285
Stew, Emerald Isle, 71
LASAGNA
Chicken Lasagna Bake, 55
Chicken Lasagna Florentine, 158
Ham-and-Chicken Lasagna,
Creamy, 88
Light Lasagna, 212
Vegetable Lasagna, 211
LEMON
Beverages
Caribbean Cooler, 203
Cubes, Lemonade, 201
Cubes, Lemon-Mint, 201
Piña Coladas, 203
Punch, Lemonade-Bourbon, 287
Sweetened Preserved Lemons, 141
Tea Tingler, Lemon, 200
Broccoli, Lemon, 53
Butter, Lemon, 32
Cheese Party Bites, Lemon-, 160
Desserts
Cake, Coconut-Lemon, 319
Cake with Blueberry Sauce, Buttermilk-
Lemon Pudding, 135
Cheesecake, Lemon Delight, 219
Crisps, Lemon, 272
Filling, Lemon, 319
Trifle, All Seasons Lemon, 219
Dressing, Honey-Lemon, 133
Main Dishes
Chicken, Lemon-Herb
Grilled, 87
Chicken, Lemon-Roasted, 24
Flank Steak, Lemon-Lime, 55
Mayonnaise, Lemon, 32
Olive Oil, Lemon-Infused, 231
Pasta, Lemon-Garlic, 181
Sauces
Barbecue Sauce, Lemony, 31
Basting Sauce, Lemon, 32
Tartar Sauce, Lemony, 32
Squeezers, Lemon, 32
Sugar, Lemon-Mint, 32
Sweetened Preserved Lemons, 141
Vinaigrette, Lemon, 31
Vinegar, Lemon, 31
LENTILS
Burgers, Lentil, 123
LIME
Cream, Ginger-Lime, 227
Desserts
Pie, Manny and Isa's Key
Lime, 118
Pies, Key Lime, 86
Flank Steak, Lemon-Lime, 55
Muffins, Key Lime, 50
Punch, Calypso Presbyterian Church Women's
Lime, 141
LINGUINE
Artichoke and Shrimp Linguine, 210
Caesar Salad Pasta, 230
Clam Linguine, 212
Favorite Pasta, My, 213
Pesto Pasta, Asian, 189
Shrimp and Pasta, Mediterranean, 286

LIVING LIGHT
Appetizers
  Eggplant Appetizer, Grilled, 198
  Plantain Chips, M203
  Sweet Potato Chips, M203
Beverages
  Caribbean Cooler, 203
  Piña Coladas, 203
Breads
  Banana Bread, Fruity, 78
  English Muffin Bread, M79
  Focaccia, Rosemary, 190
  Hush Puppies, Baked, 108
  Muffins, Granola, 78
  Swiss Cheese Loaves, Mini, 80
Chutney, Blueberry, 190
Couscous with Mixed Fruit, 232
Crab Cakes, Country, 20
Desserts
  Biscotti, Chocolate-Hazelnut, 80
  Cake Roll, Make-Ahead Chocolate-
    Mint, 220
  Cheesecake, Lemon Delight, 219
  De-Light-Ful Dessert, 220
  Fruit with Mint-Balsamic Tea,
    Fresh, 232
  Sorbet, Pink Grapefruit and
    Tarragon, 163
  Sorbet, Strawberry-Champagne, 20
  Tortoni, Apricot-Yogurt, 124
  Trifle, All Seasons Lemon, 219
  Trifle, Olde English, 331
  Trifle, Tropical, 204
Grits, Garlic-and-Herb Cheese, 122
Main Dishes
  Beef Hash, 24
  Burgers, Lentil, 123
  Casserole, Freezer Eggplant-Sausage-
    Pasta, 197
  Catfish, Oven-Fried, 106
  Chicken, Lemon-Roasted, 24
  Chicken Tostadas, 122
  Fish, Caribbean Banana, 202
  Lasagna, Creamy Ham-and-Chicken, 88
  Lasagna, Light, 212
  Orange Roughy with Herbs,
    Steamed, 189
  Pasta, Mamma Mia, 25
  Pasta with Peanut Sauce, 252
  Pork Medaillons with Port Wine and
    Dried Cranberry Sauce, 330
  Pork Tenderloin, Apple-Mushroom, 53
  Pork Tenderloin, Honey-Mustard, 52
  Pork Tenderloin, Sesame, 53
  Pork Tenderloin with Apples, Celery, and
    Potatoes, Grilled, 161
  Salmon Burgers, 24
  Salmon in Parchment, 311
  Salmon with Ginger Vinaigrette, Sesame-
    Crusted, 162
  Scallops with Tomato-Mango Salsa,
    Seared, 122
  Shrimp Enchiladas in Tomatillo
    Sauce, 310
  Spinach-and-Cheese Calzones, 310
  Swordfish with Caper Sauce,
    Grilled, 230
  Trout, Baked, 106
  Trout Fillets with Capers, 252
  Trout, Grilled, 106
  Trout, Poached, 106
  Turkey Breast with Cranberry Salsa,
    Grilled, 252

Olive Oil, Basil-Infused, 231
Olive Oil, Lemon-Infused, 231
Pasta, Asian Pesto, 189
Pasta, Caesar Salad, 230
Rice with Tomatoes and Basil, 232
Salad Dressings
  Papaya Seed Dressing, 204
  Raspberry Dressing, 202
  Vinaigrette Dressing, 231
Salads
  Black-Eyed Pea Salad, 203
  Chicken Noodle Salad, 25
  Chicken Salad, Moroccan Grilled, 231
  Chicken Salad with Raspberry Dressing,
    Grilled, 202
  Fennel and Radicchio with Orange
    Vinaigrette, Grilled, 253
  Fruit with Mint-Balsamic Tea, Fresh, 232
  Greens with Raspberry Dressing,
    Peppery, 254
  Slaw, Green Bean, 108
Sandwiches, Open-Face Eggplant, 124
Sauces
  Ginger Vinaigrette, 162
  Salsa, Cucumber-Dill, 107
  Seafood Sauce, Red, 107
  Tartar Sauce, 107
Sorbet, Pink Grapefruit and Tarragon, 163
Soups and Stews
  Bean-and-Hominy Soup, 23
  Gazpacho, Tropical, 204
  Sweet Potato-and-Sausage Soup, 23
Spice Rub, Moroccan, 231
Spread, Blue Cheese, 79
Spread, Raisin-Nut, 79
Spread, Strawberry, 79
Vegetables
  Broccoli and Walnut Sauté, 52
  Broccoli, Garlic, 54
  Broccoli, Lemon, 53
  Marinated Grilled Vegetables, 162
  Okra, Corn, and Tomatoes, 203
  Portabello Mushrooms, Grilled, 123
  Portabello Mushrooms,
    Microwave, M123
  Portabello Mushrooms, Sautéed, 123
  Potatoes, Buttermilk-Basil Mashed, 330
  Potatoes, Rosemary-Roasted, 20
  Ratatouille, Microwave, M232
  Risotto Primavera, 163
  Zucchini with Feta, Greek Grilled, 190
LOBSTER
  Crab-Stuffed Lobster Tails, 326

MACADAMIA
Crème Brûlée, White Chocolate-Macadamia
  Nut, 323
French Toast, Macadamia Nut, 282
MACARONI. *See also* Pastas.
Casserole, Mushroom-Macaroni, 180
Cheese
  Casserole, Macaroni-Cheese-Beef, 125
  Soup, Macaroni and Cheese, 264
  Tomatoes, Macaroni, Cheese, and, 213
MANGOES
Salsa, Mango, 104
Salsa, Seared Scallops with Tomato-
  Mango, 122
Vinegar, Mango-Cilantro, 190
MARSHMALLOWS
Bird's Nests, 102
Monster Mouths, 274

MAYONNAISE
Curry Mayonnaise, 66
Lemon Mayonnaise, 32
MEAT LOAF
Beef Loaves, Individual Barbecued, 242
Easy Meat Loaf, 125
Reuben Loaf, 338
MELONS
Cantaloupe-Peach Jam, 143
Salad with Orange-Raspberry Vinaigrette,
  Grilled Melon, 144
Salsa, Hot Melon, 144
Watermelon
  Daiquiri, Watermelon, 143
  Pie, Watermelon, 144
MERINGUES
Orange Meringues, 318
MICROWAVE
Appetizers
  Dip, Quick Fiesta, M237
  Plantain Chips, M203
  Sweet Potato Chips, M203
Breads
  English Muffin Bread, M79
  Muffins, Fudge Brownie, M50
Butter, Sweet Potato, M290
Fudge, Double-Good, M50
Spoons, Dipped Chocolate-Almond, M277
Turkey Scaloppine, Easy, M192
Vegetables
  Broccoli Casserole, Cheesy, M191
  Portabello Mushrooms,
    Microwave, M123
  Potatoes, Seafood-Stuffed, M192
  Ratatouille, Microwave, M232
  Sweet Potatoes, Cinnamon-
    Apple, M23
MINCEMEAT
Pie, Kentucky Mincemeat, 302
MOUSSES. *See also* Custards, Puddings.
Butter Pecan Mousse, 286
Chicken Mousse, Curried, 328
Chocolate Truffle Mousse with Raspberry
  Sauce, 327
Crab Mousse, 327
Cucumber Mousse with Dill Sauce, 216
Ham Mousse Pitas, 328
Mustard Mousse, 328
MUFFINS
Blueberry Muffins, Speedy, 135
Bran Muffins, Big Batch Moist, 214
Cheese Muffins, Dilly, 245
Coconut Muffins, 214
Corn Muffins, Sour Cream, 176
Fudge Brownie Muffins, M50
Granola Muffins, 78
Key Lime Muffins, 50
Sausage Muffins, 49
MUSHROOMS
Artichokes, Ham-Mushroom-Stuffed, 228
Casserole, Mushroom-Macaroni, 180
Garlic and Mushrooms, 165
Main Dishes
  Burgers, Brie-Mushroom, 128
  Pork Chops, Apricot-Mushroom
    Stuffed, 287
  Pork Tenderloin, Apple-Mushroom, 53
  Spinach and Mushrooms with Bow Tie
    Pasta, 341
Omelet, Golden Cheese-Shiitake, 265
Portabello Mushrooms, Grilled, 123
Portabello Mushrooms, Microwave, M123
Portabello Mushrooms, Sautéed, 123

Sauce, Filet Mignons with Shiitake
Madeira, 265
Shiitakes, Grilled, 265
Side Dishes
Baked Mushroom Rice, 84
Casserole, Mushroom, 211
Spinach and Mushrooms with Bow Tie
Pasta, 341
Soup, Cream of Shiitake, 265
Stewed Anasazi Beans with Mushrooms, 226
Tapas, Majorcan Mushroom, 159
MUSTARD
Honey Mustard, Peppered, 312
Hot Mustard, Really, 312
Jalapeño Mustard, 312
Mousse, Mustard, 328
Pork Tenderloin, Honey-Mustard, 52
Raspberry Mustard, 313
Sweet Cider Mustard, 312

NOODLES
Casserole, Sausage-and-Noodle, 255
Salad, Chicken Noodle, 25
Soup, Chicken Noodle, 45

OATMEAL
Cookies
Chocolate Morsel Cookies, Oatmeal-, 46
Chocolate-Raisin Oatmeal Cookies, 136
Fibber McGee Cookies, 72
Toasted Oatmeal Cookies, 136
Toffee Lizzies, Crispy Oatmeal-, 136
Topping, Oatmeal Cookie, 291
OKRA
Corn, and Tomatoes, Okra, 203
Skillet Okra, 179
OLIVES
Marinated Olives, Caliente, 177
OMELETS
Cheese-Shiitake Omelet, Golden, 265
Dill-Cheese-Ham Omelet, 33
ONIONS
Breads
Biscuits, Cheesy Onion, 98
Sesame Rolls, Onion-and-, 292
Caramelized Onions, Green Beans
with, 288
Crème Brûlée, Onion, 324
Dip, Swiss-Onion, 93
Patties, Potato-Onion, 269
Pudding, Kathy's Onion, 318
Salad, Roasted Onion, 65
Sweet
Casserole, French Onion, 26
Grilled Stuffed Onions, 180
Relish, Purple Onion, 253
Tarts, Sweet Onion, 229
Taters, Buck's, 72
ORANGES
Beverages
Blend, Orange, 276
Cubes, Florida, 201
Coffee Cake, Nutty Orange, 160
Cornish Hens à l'Orange, 325
Desserts
Apples with Cookie Crumbs, Orange
Baked, 271
Cake, Orange, 320
Cake, Orange Butter, 46
Candied Orange Zest, 320
Crème Brûlée, Orange, 323

Crinkles, Orange, 272
Éclairs, Miniature Orange, 92
Grand Marnier, Oranges in, 142
Meringues, Orange, 318
Shortcake, Orange-Strawberry, 100
Truffles, Orange-Pecan, 92
Glaze, Orange, 320
Salad, Orange-Buttermilk, 134
Sauce, Pears with Orange-Caramel, 281
Snack Balls, Orange-Almond, 214
Spread, Tropical Cheese, 46
Vinaigrette, Grilled Fennel and Radicchio with
Orange, 253
Vinaigrette, Orange-Raspberry, 144
Vinegar, Orange, 31
Whip, Orange-Banana, 244
ORZO
Three-Grain Rice, 166
OYSTERS
Eggplant-and-Oyster Louisiane, 196
Scalloped Oysters, 318

PANCAKES
Gingerbread Pancakes, 282
PASTAS. See also Couscous, Linguine, Macaroni, Orzo,
Spaghetti.
Asparagus, Tomatoes, and Shrimp, Garlicky
Pasta with, 82
Bow Tie Pasta, Spinach and Mushrooms
with, 341
Casserole, Freezer Eggplant-Sausage-
Pasta, 197
Cherry Tomatoes over Pasta,
Herbed, 229
Greens, Pasta with, 211
Late-Night Pasta Chez Frank, 228
Mamma Mia Pasta, 25
Mediterranean Pasta, 341
Primavera, Creamy Pasta, 167
Ravioli, St. Louis Toasted, 117
Salads
Ravioli Salad, Caesar, 183
Vegetable Salad, Pasta-, 238
Shrimp Scampi, 209
Toasted Rice and Pasta, 57
Ziti with Sausage and Broccoli, 340
PÂTÉ
Cheese Pâté, Sherry, 215
PEACHES
Cobbler, Peach, 264
Cream, Peaches and, 196
Dessert, Layered Peach, 196
Fluff, Peach, 176
Ice Cream, Fresh Peach, 195
Jam, Cantaloupe-Peach, 143
Ketchup, Peach, 306
Pies
Filling, Fresh Peach Pie, 195
Fresh Peach Pie, 195
Salsa, Fresh Peach, 195
Vinegar, Peach-Mint, 190
PEANUT BUTTER
Bird's Nests, 102
Candies
Fudge, Double-Good, M50
Fudge, Peanut Butter, 51
Cookies
Easter Basket and Eggs, 101
Macaroons, Chewy Peanut Butter, 214
Peanut Blossom Cookies, 245
Shortbread, Peanut Butter, 321
Spooky Eyes, 273

Monster Mouths, 274
Parfait, Bodacious Peanut, 167
Sauce, Pasta with Peanut, 252
PEANUTS
Beef Stir-Fry, Peanutty, 157
Cookies, Fibber McGee, 72
Dressing, Peanut-Ginger, 177
PEARS
Baked Pears à la Mode, 129
Orange-Caramel Sauce, Pears with, 281
Pie, Rhubarb-Raspberry Pear, 119
Preservation
Chutney, Pear, 251
Relish, Aunt Glennie's Pear, 305
Soda Pop Pears, 55
PEAS
Black-Eyed
Potatoes, Black-Eyed Pea-Spinach-
Stuffed, 22
Relish, Zesty Black-Eyed Pea, 56
Salad, Black-Eyed Pea, 203
Salad, Fearrington House Goat Cheese
and Black-Eyed Pea, 60
English Pea Salad, Cauliflower-, 66
Snow Pea Stir-Fry, Chicken and, 157
Special Peas, 133
PECANS. See also Praline.
Appetizers
Grapes, Blue Cheese-Pecan, 48
Pesto-Spiced Nuts, 173
Savory Southern Pecans, 240
Tarts, Toasty Southern Pecan, 329
Cakes
Coffee Cake, Nutty Orange, 160
Pound Cake, Eggnog-Pecan, 313
Coating, Salmon Bake with Pecan-
Crunch, 209
Cookies
Fudge-Pecan Chewies, Alabama, 143
Sugarplum Sticks, 321
Cornmeal Rounds, Pecan-, 99
Mousse, Butter Pecan, 286
Pork Chops with Beer Sauce, Pecan-
Breaded, 266
Spread, Raisin-Nut, 79
Topping, Butter-Pecan, 158
PEPPERMINT
Cookies, Peppermint, 322
Crème Brûlée, Peppermint, 323
Fondue, Peppermint, 35
PEPPERS
Casserole, Peppery Potato, 182
Chile
Ancho Base, 205
Ancho Cream Sauce, Boneless Pork
Chops with, 205
Chili Verde, 14
Grits with Green Chiles, Cheese, 208
Rellenos, Roasted Chiles, 64
Sauce, Red Chile, 17
Serrano Salsa, Roasted, 207
Tacos, Shrimp-and-Pepper Soft, 339
Firecrackers, Texas, 96
Jalapeño
Mustard, Jalapeño, 312
Quesadillas, Bacon-Jalapeño-
Tomato, 240
Stuffed Jalapeño Peppers, Fried, 22
Tacos, Shrimp-and-Pepper Soft, 339
Red
Bread, Roasted Red Bell Pepper, 241
Butter, Roasted Red Bell Pepper, 242
Curried Corn and Sweet Red Peppers, 47

PEPPERS
(continued)

Jam, Red Bell Pepper, 242
Soup, Cream of Roasted Sweet Red
Pepper, 65
Salsa, Roasted, 130
Sweet
Chowder, Bell Pepper-Cheese, 240
Kabobs, Summery Squash-and-
Pepper, 193
Relish, Sweet Pepper, 104
Roasted Bell Peppers in Olive Oil, 242
Sausage and Peppers, 165
Sausage, Sweet Peppery, 69
Tacos, Grilled Pepper, 340
Turkey and Peppers in Cornbread
Crust, 312
PESTOS. *See also* Relishes, Salsas, Sauces, Toppings.
Dip, Pesto, 93
Nuts, Pesto-Spiced, 173
Pasta, Asian Pesto, 189
Sauce, Pesto, 267
PIES AND PASTRIES
Apple-Bourbon Pie, 302
Apricot Pies, Fried, 215
Black Bottom Pie, Weidmann's, 118
Cobblers
Peach Cobbler, 264
Strawberry-Rhubarb Crisp, 119
Key Lime Pie, Manny and Isa's, 118
Key Lime Pies, 86
Main Dish
Calzones, All-Star Pizza, 308
Chicken Dumpling Pie, 245
Chicken Pot Pie, 54, 256
Ham-and-Cheese Pie, 256
Meat Pie, Continental, 256
Spaghetti Pie, Weeknight, 312
Mincemeat Pie, Kentucky, 302
Pastries
Calzones, Spinach-and-Cheese, 310
Chocolate-Raspberry Bags, 97
Cornucopia, Pastry, 307
Napoleons, Coffee, 276
Phyllo Bowls, 58
Phyllo Tartlet Shells, 216
Puff Pastry Bowls, 58
Shell, Water-Whipped Baked Pastry, 246
Spinach-Artichoke-Tomato Puffs, 284
Peach
Filling, Fresh Peach Pie, 195
Fresh Peach Pie, 195
Rhubarb-Raspberry Pear Pie, 119
Tarts
Midnight Delights, 278
Party Tarts, 90
Pecan Tarts, Toasty Southern, 329
Sweet Onion Tarts, 229
Tomato Tart, Fresh, 170
White Chocolate Chess Tart, 303
Vegetable
Corn Pie with Fresh Tomato Salsa,
Buttercrust, 181
Spinach Pie with Muenster Crust, 48
Watermelon Pie, 144
PINEAPPLE
Beverages
Piña Coladas, 203
Piña Colada Slush, 90
Punch, Pineapple-Gin, 140
Punch, Pineapple Sherbet, 141

Desserts
Cake, Zucchini-Pineapple, 160
Frosting, Pineapple-Cream Cheese, 160
Ham-Pineapple Nibbles, 283
PIZZA
Bayou Pizza, The Best of the, 268
Bites, Pizza, 244
Blazing Sunset Pizza, 267
Calzones, All-Star Pizza, 308
King Henry Pizza, The, 267
Sauce, Traditional Pizza, 267
Southern Classic Pizza, 268
Southwest Deluxe Pizza, 268
Tacos, Pizza-Flavored Chicken, 340
Veggie Pizza, Southwestern, 126
POLENTA
Basic Polenta, 164
POPCORN
Caramel Crunch, 165
Cheesy Barbecue Popcorn, 239
Chili Popcorn, 166
PORK. *See also* Bacon, Ham, Sausage.
Barbecue
Ribs, Barbecued Country-Style, 237
Spareribs, Barbecued, 236
Chili Verde, 14
Chops
Boneless Pork Chops with Ancho Cream
Sauce, 205
Glazed Pork Chops with Green Mole
Sauce, Tamarind-, 266
Pecan-Breaded Pork Chops with Beer
Sauce, 266
Stuffed Pork Chops, Apricot-
Mushroom, 287
Loin, Fruitcake-Stuffed Pork, 250
Pie, Continental Meat, 256
Posole, 226
Ribs
Adams' Ribs, 236
Spareribs, Southern, 116
Tenderloin
Apple-Mushroom Pork Tenderloin, 53
Cacciatore, Pork, 69
Grilled Pork Tenderloin with Apples,
Celery, and Potatoes, 161
Honey-Mustard Pork Tenderloin, 52
Medaillons with Port Wine and Dried
Cranberry Sauce, Pork, 330
Sesame Pork Tenderloin, 53
POTATOES
Baked
Buck's Taters, 72
Crabmeat-Topped Potatoes, 22
Gumbo Potatoes, 22
Rosemary-Baked Potatoes, 23
Rosemary-Roasted Potatoes, 20
Breads
Rolls, Potato Sourdough, 77
Rolls, Potato Sourdough Cinnamon, 77
Sourdough Bread Dough, Potato, 77
Sourdough Bread, Potato, 77
Sourdough Starter, Potato, 77
Starter Food, 77
Casserole, Peppery Potato, 182
Frittata, Potato-Bacon, 269
Hash, Beef, 24
Hash Brown Bake, 281
Hash Browns, Convenient, 135
Mashed
Buttermilk-Basil Mashed Potatoes, 330
Roasted Garlic Mashed Potatoes, 288
Parmesan Potato Wedges, 181

Patties, Potato-Onion, 269
Pork Tenderloin with Apples, Celery, and
Potatoes, Grilled, 161
Puff, Potato-Cheese, 269
Roasted Potatoes, Garlic-, 87, 342
Salad, Ham-and-Potato, 94
Stuffed
Black-Eyed Pea-Spinach-Stuffed
Potatoes, 22
Seafood-Stuffed Potatoes, M192
PRALINE
Buttercream, Praline, 243
Powder, Praline, 243
Torte, Lucy's Apricot Praline, 243
PRUNES
Tzimmes, 102
PUDDINGS. *See also* Custards, Mousses.
Beach, The, 168
Bread
Buttermilk Bread Pudding with Butter-
Rum Sauce, 134
Old-Fashioned Bread Pudding with
Bourbon Custard Sauce, 271
Buttermilk-Lemon Pudding Cake with
Blueberry Sauce, 135
Finger Painting Never Tasted So Good, 167
Peanut Parfait, Bodacious, 167
Savory
Corn Pudding, Tee's, 318
Onion Pudding, Kathy's, 318
PUMPKIN
Soup with Ginger-Lime Cream, Pumpkin-
Corn, 227
Waffles, Pumpkin, 282

QUICHES
Casserole, Quiche, 33
Sealed with a Quiche, 135

RAISINS
Bugs in a Rug, 178
Cookies, Chocolate-Raisin Oatmeal, 136
Spread, Raisin-Nut, 79
RASPBERRIES
Beverages
Cubes, Berry-Good, 201
Milk Shakes, Raspberry, 238
Punch, Raspberry Sherbet, 141
Shrub, Berry, 29
Tea, Rasp-Berry Good, 200
Chocolate-Raspberry Bags, 97
Crème Brûlée, Berry, 323
Crème Brûlée, Double Raspberry, 323
Dressing, Peppery Greens with
Raspberry, 254
Dressing, Raspberry, 202
Mustard, Raspberry, 313
Pie, Rhubarb-Raspberry Pear, 119
Sauce, Raspberry, 327
Shortcake, Chocolate-Raspberry, 99
Spirited Raspberries, 142
Vinaigrette, Orange-Raspberry, 144
Vinegar, Raspberry-Thyme, 190
RELISHES. *See also* Chutneys, Pestos, Relishes, Toppings.
Black-Eyed Pea Relish, Zesty, 56
Cabbage Relish, Spanish, 270
Chowchow, Nannie's, 250
Cranberry Relish, 318
Cranberry Relish, Frozen, 302
Eggplant Relish, 342
Fruit Relish, Fresh, 158

Pear Relish, Aunt Glennie's, 305
Purple Onion Relish, 253
Sweet Pepper Relish, 104
Zucchini Relish, Sweet, 159
RHUBARB
Crisp, Strawberry-Rhubarb, 119
Pie, Rhubarb-Raspberry Pear, 119
RICE
Beans and Rice
    Black Beans and Rice, 309
    Black Beans and Yellow Rice, 126
Casseroles
    Chicken and Rice, 54
    Green Rice Casserole, 181
    Mushroom Rice, Baked, 84
    Red Rice, Savannah, 27
    Squash Casserole, Creamy Rice
      and, 26
Main Dishes
    Chicken Breasts, Celebrity, 60
    Chicken with Rice, Roast, 261
Primavera, Risotto, 163
Risotto, 280
Risotto, Seafood, 280
Risotto, Tomato-Basil, 269
Stuffing, Rice, 290
Three-Grain Rice, 166
Toasted Rice and Pasta, 57
Tomatoes and Basil, Rice with, 232
Wild Rice
    Casserole, Wild Rice, 176
    Grapes, Wild Rice with, 48
    Salad, Wild Tuna, 243
ROLLS AND BUNS
Angel's Wing Rolls, 329
Caramel-Chocolate Sticky Buns, Easy, 36
Crescent Rolls, Butter, 292
Onion-and-Sesame Rolls, 292
Potato
    Sourdough Cinnamon Rolls,
      Potato, 77
    Sourdough Rolls, Potato, 77
Quick Rolls, 245
Yeast
    Hot Cross Buns, 100
    Make-Ahead Yeast Rolls, 307
    Quick Yeast Rolls, 45
RUTABAGAS
Whip, Rutabaga, 179

SALAD DRESSINGS
Creamy Dressing, 66
Honey-Lemon Dressing, 133
Papaya Seed Dressing, 204
Peanut-Ginger Dressing, 177
Raspberry Dressing, 202
Vinaigrette
    Balsamic Dressing, 281
    Dijon Vinaigrette, 301
    Garlic Vinaigrette, 65
    Lemon Vinaigrette, 31
    Orange-Raspberry Vinaigrette, 144
    Papaya Vinaigrette Dressing, 206
    Vinaigrette, 61
    Vinaigrette Dressing, 231
SALADS. *See also* Slaws.
Artichoke Salad, Marinated, 66
Beef Vinaigrette Salad, 177
Broccoli Salad, 95
Cabbage Salad, Austrian Hash
    with, 262
Cauliflower-English Pea Salad, 66

Chicken
    Crisp Salad, Crunchy, 28
    Grilled Chicken Salad, Moroccan, 231
    Noodle Salad, Chicken, 25
    Summery Chicken Salad, 138
    Thai Chicken Salad, 177
    Tortilla Salads, Mexican Chicken, 129
Congealed
    Cherry-Cola Salad, 94
    Cranberry Salad, Holiday, 301
    Fruit, Jeweled Congealed Fresh, 89
    Orange-Buttermilk Salad, 134
    Peach Fluff, 176
Cornbread Salad, Mexican, 210
Corn Salad, 214
Crab Louis, 94
Cucumber Mousse with Dill Sauce, 216
Fennel and Radicchio with Orange
    Vinaigrette, Grilled, 253
Fruit
    Berry-Citrus Twist, 100
    Gingered Fruit Salad, 95
    Melon Salad with Orange-Raspberry
      Vinaigrette, Grilled, 144
Green
    Grapefruit Salad, Greens and, 301
    Mixed Greens with Parmesan
      Walnuts, 301
    Mixed Greens with Tarragon
      Vinaigrette, 326
    Peppery Greens with Raspberry
      Dressing, 254
    Winter Salad, 280
Onion Salad, Roasted, 65
Pasta
    Caesar Salad Pasta, 230
    Mediterranean Salad, 132
    Ravioli Salad, Caesar, 183
    Vegetable Salad, Pasta-, 238
Pea
    Black-Eyed Pea Salad, 203
    Black-Eyed Pea Salad, Fearrington House
      Goat Cheese and, 60
    English Pea Salad, Cauliflower-, 66
    Special Peas, 133
Potato Salad, Ham-and-, 94
Rice
    Tomatoes and Basil, Rice with, 232
    Tuna Salad, Wild, 243
Seafood
    Shrimp Salad, Aloha, 46
    Shrimp Salad, Picnic, 182
Spinach Salad with the Blues, 66
Tomato
    Basil-Mozzarella Salad, Tomato-, 171
    Marinated Tomato and Brie Salad, 95
Tuna Salad, Wild, 243
Turkey Taco Salad, 25
Vegetable
    Healthy Salad, 133
    Pita Bread Salad, 86
    Warm Vegetable Salad, 174
Zucchini Salad, Summer, 229
SALMON
Bake with Pecan-Crunch Coating, Salmon, 209
Burgers, Salmon, 24
Parchment, Salmon in, 311
Quesadilla with Cucumber Salsa, Grilled
    Salmon, 131
Sesame-Crusted Salmon with Ginger
    Vinaigrette, 162
Smoked Salmon, 114
Smoked Salmon and Cucumber Tartlets, 216

SALSAS. *See also* Pestos, Relishes, Sauces, Toppings.
Corn Salsa, Sweet, 156
Cucumber-Dill Salsa, 107
Cucumber Salsa, 131
Fresh Salsa, 42
Mango Salsa, 104
Melon Salsa, Hot, 144
One-Minute Salsa, 93
Peach Salsa, Fresh, 195
Roasted Salsa, 130
Serrano Salsa, Roasted, 207
Tomatillo Salsa, Roasted, 64
Tomato-Mango Salsa, Seared Scallops
    with, 122
Tomato Salsa, Fresh, 181
Tomato Salsa, Roasted, 64
SANDWICHES
Chicken
    Cheese Chicken Sandwich, Ham 'n', 153
    Jamaican Chicken Sandwich, 153
    Mozzarella Melt, Italian Chicken-, 153
Eggplant Sandwiches, Open-Face, 124
Fish
    Tuna Melts, Curried, 46
    Tuna Melts, Hot, 126
    Tuna Melts, Southwestern, 127
Ham 'n' Cheese Chicken Sandwich, 153
Tomato Sandwich, Floyd's Favorite, 172
SAUCES. *See also* Desserts/Sauces, Gravies, Pestos, Salsas,
    Toppings.
Avocado-Tomatillo Sauce, 206
Barbecue Sauce, Lemony, 31
Beer Sauce, 266
Cherry-Wine Sauce, 285
Curry Sauce, 18
Custard Sauce, Bourbon, 271
Dill Sauce, 216
Garlic-Butter Sauce, 327
Garlic Sauce, Roasted, 268
Ginger Vinaigrette, 162
Green Mole Sauce, 267
Grill Basting Sauce, 236
Hollandaise Sauce, 86
Hunter Sauce, 317
Lemon Basting Sauce, 32
Maple-Cider Sauce, 288
Pesto Sauce, 267
Pizza Sauce, Traditional, 267
Red Chile Sauce, 17
Seafood Sauce, Red, 107
Shiitake Madeira Sauce, Filet Mignons
    with, 265
Tartar Sauce, 107, 155
Tartar Sauce, Lemony, 32
The Sauce, 237
Tomatillo Sauce, 206
Tomato Sauce, Chunky, 264
SAUSAGE
Casseroles
    Eggplant-Sausage-Pasta Casserole,
      Freezer, 197
    Noodle Casserole, Sausage-and-, 255
    Paella Casserole, 254
    Strata, Christmas Morning, 282
Chili, Now, Thatsa, 16
Dinner, Sausage-and-Bean, 108
Dressing, Sausage-Cornbread, 289
Muffins, Sausage, 49
Peppers, Sausage and, 165
Pizza, The King Henry, 267
Soup, Sweet Potato-and-Sausage, 23
Sweet Peppery Sausage, 69
Tacos, Breakfast, 340

SAUSAGE

(continued)

Turnovers, Turkey Sausage, 239
Ziti with Sausage and Broccoli, 340

SCALLOPS

Seared Scallops with Tomato-Mango
Salsa, 122

SEAFOOD. *See also* Clams, Crab, Fish, Lobster, Oysters,
Salmon, Scallops, Shrimp, Tuna.
Potatoes, Seafood-Stuffed, M192
Risotto, Seafood, 280
Sauce, Red Seafood, 107

SEASONINGS

Better-Than-Potpourri Brew, 271
Gremolata, 280
Lemon-Mint Sugar, 32
Lemon Squeezers, 32
Moroccan Spice Rub, 231
Olive Oil, Basil-Infused, 231
Olive Oil, Lemon-Infused, 231
Southwest Seasoning, 266

SHERBETS. *See also* Ice Creams.
Punch, Pineapple Sherbet, 141
Punch, Raspberry Sherbet, 141

SHRIMP

Bisque, Shrimp, 19
Creamed Shrimp on Pecan-Cornmeal
Rounds, 99
Creole, Easy Shrimp, 68
Enchiladas in Tomatillo Sauce,
Shrimp, 310
Gin and Ginger, Shrimp with, 205
Linguine, Artichoke and Shrimp, 210
Oven Shrimp, Vic's, 215
Paella Casserole, 254
Pastas
Asparagus, Tomatoes, and Shrimp,
Garlicky Pasta with, 82
Mediterranean Shrimp and
Pasta, 286
Scampi, Shrimp, 209
Pizza, The Best of the Bayou, 268
Salads
Aloha Shrimp Salad, 46
Picnic Shrimp Salad, 182
Sesame Shrimp, 92
Smoked Shrimp, Citrus-Marinated, 114
Stuffed Shrimp with Hollandaise Sauce, 86
Tacos, Shrimp-and-Pepper Soft, 339

SLAWS

Blue Cheese Coleslaw, 270
Green Bean Slaw, 108
Red Cabbage Slaw, 153

SOUFFLÉ

Squash Soufflé, 215

SOUPS. *See also* Chili, Chowders, Gumbo, Stews.
Bean-and-Hominy Soup, 23
Bisque, Shrimp, 19
Black, White, and Red All Over
Soup, 126
Bourbon with Molasses Sauce, Burned, 17
Butternut Squash Soup, 62
Cucumber-Buttermilk Soup, Chilled, 134
Gazpacho
Herbed Gazpacho, 175
Tropical Gazpacho, 204
Macaroni and Cheese Soup, 264
Poultry
Chicken Noodle Soup, 45
Chicken Soup, Creamy Asparagus-
and-, 82

Pumpkin-Corn Soup with Ginger-Lime
Cream, 227
Shiitake Soup, Cream of, 265
Stock, Beef, 17
Stock, Chicken, 18
Stock, Fish, 19
Stock, Quick Full-Bodied, 17
Sweet Potato-and-Sausage Soup, 23
Sweet Red Pepper Soup, Cream of
Roasted, 65
Tamale Soup, 213

SPAGHETTI

Casseroles
Casserole Spaghetti, 132
Florentine Bake, Cheesy, 131
Ham-and-Turkey Spaghetti, 19
Lemon-Garlic Pasta, 181
Peanut Sauce, Pasta with, 252
Pie, Weeknight Spaghetti, 312
Salad, Mediterranean, 132

SPICE

Rub, Moroccan Spice, 231

SPINACH

Appetizers
Filling, Spinach, 316
Puffs, Spinach, 316
Puffs, Spinach-Artichoke-Tomato, 284
Bow Tie Pasta, Spinach and Mushrooms
with, 341
Calzones, Spinach-and-Cheese, 310
Casseroles
Artichoke Bake, Spinach-, 48
Cheesy Florentine Bake, 131
Lasagna Florentine, Chicken, 158
Cornbread, Spinach, 49
Pie with Muenster Crust, Spinach, 48
Pinwheels, Flank Steak-and-Spinach, 56
Potatoes, Black-Eyed Pea-Spinach-Stuffed, 22
Salad with the Blues, Spinach, 66
Squares, Spinach, 49

SPREADS. *See also* Appetizers/Spreads.
Cheese
Blue Cheese Spread, 79
Raisin-Nut Spread, 79
Strawberry Spread, 79
Ham Spread, Buttery, 93
Tomato Sandwich Spread, Green, 172
Tuna Tapenade, 127
White Bean Spread, 279

SQUASH. *See also* Zucchini.
Butternut Squash Soup, 62
Calabacitas, 130
Chayote Squash with Cilantro, Sautéed, 227
Dressing, Squash, 290
Kabobs, Summery Squash-and-Pepper, 193
Yellow
Bake, Squash and Tomato, 180
Casserole, Chicken-Squash, 121
Casserole, Creamy Rice and Squash, 26
Soufflé, Squash, 215

STEWS. *See also* Chili, Gumbo, Soups.
Emerald Isle Stew, 71
Red Chili Stew, 226

STRAWBERRIES

Beverages
Cubes, Berry-Good, 201
Shrub, Berry, 29
Citrus Twist, Berry-, 100
Crisp, Strawberry-Rhubarb, 119
Sauce, Berry, 103
Shortcake, Orange-Strawberry, 100
Sorbet, Strawberry-Champagne, 20
Spread, Strawberry, 79

STROGANOFF

Ham Stroganoff on Cheesy Onion
Biscuits, 98

STUFFINGS. *See also* Dressings.
Apple-Walnut Stuffing, 289
Rice Stuffing, 290

SWEET POTATOES

Butter, Sweet Potato, M290
Candied Sweet Potatoes,
Nannie's, 306
Casserole, Sweet Potato-Eggnog, 291
Chips, Sweet Potato, M203
Cinnamon-Apple Sweet Potatoes, M23
Flan, Sweet Potato, 291
Peaks, Sweet Potato, 291
Soup, Sweet Potato-and-Sausage, 23
Stacked Sweet Potato Blues, 290
Tzimmes, 102

SYRUP

Rum Syrup, 313

TACOS

Breakfast Tacos, 340
Chicken Tacos, Pizza-Flavored, 340
Fish Tacos, Barbecued, 339
Pepper Tacos, Grilled, 340
Rolls, Chinese Taco, 339
Shrimp-and-Pepper Soft
Tacos, 339
Tassies, Taco, 339

TAMALES

Mozzarella Tamale, 70
Soup, Tamale, 213

TEA

Lemon Tea Tingler, 200
Mint Tea, Fresh, 88
Rasp-Berry Good Tea, 200
Sangría Tea, Pink, 200
Tropical Tea-Ser, 200

TOMATILLOS

Salsa, Roasted Tomatillo, 64
Sauce, Avocado-Tomatillo, 206
Sauce, Shrimp Enchiladas in Tomatillo, 310
Sauce, Tomatillo, 206

TOMATOES

Appetizers, Oven-Baked Tomato, 172
Basil, and Cheese, Tomato, 165
Biscuit Cakes, Tomato-Eggplant, 170
Breaded Tomatoes, 180
Canned Flavored Tomatoes, 217
Cherry Tomatoes over Pasta,
Herbed, 229
Dip, Gazpacho, 243
Dried Tomato Hummus, Creamy, 284
Gazpacho-Stuffed Endive, 287
Gratin, Tomato-Zucchini, 171
Gravy, Spicy Tomato, 172
Green
Fried Green Tomatoes, 171
Spread, Green Tomato
Sandwich, 172
Grits, Hot Tomato, 171
Okra, Corn, and Tomatoes, 203
Pastas
Asparagus, Tomatoes, and Shrimp,
Garlicky Pasta with, 82
Late-Night Pasta Chez Frank, 228
Macaroni, Cheese, and Tomatoes, 213
Puffs, Spinach-Artichoke-Tomato, 284
Quesadillas, Bacon-Jalapeño-Tomato, 240
Rice with Tomatoes and Basil, 232
Risotto, Tomato-Basil, 269

Salads
    Basil-Mozzarella Salad, Tomato-, 171
    Marinated Tomato and Brie Salad, 95
Sandwich, Floyd's Favorite Tomato, 172
Sauces
    Chunky Tomato Sauce, 264
    Pizza Sauce, Traditional, 267
    Salsa, Fresh, 42
    Salsa, Fresh Tomato, 181
    Salsa, One-Minute, 93
    Salsa, Roasted Tomato, 64
    Salsa, Seared Scallops with Tomato-
      Mango, 122
Soup, Black, White, and Red All Over, 126
Spicy Tomato Warm-Up, 328
Squash and Tomato Bake, 180
Stewed Tomatoes and Greens, 234
Tart, Fresh Tomato, 170

TOPPINGS
Savory
    Almond-Garlic Streusel, 159
    Butter-Pecan Topping, 158
    Eggs and Cheese, 165
    Ginger-Lime Cream, 227
    Mushrooms, Garlic and, 165
    Oatmeal Cookie Topping, 291
    Peach Ketchup, 306
    Sausage and Peppers, 165
    Sour Cream Topping, Spicy, 15
    Tomato, Basil, and Cheese, 165
Sweet
    Oranges in Grand Marnier, 142
    Raspberries, Spirited, 142
    Rumtopf, 142
TORTILLAS. *See also* Burritos, Enchiladas.
Bites, Tortilla, 42
Chimichangas, Apple, 43
Flour Tortillas, 44
Quesadillas, Bacon-Jalapeño-Tomato, 240
Quesadillas, Spicy Chicken, 42
Quesadilla with Cucumber Salsa, Grilled
    Salmon, 131
Quesadilla with Roasted Salsa, Northern New
    Mexican Vegetable, 130
Salads, Mexican Chicken Tortilla, 129
Tostadas, Chicken, 122
TUNA
Burgers, Tuna, 128
Creamed Chipped Tuna, 127

Curried Tuna Melts, 46
Hot Tuna Melts, 126
Nachos, Tuna, 127
Salad, Wild Tuna, 243
Southwestern Tuna Melts, 127
Tapenade, Tuna, 127
TURKEY
Cornbread Crust, Turkey and Peppers
    in, 312
Grilled Turkey Breast with Cranberry
    Salsa, 252
Hash, Turkey, 262
Roast Turkey with Herbs, 305
Salad, Turkey Taco, 25
Scaloppine, Easy Turkey, M192
Spaghetti, Ham-and-Turkey, 19
Turnovers, Turkey Sausage, 239
TURNIPS
Greens, Turnip, 306

VANILLA
Beach, The, 168
Finger Painting Never Tasted So Good, 167
Ice Cream, Honey-Vanilla, 178
Parfait, Bodacious Peanut, 167
VEGETABLES. *See also* specific types.
Calabacitas, 130
Casseroles
    Cashew Casserole, 166
    Lasagna, Vegetable, 211
    Swiss Vegetable Medley, 26
    Wine Sauce Casserole, Vegetables in, 133
Chili, Bodacious, 14
Chowchow, Nannie's, 250
Chowder, Oven-Roasted Vegetable, 229
Hash, Vegetable, 262
Marinated Grilled Vegetables, 162
Marinated Vegetable Medley, 91
Pastas
    Mediterranean Pasta, 341
    Primavera, Creamy Pasta, 167
Pizza, Blazing Sunset, 267
Pizza, Southwestern Veggie, 126
Quesadilla with Roasted Salsa, Northern New
    Mexican Vegetable, 130
Ratatouille, Microwave, M232
Risotto Primavera, 163
Roasted Vegetables, 64

Salads
    Healthy Salad, 133
    Marinated Vegetable Medley, 91
    Mediterranean Salad, 132
    Pasta-Vegetable Salad, 238
    Pita Bread Salad, 86
    Warm Vegetable Salad, 174
Sauté, Vegetarian, 69
Skillet Dinner, Fresh Vegetable, 229
Stir-Fry, Convenient Vegetable, 157
Tzimmes, 102
Yataklete Kilkil, 71
VINEGARS
Lemon Vinegar, 31
Mango-Cilantro Vinegar, 190
Orange Vinegar, 31
Peach-Mint Vinegar, 190
Raspberry-Thyme Vinegar, 190

WAFFLES
Pumpkin Waffles, 282
WALNUTS
Fillets, Blue Cheese-Walnut Stuffed, 327
Parmesan Walnuts, Mixed Greens with, 301
Sauté, Broccoli and Walnut, 52
Stuffing, Apple-Walnut, 289
WATERMELON. *See* Melons.
WOK COOKING
Beef Stir-Fry, Peanutty, 157
Chicken and Snow Pea Stir-Fry, 157
WONTONS
Bowls, Wonton Wrapper, 58
Fried Wonton Envelopes, 96

YOGURT
Tortoni, Apricot-Yogurt, 124

ZUCCHINI
Cake, Zucchini-Pineapple, 160
Crab Cakes, Mock, 159
Crispies, Zucchini, 179
Fries, Parmesan-Zucchini, 129
Gratin, Tomato-Zucchini, 171
Grilled Zucchini with Feta, Greek, 190
Relish, Sweet Zucchini, 159
Salad, Summer Zucchini, 229

METRIC EQUIVALENTS

The recipes that appear in this cookbook use the standard United States method for measuring liquid and dry or solid ingredients (teaspoons, tablespoons, and cups). The information in the following charts is provided to help cooks outside the U.S. successfully use these recipes. All equivalents are approximate.

METRIC EQUIVALENTS FOR DIFFERENT TYPES OF INGREDIENTS

A standard cup measure of a dry or solid ingredient will vary in weight depending on the type of ingredient. A standard cup of liquid is the same volume for any type of liquid. Use the following chart when converting standard cup measures to grams (weight) or milliliters (volume).

Standard Cup	Fine Powder (ex. flour)	Grain (ex. rice)	Granular (ex. sugar)	Liquid Solids (ex. butter)	Liquid (ex. milk)
1	140 g	150 g	190 g	200 g	240 ml
¾	105 g	113 g	143 g	150 g	180 ml
⅔	93 g	100 g	125 g	133 g	160 ml
½	70 g	75 g	95 g	100 g	120 ml
⅓	47 g	50 g	63 g	67 g	80 ml
¼	35 g	38 g	48 g	50 g	60 ml
⅛	18 g	19 g	24 g	25 g	30 ml

USEFUL EQUIVALENTS FOR DRY INGREDIENTS BY WEIGHT

(To convert ounces to grams, multiply the number of ounces by 30)

1 oz	=	¹⁄₁₆ lb	=	30 g
4 oz	=	¼ lb	=	120 g
8 oz	=	½ lb	=	240 g
12 oz	=	¾ lb	=	360 g
16 oz	=	1 lb	=	480 g

USEFUL EQUIVALENTS FOR LENGTH

(To convert inches to centimeters, multiply the number of inches by 2.5)

1 in				=	2.5 cm		
6 in	=	½ ft		=	15 cm		
12 in	=	1 ft		=	30 cm		
36 in	=	3 ft	=	1 yd	=	90 cm	
40 in				=	100 cm	=	1 m

USEFUL EQUIVALENTS FOR LIQUID INGREDIENTS BY VOLUME

¼ tsp						=	1 ml
½ tsp						=	2 ml
1 tsp						=	5 ml
3 tsp	=	1 tbls		=	½ fl oz	=	15 ml
		2 tbls	= ⅛ cup	=	1 fl oz	=	30 ml
		4 tbls	= ¼ cup	=	2 fl oz	=	60 ml
		5⅓ tbls	= ⅓ cup	=	3 fl oz	=	80 ml
		8 tbls	= ½ cup	=	4 fl oz	=	120 ml
		10⅔ tbls	= ⅔ cup	=	5 fl oz	=	160 ml
		12 tbls	= ¾ cup	=	6 fl oz	=	180 ml
		16 tbls	= 1 cup	=	8 fl oz	=	240 ml
		1 pt	= 2 cups	=	16 fl oz	=	480 ml
		1 qt	= 4 cups	=	32 fl oz	=	960 ml
					33 fl oz	=	1000 ml = 1 l

USEFUL EQUIVALENTS FOR COOKING/OVEN TEMPERATURES

	Fahrenheit	Celcius	Gas Mark
Freeze Water	32° F	0° C	
Room Temperature	68° F	20° C	
Boil Water	212° F	100° C	
Bake	325° F	160° C	3
	350° F	180° C	4
	375° F	190° C	5
	400° F	200° C	6
	425° F	220° C	7
	450° F	230° C	8
Broil			Grill